In the early twenty-first century, courts have become versatile actors in the governance of many constitutional democracies, and judges play a variety of roles in politics and policy making. Assembling papers penned by an array of academic specialists on high courts around the world, and presented during a year-long Andrew W. Mellon Foundation John E. Sawyer Seminar at the University of California, Berkeley, this volume maps the roles in governance that courts are undertaking and the ways in which they have come to matter in the political life of their nations. It offers empirically rich accounts of dramatic judicial actions in the Americas, the Middle East, Europe, and Asia, exploring the political conditions and judicial strategies that have fostered those assertions of power, and evaluating when and how courts' performance of new roles have been politically consequential. By focusing on the content and consequences of judicial power, the book advances a new agenda for the comparative study of courts.

Diana Kapiszewski is Assistant Professor of Political Science at the University of California, Irvine. She is the author of *High Courts and Economic Governance in Argentina and Brazil*, which draws on her PhD dissertation, winner of the American Political Science Association's Edward S. Corwin Award for Best Dissertation in Public Law, and is also coauthoring *Field Research in Political Science*, the discipline's first book-length treatment of fieldwork. Her articles have appeared in *Perspectives on Politics*, *PS: Political Science and Politics*, *Law & Society Review*, *Law and Social Inquiry*, and *Latin American Politics and Society*.

Gordon Silverstein is Assistant Dean for Graduate Programs at Yale Law School, where he is helping develop and implement a PhD in Law degree program, as well as administering the Law School's other graduate programs, including the LLM, JSD, and MSL degree programs. Silverstein is the author of *Imbalance of Powers: Constitutional Interpretation and the Making of American Foreign Policy* and *Law's Allure: How Law Shapes, Constrains, Saves, and Kills Politics*, which was awarded the 2009 C. Herman Pritchett Award for the best book published in the field of law and courts that year. Silverstein has also published work on comparative constitutionalism, with a focus on Singapore, Hong Kong, and Europe.

Robert A. Kagan is Professor Emeritus of Political Science and Law at the University of California, Berkeley. He is the author of numerous works on regulatory enforcement and compliance and on the relationships between political structures, legal systems, and courts, including *Regulatory Justice: Implementing a Wage-Price Freeze*; *Going by the Book: The Problem of Regulatory Unreasonableness*; *Adversarial Legalism: The American Way of Law*; and *Shades of Green: Business, Regulation, and Environment*. He is a Fellow of the American Academy of Arts and Sciences and recipient of the Law and Society Association's Harry Kalven Prize for distinguished sociolegal scholarship and its Stanton Wheeler Award for teaching and mentorship, as well as a Lifetime Achievement Award from the Law and Courts Section of the American Political Science Association. He has served as coeditor of *Regulation & Governance* and as director of the Center for the Study of Law and Society at UC Berkeley.

Comparative Constitutional Law and Policy

Series Editors:

Tom Ginsburg
University of Chicago

Zachary Elkins
University of Texas at Austin

Ran Hirschl
University of Toronto

Comparative constitutional law is an intellectually vibrant field that encompasses an increasingly broad array of approaches and methodologies. This series collects analytically innovative and empirically grounded work from scholars of comparative constitutionalism across academic disciplines. Books in the series include theoretically informed studies of single constitutional jurisdictions, comparative studies of constitutional law and institutions, and edited collections of original essays that respond to challenging theoretical and empirical questions in the field.

Volumes in the Series:

Comparative Constitutional Design edited by Tom Ginsburg (2012)

Consequential Courts: Judicial Roles in Global Perspective edited by Diana Kapiszewski, Gordon Silverstein, and Robert A. Kagan (2013)

Consequential Courts

JUDICIAL ROLES IN GLOBAL PERSPECTIVE

Edited by

DIANA KAPISZEWSKI
University of California, Irvine

GORDON SILVERSTEIN
Yale Law School

ROBERT A. KAGAN
University of California, Berkeley

CAMBRIDGE
UNIVERSITY PRESS

CAMBRIDGE UNIVERSITY PRESS
Cambridge, New York, Melbourne, Madrid, Cape Town,
Singapore, São Paulo, Delhi, Mexico City

Cambridge University Press
32 Avenue of the Americas, New York, NY 10013-2473, USA

www.cambridge.org
Information on this title: www.cambridge.org/9781107693746

First published 2013

Printed in the United States of America

A catalog record for this publication is available from the British Library.

Library of Congress Cataloging in Publication Data

Consequential courts : judicial roles in global perspective / [edited by] Diana Kapiszewski, Gordon
Silverstein, Robert A. Kagan.
     p.   cm. – (Comparative constitutional law and policy)
Includes bibliographical references and index.
ISBN 978-1-107-02653-7 (hardback) – ISBN 978-1-107-69374-6 (paperback)
1. Judicial power.   2. Political questions and judicial power.   3. Courts.   I. Kapiszewski, Diana.
II. Silverstein, Gordon.   III. Kagan, Robert A.
K3367.C63   2013
347′.012–dc23   2012037620

ISBN 978-1-107-02653-7 Hardback
ISBN 978-1-107-69374-6 Paperback

Contents

Contributors

Mónica Castillejos-Aragón is Assistant Professor of Law at the Centro de Investigación y Docencia Económicas (CIDE) (Mexico).

John Ferejohn is Samuel Tilden Professor of Law, New York University School of Law.

Tom Ginsburg is Leo Spitz Professor of International Law, University of Chicago Law School, and Research Professor, American Bar Foundation.

Mark A. Graber is Associate Dean for Research and Faculty Development and Professor of Law, University of Maryland, College Park.

Carlo Guarnieri is Professor of Political Science, University of Bologna (Italy).

Terence C. Halliday is Research Professor, American Bar Foundation; Co-Director, Center on Law and Globalization, American Bar Foundation and University of Illinois College of Law; Adjunct Professor of Sociology, Northwestern University; and Adjunct Professor, School of Regulation, Justice and Diplomacy, Australian National University.

Ran Hirschl is Canada Research Chair and Professor of Political Science and Law, University of Toronto.

Nick Huls is Vice Rector for Academic Affairs and Research at the Institute of Legal Practice and Development in Nyanza (Rwanda).

Heinz Klug is Evjue-Bascom Professor of Law, University of Wisconsin Law School; and Honorary Senior Research Associate in the School of Law, University of the Witwatersrand (South Africa).

Mitchel de S.-O.-l'E. Lasser is Jack G. Clarke Professor of Law and Director of Graduate Studies, Cornell Law School.

Manoj Mate is Assistant Professor of Law, Whittier Law School, and Assistant Professor of Political Science (by courtesy), Whittier College.

Amnon Reichman is Professor of Law, University of Haifa (Israel).

Druscilla L. Scribner is Associate Professor of Political Science, University of Wisconsin, Oshkosh.

Martin Shapiro is James W. and Isabel Coffroth Professor of Law (Emeritus), Berkeley Law, University of California.

Alexei Trochev is Associate Professor, School of Humanities and Social Sciences, Nazarbayev University (Kazakhstan).

Introduction

Diana Kapiszewski, Gordon Silverstein, and Robert A. Kagan[*]

In early nineteenth-century America, Alexis de Tocqueville (1835) famously observed, "[S]carcely any political question arises . . . that is not resolved, sooner or later, into a judicial question." That may have been a considerable exaggeration at the time, but today, the dynamic Tocqueville highlighted marks many constitutional democracies in which independent courts are vested with powers of judicial review. In such countries, political actors, organizations, and ordinary individuals who become enmeshed in political conflicts have strong incentives to frame their desires as constitutional or statutory claims and ask courts to vindicate them.

As a result, in the early twenty-first century, courts have become versatile actors in the governance of many constitutional democracies, and judges and justices play multiple roles in politics and policymaking. As many observers have noted,[1] politically consequential courts have emerged in new democracies from Korea to South Africa to Brazil and beyond; courts in more established democracies such as Canada and New Zealand have been given or have assumed more power to protect individual rights and invalidate government policies; and both the European Court of Justice (ECJ) and the European Court of Human Rights (ECHR) have taken on dramatic roles in European governance.

However, the political power of courts has ebbed as well as flowed. In many Latin American countries, judges are not blazing the way to robust constitutional democracy in the way many hoped they might. The Hungarian Constitutional Court, once hailed as one of the most significant new constitutional courts (Zifcak 1996), had its wings clipped less than a decade after its creation (Scheppele 1999).[2]

---

[*] Respectively, Assistant Professor of Political Science, University of California, Irvine; Assistant Dean, Yale Law School; Professor Emeritus of Political Science and Law, University of California, Berkeley.

[1] See, for example, Tate and Vallinder 1997, Stone Sweet 2000, Hirschl 2006.

[2] After another brief period of judicial independence from 2002 to 2010 (Piana 2010), the wing clipping became far more aggressive starting in November 2010 when the Hungarian government amended

There has been a sustained backlash against the growing authority of the Supreme Court in Israel. And in the last two decades, the U.S. Supreme Court has issued many rulings designed to limit the use of litigation and courts to challenge governmental decisions and policies (Staszak 2010, Siegel 2006).

This ebb and flow raises two broad questions: (1) what induces some high courts to become actively involved in politics and policy making at certain moments; and (2) in what arenas and to what effect do courts assume expanded roles in governance? During a year-long Andrew W. Mellon Foundation John E. Sawyer Seminar at the University of California, Berkeley, these questions were considered by an array of academic specialists on high courts. Much discussion dwelt on the first issue – identifying the reasons for the rise and fall of judicial power – a more traditional topic for political scientists. However, at the heart of our deliberations was the conviction that it is also vital to focus on the second question: what do empowered courts actually *do* with their power? Where, to what extent, how, and why do they become politically consequential actors in the life of a nation? Fully understanding judicial politics, our discussions indicated, requires careful attention to the functional, substantive *roles* that judges and courts play in government, politics, and policy. This book – consisting primarily of detailed studies of the roles that courts in nations from every region of the world have begun to play in politics and government – is the fruit of those conversations.

We are not the first to consider judicial roles in politics, of course.[3] This volume is distinctive, however, in its explicitly comparative method, and its mapping of the variety of roles in governance that courts are now undertaking, the political conditions and judicial strategies that have fostered those assertions of power, and the extent to which courts' attempts to play these roles have been politically consequential. With only a limited number of case studies and with numerous, often hard-to-measure causal variables in play, we cannot offer definitive explanations for variation in judicial role expansion, or make definitive claims about the broader consequences of expanded judicial governance. The volume does, however, offer a wealth of ideas about how and why diverse patterns of judicial activity in governance

---

the constitution, stripping the Constitutional Court of its power to review legislation on key economic policy issues. In part in reaction to the court's continued assertiveness, Hungarian officials rewrote the entire charter in 2011, reducing the Constitutional Court to a shadow of its former self by packing the bench, limiting the court's jurisdiction, and eliminating open access for petitions challenging the constitutionality of laws (Scheppele 2011a, 2011b, 2011c).

3 Beyond the myriad studies of judicial roles in American politics, important work has been published concerning the roles particular courts have played in other nations, for example, examining the development of constitutional courts in France (Stone Sweet 1980); the Charter of Rights and the legalization of politics in Canada (Mandel 1994); the emergence and growth of the European Court of Justice (Alter 2001); and the growth of judicial power in India (Reddy 2009). Other scholars have compared how different courts handle similar challenges – such as adjudicating social policy (Tushnet 2009, Epp 1998); constitutional design (Skach 2005); individual rights (Kende 2009); transitional justice (Teitel 2002, Elster 2004); and economic governance (Kapiszewski 2012). Other studies have examined the role of courts at particular political moments – such as democratic transition (e.g., Stotzky 1993; Czarnota, Krygier, and Sadurski 2005).

emerge and how courts have made a difference in the political life of their societies. In that respect, we believe the book advances a new agenda for the comparative study of courts.

In this chapter, we begin by discussing the concept of "judicial roles," distinguishing the political functions some courts are taking on today from the dispute-resolution and law-enforcement roles that had traditionally been their bailiwick. We then describe the various political arenas in which courts have become more active, and the types of political-judicial roles that have emerged in some polities, referencing a range of examples from the volume's empirical chapters and illustrating what we refer to as judicial role expansion. Next, we offer a three-category framework for considering the various factors and forces that impinge on judicial role expansion and contraction, again employing a range of examples from the volume's chapters. Finally, we discuss how courts have maneuvered to play (or indeed, avoid) new roles, discussing the strategies, techniques, and tactics they have adopted to do so.

EXPANDED JUDICIAL ROLES IN GOVERNANCE

The concept of a judicial role has commonly been used with reference to jurisprudential issues, characterizing how individual judges approach decision making in individual cases. Judges, it has been said, might have: (1) a *legalistic* role conception (feeling obliged to protect or adhere closely to legal texts and precedents, regardless of consequences); (2) an *activist* role conception (prioritizing judicial flexibility and substantive justice); or (3) a *deferential* role conception (convinced that judges should defer, on democratic grounds, to legislative judgments in disputes over constitutional meaning).

Our emphasis in this volume, by contrast, is on the *functional* roles courts play in politics, governance, and society. Thirty years ago in *Courts: A Comparative and Political Analysis*, Martin Shapiro (1981) pointed out several basic sociopolitical roles that courts traditionally have played in governmental systems. First, through both criminal and civil cases, courts promote the peaceful resolution of everyday disputes and reinforce widely held norms, thus helping maintain order.[4] Second, Shapiro noted that the legitimacy attached to ostensibly neutral courts enables them to play an important role in enforcing and legitimating the laws and policies promulgated by the dominant political leaders, also helping the central government control local governments, police, and bureaucrats (see also Shapiro, Ch. 16 in this volume). Third, courts traditionally have helped legitimate existing systems of economic power by enforcing rules relating to property, contract, and in many

---

[4] Courts do not provide everyday justice in all cases, of course, nor do they do so to everyone's satisfaction. There are always risks of corruption, and political and social biases are often built into the law; moreover, the costs, delays, and complexities of litigation usually give the "haves" an advantage (Galanter 1974). However, by adhering to the trappings and practices of legal neutrality, courts acquire enough legitimacy to be virtually ubiquitous in human societies.

cases, restrictions on competition. Fourth, Shapiro observed that applying generally stated laws to individual cases entails interpreting legal ambiguities in a way that draws courts into an interstitial lawmaking role. Echoing some of Shapiro's points, Ginsburg and Moustafa (2008: 4) observe that even authoritarian polities commonly establish courts and grant them some degree of autonomy, because courts perform five systemic functions or roles. Political rulers use courts, Ginsburg and Moustafa argue, to: "(1) establish social control and sideline political opponents, (2) bolster a regime's claim to 'legal' legitimacy, (3) strengthen administrative compliance within a state's own bureaucratic machinery and solve coordination problems among competing factions within the regime, (4) facilitate trade and investment, and (5) implement controversial policies."[5]

In playing the sociopolitical roles outlined by Shapiro, and Ginsburg and Moustafa, courts act primarily as agents of top political authorities. Traditionally, courts are expected to faithfully enforce the laws, not make or change them, for in principle the law is to be made by political leaders, embodying those leaders' policy preferences. However, as both established and newer democracies have empowered courts to declare laws and executive orders unconstitutional, there has been a marked increase in courts' potential to assume new roles – to make new law and apply law in new ways. When courts play these new roles in ways that depart from political leaders' preferences, they can exert a significant, independent, and distinctively judicial influence on broad realms of public policy, redistributing political authority. To mention just a few examples from the case studies in this volume, courts can decide legal disputes between political incumbents and challengers in ways that contribute significantly to the consolidation of (or, indeed, weakening of) constitutional democracy; resolve disputes between different branches of government, thus helping to decide who governs; and affect the quality of government by breaking legislative deadlocks and ordering bureaucracies to comply with statutory and constitutional law.

Why would political leaders empower courts such that they can overrule governmental decisions or otherwise function as independent political actors? Why would politicians enact constitutionally entrenched bills of rights with the potential to limit the government's own powers? Political scientists have identified a variety of explanatory scenarios. In the wake of a cruelly repressive regime, political leaders shaping a new democracy often act on the hope that strong, independent judges – armed with judicial review powers and constitutional bills of rights – will serve as barriers against re-descent into tyranny (Scheppele 2000; Klug, Ch. 3 in this volume; Ferejohn, Ch. 14 in this volume; Shapiro, Ch. 16 in this volume). Sometimes, a number of jostling political parties, none of which can count on becoming or remaining dominant (or a currently dominant political faction that is losing confidence), seek political insurance by establishing a new constitution that enshrines aspects of their

---

5 See also Ferejohn, Ch. 14 in this volume.

political program, secures political rights, and empowers a constitutional court to enforce those provisions (Ginsburg, 2003; Hirschl 2007; see also Ramseyer 1994; Magalhães 1999; Finkel 2008; and Guarnieri, Ch. 6 in this volume). However, elected leaders with a more stable power base may also obtain a range of political benefits from designating courts the ultimate interpreters of the constitution, and thus sometimes foist that power on them (Whittington 2007). For instance, judicial empowerment sometimes reflects political leaders' desire to signal their commitment to the rule of law in order to attract support from other nations, prevent capital flight, and/or encourage foreign investment (e.g., North and Weingast 1989; Farber 2002; Silverstein 2003, 2006; Moustafa 2003, 2007). In federal polities, a powerful court may promise subnational governments fairer treatment by the other subnational units and by the central government, or may provide the central government a tool to rein in subnational governments (e.g., Magaloni and Sanchez 2008; Shapiro, Ch. 16 in this volume).

Moreover, as governments empower courts, demands for judicial action can also well up from civil society. In modern states, citizens and voters expect governments to protect human rights, promote equal treatment, and provide protection from bureaucratic arbitrariness and threats to their economic liberty and security (Friedman 1984). Accordingly, political activists, legal reformers, business firms, and ordinary litigants have increasingly sought judicial remedies for a broad array of administrative, political, and policy grievances – thus calling on courts to play new roles in governance.

Judges do not invariably respond to those demands, of course. Their willingness and ability to act assertively, scholars have noted, depends on many factors, including: (a) the extent to which the constitutional text and judicial precedents give the judges a clear duty or opportunity to decide assertively in a particular case; (b) judges' own political and judicial philosophy (Segal and Spaeth 1993); (c) the current political regime's determination and capacity to squelch unwanted judicial challenges (Epstein, Knight, and Shvetsova 2001, Ginsburg 2003, Trochev 2008); (d) the extent to which an assertive court can expect political support from powerful allies (Vanberg 2001; Staton 2004, 2006, 2010); and (e) the relative strength of the national tradition of respecting judicial independence, the rule of law, and judicial creativity.[6]

As this long list of relevant factors implies, judges' willingness and ability to respond to citizens' (and politicians') demands for more assertive rulings, as well as political leaders' tolerance for such rulings, vary from polity to polity, over time, and even from issue to issue. However, where judges have grown more willing to make assertive rulings, and political leaders are more inclined to comply with their

---

[6] Judges' education or hard negative experience may have produced a judicial culture that favors a more mechanical application of legal texts and strongly discourages judicial assertiveness against political authority or involvement in politically controversial issues. See, e.g., Couso 2005, Hilbink 2007, and Huneeus 2010 on Chilean judges.

decisions, lawyers and political activists are concomitantly encouraged to bring a widening array of grievances to court. This can lead judges to adopt more expansive interpretations of constitutional ideals, further expanding their roles in governance (Stone Sweet 1999). It is these roles that our volume explores.

Before proceeding with our analysis, several caveats, qualifications, and prefatory points are in order. First, let us reemphasize that we do not mean to suggest courts have become more powerful political actors everywhere, or that all high courts follow the same developmental path toward expanding roles in governance. The courts examined in this volume – the lion's share of which have assumed important roles in society, politics, and policy making – are not fully representative of courts around the world. Rather, the countries under study were selected to illuminate the questions that inspired this project. We sought to examine a particular phenomenon – courts acting more expansively than most judiciaries did in the past – in order to identify new roles high courts have been playing in recent decades and thereby to encourage scholars to ask new questions about the place and impact of courts in politics and policy. We therefore had to examine country cases that had already become the object of serious academic attention, revealing courts' expansive actions. Simultaneously, we sought to examine courts from a broad geographic range, from both civil-law and common-law traditions, with newer as well as long-established records of judicial independence. Those goals recommended a nonrandom, targeted process for choosing country cases. We hunted where highly qualified scouts – our chapter authors – had already identified and studied the kind of quarry that fit our criteria. Given this case-selection technique, the empirical chapters do not warrant conclusions about what percentage of courts are playing more important roles throughout the world, or strong generalizations about why or when they do or do not do so. Instead, the chapters offer a broad foundation of contextually rich empirical evidence and compelling examples of courts that do play consequential roles in governance in polities around the world, and demonstrate that one cannot fully understand national politics in those contexts without paying close attention to their courts and the interaction of courts with other government institutions.

Second, we do not imply that courts will necessarily resolve (rather than exacerbate) government stasis, that they will defuse (rather than enflame) normative conflict, or that if they assume the role of delineating and enforcing individual rights they will interpret them expansively. We are not proposing that courts are everywhere and always "the good guys." Courts can play new roles in different ways, prioritizing order and authority as well as liberty or equality, endorsing local autonomy as well as central governmental power. Our volume illustrates some of that variety.

Third, we acknowledge that as passive institutions – and "the least dangerous branch" (Hamilton 1788; Bickel 1962) – courts hardly ever act alone. Just as one can think of the roles that different musical instruments play in an orchestra – with first violins carrying the melody, basses and percussion propelling the rhythm, and so forth – so, too, courts, once they are granted or assume constitutional review powers, rarely perform as soloists, instead becoming part of the ensemble of governing institutions. The more important the parts (or musical roles) assigned to courts in the orchestral score, the more forcefully courts play their parts, and the broader the range of other instruments (political and societal actors) to which they play counterpoints, the more courts affect the ensemble's overall performance – that is, the more they influence society and the output of a political system.[7] Where the "legal complex"[8] and support for constitutional norms are less developed or political cleavages too entrenched and intense, court rulings supporting constitutional democratic values, for instance, may have lesser or only short-lived effects. One of our goals in this volume, then, is to understand how courts interact with other political actors: how some actors encourage courts to play new roles and help them do so, whereas others hamper and block their efforts.

Finally, as the title of this volume suggests, asserting that courts are playing more and expanded roles in governance implies that their decisions are in some sense consequential, that they have some actual effect on the governance of the surrounding society. Making such a claim, however – even if only implied – involves an evidentiary challenge. It requires investigating what happened *after* a court issued its decisions, both in the short- and long-term, and to what extent its dictates – as opposed to other factors – actually shaped the subsequent course of events. Judicial consequentiality, therefore, can confidently be assessed – and hence a full account of judicial role expansion offered – only with the passage of time.[9] However, most of the studies in this volume focus on relatively recent court decisions, thereby limiting contributors' ability to trace the consequences of the rulings they discuss and comment on how enduring and significant expanded judicial roles in governance have been. We believe, however, that the studies represent a crucial first step toward understanding the conditions under which courts can be consequential.

POLITICAL ARENAS AND JUDICIAL ROLES

Certain kinds of political disputes, conflicts, and tensions emerge – sooner or later – in virtually all polities, and increasingly, in some countries, they are generating demands for judicial action. The empirical studies in this volume reflect five such arenas of political contention: (1) conflicts between incumbent political regimes and their challengers; (2) conflicts between proponents of secular versus religious values; (3) conflicts between competing power centers within national governments or

[7] We are indebted to Mark Graber for the orchestral image of interbranch relations.
[8] This term, as Halliday (Ch. 13 in this volume) discusses, is drawn from Halliday, Karpik, and Feeley (2007: 6–7), who use it to refer to "the system of relations among legally-trained occupations which mobilise on a particular issue." For Halliday et al., lawyers (including government lawyers and legal academics) and judges form the heart of the legal complex.
[9] To be clear, there is an important difference between courts playing a particular role successfully, and being consequential. Even when a court is not successful in the sense of outcomes exactly matching its dictates, its rulings may still be very important to the way political events play out.

between central governments and culturally or politically divergent subnational governments; (4) conflicts emerging from popular anger concerning official corruption, or governmental deadlock or stasis; and (5) conflicts reflecting government failure to recognize or implement constitutionally or legally promised rights. Because the issues with which courts grapple are complicated and multifaceted, many of the judicial roles our authors analyze fit in more than one arena. Nonetheless, we believe this typology helps us effectively summarize our chief findings concerning the expanded roles in governance that some high courts now play.

Conflict Arena I: Disputes between Political Incumbents and Challengers

Especially (but not exclusively) in new and fragile democracies, disputes often arise between political incumbents and challengers concerning the legitimacy and fairness of potentially pivotal elections, and rights of political expression and organization. Moreover, as Ginsburg (Ch. 1 in this volume) observes, after the displacement of an autocratic regime, new democracies often face controversial questions of transitional justice (construed broadly), for example, concerning the binding quality of laws or constitutional provisions promulgated by, and/or the legal immunity or punishment of officials from, the old regime. When contenders push these political controversies onto the dockets of high courts, judges face a choice between ruling for regime stalwarts or challengers, between strengthening or weakening aspirations for constitutional democracy, between entrenching the interests and values of incumbents or of new majorities. No matter what they choose, courts are thrust into a new role in governance: influencing the struggle for political power. Several chapters in this book, as summarized in the next few pages, illustrate ways in which courts have been called on to play, and have played, this new judicial role.

Facilitating Democratic Transitions

In Korea, Taiwan, and Thailand, as shown by Ginsburg (Ch. 1 in this volume), legal challenges to disputed elections (or as in Korea, impeachment proceedings) led to crucial judicial decisions that determined who shall rule and who shall not. In Ukraine, Georgia, and Kyrgyzstan, as Trochev describes (Ch. 2 in this volume, p. 68), high courts "staffed with Soviet-era judges . . . cancelled rigged elections, thus opening the way for a peaceful change of government." By resolving leadership succession crises during tense moments of constitutional challenge, high courts can strengthen – although of course not guarantee – prospects for a political regime characterized by the rule of law and respect for constitutionally defined democratic processes and procedures. Indeed, whereas Ginsburg (Ch. 1 in this volume) indicates that the Korean and Taiwanese high courts successfully played this role, acting as what he calls "downstream [democratic] consolidators," the Ukrainian, Georgian, and Kyrgyzstani high courts' success in doing so was significantly less enduring (Trochev, Ch. 2 in this volume).

More broadly, in many new democracies, independent high courts are widely viewed as symbolizing the aspiration for government characterized by constitution- alism, bound by the rule of law, and responsive to reason. Klug's chapter tells us that in postapartheid South Africa, the Constitutional Court quickly became such a sym- bol. Faced with a politically sensitive transition to majority rule, leaders managing the transformation gave the Constitutional Court an extraordinary role – helping make and legitimate the constitution itself. The 1993 interim constitution provided for a democratically elected Constitutional Assembly to draft the new constitutional text, but stipulated that the court would scrutinize the Assembly's work before certi- fying that it had abided by the principles enshrined in the interim constitution (Ch. 3 in this volume, p. 103). Amidst great political pressure, the court boldly denied certification of the new constitution drafted by the Assembly. Although it endorsed the "overwhelming majority" of its provisions, it insisted that the Bill of Rights must be further entrenched, that a controversial labor clause be subjected to (rather than insulated from) judicial review, and that the supremacy of central government law over centrifugal regional powers be protected (Id. at 104). The Constitutional Assembly complied, revising the constitution along the lines the court dictated.

Further, Klug shows that early in the postapartheid era, the court issued a series of assertive constitutional decisions that signaled its independence and commitment to constitutional principles rather than political expediency. The Bill of Rights, the court held, required invalidation of laws enacted by apartheid-era legislatures – including the death penalty and numerous other criminal laws (Ch. 3 in this volume, pp. 99–100). However, the court also invalidated some legislation that was passed by the sitting African National Congress (ANC)-dominated Parliament and signed by Nelson Mandela. The court held, for example, that newly empowered black-majority governments in South Africa – both national and regional – were bound to respect constitutionally guaranteed procedural and property rights of white citizens. The court's evenhandedness, Klug observes, enabled it to play an important political role: consolidating the core idea of constitutionalism and the rule of law in the national political culture. In so doing, he argues, judges made the constitution and court central symbols of the reconstituted nation's political identity (Ch. 3 in this volume).[10]

Sparking Antiauthoritarian Movements

In authoritarian regimes with some elements of the rule of law and measure of judi- cial independence, courts sometimes serve as what Ginsburg (Ch. 1 in this volume)

---

[10] Ginsburg's chapter describes a similar role for the Korean Constitutional Court. "Since its estab- lishment in late 1988," he suggests, the court "has become the embodiment of the new democratic constitutional order," routinely being "called upon to resolve major political conflicts and issues of social policy," including carrying out "a complete overhaul of the country's criminal proce- dure . . . prompting . . . significant amendments to the National Security Act, and (establishing) an important administrative law jurisprudence" (Ch. 1 in this volume, p. 104).

calls "upstream triggers for democratization." That is, court decisions can operate as focal points for political movements demanding democracy (or a return to democracy after authoritarian intervention). When courts label repressive governmental actions against pro-democracy advocates illegal or unconstitutional – even if doing so provokes retaliation from political leaders – their decisions "can provide clarity as to what constitutes a violation of the rules," help "legitimate regime opposition," and "raise the costs of oppression" (Ch. 1 in this volume, p. 48).

How such a process unfolded in Pakistan is recounted by Ginsburg, and Mate (Ch. 10 in this volume) discusses the Indian experience in that regard. In 1975, Indian Prime Minister Indira Gandhi, perturbed that the Supreme Court had repeatedly ruled her redistributive economic policies unconstitutional, and fearful that it would affirm a lower court ruling that she had violated electoral laws to win reelection, responded aggressively. She declared a state of emergency, assuming broad emergency powers; packed the Supreme Court with allies and drove the legislature to enact constitutional amendments and statutes that curbed judicial powers; authorized preventive detention of political opponents; and suspended fundamental political and due process rights. The Supreme Court, however, had established a record of decisions defending constitutional and legal rights, and it enjoyed the support of a lively legal complex (Halliday, Karpik, and Feeley 2007; Epp 1998). Popular and elite support for the court and constitutional values enabled previously weak opposition political parties to use Gandhi's attack on the courts and law as a rallying point. Ultimately, they pushed Gandhi to end the period of untrammeled executive rule, and then defeated her in the ensuing election.

Electoral Conflicts in Established Democracies

Even in established democracies, of course, courts are often drawn into disputes between political incumbents and their opponents, between governments and their critics, between those who regulate the boundaries of political activity and those who challenge them. The more dense the statutory and constitutional law governing democracy, the more easily political disputes can be transformed into plausible legal claims – and the more often courts have the opportunity to play a significant role in determining political winners and losers. In the United States, *Bush v. Gore* (2000) provides a widely known example. The Supreme Court resolved an extraordinarily close, intensely litigated presidential vote-counting dispute in Florida, propelling George W. Bush into office. More broadly, as Kagan (Ch. 8 in this volume) notes, in its 1962 decision in *Baker v. Carr* and a series of follow-up cases, the U.S. Supreme Court significantly reshaped the U.S. electoral process. It did so by mandating decennial redrawing of electoral district lines to equalize district population size, and by its expansive interpretation of the Voting Rights Act of 1965, which enabled the government to draw electoral district lines designed to enhance the influence of certain racial and ethnic minority voters.

Conflict Arena II: Intragovernmental Disputes about Who Governs

Conflicts over the allocation of governing power occur in every political system, but perhaps appear in more varied forms in systems with divided powers. For high courts, resolving intragovernmental conflict in ways that frustrate powerful politicians can be risky. However, as more countries have established judicial review, courts are increasingly asked to officiate tugs-of-war between the elected branches of government – and between the elected and judicial branches – over who defines policy. Likewise, many federal systems experience policy conflicts between national governments aiming to prescribe and enforce uniform rules and rights on the one hand, and subnational governments seeking to enforce their own modes of government and values on the other. Accordingly, the question of who has primary constitutional authority to govern with respect to particular issues and people is often pushed onto the agendas of national high courts, enabling them to shape the distribution of authority among government institutions.

Executive-Legislative Conflict

The authors of several of the empirical chapters in this volume describe judicial efforts to resolve heated executive-legislative conflict at the federal or national level. In Taiwan in 2004, for instance, the high court was called on to play this role in the wake of an assassination attempt against presidential candidate Chen Shui-bian one day before the presidential election (Ginsburg, Ch. 1 in this volume). After Chen's victory in the extraordinarily close contest, opposition politicians filed a case with the Taiwanese High Court alleging electoral irregularities – specifically, that the shooting had been staged to create sympathy for Chen. Soon thereafter, once the Taiwanese Executive and opposition-controlled National Assembly had established dueling committees to investigate the shooting, a second legal challenge – this one to the constitutionality of the Assembly's law creating its separate investigative committee – asked the High Court to clarify the investigative powers of each branch (and hence the ability of each to shape the political debate over the election). The court declared the act partially unconstitutional (thereby limiting the legislature's ability to encroach on either executive or judicial constitutional terrain), and also rejected the suit calling for the nullification of the election results, thus allowing Chen to retain office (Ginsburg, Ch. 1 in this volume, pp. 56–57).

Since Chile's transition to democracy in 1990, its Constitutional Tribunal (TC) has likewise been implicated in tense executive-legislative battles generated by the 1980 constitution written under the Pinochet dictatorship (1973–1990). In particular, the TC has been repeatedly called on to resolve challenges to the constitutionality of presidential decrees, requiring it to "interpret and rearticulate the power relationships set out by the authoritarian regime under the new political conditions of competitive democracy" (Scribner, Ch. 4 in this volume, p. 114). The way the court played this power-distribution role changed over the post-transition period, culminating in its articulation of a co-legislative role for the Executive (Scribner, Ch. 4 in this volume, pp. 114–115), thereby reinforcing power inequities in Chile's already strongly presidentialist system.

Judicial-Elected Branch Conflict

The more courts venture into policy-making and power-distributing roles, the greater the risk of conflict between the judiciary and chief executives or legislatures over who governs. For instance, as Reichman (Ch. 9 in this volume) explains, although the Israeli government did not adopt a founding written constitution in 1948, by 1990 it had enacted nine Basic Laws that were understood to be building blocks for a future constitution (Reichman, Ch. 9 in this volume, p. 238). Those laws established a "weak form of judicial review" in which the Knesset (Parliament) could exempt any statute from judicial review and overrule any Supreme Court ruling that had used a basic law to nullify a governmental decision (Reichman, Ch. 9 in this volume, p. 233). When the Knesset passed two additional Basic Laws concerning individual rights in 1992, it reiterated the same limited judicial review formulation. However, in the face of these limitations, Supreme Court Justice Aharon Barak (a former law professor) "launched a scholarly campaign to establish . . . that the court had in fact been granted 'unconventional' powers to strike down legislation infringing basic human rights" (Reichman, Ch. 9 in this volume). The court subsequently drew on Barak's arguments to hold "that all Basic Laws had . . . become supreme over ordinary legislation." In this way, the court dramatically expanded its own potential role in governance – for example, as Hirschl (Ch. 12 in this volume) points out, to defend liberal individual rights from the demands for religious orthodoxy (backed by the growing electoral and legislative influence of religiously passionate political parties).

The Indian Supreme Court has also assumed roles once played by elected leaders (Mate, Ch. 10 in this volume). First, although the Indian constitution authorized Parliament to enact amendments by a simple majority vote, the Supreme Court held that amendments it deemed to violate the "basic structure" of the constitution were invalid. In this way, the court appointed itself guardian of original constitutional principles against amendments it deemed to be motivated by partisan political goals. Second, following the period of emergency rule (1975–1977) and Prime Minister Indira Gandhi's ensuing electoral defeat, the court, seeking to reestablish its authority, developed a public interest litigation (PIL) regime that dramatically expanded popular access to the court and enabled it to broaden its own jurisdiction and remedial powers. In two striking PIL cases, the court, asserting that the independence of the judiciary is part of the basic structure of the constitution, ultimately wrested control over judicial appointments from the Executive, thereby ensuring a larger role for itself in the staffing process and correspondingly diminishing partisan political leaders' influence over judicial composition.

Additional conflicts have arisen between judicial and elected leaders as a result of the advancing globalization of law. In the Netherlands, for instance, Huls (Ch. 7 in this volume) describes how the Dutch high court (Hoge Raad) expanded its lawmaking role via its formal obligation to incorporate European law and supranational judicial decisions into Dutch law. For example, by interpreting ECHR opinions broadly, the court made liberal substantive changes in Dutch family law that the national Parliament had declined to enact. Similarly, in France, Lasser (Ch. 11 in this volume) shows that the Cours de Cassation interpreted European law and precedents broadly to expand fundamental rights in the French legal system. This assertive French judicial action, in turn, placed political pressure on courts in neighboring countries to do the same, and the ECJ and the ECHR endorsed member-state court decisions that followed the French lead (Lasser, Ch. 11 in this volume, pp. 301–302). The result was a "cycle of pressures" in which both domestic and supranational judges chipped away at national parliamentary control of lawmaking.

National-Subnational Government Conflict

Although many of the countries considered in this volume are unitary systems, several chapters offer intriguing examples of courts playing a role in resolving disputes about the distribution of governing power between levels of government. Kagan (Ch. 8 in this volume) recounts the well-known story of how the U.S. Supreme Court helped the federal government dramatically expand its governing reach, redefining the balance of power between Washington and state capitals. Through one set of rulings in the late 1930s reinterpreting Congress's constitutional spending power and regulatory power over interstate commerce, the court authorized construction of a much larger, increasingly dominant national administrative and regulatory state (Kagan, Ch. 8 in this volume, p. 200). In its rulings on another set of cases in the 1960s, the court reinterpreted the post–Civil War 14th Amendment to make most provisions of the federal constitution's 1791 Bill of Rights binding on both state and local governments. This enabled federal courts (as well as cooperative state courts) "to help regulate unprofessional or repressive local criminal justice systems" especially, but not only, in the South (Kagan, Ch. 8 in this volume, p. 201).

Conflict Arena III: Complaints about Government Stasis and Maladministration

In many modern societies, rising public expectations for justice, good government, and particular policies or processes generate lawsuits that call on courts to remedy perceived government nonresponsiveness or stasis, as well as maladministration of various kinds. Of course, identifying government stasis and maladministration may imply a particular notion or theory of what government should do and how it should do it. For our purposes, what matters are the new judicial roles that emerge when citizens feel their government is locked in stasis, unlawfully neglecting important issues or sources of injustice, or is being poorly run, and assert those claims in court.

Breaking Political Roadblocks

Political scientists often point out that constitutional decisions in which high courts "make policy" are not necessarily or even usually countermajoritarian. Judges can take legal or policy initiatives that political leaders support but find difficult to launch on their own owing to constitutional restrictions or political constraints (Silverstein 2009; Graber 1993; Paris 2001). Indeed, political leaders themselves often implicitly or explicitly invite courts into the political arena.

For instance, as noted previously, political leaders representing both major racial groupings instructed the South African Constitutional Court to determine whether a draft constitution complied with certain core principles (Klug, Ch. 3 in this volume). In the Netherlands, Huls (Ch. 7 in this volume) teaches us that for years, a recalcitrant minority faction in the governing parliamentary coalition had blocked demands for legislation that would shield from prosecution physicians who provide or aid in voluntary euthanasia for suffering, terminally ill patients. By deciding individual euthanasia cases to protect the treating physicians, Huls observes, the Dutch Hoge Raad played the role of political "scout" for Dutch leaders, venturing into policy territory riddled with political risk, blazing a trail politicians could follow. With the court out in front, politicians could gauge political and public reaction before moving decisively to enact legislation codifying the court's rulings (Ch. 7 in this volume).

The United States provides another (and well-known) example of political–deadlock–breaking high court action (Kagan, Ch. 8 in this volume). In the decade following the Second World War, many Northern states passed civil rights laws, and Cold War geopolitical competition pressured national political leaders to eliminate the embarrassing injustices of Southern racial apartheid. However, the Democratic majority in Congress was split: a determined minority used the Senate filibuster and their dominance of key leadership positions in the House and Senate to repeatedly block congressional civil rights legislation attacking segregation. Moreover, constitutional questions existed concerning Congress's power to regulate local school-assignment policy. In *Brown v. Board of Education* (1954), the Supreme Court gingerly grasped this political hot potato, declaring official racial segregation in public schools unconstitutional and "reflecting a moral conviction that a great many national political leaders shared but remained unable to implement through congressional legislation" (Kagan, Ch. 8 in this volume, p. 218).[11]

---

[11] The political deadlock in Southern states did not quickly end with the court's decision, of course, which met with massive and often violent resistance. Nonetheless and despite some evidence to the contrary (Rosenberg 1991), Kagan (Ch. 8 in this volume) concludes that the ruling was ultimately consequential, stimulating the Civil Rights Movement and framing the politics of civil rights in the United States. See also Klarman 2007.

Battling Corruption and Maladministration

In both Italy and India – as described by Guarnieri and Mate in Chapters 6 and 10, respectively, in this volume – courts have proactively provided new remedies against politicians and bureaucrats whose corruption and/or failure to implement national laws had generated public frustration. In Italy, the primary judicial actors were lower court judges who, in the European civil law tradition, combined investigative and prosecutorial powers with their judicial powers. The cataclysm of Fascism and World War II, Guarnieri points out, led to a postwar Italian political system that splintered power among numerous ideologically disparate parties, established a constitutional court, and greatly enhanced the independence of the judiciary. Those changes, Guarnieri shows, also weakened hierarchical controls on lower court judges and prosecutors, ultimately giving them the discretion, experience, and power to launch hundreds of corruption investigations and prosecutions against important political party leaders and government officials in the 1990s. This wave of initiatives, as Guarnieri puts it, thrust the Italian judiciary – even if not completely successfully – into the role of imposing a moralistic kind of legal accountability on the political class (Ch. 6 in this volume).

Mate's chapter shows that beginning in the 1980s and continuing into the next decades, the Indian Supreme Court sought to impose the rule of law on wayward government officials and agencies in a strikingly different way – by mobilizing private citizens to serve as enforcement agents. Indian judges reinterpreted the constitution to facilitate access to courts by dramatically expanding standing to sue, and to authorize novel judicial remedies. In the 1981 "Judges Case," Mate tells us, the court asserted that anyone with sufficient interest could file claims to redress injury to the public caused by government illegality in breach of important public duties, and pledged that the court would readily respond (Ch. 10 in this volume, pp. 272–273). The court's procedural rulings encouraged private citizens to file scores of PIL cases documenting governmental corruption and appalling maladministration. In response, the Supreme Court mandated the creation of new watchdog institutions designed to clamp down on official corruption, spur better enforcement of environmental laws, remedy mass violations of criminal defendants' rights, and more – acting, in effect, as chief "social auditor" (Mate, Ch. 10 in this volume, p. 273).

Conflict Arena IV: Cultural and Religious Cleavages

Frequently, the studies in this volume suggest, the legal issues high courts face reflect deep cultural tensions – between religious and secular values in shaping law and public policy, for example, or between preferences for national cultural or religious uniformity versus demands for subgroup or individual autonomy. Similarly, court cases often reflect conflicts between the neutrality demanded by political liberalism and the norms prized by particular religious, ethnic, or cultural subgroups. As antagonists in these clashes push their claims before the judiciary, high court judges are asked to play a balancing role: either to find points of accommodation between conflicting worldviews, or else officially prioritize one view over another in national political, legal, and social life.

Hirschl (Ch. 12 in this volume), for instance, discusses the rapid rise of fundamentalist sentiments and political pressures in a number of predominantly Islamic countries with secular rulers or ruling parties (Egypt, Kuwait, Pakistan, Malaysia). These major social changes generated cases that induced high courts – most staffed by judges professionally socialized to secular rule of law values – to adopt a new role in governance: protecting secular or moderate Islamic practices or legal preferences from subordination to fundamentalist religiosity and practices. In some cases, constitutional changes establishing Shari'a law as "the" official source of law made it even more difficult for secular courts to preserve their legal authority and their own (and political leaders') more secular values. However, the Pakistan Supreme Court, to cite one example, nevertheless held that basic constitutional principles remained supreme over Shari'a law, blocking, at least formally, a coalition of Taliban-sympathizer parties in the North-West Frontier Province from enacting laws designed to "enforce Islamic morality" (Hirschl, Ch. 12 in this volume, p. 320). The Dutch Hoge Raad could also be seen as playing a role in this arena when it blocked prosecutions of physicians for euthanizing terminally ill patients, thus bypassing a legislative deadlock between political factions defending religious beliefs in the sacredness of human life and factions committed to secular humanism (see Huls, Ch. 7 in this volume).[12]

The U.S. Supreme Court has had somewhat rougher sailing into the crosscurrents of cultural conflict between secular liberal values on the one hand and conservative traditional morality on the other. Similar to the courts described by Hirschl and Huls, the U.S. Supreme Court has tended to side with the secular position. For instance, it issued sweeping rulings banning prayer and Bible reading in all public schools (*Engel v. Vitale*, 1962; *Abington School District v. Schempp*, 1963). It also made controversial decisions restricting state laws that had criminalized pornography (*Roth v. U.S.*, 1957; *Miller v. California*, 1973), abortion (*Roe v. Wade*, 1973), and (more recently) consensual homosexual relations (*Lawrence v. Texas*, 2003). As Kagan notes in Chapter 8 in this volume, the court's decisions in these realms stimulated intense political backlash. In regions in which evangelical Christianity is politically strong, state and local legislatures have erected obstacles in the path the court "scouted" and forcefully paved, and the court has been made a symbol of secular Godlessness in the ensuing culture wars that pit local traditionalism against the tolerance preached by most national political elites. Nonetheless, the court's opinions in these areas reflect a new judicial role:

---

[12] Analogously, Huls tells us, the high court helped resolve tensions between proponents of religiously based traditional norms in Dutch family law and advocates of gender equality, holding that ECHR opinions on family law trumped Dutch family law (Ch. 7 in this volume, p. 187).

helping frame the national political debate on controversial cultural issues, and generally endorsing practices and proponents of pluralism rather than sectarian orthodoxy.

Conflict Arena V: Disputes about Rights and Equality

Many constitutions require elected governments and administrative officials to recognize individual rights to due process and equal treatment, to allow individuals to voice controversial opinions and criticize the government, and to allow freedom of worship. Conflict develops when political leaders, law enforcers, and bureaucrats in constitutional democracies seek to curtail claims to these rights and freedoms, arguing that such assertions threaten public order, national security, civility, or the realization of high-priority public objectives. Adjudicating these types of disputes compels judges to play the role of articulating critical compromises.

Moreover, since the mid-twentieth century, new constitutions have often included not only procedural, civil, and political rights but social and economic rights as well. Such "positive rights" offer citizens and groups a legal foothold to demand public goods ranging from adequate housing to a fair wage, a decent education, and healthcare. However, because these positive rights can carry a significant price tag for governments, judges sometimes face a difficult choice between fiscal prudence and constitutionalism. When courts mandate generalized provision of goods or services on the basis of these rights, political leaders must weigh the economic cost of complying against the potential political cost of, and damage to constitutionalism caused by, rejecting or ignoring such judicial mandates.

Chapters in this volume on the United States, South Africa, India, Israel, and some European countries describe critical judicial engagement with the challenges of supporting rights (and declaring their limits). To give just a few examples, in South Africa, Klug asserts, the Constitutional Court has been the "premier institution" defending human rights in the postapartheid era (Ch. 3 in this volume, p. 100). Similar to its U.S. counterpart, the South African court has played a crucial role in race relations, seeking to temper racial conflict and foster racial equality in the transition from white minority rule to democratic government dominated by black majorities. As noted earlier, the court has decided cases in favor of white litigants seeking the rights and protections afforded political minorities by the new constitution, but has also tried to eradicate the harsh legacies of apartheid. For example, it has sought to extend postapartheid governing principles to localities and remote rural areas,[13] struck down the death penalty, invalidated legislation in violation of

---

[13] In the *Zondi* case, for instance, the court considered a challenge to a set of legal provisions (the KwaZulu-Natal Pound Ordinance) that allowed landowners to seize, impound, and eventually sell animals that trespassed on their land – thereby facilitating white landowners' exploitation of rural communities who held their wealth in livestock. "Seeing in the case the perpetuation of the colonial system of exclusion and dispossession" in rural South Africa, the Constitutional Court ruled the provisions unconstitutional (Klug, Ch. 3 in this volume, pp. 107–108).

the equality clause of the constitution, expanded rights-claimants' access to courts, protected precolonial grazing rights, and reinforced rights to political participation, certain socioeconomic resources, and marriage (Klug, Ch. 3 in this volume).

Further, as Mate (Ch. 10 in this volume) summarizes, beginning in the 1977 to 1979 period, the Indian Supreme Court established a new "activist jurisprudential regime in the area of fundamental rights." It expanded the constitutionally pro-claimed "right to life and liberty" and broadened rights-based scrutiny of government action under several constitutional articles (e.g., equality before the law) (Ch. 10 in this volume, p. 271). The court also focused on procedural rights. As noted, it reinterpreted the constitution to broaden standing to sue (thereby expanding access to the judiciary). In one ensuing PIL suit filed by a crusading journalist, the court took the lead in establishing new guidelines for bail, ordered that thousands of criminal suspects be freed from extremely lengthy pretrial detention (Ch. 10 in this volume, p. 273), and helped do away with the practice of "protective custody." Over-all, Mate concludes, the Supreme Court's activism "resulted in the creation of a new corpus of constitutional rights and equitable remedies" (Ch. 10 in this volume, p. 285). Castillejos-Aragón (Chapter 5 in this volume) tells a similar story about the Mexican Supreme Court's extraordinarily proactive promotion of a new rights jurisprudence following the advent of more competitive party politics in that country in the early 2000s.

CHANGING JUDICIAL ROLES: A FRAMEWORK OF CAUSAL FACTORS AND FORCES

Taken as a whole, the examples discussed so far demonstrate significant cross-national variation in judicial roles in politics and policymaking. They also illustrate role expansion in particular country cases, suggesting that judicial roles are far from static. As Epstein et al. (2001) theorize, for instance, by repeatedly issuing decisions that fall within the "tolerance intervals" of important power centers, a constitutional court's legitimacy can increase over time, allowing it to make decisions on a broader array of issues. However, politicians' and publics' tolerance for judicial assertiveness can also quickly narrow – usually on particular issues rather than in general – but in either case shrinking the court's protective legitimacy shield and impelling it to play a role less boldly, or to reverse itself and abandon a role entirely. In short, over time, judicial roles can be added to and extended – as well as stripped, superseded, or replaced, in part or completely.

The next logical question, then, concerns what causes these shifts, expansions, and contractions in judicial roles. The answer is far from clear. Our empirical chapters point to complex constellations of political conditions, forces, and factors that encourage, enable, or even compel some high court judges to breach the constraints of judicial tradition and risk political reprisal in order to impose *their* legal solutions on controversial issues of governance. Other factors and forces discourage, impede, or prevent other courts from doing so. Indeed, as difficult as this causal question was to answer in an era when there were relatively few nations with courts deeply engaged in social policy and governance, the task has become increasingly challenging as the number of consequential courts – and the consequential roles they play – have expanded exponentially in the last twenty years. Correspondingly, we feel that at this point in the development of our collective empirical knowledge, it is not yet feasible to generate an elegant, parsimonious, and reliable theory of change in judicial roles in governance.

Instead, we suggest a three-dimensional framework for thinking about the factors and forces that help explain marked shifts in the consequential roles courts play in governance: (1) the relatively broad and enduring national institutional and political structures (such as constitutional strictures and political power configurations, and the autonomy, size and scope of judicial institutions) as well as international political and institutional structures that constrain and empower courts; (2) the contemporary political dynamics that press courts to expand their roles and take on greater responsibility for governance and public policy – or work to prevent such changes; and (3) the incentives, capacities, and motives of individual judges, and intra-court interactions. Each category includes several factors whose relative importance varies across time and contexts. We believe they resist condensation into what would inevitably be a premature and overly simplistic model.

We attempt to capture this complex framework for organizing the interacting forces and factors that influence change in judicial roles through a "nautical metaphor," schematically illustrated by Figure I.1. In our metaphor, high courts are visualized as sailing vessels navigating the political high seas. The ocean and its currents represent the first causal dimension, deep structural dynamics, defined by the type of regime that built each particular ship, and the constitutional and international context in which judicial ships sail. A second causal dimension comprises the forces that create opportunities and challenges for ships navigating these waters. These short-term political dynamics are represented in our schematic by the winds of *demand* for greater judicial participation in politics and policy, and winds of *resistance* that slow or prevent change in judicial roles. These winds can increase or decrease in intensity and change direction as political and economic squalls arise and fade. Finally, on the third causal dimension, judicial role change may be influenced by the skills of those who sail judicial ships. Structural preconditions and short-term opportunities do not dictate judicial behavior. Instead, judicial ships need a skilled and visionary captain and crew: the preferences, values, and incentives of judges are a critical dimension that must be examined.

An ocean is vast and deep, and political-structural factors below the surface (our first causal dimension) powerfully affect the choices and capacity of judicial captains

FIGURE 1.1. The Dynamics of Changing Judicial Roles: A Nautical Metaphor. Art by David Hellman

and crews. Ships built in politically stable, competitive, constitutional democracies with strong traditions of legality and judicial independence are better able to navigate rough seas and unfavorable sea lanes. Similarly, the international context – political, economic, legal, and judicial – can significantly influence the currents in the sea on which judicial ships sail.

The winds of demand for judicial role expansion (part of our second causal dimension) can arise from a number of sources. As we have seen, pluralistic states typically experience multiple types of tensions and conflicts – between political incumbents and their challengers, different political institutions and factions, secular and religious values, rights claimants and forces of order. In countries whose constitutions include rights and liberties and establish judicial review, such conflicts increasingly give rise to demands for novel judicial interventions. These strong (but still variable) winds of demand are generated by those in power as well as those in opposition. They can have their genesis with political actors who see the courts as an ally, or a means to achieve what cannot be easily accomplished through the political process alone. Alternatively, they can be the product of litigation campaigns organized by strong interest groups, or can arise from social protest movements, businesses, or other civil society actors (including what Halliday [Ch. 13 in this volume] describes as the legal complex). All of these actors can demand that courts take on new roles beyond traditional dispute resolution and law enforcement, thereby pushing for role expansion. Courts that catch the winds of demand for their involvement in politics may be driven rapidly toward the far shores of expanded roles in governance. Those that do not might be becalmed, drifting away from a course toward greater involvement in governance.

However, sometimes courts that are propelled by gusting winds of demand agree to decide cases that are so politically or culturally controversial that they stir up strong winds of resistance, roiling the seas.[14] Powerful political institutions can attack them for having acted undemocratically, illegally, and arrogantly, fighting the expansion of judicial roles in governance, criticizing the ways in which judges play new roles, denouncing the policies their rulings embody, or all three. Similar to actual winds, resistance can develop slowly and steadily or with alarming speed, particularly at moments when transformative governments sweep into power (Whittington 2007). That the winds of resistance are often both expected and unpredictable in strength is a perpetual tension that underlies judicial role expansion, even when high courts have acquired a full ballast of legitimacy.

However, calm seas and favorable winds are not enough to explain variation in the roles that courts play and how consequential they are, bringing us to our third causal dimension. Judicial captains and their crew must make critical strategic calculations when political demands push them into potentially stormy seas: should they drop anchor and wait out the storm, press forward (trusting they have the political support and institutional capacity to do so), change course, or return to safe harbor? If they decide to proceed, what strategies, tactics, and techniques should they adopt in order to do so? Even the most charismatic judicial leader must convince other judges (her crew) of the wisdom of their charted course. Judicial opinions must be shaped and reasons must be given (Shapiro 1992). Skillful captains and officers can sometimes maneuver even less-stable judicial ships through squalls of resistance. Other less-savvy, less-flexible judicial crews may be unable to extricate even well-built vessels from unexpected political storms, or may have to completely change course (or suffer damages) when they encounter them. In short, the tacks that judicial ships take – and their ability to mitigate the risks involved in making assertive, role-expanding rulings – also depend heavily on their leadership; the judicial and political values, incentives, and preferences of judicial majorities; and those majorities' navigating skills and the techniques they deploy.

In sum, the voyage of each of our courts is determined by multiple and interacting opportunities and risks, generated by structural factors and short-term political currents and winds, and ultimately dependent on the skill and capacity of the judges

---

[14] Indeed, the more the "countermajoritarian difficulty" (Bickel 1962) – the ostensible illegitimacy in a democracy of unelected judges overriding and restricting the decisions of democratically elected leaders (which Shapiro [Ch. 16 in this volume] identifies as the normative part of the "mighty problem of judicial review") – is recognized in a nation's political and legal culture, the worse resistance there may be against assertive role-expanding judicial decisions understood as illegitimate "judicial activism" or "undemocratic judicial imperialism."

who confront these challenges and embrace (or ignore) these opportunities. Admittedly, the boundaries among the three categories of factors and forces in our causal framework – particularly between deep political structures (our ships and the ocean upon which they are launched) and short-term political dynamics (our winds) – are blurry. For example, important changes in macro-political structure (such as transition from autocracy to democratic government) are often triggered by (and often, in turn, trigger) short-term political action; if regime change is recent, the two types of factors are entangled. The categories, in other words, are not mutually exclusive. Moreover, shifts in judicial roles are typically produced by an interaction among factors in at least two categories, if not all three. Hence, the implicit causal model is complex, and our attempt to disentwine causal factors and discuss them separately somewhat artificial. Further, inherent in our model is some endogeneity: each ruling that is obeyed (or at least not fully defied), particularly if it stands up to political and legal challenge, can add to a court's legitimacy – that is, increase a judicial ship's ballast – enabling it to better withstand countervailing pressures. Nevertheless, our simple framework provides a map for identifying and illustrating patterns in how different types of factors influence judicial role expansion in our empirical studies. In the rest of this section, we elaborate a bit on each of the three types of factors mentioned, providing illustrative examples drawn from the volume's chapters.

Structural Factors

Relatively enduring features of the institutional and political structure within which courts operate often influence the roles they play. We highlight three types of factors:

(a) *Major domestic political regime features* – in particular: (i) whether the regime is autocratic or democratic; and if the latter (ii) whether it is a unitary or federal system; (iii) whether it is a parliamentary or a separation of powers system; (iv) the degree to which political authority and power are concentrated or fragmented; (v) whether it is a new or established democracy; (vi) whether it is an illiberal or fully consolidated democracy;

(b) *The political status and legal powers of the judiciary* – most broadly: (i) the high court's historical degree of independence from political intervention or influence; (ii) the court's powers of judicial review of legislation (be they long-standing or only recently granted or ambiguous); (iii) the relative density and specificity of court-empowering provisions in the constitutional text; and (iv) the court's degree of support from a politically active legal complex of lawyers, judges, and legal academics;

(c) *Supranational and international forces* – demands and constraints stemming from international treaty obligations, supranational structures, and national dependencies on other states and their political, cultural, and economic actors.

Although we define structural factors as relatively enduring features of the political landscape in which courts and judges act, the empirical studies in this book portray marked changes in political structures (or indeed in entire political regimes) as salient generators of opportunities – or demands – for courts to take on expanded political roles. Most important in this regard, our studies suggest, are shifts from autocratic regimes to some form of constitutional democracy. To review just a few examples, in Taiwan and Korea (Ginsburg, Ch. 1 in this volume), and in the wake of political upheavals such as the Orange Revolution in Ukraine and the Rose Revolution in Georgia in the 2000s (Trochev, Ch. 2 in this volume), high courts were thrust into the role of resolving intense election-related disputes, thus deciding who governs. It was South Africa's dramatic transition from apartheid to a new constitutional democracy that pushed the Constitutional Court into the roles of evaluating the constitutionality of the draft constitution produced by the newly elected Constitutional Assembly and then making epochal decisions on controversial rights issues (Klug, Ch. 3 in this volume). After the 1990 transition to democracy in Chile, the Constitutional Tribunal was repeatedly asked to interpret vague constitutional provisions regarding the relative legislative power of Congress and the Executive, making consequential choices between "competing political and ideological projects" (Scribner, Ch. 4 in this volume, p. 116). The restoration of democracy after India's emergency rule period in the late 1970s created the opportunity for the Supreme Court to make a comeback from its emergency-era defeats by inviting a wave of PIL that enabled it to assume a remarkably activist social-reformer role.

It is taken as a truism among public law scholars that the fragmentation of political authority (divided government in a separation of powers system, weak multiparty coalitions, or factionalized ruling parties) decreases the likelihood that political leaders can swiftly nullify or reverse assertive judicial rulings, thus offering courts greater opportunity to play active roles in governance. One reason, therefore, that transitions to democracy stimulate judicial role expansion is that power is by definition more fragmented in democratic regimes (even fragile or partial democracies or what Trochev, Ch. 2 in this volume, labels "incomplete autocracies") than it is in any other type of political system. Transitions to democracy stimulate the creation of new governmental structures, multiple political parties, and more politically engaged news outlets – all of which can provide more potential supporters for assertive court decisions.[15] In Mexico, as Castillejos-Aragón notes, the emergence of a competitive party system in the later 1990s made it much harder for the party in power to dominate the Supreme Court, giving activist judges the political space

---

[15] Of course, more fragmentation of power, particularly in new democracies, can also generate a different kind of risk for assertive courts; that is, a greater likelihood that their decisions on controversial issues will deeply discomfit one or more power centers, even if they are pleasing others. Consider the unpleasant experience of Russia's first post-Soviet Constitutional Court in that regard, as described by Epstein et al. 2001.

to invite constitutional challenges to governmental policies and practices (Ch. 5 in this volume).

However, even in longer-established democracies with stronger traditions of judicial independence, fragmentation in ruling parties and coalitions appears to be an important factor in stimulating and sustaining judicial role expansion. To give just a few examples from this volume, division in parliamentary coalitions created the conditions under which the Dutch Hoge Raad could break political deadlocks on controversial moral "hot potato" issues without significant fear that its rulings on social policy would be reversed (Huls, Ch. 7 in this volume). Likewise, disagreements among parliamentary parties and within the governing coalition concerning completion of the Israeli constitution provided the opening for the Israeli Supreme Court – led by Justice Barak – to make bold interpretive rulings expanding its own powers of judicial review and more fully entrenching the Basic Laws as constitutionally dominant (Reichman, Ch. 9 in this volume). In another example, Guarnieri describes how the collapse of the dominant Italian political parties in the 1990s and the resulting political fragmentation enabled judge-prosecutors to launch a massive wave of corruption prosecutions against high government and party officials, for in that period the risk of parliamentary resistance or retaliation was significantly diminished (Ch. 6 in this volume, pp. 168–169, 177).[16]

Another structural factor – fragmentation of authority within or among judicial systems – can also have a significant effect on the roles courts play. Hirschl describes how in the predominantly Islamic countries he studied – and in Malaysia in particular – secular civil courts sought to erect jurisdictional barriers between secular and Islamic judicial systems in hopes of preventing Shari'a court systems from expanding their jurisdiction (Ch. 12 in this volume, pp. 321–323). In Europe, where lawmaking and adjudicative authority is fragmented among multiple European political institutions (including the ECJ and ECHR) and domestic legislatures and courts, Dutch and French courts have been able to create new rights and obligations in French and Dutch law through the expansive interpretation of European law and supranational court precedents with minimal risk of reversal or retaliation by the Dutch or French governments.[17]

---

[16] An earlier move toward political fragmentation, Guarnieri explains, had given the judge-prosecutors the capacity to mount these prosecutions. The disassembly of hierarchical, top-down control within the Italian judiciary in the late 1960s and early 1970s (in tandem with growing Communist influence on the political process and increasing terrorism and organized crime) inspired lower-court judges and prosecutors to coordinate, allowed them to play a more active investigative role, and augmented judicial influence over the police (Ch. 6 in this volume).

[17] In fact, Lasser asserts, "The simultaneous and interrelated convergence of . . . domestic and European courts on the fundamental rights idiom has made it increasingly difficult to treat the domestic and international judicial orders as truly external to each other," suggesting continuing evolution in the roles of both sets of courts (Ch. 11 in this volume, p. 309). Interestingly, Huls (Ch. 7 in this volume) suggests that being part of the European system – implying a responsibility to attend to the ECHR

Another structural factor, which might be called the formal constitutional infrastructure, can expand (or restrict) courts' opportunities to play new roles. Trochev, for example, suggests that explicitly prescribed textual barriers against nondemocratic rule and intrusions on judicial independence, bills of rights, judicial review powers, and judicial jurisdiction over electoral disputes enabled courts to play dramatic roles in critical elections in all three of the post-Soviet polities he analyzed (Ch. 2 in this volume, p. 70). Chile's constitution, Scribner tells us, specifically assigned the Constitutional Tribunal jurisdiction over legislative-executive conflicts, only vaguely prescribing the relative lawmaking authority of each branch. Thus, the constitution simultaneously drew the court into the politically sensitive role of deciding "who governs" in particular cases, and allowed it to play that role with considerable latitude (Ch. 4 in this volume, pp. 116–117).

The case-study chapters draw our attention to one final structural factor to which we have already alluded: the increasingly watchful and influential set of supranational and international actors, governmental and nongovernmental, committed to protecting and fostering democracy and expanding human rights. For instance, Klug suggests that international recognition of the South African Constitutional Court's rulings helped it develop and maintain a leading rights-defense role in that country in the postapartheid era (Ch. 3 in this volume, p. 94). Trochev suggests that attention from the West – Western election observers' and negotiators' observance and publicity of electoral irregularities and the subsequent struggle over election results in Ukraine in 2004 and Georgia in 2003 – facilitated Supreme Courts' performance of a mediating role (Trochev, Ch. 2 in this volume, p. 82).

Proximate Political Dynamics

Nested within relatively enduring structural conditions, shorter-term political pressures can also engender urgent new demands for expanded judicial action or, conversely, compel a court to retreat. We refer here to dynamics such as: (a) current political leaders' intense support for (or opposition to) a court's performance of a particular role (including efforts to appoint or eject particular judges, or to expand or retract judicial powers or independence); (b) vigorous social or political movements, including media or litigation campaigns or pressures on particular issues by what Halliday (Ch. 13 in this volume) has called the national legal complex (lawyers, law professors, and the judiciary as a whole); and (c) strong expressions of public opinion on politically, socially, or morally contentious issues.

Sometimes current political leaders push courts to assume assertive roles in governance, encouraging them to make legal decisions that might resolve politically

and UN Treaty on Civil and Political Rights, in particular – can limit the ability of domestic courts to choose and develop their own roles.

divisive issues (or at least reduce political pressures on the leaders). Both President Truman and President Eisenhower's Attorney Generals filed amicus briefs in the U.S. Supreme Court in the case of *Brown v. Board of Education*, urging the court to overrule *Plessy v. Ferguson* and declare state-mandated school segregation on the basis of race unconstitutional (Kagan, Ch. 8 in this volume). Guarnieri discusses how the Italian courts' corruption-fighting role was supported by significant segments of the political class; opposition parties in particular were enthusiastic about shifting the responsibility for highlighting and investigating politicians' transgressions to unelected judges who might be less constrained by political concerns (Ch. 6 in this volume). Even more stunningly, Trochev recounts how President Akaev of Kyrgyzstan ordered the Supreme Court to review the results of elections in districts where outcomes had led to societal outcry (Ch. 2 in this volume, p. 85). In other instances, a posteriori support for courts from government leaders can influence judicial roles. After the South African Constitutional Court struck down an act that granted the president authority to redraw regional electoral district lines and also invalidated orders in that regard that President Mandela had issued, Mandela publicly praised the court's decision as properly defending the principle of constitutional governance (Klug, Ch. 3 in this volume, p. 100), no doubt fostering its role in electoral politics. Indeed, even quite subtle signals from political leaders can influence judicial roles. Reichman highlights how a "nod" from the Attorney General and tacit approval from politicians encouraged the Israeli high court to engage in some forms of judicial review decades before the country's "constitutional revolution" in the 1990s (Ch. 9 in this volume, pp. 239–240).

Conversely, government and political leaders – driven by immediate political desires – can move aggressively to prevent, discourage, or limit judicial role expansion. Beyond overriding high court rulings that do not match their policy preferences in hopes of swatting back judicial reach into political affairs, they may seek to replace judicial personnel or alter appointment procedures, or introduce changes in a court's jurisdiction. For instance, a newly elected president in Georgia, Trochev's chapter tells us, turned on the very Supreme Court judges whose decisions helped propel him into office. He dismissed half of them, packed the court with partisan loyalists, removed its jurisdiction over electoral disputes, and constricted judicial review. Trochev tells a similar tale of court curbing by insurgent leaders whom the court had helped into power in Ukraine (Ch. 2 in this volume, p. 83). Ginsburg shows that both Thailand and Pakistan's high courts met similar fates under similar conditions (Ch. 1 in this volume).

Of course, court-curbing measures are adopted or attempted in more established democracies, as well. The Indian Supreme Court, as Mate shows (Ch. 10 in this volume), was defied, overridden, reconstituted, and weakened by Prime Minister Indira Gandhi in 1977 during the period of emergency rule. President Franklin Roosevelt's threat to expand and pack the U.S. Supreme Court and his appointment of New Deal allies as justices terminated the court's self-appointed role of policing the reach and substance of federal and state regulatory powers (Kagan, Ch. 8 in this volume). After regaining power in Italy in 2001, Prime Minister Berlusconi introduced policies designed to systematically de-emphasize judicial investigations and compromise judicial guarantees of independence – although, as Guarnieri points out, he was not successful in that regard (Ch. 6 in this volume).[18]

In addition to the pressures exerted on courts by current political authorities, upsurges in demands from civil society actors and political movements can also induce shifts in judicial roles. Hirschl's chapter describes how the rapid rise of fundamentalist Islamic sentiments in Egypt, Kuwait, Pakistan, and Malaysia led to demands for broader application of Shari'a law (Ch. 12 in this volume). As noted earlier, the resulting disputes compelled or provoked high courts to adopt a new role in governance – mediating conflicts between religious and secular groups and values. However, at the urging of moderate political leaders, statist elites, secularist elements of civil society (especially the urban intelligentsia), and powerful economic stakeholders, by and large high court judges have played that role by interpreting Shari'a law in ways that preserve the legal authority of the secular courts and their own (and political leaders') more secular values.[19] In a different context, Reichman recounts how Israel's shift toward market-based economics led business interests to demand stronger judicial protection of economic rights (property, freedom of vocation), which in turn provided support for the Supreme Court's assertion of judicial review powers and a stronger rights-protection role (Ch. 9 in this volume, p. 242). Mate describes how growing media attention to the Indian government's human rights abuses (for instance, atrocities by state and local police and abhorrent prison conditions), as well as to corruption and malgovernance, produced a surge in PIL that helped propel the Indian Supreme Court into the role of government reformer – with the support of most of India's legal complex and educated elites (Ch. 10 in this volume, p. 271).[20]

Trochev relates perhaps the most dramatic series of events, in which politicians and citizens together sought both to implicate courts in and remove them from the

---

[18] Of course, political leaders do not always have to act in order to constrain courts: courts can sometimes anticipate potential political backlash and self-restrain. For instance, Reichman asserts that in several instances in the early 2000s, the Israeli Supreme Court decided judicial review cases in ways that contrasted with its previous jurisprudence at least in part because of how it expected "relevant political forces (primarily the security establishment, the treasury department or the religious sector)" to react; the court, Reichman suggests, had "reached its political limit" (Ch. 9 in this volume, p. 257).

[19] More recently in Malaysia, however, Hirschl (Ch. 12 in this volume, p. 323) notes, mass mobilization of Islamists about the scope of Shari'a jurisdiction made playing that role in that way "no longer a feasible option for the [Federal Court]. It has opted instead for a strategy of mixed measures and vagueness."

[20] Of course, civil society can also impose limits on judicial will, or seek to do so. Kagan's chapter mentions several examples of backlashes and unintended effects stemming from civil society reactions to U.S. Supreme Court rulings (Ch. 8 in this volume). Reichman shows how in the wake of Israel's court-facilitated constitutional revolution, important facets of the legal complex together with the media grew more critical of the court (Ch. 9 in this volume, p. 256).

political scene. Following contentious parliamentary elections in February 2005, candidates who lost flooded the Kyrgyzstani courts with complaints, and a crowd of 3,000 citizens pressured the Aravan district court into hearing a case of alleged misconduct in that constituency. Soon after, about eighty protesters stormed the Supreme Court building in an effort to pressure the entire court to resign – ultimately occupying the building for more than a month before a 200-strong "people's militia" overtook the building and ejected them (Ch. 2 in this volume, pp. 83–86). These actions, Trochev suggests, almost certainly influenced the roles these courts subsequently played in politics.

Courts' Internal Incentives, Capacities, and Motives

Structural features of institutional and political systems and contemporary political dynamics can generate openings, invitations, and pressures for shifts in judicial roles in governance: these external factors may open the door and tempt judges to cross the threshold. However, judges themselves must decide whether to pass through the door, potentially risking criticism, defiance, or a reduction in authority. In other words, judges' own incentives, capacities, and motivations are crucial to judicial role expansion and contraction. Throughout this volume, authors refer to a range of intra-court sources of shifting judicial roles, including: (a) galvanizing leaders within the court; (b) evolving values and preferences of judicial majorities; and (c) judges' desires to increase (or revive) the court's status and influence or use judicial power to advance political or policy change.

With regard to judicial leadership, Mate shows us how the views, values, and influence of Justices Bhagwati and Krishna Iyer were crucial to the Indian Supreme Court's assuming the role of uplifting the poor (Ch. 10 in this volume, p. 281). Likewise, in Pakistan, Judge Chaudhry's courageous resistance to General Musharraf's attacks led the Supreme Court to assume an assertive role in seeking to trigger democracy (Ginsburg, Ch. 1 in this volume, pp. 60–62). Without the "intellectual prowess and leadership" of Israeli Supreme Court Justice Barak, Reichman argues, Israel's "constitutional revolution" would not have occurred: Barak's "scholarly campaign" arguing that the country's ambiguous Basic Laws had in fact empowered the court to invalidate legislation violating basic human rights gave the legal community an invitation to file petitions – and offered it a "comprehensive manual" for how to do so (Ch. 9 in this volume, pp. 244, 248). Just as dramatically, Castillejos-Aragón emphasizes the key role of three justices in assertively – indeed, one might say bravely – pushing for structural and procedural reforms that ultimately enabled the Mexican Supreme Court to attract constitutional litigation, reactivate the legal complex and forge a growing body of individual rights (Ch. 5 in this volume).

In addition, shifts in the stance of pivotal justices can strongly influence the roles courts play and how they play them. To offer a well-known example, it was the ostensible shift in the political motivations of one "swing" justice – Owen

Roberts's 1937 "switch in time" (Ho & Quinn 2010) – that ended the U.S. Supreme Court's efforts to block the expansion of the regulatory and administrative state. That shift was consolidated when three of the justices who had constituted a barrier to the New Deal agenda retired, another died, and President Roosevelt replaced all four (Kagan, Ch. 8 in this volume).[21] Broader changes in court majorities can also stimulate judicial role change. In the case of South Africa, Klug argues that the sharp increase in legitimacy of the justices President Nelson Mandela appointed to the Constitutional Court in the mid-1990s – compared to those who held the post previously – motivated and enabled the court to take on important symbolic, legal, and practical roles in consolidating constitutionalism and democracy (Ch. 3 in this volume, p. 97). Ginsburg notes that through the 1990s, as more and more justices born in Taiwan replaced those born on mainland China on the Council of Grand Justices, the institution's internal motivations changed, leading it to systematically disassemble barriers to democratic participation erected by the Kuomintang (KMT) regime (Ch. 1 in this volume, p. 56).

Mate points to another motivational dynamic. The Indian Supreme Court's development of PIL, he suggests, was partially inspired by several influential justices' desire to "rehabilitate and bolster the (court's) institutional legitimacy," which had been significantly damaged by its failure to block the excesses of Prime Minister Indira Gandhi's emergency rule regime in the mid-1970s (Mate, Ch. 10 in this volume, p. 264). Similarly, Scribner highlights how the Chilean Constitutional Tribunal's shift to a more flexible and pragmatic stance after 1997 was motivated not only by an evolution in the political backgrounds of the Tribunal's majority (from Pinochet-era conservatives to appointees of elected center-left governments) but also by the Tribunal's felt need – in the wake of its passivity during the dictatorship – to build legitimacy among political parties, the legal community, and the public (Ch. 4 in this volume; see also Huneeus 2010).[22] Klug, too, suggests that the South African Constitutional Court, due in great part to the failings of the judiciary under apartheid, sought to distinguish itself as "a completely new institution with a fundamentally different role in protecting individuals and promoting a culture of rights in a democratic South Africa" (Ch. 3 in this volume, p. 96).

As many of these examples demonstrate, it is usually a combination of opportunities and pressures stemming from political structures and dynamics on the one hand, and judicial motivations to seize those opportunities on the other, that produces

---

[21] Similarly, Scribner (Ch. 4 in this volume) argues that the return of Justice Valenzuela to the Chilean Constitutional Tribunal stimulated a crucial switch in its interpretation of constitutional provisions on legislative and executive lawmaking authority, thereby expanding its role in resolving institutional disputes in that realm.

[22] To add one more example, Reichman discusses how the Israeli Supreme Court's increasing protection of human rights throughout the 1990s was in part motivated by academic and human rights activists criticizing the court for missing opportunities to exercise judicial review of statutes violating the values entrenched in the country's declaration of independence, which activists believed the court should have interpreted as constitutional (Ch. 9 in this volume, p. 250).

changes in judicial roles. For instance, Mate's chapter shows that the extraordinary activism and assertiveness of the Indian Supreme Court (especially since the early 1990s) in issuing affirmative orders designed to improve various aspects of government was due in significant measure to national legal, political, intellectual, and journalistic elites' frustration with corruption and governmental ineffectiveness. The groundwork for the court's willingness to attack corruption and maladministration, however, had been laid by the justices Indira Gandhi appointed to the Supreme Court in the 1970s, who had created PIL in the 1980s in part to enhance the court's support in the wake of its mid-1970s acquiescence to emergency rule (Ch. 10 in this volume).

JUDICIAL STRATEGIES, TACTICS, AND TECHNIQUES

In hindsight, political conditions – regime change or political fragmentation or a strong legal complex – seem critical to courts playing new roles in governance. However, as we previously hinted, even when conditions seem ripe, political leaders, the legal community, or society can react negatively to judicial decisions in new areas, and the strength of those reactions can be difficult for judges to predict ex ante. The morning newspapers offer no diagrams delineating political leaders' shifting tolerance intervals, or graphs showing the depth of the court's reservoir of legitimacy. The legal complex may be supportive of expanding judicial roles, but ultimately, only to a point or only in certain areas. Influential segments of society may turn out to be unprepared for or downright resistant to particular types of judicial activism. High courts' role-expanding decisions, therefore, often require careful strategic calculation and political judgment – an assertion emphasized by Shapiro and Ferejohn (Chs. 16 and 14, respectively, in this volume) and in many of the empirical chapters.

Of course, as they are made by judges sitting on courts of law, such political judgments are generally framed and justified in "legal" ways. When high court judges do decide to make politically sensitive, role-expanding decisions, they typically strive to dampen the threat of political backlash by asserting that they are not making political judgments but merely following legal imperatives that stem from the constitutional or statutory text or from the legal principles that underlie them. Indeed, in practically every country studied in this book, judges employed a variety of legal strategies, techniques, and tactics when ruling on politically controversial matters. They exhibited striking creativity in how they interpreted constitutional texts, statutes, and judicial precedents, framed their rulings, and timed their remedial orders.

Procedural and Interpretive Creativity

Judges taking on more expansive roles in politics and governance, the chapters in this volume indicate, often engage in various kinds of legal creativity and innovation relating to procedure, remedies, case selection, and standing, as well as constitutional (re)interpretation. With regard to procedural choices, high courts have traditionally avoided politically explosive adjudication through doctrines that categorize some issues as "political questions" or "bureaucratic matters" that are inappropriate for judicial decisions, or by restricting standing to sue to escape being inundated by abstract public interest claims against the constitutionality of governmental laws and practices. However, this volume's chapters describe how some judges have extended their reach into politics by forging innovations in procedural law that invite litigation by politically or socially marginalized groups and individuals.

In the late 1950s and early 1960s, Kagan's chapter notes, the U.S. Supreme Court reinterpreted the constitution's habeas corpus clause, widening the ground for federal court review of state court decisions, thereby facilitating petitions to federal courts by prisoners in state and local prisons and jails (Ch. 8 in this volume). The court also reinterpreted the constitution's due process and right to counsel provisions to require states to provide free lawyers to indigent criminal defendants. Even more procedurally creative was the Indian Supreme Court's decision, as described by Mate, to hear (and subsequently vindicate and remedy) a claim filed not by an individual whose rights had arguably been violated, but by a journalist who had documented that the State of Bihar had been holding thousands of criminal suspects in jail for interminable periods pending trial – longer than the maximum sentence had they been tried and found guilty. Moreover, in its ruling, the court held that even a letter from an individual unable to hire a lawyer would be acceptable as a formal case filing – and in what came to be labeled "epistolary jurisprudence," went on to hear and affirm large numbers of public-interest claims that led to wide-ranging governmental reforms (Ch. 10 in this volume, p. 274).[23]

Our chapters document other types of procedural creativity, as well. As Trochev recounts in connection with Ukraine's Orange Revolution, following the 2004 runoff presidential election between Viktor Yushchenko and Viktor Yanukovych, opposition and government actors filed multiple court cases accusing each other of voter fraud. The dispute eventually reached the Supreme Court. Departing from the three-judge panel norm, the court announced that the entire twenty-one–member Civil Chamber would hear the plaintiffs' claims. The court also aired the proceedings on national television, thereby displaying the formally legal (rather than politically partisan) nature of the hearings. Further, in ruling on the case, the court "discovered" a new remedy it asserted derived from the people's constitutional right to vote: the holding of another second-round presidential election. That decision, as Trochev perhaps understates, "relied as much on the spirit as the letter of the law" (Ch. 2 in this volume, pp. 78–83). Yushchenko's lawyers hailed the solution for its "creative" and "innovative" nature. Ginsburg (Ch. 1 in this volume) describes another

---

[23] The court's procedural creativity extended beyond its manipulation of standing; for instance, it also developed other procedural tools such as "continuing mandamus," which allowed it to maintain jurisdiction over PIL cases indefinitely by issuing orders and directives before final adjudication.

form of procedural creativity. In both South Korea and Taiwan, courts bifurcated politically sensitive legal claims into smaller, more manageable cases that could be decided somewhat independently. For example, by treating a linked series of cases surrounding the 2004 elections as discrete legal issues, Taiwanese judges and justices ensured that they would be decided by different courts using different procedures. As a result, different outcomes obtained, some favoring challengers and some incumbents, helping maintain political balance and foster democratic consolidation (Ch. 1 in this volume, p. 57).

Much has been written, of course, about the interpretive strategies courts employ in reading constitutions, such as the discernment of non-textual fundamental principles, implied rights, balancing tests, and structural imperatives (see, e.g., Silverstein, 2003). Hirschl's chapter highlights a different kind of interpretive creativity in both Egypt and Pakistan. In 1980, Egyptian leaders amended the country's constitution, introducing Shari'a as "the" (rather than "a") primary source of legislation. To help courts grapple with the status of Shari'a as a "potentially determinative source of authority," the Supreme Constitutional Court developed an "innovative interpretive matrix of religious directives" that sought to distinguish between "undisputed, universally binding principles of Shari'a and flexible *applications* of those principles" (emphasis added) – the first such rubric to be created by a secular tribunal (Ch. 12 in this volume, p. 315). In Pakistan, the Supreme Court developed what Hirschl refers to as a "harmonization doctrine" that entailed interpreting the constitution "holistically" – such that no provision stood above any other – again allowing justices significant latitude to limit the influence of a constitutional amendment requiring the nullification of all laws repugnant to the "injunctions of Islam" (Ch. 12 in this volume, pp. 318–319).

Strategic Assertiveness

For decades, political scientists have argued that courts often decide highly controversial cases strategically (rather than in strict adherence to legal principle) in order to minimize the risk of governmental, political, and even judicial criticism or backlash (Murphy 1964; Ferejohn, Ch. 14 in this volume). That propensity is evident in many of the empirical studies in this volume. In politically controversial cases, one common conflict-defusing judicial tactic is to assert a constitutionally important principle and hold that the government has violated it, but then temper or delay the legal remedy sought by the government's challengers. For instance, Ginsburg tells us that in 2004, the opposition-dominated Korean National Assembly brought an impeachment charge against the popular president, Roh Moo-hyun, claiming he had violated election laws requiring presidential neutrality in election campaigns for the Assembly. The Korean Constitutional Court disaggregated the case, ruling first that Roh had violated the law (the basis for impeachment), but second that removal from office (the demanded remedy) would be disproportionate to the offense.[24] In so deciding, the court provided partial validation for both sides in the dispute (Ch. 1 in this volume, pp. 54–55). In another example, the historically deferential Ukrainian Supreme Court split the difference when deciding a case concerning the closely contested 2004 election. It annulled the politically docile election commission's certification of victory by the incumbents, ruling that they had engaged in extensive fraud, thus giving the challengers an important legal and political victory. But rather than handing victory to the challengers, the court mandated that a new election be held, thus affording incumbents a chance to compete again and perhaps survive (although in the event they lost).[25]

On other occasions, courts postpone publication of bold remedies against the government or delay their implementation in an effort to head off tensions. This tactic is illustrated by the U.S. Supreme Court decision in *Brown v. Board of Education* (Kagan, Ch. 8 in this volume). After ruling mandatory racially segregated schools unconstitutional, the court postponed its decision on the mandatory remedy until the following year's term, and then ordered that racially segregated school districts must dismantle discriminatory systems not immediately but "with all deliberate speed," enabling recalcitrant school boards to temporize, often for years (Rosenberg 1991).

A different postponement-of-remedy tactic is illustrated by Klug's account of the 1995 *Western Cape* case. In that case, the South African Constitutional Court was confronted with a potentially explosive challenge to the constitutionality of a law passed by the recently elected ANC-controlled Parliament and signed by the immensely popular President Mandela, granting him authority to redraw the electoral district lines for local government elections. The existing lines had been established by an earlier act "negotiated by all parties as part of the transition to democracy," and thus represented a crucial consensual compromise (Ch. 3 in this volume, p. 105). However, a court ruling striking down the new law and Mandela's district lines could have impeded local government elections across the country and "halted the very process of democratic transition away from apartheid" (Ch. 3 in this volume, p. 18). To reassert the primacy of basic principles, the court gave challengers an important victory: it held that the law and Mandela's implementing orders represented an unconstitutional delegation of essential legislative power to

---

[24] Ginsburg emphasizes that by refusing to endorse the National Assembly's factual findings, the court assumed the role of "reviewing the *political* assessment of the impact that the removal of the President would have on Korean democracy, establishing itself (rather than the Assembly) as the final arbiter of whether removal was actually warranted" (emphasis added); that is, of saying what law is (Ginsburg, Ch. 1 in this volume, p. 54).

[25] Our authors also suggest that courts sometimes split the difference through their rulings across a series of cases. Hirschl illustrates this dynamic in his discussion of a set of crucial cases in Malaysia concerning whether Shari'a courts are subject to fundamental principles of administrative and constitutional law. Whereas overall the Malaysian court tended to bolster secular values, in these sorts of controversial, highly publicized and politicized cases, it often sided with religious authorities and tribunals to some degree, in hopes of retaining relevance and reducing the steadily increasing risk of backlash (Ch. 12 in this volume, pp. 323–325).

the President. However, it also offered the ANC-dominated Parliament a period of time to correct the violations, ultimately allowing the elections to go forward as outlined in the newer regulations (Ch. 3 in this volume).

Finally, in a case discussed by Reichman (Ch. 9 in this volume) and then by Ferejohn (Ch. 14 in this volume), the Israeli court employed a strategy reminiscent of that famously used by the U.S. Supreme Court in *Marbury v. Madison* (1803): strategically manufacturing an extraordinary role for itself and simultaneously pre-empting retaliation by playing that role so as to support the government's position in the particular case at hand. In the 1995 *Bank Hamizrachi* case, discussed earlier, creditors claimed that their "right to property," established by a Basic Law, should override a statute that granted a government agency the power to forgive the debts of nearly bankrupt rural settlements. Until then, the prevailing doctrine had been that even if the courts found a statute in conflict with a previously enacted Basic Law, the Knesset (Parliament) could explicitly authorize the statute's implementa-tion. In boldly asserting "that all Basic Laws had . . . become supreme over ordinary legislation," the Supreme Court empowered itself to exercise judicial review on the basis of all Basic Laws (Reichman, Ch. 9 in this volume, pp. 234, 246). However, in deciding the particular dispute, the court upheld the questioned statute's constitu-tionality, holding that its infringement of the right to property was "proportionate," and adding that the state should be given some leeway as the issue had not been seri-ously litigated previously (Reichman, Ch. 9 in this volume, p. 247). In part because the case was a relatively technical one concerning an issue that did not implicate the main rifts in Israeli society (and in part because the court strategically delayed publishing the ruling, ultimately "burying" it by publishing it in the wake of Yitzhak Rabin's assassination in 1997), the government did not attack or protest the decision (Reichman, Ch. 9 in this volume, p. 247). The *Bank Hamizrachi* opinion, however, could be and was used by the court in subsequent cases to entrench its self-assigned powers of legally and politically authoritative judicial review.

Judges can also sequence their rulings strategically. For example, some courts sequence involvement in new policy areas carefully, testing the waters by first assert-ing their powers in cases involving issues of low political salience, gradually building on those precedents before applying them to cases with higher political stakes. Reich-man suggests the Israeli court strove to ensure that the cases on which the country's "constitutional transition" was founded were of low political visibility (Ch. 9 in this volume, p. 249). Another form of sequencing entails initially targeting subnational levels of government. Mate shows that when the Indian Supreme Court began to use public interest litigation in the 1980s to issue bold reform orders to government bureaucracies for failing to implement national laws, its targets were state and local bureaucracies, not central government agencies. Only in the 1990s, facing more unstable, short-lived central government ruling coalitions in Parliament did the court, less worried about central government resistance, begin issuing bold reform orders to national bureaucratic bodies (Ch. 10 in this volume).

A related role-expansion tactic involves what Mate refers to as "strategic assertiveness." Strategic assertiveness entails a court undertaking a new role by announcing a general principle that constrains governmental power, initially applying that principle in selective or qualified ways so as to avoid outcomes in individual cases that might invoke governmental resistance or retaliation, but ultimately moving step by step – as political conditions permit – to apply it more boldly and against more important targets. Thus, Mate describes the 1981 "Judges Case," in which senior lawyers from various states in India challenged the central government's control over judicial transfers and appointments, and in particular, the law minister's asserted power to transfer state high court judges to other jurisdictions, bypassing the normal consultation procedures. The central government maintained that the lawyers did not have standing to file the case, as they had not suffered any legal harm, and asserted that only judges could bring such claims. The Indian Supreme Court dismissed the government's objections to the lawyers' standing, asserting that as "officers of the court" they had a strong interest in the maintenance of judicial independence, which the court held was part of the "basic structure" of the constitution and hence immune from infringement by the government – and which the government's judicial transfers arguably compromised. On the merits of the case, the justices ruled that the constitutional principle of judicial independence required the Executive to consult in advance with the chief justice and at least one other Supreme Court and high court justice concerning judicial appointments and transfers. The court qualified the ruling, however, by stipulating that the Executive was not constitutionally required to abide by the advice of the consulted judges (Ch. 10 in this volume, pp. 272–273).

In sum, the court strategically extended its own jurisdiction (by endorsing standing for public interest litigation to the advocates) and laid down a basic precedent (constraining unfettered executive discretion in dealing with judicial staffing) enabling the minister to achieve the outcomes he had sought in the case at hand. Twelve years later in the "Second Judges Case" (1993), the Supreme Court – buoyed by a decade of successfully asserting its power and facing a politically weaker governing coalition – reinterpreted the same constitutional provisions even more assertively, ruling that the chief justice of India (in consultation with the other two senior justices on the Supreme Court), not the Executive, had the final say in judicial appointments and transfers (Mate, Ch. 10 in this volume, p. 276).

CONCLUSION

In the countries examined in this volume – and undoubtedly in others, as well – courts are playing consequential new roles in governance. They do so in multiple arenas of political conflict: deciding disputes between political incumbents and challengers and between units of government about who governs; addressing tensions between secular and religious beliefs; and responding to popular outcry about government corruption, deadlock, or stasis. Courts are playing such new roles – our country studies suggest – because macrostructural conditions more often offer them the opportunity to do so; because political actors increasingly urge, encourage, and sometimes insist that they do so; and because judges themselves are motivated to assume new functions in governance. Because they often (although not always) do so at the risk of criticism and resistance from some political leaders, institutions, certain segments of the public, and even some judges and other members of the national legal complex, judges often proceed toward new roles in governance carefully and strategically – picking and choosing their battles, linking bold rulings to constitutional texts via creative interpretation, and seeking to avoid political backlash by tempering the remedies they order in particular cases. We sought to illustrate this complex mix of factors and forces impinging on courts and the roles they play with a nautical metaphor depicting judicial ships sailing on an ocean of multifaceted opportunity and risk, propelled by winds of demand and ever watchful for winds of resistance. The chapters following this introduction take us on a fascinating array of judicial voyages.

We hasten to highlight that neither we nor the volume's contributors wish to exaggerate the roles courts are playing in politics and policymaking around the world. Even where courts play enormously important roles, factors and forces with the potential to limit those roles or the way courts play them can arise without warning. Indeed, far from being power maximizers, courts are often successful because they are careful balancers. Few judicial ships seek to cross the high seas at full sail as quickly as possible, taking on ever-more cargo (judicial roles); instead, courts often tack carefully, assuming new roles judiciously. As a result, courts are rarely monolithically strong. They are called on selectively to resolve particular types of disputes, and they generally respond selectively, ultimately playing more roles in certain spheres of politics and policy than in others.

Likewise, our case studies call into question the assumption that political power is zero-sum – that the power gained by courts must come at the expense of that possessed by the other branches of government, or that a loss of power by judges must mean the other branches have become more powerful. As our authors show quite clearly, powerful courts can strengthen and legitimate the authority of the executive and legislative branches alike. Courts and politicians coordinate in myriad ways, and affording courts more power can simultaneously strengthen a political regime: the power of all of the branches can grow together in something of a virtuous cycle. However, the fact that courts have not commandeered politics in any country – even where they have long been powerful – suggests that judicial power is asymptotic to political power: the former may grow to the outer boundaries of the latter but will never eclipse it. Indeed, our case studies demonstrate repeatedly that courts rarely act alone. This is true in part because they are structurally passive institutions, but also because they are often most consequential when they exercise power in concert with, rather than in opposition to, other important actors.

This volume is an effort to begin a new conversation in the field of comparative judicial politics. It suggests an agenda, and a direction in which scholars of courts around the world might move – one that we hope will lead to a more nuanced discussion of the roles courts play and how those roles change over time. It is precisely because we see this book as an effort to open new avenues of inquiry that – following the eleven empirical chapters that form the heart of the volume – it includes a quartet of chapters in which distinguished authors (whom we have called our *provocateurs théoretiques*) offer their own perspectives on the general project, our discussion of the expansion of judicial roles in governance, and the analytic framework we have outlined here. We reserve the final word, however, for our own concluding chapter, in which we take up some of their arguments and challenges.

REFERENCES

Ackerman, Bruce A. 1991. *We the People: Foundations.* Cambridge, MA: Harvard University Press.

Alter, Karen J. 2001. *Establishing the Supremacy of European Law: The Making of an International Rule of Law in Europe.* New York: Oxford University Press.

Baum, Lawrence. 2006. *Judges and Their Audiences: A Perspective on Judicial Behavior.* Princeton: Princeton University Press.

Bickel, Alexander. 1962. *The Least Dangerous Branch: The Supreme Court at the Bar of Politics.* Indianapolis: The Bobs-Merrill.

Couso, Javier A. 2005. "The Judicialization of Chilean Politics: The Rights Revolution that Never Was." In *The Judicialization of Politics in Latin America*, edited by Rachel Sieder, Line Schjolden, and Alan Angell. New York: Palgrave.

Czarnota, Adam, Martin Krygier, and Wojciech Sadurski, eds. 2005. *Rethinking the Rule of Law after Communism.* New York: Central European University Press.

Dunoff, Jeffrey and Joel Trachtman, eds. 2009. *Ruling the World? Constitutionalism, International Law and Global Governance.* New York: Cambridge University Press.

Dupre, Catherine. 2003. *Importing the Law in Post-Communist Transitions: The Hungarian Constitutional Court and the Right to Human Dignity.* Portland: Hart Publishers.

Elster, Jon. 2004. *Closing the Books: Transitional Justice in Historical Perspective.* New York: Cambridge University Press.

Epp, Charles. 1998. *The Rights Revolution: Lawyers, Activists, and Supreme Courts in Comparative Perspective.* Chicago: University of Chicago Press.

Epstein, Lee, Jack Knight and Olga Shvetsova. 2001. "The Role of Constitutional Courts in the Establishment and Maintenance of Democratic Systems of Government." *Law & Society Review* 35: 117–63.

Farber, Daniel A. 2002. "Rights as Signals." *The Journal of Legal Studies* 31(1): 83–98.

Finkel, Jodi. 2008. *Judicial Reform as Political Insurance: Argentina, Peru and Mexico in the 1990s.* Notre Dame: University of Notre Dame Press.

Friedman, Lawrence. 1984. *Total Justice.* New York: Russell Sage Foundation.

Galanter, Marc. 1974. "Why 'the Haves' Come Out Ahead: Speculations on the Limits of Legal Change." *Law & Society Rev.* 9: 95.

Gargarella, Roberto, Pilar Domingo, and Theunis Roux, eds. 2006. *Courts and Social Transformation in New Democracies: An Institutional Voice for the Poor?* Aldershot: Ashgate.

Gauri, Varun and Daniel M. Brinks. 2008. *Courting Social Justice: Judicial Enforcement of Social and Economic Rights in the Developing World.* New York: Cambridge University Press.

Ginsburg, Tom. 2003. *Judicial Review in New Democracies: Constitutional Courts in Asian Cases.* New York: Cambridge University Press.

Ginsburg. Tom and Tamir Moustafa, eds. 2008. *Rule by Law: The Politics of Courts in Authoritarian Regimes.* New York: Cambridge University Press.

Goldstein, Judith et al. 2001. *Legalization and World Politics.* Cambridge: MIT Press.

Graber, Mark. 1993. "The Nonmajoritarian Difficulty: Legislative Deference to the Judiciary." *Studies in American Political Development* 7(1): 35–73.

Halliday, Terry, Lucien Karpik, and Malcolm Feeley, eds. 2007. *Fighting for Political Freedom: Comparative Studies of the Legal Complex and Political Change.* Portland: Hart Publishing.

Hamilton, Alexander. 1788. "The Federalist No. 78: The Judiciary Department." *Independent Journal,* June 14.

Hasen, Richard. 2006. *The Supreme Court and Election Law: Judging Equality from Baker v. Carr to Bush v. Gore.* New York: New York University Press.

Helmke, Gretchen. 2005. *Courts under Constraints: Judges, Generals, and Presidents in Argentina.* New York: Cambridge University Press.

Hilbink, Lisa. 2007. *Judges beyond Politics in Democracy and Dictatorship: Lessons from Chile.* New York: Cambridge University Press.

Hirschl, Ran. 2006. "The New Constitutionalism and the Judicialization of Pure Politics Worldwide." *Fordham Law Review* 75(2): 721–54.

Hirschl, Ran. 2007. *Towards Juristocracy: The Origins and Consequences of the New Constitutionalism.* Cambridge: Harvard University Press.

Ho, Daniel and Kevin Quinn. 2010. "Did a Switch in Time Save Nine?" *Journal of Legal Analysis* 2(1), 69–113.

Huneeus, Alexandra. 2010. "Judging with a Guilty Conscience: The Chilean Judiciary's Human Rights Turn." *Law and Social Inquiry* 35 (Winter): 99–135.

Kapiszewski, Diana. 2011. "Power Broker, Policy Maker, or Rights Protector? The Brazilian Supremo Tribunal Federal in Transition." In *Courts in Latin America,* edited by Gretchen Helmke and Julio Ríos-Figueroa. New York: Cambridge University Press.

Kapiszewski, Diana. 2012. *High Courts and Economic Governance in Argentina and Brazil.* New York: Cambridge University Press.

Kende, Mark. 2009. *Constitutional Rights in Two Worlds: South Africa and the United States.* New York: Cambridge University Press.

Klarman, Michael J. 2007. *Brown v. Board of Education and the Civil Rights Movement.* Oxford: Oxford University Press.

Lasser, Mitchel de S.-O.-l'E. 2009. *Judicial Transformations: The Rights Revolution in the Courts of Europe.* New York: Oxford University Press.

Magalhães, Pedro C. 1999. "The Politics of Judicial Reform in Eastern Europe." *Comparative Politics* 31(4): 43–62.

Magaloni, Beatriz and Arianna Sanchez. 2008. "Institutional Origins of Supreme Court Power: Mexico 1994–2007." Presented at "The Dilemmas of Judicial Power: A Sawyer Seminar at the University of California Berkeley," February 14, 2008.

Mandel, Michael. 1994. *Charter of Rights and the Legalization of Politics in Canada.* Toronto: Thompson Educational Publishing.

Moustafa, Tamir. 2003. "Law versus the State: The Judicialization of Politics in Egypt." *Law and Social Inquiry* 28: 883–928.

Moustafa, Tamir. 2007. *The Struggle for Constitutional Power: Law, Politics, and Economic Development in Egypt*. New York: Cambridge University Press.

Murphy, Walter. 1964. *Elements of Judicial Strategy*. Chicago: University of Chicago Press.

Nonet, Philippe and Philip Selznick. 1978. *Law and Society in Transition: Toward Responsive Law*. New York: Harper Colophon [reprinted, 2001, Transaction Books].

North, Douglas and Barry Weingast. 1989. "Constitutions and Commitment: The Evolution of Institutions Governing Public Choice in 17th C. England." *Journal of Economic History* 49: 803–32.

Nunes, Rodrigo. 2010. "Politics without Insurance: Democratic Competition and Judicial Reform in Brazil." *Comparative Politics* 42(3): 313–31.

Paris, Michael. 2001. "Legal Mobilization and the Politics of Reform: Lessons from School Finance Litigation in Kentucky." *Law and Social Inquiry* 26: 631–84.

Piana, Daniela. 2010. *Judicial Accountabilities in New Europe: From Rule of Law to Quality of Justice*. Aldershot: Ashgate.

Ramseyer, J. Mark. 1994. "The Puzzling Independence of Courts: A Comparative Approach." *Journal of Legal Studies* 23(2): 721–47.

Reddy, O. Chinnappa. 2009. *The Court and the Constitution of India: Summits and Shallows*. New York: Oxford University Press.

Rosenberg, Gerald. 1991. *The Hollow Hope: Can Courts Bring about Social Change?* Chicago: University of Chicago Press.

Sadurski, Wojciech, ed. 2002. *Constitutional Justice, East and West: Democratic Legitimacy and Constitutional Courts in Post-Communist Europe in a Comparative Perspective*. The Hague: Kluwer Law International.

Scheppele, Kim Lane. 1999. "The New Hungarian Constitutional Court." *Eastern European Constitutional Review* 8(4): 81–87.

Scheppele, Kim Lane. 2000. "Constitutional Interpretation after Regimes of Horror." University of Pennsylvania Law School, Public Law Working Paper No. 05.

Scheppele, Kim Lane. 2011a. "Hungary's Constitutional Revolution." *New York Times* December 19, 2011. Retrieved from http://krugman.blogs.nytimes.com/2011/12/19/hungarys-constitutional-revolution/

Scheppele, Kim Lane. 2011b. "Update: Depression and Democracy Revisited." *New York Times,* December 20, 2011. Retrieved from http://krugman.blogs.nytimes.com/2011/12/20/more-hungary/

Scheppele, Kim Lane. 2011c. "The Unconstitutional Constitution." *New York Times,* January 2, 2012. Retrieved from http://krugman.blogs.nytimes.com/2012/01/02/the-unconstitutional-constitution/

Schwartz, Herman. 2000. *The Struggle for Constitutional Justice in Post-Communist Europe*. Chicago: University of Chicago Press.

Segal, Jeffrey A. and Harold J. Spaeth. 1993. *The Supreme Court and the Attitudinal Model*. New York: Cambridge University Press.

Shapiro, Martin. 1981. *Courts: A Comparative and Political Analysis*. Chicago: University of Chicago Press.

Shapiro, Martin. 1992. "The Giving Reasons Requirement." *University of Chicago Legal Forum,* 179–221.

Shapiro, Martin and Alec Stone Sweet. 2002. *On Law, Politics and Judicialization*. New York: Oxford University Press.

Sieder, Rachel, Alan Angell, and Line Schjolden. 2005. *The Judicialization of Politics in Latin America*. New York: Palgrave Macmillan.

Siegel, Andrew. 2006. "The Court Against Courts: Hostility to Litigation as an Organizing Theme in the Rehnquist Court's Jurisprudence." *Texas Law Review* 84(5): 1097–202.

Silverstein, Gordon. 2003. "Globalization and the Rule of Law: A Machine that Runs of Itself?" *International Journal of Constitutional Law* 1: 427–45.

Silverstein, Gordon. 2006. "Singapore: The Exception that Proves Rules Matter." In *Rule by Law: The Politics of Courts in Authoritarian Regimes*, edited by Tom Ginsburg and Tamir Moustafa. New York: Cambridge University Press, 73–101.

Silverstein, Gordon. 2009. *Law's Allure: How Law Shapes, Constrains, Saves and Kills Politics.* New York: Cambridge University Press.

Simmons, Beth. 2009. *Mobilizing for Human Rights: International Law in Domestic Politics.* New York: Cambridge University Press.

Skach, Cindy. 2005. *Borrowing Constitutional Designs: Constitutional Law in Weimar Germany and the French Fifth Republic.* Princeton: Princeton University Press.

Slaughter, Anne-Marie, Alec Stone Sweet, and Joseph Weiler. 1998. *The European Courts and National Courts.* Portland: Hart Publishing.

Solyom, Laszlo and Georg Brunner. 2000. *Constitutional Judiciary in a New Democracy: The Hungarian Constitutional Court.* Ann Arbor: University of Michigan Press.

Staszak, Sarah. 2010. "Institutions, Rulemaking and the Politics of Judicial Retrenchment." *Studies in American Political Development* 24: 168–80.

Staton, Jeffrey K. 2004. "Judicial Policy Implementation in Mexico City and Mérida." *Comparative Politics* 37(1): 41–60.

Staton, Jeffrey K. 2006. "Constitutional Review and the Selective Promotion of Case Results." *American Journal of Political Science* 50(1): 98–112.

Staton, Jeffrey K. 2010. *Judicial Power and Strategic Communication in Mexico.* New York: Cambridge University Press.

Stone Sweet, Alec. 1980. *The Birth of Judicial Politics in France: The Constitutional Council in Comparative Perspective.* New York: Oxford University Press.

Stone Sweet, Alec. 1999. "Judicialization and the Construction of Governance." *Comparative Political Studies* 31: 147–84.

Stone Sweet, Alec. 2000. *Governing with Judges: Constitutional Politics in Europe.* New York: Oxford University Press.

Stotzky, Irwin P., ed. 1993. *Transition to Democracy in Latin America: The Role of the Judiciary.* Boulder: Westview Press.

Tate, C. Neal and Torbjorn Vallinder. 1997. *The Global Expansion of Judicial Power.* New York: New York University Press.

Teitel, Ruti. 2002. *Transitional Justice.* New York: Oxford University Press.

de Tocqueville, Alexis. 1835 (1899). *Democracy in America* (Book I, Chapter XVI) New York: D. Appleton and Company.

Trochev, Alexei. 2008. *Judging Russia: The Role of Constitutional Courts in Russian Politics 1990–2006.* New York: Cambridge University Press.

Tushnet, Mark. 2009. *Weak Courts, Strong Rights: Judicial Review and Social Welfare Rights in Comparative Constitutional Law.* Princeton: Princeton University Press.

Vanberg, Georg. 2001. "Legislative-Judicial Relations: A Game-Theoretic Approach to Constitutional Review." *American Journal of Political Science* 45(2): 346–61.

Waltz, Kenneth. 1964. *Man, the State and War.* New York: Columbia University Press.

Whittington, Keith E. 2005. "Interpose Your Friendly Hand: Political Supports for the Exercise of Judicial Review by the United States Supreme Court." *American Political Science Review* 99(4): 583–96.

Whittington, Keith. 2007. *Political Foundations of Judicial Supremacy: The Presidency, the Supreme Court, and Constitutional Leadership in U.S. History.* Princeton: Princeton University Press.

Wolfensohn, James. 2001. "Keynote Address to the Law and Justice Conference: Empowerment, Security and Opportunity through Law and Justice." Retrieved from http://www.worldbank.org/html/extdr/extme/jdwspo70901.htm.

Zifcak, Spencer. 1996. "Hungary's Remarkable, Radical, Constitutional Court." *Journal of Constitutional Law in Eastern and Central Europe* 3: 1–56.

PART I

Expanding Judicial Roles in
New or Restored Democracies

1

The Politics of Courts in Democratization
Four Junctures in Asia

Tom Ginsburg*

Scenario One: In a country with only a decade-old democracy, the country's newly elected president is the ultimate political outsider – an activist lawyer, relatively young, whose party does not hold a majority in the parliament. His opponents launch fierce political attacks, and then impeach him for seemingly trivial offenses. The country's widely respected Constitutional Court is called on to decide whether to uphold the impeachment and decides that, although the president violated the law, he can retain office.

Scenario Two: In a hotly contested presidential campaign he looks certain to lose, the incumbent (another former activist lawyer) is shot the day before the election. He wins by a razor-thin margin, and the election is contested. Meanwhile, the executive and legislative branches set up competing investigative committees to determine the source of the shooting. The election case is sent to the courts to resolve, along with constitutional disputes about the investigative committees. The court holds that the election is valid, the investigation constitutional, and the leader takes power.

Scenario Three: In a country with a long history of political instability, a new constitution is adopted, considered the most democratic in the country's history and featuring several new independent institutions to regulate the political process. Soon thereafter, a billionaire who earned a fortune in the telecommunications sector enters politics, creates a party, and develops a populist political program. His party wins a majority of parliamentary seats outright, the first time that has occurred in the country's history. However, he is accused of campaign finance violations and the country's new Constitutional Court is called on to decide whether he should be allowed to take office. The Court holds that he can. Five years later, the leader is deposed by a military coup d'état and a new constitution drafted; after new elections, the courts again find themselves in the midst of repeated challenges to civilian politicians.

* Leo Spitz Professor of International Law, University of Chicago Law School; Research Professor, American Bar Foundation. Many thanks to T. J. Cheng, Javier Couso, Michael Dowdle, and Diana Kapiszewski for comments.

Scenario Four: A country's long-serving military ruler decides to extend his tenure by running for president. The country's Supreme Court, which has been engaged in a struggle with him over various issues, decides that he can run, but then agrees to hear a political challenge to his reelection. The Court announces that it will issue a decision clarifying whether the election is valid after it is held. A few days before the decision is due, the ruler declares a state of emergency, arrests several of the judges, and decries judicial activism as a threat to the nation. Riots ensue; a crackdown follows and opposition politicians are arrested. Within a few months, the ruler is forced from power and elections are held, returning civilians back to power.

These four scenarios took place in recent years in various countries in Asia: Korea, Taiwan, Thailand, and Pakistan, respectively. In all four cases, courts were called on to decide whether or not an elected political leader could take or continue to hold office. In all four cases, the threat of constitutional crisis lurked in the background, for the military has had an active role in all four polities and democracy was perceived to be fragile. Deciding such cases is difficult enough for an established court with a deep cache of institutional capital, as the U.S. Supreme Court learned in *Bush v. Gore*.[1] It is all the more challenging for a court that is itself relatively new.

These types of decisions are critical junctures for the political and constitutional system; they are moments of choice when everything may be at stake, including whether the country will remain a democracy. Examining how these courts handled these opportunities and challenges has the potential to inform theories of the causes and consequences of judicial empowerment, as well as our understanding of the roles of courts in democratization. It is also important to try to understand these critical decisions simply because they seem to be arising with greater frequency, a result of increased judicial power in general, and, more specifically, of the assignment of ancillary powers beyond judicial review to constitutional courts (Ginsburg 2004).

Being forced to pick a leader, either to take or retain power, presents the courts with an enormous institutional challenge. Recall Shapiro's (1981: 1) classic framework suggesting that much of judicial legitimacy comes from the (false) image of an independent judge applying preexisting rules after adversary proceedings to reach a dichotomous solution. One way in which courts deal with the disjuncture between this imagery and the need to secure compliance is by providing mediate solutions. The problem for courts in cases where they must pick leaders is obvious: there is no way to split the proverbial baby, so one or the other of the two parties is going to be very upset.

One can imagine several possible responses to this state of affairs. Perhaps courts will fall back on other devices from the legitimating imagery, emphasizing preexisting rules or the procedural integrity of the process, so as to convince the loser to comply. These solutions may work up to a point. Ultimately, however, a decision must be rendered, and if courts are to retain authority, it must be complied with. Because judicial power to force compliance is minimal, courts rely on other agents to

---

[1] 531 U.S. 98 (2000).

ensure that decisions are effectuated. Why do these other agents enforce compliance? Ultimately, in a democracy, the issue comes down to whether or not citizens are willing to enforce the terms of a constitutional bargain, or to demand that their agents do so (Hardin 1989; see also Vanberg 2004). This suggests that, when faced with the binary question of whether a prospective leader can hold office, the courts ought to ask: which decision is likely to command the support of the citizenry? Taking a majoritarian approach may make sense, particularly in a democracy, for it ensures the greatest likelihood of compliance.

This simple framework is somewhat complicated by introducing dynamic considerations. In a new democracy, the issues are likely to implicate not just which group of elites runs the country, but whether democratization proceeds at all. Consider the "Przeworski moment," when the incumbent party has lost an election for the first time but retains power until the legal transfer of power occurs (Przeworski 1991). Such moments are crucial junctures at which many new democracies fail, when incumbents refuse to transfer power. Courts called on to pick winners at such junctures are caught between a proverbial rock and hard place in seeking compliance. The logic of dictatorship says to bless the incumbents; the logic of democracy says to side with the new majority. Choosing one side or the other will determine the character of the political regime for years to come (see also Trochev, Chapter 2 in this volume).

Even after an initial transfer of power has occurred, courts may find themselves to be arenas in which those out of power challenge the rulers' authority, either in new elections or in attempts to recall the leaders. They are thus in the position of distributing political goods to one or the other contentious party. How courts handle such situations is worthy of further investigation. Should they side with one side consistently? Should they seek solutions that deliver gains for both sides? These are issues of judicial role and strategy that may be illuminated in studying decisions that require courts to choose a national political leader.

THE POLITICS OF COURTS IN DEMOCRATIZATION

To understand the role of courts in democratization, let us begin by distinguishing three alternative scenarios: courts as upstream triggers for democratization; courts as downstream guarantors of authoritarian position; and courts as downstream democratic consolidators, in which courts follow the initial decision to democratize and facilitate the process. A fourth possibility is judicial irrelevance, in which courts play no discernible role as guarantors, triggers, or consolidators.

Upstream Triggers of Democracy

In very rare instances, courts play a central role triggering democratization when the autocrat is not seeking to withdraw, and opposition arises. In these situations, courts are in fact at the center of the transition decision, providing *focal points* for mobilization (Weingast 1997; Schelling 1960). These are situations of conflict and contingency, in which democratization has not yet been embarked on. The basic idea is that an authoritarian regime can only be restrained if the public can coordinate to overturn its action. Coordination is very difficult to achieve. The difficulty is that citizens may not agree on what exactly constitutes a violation of the rules, and may not know whether other citizens will join in an effort to take power. Any subset of citizens thinking of rising up to challenge the regime can only succeed if others join them. Otherwise, the opponent ends up in jail or worse, and the regime maintains power. Being uncertain as to what other citizens will do, the prospective mobilizers will likely stay quiescent and authoritarianism will be sustained. Only when there is agreement on what constitutes a violation and mutual expectations that citizens will in fact enforce the rules will democracy emerge and be sustained. My argument is that, in some limited conditions, court decisions can serve as focal points in helping citizens coordinate, and force the autocracy to liberalize.

Why might citizens focus on a court decision? First, a court decision can provide clarity as to what constitutes a violation of the rules by the government. Lacking an authoritative pronouncement, regime opponents might disagree about whether a violation occurred and may thus fail to coordinate to enforce the rules. However, a court decision can frame the issue and crystallize it in the public imagination, as well as provide persuasive evidence for agreement among citizens. By creating common knowledge that a violation of the rules has in fact occurred, a court decision can help citizens overcome the collective-action problem.

Second, a court decision against the government transmits information. It communicates the view that the government apparatus is not completely unified on policy. It also indicates, at a minimum, that judges do not believe their personal safety is in jeopardy from challenging regime rules, and so may allow opponents to update their own assessments of the risks of challenge.

Third, a court decision raises the cost of repression, and is a resource that can be used by activists to rally supporters to their cause (Silverstein 2009). A regime that arrests citizens after an unfavorable court decision will suffer greater reputational loss than it would have done had the court said nothing. This is not to say that the court decision guarantees implementation – only that it can facilitate mobilization and raise costs for noncompliance.

The incentives for courts to produce "trigger" decisions are not obvious ex ante. Courts have an institutional incentive in ensuring that their decisions are implemented rather than ignored, which requires predicting that citizens will actually respond to calls for change. Attempting to provide a focal point for regime opposition carries grave institutional risks in the event that the citizenry does not enforce the decision. The regime can respond in myriad ways to punish the courts. We should expect, then, that courts will engage in providing focal points only when they have strong institutional and political links to outside institutions that can defend them from punishment, or are sufficiently confident for other reasons that their decisions will be implemented. These conditions are not always present.

A dramatic juncture in which courts appeared to play a triggering role occurred during Ukraine's Orange Revolution (2004–2005), as Trochev discusses in Chapter 2. President Kuchma had sought to use his position to promote the candidacy of his chosen successor, Viktor Yanukovych. The opposition mobilized to protest a rigged election in November 2004, holding widespread demonstrations and initiating a court case to annul the results. Dramatically, on December 3, 2004, the Supreme Court resolved the immediate political deadlock when it ordered a revote for the presidential election later that month. Held under intense international scrutiny, the opposition candidate, Victor Yushchenko, won the second election handily and the court dismissed Yanukovych's various legal challenges. The court was thus at the center of forcing a change in power, providing the capstone to a broad movement and turning back continued dictatorship.

The decision served as a trigger because of its temporal proximity to broader efforts at social mobilization. The Ukrainian decision emboldened the opposition and buried the regime. The court did not pick the leader directly, but was involved in structuring political competition to ensure that the choice was made in a transparent manner, providing an opportunity for the opposition forces to exploit. This illustrates, again, one of the themes of how courts can assist with democratization: holding the regime to its nominal promises and providing fora for political forces to pursue their agendas. It also reminds us that courts do not act in a vacuum but are embedded in broader political environments.

In very rare cases, then, courts may make crucial decisions that become focal points around which broader oppositional coalitions mobilize. That is, court decisions can represent the critical juncture at which regime change coalesces. However, court decisions are neither necessary nor sufficient for democratic transition to occur, and a historical review suggests that courts are rarely the crucial actors in such transitions.

Downstream Guarantors

A more common scenario occurs when the authoritarian regime seeks to withdraw from active involvement in politics rather than maintain power indefinitely. This may be typical of some coup-makers, or a regime that relied on a short-term emergency to justify repressive policies. It may also be a rational decision once a regime realizes it cannot survive. In such cases, the autocrat faces the problem of guaranteeing that his or her core policies will not be overturned after a transition back to majoritarian rule. The autocrat may also be concerned with the property and liberty of his or her supporters, who are likely threatened by a change in power.

In this type of situation, the autocrat may seek to empower courts to act as downstream guarantors of the bargain for exit, providing policy security after the dictator goes. Hirschl (2004), writing in the context of industrial democracies, calls this function "hegemonic preservation," in which a declining powerful group uses courts to secure its policies and limit downstream actors. My version of this argument (Ginsburg 2003) focuses on minorities in general (which can include but is not limited to departing autocrats) and suggests that courts provide political insurance to prevent policy reversal and minimize the risks of the future. This should not, strictly speaking, be seen as an antidemocratic function – sometimes it can be necessary to induce the autocrat to give up power in the first place. However, the court plays a basically conservative role of preserving a bargain against future disruption.

This scenario is only likely for certain kinds of transitions, typically gradual ones in which the autocrat is able to write the rules of the game and negotiate the terms of exit. Perhaps the paradigmatic example is modern-day South Africa, in which the National Party negotiated an extensive set of judicially enforceable rights as a condition of turning over power to majoritarian institutions (Hirschl 2004). This allowed the white minority to protect their economic interests. To be sure, the judges themselves must not be so tied to the old regime as to provoke the ire of the majority. In some circumstances, however, the judges may have enough autonomy to credibly uphold the rights of former dictators, and this serves democratization because such institutional guarantees can induce resignation without revolution.

Downstream Democratic Consolidators

In other times and places, courts may serve as instruments of the newly democratic regime, becoming central to the process after the crucial transition takes place. In these scenarios, the change from autocracy to democracy involves a removal of constraints on the legal system, or in some cases affirmative empowerment of legal actors. In these instances, the courts can become important sites of contestation between elements of the old regime and new, devices for facilitating transitional justice, allies of the new order, or systematic dismantlers of the legal infrastructure of the old regime. In such cases, the court's role is essentially one of building up its own power through cleaning up the legacies of authoritarian rule. However, the timing is one of follower rather than leader in democratization.

To state the matter this way is not to assert that judges and law are unimportant to transition. On the contrary, courts play an essential role in structuring an environment of open political competition, free exchange of ideas, and limited government. It is only to point out that in most instances, legal actors are not at the very center of the transition decision, but rather are involved in the consolidation phase. Often, this scenario results from a reinvention of the judicial role post democratization. Formerly quiescent institutions can become more powerful and capable should they choose to do so, and skillful judges can adjust to the new era. Furthermore, as judicial personnel change, they are likely to become more daring and serve as the expression of a new era.[2]

---

[2] It is not surprising that the South African negotiations called for the creation of a new constitutional court, rather than relying on institutions affiliated with apartheid. In general, however, new elites lack

One area in which one sees particularly intense judicial involvement is criminal procedure, which constitutes the legal apparatus of social control. Democracies and dictatorships differ in their use of legal tools in this regard. Typically, judges have a much greater role in democracies than they do in dictatorships, in which prosecutors and police operate with less judicial scrutiny. Judges asserting the need for greater judicial oversight of criminal procedure are at once advancing their institutional self-interest and ensuring conformity of the new regime with international standards.

Another zone of frequent judicial activity in new democracies involves administrative law. In many authoritarian regimes, administrative law is relatively underdeveloped as a discipline on bureaucratic discretion. Because dictators have lots of other tools for controlling bureaucrats, they do not always need to rely on courts to do so. A typical configuration involves loosely drafted statutes, within which bureaucrats exercise a good deal of discretion, subject to political rather than legal oversight. When new democratic governments take over, they are frequently stuck with the bureaucrats appointed by the authoritarian regime, and may lack sufficient personnel with technical expertise capable of running the government. In such circumstances, it is imperative to find ways to control bureaucrats, and courts can play a useful role in this regard. We often see an increase in the use of delegation doctrines, requiring a tight linkage between legislative command and bureaucratic action, in the early years of new democracy (see Ginsburg 2003, chapters 5 and 7).

Another consolidation function quite particular to new democracies involves dealing with the legacy of the past. Where the old forces are not totally defeated but retain a powerful position in politics, demands for transitional justice are likely to be suppressed (and appropriately so, given that pushing too hard can undo the democratic turn.) On the other hand, if the old forces are defeated, there will be significant demands for coming to terms with the past, and this frequently – albeit not always – involves the legal system.

There is a vast literature on lustration, judicial rehabilitation, truth commissions, and retroactive justice. When courts and the legal process are involved, complex technical issues arise involving, inter alia, proscriptions on ex post facto laws, statutes of limitations, and command responsibility. Frequently the rule of law, as classically defined, suffers when courts ignore legal formalities to hold elements from the past regime accountable for their actions. Nevertheless, from a political rather than formalist perspective, such a role can be helpful in furthering democratic consolidation and legitimation of the new regime in the eyes of the victims of the former regime. It also can provide a kind of mediating political function, in which the past forces are held responsible but not completely devastated. Law can mediate vengeance somewhat.

---

the breadth and depth of personnel to staff a full judiciary after transition, so that of necessity low-level judicial staff may remain who have been appointed by the previous regime. This can have significant downstream effects at low levels of policy conflict, in which judges can hamper the new regime.

Judicial Irrelevance

A fourth possibility can also be observed. This is where the courts, for whatever reason, remain on the sidelines without either supporting or hindering democratization. Hilbink's (2007) account of Chilean judges during and after the Pinochet dictatorship seems to fit this story. The courts in Chile had internalized an ideology of "apoliticism" along with a hierarchical, self-reproducing institutional structure that rendered judges unequipped and disinclined to take stands in defense of liberal democratic principles before, during, and after the authoritarian interlude. Nor have courts been particularly effective enforcers of the policies put in place at the end of the Pinochet regime, failing to strike infringements on property rights, as well (Couso 2003). This seems to be a case where the courts were not agents of either the past or the future. To be sure, after two decades they began to play a role in transitional justice, indicting General Pinochet before his death in 2006, but overall, the story seems to be one of general irrelevance.

Summary

We have identified four different roles that courts can play in democratic transition. Sometimes they serve as agents of the past, policing a transition or even preserving policies of the authoritarian regime. Sometimes they act as agents of the future, helping transform the political process and encouraging the consolidation of democracy. In some rare instances, courts themselves trigger the democratization process, encouraging mobilization and tipping the regime into transformation. Finally, courts can be merely marginal players who neither facilitate nor hinder a transition to democracy.

FOUR CASES

Impeachment in South Korea, 2004

In 1987, after thirty-five years of more or less continuous authoritarian rule by military strongmen, South Korea established its Sixth Republic. The immediate trigger had been large-scale demonstrations on the streets of Seoul, in which a growing middle class had joined students and labor activists to force political liberalization. The military leader, Chun Doo-hwan, stepped down; his successor, Roh Tae Woo, negotiated a deal with the two leading opposition parties, led by Kim Young Sam and Kim Dae Jung. The three major forces negotiated a new Constitution establishing a democratic order.

The major issues in constitutional negotiation concerned elections and the role of the military. Relatively little thought was given to the new Constitutional Court. In the years since its establishment in late 1988, however, the Court has become the embodiment of the new democratic constitutional order of Korea. The Constitutional Court is routinely called on to resolve major political conflicts and issues of social policy, and has rendered many thousands of decisions.[3] This reflects both growing demand from newly empowered civil society, as well as a willingness on the part of the justices to advance constitutional justice. Among the Court's many achievements are a delicate navigation of issues of retroactive justice, a complete overhaul of the country's criminal procedure, the prompting of significant amendments to the National Security Act, and an important administrative law jurisprudence (see, generally, Ginsburg 2003; Chapter 7 in this volume; Cho 1997). It is a classic downstream consolidator.

I have argued elsewhere that the Korean Court's powerful design, and its effective exercise of power, were facilitated by the fact that Korean politics were quite divided at the time of the constitutional founding (Ginsburg 2003). Three major political forces vied for power; they concluded a deal in which presidents would be elected for a single five-year term. This maximized the chances that each of the major leaders (Roh Tae Woo, Kim Young Sam, and Kim Dae Jung) would get to hold office, and they proceeded to win the presidency in three successive cycles. However, because no party could anticipate that it would be able to dominate the political system, each had an incentive to empower a constitutional court as well, to minimize the harm it might suffer when out of power, and allow for opportunities to challenge legislation and government action.

An unanticipated by-product of this constitutional bargain was weakness in the major political institutions. Because the Constitution provides that presidents cannot be reelected, leaders became lame ducks almost from the beginning of their terms. Furthermore, divided government has not been uncommon, as the National Assembly is often controlled by coalitions of parties that did not include the president's party. Each Korean president has ended his term in scandal and quite unpopular. In such a circumstance, the Constitutional Court was seen as a relatively trustworthy institution and enjoyed a good deal of institutional capital. Other government institutions are not as respected, and there is even talk at the moment about the need for constitutional reform. The legitimacy of the Court, and its active role, has been relatively stable since it emerged in the early years after democratization.

A key factor here was the emergence of a vigorous civil-society movement, in which lawyers played a crucial role. Influenced by cause litigation in the United States and elsewhere, these lawyers sought to press for liberal transformation through law. Courts were one among many milieu used in these campaigns. This legal complex represented an important external influence on the court, and provided the needed demand referenced in the Introduction of this volume.

In December 2002, a major step in the country's democratic history came with the election of activist labor lawyer Roh Moo-hyun as president, the first person

---

[3] Constitutional Court statistics. Retrieved from http://www.ccourt.go.kr/home/english/statistics.jsp#.

to hold that office after the three who had negotiated the 1987 Constitution. Roh represented a new set of social forces. A farmer's son who had passed the country's notoriously difficult bar exam without a college degree, he represented meritocracy, liberal activism, and, as the first president born after World War II, generational change. Roh's ability to pursue his ambitious agenda, however, was complicated by the fact that his party did not win a majority in the National Assembly. His position became even less tenable when the party split as a result of generational tensions in September 2003, and a corruption scandal related to campaign contributions erupted that October. Roh staked his future on a mid-term legislative election to be held in April 2004, but – in violation of South Korean law – appeared to campaign for his new Uri party by urging voters to support it. The majority in the National Assembly responded with a motion for impeachment that easily achieved the necessary two-thirds vote (Lee 2005). The impeachment was sent to the Constitutional Court for confirmation, as required under the Constitution.[4] This was the first time any court in South Korea had been called on to pick a ruler or allow one to be impeached, and the Court held a series of trial-like hearings at which the issues were argued.

Surprisingly, Roh's approval rating skyrocketed in the wake of the impeachment, and his party received overwhelming support at the April 2004 polls, winning an absolute majority in the National Assembly with 152 out of 299 votes. It is speculative but generally believed that this indicator of the public's preferences influenced the court in its decision. On May 14, the Court rejected the impeachment motion. In addressing the issue, the Court bifurcated the issue into the question of whether there was a "violation of the Constitution or other Acts" – the predicate for impeach-ment – and whether those violations were severe enough to warrant removal. Although the Court found that Roh had violated the election-law provisions that public officials remain neutral – along with other provisions of law – they decided that it would not be proportional to remove the president for the violation. Instead, they asserted that removal is only appropriate when the "free and democratic basic order" is threatened. Roh's violations were not a premeditated attempt to undermine constitutional democracy, said the Court.

The incident illustrates two themes in the study of judicial politics. Most obvi-ously, the Court demonstrated great sensitivity to signals from the broader political environment. By splitting the difference in a manner that responded to recent signals from the electorate, the Court gave both sides what they wanted, at the same time avoiding a constitutional crisis. Second, and more importantly, was the subtle way in which the Court aggrandized its own power in making the decision. By failing to simply confirm the National Assembly's factual findings, the Court placed itself in the position of reviewing the political assessment of the impact the removal of the president would have on Korean democracy. The Court established itself, and not the Assembly, as the final arbiter of whether removal was actually warranted.

---

[4] Art. 112.

In this sense, the Court ended up enhancing its ability to say what the law is, and did so in a manner that ensured it would be accepted by the majority of the public.

Roh's political redemption at the hands of the Court proved short-lived. In October 2004, his ambitious plan to move the capital of the country from Seoul was rejected by the Court as a violation of an unwritten customary constitution of Korea. Roh's popularity continued to decline, and his other initiatives foundered. He ended his term in disgrace, and hounded by a corruption scandal, took his own life in 2009. The Court, on the other hand, is consistently rated one of the most effective institutions by the Korean public. In a recent poll, for example, it received the highest rating of any government body (and just behind several large corporations) in terms of influence and trust.[5]

In considering this juncture two themes jump out. First, the Court did seem to generate a kind of mediate solution by finding that Roh had both broken the law but also deserved to remain in power. This left him as a weakened president and enhanced the Court's status. The addition of a political criterion for determining impeachment cases means the Court will have the final word should similar cases arise in the future. Second, the Court seemed to clearly respond to electoral signals. The popular support Roh enjoyed as a result of the impeachment meant that removing him from office would provoke a major political crisis. The Court avoided this by listening to the electorate. It was not constraining the new rising forces on behalf of the old, as in the guarantor model.

There has been no major shift in the Court's role since this watershed case. It remains a major player in Korean politics, with enhanced legitimacy. The Court's caseload has gradually and somewhat seamlessly shifted from transitional issues associated with democratic consolidation to more conventional issues of guarding constitutional democracy, and remains a major player. Continuity, rather than change in the judicial role, is the trope in this case study.

Adjudicating the Election in Taiwan, 2004

Taiwan's remarkable transformation from Leninist party-state authoritarianism to multiparty democracy has been rightly celebrated as a central case in understanding the third wave of democracy. It also provides insights into the role that courts can play in democratic politics.

As in many authoritarian regimes, courts did exist during the one-party period. Although courts provided some outlet for contesting policies during the authoritarian period, they never challenged core policies of the regime, preferring to remain in a discrete zone of apoliticism (compare Toharia 1975; Hilbink 2007). The crucial

---

[5] See, e.g., *JoongAng Daily*, July 3, 2007. Retrieved from http://joongangdaily.joins.com/article/view .asp?aid=2877553.

decisions to embark on democratization were not taken in courtrooms. Rather, they were taken in the backroom discussions during and after 1985, when President Chiang Ching-kuo decided to save the Kuomintang (KMT) regime by "returning power to the people."

Only once the direction of democratization was absolutely clear did the courts begin to act, around 1989. Much attention has been given to a dramatic decision in the democratization process, Interpretation Number 261 of the Council of Grand Justices. In this case, the Council was called on to determine whether the "Old Thieves" (legislators who had been elected on mainland China some forty years previously) could be forced to retire in 1990. This was certainly a watershed, but as I explore at length elsewhere (Ginsburg 2003), the decision cannot be seen as having been independently determined by judges. Rather, the Council served as part of Lee Teng-hui's faction within the KMT, helping reform to proceed over the objections of an intraparty obstacle. Judges were not the triggers.

Once democratization occurred, however, the courts played an absolutely crucial role as consolidator. As in Korea, lawyer-activists played an important role in the process, as a new generation sought to enact a liberal transformation through law. The internal motivations of courts themselves were also affected by generational change, as a new generation of Taiwanese judges rose in the judicial hierarchy.

At the apex of the judicial system, Taiwanization of personnel (meaning the rise of Taiwan-born justices to replace those born on the mainland) changed the internal motivation of the Council of Grand Justices. This top court systematically removed many of the barriers to participation set up by the KMT. The Court began a pattern of deciding cases against administrative agencies, using a nondelegation doctrine to require tighter links between a reinvigorated political process and administrative action. Leninist institutions that had been used to ensure ideological conformity of teachers and the media were cast aside as unconstitutional. The Council also instituted a total reform of criminal procedure, ensuring that police and prosecutors were henceforth under greater judicial scrutiny. After the "Przeworski moment" occurred and the presidency of the country shifted to the opposition Democratic Progressive Party (DPP) with the election of Chen Shui-bian in 2000, a period of divided government ensued, with the Council playing a key mediating role.

The expanded role for courts came to a head in the heated presidential election of 2004. The incumbent was Chen, a former activist lawyer. Similar to Korea's Roh Moo Hyun, he came from a poor background and was something of a political outsider; he had won election in 2000 with only 39 percent of the vote and, similar to Roh, had to govern without control of the legislature. His first term was marked by significant controversy and ineffectiveness, and polls predicted he would lose his bid for reelection. On March 19, 2004 – the day before the election – Chen and Vice President Annette Lu were shot while riding in an open jeep in Tainan City. The next day, they were elected by the razor-thin margin of 30,000 votes out of nearly

13 million cast.[6] The losing candidates charged that the shooting had been staged to elicit sympathy, and filed a suit the next day in the Taiwan High court challenging the election for legal irregularities. The High Court began to hear the case, and the political parties agreed to a recount under court auspices.

Meanwhile, competing investigations were launched to examine the shooting incident. The government set up its independent investigative committee in early July. The opposition-controlled legislature, however, thought this would not generate an accurate account, and passed a law on August 24 to set up a special seventeen-member "March 19 Shooting Truth-Finding Commission." The Commission members were to be nominated by political parties on the basis of proportional representation, and it was granted wide investigatory and prosecutorial powers.

On September 15, 2004, legislators from the DPP requested the Council of Grand Justices to enjoin the Truth Commission Act and provide an interpretation of its constitutionality, pursuant to provisions allowing any group of one-third of legislators to challenge acts as unconstitutional. In early November, the Taiwan High Court rejected the lawsuit, calling for nullification of the electee status of the president and vice president. The Court found that the recount had upheld Chen's victory, this time by a margin of 25,563 votes. Although this was a smaller margin than the figure announced by the Central Election Commission in March, the difference was not of a magnitude to affect the outcome, said the Court.

All eyes then turned to the constitutional case. On December 15, 2004, the Council of Grand Justices issued Interpretation Number 585, holding parts of the "Special March 19 Shooting Truth-Finding Commission Act" Unconstitutional. In particular, provisions granting the Commission the exclusive power to investigate the incident and Commission members full prosecutorial powers were seen to violate the constitutional separation of powers scheme.[7] Provisions setting aside the National Secrets Act and other generally applicable rules also did not pass constitutional muster. A provision purporting to allow the Commission to order a retrial of a final judicial decision on the case was held to violate rule-of-law principles. In short, the legislature was limited in its investigatory powers to those related to its own constitutional functions, and could not encroach on Executive or judicial powers.

At the very end of 2004, the Taiwan High Court rejected the suit, seeking to nullify the election results. The Executive investigation continued, eventually holding that the shooter was a disgruntled citizen who had suffered financial problems he attributed to Chen. Because he had committed suicide shortly after the shooting, no criminal prosecution went forward.

This series of cases placed the Taiwan courts at the very center of the political controversy surrounding the 2004 election. The courts ended up allowing Chen Shui-bian to retain office, a decision that was no doubt legally sound and also

---

[6] The referendum failed for lack of 50 percent of the electorate voting on it.
[7] Interpretation 585, Sec. 5.

deferential to public preferences. As in South Korea, however, the decision did not prevent Chen's popularity from continuing to plummet. A series of scandals implicated his wife and son, and he is currently appealing a life sentence for corruption. The Council, however, continued to remain a popular branch.

As a matter of judicial strategy, the Taiwan court system acquitted itself well in this series of events. They broke up a potential crisis into several discrete legal issues, to be decided by different courts using different procedures. The Council of Grand Justices turned an egregiously unconstitutional statute into an ongoing opportunity for constitutional dialogue by framing the issue as the general scope of legislative powers to conduct investigations. A crisis was averted, judicial power enhanced, and consolidation was furthered. As its counterpart in Korea, the Court was a consolidator.

The aftermath of the case has not seen a major shift in judicial role, but some concerns about judicial legitimacy emerged in 2010 with the discovery of some instances of judicial corruption. This led to the reinvigoration of debates over judicial reform, as members of the bar and others called for a more responsive, accountable, and independent judiciary. No doubt the courts' roles will evolve in response to these events.

Picking and Rejecting a Populist in Thailand, 2001 and 2008

Thailand's politics have been notoriously unstable, with a history of coups and short-lived civilian government. The country's overall stability, however, has been maintained by a stable bureaucratic structure. Consistent with many other civil-law jurisdictions, the judiciary was seen essentially as a bureaucratic structure. Judges saw themselves as technocrats, staying away from politics.

After a large set of demonstrations protesting one of the countries many coups, the Constitution of 1997 was a major effort to resolve the country's chronic political instabilities; it was the first time that a constitution was adopted with widespread public involvement. The Constitution included a plethora of independent agencies to oversee politics: the Electoral Commission, Audit Commission, Human Rights Commission, Ombudsman, Supreme Court, Supreme Administrative Court, Constitutional Court, and National Counter-Corruption Commission. A new Constitutional Court was a central institution in this scheme, as it was charged with policing the other independent bodies in addition to its role in interpreting the Constitution and resolving jurisdictional disputes among governmental authorities. Among other powers, it could confirm findings of and evaluate disclosures submitted to the National Counter-Corruption Commission (NCCC).

This power became crucial with the 2001 election bringing Thaksin Shinawatra to power, a billionaire-turned-politician. Described as Thailand's Berlusconi, Thaksin had little in the way of a substantive policy platform other than populist promises of wealth for the countryside. Similar to his Italian counterpart, he had long been linked with corruption. In early 2001, when Thaksin was still running, he was found by the NCCC to have filed a false asset report. After Thaksin's party subsequently won the elections, the Constitutional Court was put in a difficult position when it was called on to confirm the NCCC decision. The Court found that the false report had not been filed deliberately, and thereby allowed Thaksin to take the post of prime minister. As in South Korea, the Thai Court seemed to respond to democratic signals and found that the violation, however serious, did not justify overturning the election.

Thus began a long chapter that ultimately led to the Constitution's demise. Thaksin subsequently consolidated his hold on power, acquiring political parties by merger and acquisition. Gradually, he began to influence all the independent institutions, including the very ones designed to oversee corruption, as well as the Constitutional Court itself. He did this through a combination of appointments, intimidation, and bribery. The independent NCCC, which refused to acquiesce to Thaksin's demands, was disbanded and new appointments left in limbo. In early 2005, Thaksin won reelection when his Thai Rak Thai Party captured an overwhelming majority of parliamentary seats, making it impossible for the opposition to mount a vote of no confidence. Soon thereafter, mass protests erupted in the wake of Thaksin's manipulation of law to allow the tax-free sale of his company, and Thaksin was investigated for corruption. Because the NCCC was not operative, the case went to the Constitutional Court. The Court's pro-Thaksin reputation seemed confirmed when it found that there was no justiciable case.

With no help from any political institutions, anti-Thaksin members of the public began to demonstrate in the streets, calling for his resignation or impeachment. Thaksin then dissolved Parliament and called a snap election for April 2, 2006, but the opposition chose to boycott it, saying Thaksin should step down first. The election went ahead anyway. Thaksin's party won 80 percent of the seats, running unopposed in many districts. However, a series of irregularities led the Election Commission to set aside the election, and Thaksin continued in office only as a caretaker. Shortly thereafter, the king met with the leaders of the Constitutional, Supreme, and Administrative Courts and publicly called for them to resolve the problem. However, it was unclear exactly what sort of judicial resolution was possible, with demonstrators on the streets both in support of and against Thaksin.

The Constitutional Court responded by annulling the April election, and three election commissioners were jailed on the grounds that the time allowed for the election campaign had been too brief and that some polling booths had been positioned to allow others to view the ballots as they were cast. Five new election commissioners, who had just been chosen after months of deadlock, would be replaced. Nevertheless, with the Senate and other political institutions at a standstill, the appointment process could hardly operate. The Constitutional Court had failed to resolve the problem completely.

A few months later, before a new vote could be held in November, the military staged a bloodless coup and abolished the 1997 Constitution. An Interim Constitution disbanded the Constitutional Court, although many of the other guardian institutions were able to continue to function. The power of judicial review was transferred to a new Constitutional Committee, consisting of the Chair of the Supreme Court and the Chair of the Administrative Court, along with five justices of the Supreme Court elected by their colleagues. No doubt this reflects disappointment in the Constitutional Court that had allowed Thaksin to take power in the first place and later seemed to serve his interests.

The Interim Constitution also outlined a process for constitutional reform and, in August 2007, a referendum approved the country's eighteenth Constitution, bringing the first chapter to a close. When subsequent elections returned Thaksin's new party to power, even as he was in exile, a new round of electoral disputes broke out, requiring intervention by the Electoral Commission and a new Constitutional Court. Competing street protests ensued. In September 2008, the Court was called on to decide if the new leader, Thaksin's handpicked successor Prime Minister Samak Sundaravej, had to leave office because of a paid appearance on a television cooking show in violation of the Constitution. Again faced with a de minimis legal violation, this time the Court sided against the electoral majority and in favor of the opposition anti-Thaksin forces, who had supported the coup d'état.

The Thai story involves two different key junctures. In the first, the Court deferred to a democratic majority to allow Thaksin to take power despite his corruption. The Court was playing the role of democratic consolidator, allowing a popular leader to take power. In contrast with the Taiwan and South Korean examples, the person the court delivered power to was neither democratic nor ineffective. He methodically undermined the country's independent institutions, including the Constitutional Court itself, so that it was not in a position to deliver benefits to the opposition or Thaksin. However, the risk taking that had earned Thaksin a fortune led him to step over the line, provoking demonstrations and political crisis. This led the king to call on the Constitutional Court to resolve the problem, but it was unable to, and was itself disbanded after the 2006 coup.

The second juncture took place in 2008 under the new Constitution drafted under military rule. This time, the Court appeared to be playing the role of downstream guarantor for the coup makers and their political allies. It appeared to be completely willing to constrain the new forces around Thaksin. This case suggests a generalizable hypothesis: consolidator courts that are subjected to democratic reversal may play the more cautious role of guarantor in the next iteration of democracy.

Triggering Democracy in Pakistan, 2007

In March 2007, Pakistan's General Pervez Musharraf attempted to suspend the chief justice of the Supreme Court, Iftikhar Mohammad Chaudhry for "abuse of power and nepotism." Analysts tied the decision to Chaudhry's resistance to the establishment of military rule in the restive North-West Frontier Province and the willingness of courts to take cases involving disappearances affected by the military. The courts had gradually enhanced their power (Ghias 2008). The timing was also related to a series of cases in which Musharraf's rule was challenged in courts. Pakistan's courts have a long history of dealing with the legality of exceptional rule, generally being supportive but also trying to limit the temporal duration of states of emergency (Mahmud 1993; Newberg 1995).

Justice Chaudhry responded by resisting the attack and framing it as directed against the judiciary as a whole (Sanchez Urribarri 2007). The attack prompted broad demonstrations from the bar, which took to the streets to protest the decision and was joined by a broad coalition of supporters of the civilian political parties. The legal complex was mobilized. The legal controversy ended in the courts, and featured the remarkable spectacle of the Supreme Court reinstating Chaudhry on the grounds that his dismissal violated the law. No doubt this reflected the overall position of the courts in common-law Pakistan, however, it also marked a sharp departure from earlier incidents in which the courts blessed dictatorship. In terms of internal motivational factors in the courts, many ascribe the change to Chaudhry's leadership, suggesting contingency rather than structure.

Pressure continued to build on Musharraf's regime and he was forced to allow former Prime Minister Benazir Bhutto to return to the country through a combination of judicial decision and pressure from his most important ally, the United States. The Supreme Court found that Ms. Bhutto and Former Prime Minister Nawaz Sharif had, as citizens, an inalienable right to return to the country. Sharif, however, who had been in exile in Saudi Arabia after fleeing corruption charges, was not permitted to reenter the country until mid-November.[8]

Musharraf then announced that he would run for office. This seemed a facial violation of the Constitution, which prohibits the president from holding any other position[9] and requires military officers to take an oath not to engage in politics.[10] In late September, however, the Court surprised observers by holding that Musharraf himself could run for office, by a vote of 6:3. This decision prompted protests from the bar association. Without getting into the legal merits of the decision, the effect was certainly to signal to Musharraf that the Court was not inexorably opposed to him. The Court appeared to be avoiding a crucial mistake of the Thai Court – consistently siding with only one side in a deeply divided political scene. The decision seemed to suggest that the role of the court was not to pick winners and losers, but to structure, to the extent possible, a fair contest for leadership of the country. Before Musharraf was reelected by the Parliament, however, the Court announced that it would hear

---

[8] "Home and Away," *The Economist*, September 15, 2007, pp. 31–33.
[9] Constitution of Pakistan 1973, Art. 43.
[10] Constitution of Pakistan 1973, Art. 244; Third Schedule.

a new constitutional challenge and announce whether the election was valid after the fact. The Court reasserted its role as the final arbiter.

On November 3, 2007, before the Supreme Court could rule, Musharraf declared a state of emergency, and arrested thousands of activists, lawyers, and political party workers. Taking a page from his American counterparts, he decried judicial activism and terrorism in the same breath. Bhutto and other political leaders were put under house arrest; a Provisional Constitutional Order (PCO) was issued prohibiting any court issuing an order against the president, prime minister, or any person exercising powers under their authority. The PCO further put the Constitution in abeyance, saying that the country would be governed "as nearly as may be by the Constitution."[11] Only the five Supreme Court justices who took an oath to uphold the PCO would be allowed to remain; the other twelve were placed under house arrest, along with a number of Provincial High Court justices. Chaudhry called for resistance, from his house arrest (Ghias 2008).

Musharraf was eventually forced to resign his military post through the intervention of the United States. After Bhutto's December assassination, elections returned a coalition of civilian parties to office. Despite campaigning on a promise to restore the judges to the Supreme Court, the civilians dithered, largely because of tensions between the judiciary and Pakistan People's Party leadership (chiefly Bhutto's widower, President Zardari), and it took another round of struggle before the judiciary was fully restored. In the end, however, the judiciary emerged with significantly enhanced status.

The story of Pakistan's courts thus involves shifting judicial roles. Historically, courts had blessed and rationalized authoritarian rule in Pakistan. Although the basic structural conditions of Pakistan's courts and lawyers were not fundamentally different in the early twenty-first century than in earlier rounds of dictatorship, there was a slightly different international environment, and different leadership in the person of Chief Justice Chaudhry. This changed the internal motivation of the courts, leading them to play – for the first time – a triggering role for democracy leading to a new equilibrium of enhanced judicial power. Perhaps the major lesson to be drawn from this case study is the important and contingent role of judicial leadership in helping the courts navigate political junctures and evolving roles.

Pakistan's key juncture may well be viewed by historians as having been at the very center of the return to democracy. However, the drama reminds us that seeking a place in history is fraught with danger for courts as institutions. The Supreme Court itself has suffered, although as of this writing it is again engaged in high-profile disputes with the government and army. Courts need allies, and sometimes from unexpected places. The domestic legal complex was not enough to mobilize a popular movement to overthrow Musharraf, and outside intervention was the decisive factor in democratization. All that said, however, Pakistan seems to be a

---

[11] Provisional Constitutional Order No. 1 (2007) Art. 2.1.

case of an upstream trigger, and serves as somewhat of a caution to other courts considering this risky role.

LEGACIES AND ROLES

In each case described in this chapter, courts had developed some sort of established role in the political system, and then were confronted with pressure to play a new, very central role: picking a leader in a highly contested situation. These cases also involved varying roles in terms of democratization. We observed two (and a half) cases of a court playing a consolidation-type role (Korea and Taiwan, with Thailand 1997–2006 also falling into this category), one case where the court served as a trigger (Pakistan), and one in which the Court appeared to be a guarantor (Thailand after the 2006 coup).

We have focused on how these cases affected democratization, but what were the effects on the judicial roles that are the focus of this volume? Do the four cases tell us anything about the conditions under which we might see different roles being played, particularly in situations of picking leaders? I do not seek here to articulate a complete theory, and my sense is that individual trajectories will be determined in large part through the skill and choices of judges themselves, as well as the inclinations of other political actors. That is, there is a significant role for judicial agency in accounting for variation across cases. Nevertheless, I can offer some speculative thoughts.

First, consider the authoritarian legacy. In our four cases, judiciaries in general had a relative degree of autonomy in the authoritarian period. However, two of our cases (Korea and Thailand) involved Constitutional Courts that had not existed in the initial authoritarian period and were products of the new democratic constitutional scheme. Instead of giving constitutional jurisdiction to the ordinary Supreme Court, both new democracies created new courts. Neither new court played a role as a guarantor. In neither case, in other words, was judicial empowerment associated with hegemonic preservation (cf. Hirschl 2004). The insurance argument works better in the Korean context, in which the Court was part of a constitutional agreement among three parties of equal strength. However, the courts were not agents of the past: when presented with cases to choose leaders, both courts chose to issue majoritarian decisions that overlooked technical violations of the law to reflect recent electoral results.

The outcomes in terms of judicial role, however, were quite different across these two cases. The Korean Court, very similar to the Taiwanese Grand Justices, has seen its role steadily grow, even as it moves from a phase of democratic consolidation to more conventional protection of constitutional democracy. At no time after democratization was well along did the role dramatically change. The Thai case, on the other hand, illustrates how picking the leader can lead to crises that force a shift in the judicial role. The court initially attempted to facilitate consolidation by allowing the newly minted majority of Thaksin Shinawatra to take over. It subsequently sought to balance various political forces and encourage constitutional dialogues. For reasons largely beyond the Court's control, the country's political institutions gridlocked, and the Court died in the 2006 coup. The new Constitutional Court that was established in 2007 has played a more aggressive role in constraining elected institutions on behalf of the more conservative urban elite, a shift from democratic consolidation to downstream guarantor. The suggestion is that the proximity of the disbanding of the first court led the second court to be more cautious. A shock to the system, in other words, can lead to a reformulation of judicial roles.

Pakistan's own long history of judges constraining power at the margin but giving sanction to states of emergency seems to have drawn to a close in the most recent iterations of government-court conflict. Judges seem to have sought to play a triggering role, and were ultimately successful. Their stature certainly emerged greatly enhanced through the sequence of events discussed here, although it remains too early to predict whether their enhanced legitimacy represents even a temporary equilibrium.

CONCLUSION

This essay has provided a framework for thinking about the political role of courts and law in democratization, through the lens of four cases involving choosing leaders. These cases seem fraught with danger for courts, as they risked alienating major political forces, and a major technique of judicial craft – namely issuing mediate decisions – is not always available.

The cases indicate that successful approaches depend on the broader role of courts in the political system. In autocratic settings, courts may on occasion seek to trigger a democratic tipping, but this is a dangerous course that rarely succeeds. Once democracy is relatively entrenched, the successful courts combined sensitivity to majoritarian pressures, with an ability to transform the dispute from one about personnel into one of principle. Serving as an agent for one of the parties, as in the hegemonic preservation model and Thai examples, does not seem to be a successful strategy, at least not in a period of pressure on the constitutional bargain. Although the particular role of courts must of course depend ultimately on the decisions of individual judges, the ultimate conclusion is a modest one: courts seem to play an important but second-order role in democratization.

REFERENCES

Cho, Kuk. 1997. "Tension between the National Security Law and Constitutionalism in South Korea: Security for What?" *Boston University Law Review* 15: 125–65.
Couso, Javier. 2003. "The Politics of Judicial Review in Chile in the Era of Democratic Transition 1990–2002." *Democratization* 10(4): 70–91.

Ghias, Shoiab. 2008. "Miscarriage of Chief Justice: The Rise and Fall of Judicial Power in Pakistan." *Law and Social Inquiry* 35(4): 985–1022.

Ginsburg, Tom. 2003. *Judicial Review in New Democracies: Constitutional Courts in Asian Cases*. New York: Cambridge University Press.

Ginsburg, Tom. 2004. "Ancillary Powers of Constitutional Courts" in Tom Ginsburg and Robert Kagan, eds. *Institutions and Public Law: Comparative Approaches*, pp. 225–49. New York: Peter Lang Publishing.

Ginsburg, Tom and Tamir Moustafa, eds. 2008. *Rule By Law: The Politics of Courts in Authoritarian Regimes*. New York: Cambridge University Press.

Halliday, Terry et al. 2007. *Fighting for Freedom: Comparative Studies of the Legal Complex and Political Liberalism*, Oxford: Hart Publishing.

Handley, Paul. 2006. *The King Never Smiles: Thailand's Bhumibol Adulyadej*. New Haven: Yale University Press.

Hardin, Russell. 1989. "Why a Constitution?" In Bernard Grofman and Donald Wittman (eds.), The Federalist Papers and the New Institutionalism, pp. 100–20. New York: Agathon Press.

Helmke, Gretchen. 2004. *Courts under Constraints: Judges, Generals and Presidents in Argentina*. New York: Cambridge University Press.

Hilbink, Lisa. 2007. *The Politics of Judicial Apoliticism: Chile in Comparative Perspective*. New York: Cambridge University Press.

Hirschl, Ran. 2004. *Towards Juristocracy*. Cambridge: Harvard University Press.

Lee, Youngjae. 2005. "Law, Politics and Impeachment: The Impeachment of Roh Moo-Hyun from a Comparative Constitutional Perspective." *American Journal of Comparative Law* 53: 403–32.

Mahmud, Tayyab. 1993. "Praetorianism and Common Law in Post-Colonial Settings: Judicial Responses to Constitutional Breakdowns in Pakistan." *Utah Law Review* 1225–305.

Maravall, José María and Adam Przeworski. 2003. "Introduction," in *Democracy and the Rule of Law*, pp. 1–16. New York: Cambridge University Press.

Newberg, Paula. 1995. *Judging the State: Courts and Constitutional Politics in Pakistan*. New York: Cambridge University Press.

Ockey, James. 2007. "Thailand in 2006." *Asian Survey* 47:133–42 (Jan/Feb).

Pereira, Anthony W. 2005. *Political (In)Justice: Authoritarianism and the Rule of Law in Brazil, Chile and Argentina*. Pittsburgh: University of Pittsburgh Press.

Przeworski, Adam. 1991. *Democracy and the Market: Political and Economic Reforms in Eastern Europe and Latin America*. New York: Cambridge University Press.

Ramseyer, J. Mark and Eric Rasmusen. 2003. *Measuring Judicial Independence*. Chicago: University of Chicago Press.

Roy, Denny. 2003. *Taiwan: A Political History*. Ithaca: Cornell University Press.

Sanchez Urribarri, Raul. 2007. "News from the Comparative Realm." *Law and Courts Newsletter*, 11–13.

Schelling, Thomas. 1960. *The Strategy of Conflict*. Cambridge: Harvard University Press.

Shapiro, Martin, 1981. *Courts: A Comparative and Political Analysis*. Chicago: University of Chicago Press.

Silverstein, Gordon. 2008. "Singapore: The Exception that Proves Rules Matter" in Tom Ginsburg and Tamir Moustafa, eds. *Rule by Law: The Politics of Courts in Authoritarian Regimes*. New York: Cambridge University Press, 73–92.

Silverstein, Gordon. 2009. *Law's Allure: How Law Shapes, Constrains, Saves and Kills Politics*. New York: Cambridge University Press.

Toharia, Juan. 1975 "Judicial Independence in an Authoritarian Regime: The Case of Spain" *Law and Society Review* 9: 475–96.

Vanberg, Georg. 2004. *The Politics of Constitutional Review in Germany*. New York: Cambridge University Press

Weingast, Barry. 1997. "The Political Foundations of Democracy and the Rule of Law." *American Political Science Review* 91: 245–63.

2

Fragmentation? Defection? Legitimacy?
Explaining Judicial Roles in Post-Communist "Colored Revolutions"

*Alexei Trochev**

One of the key insights of research on comparative judicial politics is that judicial power moves in mysterious ways: strong courts sometimes fail to command the obedience of other political actors, and weak courts sometimes compel rulers to obey adverse rulings. Neither the trajectory nor destination of judicial power is set in stone: the de facto power of courts moves in a nonlinear fashion and shrinks as often as it expands (Chavez 2004; Vanberg 2005; Moustafa 2007; Trochev 2008; Staton 2010). As the editors remind us in the Introduction to this book, judges' internal motivations as well as the external influences on courts interact in complex ways, leading courts to play very different roles. Drawing on judicial experiences in resolving highly contested electoral disputes in three post-Soviet countries (unique occurrences in this region),[1] this chapter provides empirical evidence of this variation.

Georgia, Ukraine, and Kyrgyzstan are the only post-Soviet states that underwent "colored revolutions" – peaceful mass protests against fraudulent national elections that toppled incumbent presidents – between 2003 and 2005 (Wheatley 2005; Wilson 2005; Radnitz 2010). One factor that appears to be of central importance to these conflicts, but that so far has received little attention, is the differing role assumed by the courts in supporting these revolutions.[2] Unexpectedly, the political opposition – in addition to street protests – actively used litigation to expose electoral fraud.

* Associate Professor, School of Humanities and Social Sciences, Nazarbayev University, Kazakhstan. Author is grateful to the Social Science and Humanities Research Council of Canada for the financial support and to the Tinatin Tsereteli Institute of State and Law of Georgia's Academy of Sciences for the logistical support. The author thanks Aleksander Rusetsky, Anna Dolidze, Oksana Syroid, and Vasyl Hubarets for their insights and kind help.

[1] Although the Kazakhstan Constitutional Court canceled parliamentary election results in 1995 (Olcott 2010: 109–111) and the Yugoslav Constitutional Court canceled presidential election results in 2000 (Thompson and Kuntz 2004), these decisions were believed to be in favor of incumbent presidents Nazarbayev and Milosevic.

[2] For example, in their comparative analysis of these electoral breakthroughs, Bunce and Wolchik (2011: 115, 141) only note the importance of the judicial role in Ukraine, and do not explain it.

Unexpectedly, Supreme Courts – which are staffed with Soviet-era judges – canceled rigged elections, thus opening the way for a peaceful change of government. Also unexpectedly, the incoming governments did not embrace judicial independence, instead pressuring and eventually emasculating judiciaries, a move voters did not seem to resist.

Why and how did these Supreme Courts join the protesters and support the opposition? More generally, why would Soviet-era judges assume a role in electoral politics at key points during regime change – and challenge the rulers? Under what conditions do judges in incomplete autocracies deal crushing blows to authoritarian presidents during national elections – events incumbents try to use to solidify their rule? Why are such judge-made outcomes often short-lived in such contexts?

To address these questions, this chapter begins by theorizing the conditions that enable antigovernment judicial behavior and argues that more fragmented autocracies may allow judicial roles to be played more boldly. It then explores the range of strategies judges may use to rule against incumbent Executives and the functional roles judges play when they challenge the legality of elections in incomplete autocracies. It argues that although politics in these regimes may provide opportunities for judges to rule against the rulers at crucial moments, such rulings may neither reflect nor result in political leaders' broader acceptance of judicial power or expanded judicial roles. The chapter proceeds by summarizing the unexpected roles the Supreme Courts played in the colored revolutions in Georgia, Ukraine, and Kyrgyzstan between 2003 and 2005. It argues that by creatively mixing law and politics and building on the weakness of nondemocratic leaders, judges were able to prevent them from stealing elections. It concludes by assessing the effects of these risky and bold antigovernment judicial decisions. Although these moments of judicial courage were accepted by both outgoing and incoming governments in each country, they alone were not sufficient to expand and entrench judicial power. Landmark court rulings may have limited effects because ruling elites want no constraints on their rule, including those imposed by independent and assertive courts. In short, judicial boldness at regime change does not necessarily lead to expanded judicial power or independence, or to expanded judicial roles in governance in the new regimes. As Table 2.1 shows, judicial boldness in all three countries failed to improve judicial independence.

THREE CONDITIONS THAT MAY ENABLE JUDGES TO DECIDE CONTESTED ELECTIONS IN SEMI-AUTHORITARIAN REGIMES

Under what conditions do seemingly dependent judges rule against authoritarian leaders? The political and legal conditions that enable judges to rule against the rulers in authoritarian and semi-authoritarian regimes – regimes that persist despite the third wave of democratization (Magaloni and Krichelli 2010) – have received greater attention in recent years, as students of comparative politics have increasingly

TABLE 2.1. *Judicial framework and independence in Georgia, Kyrgyzstan, and Ukraine, 2000–2011*

	2000	2001	2002	2003	2004	2005	2006	2007	2008	2009	2010	2011	2012
GEO	4	4	4.25	**4.5**	4.5	5	4.75	4.75	4.75	4.75	4.75	5	5
KYR	5	5.25	5.25	5.5	5.5	**5.5**	5.5	5.5	6	6	6	6.25	6.25
UKR	4.5	4.5	4.75	4.5	**4.75**	4.25	4.25	4.5	4.75	5	5	5.5	6

Source: Freedom House (2012). The ratings are based on a scale of 1 to 7, with 1 representing the highest level of judicial independence and 7 the lowest. Ratings in bold are for the years in which supreme courts canceled fraudulent elections.

explored the power of various institutions, including courts, which were assumed to shape politics and policies (Levitsky and Murillo 2009). I outline three conditions here: political fragmentation; elections (at least semi-competitive ones) and constitutionally defined barriers against nondemocratic rule (e.g., accessible judicial review); and judicial jurisdiction in politically salient areas (which tends to be awarded when authoritarian Executives have multiple mechanisms to control the courts).

In seeking to address important questions about the role of courts in nondemocratic regimes, court watchers noted that opposition groups actively used law and courts to fight authoritarian Executives and succeeded in some cases (Newberg 1995; Widner 2001; Shambayati 2004; Helmke 2005; Moustafa 2007; Ginsburg and Moustafa 2008; Popova 2012). Without pretending to have found the key to unlock the black box of judicial power, scholars concluded that one of the crucial conditions that enabled the opposition to use law and courts as a weapon against incumbents was the fragmentation of the ruling regime as reflected in leaders' declining popularity, growing divisions within the governing coalition, economic crises, civil wars, and so on. The inherently fragmented nature of incomplete autocracies allows courts to preserve some degree of judicial integrity and use their powers to challenge rulers and influence political change. In particular, fragmentation in these regimes allows judges to shield the judiciary's informal system of promoting and sanctioning judges from interference by authoritarian rulers, and defect from the ruling regime when they sense that the incumbents are too weak to punish them and incoming leaders are strong enough to protect them.

The fragmented nature of incomplete autocracy in Georgia (Jones 2006), Ukraine (Carothers 2002: 11), and Kyrgyzstan (Collins 2006) facilitated successful (colored) revolutions and the downfall of unpopular presidents (Kuzio 2005a; Way 2005; Areshidze 2007; Huskey 2007) who had failed to consolidate their power, prepare their successors, or maintain control over important segments of political and business elites, media, and security services.[3] As I show in this chapter, Georgian

[3] Political fragmentation is also exacerbated by the breakaway regions in Georgia, the East-West divide in Ukraine, and the North-South split in Kyrgyzstan.

President Shevardnadze, Ukrainian President Kuchma, and Kyrgyzstani President Akaev failed to fully control their judiciaries, which allowed Supreme Courts to cancel the results of national elections that these autocrats had attempted to steal. The level of judicial challenge, however, varied among the three countries. Kyrgyzstan had the smallest number of antigovernment judicial decisions, and only a handful of its judges displayed autonomy from President Akaev (BBC News 2000; Collins 2006: 183–184, 229–231). By contrast, Ukraine's President Kuchma repeatedly complained about judges issuing unfavorable rulings.[4]

Second, the existence of institutionalized sites of contestation, such as regularly held elections and courts, provided an opportunity both for the opposition to demonstrate these regimes' weaknesses and for the rulers to legitimize their regime. The fact that Georgia, Ukraine, and Kyrgyzstan held elections regularly after the fall of the Soviet Union – and that opposition candidates were allowed to run for office and complain to courts against violations of electoral law – shows that having constitutionally defined barriers against nondemocratic rule is another condition that enables judges to rule against the rulers. To be sure, these barriers both have to be stronger than the paper on which they are written and be activated by the opposition. They may also matter less when authoritarian leaders are able to define them and manipulate them in their favor by rigging elections and creating obstacles for the opposition to compete in them and survive between them (Brownlee 2009; Gandhi and Lust-Oskar 2009; Levitsky and Way 2010).

By the time of their colored revolutions, Georgia, Ukraine, and Kyrgyzstan each had long-serving presidents: Shevardnadze had headed Georgia since March 1992; ex-Prime Minister Kuchma had won Ukraine's presidential elections twice in 1994 and 1999; and President Akaev had ruled Kyrgyzstan since 1990 and showed no signs of leaving the office to anyone other than his relatives. However, all three countries are invariably counted in the global wave of judicial empowerment (Ginsburg 2003: 7–8). All three ratified constitutional bills of rights, enshrined standard safeguards of judicial independence in their constitutions, and activated Constitutional Courts in the mid-1990s (Trochev 2008: 3). All three countries kept Supreme Courts from the time of the USSR in place (although Georgia and Kyrgyzstan passed new laws on the Supreme Court in the spring of 1999), and none purged the Soviet-era judiciary. These top courts, created and reformed by authoritarian presidents who had already consolidated their power, rarely disagreed with powerful Executives.

Finally, the third condition that gives courts a chance to exercise real power is having jurisdiction in politically salient areas, and over electoral disputes in particular. Without such jurisdiction, judges do not have a chance to intervene in heavyweight politics. In theory, authoritarian leaders can keep jurisdiction over electoral

---

4 According to Kuchma, then-Supreme Court Chief Justice Vitalii Boyko was an "underhanded bastard" who needed to be dealt with, and local judge Aleksandr Tupitskii in Donetsk (home base of Kuchma's anointed successor, Viktor Yanukovych) should be hung "by the [expletive] for one night" just for ordering Kuchma to testify as the victim in a libel case (Wilson 2005: 57, 147).

disputes to themselves or grant it to the handpicked Central Election Commission. In practice, rulers use delegating the authority to resolve electoral disputes to the judiciary as a mechanism to enhance their legitimacy and demand judicial loyalty in return. By securing the judicial stamp of approval on elections, authoritarian rulers demonstrate that the opposition's complaints about electoral outcomes are groundless and elections were lawful. Autocrats know that they can score points at home and abroad when they expand jurisdiction of the judicial branch and praise judicial authority. Autocrats have plenty of tools and resources to ensure that judges are on their side. In the countries under study, as the political battle between the increasingly unpopular authorities and the opposition intensified, the pressure on courts became more blatant (Civil.GE 2003a; Popova 2012; ABA CEELI 2004). At the same time, presidents in these countries raised judicial salaries and appointed trusted persons to head the top courts, believing that they would control the judiciary in the same way that generals control an army.

Authoritarian Executives delegated the power to review election results to courts in each of the three countries under study because they planned on courts being neither veto points nor window dressing, but instead tame and resilient workhorses in legitimating their rule (Schedler 2010: 71). These rulers knew that they (not judges) ultimately controlled whether judicial decisions were implemented, in case judges unexpectedly issued unfavorable judgments (Trochev 2008). They knew that they could punish recalcitrant judges and face no retribution for doing so. They also knew that their judiciary could perform miracles for them like a genie that has been let out of the bottle (ruling against political opponents, banning them from running in elections, shutting down recalcitrant media outlets, etc.). However, the autocrats were also confident that they could put the judicial genie back in the bottle when it was no longer needed (Nodia 2005: 42–43). Just as importantly, if the genie tried to resist, they had enough tools to discipline it (Moustafa and Ginsburg 2008).

In Georgia, the Justice Council in charge of recruiting judges and enforcing judicial discipline was a part of the presidential administration. In June 1999, four months prior to legislative elections, President Shevardnadze nominated and the Georgian parliament unanimously confirmed a new Supreme Court Chair, Lado Chanturia. The Supreme Court was authorized to review the legality of administrative actions, including decisions of the Central Election Commission (CEC). In July 2001, following his 2000 reelection, Shevardnadze appointed his parliamentary secretary, Joni Khetsuriani, to the Constitutional Court, and he quickly became its chief justice. Under Article 89 (d) of the 1995 Constitution, the Constitutional Court had the power to resolve disputes arising with the constitutionality of elections.

Concerning Executive tools to discipline courts in Ukraine, in February 2002 – seven weeks before parliamentary elections – President Kuchma grabbed the power to create courts, define their size, and appoint their chairs and vice-chairs (i.e., chief justices), except for the Supreme and Constitutional Court. In November 2002, after a massive PR campaign and Kuchma's promises to double judicial salaries, the eighty-two–member Supreme Court elected (with forty-nine votes) Vasyl Malyarenko as its chief justice, Kuchma's pick for the post. Secretly recorded conversations of Kuchma revealed that Malyarenko was on much better terms with him than was outgoing Chief Justice Boyko (Kyiv Post 2002). As in Georgia, the Supreme Court was the trial-level court in lawsuits against decisions of the CEC. Kuchma's cronies, Serhiy Kivalov and Viktor Medvedchuk, held a tight grip over the Ukrainian High Council of Justice, the body in charge of selecting and disciplining judges, and masterminded the rigging of the 2004 presidential elections. Since its activation in 1996, the Ukrainian Constitutional Court grew increasingly loyal to President Kuchma and "became instrumental in eroding legislative power and shifting it to the executive" (Wolczuk 2002: 328). For example, this tribunal approved most constitutional amendments sponsored by Kuchma and allowed him to run for a third term in office despite the constitutional two-term limit (Kuchma chose not to run) (Wolczuk 2001: 258–260, 273–277; D'Anieri 2007: 90–91, 95).

Finally, Kyrgyzstani President Akaev's pattern of controlling the courts was more blatant than in Georgia or Ukraine (ABA CEELI 2004). Unlike Shevardnadze and Kuchma, he did not allow for any meaningful judicial self-governance, and reshuffled local judges and Supreme Court Chief Justices in the same way as he reshuffled government ministers. As a result, during Akaev's fourteen years in office, the Kyrgyzstan Supreme Court – which has the power to resolve elections disputes – was headed by five chief justices. In January 2004 – a year before the fraudulent parliamentary elections that triggered the Tulip Revolution and Akaev's downfall – the Kyrgyzstan Parliament appointed Akaev's nominee, Deputy Prime Minister Kurmanbek Osmonov (who, similar to his predecessors, was widely believed to be in Akaev's pocket [RFE/RL 2004a]), to head the nation's Supreme Court. In contrast, the same person, Cholpon Baekova, who was connected to Akaev by kin, headed the Constitutional Court (which can review the constitutionality of Supreme Court's decisions) throughout Akaev's presidency and well beyond his ouster. Similar to Ukraine, in 1998, the Constitutional Court allowed Akaev to run for a third term in office despite the constitutional two-term limit: Akaev was reelected in 2000 in a vote marred by fraud. In September 2004, this Court ruled that it was up to the parliament to decide whether Akaev could run again in the 2005 presidential elections. Prior to the Tulip Revolution, this tribunal displayed no signs of "strategic" defection, although Akaev's regime had been steadily losing its support at home and abroad (Collins 2006: 231).

In short, three conditions – failing to tame the political opposition (which manifests itself in fragmentation), allowing the opposition to compete in regular elections and complain to courts, and granting courts the power to review the conduct of election officials – appear to be necessary for judges to rule against incumbents during highly contested and fraudulent elections. Facing these conditions, judges may choose to expose electoral fraud or condone it either explicitly or quietly. How and why did the Supreme Courts in Georgia, Ukraine, and Kyrgyzstan choose the extreme and untested route of canceling the results of rigged elections? The answer to this question requires careful examination of both judicial strategies and the roles judges sought to play when they chose, against all odds, to rule against powerful presidents at the most controversial moments. To be sure, these strategies are context specific, as judges on different courts in different countries face different kinds of pressures, have different loyalties to the regime, and experience different intra-court dynamics.

JUDGING CONTESTED ELECTIONS IN SEMI-AUTHORITARIAN REGIMES: JUDICIAL STRATEGIES AND ROLES

With the benefit of hindsight, we now know that authoritarian leaders may miscalculate. They may overestimate their own capacity to keep judges (and other elements of the ruling regime) in line and the strength of the opposition and its ability to mobilize street protesters and attract elements of the ruling regime. By exploiting the miscalculations and weakness of nondemocratic Executives, and by creatively mixing law and politics, Supreme Court judges in Georgia, Ukraine, and Kyrgyzstan did not let authoritarian presidents steal elections. Unexpectedly, these judges chose to switch sides and play three important roles: resolving crucial election disputes; monitoring election officials and exposing massive vote fraud; and resolving deadlocks during regime change. Was this a display of genuine judicial independence that could potentially lead to fairer elections and more accountable government?

The answer is yes, according to the opposition groups that were victorious in these disputes, and the judges themselves. Opposition groups argued that they had a strong case: they had obeyed electoral law; collected evidence of vote fraud; and sued the authorities for violations of their electoral rights. Supreme Court Judges likewise claimed that they had simply followed the law: they heard both sides of the electoral dispute; examined the evidence; applied preexisting electoral laws; determined numerous elections irregularities; and consequently overturned election results. This, however, does not answer the question of why judges switched sides and followed the law at these moments and not others. As we shall see, judges did so in part because they found a way to engage in creative decision making that went well beyond the letter of law.

Another more cynical answer, preferred by the losers of the colored revolutions, is that judges were prepared to defect to the opposition once they realized that the incumbent regime was losing power. Arguably, Argentinean judges often "strategically" defected this way, even before the incumbents actually lost their power (Helmke 2005). According to this view, canceling the results of rigged elections reflects continued judicial dependency: it has nothing to do with law and everything to do with the balance of power between the rulers and the opposition.[5] The stronger

---

[5] On the crucial importance of the distribution of power between the rulers and the opposition, see McFaul (2002).

the opposition, the more likely judges are to abandon the incumbent regime. However, as I have argued, the top courts in Georgia, Ukraine, and Kyrgyzstan grew increasingly loyal to authoritarian rulers precisely when the popularity of the latter began to crumble. There were no signs of strategic defection by judges and no signs of them strategically currying favor with the opposition. Whenever there were judicial decisions inconvenient to Shevardnadze, Kuchma, or Akaev, their top courts intervened and reversed them and tried their best to punish recalcitrant judges.

Rather than defecting to an increasingly popular opposition gradually as in the Argentine case, Supreme Courts in Georgia, Ukraine, and Kyrgyzstan defected "on the spot" through the creative use of legal resources. The courts in all three countries were able to use this strategy precisely because they had not engaged in strategic defection and were thus trusted by the rulers to hand down verdicts against the opposition. Judges preferred to use this strategy in all three countries because incumbent presidents – although widely unpopular[6] – retained sufficient resources to punish recalcitrant judges. The unwillingness of the Constitutional Courts to intervene in these electoral breakthroughs shows that many judges chose to play it safe and wait and see who would win in these rigged, chaotic (and in Kyrgyzstan, violent) elections.

Defecting judges may deliver tangible benefits to the opposition that it should consider helpful to its cause of overthrowing the ancien régime. However, judicial invalidation of election results or mandated recounting of ballots may not help the opposition if it allows the status quo to continue: incumbents (unless they fled the country) remain in office and retain control of scheduling new vote or recounting ballots. As I will explain, because of the presence of the three conditions outlined, Ukraine's judges delivered the most benefits to the opposition; Kyrgyzstan's judges delivered the fewest.

Judicial Roles in Georgia's 2003 Rose Revolution: Exposing Vote Fraud

Georgia's parliamentary elections were held on November 2, 2003. Seventy-five legislative seats were contested in single-member districts and 150 seats were to be allocated according to party lists on a proportional basis.[7] Then-U.S. Ambassador to Georgia Richard Miles called the vote "a mess from start to finish" (Areshidze 2007: 149). The U.S.-based National Democratic Institute together with the Georgian NGO International Society for Fair Elections and Democracy (ISFED) quickly produced parallel vote tabulations, announcing that six electoral blocs had gained parliamentary representation; the National Movement, a party led by the

---

[6] President Shevardnadze (Georgia) and President Kuchma (Ukraine) enjoyed the same (13%) approval ratings several months prior to fraudulent elections. This is why I treat their lack of popularity as constant.

[7] At the time, the Georgian Parliament consisted of 235 seats with 10 seats reserved to the secessionist regions of Abkhazia and South Ossetia, neither of which Georgia controlled.

head of the Tbilisi City Council Mikheil Saakashvili, had gained 26 percent of the vote; and pro-government blocs had received 27 percent of the vote. Saakashvili called his supporters to the streets to allege that the elections had been rigged and demand the resignation of President Shevardnadze. The CEC announced the official election results only on November 20, the last day of vote counting as allowed by the election code: pro-government blocs received 40 percent of the vote and Saakashvili's National Movement 19 percent (Areshidze 2007: 153–170).

Throughout this "vote-counting" period and the whole election campaign, the ISFED actively used courts to fight against electoral violations. Prior to the election, courts heard more than fifty election-related complaints concerning changes to the composition of precinct election commissions, inaccuracies in voter lists, reinstatement of de-registered opposition candidates, and so on (OSCE/ODIHR 2004a: 14; Georgian Times 2003: 6). The judiciary was extremely active in hearing election disputes, sometimes working well into the night to meet tight deadlines (OSCE/ODIHR 2003: 7). These legal battles in the local courts produced mixed results. In some cases the courts took bold decisions and ruled against the government (Caucasian Knot 2003; Civil.Ge 2003b). In other cases, they deferred to the CEC or declined to consider cases on the merits (OSCE/ODIHR 2003: 7; International Crisis Group 2003: 10). As of November 18, there were more than three dozen cases pending before various courts contesting election results in single-member districts (Areshidze 2007: 168). Although the ISFED insisted that legal battles were more effective than street protests, it did not expect the courts to annul election results because "neither the Constitution nor election law" gave them the power to do so (Hedges 2003: 5).

On the evening of November 21, a day after the CEC announced the election results, the ISFED asked the Supreme Court to order a recount of the ballots cast for 150 seats under the proportional system. The Court accepted the complaint, and the judge-reporter (who prepares the case and drafts the decision) informed the CEC about the lawsuit. CEC officials told the judge that the recount was impossible because of the disorderly tabulation of the voting protocols coming from the electoral precincts and the CEC's falsified calculations. On visiting the CEC offices, the judge-reporter saw that they were full of voting protocols piled up in a chaotic manner in addition to opened bags with voters' ballots. The judge scheduled a hearing on the case for November 24 and announced that it would be heard by a three-judge panel.[8] The election code gave the Supreme Court five days to issue its decision.

However, neither President Shevardnadze nor Saakashvili (the former justice minister who led the party that had gained the most votes) waited for the Supreme Court's decision. The next day – November 22 – was the last day of the twenty-day post-election period within which the Constitution (Art. 51) required the first sitting of the newly elected Parliament, the final step required to recognize its authority. Using the Constitution's silence on whether this session had to await any judicial decisions on electoral irregularities – and choosing not to condemn the alleged election fraud (which might have disarmed the protesters) – Shevardnadze attempted to convene the new parliament. In response, Saakashvili led the protesters, holding red roses, into the parliament building, disrupting the session (Eurasianet 2003; Fairbanks 2004: 116; Areshidze 2007: 175–180).

Shevardnadze's bodyguards whisked him to his residence outside Tbilisi; Saakashvili's supporters roamed the Parliament building and stormed other government buildings. They faced almost no resistance, as many of Shevardnadze's ministers and advisers had resigned and joined the opposition a few days earlier (Eurasianet 2003). After intense negotiations mediated by Supreme Court Chief Justice Lado Chanturia and the Russian Foreign Minister Igor Ivanov, President Shevardnadze resigned the following day, completing the Rose Revolution (or coup d'état).

On November 24, after opposition leader Saakashvili's team took over the actual power in the country, the Supreme Court heard the case concerning the election results. At the start of the hearing, the plaintiff (ISFED) changed its complaint and asked the Supreme Court to cancel the results of the elections for the 150 seats allocated under the proportional system, rather than simply order a ballot recount. Clearly, this new demand was motivated by the opposition's desire to hold new parliamentary elections for these seats in conjunction with new presidential elections, which had to be held within forty-five days of Shevardnadze's resignation according to the Constitution (Art. 76). At the trial, CEC officials admitted numerous electoral violations and accepted all charges against the CEC. The next day, the Supreme Court canceled the results of the elections for the 150 seats allocated under the proportional system, reasoning that the widespread fraud committed by election officials at all levels made it impossible to recount the ballots or determine the will of the people.[9] However, the Court did not say anything on the legality of the remaining seventy-five legislative seats contested in head-to-head races, because ISFED had not asked the Court to cancel the elections for these seats. Chief Justice Chanturia, who did not take part in the hearing, repeatedly asserted that his Court acted according to law and had the right to review actions and decisions of the high government bodies, and that the Rose Revolution was constitutional (Baiandurlu 2004).

The Georgian Constitutional Court – by contrast – did not switch sides, probably because justices remained loyal to Shevardnadze and viewed the Rose Revolution

---

[9] Specifically, the judges compared the data from the protocols of nine randomly selected district electoral commissions with the figures in the nationwide CEC protocol, found numerous discrepancies, concluded that the CEC had violated electoral law, and invalidated the CEC protocol of election results. Decision of the Supreme Court of Georgia No. B-11–36-54–03 of November 25, 2003 (on file with author).

as a coup d'état. On November 27, a group of more than eighty MPs, fearing that the Supreme Court lacked the power to cancel elections results,[10] petitioned the Constitutional Court to rule the results of the 2003 elections unconstitutional (OSCE/ODIHR 2004a: 21). The Constitutional Court found that the complaint did not satisfy technical requirements and gave the plaintiffs three days to correct their petition. On December 1, the complaint was resubmitted, but the Court found the petition inadmissible because its signatories had fallen below the required number (forty-seven) of MPs.[11] Interim President Nino Burjanadze chose not to bring a case, and as a result the results of the single-member elections stood, although many believed that these elections had also been rigged.[12] In fact, the newly constituted CEC certified those elections, allowing the newly elected MPs from those districts to retain seats in the new parliament (OSCE/ODIHR 2004a: 22).

Whereas international observers hailed the Supreme Court's boldness, domestic politicians criticized it. Ironically, it was the opponents of the outgoing president, rather than pro-Shevardnadze groups, who blasted the Supreme Court. A left-wing Labor Party leader charged that the Court had overstepped its authority (Chikhladze 2003). By contrast, Mikheil Saakashvili – who won the January 2004 presidential elections with 96 percent of the vote – openly accused the Court of doing too little: judges should have canceled the election results for all 225 parliamentary seats, not just the ones from the party lists (RFE/RL 2004b). These accusations may have prompted the prediction made by one judge: "I don't think the Supreme Court will issue such a decision ever again!"

To sum up, fragmentation and competitive elections and judicial review of election results made the Georgian Supreme Court's partial cancelation of the 2003 election results possible. It was as legal as the Rose Revolution. The Court exposed electoral fraud and annulled the results of rigged parliamentary elections only after it became clear that the opposition had won. Prior to the Rose Revolution, the opposition did not expect the Court to cancel election results wholesale and thus only called on it to order a ballot recount. However, following Shevardnadze's resignation and the transfer of power to Saakashvili's team, the opposition changed its legal claim, requesting that the Court cancel the election results, and faced no objections from CEC officials. The Court was no longer resolving a dispute, as both plaintiffs and defendants agreed on all counts. However, the Court's invalidation of the CEC's certification of the vote was the necessary legal formality to re-hold party-list elections. At the same time, the chief justice served as an intermediary

[10] Indeed, the Constitution (Article 89d) states that disputes over the constitutionality of elections fall into the exclusive jurisdiction of the Constitutional Court.

[11] Under Art. 89 of the Georgian Constitution, the constitutionality of elections can only be challenged by one-fifth of parliament (forty-seven MPs) or the president.

[12] According to a survey conducted immediately after the elections, 92% of Tbilisi residents believed the elections had been rigged and 68% favored the annulment of the results of the vote (Sumbadze and Tarkhan-Mouravi 2004).

between the rulers and the opposition during the revolution, reflecting his moral authority in the eyes of politicians and judges.

The new rulers of Georgia (Saakashvili won presidency with 96 percent of the vote, and his party won the party-list elections with 67 percent of the vote), however, made sure that the courts would not continue to intervene in politics. President Saakashvili – whose governing style reflected little tolerance for either accountability or anything inherited from the ancien régime – purged the Supreme Court, shrunk its size from forty-four to nineteen justices, forced Chief Justice Lado Chanturia into honorary exile in Germany, and transferred jurisdiction over electoral disputes to the Tbilisi Court of Appeals without the possibility of appeal to the Supreme Court. This lowered the visibility of complaints against electoral violations and helped the regime cover up vote fraud. In 2008, when Saakashvili was reelected with 53 percent of the vote and his party won parliamentary elections with 59 percent, only three out of ten Georgians believed that the elections were fair (Sumbadze 2009: 192). International election monitors criticized the courts in Saakashvili's Georgia for turning a blind eye on claims of irregularities in subsequent national and local elections (OSCE/ODIHR 2008a: 23–24, 29; 2008b: 19–22, 27–28; 2010: 23–24). Numerous experts noted that judicial involvement in protecting human rights remained "inadequate" or raised cause for concern (ABA ROLI 2009: 3; Freedom House 2012; Hammarberg 2011). The December 2009 survey commissioned by the United Nations Development Program (UNDP 2010) found that 73.2 percent of respondents said the government either fully or partially controlled the judiciary. With regard to elections or other sensitive issues, the courts ruled in a partisan manner under Saakashvili's one-party regime.

Judicial Roles in Ukraine's 2004 Orange Revolution: Deciding Election Disputes and Resolving High-Stakes Deadlocks

Ukraine's Orange Revolution took place a year after Georgia's Rose Revolution, and there is considerable evidence that both the authorities and the opposition in Ukraine learned a great deal from peaceful regime change in Tbilisi (Bunce and Wolchik 2011). On October 31, 2004, Ukraine held presidential elections, which outgoing president Kuchma had predicted would be its "dirtiest" (Kuzio 2005b: 30). The CEC announced that Viktor Yushchenko – a former prime minister and the leader of the opposition that used the color orange in its campaign – received 39.9 percent of the vote; then-Prime Minister Viktor Yanukovych – Kuchma's protégé – received 39.3 percent. As neither captured a majority (the threshold needed to win office), the two advanced to a runoff, scheduled for November 21. This second round was marred by blatant voter fraud, which received worldwide attention thanks to thousands of domestic and international election observers. On November 22, the CEC announced that – with 98 percent of the ballots counted – Yanukovych was leading the polls, and two days later officially declared him the winner with

49.5 percent of the vote against Yushchenko's 46.6 percent. By this time, Yushchenko had called for street protests – heeded by hundreds of thousands of Ukrainians (far more than in Georgia) – and taken a symbolic oath as the next Ukrainian president in the half-empty parliament building.

As in Georgia's Rose Revolution, courts were actively involved in election disputes. Both the opposition and the government resorted to courts to accuse each other of vote fraud throughout the campaign (Committee of Voters of Ukraine 2005). On the day of the first-round presidential election (October 31), judges heard 42,561 complaints concerning irregularities in voter lists (Korrespondent.net 2004a). Following the runoff, regional courts handled some 11,000 complaints about alleged vote fraud (BBC News 2004; Guardian 2004). Similar to Georgia, the results of these court battles were mixed. On the one hand, several regional courts reinstated representatives of the opposition to local election commissions, corrected voter lists, made it easier for Ukrainians living in the West to vote, and dismissed lawsuits filed by Yanukovych's lawyers (Wilson 2005: 110). On the other hand, local courts ruled in favor of the authorities on many occasions (OSCE/ODIHR 2004b, 2004c), even canceling the results of the vote in two election districts (200 and 203) where Yushchenko was ahead (ProUA 2004a). For the Yushchenko camp, battles in regional courts – which many assumed to be controlled by the authorities (Wilson 2005: 146) – were very important, as the only legal recourse open to the opposition was to lodge legal complaints against vote fraud in polling stations before regional courts, and then appeal them to the Supreme Court. However, jurists from both political sides agreed that the courts, including the Supreme Court, lacked the power to cancel district or nationwide election results, let alone to order new elections across the nation (Krushelnycky 2004; Peuch 2004; Ukrayinska Pravda 2004a; Katerinchuk 2006: 91).

However, as in Georgia, the Ukrainian Supreme Court proved these experts wrong. Chief Justice Vasyl Malyarenko charged his deputy, Anatoly Yarema, with overseeing the legality of the elections. Justice Yarema, who had risen through the judicial ranks in Western Ukraine, headed the Court's twenty-one–member Civil Chamber, which was in charge of hearing election disputes. Justice Yarema took his job seriously and publicly admonished election officials for poor handling of voter lists. More importantly, the Court upheld Yushchenko's complaints against the cancelation of the vote count in three election districts – 100, 200, and 203 – in which he was ahead (ProUA 2004c, 2004b; Wilson 2005: 112).

Shortly after the CEC's November 22 announcement that the preliminary results of the runoff showed Yanukovych in the lead, Yushchenko's legal team asked the Supreme Court to overturn the announcement.[13] Submitting numerous examples of the falsified vote in eastern Ukraine, Yushchenko's lawyers argued that the CEC

---

[13] Katerinchuk (2006), one of Yushchenko's legal advisors, provides an account of the role of lawyers in the Orange Revolution.

could not declare Yanukovych the winner owing to the massive vote fraud in the second round of voting. The next day, however, the Supreme Court Justice Olexandr Potylchak refused to hear this complaint on procedural grounds (Korrespondent.Net 2004b), much as the Georgian Constitutional Court did during the Rose Revolution. In response, overnight, Yushchenko's lawyers assembled ten bags of documentary evidence of massive violations of voting rights and electoral procedures.[14] They resubmitted their lawsuit on November 25 – "the key day of transition" (Wilson 2005: 127) – asking the Supreme Court to: (1) declare that the CEC acted unlawfully during the vote counting; (2) invalidate the CEC's announcement that Yanukovych had won the runoff; (3) declare that serious violations of election law had occurred during the runoff; (4) invalidate the results of the runoff in Yanukovych's home region; and (5) indicate that the winner should be elected on the basis of the results of the first round alone (Prescott 2006: 228).

Unexpectedly, Supreme Court Justice Ivan Dombrovskii – who made his judicial career in Western Ukraine – accepted the lawsuit, scheduled the hearing for November 29, and banned the CEC from publishing the official election results, the final step in the confirmation of the vote. The outcome of the case was anything but predictable. Whereas there were hundreds of thousands of people on the streets of Kyiv, it was not evident that the opposition had won the election. Indeed, the main entrance of the Supreme Court building was decorated with the slogan "Yanukovych – the Choice of 2004."[15] The Cabinet of Ministers met as if nothing was happening (as did the Parliament), and ordered the election results to be published (Wilson 2005: 134).[16] The CEC, security forces, law-enforcement agencies, and media remained on the government's side; European Union mediators had yet to land in Kyiv (Wilson 2005: 140). Kuchma, who wanted to extend his term in office and prepare a safer retirement, insisted that the Court could issue only "some recommendations" to the government (Wilson 2005: 147), and Yanukovych's lawyers and the CEC likewise claimed that the Court lacked the authority to cancel election results across the country, let alone order new elections. Ordinary Ukrainians expected little from the judiciary, known for its toothless, biased, and corrupt decisions; even Yushchenko's team was not sure what the Court could really do for their leader.[17] Justice Anatoly Yarema was allegedly taken to the presidential villa and "instructed" on how to handle the case (Katerinchuk 2006: 291). Meanwhile, Chief Justice Malyarenko actively lobbied for cancelation of the election results from both rounds and for the holding of new elections within three months, the solution preferred by outgoing President Kuchma (Mostova 2004).

---

[14] Author's interview with lawyers on Yushchenko's team, Kyiv, April 2008.

[15] Yushchenko's lawyer, Svitlana Kustova, who delivered the lawsuit to the courthouse, managed to tear down the banner (Katerinchuk 2006: 69).

[16] The results were not published only because opposition MPs physically occupied the government printing house.

[17] Interview with lawyers on Yushchenko's team, Kyiv, April 2008.

However, the authorities would prove to have been overconfident in their ability to control the Supreme Court. On November 29, when the judges assembled for the first time to hear Yushchenko's case, they unexpectedly decided that the whole Civil Chamber (twenty-one judges) – headed by Justice Yarema – would hear the new claim to cancel the results of the nationwide vote and allowed live TV cameras in the courtroom. Although according to the law the Court hears cases in three-judge panels, this case required unprecedented solidarity and transparency: justices needed protection from political pressure and threats by the government in order to expose electoral fraud. By that time, the judges surely sensed that the opposition was gaining strength because of numerous defections in the security services, Parliament, media, and business elite. Indeed, Yushchenko's bodyguards protected judges who leaned toward his side, and their family members (Moyer 2005: 7–8; Katerinchuk 2006: 291).[18]

To the surprise of many, in the course of the hearing, judges threw out most of the requests made by the CEC and Yanukovych's lawyers. At the same time, judges demanded more factual evidence of voter fraud from Yushchenko and agreed with many of his lawyers' requests despite their numerous legal blunders.[19] Judges went to the deliberation room to discuss every motion brought by the parties, thereby reaching their decisions in secret, as the law required. Even Chief Justice Malyarenko was barred from entering the deliberation room (Katerinchuk 2006: 276).

On December 3, after five days of the full-blown televised trial – in which judges reviewed several thousand pages of documentary evidence and heard the oral testimony of election officials – the Supreme Court ruled for Yushchenko on almost all counts (Ukrayinska Pravda 2004b). The Court slammed the CEC for failing to check regional election protocols, handle complaints in a timely manner, or control the processing of absentee ballots, and for allowing mass violations of electoral law. Relying on evidence produced by grassroots activists in the Yushchenko camp and the security services who taped the conversations of Yanukovych and CEC officials, the Court declared that these mass violations infringed on the constitutional principle of free elections and precluded the possibility of determining the will of the electorate in the whole country.

However, judges also refused Yushchenko's request to declare him the winner on the basis of the results of the first round of voting alone. The Court argued that because none of the candidates gained more than fifty percent of the vote in the first round, Yushchenko could not be declared the winner. Instead, the Court "discovered" a new remedy for Yushchenko and voters: a repeat second-round presidential election to be held on December 26. Yushchenko's lawyers insisted that the "creative" and "innovative" nature of this judge-made discovery was necessary to uphold the people's constitutional right to vote.[20] Thus, against all odds, the Court

[18] My interviews with lawyers in Yushchenko's team confirmed this as well as Yushchenko's protection.
[19] Rakhmanin (2004) offers critical analysis of Yushchenko's legal team.
[20] Interview with lawyers in Yushchenko's team, Kyiv, April 2008.

canceled the election results, and ordered and scheduled a new runoff between Yushchenko and Yanukovych.

This Ukrainian verdict was bolder than the Georgian Supreme Court's ruling, discussed previously. Simply canceling the election results, as the Georgian judges did, would have been a "weak" decision tantamount to deferring to the incumbents. Instead, Ukraine's top judges – working under enormous pressure from both sides – sided with the opposition. By liberally interpreting the Elections Act and directly applying constitutional provisions, judges set the date and format of elections against the wishes of both the Executive and chief justice (who advocated a whole new election in three months). Moreover, post-decisional dynamics show that the opposition was also deadlocked over the issue of conducting the new runoff. Thus, there were few signs that politicians were ready to reach a consensus on the timing and procedure of new elections, if the Court were to defer to political elites. In short, by setting a date for the runoff, the Court "completely changed the political game" (Wilson 2005: 147).

As in the Georgian case, this judicial role was met with criticism. Yanukovych lashed out at the Supreme Court for overstepping its jurisdiction, issuing an unlawful decision, and intruding in the domain of the Constitutional Court, the only tribunal that could draw directly on the constitutional principles of free elections, in his opinion (Prescott 2006: 228–230). On December 7, Yanukovych's team petitioned the Constitutional Court to annul this Supreme Court judgment. Meanwhile, the opposition, defectors, and Western negotiators applauded the Supreme Court (Romovska 2004). In fact, close attention from the West restrained Ukrainian authorities from using force against protesters and defying the Supreme Court. On December 8, five days after the Court spoke, Parliament reached a compromise and amended the election law, paving the way for the repeat second round on the date set by the Supreme Court. On December 15, the Constitutional Court refused to hear petitions against the Supreme Court verdict on the grounds that it lacked jurisdiction to oversee the constitutionality of judicial decisions. Contributing to its reluctance was the fact that at the time, the eighteen-member Court barely had a twelve-member quorum to make decisions (two judges were on sick leave and four judgeships were vacant thanks to the skillful sabotage of pro-Yushchenko groups in Parliament), and was unlikely to arrive at the ten votes needed to issue a judgment on the merits of the case (ProUA 2004d). However, more importantly, by that time the Constitutional Court realized that the Orange Revolution had won and chose to go with the flow. Its judges prudently chose to stay on the sidelines of this historic electoral dispute: judges had several months left on the bench before their term expired and they did not want to take any chances of losing their generous retirement packages.[21]

In sum, political fragmentation and competitive elections allowed the Supreme Court to set the rules of this electoral breakthrough. By handing down an explicitly

---

[21] Interview with a clerk of the Ukrainian Constitutional Court, Kyiv, April 2008.

political decision building on both the spirit and letter of the law, the Court played three important roles during regime change. First, it resolved a bitter electoral dispute in a unique decision that humiliated the incumbent Executive and remained in the national memory. Second, judges monitored the CEC, discovered numerous blatant violations of electoral law, protected the whistleblowers (CEC members who openly spoke out against vote fraud), and vetoed its illegal behavior. Third, judges resolved political deadlocks, stepping in to tell embattled elites who were unable to compromise what to do. Expecting totally new elections, outgoing President Kuchma delegated the resolution of this hot potato dispute to the Court in order to avoid blame for an unpopular decision. Only five days after the Supreme Court judgment, the Ukrainian parliament managed to reach consensus on how to conduct the Court-ordered runoff election. The CEC organized the new runoff in order to repair its reputation and avoid its own dissolution. On December 26, Viktor Yushchenko won the runoff with 52 percent of the vote against Yanukovych's 44 percent. On January 20, 2005, the Court rejected Yanukovych's allegations of vote fraud and confirmed that Yushchenko had won in a free and fair election.

As in Georgia, however, incoming rulers tried their best to minimize judicial constraints on their power and successfully weakened courts. President Yushchenko promptly transferred the Supreme Court's power to review election results to the newly created High Administrative Court and repeatedly accused the Supreme Court of thwarting Ukraine's democratic development. Both incumbents and the opposition pressured the courts, particularly during national elections. Meanwhile, public approval ratings of Ukraine's judiciary fell from of 21 percent to 4 percent in the course of Yushchenko's presidency (Trochev 2010). His successor, Viktor Yanukovych (elected in 2010), narrowed the Supreme Court's jurisdiction even further and purged the Court (Kyiv Post 2011). At that time, 4 percent of Ukrainians approved of the performance of courts with 57 percent disapproving (Razumkov Centre 2011). Judicial empowerment did not stick because incoming rulers learned from their predecessors that courts had to be kept under tight control.

Judicial Roles in Kyrgyzstan's 2005 Tulip Revolution: Legalizing the Unexpected Transfer of Power

Kyrgyzstan's Tulip Revolution, named for the color of the country's national flower, took place in March 2005 in the wake of rigged parliamentary elections (that were nonetheless the freest and fairest in Central Asia to that point) (Radnitz 2010: 135). This revolution was quicker, less organized and even less expected than Georgia's and Ukraine's. Looking back, its achievements are also much more ambiguous. Politicians' reactions to the roles courts sought to play during and after this electoral breakthrough reflect this ambiguity. President Akaev repeatedly warned that he would not allow a revolution similar to Georgia's and Ukraine's to occur. Some 388 candidates competed for 75 legislative seats but only 31 seats were filled in the first round of voting on February 27, 2005.[22] Opposition candidates ran in only two dozen districts, and only seven were elected either in the first or second round of voting, held on March 13. The CEC took its time, and on March 22, registered sixty-nine newly elected MPs.

Just as in Georgia and Ukraine, courts in Kyrgyzstan were actively involved in the resolution of election disputes throughout the campaign, and their work produced mixed results. According to the OSCE/ODIHR (2005), in disputes over candidate registration, some courts applied the Election Code inconsistently and appeared to be biased in favor of particular candidates. In a number of instances, courts disregarded petitions by CEC representatives against de-registration of candidates; the Supreme Court likewise upheld several de-registrations, even when the grounds for de-registration were not well evidenced or concerned minor infractions and the CEC argued against them. The Supreme Court also de-registered two candidates shortly before the elections, a violation of Article 56 of the Election Code, which established a five-day moratorium on candidate de-registration prior to election day. Finally, there were cases where court decisions were ignored, and election commissions made decisions contradicting both court rulings and the law. OSCE/ODIHR monitors suggested that "the practice of ignoring court decisions appears to be a direct result of politically motivated decisions by courts and election commissions." Following the vote, courts invalidated results reported by individual polling stations in a number of constituencies, leading to repeat voting in order to determine the winner and even to the replacement of the winning candidate – sometimes after candidates had already received their mandate (OSCE/ODIHR 2005: 10–11, 18–19, 24).

Unlike in Georgia and Ukraine, however, in Kyrgyzstan de-registered candidates usually brought hundreds of their supporters to protest at local courthouses and even at the Supreme Court (Radnitz 2010: 131–166). The crowds were peaceful and dispersed in an orderly fashion following court rulings, and this tactic worked well for the losing candidates, who flooded the courts with complaints despite the lack of trust in the judiciary. For example, former Minister Jeenbekov, who ran against President Akaev's sister-in-law, brought out hundreds of protesters to surround the local courthouse and succeeded in foiling attempts to de-register him. On February 28, a crowd of 3,000 gathered in Aravan village in southern Kyrgyzstan to demonstrate against alleged misconduct by Mahamadjan Mamasaidov, the rector of Osh Kyrgyz-Uzbek University, who had received the most votes in the first round. They blocked the Aravan-Osh highway until the next day, when the Aravan district court agreed to hear the case (International Crisis Group 2005: 4–5).

Indeed, this tactic would eventually succeed in unseating President Akaev. Feeding on their unexpected successes, by March 2005, public protestors had captured numerous government buildings in key southern cities and were demanding the

---

[22] Kyrgyzstani MPs were then elected in seventy-five single-member districts. Election law required a runoff between the top two vote getters when no candidate received a first-round majority. Most candidates ran as independents.

resignation of President Akaev, whose home base was in northern Kyrgyzstan. On March 21, Akaev ordered the Supreme Court to review the results of elections in districts where results had elicited a "sharp reaction in society." He clearly trusted the Court and did not sense that its judges would defect to the opposition – which did not trust the Court and did not expect judges to change the result of the ballot (Blua 2005; Peuch 2005). The next day, the CEC registered sixty-nine newly elected MPs, and the new parliament held its opening session immediately thereafter. During this session, president Akaev repeated that he would not resign and ordered law-enforcement agencies to maintain law and order in the capital. On March 23, police dispersed a crowd of hundreds of protesters in central Bishkek and the opposition repeated its call for Akaev's resignation as well as that of the Supreme Court, CEC, and other central government officials. Meanwhile, Cholpon Baekova, the chief justice of the nine-member Constitutional Court, spent two days fruitlessly trying to see Akaev to attempt negotiations (International Crisis Group 2005: 8). On March 24, the opposition held a major rally in Bishkek's central square, during which protestors unexpectedly stormed and captured the headquarters of central government. Conflicting reports suggested that President Akaev fled to Moscow or Kazakhstan. Meanwhile, Chief Justice Baekova announced on TV that the prime minister resigned.

At 10:00 P.M. that day, Supreme Court Chief Justice Kurmanbek Osmonov announced the thirty-three–member Supreme Court's (unanimous) decision. It canceled, on procedural grounds, the CEC's registration of the new members of Parliament, and returned the mandate to the "old" parliament until April 14, the constitutionally set date for the expiration of its mandate. However, Osmonov insisted that the ruling (which he described as both a "political" and a "legal" decision) did not represent a cancelation of the results of the first- or second-round parliamentary elections, thus creating the possibility for politicians to find a way out of the deadlock (OSCE/ODIHR 2005: 24; RFE/RL 2005a). The judgment was made in an atmosphere marked by extraordinary uncertainty: the opposition was unprepared for Akaev's regime to crumble, and unaware of his whereabouts and ability to launch a forcible comeback. In contrast with Georgia and Ukraine, the Kyrgyzstani Court did not expose vote fraud or broken vote-counting procedures. Its chief justice masterminded the judgment without hiding its political nature and paved the legal way for the outgoing Parliament to fill the void created by the disappearance of President Akaev.

The outgoing parliament immediately appointed opposition leader Kurmanbek Bakiev as both an acting president and acting prime minister. On March 28, the CEC registered the newly elected MPs again, but several seats remained contested in courts. Newly registered MPs forced the old Parliament to disband. Meanwhile, courts continued to hear cases concerning election disputes. In one case, a Bishkek court determined electoral fraud, ruled against a pro-government candidate, and declared the losing candidate the winner (RFE/RL 2005b). In another case, some

800 supporters occupied regional government buildings in Naryn, a town in central Kyrgyzstan, demanding that the Naryn regional court overturn its decision to annul the results of a tight race in the town (RFE/RL 2005c).

Cases concerning five additional contested parliamentary seats ultimately paralyzed the Supreme Court. On April 26, 80 protesters stormed and occupied the Supreme Court building (300 more surrounded the courthouse) and demanded that their 5 candidates be declared winners in the parliamentary elections. They also demanded that the whole Court resign for aiding and abetting electoral fraud. Supreme Court Chief Justice Osmonov submitted his resignation only to withdraw it two weeks later; other judges refused to resign. The police were nowhere to be found, and the protesters occupied the courthouse until June 1, despite judges' repeated pleas that they leave. That day, a 200-strong people's militia – mostly supporters of the election winners in the five districts in which parliamentary seats were being contested – stormed the Supreme Court and evicted the protesters (Pannier 2005; Toktogulov 2005). However, protesters continued to block Chief Justice Osmonov and judges in the Civil Chamber (which handles election disputes) from entering the courthouse until July (Slovo Kyrgyzstana 2005).

Osmonov claimed that the incoming government did not offer any protection to the Supreme Court against the protesters because the Court refused to obey Bakiev's requests to award parliamentary seats to his cronies (Slovo Kyrgyzstana 2010). Having won presidential elections in July 2005 with 89 percent of the vote, Bakiev pressured the Supreme Court to uphold the 2007 fraudulent parliamentary elections, packed the judiciary with at least 100 cronies, and fired the chief justice in January 2008. Other judges also felt ever-increasing pressure from the powerful and grassroots protesters (International Crisis Group 2008). The interim government that came to power as a result of the 2010 uprising against Bakiev adopted a new Constitution, purged the Supreme Court, abolished the Constitutional Court, and brought criminal charges against top judges.

To sum up, political fragmentation and highly contested elections enabled Kyrgyzstan's Supreme Court to participate in the Tulip Revolution. In contrast to Georgia and Ukraine, Kyrgyzstan's Supreme Court admitted that it had to mix law with politics and act quickly but cautiously to pave the way for the transfer of power to new government without upsetting election winners. However, judges did not become the heroes of the Tulip Revolution because weaker but more violent opposition in Kyrgyzstan did not see the behavior of the Supreme Court as defection from the outgoing regime, and the incoming government tried its best to keep judges under its tight control.

CONCLUSION

Judicial power moves in mysterious ways partly because of the nature of the political regimes within which judges operate, and partly because of the strategies they adopt as they assume new roles in governance. Three cases of unexpected electoral breakthroughs and peaceful government change in Georgia, Ukraine, and Kyrgyzstan revealed that judges sometimes choose to perform important functions in regime transition. Politically, the inherent fragmentation of power in semi-authoritarian regimes allowed some judges to develop both formal and informal protections of their personal independence and that of their court. Authoritarian rulers appeared over-confident in entrusting judiciaries with settling crucial election disputes. Legally, jurisdictional rules (which Supreme Courts in the three cases under study skillfully bent) and intense pressure from parties to electoral disputes mattered. Opposition candidates in semi-authoritarian regimes such as Ukraine, failing states such as Georgia, and clan-based societies such as Kyrgyzstan used litigation very actively and gained favorable results.

Facing unpopular rulers in contexts marked by blatant electoral fraud and rising street-level protests, Supreme Courts in all three countries unexpectedly switched sides and ruled in favor of the opposition. They canceled election results by over-stepping their jurisdiction. By mixing law and politics and appealing to the spirit as much as the letter of the law, Supreme Courts monitored the functioning of election commissions, and denounced the manipulation of elections by the out-going regime. Thus, the Supreme Courts boldly delegitimized the ruling regimes in all three countries. In Ukraine, the Supreme Court also resolved the deadlock between the authorities and opposition by setting the date for a repeat runoff of a highly contested presidential election. In all three cases, judges were able to get away with playing a crucial role in electoral governance partly because they calculated correctly and partly because they knew how to twist legal rules.

This does not mean, however, that these Courts will continue performing these functions happily ever after or that the demand for independent judicial authority among politicians and society will increase. Indeed, agile politicians learn from their predecessors that they should keep judges under control and that they face no punishment for making the courts pliant. The fact that the perpetrators of electoral fraud were never brought to account in Georgia and Kyrgyzstan and in Ukraine they even managed to regain high government positions through competitive elections shows that pliant courts may persist because they provide important benefits to the powers that be.

REFERENCES

ABA CEELI. 2004. "Judicial Reform Index for Kyrgyzstan." *ABA*, June. Retrieved from http://apps.americanbar.org/rol/publications/kyrgyzstan-jri-2003.pdf.

ABA CEELI. 2005. "Judicial Reform Index for Georgia." *ABA*, September. Retrieved from http://apps.americanbar.org/rol/publications/georgia-jri-2005-eng.pdf.

ABA ROLI. 2009. "Judicial Reform Index for Georgia. *ABA*, April. Retrieved from http://apps .americanbar.org/rol/publications/georgia_judicial_reform_index_volume_ii_2009_en.pdf.

Areshidze, Irakly. 2007. *Democracy and Autocracy in Eurasia: Georgia in Transition.* East Lansing: Michigan State University Press.

Baiandurlu, Ibragim. 2004. "Lado Chanturia: Prezident Saakashvili byl initsiatorom sudebnoi reformy v Gruzii." *Zerkalo*, February 10. Retrieved from http://dlib.eastview.com/browse/doc/5872571.

BBC News. 2000. "Kyrgyz Opposition Leader Cleared." *BBC News Asia-Pacific*, August 7. Retrieved from http://news.bbc.co.uk/2/hi/asia-pacific/870371.stm.

BBC News. 2004. "Judges Step into Ukraine Crisis." *BBC News*, November 29. Retrieved from http://news.bbc.co.uk/2/hi/europe/4050633.stm.

Blua, Antoine. 2005. "Kyrgyz President Says Elections Were Valid." *RFE/RL Newsline*, March 22. Retrieved from http://www.rferl.org/content/article/1058071.html.

Brownlee, Jason. 2009. "Portents of Pluralism: How Hybrid Regimes Affect Democratic Transitions." *American Journal of Political Science* 53: 515–532.

Bunce, Valerie and Sharon Wolchik. 2011. *Defeating Authoritarian Leaders in Postcommunist Countries*. New York: Cambridge University Press.

Carothers, Thomas. 2002. "The End of the Transition Paradigm." *Journal of Democracy* 13: 5–21.

Caucasian Knot. 2003. "Election Results Outside Georgia Declared Invalid." *Caucasian Knot*, November 14. Retrieved from http://www.eng.kavkaz-uzel.ru/articles/1462.

Chavez, Rebecca Bill. 2004. *The Rule of Law in Nascent Democracies: Judicial Politics in Argentina*. Stanford: Stanford University Press.

Chikhladze, Giga. 2003. "Labor Party Leader: Georgia Faces 'Real Threat' of Civil War." *Eurasianet*, December 3. Retrieved from http://www.eurasianet.org/departments/recaps/articles/eav120303.shtml.

Civil.Ge. 2003a. "Civil Rights Activists Say Shevardnadze Threatens Judicial System." *Civil.Ge*, August 15. Retrieved from http://www.civil.ge/eng/article.php?id=4772.

Civil.Ge. 2003b. "Court Canceled CEC's Controversial Ruling." *Civil.Ge*, November 18. Retrieved from http://www.civil.ge/eng/article.php?id=5545.

Collins, Kathleen. 2006. *Clan Politics and Regime Transition in Central Asia*. New York: Cambridge University Press.

Committee of Voters of Ukraine. 2005. "Report of the Committee of Voters of Ukraine on Results of Work During the Presidential Elections in Ukraine in 2004," February 5. Retrieved from http://www.cvu.org.ua/?lang=eng&mid=fp&id=929&lim_beg=60.

D'Anieri, Paul. 2007. *Understanding Ukrainian Politics: Power, Politics, and Institutional Design*. Armonk, NY: M.E. Sharpe.

Eurasianet. 2003. "Pressure Builds on Shevardnadze as Georgian Crisis Boils." *Eurasianet*, November 21. Retrieved from http://www.eurasianet.org/departments/insight/articles/eav112103a.shtml.

Fairbanks, Charles. 2004. "Georgia Rose Revolution." *Journal of Democracy* 15: 110–124.

Freedom House. 2012. "Nations in Transit 2012." *Freedom House*. Retrieved from http://www.freedomhouse.org/report/nations-transit/nations-transit-2012.

Gandhi, Jennifer and Ellen Lust-Okar. 2009. "Elections under Authoritarianism." *Annual Review of Political Science* 12: 403–422.

Georgian Times. 2003. "Nongovernmental Organization Filed Cases at Different Regional Courts of Georgia." *Georgian Times International Edition*, November 10.

Ginsburg, Tom. 2003. *Judicial Review in New Democracies: Constitutional Courts in Asian Cases*. New York: Cambridge University Press.

Ginsburg, Tom and Tamir Moustafa, eds. 2008. *Rule By Law: The Politics of Courts in Authoritarian Regimes*. New York: Cambridge University Press.

Guardian. 2004. "Ukraine Crisis Simmers." *Guardian*. November 27.

Hammarberg, Thomas. 2011. "Administration of Justice and Protection of Human Rights in the Justice System in Georgia." *Commissioner for Human Rights*, April 20. Retrieved from https://wcd.coe.int/ViewDoc.jsp?id=1809789.

Hedges, Warren. 2003. "CEC Decree Overturned by Court." *The Messenger*, November 19.

Helmke, Gretchen. 2005. *Courts under Constraints: Judges, Generals, and Presidents in Argentina*. Cambridge: Cambridge University Press.

Huskey, Eugene. 2007. "Eurasian Semi-Presidentialism? The Development of Kyrgyzstan's Model of Government." In *Semi-Presidentialism Outside Europe*, edited by Robert Elgie. London: Routledge.

International Crisis Group. 2003. "Georgia: What Now? Europe Report No. I51." *International Crisis Group*, December 3. Retrieved from http://www.crisisgroup.org/~/media/Files/europe/151_georgia_what_now.pdf.

International Crisis Group. 2005. "Kyrgyzstan: After the Revolution. Asia Report No. 97." *International Crisis Group*, May 4. Retrieved from http://www.crisisgroup.org/~/media/Files/asia/central-asia/kyrgyzstan/097_kyrgyzstan_after_the_revolution.pdf.

International Crisis Group. 2008. "Kyrgyzstan: The Challenge of Judicial Reform. Asia Report No. 150." *International Crisis Group*, April 10. Retrieved from http://www.crisisgroup.org/~/media/Files/asia/central-asia/kyrgyzstan/150_kyrgyzstan_the_challenge_of_judicial_reform.pdf.

Jones, Stephen. 2006. "Georgia: Nationalism from under the Rubble." In *After Independence: Making and Protecting the Nation in Postcolonial and Postcommunist States*, edited by Lowell W. Barrington. Ann Arbor: University of Michigan Press, 248–276.

Katerinchuk, Mykola. 2006. *Advokati pomaranchevoi revoliutsii*. Kyiv: Iustinian.

Korrespondent.Net. 2004a. "V den' vyborov sudy rassmotreli bolee 42,5 tys. zhalob grazhdan." *Korrespondent.net*, November 2. Retrieved from http://www.korrespondent.net/main/105779.

Korrespondent.Net. 2004b. "Verkhovnyi sud otkazalsia rassmatrivat' zhaloby Yushchenko na rezultaty vyborov." *Korrespondent.Net*, November 24. Retrieved from http://www.korrespondent.net/main/107627.

Krushelnycky, Askold. 2004. "Ukraine: Rivals for Ukraine's Presidency Seek Peaceful Solutions." *RFE/RL*, November 24. Retrieved from http://www.rferl.org/featuresarticle/2004/11/EAED46D0-8D2D-484A-9EFD-E02F2618EC48.html.

Kuzio, Taras. 2005a. "Regime Type and Politics in Ukraine under Kuchma." *Communist and Post-Communist Studies* 38: 167–190.

Kuzio, Taras. 2005b. "From Kuchma to Yushchenko: Ukraine's 2004 Presidential Elections and the Orange Revolution." *Problems of Post-Communism* 52: 29–40.

Kyiv Post. 2002. "Supreme Court Elects Chairman in Fractious Campaign." *Kyiv Post*, November 14. Retrieved from http://www.kyivpost.com/content/ukraine/supreme-court-elects-chairman-in-fractious-campaig-12273.html.

Kyiv Post. 2011. "Yanukovych Signs Law that Broaden Functions of Supreme Court." *Kyiv Post*, November 11. Retrieved from http://www.kievpost.net/news/nation/detail/116778.

Levitsky, Steven and María Victoria Murillo. 2009. "Variation in Institutional Strength." *Annual Review of Political Science* 12: 115–133.

Levitsky, Steven and Lucan Way. 2010. *Competitive Authoritarianism: Hybrid Regimes After the Cold War*. New York: Cambridge University Press.

Magaloni, Beatriz and Ruth Krichelli. 2010. "Political Order and One-Party Rule." *Annual Review of Political Science* 13: 123–143.

McFaul, Michael. 2002. "The Fourth Wave of Democracy and Dictatorship: Noncooperative Transitions in the Postcommunist World." *World Politics* 54: 212–244.

Mostova, Yulia. 2004. "Maidany i Kabineti." *Dzerkalo tyzhnia*, November 27. Retrieved from http://dt.ua/ARCHIVE/maydani_i_kabineti-41869.html.

Moustafa, Tamir. 2007. *The Struggle for Constitutional Power: Law, Politics, and Economic Development in Egypt*. Cambridge: Cambridge University Press.

Moustafa, Tamir and Tom Ginsburg. 2008. "Introduction: The Functions of Courts in Authoritarian Politics." In *Rule by Law: The Politics of Courts in Authoritarian Regimes*, edited by Moustafa and Ginsburg. New York: Cambridge University Press, 1–22.

Moyer, Thomas. 2005. "Speech at the Ohio State Bar Annual Meeting." *Ohio State Bar Association*, May 12. Retrieved from http://www.ocraonline.com/pdf/osba5-12-05.pdf.

Newberg, Paula R. 1995. *Judging the State: Courts and Constitutional Politics in Pakistan*. Cambridge: Cambridge University Press.

Nodia, Ghia. 2005. "The Dynamics and Sustainability of the Rose Revolution." In *Democratisation in the European Neighbourhood*, edited by Michael Emerson. Brussels: Centre for European Policy Studies. Retrieved from http://www.ceps.eu/system/files/book/1267.pdf.

Olcott, Martha. 2010. *Kazakhstan: Unfulfilled Promise?* Washington, DC: Carnegie Endowment for International Peace.

OSCE/ODIHR. 2003. "Election Observation Mission, Georgia, Parliamentary Elections 2003: Post-Election Interim Report." *OSCE/ODIHR*, November 3–25. Retrieved from http://www.osce.org/odihr/elections/georgia/17822.

OSCE/ODIHR. 2004a. "Election Observation Mission, Georgia, Parliamentary Elections 2003, Final Report." *OSCE/ODIHR*, January 28. Retrieved from http://www.osce.org/documents/odihr/2004/01/1992_en.pdf.

OSCE/ODIHR. 2004b. "Preliminary Statement on the First Round of the Presidential Election in Ukraine." *OSCE/ODIHR*, November 1. Retrieved from http://www.osce.org/odihr/elections/ukraine/35656.

OSCE/ODIHR. 2004c. "Preliminary Statement on the Second Round of the Presidential Election in Ukraine." *OSCE/ODIHR*, November 22. Retrieved from http://www.osce.org/odihr/elections/ukraine/16565.

OSCE/ODIHR. 2005. "Election Observation Mission Final Report, The Kyrgyz Republic Parliamentary Elections 2005." *OSCE/ODIHR*, May 20. Retrieved from http://www.osce.org/documents/odihr/2005/05/14456_en.pdf.

OSCE/ODIHR. 2008a. "Election Observation Mission, Georgia, Final Report on Extraordinary Presidential Election." *OSCE/ODIHR*, March 4. Retrieved from http://www.osce.org/odihr/elections/georgia/30959.

OSCE/ODIHR. 2008b. "Election Observation Mission Final Report, Georgia, Parliamentary Elections." *OSCE/ODIHR*, September 9. Retrieved from http://www.osce.org/odihr/elections/georgia/33301.

OSCE/ODIHR. 2010. "Election Observation Mission Final Report, Georgia, Municipal Elections." *OSCE/ODIHR*, September 13. Retrieved from http://www.osce.org/odihr/elections/71280.

Pannier, Bruce. 2005. "Kyrgyzstan: Police Evict Occupiers from Supreme Court Building." *RFE/RL*, June 1. Retrieved from http://www.rferl.org/content/article/1059073.html.

Peuch, Jean-Christophe. 2004. "Ukraine: What Legal Recourse is Open to the Opposition?" *RFE/RL*, November 24. Retrieved from http://www.rferl.org/content/article/1056039.html.

Peuch, Jean-Christophe. 2005. "Kyrgyz Protests Continue." *RFE/RL*, March 22. Retrieved from http://www.rferl.org/content/article/1058065.html.

Popova, Maria. 2012. *Politicized Justice in Emerging Democracies: A Study of Courts in Russia and Ukraine*. New York: Cambridge University Press.

Prescott, Natalie. 2006. "Orange Revolution in Red, White, and Blue: U.S. Impact on the 2004 Ukrainian Election." *Duke Journal of Comparative & International Law* 16: 219–248.

ProUA. 2004a. "Cherkassy: vybory priznany nedeistvitelnymi v dvukh orugakh." *ProUA.Com*, November 8. Retrieved from http://proua.com/news/2004/11/08/174819.html.

ProUA. 2004b. "VSU: rezultaty vyborov v okruge No 203 deistvitelny." *ProUA.Com*, November 15. Retrieved from http://proua.com/news/2004/11/15/165414.html.

ProUA. 2004c. "VSU: vybory v okruge No 200 Cherkasskoi oblasti deistvitelny." *ProUA.Com*, November 16. Retrieved from http://proua.com/news/2004/11/16/115221.html.

ProUA. 2004d. "Shufrich obratilsia v KS otnositelno resheniia VSU, no poluchit otvet neskoro." *ProUA.Com*, December 7. Retrieved from http://proua.com/news/2004/12/07/122920.html.

Radnitz, Scott. 2010. *Weapons of the Wealthy: Predatory Regimes and Elite-Led Protests in Central Asia*. Ithaca: Cornell University Press.

Rakhmanin, Serhiy. 2004. "Dukh i bukva." *Dzerkalo tyzhnia*, December 4. Retrieved from http://dt.ua/ARCHIVE/duh_i_bukva-41926.html.

Razumkov Centre. 2011. "Recurrent Sociological Poll." *Razumkov Centre*. Retrieved from http://www.uceps.org/eng/poll.php?poll_id=169.

RFE/RL. 2004a. "Kyrgyz President Shakes up the Government." *RFE/RL Newsline*, February 10. Retrieved from http://www.rferl.org/content/article/1143094.html.

RFE/RL. 2004b. "Georgian President Says He Does Not Need Opposition Representation in Parliament." *RFE/RL Newsline*, March 26. Retrieved from http://www.rferl.org/content/article/1143125.html.

RFE/RL. 2005a. "Supreme Court Affirms Mandate of 'Old' Kyrgyz Parliament." *RFE/RL Newsline*, March 25. Retrieved from http://www.rferl.org/content/article/1143365.html.

RFE/RL. 2005b. "Court Begins to Review Election Disputes." *RFE/RL Newsline*, March 30. Retrieved from http://www.rferl.org/content/article/1143367.html.

RFE/RL. 2005c. "Demonstrators Seize Regional Administration Offices." *RFE/RL Newsline*, April 7. Retrieved from http://www.rferl.org/content/article/1143373.html.

Romovska, Zoryslava. 2004. "Rishennya Sudovoi palaty Verkhovnogo Sudu Ukraini: pogliad naukovtsa i gromadianina." *Visnyk Verkhovnoho Sudu Ukraini* no. 12: 5–8.

Schedler, Andreas. 2010. "Authoritarianism's Last Line of Defense." *Journal of Democracy* 21: 69–80.

Shambayati, Hootan. 2004. "A Tale of Two Mayors: Courts and Politics in Iran and Turkey." *International Journal of Middle East Studies* 36: 253–275.

Slovo Kyrgyzstana. 2005. "Kurmanbek Osmonov: Moi gospodin – zakon." *Slovo Kyrgyzstana*, July 1.

Slovo Kyrgyzstana. 2010. "Moe kredo: zakon i poriadok." *Slovo Kyrgyzstana*, August 16.

Staton, Jeffrey. 2010. *Judicial Power and Strategic Communication in Mexico*. New York: Cambridge University Press.

Sumbadze, Nana. 2009. "Saakashvili in the Public Eye." *Central Asian Survey* 28: 185–197.

Sumbadze, Nana and George Tarkhan-Mouravi. 2004. "Public Opinion in Tbilisi." *NISPAcee News* 11 (Winter): 1–14.

Thompson, Mark and Philipp Kuntz. 2004. "Stolen Elections: The Case of the Serbian October." *Journal of Democracy* 15: 159–172.

Toktogulov, Kadyr. 2005. "Several Hundred People Break into Kyrgyz Supreme Court," *Pravda.Ru*, June 1. Retrieved from http://english.pravda.ru/news/world/ussr/01-06-2005/63097-0.

Tribuna. 2004. "V den' vyborov sudy zavalili zhalobami." *Tribuna*, November 1. Retrieved from http://tribuna.com.ua/news/129996.htm.

Trochev, Alexei. 2008. *Judging Russia: The Role of Constitutional Court in Russian Politics*. New York: Cambridge University Press.

Trochev, Alexei. 2010. "Meddling with Justice: Competitive Politics, Impunity, and Distrusted Courts in Post-Orange Ukraine." *Demokratizatsiya* 18: 122–147.

Ukrayinska Pravda. 2004a. "Sud, kotoryi zabral golosa u Yushchenko, byl nechestnyi?" *Ukrayinska Pravda*, November 8. Retrieved from http://pravda.com.ua/ru/news/2004/11/8/13341.htm.

Ukrayinska Pravda. 2004b. "Postanova Verkhovnogo Sudu Ukraini [Decision of the Supreme Court of Ukraine]." *Ukrayinska Pravda*, December 3. Retrieved from http://www.pravda.com.ua/articles/2004/12/3/3004988.

UNDP. 2010. "Basic Knowledge and Perception Survey about the Judicial System of Georgia." *UNDP*, March 25. Retrieved from http://www.undp.org.ge/files/24_861_740597-judiciary-survey-eng.pdf.

Way, Lucan. 2005. "Authoritarian State Building and the Sources of Political Competition in the Fourth Wave: The Cases of Belarus, Moldova, Russia, and Ukraine." *World Politics* 57: 231–261.

Wheatley, Jonathan. 2005. *Georgia from National Awakening to Rose Revolution: Delayed Transition in the Former Soviet Union*. Burlington, VT: Ashgate.

Widner, Jennifer. 2001. *Building the Rule of Law*. New York: W.W. Norton & Company.

Wilson, Andrew. 2005. *Ukraine's Orange Revolution*. New Haven: Yale University Press.

Wolczuk, Kataryna. 2001. *The Moulding of Ukraine: The Constitutional Politics of State Formation*. Budapest: Central University Press.

Wolczuk, Kataryna. 2002. "The Constitutional Court of Ukraine: The Politics of Survival." In *Constitutional Justice, East and West: Democratic Legitimacy and Constitutional Courts in Post-Communist Europe in a Comparative Perspective*, edited by Wojciech Sadurski. The Hague: Kluwer Law International, 327–348.

Vanberg, Georg. 2005. *The Politics of Constitutional Review in Germany*. New York: Cambridge University Press.

3

Constitutional Authority and Judicial Pragmatism
Politics and Law in the Evolution of South Africa's Constitutional Court

*Heinz Klug**

Judging from comments in judicial opinions and academic journals, South Africa's Constitutional Court is held in high esteem around the world. Although this might seem an unsurprising response to the highest court in a post-apartheid South Africa, this chapter argues that the Court's image as well as its judicial authority are the product of a very particular set of conditions and politics and cannot be taken for granted now or in the future. Implicit in this argument is the idea that the Constitutional Court plays a number of different roles that vary over time. In order to understand the evolution of the Constitutional Court and of its roles in the governance of the country, it is important to explore three dimensions of the Court's history and function, which taken together, provide insight into the way in which the courts and judges have entered into national political life, and what difference their participation has made in the construction of constitutional democracy in South Africa. These three dimensions are: (1) the sources of judicial authority; (2) the practice of the judiciary in exercising this authority; and (3) the challenges faced by the court as political conditions shift, and as it is confronted with increasingly difficult cases rooted in seemingly intractable socioeconomic and political conditions.

In terms of the causal framework this volume employs, we can identify three distinct sets of factors that have helped to define the roles the South African Constitutional Court has performed: (1) the original conditions that enabled the Court to issue the rulings for which it has become famous; (2) the internal motivations or actions of the Court; and (3) the external influences that encouraged the Court to adopt the stance it has taken. These three factors provide a means to identify and evaluate how particular cases and events have shaped each of the three dimensions that need to be explored in order to understand the roles the Court has and

* Evjue-Bascom Professor of Law, University of Wisconsin Law School, Honorary Senior Research Associate in the School of Law, University of the Witwatersrand.

continues to play in governance. In practice, these factors – and the various roles they enable or provoke – are not distinct or separate from one another. At any moment the Court is both tackling a particular set of cases defined by a host of factors that are mostly beyond its control, as well as managing its own broader role in the polity with respect to other institutions and the public more generally. Understanding how the Court's various roles have evolved thus requires both identifying particular strands within the general functioning of the Court, as well as appreciating the continuous change that marks the life of an institution seeking to build its own jurisprudential body of doctrine at the same time its primary decision makers are being periodically replaced, and it is being reshaped as a working entity adopting principled and strategic responses to the world.

To build an understanding of the Constitutional Court's evolving roles, this chapter begins by discussing the sources of judicial power, including the historical legacies of law and practice; the Court's origins and the appointment of justices; the Court's early decisions and the triumph of rights; international recognition; and finally, the efforts to promote a constitutional patriotism around the court. Second, the chapter explores the ways in which the Court has pursued its task: both its strategic engagement with issues and a degree of judicial pragmatism help to account for the Court's success in institutionalizing its role within the political system. Finally, the chapter turns to discuss a series of cases that brings the Court to the margins of its power, raising a number of concerns about the limits of its power and the growing struggle and debate about the role of law – and constitutional adjudication in particular – in the politics of South Africa today. Although the Constitutional Court continues to play a central role in the legal system, the political tensions that are inevitable in a country facing enormous social, political, and economic challenges have not left the judicial system unaffected. The chapter will conclude with a discussion of these tensions and the continuing attempts by the government and the Court to find a way forward that both protects the legitimacy of the Court and addresses the tensions inherent in the relationship between a powerful political center and a Court with unique constitutional authority.

Before addressing these specific dimensions of the Constitutional Court's experience, it will be useful to give a brief snapshot of the history and practice of the Court. As a direct product of the political negotiations that ended apartheid, the Constitutional Court – provided for in the 1993 "interim" Constitution – was established in the first half of 1995, about a year after South Africa's first democratic election, with the appointment of eleven justices to the Court. The Court was formally opened in October 1995. Empowered to exercise both concrete and abstract review, as well as to take direct applications and serve as a court of final review, the Constitutional Court has had a broad scope of authority within which to establish its role. On average, the Court decided about twenty-five cases per year during its first decade and ruled against the government in about 40 percent of cases. Of the cases that the Court decided, approximately 60 percent were on the basis of claims of violations of rights, and 30 percent arose out of criminal cases. About 78 percent of all cases were decided by a unanimous Court.

SOURCES OF JUDICIAL POWER AND THE EMERGENCE OF MULTIPLE ROLES FOR THE COURT

The South African Constitutional Court has wielded significant power over the first fifteen years of constitutional democracy in South Africa, despite the well-rehearsed notion that the judiciary is the "least dangerous branch" of government (Bickel 1962). In making this claim, it is useful to identify the particular sources of power that any judiciary may draw on, including formal and informal sources of power as well as popular support and legitimacy. Apart from formal constitutional recognition of the judiciary's power to decide cases and even exercise its jurisdiction over the Executive and Legislature through administrative and constitutional review, I will argue that judiciaries – and Constitutional Courts in particular – are empowered or constrained by a number of specific conditions. These include specific processes, legacies, roles, and even public campaigns, such as: the origins of the Court and the processes through which justices are appointed; the specific historical legacy of the courts and judiciary; the Court's handling of major cases, particularly in the early years of a new jurisdiction; recognition of the Court's decisions both internally and by an increasingly interested international audience; and finally, the ways in which the Court works to establish its place within the political life of the society, for example through the promotion of a constitutional patriotism or other strategies to enhance the role of the Court, law, and constitution in particular.

Historical Legacies

Although the rejection of tyranny and embracing of rights may seem a logical reaction to a period in which rights have been systematically violated, this does not explain why a particular society would choose to turn toward the judiciary as the ultimate protectors of such rights. This is particularly so when the judiciary and the law in general were intimately associated with the construction and maintenance of a prior oppressive regime. In South Africa, judicial review of legislative authority had historically been explicitly rejected, and in the period just prior to the democratic transition all the major parties remained committed to notions of democracy that assumed a future democratic South Africa would continue to embrace parliamentary sovereignty (Klug 2000). In fact, the struggle against apartheid was always understood as a struggle against racial oppression and minority rule, and conversely, as a struggle for majoritarian democracy. This history makes the empowerment of judges not just unnecessary to the original goals of democratization, but an interesting development that reflects both global dynamics around judicial empowerment and internal notions of the proper role of the judiciary in the new South Africa.

Despite attempts by participants in the antiapartheid struggle to defend themselves
in the courts against the abuses of the state, it was only in the last decade of the
apartheid era that they began to actively engage the judiciary in an attempt to
challenge apartheid laws and create legal spaces for contesting the policies and
actions of the apartheid state (Abel 1995; Harris 2008). Although there were significant
victories in the Supreme Court against the States of Emergency, such as requiring
the police to account for their actions (Haysom and Kahanovitz 1987), it is important
to distinguish the Supreme Court from the lower courts. In both highly publicized
inquest hearings and what came to be described as a system of "punishment by
process" in the lower courts, the experience of the majority of participants in the
legal system provides a completely different perspective. Although more than seventy
political detainees are known to have died in security police detention between
1963 and 1990, the courts repeatedly exonerated their torturers "either because the
conspiracy of silence and outright lying by police officers made it impossible to
reach the truth or because the courts too readily believed the fairytales proffered as
fact... [and] in the face of glaring evidence to the contrary, they resolutely declared
that no one was to blame" (Bizos 1998: 6–7).

Even the superior courts came under direct criticism after antiapartheid lawyers
in the mid-1980s – who had gained early judicial victories against the worst
restrictions of the state of emergency – experienced a wave of successive judgments by the Appellate Division that held that the state had virtually unlimited
power under emergency provisions (Haysom and Kahanovitz 1987; Rickard 1988).
Criticism came particularly from external bodies such as the International Commission of Jurists, whose observer at the treason trial of Helene Passtoors in 1986
concluded that there is "justification to the viewpoint of black people and concerned
whites that most South African courts in their uncritical and 'positivist' approach
to apartheid legislation merely serve as instruments of repression" (Sidley 1986: 2).
Thus, although it may be reasonable to believe that the victims of apartheid would
support the introduction of a bill of rights in response to the massive denial of rights
under apartheid, there is less reason to believe that there should be an equivalent
faith in the judiciary as the upholder of such rights.

Given this historical experience it is difficult to conclude that the new Constitutional Court was in a position to draw on either a vast reservoir of judicial
legitimacy or respect for past law. Instead, it is easier to see how the new court would
be able to use the past to distinguish itself as a completely new institution with a
fundamentally different role in protecting individuals and promoting a culture of
rights in a democratic South Africa. In fact, the Constitutional Court has treated
the country's colonial and apartheid history and its continuing legacy as a constant
backdrop and justification for its generous interpretations of rights. In their first
major judgment striking down the death penalty (*Makwanyane*), the justices of the
new Constitutional Court made repeated reference to the country's recent history
as a justification for both their own role as interpreters of the Constitution as well as

their purposive approach to interpretation. Justice Mahomed, for example, argued that:

> In some countries, the Constitution only formalizes, in a legal instrument, a historical consensus of values and aspirations evolved incrementally from a stable and unbroken past to accommodate the needs of the future. The South African Constitution is different: it retains from the past only what is defensible and represents a decisive break from, and a ringing rejection of that part of the past which is disgracefully racist, authoritarian, insular and repressive.... What the Constitution expressly aspires to do is to provide a transition from these grossly unacceptable features of the past to a conspicuously contrasting "future founded on the recognition of human rights, democracy and peaceful co-existence and development opportunities for all South Africans, irrespective of colour, race, class, belief or sex." (*State v Makwanyane and Another*: para. 262)

In this way, history has been used by the justices of the new Constitutional Court as a way to repeatedly assert the Court's role in building a new culture of rights and distinguish the past, including past law, as a counterexample or anti-model to itself.

The Court's Origins and the Appointment of Justices

Prior to the 1993 interim Constitution, the architecture of the South African high court system (the Supreme Court) was composed of a number of provincial and local divisions of the Supreme Court – which had both original and review jurisdiction – from which a final appeal was made to the Appellate Division of the Supreme Court. The judiciary was appointed by the executive, and as a matter of custom its members were drawn from the ranks of senior advocates – the equivalent of barristers – in South Africa's divided bar. As a result of both the reluctance of a number of senior advocates – who considered the apartheid judiciary to be tainted – as well as the increasing tendency of the apartheid regime to appoint judges sympathetic to its world view, the integrity of some justices – particularly the very conservative Chief Justice Rabie – had been increasingly brought into question. F. W. De Klerk's appointment of the more liberal Justice Corbett at the very beginning of the democratic transition in 1989 seemed to acknowledge the importance of shoring up the legitimacy of the judiciary during this period. At the same time, the liberation movement was suggesting that there needed to be a complete replacement or at least vetting of apartheid judges. In stark contrast to this negative and contested historical legacy, the origins of the Constitutional Court as well as the legitimacy of the justices appointed by the newly elected President Nelson Mandela brought an extraordinary degree of legitimacy to this emerging institution.

As attention shifted in the early 1990s to the negotiation of a new Constitution, a debate began over the role of the judiciary in a postapartheid South Africa. Although there was early agreement in constitutional negotiations at Kempton Park in 1993 on the principle that there should be a competent, independent, and impartial judiciary that should have the "power and jurisdiction to safeguard and enforce the Constitution and all fundamental rights" (Third Report, 1993: 2), the parties remained far apart in their proposals for the structure, functioning, and means of appointing judges to a new court. Resolution of this conflict involved an elaborate compromise requiring the newly elected president to follow three distinct processes in appointing members of a new Constitutional Court for a nonrenewable period of seven years (1993 Const.: s99[1]). First, the president appointed a president of the Constitutional Court in consultation with the cabinet and chief justice (1993 Const.: s97[2][a]). Second, four members of the court were appointed from among the existing judges of the Supreme Court after consultation between the president, cabinet, and chief justice (1993 Const.: s99[3]). Finally, the president, in consultation with the cabinet and the president of the Constitutional Court, appointed six members from a list submitted by the Judicial Service Commission (JSC) (1993 Const.: s99[3]), a newly created body dominated two-to-one by lawyers (1993 Const.: s105[1]).

The "final" Constitution extended the period of nonrenewable appointment from seven to twelve years but also imposed a mandatory retirement age of seventy years. A subsequent constitutional amendment provides that the term of an individual justice may be extended by an act of Parliament (1996 Const.: s176[1]). Appointments to the court are now made by the president, either in consultation with the JSC and the leaders of the political parties represented in the National Assembly (in the case of the chief justice and the deputy chief justice), or from a list of nominees prepared by the JSC after the president consults with the chief justice and the leaders of political parties (for the remaining positions on the court). The JSC is required to provide three more nominees than the number of appointments to be made and the president may refuse to appoint any of these by giving reasons to the JSC why the nominees are unacceptable – requiring the JSC to provide a supplemental list. The president's power of appointment is further restricted by the requirement that "at all times, at least four members of the Constitutional Court must be persons who were judges at the time they were appointed" (1996 Const.: s174[5]).

Appointment to the Constitutional Court is also determined by the requirement that justices must be South African citizens and consideration must be given to the "[n]eed for the judiciary to reflect broadly the racial and gender composition of South Africa" (1996 Const.: s174[1] and [2]). In practice, the Constitutional Court has, despite its young age, experienced regular changes in composition. This has occurred as a result of a number of developments, including the transfer of the first deputy president of the Court to become chief justice (a position at the helm of the Supreme Court of Appeal exercising final appeal jurisdiction over nonconstitutional matters), the death of Justice Didcott, numerous retirements, and the fairly frequent use of acting (temporary) justices when permanent members were either on temporary assignment to international organizations or on leave. The Judges

Remuneration and Conditions of Employment Act of 2001 now provides that whereas the formal length of a justice's term remains twelve years, justices may continue until they have completed fifteen years of total judicial service or reached the age of seventy-five – whichever comes first – in order to ensure that those who have not previously held judicial office may still retire from the Court with a full judicial pension. Although the first appointments to the Constitutional Court were dominated by lawyers, judges, and legal academics who had gained high stature during the struggle against apartheid or whose integrity was recognized nationally and internationally, concern for the need to achieve or maintain racial and ethnic representation seems to have determined more recent appointments. Fifteen years after its inauguration, the justices of the Constitutional Court reflected the diversity of South Africa with two female, three white, seven African, one Indian, and one physically disabled justice on the eleven-person panel.

Early Decisions and the Triumph of Rights

In its first politically important and publicly controversial holding, the South African Constitutional Court struck down the death penalty (*Makwanyane* 1995). Although there had been a moratorium placed on executions from the end of 1989, as part of the initial moves toward a negotiated political transition, possibly as many as 400 persons were awaiting execution at the time of the Court's ruling. In declaring capital punishment unconstitutional, the Court emphasized that the transitional Constitution established a new order in South Africa, one in which human rights and democracy are entrenched and in which the Constitution is supreme. The Court's declaration of a new order on the basis of constitutional rights was forcefully carried through in the adoption of a generous and purposive approach to the interpretation of the fundamental rights enshrined in the Constitution (Klug 2006).

The unanimous opinion, authored by Justice Arthur Chaskalson, the president of the Court, was judiciously tailored. Finding that the death penalty amounted to cruel and unusual punishment under most circumstances, Chaskalson's opinion declined to engage in a determinative interpretation of other sections of the bill of rights that may also have impacted on the death penalty, such as the right to life, dignity, and equality. Although the individual concurring opinions of the remaining ten justices were not as restrained, they all joined Justice Chaskalson in giving explicit and great weight to the introduction of constitutional review. They emphasized that the Court "must not shrink from its task" of constitutional review (*Makwanyane*: para. 22), otherwise South Africa would be back to parliamentary sovereignty and by implication back to the unrestrained violation of rights so common under previous legislatures (Id.: para. 88). Even the recognition that public opinion seemed to favor the retention of the death penalty was met with a clear statement that the Court would "not allow itself to be diverted from its duty to act as an independent arbiter of the Constitution" (Id.: para. 89) and that public opinion in itself is "no substitute for the duty vested in the Courts to interpret the Constitution and to uphold its provisions without fear or favor" (Id.: para. 88). If public opinion were to be decisive, Chaskalson argued, "there would be no need for constitutional adjudication" (Id.).

The Court took a similarly strong stand in its other early rulings striking down legislation in violation of the equality clause, and numerous criminal cases involving both procedural and substantive rules that the Court found in violation of the Bill of Rights. In its first year, more than 64 percent of the Court's caseload involved criminal matters, although this dropped to around one-third in the following two years. In considering the willingness of this new court to strike down legislation and reverse official decisions, it is important to note that the vast bulk of the legislation it struck down in this early period, and most of the official decisions and acts it reversed, were inherited from the apartheid era. Although the old regime had insisted on legal continuity – the idea that all laws would remain in place until either reversed by new legislation or found to be inconsistent with the new Constitution by the Court – the outcome of this approach was to indirectly empower the new Constitutional Court as it proceeded to strike down old laws and regulations without any resistance from the new democratic government. What might under other circumstances have been perceived as a countermajoritarian and hence antidemocratic exercise of power was instead embraced as the triumph of human rights standards over the legacies of apartheid.

International Recognition

It was this boldness in the upholding of rights that brought international attention to the new Court. From the moment the Court struck down the death penalty it was held up around the world as a shining model, a new and progressive institution arising out of the ashes of apartheid. When it first reversed a decision made by President Mandela, he welcomed the ruling and publicly thanked the Court for doing its duty. By the time the court was faced with making decisions at odds with the policies of the new government, it had garnered a significant amount of international support and recognition. The international recognition achieved by the Court has helped secure its role as the premier institution defending human rights in postapartheid South Africa.

The Old Fort and Constitutional Patriotism

Adding to the symbolic stature of the new Constitutional Court has been the project of renovating and transforming the site of a cluster of prisons, known as the "Old Fort," located in the center of Johannesburg. The Constitutional Court was first housed in a Johannesburg business park. Placing the new Court building in the center of the Old Fort site – along with the renovation of the Old Fort and related prison buildings as historical monuments to the history of the "lawful" violation of rights – placed the Court in the midst of a project to build what has been termed in the German context "constitutional patriotism." This project, pursued more vigorously by some justices than others, seems to be aimed at solidifying the historic role of the Court in the building of a new South Africa. Despite continuing social inequalities and periodic examples of blatant disrespect for rights by some government officials, the notion that South Africa is building a culture of rights on the basis of the new Constitution is consistently asserted by the government. As long as the political leadership in all branches of government continues to assert that the Constitution is South Africa's highest achievement in the transition away from apartheid, the Court will be able to pursue its role of publicly promoting a culture of rights and constitutional supremacy, both through its decisions and the articulation of a project of constitutional patriotism.

A Powerful Court?

There can be little doubt that the Constitutional Court is one of the most successful institutions to emerge in postapartheid South Africa. Not only is it the guardian of the political transition's most explicit symbol – the final Constitution – but unlike all other branches of government, it began its life as a brand-new institution, its personnel largely untainted by apartheid. Further, its most explicit task is to uphold the promise of rights that embody the hopes and aspirations of those who struggled against apartheid. These attributes do not, however, guarantee power or authority given the inherent institutional limits of an apex Court. Instead, the Court has used its symbolic authority to publicly engage in what has been termed a "post-liberal" or "transformative constitutionalism" – a rejection of the negative past, a generous interpretation of rights, and a commitment to "inducing large-scale social change through nonviolent political processes grounded in law" (Klare 1998: 150). At the same time, however, the Court has always wielded this power conscious of what this assertion suggests about its broader roles in governance – in what may be viewed paradoxically as a form of judicial pragmatism rather than the symbolic judicial activism the Court's rights jurisprudence has led most international observers to applaud.

STRATEGIC ENGAGEMENT AND JUDICIAL PRAGMATISM IN DEFINING THE COURT'S ROLE

Asserting a constitutional patriotism and declaring a culture of rights have been the hallmarks of the early life of the Constitutional Court. However, at the same time, the Court has always been concerned about its own role in the new political order (Klug 2011). Aware of their unique status within the new constitutional order, the justices of the Constitutional Court have been careful to define their role as simply upholding the law and have denied claims they might be substituting their own political decisions for those of the democratically elected branches of government through their formal role as interpreters of the Constitution. Furthermore, the Court has in fact had to manage a number of quite explicit challenges to its role. In one case concerning the appointment of a commission of inquiry by the president, for example, one party demanded that all of the justices recuse themselves because they had been appointed by President Mandela. More recently, the Johannesburg High Court upheld a claim that the justices of the Constitutional Court had violated the constitutional rights of Cape Judge President John Hlophe, whom the justices had publicly accused of attempting to interfere in the Court's decision making on pending appeals by then-ANC President Jacob Zuma. The Court also came under direct political attack by senior ANC politicians who objected to legal processes involving Jacob Zuma before his election as president of the country in 2009. Despite these setbacks, the Court has remained quite conscious of the different ways in which it is responsible for ensuring the transition to democracy. Moreover, in response to these attacks, President Kgalema Motlanthe (who was installed by Parliament after the resignation of President Mbeki in September 2008) as well as his newly appointed minister of justice – Enver Surty – publicly reasserted the importance of judicial independence and respect for the Constitutional Court. In contrast to the history of other Constitutional Courts – including those of Hungary and Russia – where judges were replaced at the end of their terms in office by more–government-friendly judges or the Court was simply closed down by the government, the South African Constitutional Court has thus far managed – through both its strategic engagement and a pragmatic jurisprudence – to retain its authority and survive strong political attacks.

Jurisdiction and Authority

The Court's formal power is on the basis of the Constitution's proclamation that it is the supreme law of the land, and on its explicit grant of authority to the Constitutional Court to be the final arbiter of the meaning of the Constitution. Despite distrust of the old judicial order, the idea of superimposing a constitutional court as the final interpreter of a new constitution gained early acceptance among participants in the political transition and the exact parameters of this power were left to subsequent negotiation. The Constitutional Court first created under the 1993 interim Constitution was given exclusive jurisdiction over constitutional appeals, and was placed in an equal position with the old appellate division of the Supreme Court, which retained final jurisdiction for all nonconstitutional matters but had no jurisdiction over constitutional questions. The 1996 final Constitution retained this basic jurisdictional division. However, the Supreme Court of Appeals, which hears appeals from the High Courts, was awarded appellate jurisdiction over all matters, including constitutional issues (1996 Const.: s168[3]), with the Constitutional Court retaining original jurisdiction over direct applications (Id.: s167[6]) and serving as the final court of appeal on constitutional cases (Id.: s167[3]-[5]). Constitutional jurisdiction is, however, very far-reaching, as it not only deals with all government-related activity (Id.: s8[1]) but also certain private activity (Id.: s8[2]-[3]) as well as the duty to develop the common law and indigenous law in conformity with the requirements of the Bill of Rights (Id.: s39[2]).

Certification Judgments

The most extraordinary role given to the new Constitutional Court was certifying that the Constitutional Assembly had abided by the thirty-four constitutional principles contained in Schedule 4 of the 1993 interim Constitution. Thrust into the unique role of arbiter in this second and final phase of the constitution-making process, the Constitutional Court faced a number of distinct pressures. First, the democratically elected Constitutional Assembly represented the pinnacle of the country's new democratic institutions empowered with the task of producing the country's final Constitution – the end product of the formal transition from apartheid. Given a history of parliamentary sovereignty and the failure of the courts to check the antidemocratic actions of the executive in the dark days of apartheid and during the States of Emergency, how could a newly appointed Constitutional Court stand up against the first truly democratic legislature and constitution-making body in South African history?

Second, the credibility of the Constitutional Court was at stake. As the Court heard argument on the certification of the Constitution, numerous sectors – including important elements within the established legal profession – openly speculated whether the Court had sufficient independence to confront the Constitutional Assembly, particularly over the key issue of the entrenchment of the Bill of Rights. In this view, failure to refuse certification on at least this ground would have amounted to a failure of the certification function and proof that the Court lacked the independence necessary to play this role.

Third, the Constitutional Court's certification powers were not only unique but were to be exercised on the basis of a set of Constitutional Principles negotiated in the preelection transition. The Principles had – in the dying days of the multiparty negotiations and context of a rebellion by various conservative groups who came together as the Concerned South Africans Group – become the focus of unresolved demands. This led to the last-minute inclusion of a number of contradictory Principles designed more to encourage contending groups to continue participating in the process than to establish a coherent set of Constitutional Principles by which a future draft Constitution could be judged. Significantly, however, the basic framework of Principles – which traced their heritage to the ANC's Constitutional Principles of 1988, the Harare Declaration, and the United Nations General Assembly Resolution on Apartheid, and were finally adopted by the major parties at the Convention for a Democratic South Africa (CODESA) – remained at the core of the Constitutional

Principles. It was this basic framework, guaranteeing broad democratic participation, a justiciable Bill of Rights, and an independent judiciary that provided the fundamental basis for the Constitutional Court's analysis of the content of the text and its role in the certification process.

Fourth, the Constitutional Court's review of the text was permeated with the Court's own unarticulated assumptions about the institutional implications of the new constitutionalism. These assumptions are evident in the Court's response to those elements of the text that had implications for its own institutional role. In fact, many of the grounds on which the Court declined to certify the text had institutional implications for the Court, including: the Court's demands to strengthen the procedures and threshold for amendment of the Bill of Rights; its striking down of attempts to insulate the labor clause from judicial review; and the Court's argument that the provision – that a bill passed by the National Council of Provinces is presumed to indicate a national interest overriding a separate regional interest – tipped the balance against the adequacy of the basket of regional powers guaranteed in the Constitutional Principles. Thus, the Court's approach to the new text indicated a profound concern with guaranteeing its own institutional prerogatives – establishing itself as the institutional repository of the power to decide who decides. The imperative to secure this role for the Court – guardian of a constitutional democracy on the basis of the explicit foundations of constitutional supremacy – weighted the balance in the first certification judgment.

Despite this imperative, refusing to certify the text of a constitution adopted after last-minute political compromises by 86 percent of the democratically elected Constitutional Assembly was, on its face, a bold assertion of the power of constitutional review. However, the Constitutional Court's denial of certification was far more measured and subtly crafted than this bold assertion of unconstitutionality implies. In fact, the Constitutional Court was careful to point out in its unanimous and unattributed opinion that "in general and in respect of the overwhelming majority of its provisions" the Constitutional Assembly had met the predetermined requirements of the Constitutional Principles (*First Certification Judgment*: para. 31). In effect, then, the ruling was very limited and circumscribed. This analysis was confirmed when the major political parties rejected any attempt to use the denial of certification as a tool to reopen debates; instead, the Constitutional Assembly – in producing a new text – focused solely on the issues raised by the Constitutional Court (Madlala 1996).

Rights and Structure in the Court's Jurisprudence

South Africa's Bill of Rights is often heralded as the crowning achievement of the democratic transition and as having produced "some of the most progressive decision-making in the world, including the prohibition of the death penalty and the legalization of abortion" (Sparks 2003: 47). Discussing the new Constitution and the Bill of Rights first introduced in the interim Constitution, the late Etienne Mureinik argued that both must serve as a "bridge away from a culture of authority," and lead the country toward a "culture of justification – a culture in which every exercise of power is expected to be justified" (Murienik 1994: 32). Although there is a great deal of continuity between the Bill of Rights in the interim and final Constitutions, it is the inclusion of a commitment to the rule of law, in addition to constitutional supremacy, in the founding provisions of the final Constitution that highlights postapartheid South Africa's formal commitment to a particular culture of justification.

Despite the boldness of the Courts rights jurisprudence – especially its early decisions interpreting the Bill of Rights and assertion of constitutional powers in the death penalty case – its approach in cases involving the distribution of power among different parts of government is markedly different. The first such case, involving the demarcation of local government boundaries and constituencies (the Western Cape case, *Executive Council of the Western Cape*), came to the Court within three months of the death penalty decision. Differences between the death penalty case and the demarcation case are clear. The death penalty case involved the interpretation of fundamental rights and the striking down of law and practice closely associated with the violations and inequalities of the apartheid era. The demarcation case involved the allocation of powers between levels of government under an act negotiated by all parties as part of the transition to democracy. The salience of this difference lies in the distinction between two judicial roles: adjudicating rights and allocating powers. In deciding on the relative powers of the legislature and executive and the national and provincial, the Court faces the threat that any of these sites of governmental power could simply ignore or publicly disregard its decisions.

In rejecting the Western Cape's claim that President Mandela had exceeded his powers in issuing a proclamation on the demarcation of local government boundaries in the province, the Provincial Division of the Supreme Court had argued that Parliament's amendment of the Local Government Transition Act had effectively transferred Parliament's highest legislative powers to President Mandela by "allowing the President to make laws in its place." On appeal, the Constitutional Court was faced with resolving a crisis that by early September 1995 was threatening to prevent the holding of nationwide local government elections and halt the very process of democratic transition. Deflecting the potentially explosive issue of provincial autonomy and avoiding the politically sensitive issue of local government demarcation, the Constitutional Court focused on the constitutionality of the legislature's delegation of amending powers to the executive, calling into question the constitutionality of section 16A of the act, which was the legal basis on which President Mandela had acted.

In reversing the lower court – striking down Mandela's proclamations and Parliament's amendment of the Local Government Transition Act – the Constitutional Court was hailed by opponents of the government for defending the Constitution, standing up to the ANC-dominated executive and legislature, and fulfilling the promise of judicial review. However, when President Mandela publicly praised the Constitutional Court's decision, stating that "this judgment is not the first, nor will it be the last, in which the Constitutional Court assists both the government and society to ensure constitutionality and effective governance," it became clear that the Court had effectively traversed the "fundamental questions of constitutional law" and "matters of grave public concern" that Justice Chaskalson had raised in the opening paragraphs of the Court's decision (*Executive Council of the Western Cape*: para. 1). The sting of the ruling against the legislature was removed, in part, by the remedy granted (giving the legislature a period of time to correct the defect in the act), whereas executive concern was addressed by the Court's tacit prioritization of the powers of the central government over the provinces in controlling the restructuring and regulation of local government. In the end, however, the Constitutional Court had for the first time, in a most judicious manner, struck down intensely politicized legislation passed by a democratically elected Parliament and a highly popular president.

RIGHTS, POLITICS, AND THE MARGINS OF JUDICIAL POWER

Although the Constitutional Court has continued to receive acclaim for its jurisprudence, there was concern that it had still not addressed a range of difficult issues affecting the legal lives of a majority of ordinary South Africans; issues with the potential to confront some of the more ingrained aspects of inequality and conflict that continue to pervade postapartheid society. At the same time, there has been increasing political tension over the judiciary, including the Constitutional Court. These tensions have diverse origins, including concern over the rate of crime, case management in the courts that at times seems chaotic, attempts by the government to take greater control over the administration of the courts, accusations of racism among judges, complaints over the appointment process and against individual judges, and an open conflict between the justices of the Constitutional Court and the Judge President of the Cape High Court. These varied circumstances directly raise questions about the capacity of the courts, and the Constitutional Court in particular, to continue to play the role they have been playing in the political life of the country. At the same time, it is clear from the responses of the highest state officials that they do not wish to lose the legitimacy, both international and local, that the prominent role of courts has brought to the new South Africa.

A Problem of Rights and Expectations

Over the last few years, the Constitutional Court has decided a group of cases that hold profound consequences for the hopes and aspirations of the majority of South Africans. These cases include challenges to the "customary" laws of succession on grounds of gender discrimination (*Bhe*); the KwaZulu-Natal Pound Ordinance on the grounds that it denied cattle owners' rights of equality and access to the courts (*Zondi*); and the Land Claims Court's decision that a community claiming land under the Restitution of Land Rights Act had failed to prove that their dispossession was the result of discriminatory laws or practices (*Richtersveld*). In each of these cases, the decision of the Court would hold important consequences for power relations between: men and women living under indigenous law; landowners (usually white) and landless or land-hungry stock owners (usually black); as well as landowners and land-claiming communities whose claims did not self-evidently fall within the terms of the Restitution of Land Rights Act.

In both the *Bhe* and *Richtersveld* cases, the majority of the Court acknowledged the constitutional status of indigenous law. In the first instance, the Court struck down a rule of customary law that discriminated on the basis of gender; in the second instance the Court held that "indigenous law is an independent source of norms within the legal system, [but like all other] law is subject to the Constitution and has to be interpreted in light of its values" (*Richtersveld*: para. 51). In *Bhe*, the Constitutional Court directly struck down – at least with respect to intestate succession – the customary rule of primogeniture held by many traditionalists and others to be a key element of the customary legal system. In effect, the Court's decision will profoundly impact the rights of wives and daughters who until now relied on the system of extended-family obligation historically inherent in indigenous law, long disrupted by social and economic change. On the other side, the Court's decision in *Richtersveld* recognized indigenous law as a source of land rights, thus strengthening the claims of those who have argued that their land rights – including rights to natural resources – were not automatically extinguished by the extension of colonial sovereignty over their territories. Their dispossession, through means other than the direct application of specific, discriminatory, apartheid land laws will also be recognized for the purpose of claiming restitution of their land rights. Although of somewhat limited impact, the symbolic value of this recognition of indigenous land rights makes an important contribution to legitimizing the new constitutional order among ordinary South Africans.

Finally, the *Zondi* case involved a challenge to a set of legal provisions that formed a central plank of the system of control and dispossession in the rural areas of apartheid South Africa. Under the Pound Ordinance, landowners were historically empowered to seize and impound animals trespassing on their land without notice to the livestock owner, unless the owner was a neighboring landowner. Subsequently, the livestock would be sold in execution if the owners could not afford the impounding fees and damages claimed by the landowner or if the owners of the livestock could not be readily identified. Without notice requirements or judicial process, the effect was that white landowners used these rules to exert power over rural communities who lived on the land as sharecroppers, labor tenants, or wage laborers and held what little wealth or economic security they had in livestock. In effect, these rules, although not racially based, interacted with the racially based landownership rules to both structure rural social relations and perpetuate a continuing process of dispossession, as the ownership of livestock continually shifted at below-market prices from black to white farmers.

Facially race neutral, the Pound Ordinance survived the dismantling of apartheid laws, but nevertheless continues to have a predominantly racial effect because rural landownership remains, even a decade and a half after apartheid, largely in white hands. On the other side, as Justice Ngcobo noted in his opinion, are people such as "Mrs. Zondi, who belongs to a group of persons historically discriminated against by their government . . . which still affects their ability to protect themselves under the laws of the new order" (*Zondi*: para. 51). With respect to the question of notice, the Court noted that the statute did not even require anyone to tell the livestock owner of the impending sale, and Justice Ngcobo pointed out that even a general public notice in government publications or newspapers is likely to be insufficient "where a large portion of the population . . . is illiterate and otherwise socially disadvantaged. Mrs. Zondi is indeed illiterate. The thumbprint mark she affixed to her founding affidavit bears testimony to this" (Id.). Furthermore, the statute permitted the landowner to "bypass the courts and recover damages through an execution process carried out by a private businessperson or an official of a municipality without any court intervention" (*Zondi*: para. 75). Holding the statutory scheme unconstitutional – among other reasons because its effect is to limit the right of access to the courts – Justice Ngcobo noted that the scheme removes "from the court's scrutiny one of the sharpest and most divisive conflicts of our society. The problem of cattle trespassing on farm land . . . is not merely the ordinary agrarian irritation it must be in many societies. It is a constant and bitter reminder of the process of colonial dispossession and exclusion" (*Zondi*: para. 76).

Enforcing Rights, Remedies and Judicial Authority

Although the Constitutional Court has been held in high regard and the government has repeatedly acknowledged its authority and accepted its decisions,[1] a period of heightening political tensions has seen the law increasingly used as a weapon in internecine conflict among government officials and within political parties. Along with this atmosphere of legal conflict has come increasing tension over the work of the judiciary, individual judges, and the judicial appointment process. Although the Ministry of Justice has proposed statutory reforms and constitutional amendments designed to improve the functioning of the courts and administration of justice, these have raised fears that government is undermining the independence of the judiciary. Even as the government was forced to withdraw some of these proposals, the JSC

---

[1] In its ruling on *Minister of Health v Treatment Action Campaign*, para. 129, the Court stated, "The government has always respected and executed orders of this Court. There is no reason to believe that it will not do so in the present case."

publicly acknowledged that it was unable to attract sufficient numbers of highly qualified individuals as candidates for judicial appointment. It is in this context then that the courts – and the Constitutional Court in particular – are confronting growing concern at the failure of government officials to effectively implement court orders requiring public officials to resolve systemic problems of public administration and corruption, especially at the local level.

In response, there has been intense debate about the types of remedies the courts should provide (Roach and Budlender 2005), including demands for bolder judicial action: that the courts award mandatory relief and retain supervisory jurisdiction. The Constitutional Court, however, has been very careful to frame its orders in ways that encourage compliance but also attempt to bring the democratic organs of government into the decision-making process. Whereas the Court has asserted its right to provide appropriate relief – including mandatory orders and structural relief – it has also used its ability to suspend declarations of invalidity to give the legislature or executive the time and flexibility to formulate constitutional alternatives (Id.). In this way, the Court has effectively engaged in a dialogue with the other branches of the government in its attempt to both assert its power and preserve and protect its own institutional authority against potential popular and political backlashes.

CONCLUSION

The creation and legitimation of a Constitutional Court in South Africa has provided a unique institutional site within which a process of mediation between alternative constitutional imaginations has occurred. The Court's existence and legitimacy also created the possibility that the judiciary – in its role as primary interpreter of the Constitution – would be able to sustain and civilize the tensions inherent in the repeated referral and contestation of political differences in the postapartheid era. However, there has been growing concern among nongovernmental organizations and human rights bodies that the social crisis in the country – including the continuing disparities in wealth (and their racial character) as well as the levels of violence and criminal activity – may pressure the government into eroding some of the exemplary human rights gains of the democratic transition. In this sense, debates over the funding of constitutionally mandated bodies designed to protect and further democracy such as the Independent Electoral Commission, the Human Rights Commission, and the Commission on Gender Equality have focused on the relationship between their fiscal dependence and the potential threat to their autonomy posed by the ruling party and government. Those concerned with the autonomy of these institutions have expressed their concerns in terms of these institutions' importance both to implementing the Constitution's human rights guarantees and the future of democracy itself. Others – including most notably the ruling ANC – argue that it is the socioeconomic disparities and their continuing racial character that need to be addressed if the future of democracy and human rights is to be secured.

Although the Constitutional Court has played a fundamental role in enabling the democratic transition in South Africa, the conditions of its emergence as well as the strategies of its justices have allowed the institution to play a number of other roles, from promoter and symbol of a transformed justice to the more traditional role of conflict resolution and absorber or deflector of intense interregional political conflict. Whereas the initial conditions of its creation and caliber of its justices enabled the Court to build significant legitimacy among a range of constituencies – from the bar to government officials and the ruling party – the changing conditions of the country have begun to reshape the terrain on which the Court functions. At first, it was the persistence of inequality and the tragic HIV/AIDS pandemic that saw the court increasingly confront the government. More recently, the political struggle within the ruling party has created a political vortex into which an increasing array of constitutional and public institutions – including the Public Protector, National Prosecuting Authority, and its investigative arm, the Directorate of Special Operations (Scorpions) – have been sucked. Although in the past the dominant motivation of Constitutional Court justices may have been to enhance the power and legitimacy of their institution, more recently they have found themselves, as a body, defending their own integrity after a lower court found that they had violated the rights of a senior judge of the High Court by publicly announcing their complaint to the JSC that he had attempted to interfere in the outcome of a case against Jacob Zuma – soon to become the nation's fourth president.

When we consider the brief history of the South African Constitutional Court, it is possible to identify a number of very important political and social roles it has been called on to play or has taken on itself as South Africa's democratic transition has proceeded. First, the Court played a key role in the democratic transition by certifying that the Constitutional Assembly had, in writing a new final Constitution, abided by the Constitutional Principles that were the essence of the negotiated deal to end apartheid. Second, the Court has continued to serve as the one legitimate alternative to the ANC government when that government has failed to uphold or promote the rights guaranteed in the Bill of Rights. Third, the Court has played at least a symbolic (if not substantive) role as an independent institution upholding the rule of law, despite claims by the vociferous political opposition that the ANC has colonized the state through its policy of cadre deployment and thereby undermined the Constitution and democratic order. Fourth, the Court has played an important role in prompting legislative action by suspending its own orders of constitutional invalidity and referring the affected legislation to the legislature for amendment. This has both stimulated democratic engagement with issues the majority in the legislature would otherwise have preferred to ignore and created an implicit dialogue between the Court and other branches of government. Finally, the Court has played an important role in protecting the legitimate claims of regional authorities and stemming overreaching by regional governments controlled by opposition parties who have asserted greater autonomy than the constitutional framework or political support has provided.

In short, the South African Constitutional Court's roles in politics and governance have evolved significantly over the past fifteen years. Initially, the Court was called into the political arena in order to play handmaiden to the negotiated agreement that enabled the democratic transition. Although this role was formally accomplished with the certification judgments, the related but more substantive role of guaranteeing the rule of law and constitutional supremacy as key features of the new order persisted. The Court continued to break new jurisprudential ground into the late 1990s, but its decisions were consistent with the steady implementation of an extensive Bill of Rights, and it has continued to play the role of interpreting a supreme Constitution. The Court's roles seemed to be increasingly challenged at the end of the 1990s and into the first half of the first decade of the new millennium, and its approach of strategic engagement and judicial pragmatism gave way to confrontation and political brinkmanship. The Court was perceived as taking sides in internal political conflicts within the ANC as well as challenging the executive and legislature more directly. Apart from the cases involving ANC President Jacob Zuma and the related conflict with Judge President Hlophe, the Court also weighed into the intense conflict over the provision of antiretroviral treatment to mothers giving birth in public-sector hospitals, and in the case of highly controversial attempts to alter municipal boundaries, struck down both legislation and a constitutional amendment on the grounds that the legislature in both cases had failed to provide the required amount of democratic participation. It could be argued that by aggressively expanding rights to democratic participation, socioeconomic resources, and gender equality – including challenging indigenous law as patriarchal and recognizing the equality rights of gays and lesbians, including the right to marry – the Court was overreaching. However, the reaction of the government to instability in the Court, including the controversy over Juge Hlophe as well as tensions over judicial appointments and the Court's management of its caseload, seems to have led the Court to settle into a more tractable set of roles, demonstrating how occasional confrontation with other parts of the state or internal divisions affect the roles it plays.

South Africa's experiment in constitutionalism is still young, and the conditions that gave rise to the new constitutional order – as well as the continuing problems of a postcolonial society facing the dual challenges of extreme inequality and a devastating HIV/AIDS pandemic – have brought domestic tension as well as global interest to the work of the Constitutional Court. Caught in the crosshairs of struggles for the realization of the extensive promise of rights entrenched in the Constitution and the limitations of governmental capacity and resources, the Court has thus far tread a careful path, avoiding the easy declaration of rights but continuing to question government failings (Klug 2011). At the same time, the broader judiciary is undergoing transformation. Tensions over this process continue to simmer within the courts, and among the courts, government, and legal profession (See National Judges Symposium 2003). In this regard, it is the government's responsiveness to the courts and public claims of right that are of greatest concern, both for the role of the Constitutional Court and the constitutional system more generally. The Constitutional Court has repeatedly sought to remind government and its lawyers of their duty to be responsive to litigants and ensure that statutes of limitation and other barriers that inhibit either access to justice or other means of making government transparent and accountable are not unduly burdensome. In one striking example, the Court castigated the state for failing to respond to a case before the Constitutional Court, stating that it "is regrettable" because the "state has an obligation to respond to court processes." Noting that "[t]his is not the first time that the state has not responded to a matter that is before this court," the Court, in its per curium opinion, described the failure of the State Attorney's Office in Johannesburg as "cause for grave concern in a country governed by the rule of law" (*Van Straaten*: para. 9). In order to prevent such neglect in the future, the Court requested that the registrar of the Court to send a "copy of [the] judgement to the offices of the President and the Minister of Justice and Constitutional Development. We are confident that these offices will take appropriate steps to prevent a situation like this from occurring again" (Id.: para. 10).

Indeed, the greatest threat for the Court is that it may be ignored. Although *van Straaten* illustrates that the Court itself experienced the failures of governmental capacity – so evident in many of the cases that it has been called on to decide and which may truly threaten the rule of law – there is no evidence to date that the government has actively attempted to circumvent or undermine the Court. Instead, the government has repeatedly declared its allegiance to the constitutional order and the roles the Constitutional Court plays within that order. Whereas elements within the ruling party and its alliance partners have at times leveled criticism at the Court, this has often produced a healthy public response in defense of the Court and the Constitution more generally. It is this continuing and vociferous support for constitutional democracy that is providing the space for the Constitutional Court to play its multiple roles in South Africa's young democracy.

REFERENCES

Abel, R. L., *Politics by Other Means: Law in the Struggle Against Apartheid, 1980–1994*, New York: Routledge (1995).

Bickel, Alexander, *The Least Dangerous Branch: The Supreme Court at the Bar of Politics*, Indianapolis: Bobbs-Merrill (1962).

Bizos, George, *No One to Blame?: In Pursuit of Justice in South Africa*, Cape Town, Bellville: David Philip, Mayibuye (1998).

Harris, Peter, *In a Different Time: The Inside Story of the Delmas Four*, Roggebaai: Umuzi, Struik Publishers (2008).

Haysom, N. & S. Kahanovitz, "Courts and the State of Emergency," *South African Review* 4: 187 (Moss & Obrey, eds., 1987).

Klare, Karl, "Legal Culture and Transformative Constitutionalism," *South African Journal on Human Rights* 14: 146 (1998).

Klug, Heinz, *Constituting Democracy: Law, Globalism and South Africa's Political Reconstruction*, Cambridge, UK: Cambridge University Press (2000).

Klug, Heinz, "South Africa: From Constitutional Promise to Social Transformation," in *Interpreting Constitutions: A Comparative Study* (Goldsworthy, Jeffrey, ed.) New York: Oxford University Press (2006).

Klug, Heinz, "Finding the Constitutional Court's Place in South Africa's Democracy: The Interaction of Principle and Institutional Pragmatism in the Court's Decision Making," *Constitutional Court Review* 3: 1–32 (2011).

Madlala, C., "Final Fitting for the Cloth of Nationhood," *Sunday Times* p. 4. col. 2 (Oct. 13, 1996).

Murienik, Etienne, "A Bridge to Where? Introducing the Interim Bill of Rights," *South African Journal on Human Rights* 10: 31 (1994).

"National Judges Symposium," reported in *The South African Law Journal*, 120(4): pp. 647–718 (2003).

Republic of South Africa Constitution Act (hereafter 1993 Const.) 200 of 1993.

Republic of South Africa Constitution Act (hereafter 1996 Const.) 108 of 1996.

Rickard, C., "This Year's Message to Despondent Civil Rights Lawyers: Pack Your Bags," 3 Weekly Mail No. 51, p. 8, col. 3 (Dec. 24, 1987–Jan. 14, 1988).

Roach, Kent and Geoff Budlender, "Mandatory Relief and Supervisory Jurisdiction: When is it appropriate, Just and Equitable?" *South African Law Journal* 122(2): 325 (2005).

Sidley, P., "World Jurists Slam S.A. Courts," 2 Weekly Mail No. 45, p. 2, col. 1 (Nov. 14–20, 1986).

Sparks, Allister. *Beyond the Miracle: Inside the New South Africa* Johannesburg, Jeppestown: Jonathan Ball Publishers (2003).

Third Report to the Negotiating Council (hereafter Third Report), Kempton Park, May 28, 1993.

COURT CASES

Alexkor Ltd et al v The Richtersveld Community and Others (hereafter *Richtersveld*), 2004 (5) SA 460 (CC).

Bhe et al v Magistrate, Khayelitsha et al. (hereafter *Bhe*), 2005 (1) SA 563 (CC).

Ex parte Chairperson of the Constitutional Assembly: In re Certification of the Constitution of the Republic of South Africa (hereafter *First Certification Judgment*), 1996 (4) SA 744 (CC).

Executive Council of the Western Cape Legislature v President of the Republic of South Africa (hereafter *Executive Council of the Western Cape*), 1995 (4) SA 877 (CC).

State v Makwanyane and Another (hereafter *Makwanyane*), 1995 (3) SA 391 (CC); 1995 (6) BCLR 665 (CC).

Minister of Health v Treatment Action Campaign (No. 2) (hereafter *TAC*), 2002 (5) SA 721 (CC).

Van Straaten v President of the Republic of South Africa (hereafter *Van Straaten*), 2009 3 SA 457 (CC); 2009 5 BCLR 480 (CC).

Xolisile Zondi v Member of the Traditional Council for Traditional and Local Government Affairs et al. (hereafter *Zondi*]), 2005 (3) SA 589 (CC).

4

Distributing Political Power
The Constitutional Tribunal in Post-Authoritarian Chile

*Druscilla L. Scribner**

Democratic transition and consolidation in Chile are bounded by four important events: 1) constitutional reform under the military culminating in the 1980 Constitution; 2) the transfer of power to a newly elected democratic government in 1990; 3) significant reform of the Constitution in 2005; and 4) the successful transfer of power to an opposition government in 2010. With respect to each of these events, the contribution of the Chilean courts has been minimal. In fact, Ginsburg (Ch. 1 in this volume) classifies Chile as a case of "judicial irrelevance, in which courts play no discernible role, either as guarantors, triggers or consolidators" of democratic transition. It is widely accepted that neither the ordinary courts nor Chile's Constitutional Court, the Tribunal Constitucional (TC), have aggressively played a rights-based role (Couso 2003, 2004, 2005; Hilbink 2007). However, less often explored is the TC's power-distribution role – despite it being a court expressly designed to adjudicate separation of powers conflicts.

Once democracy was reestablished in 1990, political supporters of the former military regime – represented by the Alianza, an alliance of right and center-right parties – formed a formidable opposition to the center-left-governing Concertación coalition, and turned to the courts as one of multiple political strategies to defend the status quo and promote their political agenda. Over the next fifteen years, the TC was called on to interpret and rearticulate the power relationships set out by the authoritarian regime under new political conditions of competitive democracy. Constitutional ambiguity with respect to the relationship between Legislative and Executive authority produced a series of separation-of-powers conflicts. This chapter is concerned with how the TC exercised its assigned functional role of distributing power in these controversies and how (and why) this role evolved.

The first section of the chapter briefly outlines the nature of Executive-Legislative conflict generated by the 1980 Constitution and the power-distribution role that

* Associate Professor of Political Science at the University of Wisconsin Oshkosh.

the TC is tasked with performing in Chile's mixed system of constitutional review. The chapter examines how the TC played this role over time within a specific type of constitutional controversy arising between laws (legislative power) and decrees (executive power).[1] In Chilean jurisprudence, these controversies are termed *ley vs. reglamento* cases (or law vs. decree cases).[2] These kinds of cases primarily concern the question of who governs: who (the Legislative or Executive branch) may impose duties on citizens and restrict constitutional rights, and under what conditions. In law vs. decree cases, the petitioners (legislators) typically charge that the Executive (represented by the office of the president) has unconstitutionally encroached on the lawful authority of the legislature or has ignored congressional authority altogether. These cases are of additional political importance because they often concern economic policies: they represent policy disputes reframed by legislators (most often from the opposition) as constitutional or statutory claims about the reach of decree-making authority and the relationship between regulations and their enabling statutes. As a result, the law vs. decree cases under study here have drawn the TC into adjudicating the competing political projects of the center-right opposition associated with the previous authoritarian regime and the center-left governing coalition that held the presidency from 1990 to 2010. Law vs. decree cases thus provide the TC an opportunity to shape the distribution of power and position the Court to adjudicate substantive policy conflicts.

Importantly, TC judgments in these cases feature competing interpretations of legislative and executive power and competing visions of the extent to which the TC should exercise its power-distribution role. The second section examines all law vs. decree conflicts decided between 1990 and 2005, highlighting how TC doctrine on two key issues (the reach of presidential power and the reach of the TC's authority) evolved over time. This systematic analysis provides the inferential leverage to articulate an account of how and why the TC's power-distribution role (and the modes of constitutional reasoning the Court employed) changed, ultimately settling on an interpretation of the Constitution that articulates a collaborative role for the Executive branch in policy making. Through ruling on these law vs. decree cases, the Court adapts its interpretation of the 1980 Constitution to the changing political context and moderates political conflict during the transition years. Section three of the chapter turns to the question of causes: how can we best understand why TC rulings on separation of powers cases reach a relatively stable equilibrium when

---

[1] The chapter draws heavily on a prior analysis in the *Journal of Politics in Latin America* (Scribner 2010) concerning the judicialization of separation-of-powers conflicts.

[2] The term "decree" describes a number of different practices: "executive rule-making in the implementation of legislation, decree authority delegated by legislatures, decree authority established in constitutions, and powers allotted to presidents under constitutional states of emergency or exception" (Carey and Shugart 1998: 5). Although Chilean presidents enjoy all of these types of decree power, law vs. decree cases typically concern the first type (rule making). These regulatory decrees or orders are technically subordinate to the law, but what is generally questioned in these cases is precisely these decrees' relationship to law and the scope of statutory authority.

they do? The analysis points to the importance and interaction of changes internal to the Court and the political context of transition.

At the end of the transition to democracy in 2005, the TC was a more broadly politically relevant institution than it was fifteen years previously. On the one hand, in exercising its power-distribution role, the TC clearly structured the policy-making context itself, such that TC doctrine on the relationship between legislative and executive authority informed the strategies of political actors (Scribner 2010). On the other hand, the TC's jurisdiction was expanded by the 2005 constitutional reform. The 1980 Constitution had contained a number of antidemocratic provisions, such as unelected senators, that were considered long-standing obstacles to the consolidation of democracy. In 2005, the Constitution was reformed to remove several of these elements, prompting then-President Lagos to declare the transition to democracy complete. Although the 2005 reforms did not alter the relationship between laws and decrees, they did open access to the TC to individual petitioners with rights-based claims. The concluding section of the chapter reflects on how the TC has renegotiated its position in Chilean democracy since 2005 and begun, perhaps, to take on new roles.

DISTRIBUTING POWER: INSTITUTIONAL AND POLITICAL BEGINNINGS

Chile's TC was created in 1970 to resolve constitutional separation of powers conflicts. It was then dissolved following the 1973 military coup. The TC was revived by the 1980 Constitution and given an expanded mandate to judge the constitutionality of executive action and, specifically, to adjudicate conflicts between branches of government. Once democracy was reestablished in 1990, the TC was drawn into adjudicating competing political and ideological projects of government and opposition.[3] The center-left governing Concertación coalition faced clear and often strident opposition from supporters of the former military regime, particularly in the Senate. In this competitive political environment, in which the Concertación held the presidency but faced a divided legislature, referral to the TC (and litigation in the ordinary courts) became a political strategy to block or delay policy change. This contentious political environment and the constitutional rules established by the military government characterized the macro conditions in which the TC would be called on to delineate the boundaries of power.

Constitutional Boundaries of Power

From 1973 through 1989, Chile was governed by a military dictatorship under the leadership of General Augusto Pinochet. Shortly after taking power, the military

---

[3] In practice, the executive and legislative branches were substantially fused during the military regime; interbranch controversy did not manifest in law vs. decree challenges until the practical separation of power under democratic conditions.

regime convened a constitutional committee to begin work on a new constitution that would address the perceived failures of the previous democratic regime. The new Constitution was approved by public referendum in 1980, roughly ten years prior to the democratic transition. Written by a military government expecting to retain control of the Executive branch, the 1980 Constitution altered the relations between the Executive and Legislative branches, increasing and reinforcing presidential power in an already strongly presidential system. Specifically, the Constitution significantly strengthened and widened executive authority to act administratively and legislatively through presidential decrees. This represented an important departure from the 1925 constitutional order that had structured Chile's fragmented presidential democracy (Caldera Delgado 1980; Blanc Renard and Pfeffer Urquiaga 1989; Cea Egaña 1988, 1989; Nogueira Alaclá 1994; Frei Ruiz-Tagle 2000).[4]

This clear shift toward greater presidential decree authority was based in two key provisions of the 1980 Constitution, provisions that are at the heart of law vs. decrees judgments. First, the Constitution established a maximum legal reserve (*reserva legal maxima*) that lists the kinds of matters, such as fundamental rights, that explicitly require congressional action. Matters outside of this legal reserve are left to the autonomous decree power of the president, forming a decree reserve (Cea Egaña 1998).[5] Second, within this reserve of legislative authority (hereafter "the legal reserve"), the 1980 Constitution restricted the reach of legislative action to establishing the "basic legal framework" in matters reserved for the legislature (the so called *leyes de base*).[6] Accordingly, the legislature is to concern itself only with the essential nucleus and fundamental framework of law within the legal reserve; the executive is given the task of developing, fine-tuning, and implementing the law by presidential decree (a *decreto supremo*). Both of these mechanisms (the legal reserve and the limitation of legislative activity implied by the *leyes de base*) extend presidential authority beyond the typical power to dictate executive orders necessary to implement the law.[7] Under the 1980 Constitution, the Chilean president is theoretically empowered with three general types of decree power: rule making, autonomous, and that emanating expressly from legislative delegation (Caldera Delgado 1980). These

[4] The faculties exclusive to the President are enumerated in Art. 32 of the 1980 Constitution.
[5] See the *Actas Oficiales de la Comisión de Estudio de la Nueva Constitución*, Session 345, p. 2094 and Session 355, p. 2278. The maximum legal reserve is outlined in Art. 60 of the 1980 Constitution and Art. 63 of the reformed 2005 Constitution. The maximum legal reserve was a significant innovation with respect to presidential decree powers. The 1925 Constitution had followed a system of a minimum legal reserve (*reserva legal mínima*), in which certain matters necessarily had to be decided by law, but other matters could also be the subject of legislative (congressional) activity. The change from a minimum to maximum legal reserve responds in part to the concern that the minimum legal reserve had produced an excessive amount of personalistic legislation (Tapia Valdés 1993). With the maximum legal reserve, only matters that figure in a closed list may be the object of legislative action (*Actas Oficiales de la Comisión de Estudio de la Nueva Constitución*, Session 355, p. 2278). Those matters excluded from the maximum legal reserve fall to presidential decree power (*Actas Oficiales de la Comisión de Estudio de la Nueva Constitución*, Session 345, p. 2094).
[6] The *leyes de base* restriction is found in numbers 4, 18, and 20 of Art. 60 of the 1980 Constitution.
[7] Art. 32, No. 8 of the 1980 Constitution.

key constitutional changes formalized a vague but collaborative policy-making role in a system that was – to emphasize – already heavily presidential.

These constitutional provisions, particularly the meaning and extension of the legal reserve, are sufficiently ambiguous to invite opposing views about the boundaries of decree authority vis-à-vis legislative authority.[8] According to the Executive branch, the maximum legal reserve and leyes de base constitutionality provide for executive decree faculties that do not require express authorization, remission, or delegation and are considered as additional to the classical and subordinated power to implement the law (Soto Kloss 1980; Carmona Santander 1998, 2001; Cea Egaña 1998; Alliende Crichton 2000; Frei Ruiz-Tagle 2000).[9] Beginning in 1990 and continuing across the transition time frame, this constitutional ambiguity produced a series of important law vs. decree controversies that were referred to the TC for resolution.

The Constitutional Review of Decree Authority

The TC is a juridical-political body; it sits at the nexus of separation of powers conflicts, and during the time period under study (1990–2005), could only be accessed by the other branches of government. The TC exercises obligatory abstract review of organic constitutional laws and laws that interpret the Constitution, and can also engage in abstract review of ordinary laws at the request of congress (or the president) and a posteriori review of executive decrees at the request of a portion of congressional membership. A decision by the Court that a disposition of a bill is unconstitutional prevents its promulgation; for a decree, a ruling of unconstitutionality invalidates the decree. Most cases decided by the TC prior to 2006 entailed obligatory abstract review of legislation (Zapata Larraín 1991, 1993, 1994, 2002; Bertelsen Repetto 1993); it decided just a couple of law vs. decree cases each year. These latter cases, however, are politically contentious and identified by the Court as consequential for interbranch relations (Couso 2004).[10] The 2005 constitutional reforms shifted the jurisdiction of direct constitutional challenges filed by individuals (under the writ of inapplicability for unconstitutionality) from the Supreme Court to the TC.[11] This reform further concentrated constitutional review

[8] Not surprisingly, the ambiguity surrounding the borders of decree power was the subject of debate even before the Constitution took effect. Caldera Delgado (1980), for example, criticized the lack of definition between law and decree, arguing that Art. 60, No. 20 effectively restored the legal reserve to the 1925 Constitutional definition of a minimum reserve.

[9] Additionally, Art. 61 of the 1980 Constitution expressly recognizes the delegation of legislative power to the executive and establishes limits on the dictation of decrees with the force of law. The Constitution of 1925 discarded the possibility of legislative delegation, in practice; however, the legislature on a number of occasions delegated to the president under the 1925 constitution (Scribner 2004).

[10] See also *Memoria del Tribunal Constitucional 2006.*

[11] The 1925 Constitution provided the Chilean Supreme Court with a limited concentrated judicial review power through the writ of inapplicability for unconstitutionality (*recurso de inaplicabilidad*). Until 2006, when the writ of inapplicability for unconstitutionality is passed to the TC, the Supreme

in the TC, and as a result its overall caseload increased nearly fourfold beginning in 2006.[12]

Chile has a mixed system of constitutional review. The legal and constitutional review of executive decrees is carried out by three main institutions: the Controller General of the Republic (CGR), the ordinary judiciary, and the TC as described. Before decrees are considered legally valid, they must be formally reviewed and approved (registered) by the controller general. The CGR returns decrees that are rejected to the Executive branch for modification (Soto Kloss 1977, 1999; Aylwin Azócar 1984).[13] The CGR does not have the final word on the legality and constitutionality of decrees, however. Decrees may be subsequently challenged before the ordinary judiciary at any time (Aróstica Maldonado 1989, 1991), and before the TC within thirty days of taking effect.

In practice, decrees are challenged in all three of these venues (the CGR, ordinary courts, and the TC), often simultaneously. Early opposition to a specific government decree may be voiced when review of the decree is pending in the CGR. Political pressure on the controller general to reject a controversial decree or force modifications to the decree before registration can be intense, ranging from attacks in the media to legislative threats of impeachment of the controller general (Scribner 2007). Law vs. decree conflicts that are referred to the TC are often adjudicated previously – or simultaneously – in the appellate courts using the writ of protection or – prior to 2006 – before the Supreme Court under the writ inapplicability for unconstitutionality.[14] Concurrently, or when these political and litigation strategies fail to produce the intended effect, legislators (rather than individuals) can refer the Executive-Legislative conflict to the TC. This referral may be solicited by either house in the legislature or by more than one quarter of congressional members within thirty days of the official publication of the decree.[15]

Court could hear direct constitutional challenges at any stage of court proceedings, by petition by one of the parties or *de oficio*, and could suspend the lower-court proceedings until a decision on the constitutionality of the law in question had been reached (Frei Ruiz-Tagle 2000; Verdugo Marinkovic and Pfeffer Urquiaca 1993). However, under both the 1925 and 1980 Constitutions the writ of inapplicability was infrequently used and rarely accepted by the Supreme Court (Bertelsen Repetto 1985; Valenzuela Somarriva 1990; Vargas Viancos and Correa Sutil 1995).

[12] See the annual reports of the TC available on the Court's Web site: www.tribunalconstitucional.cl.

[13] The GCR rejects and returns very few decrees; in part, this low rejection rate reflects informal practices of consultation between CGR and administration staff that result in modifications before formal review is initiated (Interview, CGR staff, Santiago, August 9, 2001).

[14] The writ of protection (*recurso de protección*) was established under the military government as a legal action giving individuals the ability to challenge state or private conduct that harms, or threatens to harm, a constitutionally guaranteed right. The writ of protection operates in the appellate courts and on appeal before the Supreme Court (Soto Kloss 1982; Nogueira Alcalá 2007).

[15] These two different requirements – one-quarter of membership versus the whole house (Art 82 No. 5 and No. 12 of the 1980 Constitution, respectively) – created uncertainty and conflict between 1990 and 2005 over standing in law vs. decree referrals. The constitutional reforms of 2005 combined the two requirements for standing into a single rule (Art. 93 No. 16); an innovation that generates greater coherency in the review of presidential decrees.

EVOLVING LAW VS. DECREE DOCTRINE

In law vs. decree cases, the TC is called to delineate the boundaries of legislative and executive power. Petitions claiming unconstitutional use of decree authority primarily center on encroachment issues: the president has trespassed, invaded, or encroached on the legal reserve (matters that explicitly require congressional action). TC decisions in these cases turn on the Court's interpretation of the legal reserve relative to other constitutional provisions, and on the hierarchical relationship between the decree, enabling statute, and Constitution. This section of the chapter describes how the TC's power-distribution role evolved across the law vs. decree cases it decided from 1990 to 2005. It discusses the two doctrinal positions that crystallized on the Court beginning in 1990 – which reflect clearly different definitions of the legal reserve, conceptions of the role of the Court, and modes of constitutional reasoning – and demonstrates how the Court came to settle (at least temporarily) on a majority doctrine that articulates a collaborative policy-making role for the Executive branch and a limited role for the TC.

The contrast between the doctrinal positions that characterize law vs. decree adjudication has two defining features. First, there is disagreement about how the TC should exercise constitutional review of administrative action and thus exercise its power-distribution role. The crux of this division is whether, and under what conditions, decrees are justiciable; this in turn depends on whether or not the Court can exercise direct constitutional review of a legal decree (one that validly executes the law). Second, there is clear divergence in opinion among the political branches and on the Court about the character of the maximum legal reserve in the context of other constitutional provisions, and thus divergent constitutional interpretations about the relationship between law (legislative power) and decree (executive power) given by the 1980 Constitution. Table 4.1 lists all law vs. decree cases filed with the TC between 1990 and 2005. These cases, which generally involve regulations that impact economic policy, are referred to the TC by legislators (primarily from the center-right opposition parties). Further, the table characterizes the TC's decisions on these cases with respect to these two issues. First, the table indicates whether the majority opinion asserts the TC's authority to review decrees generally – *wide scope of authority* – or limits the reach of its constitutional review power to illegal decrees that depart from the enabling statute – *narrow scope of authority*. Second, the table identifies how the majority opinion distributes power: to the legislature, finding for the petitioners that the Executive exceeded its authority or encroached on Legislative terrain, thus invalidating the decree; or to the Executive, allowing the executive action to stand.

Concurrent with the substantive changes in the TC's decisions summarized in Table 4.1, there is a shift in modes of constitutional reasoning from an interpretive model that is originalist, literal, and rigid to a more structuralist model in which the Constitution is interpreted holistically and its text, inherent principles, and values

TABLE 4.1. *Law vs. decree decisions 1990–2005*

Case summary	Scope of authority		To whom power distributed	
	Wide	Narrow	Legislature	Executive
Rol 116 (Dec. 27, 1990) rejects a challenge to a decree regulating housing applications.	√			√
Rol 124 (Jun. 18, 1991) rejects a challenge to a decree dissolving the *Sociedad Benefactora y Educacional Dignidad*.	√			√
Rol 146 (Apr. 21, 1992) upholds a challenge to a decree prohibiting the placement of billboards within a certain proximity to public roadways.	√		√	
Rol 153 (Jan. 25, 1993) upholds a challenge to a decree implementing intercommunal regulations.	√		√	
Rol 167 (Apr. 6, 1993) upholds a challenge to a decree prohibiting the placement of billboards within a certain proximity to public roadways.	√		√	
Rol 183 (May 17, 1994) rejects a challenge to a decree establishing transportation tolls.	√			√
Rol 245 and 246 (Dec. 2, 1996) upholds a challenge to a decree requiring property owners to provide public access to beaches, rivers, and lakes.	√		√	
Rol 253 (Apr. 15, 1997) rejects a challenge to a decree requiring that urban construction cede a proportion of land for green space, access, and equipment.		√		√
Rol 254 (Apr. 26, 1997) rejects a challenge to a decree introducing modifications to the budget law approved by Congress.		√		√
Rol 282 (Jan. 28, 1999) rejects a challenge to a decree promulgating the Additional Protocol and Appendix of the Complementary Economic Agreement with Bolivia.		√		√

(continued)

TABLE 4.1 *(continued)*

Case summary	Scope of authority		To whom power distributed	
	Wide	Narrow	Legislature	Executive
Rol 325 (Jun. 26, 2001) rejects a challenge to a decree restricting the circulation of vehicles with catalytic converters on days of high ambient contamination.	✓			✓
Rol 370 (Apr. 9, 2003) upholds a challenge to a decree requiring an impact study of construction projects.	✓		✓	
Rol 373 (Jul. 22, 2003) rejects a challenge to a decree regulating construction in green space.	✓			✓
Rol 388 (Nov. 25, 2003) rejects a challenge to a decree regulating public transport; upholds one aspect of the challenge concerning penalties.	✓			✓

seen as coherent, harmonious, and consistent.[16] The shift to this interpretation is evident in the majority and minority opinions in the examples given and informs the two divergent positions on the nature of the legal reserve.

The first seven decisions (roughly 1990–1996) in Table 4.1 demonstrate a doctrinal position that interprets the maximum legal reserve (the Constitution's reservation of particular matters for formal legislation and congressional action) as *absolute*. According to this position, matters within the legal reserve (such as fundamental rights and duties) cannot be regulated by presidential decree. The details of these matters should be specified by congress, formal law, and not left to the discretion or complementary decree power of the Executive. This same position articulates a wide scope of review and sustains that the TC has ample competency to consider the constitutionality of decrees, even in cases in which the decree is consistent with the enabling statute and thus legal. The TC majority asserted its authority to directly review the constitutionality of executive decrees, and argued for an interpretation of the legal reserve that significantly restricted executive and administrative discretion and action. This literal interpretation of the legal reserve as absolute seals off and protects fundamental rights at the heart of Pinochet's neoliberal economic

---

[16] "Structuralism" is the term that would be used in the U.S. context; in Chile, this mode of constitutional interpretation is referred to as *finalista*.

reforms – such as the right to property and to engage in an economic activity – from potential administrative discretion and state regulation.

The interpretation of the legal reserve as absolute characterized the majority opinions of the Court in law vs. decree judgments from 1990 to 1996 as summarized in Table 4.1. Of these cases, *Letreros Camineros I* (Rol 146; Apr. 21, 1992) demonstrates well what is at stake in law vs. decree cases, and provides a good summary of this first doctrinal position. On March 19, 1992, thirty members of the lower house (more than a quarter of the membership) petitioned the TC seeking a declaration of unconstitutionality of Supreme Decree No. 357 signed by the minister of public works and published one month prior to the petition. The decree prohibited installation of commercial signage (billboards) within 300 meters of the roadside on public roads. The decree also altered the administrative procedure governing billboard authorization. This case (and several others that were pursued at the same time in the ordinary courts) was important both politically and economically, pitting large advertising companies and their right-of-center congressional allies against a relatively new left-of-center democratically elected government.

The position of the congressional members who brought the case to the TC was that the decree infringed the constitutional right to develop an economic activity and the property rights of those who owned land adjacent to public roadways (i.e., the right to develop, rent out, or use their property as they wished). The power-distribution issue before the Court concerned the constitutionality of limiting a fundamental right via executive decree rather than by law (because matters pertaining to fundamental rights are reserved exclusively for legislative action). The president and the CGR (which reviews decrees for legality prior to publication) defended the decree on the basis of the legal history of signage restrictions, improved highway safety, and preservation of the natural beauty of public roads. They emphasized that the enabling statute explicitly conferred regulatory authority with respect to signage, and in this manner allowed limited restrictions on property rights. Arguments for both sides were bolstered by "friend of the court" letters and expert opinions submitted to the TC by legislators, members of the legal community including legal scholars, and cabinet members. Some of these letters cited the decisions of ordinary courts (appellate and Supreme Court – venues in which the same decree was previously or concurrently contested).

The majority opinion, written by Justice Luz Bulnes, declared the decree an unconstitutional invasion of the legislative sphere. The decision was on the basis of several related points. First, the original intent of the founders was to give the legislature the power to regulate economic activities and impose limitations on individual rights. Second, according to a strict reading of the Constitution, limitations on the right to develop an economic activity are justified only by reasons of public order, morality, or national security, not the protection of the environment as the president and CGR argued. Third, the restriction, limitation, or prohibition of the enjoyment of constitutional rights (such as those imposed by Supreme Decree No. 357) can only be carried out by law, not by decree. In short, the opinion established the existence of a legal reserve that is absolute in matters regulating economic activity, and reiterated a wide scope of review, sustaining the TC's competency to consider the constitutionality of decrees.

The dissent in this case clearly outlines the opposing doctrinal position in law vs. decree cases. The minority opinion argued that in dictating Supreme Decree No. 357, the president had merely made use of a faculty that the enabling statute conferred on the Executive – to dictate norms regulating the location of signs on the edge of public roadways. The Executive (the minister of public works in this case) acted within the regulatory powers given by the Constitution and the enabling statute. The dissenting opinion added that such decree power was increased in the 1980 Constitution with the addition of a closed and maximum legal reserve in which the Legislative branch attends to only the basic outline of the law, leaving other matters to the decree power of the president. In sum, the dissent interpreted the legal reserve relative to other constitutional provisions defining legislative and executive powers, rejecting the absolutist view of legislative power, thus shifting the interpretation of the bounds of power in favor of a complementary but subordinated role for the Executive branch.

This alternative interpretation became the majority position on the TC in 1997 with the decision in *Cesión Gratuita de Terrenos* (Rol 253; Apr. 15, 1997). Table 4.1 clearly demonstrates this shift. As with the previous example, the *Cesión Gratuita de Terrenos* case was important politically and economically, as well as constitutionally. Twelve senators challenged the constitutionality of a presidential decree that set the proportion of land that developers would need to cede to public use for green space, access, and equipment. The senators characterized the decree as a privation of property rights and claimed that in dictating the decree the president had invaded the Legislative sphere. Indicative of the contentious nature of these kinds of conflicts, legislators, legal scholars, and interest groups sent the TC friend of the court letters and supplemental information calling attention to the opinion of the appellate courts and CGR. Those submitted in support of the president's position highlighted a series of writ of protection cases that had favorably recognized the ceding of land for green space.

The TC majority concluded that the Executive branch had executed the law rigorously and faithfully and had acted well within its powers to implement law. The decision elaborated on the nature of the relationship between decrees and the law they execute, arguing that decrees and law form a juridical whole, "harmonious, united and insoluble." This interpretation views the relationship between laws and decrees as complementary and collaborative. The decision interpreted the role of the legislature as limited to defining the essential bases or fundamentals of the law, leaving the details to decree power. Decrees are understood to be the instrument by which the Executive collaborates with the Legislature in the specification and execution of law. The *Cesión Gratuita de Terrenos* judgment marks the ascendancy of a view of the legal reserve as relative and relational to other constitutional provisions rather than absolute. This position tilts the balance of power in these kinds of conflicts toward the Executive branch and is associated with written opinions of Justices Eugenio Valenzuela, Colombo Campbell, and Cea Egaña.

With respect to justiciability, this second position is restrictive, maintaining that the TC may only rule on the constitutionality of decrees when the decree departs from the enabling statute, or from the constitutional bounds of presidential decree power, and is therefore illegal. When faced with a *legal decree* – one that faithfully executes the law, as in the *Cesión Gratuita de Terrenos* case – the true object of the constitutional question is the law in which the decree is founded, and the TC cannot exercise review over laws already in force. Moreover, the majority established in *Cesión Gratuita de Terrenos* that a legal decree can be presumed constitutional because a reasonable legislature would not remit or delegate powers that could result in unconstitutional administrative action. As a result, the *Cesión Gratuita de Terrenos* judgment reinforced the presumption of constitutionality of formal statutory law, and limited the reach of the TC's authority. Moreover, because the majority block turned out to be enduring, the ruling established a new dominant mode of constitutional interpretation.[17] This doctrine (relative legal reserve and limited scope of review) is reiterated in *Ley de Presupuestos* Rol 254 (Apr. 26, 1997) and *Décimo Protocolo con Bolivia* Rol 282 (Jan. 28, 1999); the dissents in these same cases reiterate the opposing doctrine (absolute legal reserve and wide scope of constitutional review).

As demonstrated in Table 4.1, between 1997 and 2001, the TC played its power-distribution role in law vs. decree conflicts roughly consistently. It reinforced the presumption of constitutionality that formal law enjoys in the Chilean system and limited the reach of TC authority to hold presidents accountable for the constitutionality of their actions.[18] This position – which emphasized legal control of decrees (recognizing that constitutional review only proceeds if the decree is illegal) – elicited criticism about the ability of Chile's mixed system to protect fundamental rights (Couso 2004).

In the first half of the 2000s, the TC majority refined and further clarified its view that the boundaries of the legal reserve should be interpreted relative to other constitutional provisions. In particular, it argued that the legal reserve is more intense in matters concerning individual rights and, consequently, that there is less room for administrative discretion. Leading cases include *Restricción a Catalíticos* Rol 325 (Jun. 26, 2001) and *Plan de Impacto Vial Rol* 370 (Apr. 9, 2003). In the first of these,

---

[17] The minority opinion in *Cesión Gratuita de Terrenos* (written by Luz Bulnes) objected vehemently to the possibility that the mere "legality" of a decree (which in turn presumed that the legislature acts constitutionally) served to justify a constitutional violation.

[18] The TC has developed a doctrine of reasoned deference (*deferencia razonada*) that respects the will and autonomy of the legislature as well as presumes the constitutionality of legislative acts (Peña Torres 2006: 176; Zapata Larraín 2002: 72).

the TC established that legislation concerning rights must explicitly determine what constitutional rights may be affected or restricted by administrative power and specify the measures the Executive may take to restrict rights and under what conditions. The TC then applied these constitutional tests of specificity and determination to subsequent cases. The TC's rulings in this vein sought to limit the Executive's discretion by requiring the legislature to provide greater direction to the administration in statutes involving fundamental rights (Hernández Emparanza 2006). Between 2000 and 2005, the TC established and refined the relative reserve doctrine, and by the end of the transition period, it had established a clear framework for interpreting the relationship between law and decree depending on the intensity of the legal reserve and the legislature's design of statutory law.[19]

In sum, this analysis of law vs. decree cases demonstrates that the way in which the TC exercised its power-distribution role shifted significantly during Chile's long transition to democracy. The early 1990s were dominated by a majority position that asserted wide original TC authority to directly review the constitutionality of executive decree authority and argued for a rigid originalist interpretation of the legal reserve that significantly restricted executive and administrative action and potentially protected the economic project of the previous regime. As the transition to democracy matured, the Court rearticulated the constitutional boundaries of power pragmatically and flexibly, recognizing a collaborative relationship between law and decrees that facilitated administrative action. Arguably, this shift resulted in a more limited role for the Court and tipped the balance of power toward the Executive, albeit setting some clear and consistent limits on Executive and Legislative discretion. How can we best understand this shift?

CAUSES: INTERNAL MOTIVATIONS AND EXTERNAL INFLUENCES

The comparative judicial-politics literature highlights two broad explanations to account for judicial behavior: one stresses external influences (factors in the political environment); and one focuses on factors internal to courts (legal culture, institutional structure, and court composition). The first of these explanations views judges as constrained by political forces, either explicitly because of court-curbing policies or intrinsically by the desire of judges to maintain the institutional legitimacy of the Court. Facing these kinds of constraints, courts do not venture far from majority political preferences (Dahl 1957).

Separation-of-powers explanations for judicial behavior center on the idea that legal policy outcomes are a function of the dynamic interaction of all three branches of government (Epstein and Knight 1998; Epstein, Knight and Shvetsova 2001; Iaryczower, Spiller and Tommasi 2002; Chavez 2004; Scribner 2004; Helmke 2005;

---

[19] Hernández Esparanza (2006) provides a fuller discussion of the TC's use of precedent.

Ríos-Figueroa 2007). Judges face incentives to decide cases within the policy "comfort zone" of the Legislature and Executive, who may overturn, ignore, or refuse to implement judicial decisions and thus thwart the ability of the Court to attain its objectives. One of the key findings in this literature is that political fragmentation affords judges greater room for maneuvering.

Chile during the transition to democracy presents us with a case of political fragmentation in the context of stable coalition politics. In this environment, the external political pressures highlighted by separation-of-powers accounts are relatively weak. Roughly the same center-left coalition of parties that took over government from the military remained in power over the entire time period under study, and faced significant opposition from the same coalition of opposition parties (mainly in the Senate, where political allies of the former military regime were overrepresented). In this context, neither the government nor the opposition could mount a politically credible threat against the TC. The cases outlined in Table 4.1 were quite contentious, pulling the TC squarely into policy battles. The losers (the Executive branch in the early period, center-right opposition legislators after 1997) grumbled publicly about the TC's decisions, questioned the motivation of some TC justices, and sometimes even challenged the legitimacy of the Court itself. However, despite this political wrangling and posturing about TC judgments, much of the negotiation over its power-distribution role was really internal to the Court itself.

A second broad approach to understanding judicial behavior stresses factors internal to courts such as judicial culture and ideological, political, or legal policy preferences. The core insight of cultural approaches, such as the attitudinal model, is that the composition of the court, and the resulting mix of political and/or ideological attitudes with respect to constitutional review and the relationship between the state and individual, best explain decision making (Segal and Spaeth 2002).

Along these lines, this chapter argues that the construction of a new majority position on the TC concerning the relationship between law and decree power resulted from a change in the composition of the Court.[20] That is, owing to transition politics (the electoral successes of the left-of-center Concertación coalition, which held the presidency and a majority in the lower house from 1990 to 2005), the composition of the TC slowly changed, and with it the dominant model of constitutional interpretation and thus TC doctrine on the distribution of power.

For a broader range of constitutional controversies than I review here, Zapata Larraín (1991) suggests that the TC's composition best accounts for changes in its decision making during the decade preceding the democratic transition (1981–1989). He finds that during the first half of that period, TC decision making was dominated by the strict originalist jurisprudence of Enrique Ortúzar (a key member of the commission that penned the 1980 Constitution),[21] supported by Marco Aburto

---

[20] Interview, presidential lawyer, August 2001.
[21] Originalism is facilitated in Chile by the existence of tomes of documents from the Comisión de Estudios de la Nueva Constitución (known as Comisión Ortúzar) as well as from the Consejo del

and Eduardo Urzúa. In the second half of the decade, leading up to the moment of transition, an alternative model of constitutional interpretation began to take shape under the leadership of Eugenio Valenzuela, and supported by Julio Philippi and Luis Maldonado. During the 1980s, Justices Ortúzar and Valenzuela represented opposing views on constitutional interpretation. The existence of alternative contested modes of constitutional reasoning and a trend toward a structural method of interpretation mirrored regional developments in legal theory in which "textualism and literalism" were increasing supplanted (Couso 2010: 147, citing López Medina; Núñez Poblete 2010). Couso (2010: 147) describes this regional shift, beginning roughly in the 1980s, as the "path from a 'formalist and anti-judicial review' position, to a 'quasi-natural law and pro-judicial review' new orthodoxy."[22]

Indications of this broader trend can be found in some early TC decisions. For example, in 1985 Valenzuela employed a systemic, structuralist approach to constitutional interpretation in one of the most politically consequential decisions of the pre-democratic period (Zapata Larraín 2002). The 1980 Constitution mandated that a plebiscite be held in 1988 to move the country toward civilian government. The judgment in *Tribunal Calificador de Elecciones* (Rol 33, 1985) required that the 1988 plebiscite be held according to the organic constitutional law governing elections. The decision ostensibly gave the pro-democracy opposition a legal leg to stand on in organizing and advertising a campaign to vote no in the plebiscite. Pinochet narrowly lost the 1988 plebiscite, setting in motion the democratic elections in December 1989 and the inauguration of a new government in March 1990. In 1989, just prior to the transition to democracy, Eugenio Valenzuela left the TC and was replaced by Luz Bulnes, one of the members of the Ortúzar Commission that wrote the 1980 Constitution. On the eve of the transition to democracy in 1990, the TC was dominated by military government appointees and justices who tended to utilize an originalist model of constitutional interpretation. Originalism informs the majority opinions of the 1990–1997 law vs. decree cases.

The composition of the TC gradually changed during the second half of the 1990s, as some justices were replaced by the center-left governing coalition. Many of these new appointments represented political compromises with the opposition and did not necessarily represent the political left. Eugenio Valenzuela, who left the TC in 1989 as the transition to democracy began, returned to the Court in March 1997 and revived and nurtured a structural and finalist model of constitutional interpretation that calls for a holistic interpretation of the Constitution. At the end of the decade and into the new century, Valenzuela (1997–2006) was joined by several more

---

Estado, which make it possible to discern (and legitimize) the original intent of the framers of the 1980 Constitution.

[22] Couso (2010: 158) uses the term *neoconstitutionalism* to describe a natural-law approach that emphasizes the "preeminence of human rights and constitutional principles over legislated law, as well as an activist conception of the role of courts in a democracy." See also Núñez Poblete (2010) for a discussion of neo-constitutionalism in the Chilean context.

centrist and moderate members, such as Mario Verdugo Marinkovic (1997–2001), Hernán Alvarez García (1997–2005), and Juan Colombo Campbell (1993–2009). The appointments of José Luis Cea Egaña (2002–2010), Jorge Sutil Correa (2006–2009), and more recently, Carlos Carmona Santander (2009–2018), all of whom had been involved in the development of law vs. decree doctrine in various capacities, also followed this moderate trend.[23] These appointments have helped shift the TC away from formalism and solidify the relative position on law vs. decree jurisprudence. In sum, shifts in composition, politically driven or otherwise, and the accompanying shift in dominant models of constitutional interpretation influenced how the TC performed its power-distribution role.

However, changes in models of constitutional interpretation on the Court and in the way it constructed its power-distribution role are also tied to a related set of internal factors: judicial culture and identity. It is widely argued and generally accepted that judicial resistance to engage in constitutional (rather than legal) review across Chilean history is the result of Chile's legal culture. A rigid judicial hierarchy and formalistic and positivist legal training reinforced a judicial culture of legalism and institutional and ideological conservatism. The result is antipathy toward constitutional review, a persistent understanding of statutory law as supreme, and a private law perspective on questions of constitutional rights (Correa Sutíl 1988; Peña González 1997; Couso 2004; Hilbink 2007; Faundez 2010). The Supreme Court has figured prominently in the composition of the TC, thus inculcating the latter with these aspects of judicial culture.[24] Consistent with the explanations of conservatism on the Chilean Supreme Court and in the ordinary judiciary, accounts of TC decisions have often emphasized the negative influence of judicial culture (Couso 2005). The predominance of a private law approach to constitutional adjudication and the de facto presumption of the constitutionality of law by ordinary and constitutional judges in Chile have justified the construction of a narrow scope of TC authority.

This discussion suggests that the gradual (re)construction, refinement, and limitation of the judicial role during Chile's political transition was largely internally driven rather than forged through the kind of intense conflict with the political branches that Trochev describes in his chapter (Ch. 2 in this volume).[25] Nonetheless,

---

[23] Cea Egaña has written extensively on doctrine in this area, and Carmona had served, since 1990, in the executive branch as a legal advisor to the president. Colombo and Cea Egaña had supported a relative view of the legal reserve and the thesis of intensity of the legal reserve before their appointments to the TC. Moreover, Correa has been a critic of the disappointing performance of Chile's mixed system (particularly the writ of protection) in protecting fundamental rights.

[24] Until constitutional reforms were enacted in 2005, the TC was a seven-member body with three members selected by the Supreme Court, two by Chile's National Security Council, one by the president, and one by the Senate. The last two were additionally required to have previously served as substitute justices for the Supreme Court for at least three consecutive years. As a result, the choices of the president and Senate were restricted in ways that promoted greater Supreme Court influence (Nogueira Alcalá 1995).

[25] This is consistent with accounts of the Chilean judiciary generally as less assertive and more politically insulated (Couso 2005; Hilbink 2007; Huneeus 2010).

these processes do not occur in political isolation. In fact, to best understand change in the Court's doctrine on law vs. decree decisions, we need to view the internal changes on the court in the context of transition politics in which the TC needed to establish its legitimacy as a political and judicial actor in a newly competitive environment and within broader regional shifts in judicial culture (Couso and Hilbink 2011).

The separation-of-powers approach briefly outlined has important insights for understanding the proclivity of courts to defer to the political branches, favor one branch over another, or auto-restrict the scope of their review authority (and thus duck contentious separation-of-powers questions). For example, Epstein et al. (2001; 138), argue that in new or transitioning democracies a new court may prefer to "promote its legitimacy and adjust the status quo policy slowly" by adopting a strategy of "soft" or semi-deferential review. Soft review is certainly rational when courts face cohesive political majorities. However, a strategy of deliberate passivity with respect to various judicial functions is also logical, even in politically fragmented contexts, when a court's legitimacy is not well-established, is contested or damaged, or when legal culture significantly and conservatively circumscribes the definition of legitimate judicial action. This is arguably the case for the TC, particularly during the first decade of the transition to democracy.

The TC played a pivotal role in events that led to the end of the military regime, and expectations surrounding its role in the new democratic framework were high (Couso 2005). However, it is not surprising that the TC (or the Supreme Court) did not embrace a new activist role with respect to constitutional review. At the beginning of the transition period, the TC was not well-established, the political context was in flux, and the judiciary as a whole (in which members of the TC were deeply embedded) was being heavily criticized politically and publicly for its record on human rights adjudication (Huneeus 2010). As Murphy (1964) notes, judges will neither knowingly injure or destroy judicial power nor attempt to expand their power beyond the limits that would be legitimate under accepted theories of the judicial function. Without a public consensus in Chile about what alternative principles to traditional legal positivism and reasoning should govern judicial activity, judges (even constitutional judges aware of their political role) were unlikely to leave the safety of the traditional model of legitimacy, especially in politically contentious cases (Scribner 2004, 2010). In other words, the judicial advancement of strong countermajoritarian rights protections (a "rights revolution") or assertively checking the elected branches would not have served the institutional goals of the TC (or the ordinary judiciary) during the transition period.

In contrast to the 1990–1997 period, from roughly 1997 to 2001 the TC rulings rearticulated the bounds of power to favor presidential governance and limit its own authority. Post-2001, the TC articulated limits on Executive (and Legislative) discretion by refining the intensity of the legal reserve. We might best appreciate this shift in the TC's exercise of its power-distribution role (from rigid and confrontational toward Executive authority to flexible, pragmatic, and somewhat more deferential after 1997) in light of the changes in court composition and the Court's need to build institutional legitimacy in a political context in which it faced many audiences (Baum 2008). Facing a complex political and judicial environment with multiple judicial actors and multiple audiences – including the other branches of government as well as interest groups, the press and public, the legal community and political parties – the TC avoided engaging in review outside of its jurisdiction and tailored its own competency in law vs. decree cases narrowly. A strategy of subtly redefining its power and doctrine in separation of power cases allowed the TC to navigate its relations with the co-legislative branches as well as the Supreme Court and the CGR, at the same time protecting and advancing its long-term legitimacy and political relevancy. The TC's development of the doctrine of reasoned deference (*deferencia razonada*) is consistent with this view.[26] Deference allowed the TC to exercise its power-distribution role "vigorously and creatively," avoiding confrontation and politicization (Zapata Larraín 2002: 71). The pattern of nonconfrontational rulings that incrementally developed the TC's power-distribution role was facilitated by changes in composition and the ascendency of a less formalistic and more pragmatic model of constitutional interpretation among a majority of justices.

CONCLUSION: NEGOTIATING NEW ROLES

As discussed, the changing composition of the TC and the impact of judicial culture in the context of transition politics help to explain why the TC embraced a doctrinal strategy of soft review in law vs. decree cases that limited administrative discretion and recognized a collaborative policy-making role for the Executive. The use of judicial strategies (such as the doctrine of reasoned deference) is rational for protecting and advancing judicial power. The way the TC exercised its power-distribution role served to strengthen the institutional position of the court vis-à-vis other institutional actors: The TC emerged in 2005, at the end of the transition to democracy, a much stronger, legitimate, and politically relevant institution. In particular, the TC was successful in its bid to expand its jurisdiction and further concentrate judicial review as part of the 2005 constitutional reforms negotiated during the administration of Ricardo Lagos (2000–2006).

As a result of the 2005 constitutional reforms, the president gained full authority over armed-forces personnel decisions, nonelected Senate seats were eliminated, and the presidential term was shortened to four years. Less publicized but substantial changes were made to the appointment procedures for the TC and to its jurisdiction. TC membership was increased to ten and appointment procedures altered; the reforms reduced the influence of the more conservative Supreme Court

---

[26] Zapata Larraín (2002) discusses the constitutive elements of the doctrine of reasoned deference (presumption of legality and constitutionality of legislative acts, and autonomy of the legislature) in Chilean and comparative jurisprudence.

and immediately resulted in personnel changes on the Court.[27] The president now chooses three members, the Supreme Court chooses three, and Congress chooses four. Justices now serve nine-year terms.[28] Importantly, the 2005 reforms (for which the TC had long lobbied) shifted jurisdiction over writ of inapplicability for unconstitutionality cases (which are filed by individuals or by lower court judges) from the Supreme Court to the TC. The move ostensibly concentrated constitutional review in the TC and expanded access to it, broadening the kinds of claims it could be asked to judge and potentially expanding the roles it can play (Fernández González 2006).

We might ask whether the evolution of judicial roles in Chile will be consistent with Shapiro's (2004: 21–25) two-step evolution of rights-based constitutional review, where narrow rule of law jurisprudence establishes the foundations for more confrontational rights-based constitutional review in the future. How might the roles the TC plays in Chilean democracy expand and evolve? Institutional reform coupled with changes to judicial culture could support an emerging rights-based jurisprudence in Chile.

Along with expanded access to the TC, the shift in constitutional interpretation toward a model that supports the incorporation of natural-law principles and human rights instruments appears to be gaining support and legitimacy among multiple audiences, including within academic circles (Nogueira Alcalá 1997, 2003; Couso 2010; Núñez Poblete 2010; Couso and Hilbink 2011). Just as public support resources available to courts can affect their ability to challenge the Executive and Legislature (Caldeira and Gibson 1992; Staton 2002; Vanberg 2005), broad changes to judicial culture may support a move away from the historically dominant positive law model of constitutional interpretation. Changes to the Court's jurisdiction and a broader transformation of constitutional discourse in Chile and regionally (Couso 2010; Couso and Hilbink 2011) indicate that the type of roles the TC has been assigned, and may assume for itself in the future, is in flux.

In fact, the equilibrium reached in law vs. decree jurisprudence prior to the institutional and composition changes on the TC may have become less stable. Table 4.2 summarizes the post-2005 law vs. decree cases along the same lines as Table 4.1. Significantly, all of the cases decided after the constitutional changes have been closely divided, demonstrating shifting majorities on the TC. Moreover, the docket of the Court has become more complex and varied. The first writ of inapplicability cases were decided by the TC in 2006 and the number of such cases has soared from that time, significantly increasing the overall caseload of the Court.[29]

---

[27] As a result of new appointments in the wake of the reform, only Cea Egaña, Colombo Campbell, and Libedinski Tschorne remained on the TC; 70 percent of the positions were newly appointed (Fernández González 2006).

[28] Art. 92 of the Constitution promulgated in 2005.

[29] Inapplicability cases represented roughly 87 percent of the TC's docket in 2006 and 2007; 85 percent in 2008; and 84 percent in 2009. As reported in the annual reports from 2006 to 2009 available on the Court's Web site at: http://www.tribunalconstitucional.cl/index.php/documentos/memorias_cuentas.

TABLE 4.2. *Law vs. decree decisions 2005–2008*

Case summary	Scope of authority		To whom power distributed	
	Wide	Narrow	Legislature	Executive
Rol 465 (Mar. 30, 2006) rejects a challenge to a decree that regulates state requirements for school accreditation.		✓		✓
Rol 591 (Jan. 11, 2007) upholds a challenge to an administrative resolution (health ministry) approving the distribution of the morning-after-pill through the public health system.	✓		✓	
Rol 577 (Apr. 26, 2007) rejects a challenge to a decree that sets effluent emissions standards for CODELCO's El Teniente mining operation.	[Not a key issue]		✓	
Rol 740 (Apr. 18, 2008) upholds a challenge to decree approving the distribution of the morning-after-pill.	✓		✓	
Rol 1035 (May 22, 2008) rejects a challenge to administrative actions and a decree that secured a line for credit to finance the Transantiago public transportation project.		✓		✓
Rol 1153 (Sep. 30, 2008) upholds challenges to decrees that modify lines of credit (to finance the Transantiago project) with the IDB and the Banco del Estado.	✓		✓	

Moreover, petitioners are increasingly making rights-based claims, providing the TC opportunities to take on new roles.

Some TC judgments in this period indicate that a rights-based jurisprudence is developing.[30] For example, a 2007 writ of inapplicability case recognized the right of access to information (as essential for freedom of expression and a democratic regime broadly). However, there are also counterexamples, such as the 2008 decision overturning public provision of the morning-after pill, which suggest the pragmatism that characterized the later transition period is giving way. The judgment, roundly

---

[30] *Casas Cordero et al v. The National Customs Service* (Rol No. 634, Aug. 9, 2007), written by Marisol Peña Torres. See also Peña Torres (2006).

criticized as ideological and non-neutral, was greeted by large public protests, and signaled to the TC that the interaction between litigation, legislation, and political praise/threat in a context of increased individual access to the court would be much more public – and perhaps more contentious – than it had been in the past. In sum, since 2006, the Court appears to be negotiating and constructing its new powers and the kinds of roles it will play in Chilean politics and society. Couso and Hilbink (2011: 117) describe for the 2006 to 2009 period a "more activist and politically influential constitutional court;" one that has "assertively defended and expanded" its own powers, "engaged in rights-based and value-laden" constitutional interpretation, and "issued an impressive set of visible and activist decisions."

REFERENCES

Alliende Crichton, Fernando José. 2000. *La Reserva de Ley. Memoria para optar al grado de licenciado en ciencias jurídicas y sociales*. Facultad de Derecho, Departamento de Derecho Público, Universidad de Chile, Santiago.

Aróstica Maldonado, Iván. 1989. "Impugnabilidad de los Actos Administrativos," *Revista Chilena de Derecho* (Universidad Católica) 16: 455–464.

Aróstica Maldonado, Iván. 1991. "¿Qué Queda de la 'Presunción de Legalidad'?" *Revista de Derecho y Jurisprudencia* 88(1): 1–7.

Aylwin Azócar, Arturo. 1984. "Límite de la Potestad Reglamentaria del Presidente de la República," *Revista Chilena de Derecho* (Universidad Católica) 11: 449–453.

Baum, Lawrence. 2008. *Judges and Their Audiences A Perspective on Judicial Behavior*. Princeton, N.J.: Princeton University Press.

Bertelsen Repetto, Raúl. 1985. "La Jurisprudencia de la Corte Suprema sobre el Recurso de Inaplicabilidad," *Revista de Derecho Público* (Universidad de Chile) 37–38 (Enero-Diciembre): 167–185.

Bertelsen Repetto, Raúl. 1993. "Sistemas de Control de Constitucionalidad entre 1960–1989," in *Diagnostico Histórico Jurídico del Poder Legislativo en Chile*. Valparaíso: Centro de Estudios y Asistencia Legislativa, Universidad Católica de Valparaíso, Ediciones Universitarias de Valparaíso.

Blanc Renard, Neville and Emilio Pfeffer Urquiaga. 1989. *Reflexiones en Torno al Equilibrio Ejecutivo – Parlamento, Documento de Trabajo No. 8*. Santiago: Corporación de Estudio Liberales.

Caldeira, Gregory A. and James L. Gibson. 1992. "The Etiology of Public Support for the Supreme Court," *American Journal of Political Science* 36: 635–664.

Caldera Delgado, Hugo. 1980. "Bases para el Control Jurídico de la Potestad Reglamentaria Autónoma Contemplada en el Anteproyecto de la Nueva Constitución," *Décimas Jornadas Chilenas de Derecho Público* (Edeval, 1980): 187–191.

Carey, John M. and Matthew Soberg Shugart (eds.). 1998. *Executive Decree Authority*. Cambridge: Cambridge University Press.

Carmona Santander, Carlos. 1998. "Tendencias del Tribunal Constitucional en al Relación Ley-Reglamento," *Revista de Derecho Público* 61 (1998–1999): 180–192.

Carmona Santander, Carlos. 2001. "Tres Problemas de la Potestad Reglamentaria: Legitimidad, Intensidad y Control," *Revista de Derecho* (Consejo de Defensa del Estado) 1(3): 29–62.

Cea Egaña, José Luis. 1988. "Visión de la Presidencia y el Congreso en la Constitución de 1980," in *Constitución 1980: Estudio Crítico*. Santiago: Editorial Jurídica Ediar – ConoSur Ltda.

Cea Egaña, José Luis. 1989. "La Separación de Poderes en la Democracia Constitucional Chilena," in *La Experiencia Constitucional Norteamericana y Chilena sobre la Separación de Poderes*, Instituto de Estudios Judiciales (ed). Santiago: Ediar – Conosur.

Cea Egaña, José Luis. 1998. "Los Principios de Reserva Legal y Complementaria en la Constitución Chilena," *Revista de Derecho* (Universidad Austral) IX: 65–104.

Chavez, Rebecca Bill. 2004. *The Rule of Law in Nascent Democracies: Judicial Politics in Argentina*. Stanford: Stanford University Press.

Correa Sutíl, Jorge. 1988. "La Cultura Jurídica Chilena en Relación a la Función Judicial," in *La Cultura Jurídica Chilena*, A. Squella (ed). Santiago: Corporación de Promoción Universitaria.

Couso, Javier. 2003. "The Politics of Judicial Review in Chile in the Era of Democratic Transition 1990–2002," *Democratization* 10(4): 70–91.

Couso, Javier A. 2004. "The Politics of Judicial Review in Chile in the Era of Domestic Transition, 1990–2002," in *Democratization and the Judiciary: The Accountability Function of Courts in New Democracies*, Gloppen, Siri, Robert Gargarella, and Elin Skaar (eds.). Portland, OR: Frank Cass Publishers: 70–91.

Couso, Javier A. 2005. "The Judicialization of Chilean Politics: The Rights Revolution that Never Was," in *The Judicialization of Politics in Latin America*, Rachel Sieder, Line Schjolden, and Alan Angell (eds.). New York: Palgrave: 105–129.

Couso, Javier. 2010. "The Transformation of Constitutional Discourse and the Judicialization of Politics in Latin America," in *Cultures of Legality: Judicialization and Political Activism in Latin America*. New York: Cambridge University Press: 141–160.

Couso, Javier and Lisa Hilbink. 2011. "From Quietism to Incipient Activism: The Institutional and Ideational Roots of Rights Adjudication in Chile," in *Courts in Latin America*, Gretchen Helmke and Julio Ríos-Figueroa (eds.). Cambridge: Cambridge University Press: 99–127.

Dahl, Robert. 1957. "Decision-Making in a Democracy: The Supreme Court as a National Policy-Maker," *Journal of Public Law* VI(2): 279–295.

Epstein, Lee and Jack Knight. 1998. *The Choices Justices Make*. Washington, DC: Congressional Quarterly Press.

Epstein, Lee, Jack Knight, and Olga Shvetsova. 2001. "The Role of Constitutional Courts in the Establishment and Maintenance of Democratic Systems of Government," *Law & Society Review* 35(1): 117–164.

Faundez, Julio. 2010. "Chilean Constitutionalism before Allende: Legality without Courts," *Bulletin of Latin American Research* 29(1): 34–50.

Fernández González, Miguel Ángel. 2006. *Los Derechos Fundamentales en 25 Años de Jurisprudencia del Tribunal Constitucional 1980–2005*. Santiago: Tribunal Constitucional. Retrieved from http://www.tribunalconstitucional.cl.

Frei Ruiz-Tagle, Eduardo. 2000. *Doctrina Constitucional de Presidente Eduardo Ruiz-Tagle Frei*. Vol. Tomos 1 y 2. Santiago: División Jurídico Legislativo, Ministerio Secretaria General de la Presidencia.

Helmke, Gretchen. 2005. *Courts under Constraints: Judges, Generals, and Presidents in Argentina*. Cambridge, MA: Cambridge University Press.

Hernández Emparanza, Domingo. 2006. "Control de Constitucionalidad de Actos Administrativos por el Tribunal Constitucional. Precedentes Constitucionales," *Estudios Constitucionales* 4(001): 207–222.

Hilbink, Elisabeth C. 2007. *Judges beyond Politics in Democracy and Dictatorship: Lessons from Chile*. Cambridge: Cambridge University Press.

Huneeus, Alexandra Valeria. 2010. "Judging from a Guilty Conscience: The Chilean Judiciary's Human Rights Turn," *Law & Social Inquiry* 35(1): 99–135.

Iaryczower, Matías, Pablo T. Spiller, and Mariano Tommasi. 2002. "Judicial Decision Making in Unstable Environments, Argentina 1935–1998," *American Journal of Political Science* 46(4): 699–716.

Murphy, Walter F. 1964. *Elements of Judicial Strategy*. Chicago: University of Chicago Press.

Nogueira Alcalá, Humberto. 1994. "Forma de Gobierno, Distribución de Funciones y Controles Inter-órganos en el Régimen Político Chileno," in *División de Poderes*, C. Jackisch (ed.). Buenos Aires: Fundación Konrad Adenauer.

Nogueira Alcalá, Humberto. 1995. "El Tribunal Constitucional Chileno," in *Una Mirada a los Tribunales Constitucionales: Las Experiencias Recientes*. Lima: Comisión Andina de Juristas.

Nogueira Alcalá, Humberto. 1997. "Los Tratados Internacionales en el Ordenamiento Jurídico Chileno," *Ius et Praxis* 2(2): 7–62. Retrieved from http://enj.org/portal/biblioteca/ principios_fundamentales/convenios_internacionales/24.pdf.

Nogueira Alcalá, Humberto. 2003. "Los Derechos Esenciales o Humanos Contenido en los Tratados Internacionales y su Ubicación en el Ordenamiento Jurídico Nacional: Doctrina y Jurisprudencia," *Ius et Praxis* 9(1): 403–466. ISSN 0718–0012. Retrieved from http://www.scielo.cl/scielo.php?pid=S0718-00122003000100020&script=sci_arttext.

Nogueira Alcalá, Humberto. 2007. "El Recurso de Protección en el Contexto del Amparo de los Derechos Fundamentales Latinoamericano e Interamericano," *Ius et Praxis* 13(1): 75–134. ISSN 0718–0012. Retrieved from http://www.scielo.cl/scielo.php?pid=S0718-00122007000100005&script=sci_arttext.

Núñez Poblete, Manuel A. 2010. "El Neoconstitucionalismo y el Recurso a los Valores en la Jurisprudencia del Tribunal Constitucional Chileno," *Revista de Derecho de la Pontificia Universidad Católica de Valparaíso* 34: 523–541. ISSN 0718–6851. Retrieved from http://www.scielo.cl/scielo.php?pid=S0718-68512010000100016&script=sci_arttext.

Peña González, Carlos. 1997. *Práctica Constitucional y Derechos Fundamentales*. Santiago: Corporación Nacional de Reparación y Reconciliación.

Peña Torres, Marisol. 2006. "El Precedente Constitucional Emanado del Tribunal Constitucional y su Impacto en la Función Legislativa," *Estudios Constitucionales* 4(001): 173–184.

Ríos-Figueroa. 2007. "The Emergence of an Effective Judiciary in Mexico, 1994–2002," *Latin American Politics & Society* 49(1): 31–57.

Scribner, Druscilla L. 2004. "Limiting Presidential Power: Supreme Court Executive Relations in Argentina and Chile." PhD Dissertation, Political Science, University of California, San Diego.

Scribner, Druscilla. 2007. "The Political Dynamics of Vehicle Emissions: A Constitutional Tale of Public Policy in Santiago," *Journal of Latin American Urban Studies* 8: 1–16.

Scribner, Druscilla. 2010. "The Judicialization of (Separation of Powers) Politics: Lessons from Chile," *Journal of Politics in Latin America* 2(3): 71–97.

Segal, Jeffrey A. and Harold J. Spaeth. 2002. *The Supreme Court and the Attitudinal Model Revisited*. Cambridge: Cambridge University Press.

Shapiro, Martin. 2004. "Judicial Review in Developed Democracies," in *Democratization and the Judiciary: The Accountability Function of Courts in New Democracies*, Siri Gloppen, Robert Gargarella, Elin Skaar (eds.). Portland, OR: Frank Cass: 7–26.

Soto Kloss, Eduardo. 1977. "La Toma de Razón y el Poder Normativo de la Contraloría General de la República," in *La Contraloría General de la República, 50 Años de Vida Institucional (1927–1977)*. Santiago: Universidad de Chile, Facultad de Derecho.

Soto Kloss, Eduardo. 1980. "Estado de Derecho y Procedimiento Administrativo," *Revista de Derecho Público* (Universidad de Chile) 27–28: 101–124.

Soto Kloss, Eduardo. 1982. *El Recurso de Protección: Orígenes, Doctrina y Jurisprudencia*. Santiago: Editorial Jurídica de Chile.

Soto Kloss, Eduardo. 1999. "Ley y Reglamento: Sus Relaciones en el Derecho Chileno," *Ius Publicum* 3: 33–47.

Staton, Jeffrey. 2002. "Judicial Activism and Public Authority Compliance: The Role of Public Support in the Mexican Separation-of-Powers System." PhD Dissertation, Department of Political Science, Washington University.

Tapia Valdés, Jorge. 1993. "Funciones y Atribuciones del Parlamento entre 1960–1990," in *Diagnostico Histórico Jurídico del Poder Legislativo en Chile*. Valparaíso: Centro de Estudios y Asistencia Legislativa, Universidad Católica de Valparaíso, Ediciones Universitarias de Valparaíso: 85–132.

Valenzuela Somarriva, Eugenio. 1990. "Labor Jurisdiccional de al Corte Suprema," *Estudios Políticos* 40(Primavera): 137–169.

Vanberg, Georg. 2005. *The Politics of Constitutional Review in Germany*. Cambridge: Cambridge University Press.

Vargas Viancos, Juan E. and Jorge Correa Sutil. 1995. *Diagnóstico del Sistema Judicial Chileno*. Santiago de Chile: Corporación de Promoción Universitaria.

Verdudo Marinkovic, Mario and Emilio Pfeffer Urquiaca. 1993. *Constitución Política de la República de Chile 1980*. Santiago: Editorial Juridica de Chile.

Zapata Larraín, Patricio. 1991. "Jurisprudencia del Tribunal Constitucional: 1981–1991," *Revista Chilena de Derecho* 18(2): 261–330.

Zapata Larraín, Patricio. 1993. "El Precedente en la Jurisprudencia Constitucional Chilena y Comparada," *Revista Chilena de Derecho* 20: 449–508.

Zapata Larraín, Patricio. 1994. *La Jurisprudencia del Tribunal Constitucional*. Santiago: Imprenta VIS Ltda.

Zapata Larraín, Patricio. 2002. *La Jurisprudencia del Tribunal Constitucional*. Santiago: Biblioteca Americana.

5

The Transformation of the Mexican Supreme Court into an Arena for Political Contestation

Mónica Castillejos-Aragón*

"In the process of transformation of a post-colonial regime, judicial leadership matters. Public Interest Litigation began with a letter addressed to the Supreme Court from an inmate imprisoned in the South of India. After I read the communication, I decided to visit the poorest areas in India. I spoke with the less advantaged citizens and I got to know their needs. Based on those needs, I developed my own social philosophy and promoted important changes within the Supreme Court."

> – From my interview with Chief Justice N.P. Bhagwati in New Delhi, India, on July 17, 2010

Between 1929 and 2000, the legislative and judicial branches of the Mexican government were subordinated to the executive's control. In theory, the separation of powers was recognized by the dominant political party, the Partido Revolucionario Institucional (PRI), as a leading tenet defining the governmental structure. However, in practice, the president limited the powers of the other branches through various constitutional reforms. These institutional reforms effectively restricted the Mexican Supreme Court from properly functioning as arbiter between the presidential and congressional powers, and from protecting fundamental rights. The court system essentially preserved authoritarian rule and the Mexican Supreme Court turned into a passive and unimportant institution. Judges aligned themselves with the executive in an effort to avoid any kind of confrontation. As Domingo (2004)

* This chapter draws on my doctoral dissertation, "Judges as Institutional Builders: The Transformation of the Mexican Supreme Court into an arena for Political Contestation." I am deeply grateful to my dissertation advisors Malcolm M. Feeley, Martin M. Shapiro and Diana Kapiszewski for helping me develop and frame the ideas in both my doctoral dissertation and this chapter. I am also thankful to Robert A. Kagan for his insightful comments and feedback on earlier drafts of this document, and to Peter W. Williams for his invaluable input and support as I wrote the final version. I extend my sincere gratitude to my mentor, Justice José Ramón Cossío Díaz, for giving me the opportunity to witness and participate in his project of judicial transformation. The chapter also draws on my experiences as a clerk on the Mexican Supreme Court from 2004 to 2007.

describes, the judiciary responded to the wishes of the executive as expressed through a number of formal and informal pressures and incentives such as political rewards and career incentives.

Mexico's judicial inadequacies sprung many sources, including weak judicial independence, thousands of inconsequential cases, and corrupt and incompetent judges. Because of these inadequacies, myriad serious violations of fundamental rights went unpunished during the seven decades of authoritarian rule. Human rights violations were condoned or suppressed by the PRI authorities responsible for prosecuting and investigating them. For its part, the Supreme Court addressed the few cases that produced strident public outcry, and created commissions allegedly responsible for investigation. However, these commissions rarely established the facts (Rubio 1990). Moreover, the Court often refused to hear *amparo* lawsuits that challenged violations of rights presumably committed by the PRI authorities (Cossío Díaz 2001). Consequently, judicial decisions received very little media attention and were rarely mentioned by rights advocates and activists in their struggles. In sum, the Mexican Supreme Court's influence over the battle for the protection and recognition of the fundamental rights of citizens was futile.

However, from 1995 to 2010, the Mexican Supreme Court initiated a fascinating process of institutional transformation, which positioned justices to develop novel fundamental-rights jurisprudence. Since 2007, the Court has come to be viewed not merely as a forum to settle disputes but as an instrument of societal change. It has issued decisions that were unthinkable during the authoritarian rule, and engaged in unprecedented constitutional interpretation of women's rights, indigenous rights, decriminalization of abortion, transgender rights, HIV rights, labor rights, and health rights; freedom of expression, freedom of press, and freedom of privacy rights, the right to information, same-sex marriages, DNA rights, children's rights, property rights, and freedom of association, among many others. Why has the Mexican Supreme Court begun to serve as an arena for political contestation?

Most students of the Mexican Supreme Court point to two causal factors to explain the Court's political awakening: (a) the 1994 judicial reform (Inclán Oseguera 2009; Fix Fierro 2003; Finkel 2000; Staton 2010); and (b) the advent of a new competitive political party system in 2000 (Magaloni and Sánchez 2006; Ríos-Figueroa 2007). First, in December 1994, during the last PRI administration (1988–1994), President Ernesto Zedillo proposed a judicial reform that restructured the entire judiciary; changed the judicial appointment process and appointed all new justices to the high court; granted the Court the power to review constitutional or substantial challenges to the state (not simply legal or procedural questions) in *amparo* lawsuits (Magaloni 2003); and more generally sought to convert the court into a constitutional tribunal according to the Kelsenian model (Ferejohn 2002; Castillejos 2005; Fix Zamudio 1993; Finkel 2003; Gudiño Pelayo 2005; Góngora Pimentel 2005). According to this first account, this restructuring granted the Court a higher degree of independence that enabled justices to rule against the government.

Research in the second vein claims that in addition to the 1994 legal reform, the new competitive party system that emerged in 2000 constituted a turning point for the institutional operation of the Supreme Court. It also suggests that the new political atmosphere provided the Supreme Court with institutional autonomy to address issues that were systematically neglected during the PRI regime.

In this chapter, I argue that although legal reform and the new competitive political party system played a role in the Court's empowerment and its higher degree of independence, they are not sufficient to explain the Court's new role as an "arena for political contestation," or its new approach to interpreting fundamental rights. In addition, we must pay special attention to progressive judicial leadership. By implementing substantial institutional changes within the Court and converting the courtroom into an individual-state forum, over the last four Supreme Court terms (from 1995 to 2010) judicial leaders provided political and social advocates an opportunity to convert grievances into legal claims (Moustafa 2007). In brief, progressive justices converted the Court into an arena for political contestation to propel political change by cultivating bonds between the Supreme Court and various agents (see Figure 5.1): the executive and the legislature (1995–1999 and 1999–2003); mass media and the legal complex (see Halliday, Ch. 13 in this volume) (2003–2007); and civil society organizations and interest groups (2007–2010). Importantly, and in contrast to the United States' Warren Court (see Kagan, Ch. 8 in this volume) and India's Bhagwati Court (see Mate, Ch. 10 in this volume), these institutional changes were not carried out exclusively by chief justices, but also by associate justices who followed their own incentives. The justices cultivated those connections because the type of social change they envisioned required building synergies with agents who, by working together, would produce results not obtainable by any one of them alone. As a result of these synergies, the Court began issuing an increasing number of fundamental-rights decisions by 2007.

This finding is in line with much of the judicial impact literature, which suggests that courts alone can rarely do much to advance progressive social agendas (Scheingold 1974; Rosenberg 1991). However, it calls into question propositions developed in the rights-revolution literature that suggest the transformation of supreme courts into guardians of individual rights occurs as a result of pressure from below (i.e., through deliberate, strategic, organized effort by rights advocates; Epp 1998). It also departs from most studies of courts, which analyze judicial behavior primarily on the basis of judicial rulings. Indeed, focusing on judicial decision making, scholars of the Mexican Court have been unable to explain why the Court began to pay more attention to fundamental-rights cases after the end of the PRI era, and have missed the larger political role the Court has developed and begun to play.

This chapter proceeds in three sections. Section I describes and explains the absence of fundamental-rights interpretation by the Mexican Supreme Court during the PRI regime. Section II discusses the three variables that I argue combined to produce the Court's new role as an arena of political contestation: the 1994 legal reform; the new competitive party system that emerged since 2000; and most importantly,

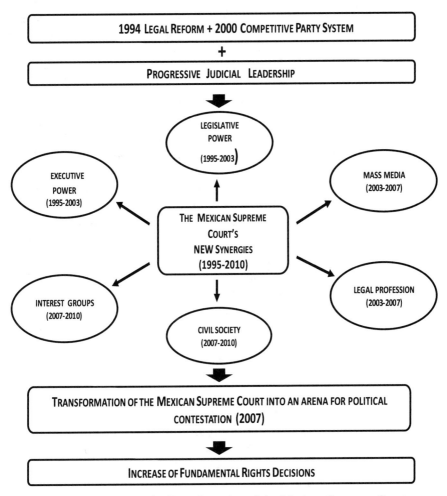

FIGURE 5.1. Mapping the Transformation of the Mexican Supreme Court.

progressive leadership on the Court after 1995. Section III analyzes the past four Supreme Court terms and shows how the work of three energetic and progressive justices – Justice Juventino Castro y Castro, Chief Justice Genaro Góngora, and Justice José Ramón Cossío – helped the Court build synergies with new audiences, emerge as an arena for political contestation, and develop a new rights role.

FACTORS INHIBITING FUNDAMENTAL RIGHTS INTERPRETATION DURING PRI RULE

The overt reluctance of the Mexican Supreme Court to address fundamental-rights challenges during the PRI era frequently attracted public criticism. This judicial unwillingness eventually provoked Mexican intellectuals to harshly scrutinize the Court's work – however, the justices remained apathetic to such critiques throughout

PRI rule (1929–2000) (Cossío Díaz 2001; Magaloni and Zaldívar 2006; Raphael 2006). Although the Mexican Constitution of 1917 fully protects a range of rights and freedoms, the Court's actions undermined these protections, and the entire judicial system was known for delay and unpredictability, especially in lower courts and rural areas.

There are five major explanations for this weak judicial commitment to fundamental rights. First, under the PRI regime, government officials severely limited the judiciary's latitude – effectively preventing courts from vindicating rights or challenging the PRI's abuses of power. Second, the procedural mechanism available to challenge state action, including human rights violations, before federal courts – the amparo writ (*juicio de amparo*) – was laden with technicalities and antiquated rules that made rights litigation costly and inefficient. Third, as a result, legal professionals rarely sought to use the courtroom to seek societal change. Fourth, civil society and rights advocates discounted the Supreme Court as a trustworthy institution, and thus brought their claims before the Inter-American Court of Human Rights. Fifth and finally, the absence of support structures such as mass media, the legal profession, civil society, and interest groups limited the justices' opportunity to issue more progressive rights decisions. I develop each of these reasons in turn.

The first explanation can be extracted from the literature on the judicialization of politics, originally advocated by Martin M. Shapiro (1981, 1994; Shapiro and Stone Sweet 2002). Shapiro claims that under specific political circumstances, courts are able to make enduring policies. However, despite the empowerment of the Supreme Court in 1994, justices did not immediately exert their power because they were hesitant to challenge their appointer (PRI President Zedillo [1994–2000]), and because Mexico continued under one-party rule through 2000. From 1995 to 2000, politicians used methods of discipline such as dismissals and impeachments to discourage justices from deciding significant constitutional issues and challenging the PRI's status quo (Fix Fierro 2003).

The second explanation concerns the nature and design of writ of amparo. The amparo procedure allows citizens to take specific constitutional questions concerning rights to federal courts, including the Supreme Court. However, historically in Mexico, the amparo procedure did not allow citizens to effectively challenge human rights violations (Fix Zamudio 1981), but rather served primarily as a set of rules that protected and legitimated existing political and social hierarchies (Galanter 1974). It is well documented that this procedure is an ineffective, costly, and inefficient legal recourse, and embedded with legal uncertainty and complex technicalities that made it inaccessible to the majority of the population. Moreover, scholars have documented that under the PRI, the Supreme Court often denied judicial review in constitutional cases that explicitly challenged the PRI by focusing on scrutinizing procedural technicalities in the amparo lawsuits as grounds to deny judicial review (Cossío Diaz 2001). Consequently, no standards of review were developed and litigants were generally unable to unravel the rationale behind the Court's dismissal of amparo cases. In short, the amparo procedure neither served as an instrument of societal progress nor a legal tool to subject the preferences of the powerful to the constraints of the law. In this way, the PRI's control over the courts delayed the emergence of rights litigation.

The third reason for weak judicial protection of fundamental rights draws on the legal-complex literature (see Halliday, Karpik, and Feeley 2007; Halliday, Chapter 13 in this volume). The "legal complex" refers not only to the activity of judiciaries and lawyers, but also prosecutors, civil servants, and academics, and work on this phenomenon analyzes the way these actors advance and defend – and in some cases inhibit – political liberalism in a state. In PRI-led Mexico, the party's institutionalization of its rule and the top-down discipline it established through the legal system (Moustafa 2008) kept political parties, the legal profession, interest groups, and business interests – and the Supreme Court – "aligned" with the regime and inhibited legal and societal efforts to challenge the PRI's policies and advance political liberalism (Schatz 2000; Fix Fierro 2007).

The fourth and fifth explanations are illustrated in the literature addressing judicial transparency and legal mobilization (e.g., Kahn Zemans 1980; Kessler 1990; Lasser 2004). Weak transparency and accountability during PRI rule also hampered rights litigation. During the PRI regime, the Supreme Court drafted lengthy opinions that were often many hundreds of pages long. These contained endless transcriptions of articles, precedents, and judgments of lower courts (*Vistos y Resultandos*). In the central part of the decision or *ratio decidendi* (*Considerandos*) justices drafted convoluted paragraphs supposedly arguing why they granted or dismissed amparo review (Shapiro 1992). Voids in legal literacy not only constrained litigants' ability to access and critique judicial outcomes, but also simultaneously hampered public dialogue and debate between justices and the legal profession to bring about social change.

Also as a result of this lack of transparency, civil society and interest groups avoided using the courts. In the late 1980s, Mexico experienced high levels of corruption, causing massive societal distrust in state institutions; however, the PRI's corporatist model provided no opportunity for civil society to pursue an agenda contrary to the one already established by the ruling party. Even once civil society groups began to emerge as important actors in the 1960s and 1970s activists were often subjected to various forms of harassment and repression, and were persuaded to show restraint in their criticisms of PRI public officials (Redding 1995). To denounce these violations, NGOs and activists united with international organizations to litigate before international tribunals such as the Inter-American Court of Human Rights rather than making demands directly within the Mexican court system (Cossío Díaz 2005).

VARIABLES THAT TRIGGERED THE NEW ROLE OF THE MEXICAN SUPREME COURT

As briefly explained, legal and political science research points out that as a result of legal reform in 1994 – which involved structural and jurisdictional changes within the Supreme Court – justices became more independent from political pressures.

Additionally, scholars suggest that the emergence of a new competitive political party system in 2000 enabled justices to rule against the government's interests without being systematically challenged or ignored (Ríos-Figueroa 2007). These two variables alone arguably expanded the Court's formal power and empowered justices to safeguard the rights and liberties mandated in the Constitution. However, they are not sufficient to explain the new role of the Mexican Supreme Court. A third and essential variable – progressive judicial leadership – enabled the Court to convert itself into an arena for political contestation.

Variable I: The 1994 Judicial Reform

When President Ernesto Zedillo assumed office in 1994, Mexico was undergoing political, economic, and social struggle. In December 1994, President Zedillo assembled the main political party leaders to discuss and pass a constitutional reform to restructure the Mexican judiciary, one step in broader efforts to address the multi-faceted crisis. This judicial reform, subsequently enacted by the legislature,[1] implemented three main proposals: (1) it granted and strengthened the Supreme Court's powers to function as an authentic constitutional tribunal, according to the European model of judicial review; (2) it modified the judicial appointment process, decreased the number of justices from twenty-one to eleven, and appointed all new justices to the bench; (3) it created a Judicial Council to alleviate the need for justices to perform administrative tasks and allow them to focus on jurisdictional issues (Jiménez Remus 1996). The 1994 judicial reform established the institutional conditions for the Supreme Court to become independent from the Executive and Legislative branches' influence. Of course, such a reform could not induce an immediate change in justices' attitudes toward the adjudication of fundamental rights, and the Court's constitutional engagement on fundamental rights continued to be extraordinarily weak through 2000 (Cossío Díaz 2000). In sum, the 1994 judicial reform was necessary to expand the Supreme Court's powers, but it was not sufficient to motivate the newly appointed justices to pay sustained attention to fundamental rights and liberties issues in their first years on the new Court.

Variable II: The Emergence of a New Competitive Party System in 2000

According to *fragmentation theory*, in countries where there is a dominant party that can subordinate courts, courts tend to be weaker; by contrast, when there are multiple competing parties, those parties are less likely to override judicial decisions through legislation or reshape the courts through changing personnel, allowing courts to become powerful and act as an autonomous branch of government (see Ferejohn, Ch. 14 in this volume). Thus, the greater the fragmentation in the Executive and

[1] *Exposición de Motivos de la Reforma Constitucional*, December 1994.

Legislative branches, the more likely it is that courts will rule against the government and engage in policy-making (Finkel 2005; Ríos-Figueroa 2007). This theory has been applied to the Mexican case, arguing that the Supreme Court has gradually moved from being a weak institution during the PRI regime to becoming a powerful one after the PRI was defeated by the conservative Partido Acción Nacional (PAN) in 2000. President Vicente Fox (2000–2006) established two important conditions that influenced the Supreme Court's operation in the first three years of his presidential administration. First, his judicial appointments dramatically changed the judiciary's internal dynamics and debates. Second, his enactment of the Law of Transparency and Access of Governmental Information provided justices with opportunities to gain institutional legitimacy through various channels.

These first two variables set the stage for the Mexican Supreme Court's institutional conversion into a space for political activism. However, they only gained significance when progressive justices embraced them and advocated for institutional change within the Court in the later 1990s.

Variable III: Progressive Judicial Leadership

Much political and legal research on how courts operate and change focuses on legalistic and jurisprudential issues, neglecting the human factor. As with all types of institutions, however, without effective leadership viable innovation and reform are impossible (Mahoney 1988; Wice 1995). Indeed, the literature on judicial leadership assumes that when highly motivated and liberal justices commit to court reform and combine intelligence with effective leadership, they can make significant improvements within their justice systems (Wice 1995). We must carefully define "leadership," however. In contrast to the United States and Indian examples mentioned, the type of progressive judicial change witnessed in the past fifteen years in Mexico did not derive exclusively from the vision and actions of the chief justice. Rather, during specific periods after the 1994 judicial reform, highly motivated justices – and especially Justice Juventino Castro (1995–1999), Chief Justice Genaro Góngora (1999–2003), and Justice José Ramón Cossío (2004–2010) – developed and promoted various landmark institutional changes in order to develop a new role for the Court. In particular, they built connections (synergies) with new agents – the Executive, Legislative, mass media, legal complex, civil society, and interest groups. The resulting judicial forum (the Court itself) fomented a public dialogue and debate among these new audiences and encouraged them to bring fundamental-rights cases.

LEADERSHIP ON THE MEXICAN SUPREME COURT AND ITS NEW SYNERGIES: 1995–2010

This section explores how the contributions and agendas of three key justices – Justice Juventino Castro y Castro (1995–1999), Chief Justice Genaro Góngora Pimentel

(1999–2003), and Justice José Ramón Cossío (2004 to 2010) – led to the development of the Mexican Supreme Court's new role.

Justice Juventino Castro y Castro and the Establishment of the SC's Agenda, 1995–1999

When the newly appointed Supreme Court initiated its operation in January 1995, Mexico was experiencing multifaceted crisis. Further, the PRI was still the major force in the federal executive and legislature. The judiciary was marked by high levels of corruption, public distrust, and a lack of legitimacy, and the PRI's legal formalism continued to prevail in judicial ideolosgy. Judicial independence was rhetorically recognized by the other branches, but in practice was very weak. For its part, the Mexican Supreme Court rarely heard cases concerning political matters such as elections or electoral legitimacy. In interviews Schatz (2000) conducted with various justices, they discussed the PRI's continued influence on the Court. Justice Juventino Castro y Castro, for example, referenced the Supreme Court's continuing weakness and the executive's ongoing intervention in judicial affairs during the 1995–1999 term. Justice Mariano Azuela explained the Court's continued tendency to subordinate its operation to the executive's wishes. These statements help explain why the Court continued to be unable to act as a genuine constitutional tribunal to protect the rights of individuals.[2]

Given the PRI's continued dominance, the Court focused on developing its organizational structure and, much more urgently, setting the agenda for the future. In view of the overload of existing and pending cases, the deficiency of the Court's automated management systems (i.e., databases), and insufficient standards of procedures and training of judicial personnel (Aguinaco Alemán 1997), the justices mostly confronted issues of case management and processing.

With regard to setting the new judicial agenda, the leadership of Justice Juventino Castro y Castro was particularly critical. He promoted a respectful attitude toward rights and liberties mandated in the Constitution, and sought to recognize the important role the Court played in constitutional interpretation and creating conditions under which the rule of law could be fully realized in Mexico (Staton 2010). Justice Castro y Castro also advocated for a real political party system to tip the balance among the executive, legislature, and judiciary, and openly criticized President Zedillo's Annual Presidential Report, which suggested that Mexico's system was characterized by a division of powers.[3] The justice highlighted that despite legal reforms, the Executive remained reluctant to delegate power to the other branches of government in a meaningful way, continuing to serve as commander in chief of

---

[2] Justice Juventino Castro y Castro served fifteen years on the Supreme Court, from 1995 to 2003.
[3] Agustin Ambriz, "El ministro Juventino Castro refuta a Zedillo: hay desequilibrio de poderes," *Proceso* September 5, 1999.

the Mexican army, head of foreign affairs, chief architect of economic policy, as well as the head of the administrative tribunals. The executive's veto powers and his ability to initiate legislation preserved the political hegemony that such reforms aimed to dispel.

Over the years, in his publications and speeches, Castro y Castro delineated the many obstacles facing the nation's administration of justice and proposed ideas for improvement (Castro y Castro 2003).[4] First, he advocated for reform of the legislation guiding the amparo procedure, which he alleged was designed to obstruct the administration of justice in Mexico. Originating in 1847, these antiquated rules and formalistic principles fostered high levels of corruption and distrust in the judiciary, and allowed the more powerful to profit at expense of the less advantaged. He also proposed to grant the Court the power to present initiatives before Congress and thus to participate in the political process in areas directly related to judicial activity. Third, he suggested the Court be given financial autonomy and the ability to request an annual budget (subject to congressional approval). He also advocated incorporating administrative tribunals into the judicial structure, and proposed constitutional reform to establish oral trials (*juicios orales*) to make the justice sector more expeditious, transparent, and efficient (Castro y Castro 2004). Finally, he initiated alliances between the Court and media, speaking with journalists to inform them of judicial outcomes in a timely fashion, thus joining the national debate.[5]

In sum, during this first term on the Court, Justice Castro y Castro played a pivotal role in setting the agenda for and scope of judicial activity. Indeed, each of his proposals was undertaken and promoted in the following judicial terms.

Chief Justice Genaro Góngora Pimentel: Lobbying for Institutional Emancipation, 1999–2003

On July 2, 2000, Mexico's political system experienced the unthinkable: the PRI lost the presidential election for the first time since the political party was founded in 1929. President Ernesto Zedillo announced Vicente Fox's historical victory in a televised speech, and claimed to be the president who had made democratic change possible in Mexico. In the wake of this political earthquake, the close ties between the state and the PRI collapsed (Bell and Pansters 2001), and a new competitive party system emerged that provided justices with the opportunity to situate the Supreme Court as an autonomous institution (Góngora Pimentel 2000).[6] The Court's main goals during this period – championed by Chief Justice Genaro Góngora – were

---

4 Justice Juventino Castro y Castro, "Retirement Speech" delivered at the Mexican Supreme Court on November 28, 2003.

5 Interview I conducted with Licenciada Rosalba Rodríguez Mireles, a former staff attorney of Justice Castro y Castro, in December 2010 in Mexico City.

6 Genaro Góngora, "Sin Independencia no somos nada" (México: Suprema Corte de Justicia de la Nación, August 2000).

emancipation from executive and legislative influence, and the promotion of a new kind of interaction with elected leaders (Góngora Pimentel 2000).[7]

The central tenet of Chief Justice Góngora Pimentel's judicial term was, "Let's simplify the law."[8] He strongly advocated for interbranch collaboration on reform proposals,[9] and more generally, promoted a new political dialogue between the Supreme Court and the other branches of government. The newly established competitive party system empowered Góngora Pimentel to position the Court as an autonomous branch of government and push for the dismantlement of the PRI's subordination and control. This increase of autonomy allowed him to advocate for three landmark constitutional reforms during the 1999–2003 term: (a) reforming the Amparo Law; (b) granting financial autonomy to the Supreme Court; and (c) granting the Supreme Court the power to present reform initiatives before Congress.

The Amparo Law Reform

The reform of the amparo law constituted the most important debate of this judicial term, and of subsequent terms, as well. In 1999, Chief Justice Góngora Pimentel appointed a committee to help carry out the New Amparo Law Project (Proyecto de la Nueva Ley de Amparo). Through this committee, the Supreme Court invited judges and other members of the legal profession, academic institutions, and civil society to submit proposals for the Amparo Law reform. Ultimately, 1,430 proposals were submitted by civil society groups, political parties, academic institutions, and litigants. Most proposals focused on improving the mechanism's effectiveness at protecting human rights. The proposals were discussed in various forums led by intellectuals and justices, and the outcomes of these debates were ultimately published in August 2006 in the form of The White Book of the Judicial Reform (El Libro Blanco de la Reforma Judicial). Supreme Court justices distributed The White Book to executive and legislative authorities, and its contents were broadly disseminated in various forums at the federal and state levels. After twelve years of political debate, the Senate passed the reform of the Amparo Law in October 2011.[10] The new law incorporates novel provisions to facilitate the filing of amparo lawsuits by citizens, groups, and organizations that have experienced violations of their fundamental rights by state authorities. As such, the new law will facilitate access to justice in Mexico.

---

[7] Justice Genaro Góngora served on the Supreme Court from 1995 to 2009.
[8] Góngora sold this idea to the legislature as a means to promote economic growth and encourage foreign investment. See his speech delivered in April 2001, "Urge Simplificar Nuestras Leyes" (The Mexican Supreme Court Speeches Collection); see also a speech delivered in November 2000, "Por qué debemos invertir en la Justicia" (The Mexican Supreme Court's Speeches Collection).
[9] The Mexican Supreme Court of Justice, Annual Report, 2000.
[10] Horacio Jiménez y Ricardo Gómez, "Aprueba Senado La Nueva Ley de Amparo," *El Universal*, October 13, 2011.

Financial Independence and the Power to Present Reform Initiatives

In addition to the Amparo Law reform, in February 2002, Chief Justice Góngora Pimentel held various meetings with President Vicente Fox to seek his support for other reform proposals that would affect the Court's independence. One such proposal concerned guaranteeing the judiciary 3 percent of the federal budget. President Fox agreed to create a commission to consider Chief Justice Góngora Pimentel's proposal. This proposal aimed to avoid the cutting of the judicial budget that had occurred in the past, and to tackle the workload and corruption issues that plagued the administration of justice. According to newspaper reports, the chief justice had already secured the support of the two opposition parties – the PRI and Partido de la Revolución Democrática (PRD) – when he began these unprecedented negotiations with President Fox.[11] In addition, in June 2001 Chief Justice Góngora Pimentel appeared before Congress to call for amending Article 71 of the Constitution to award the Supreme Court the power to propose reforms to the Organic Law of the Judicial Power of the Federation and other legislation closely related to judicial activity, arguing that the Court knew better than any other actor what judicial reforms were necessary (Staton 2008).

These two proposals encountered strong opposition from political party leaders, mostly because they were advanced at an inopportune political moment (in advance of state-level elections). Nonetheless, Chief Justice Genaro Góngora Pimentel's leadership is significant in terms of explaining how the Supreme Court began functioning as a political actor, seeking legal reform and institutional autonomy. Whereas pursuing the recognition of the Court as truly a third branch of government, he strategically established new synergies with the Executive and Congress, fundamentally altering the relationship between the Supreme Court and elected leaders.

Justice José Ramón Cossío Diaz and His Fundamental Rights Program, 2004–2007

The 2004–2007 judicial term was the most controversial in the history of the Mexican Supreme Court. On the eve of the 2006 presidential election – which would be the second most competitive in the country's history – the media reported a private meeting between President Vicente Fox (of the PAN party) and Supreme Court Chief Justice Mariano Azuela. The two allegedly discussed the political fate of Andrés Manuel López Obrador, the left-wing presidential candidate of the PRD.[12] The meeting unleashed serious accusations against Chief Justice Azuela and

---

[11] Jorge Teherán, "Pide Poder Judicial Autonomía Financiera," *El Universal*, June 27, 2001; Carlos Avilés and Julián Sánchez, "Solicita la SCJN a Fox autonomía financiera," *El Universal*, February 2002.

[12] Jorge Ramos, "Desafuero y Azuela, en agenda del PRD," *El Universal*, September 22, 2004; Carlos Avilés, "Legal, reunión con Fox dice titular de la Corte," *El Universal*, September 22, 2004.

negatively impacted the Supreme Court's image.[13] Somewhat paradoxically, this judicial term proved crucial for the Supreme Court's efforts toward incorporating principles of transparency into its operation through its Fundamental Rights Program, championed by Justice José Ramón Cossío. The program included three facets: (1) judicial transparency; (2) interaction with the legal profession; and (3) utilizing judicial remedies to increase rights decisions.[14]

The Supreme Court benefitted from two conditions created during the Fox administration. First, President Fox appointed four new justices: José Ramón Cossío Díaz (2003), Margarita Luna Ramos (2004), Sergio Valls Hernández (2004), and Fernando Franco Gonzalez Salas (2006). These judicial appointments raised the quality of judicial debates and changed the dynamic of the Supreme Court's decision making. Second, President Fox presented to Congress a proposal for a Federal Law of Transparency and Access to Public Governmental Information. This law, which was successfully passed and entered into effect on June 11, 2002, represented an opportunity for the Supreme Court to build synergies with the mass media and legal profession.

Judicial Transparency and Access to Information, 2005

The 2002 Transparency Law expressly mandated that the Supreme Court and Judicial Council adjust the judiciary's institutional structure to the principles and regulations contained in the law. In response, in 2003 the Supreme Court issued various administrative rules or Acuerdos Generales to regulate access to information stored in the Supreme Court's archives.[15] Ultimately and more indirectly, the law led to the implementation of other important measures including increased access to judicial decisions (both hard copies and electronic versions), the establishment of a television channel (Canal Judicial) dedicated to the judiciary, the creation of the Supreme Court's Web site, and initiation of a public radio station to educate the public on matters of important social concern decided by the Court.[16] In addition, Chief Justice Azuela, Justice Cossío Díaz, and Justice Valls created a Committee of Social Communication to set the rules, procedures, and objectives of the judicial channel.[17] The justices also organized training programs for journalists responsible

---

[13] Aranda, Jesús, "La Corte debe resolver aun en contra del interés del Estado: Góngora Pimentel," *La Jornada*, November 16, 2009.

[14] Justice Cossío joined the Supreme Court in November 2003, and will serve until 2018.

[15] Acuerdo General 9/2003 (May 27, 2003); "Lineamientos de la Comisión de Transparencia y Acceso a la Información Pública de la Suprema Corte de Justicia de la Nación, relativos a la organización, catalogación, clasificación y conservación de la documentación de este Alto Tribunal" (June, 2, 2003); Acuerdo General 12/2003 and Reglamento de la Suprema Corte de Justicia de la Nación y del Consejo de la Judicatura Federal para la Aplicación de la Ley Federal de Transparencia y Acceso a la Información Pública Gubernamental (April 4, 2004).

[16] *El Universal*, "Inicia transmisiones Canal Judicial," May 29, 2006.

[17] Acta Extraordinaria del Comité de Comunicación Social de la Suprema Corte de Justicia de la Nación, September 2005.

for covering the judiciary in an effort to keep civil society informed of the Court's decisions.[18] "Going public" in these ways allowed the general public, litigants, and civil society to witness the judicial decision-making process and participate in the national debate (Staton 2003).

In addition to promoting these institutional changes, Justice Cossío Díaz emphasized the importance of integrating principles of transparency and access to information into judiciary's daily operations, proposing the following agenda (Cossío Díaz 2005).[19] First, Cossío Diaz promoted a simplified format for judicial opinions. Under the PRI, the Court issued lengthy opinions loaded with inconsequential transcriptions and legal jargon that were incomprehensible to nonlegal audiences. To correct this deficiency, Justice Cossío Díaz proposed the adoption of the *Manual of Style for Judicial Opinions*,[20] in hopes of homogenizing forms of drafting opinions and noting citations. Adoption of the manual's format resulted in better organized and more concise rulings that could be evaluated by the general public. This change was perceived by the legal profession and society as the beginning of a new public dialogue between the Court and members of the legal profession. Second, the Court began to publish its rulings and transcriptions of its deliberations (*versiones estenográficas*) on its Web site to inform the public about the judicial decision-making process. Third, Justice Cossío Diaz encouraged the participation of interest groups in the judicial decision processes through amicus curiae briefs. Finally, the justice invited litigants, academics, and the media to utilize the new channels opened by the Supreme Court to formulate well-informed and high-quality critiques as an effort to build Mexico's democratic society. These institutional changes regarding judicial transparency dismantled former PRI practices of secrecy and obscurity within the judicial decision-making processes.

Inviting the Legal Complex to Participate with the Supreme Court, 2006

Justice Cossío Díaz also launched an immensely influential "legal education campaign" in hopes of encouraging members of the legal profession to work in conjunction with the Supreme Court in an effort to consolidate democratic principles in Mexico. In July 2006, Cossío Díaz delivered a presentation before the Mexican Bar in which he encouraged lawyers to participate in articulating a constitutional theory supporting the aspirations of the fundamental rights listed in the Constitution, the first time in the Court's history it reached out to members of the legal profession in such a way.[21] However, Cossío Díaz also called on lawyers to serve as social engineers,

---

[18] "Capacitación a Periodistas en Temas Jurídicos," Supreme Court Press Release, 2010.

[19] José Ramón Cossío, "Un año de apertura," *El Universal*, October 13, 2005.

[20] "Propuesta para la Elaboración de Proyectos de Sentencia en la Primera Sala derivada del Consenso adoptado en la reunión de fecha 12 de Septiembre del año en curso entre el Ministro José Ramón Cossío Díaz y los Coordinadores de las Ponencias de esta Sala."

[21] "The Role of Lawyers and the Necessity of Building a Constitutional Theory in Mexico" (Cossío 2006).

bringing claims concerning policy making to the courts. Overall, Cossío Díaz highlighted that increasing the Court's fundamental-rights docket and fomenting rights jurisprudence was a collective responsibility involving justices and the legal profession.[22] As president of the Court's First Chamber,[23] Justice Cossío Díaz also reinforced the idea of strengthening bonds with the legal community and improving the constitutional questions posed by its members. Most broadly, he portrayed the Court not as a mere problem solver but as an arena in which political struggles could be waged to change the fundamental nature of society by interpreting the scope of the fundamental rights incorporated in the Constitution.[24]

Judicial Remedies to Increase Fundamental Rights Decisions, 2007

Despite substantial improvements in judicial transparency and the Court's emerging public dialogue with members of the legal profession, the Court's fundamental-rights jurisprudence continued to be weak. To address this ongoing problem, in 2007 Justice Cossío Díaz promoted the Fundamental Rights Program. He also employed an unusual strategy: using the Court's Facultad de Atracción (Attraction Power) to bring fundamental-rights cases to the Court. The Facultad de Atracción grants the Supreme Court the power to hear amparo cases – whose original jurisdiction corresponds to circuit courts – by request of any justice, circuit court magistrate, or the attorney general because of the "importance or transcendence" of the case.[25] Once a case is "attracted" to the Court from the circuit court, the justices decide whether or not the case deserves to be heard by the Supreme Court on the basis of the importance and transcendence standard.

This power, which is unique to Mexico, granted the Court enormous leverage (which, for obvious reasons, it rarely used during the PRI regime). After 2007, the Court used the power to identify "potential" fundamental-rights challenges in amparo cases in circuit courts across the country.[26] In order to effectively track these cases, on July 3, 2007, the Judicial Council created the Integral System for Tracking

---

[22] Justice Cossío reiterated this mutual responsibility in his 2006 and 2007 First Chamber's Annual Reports.

[23] The Mexican Supreme Court functions in two Chambers. The First Chambers reviews civil and criminal cases and the Second Chamber reviews administrative and labor cases. Each chamber is composed by five justices; the Chief Justices belongs to neither.

[24] *Informe de Labores de la Primera Sala de la Suprema Corte de Justicia de la Nación del 2006* and *Informe de Labores de la Primera Sala de la Suprema Corte de Justicia de la Nación del 2007.*

[25] A legal reform in 1988 originally empowered justices to "attract" amparo cases that deserved to be heard by the Court because of fulfilling the "special characteristics" standard. In the 1994 legal reform, the "importance and transcendence" standard replaced the special characteristics standard. Over the years, the Supreme Court had significant discretion in applying the "importance" standard; the "transcendence" standard was determined in terms of the case's consequences.

[26] "La Suprema Corte atrae asuntos sobre presuntas violaciones a los derechos humanos," Mexican Foreign Affairs Minister, Press Release, March 2010; "Conocerá la Suprema Corte amparo promovido por Amalia García Medina sobre el derecho fundamental a la no incriminación," The Supreme Court, Press Release, June 2011.

Judicial Files database (Sistema Integral de Seguimiento de Expedientes; SISE).[27] This database contains statistical data on circuit court cases, including the number of cases each court has, the challenge involved in each, and the timing of their resolution. The Facultad de Atracción has become a major "judicial remedy" that the Supreme Court has utilized to fill the void of fundamental-rights challenges. Using this power, the Court has attracted cases concerning people's right to their own image, children's best interest, due process for indigenous people, protection from domestic violence, privacy rights and personal data, right to health, and transgender rights, among many others.

Implementing these various institutional changes succeeded in validating the Court's transparency and increasing access to information for society. Further, using the Facultad de Atracción (together with the SISE database) represented an innovative judicial strategy to increase the number of fundamental-rights challenges at the Supreme Court. Justice Cossío Diaz's legal education campaign – for the first time in the Supreme Court's history – highlighted the legal profession's shared responsibility in setting the rights agenda and consolidating democratic principles in Mexico.

Justice José Ramón Cossío Diaz and the New Role of the Mexican Supreme Court, 2007–2010

By 2007, the Mexican Supreme Court's transformation was almost complete: the Court had promoted synergies with the Executive and Congress (1999–2003), and with mass media and the legal profession (2003–2007). However, synergies with support structures (civil society, interest groups, and international organizations) still needed to be established. The leadership of Justice José Ramón Cossío Díaz would again prove crucial to the implementation of significant institutional changes that allowed the Court to fully adopt its new role. Indeed, the 2007–2010 judicial term represented one of the Court's most flourishing moments.

At the beginning of this new judicial term, the Court's strategy was to divide the judicial calendar by year – the year of transparency and access to information (2008), the year of society (2009),[28] and the year of access to justice (2010)[29] – in order to cultivate and strengthen bonds with new audiences – the mass media (2008), civil society groups (2009), and interest groups, such as the Mexican scientific community (2010). Further, Justice Cossío Díaz sought to democratize the judicial

---

[27] *Acuerdo de la Comisión de Administración del Consejo de la Judicatura Federal, que establece el procedimiento de asignación, certificación y uso de la Firma Electrónica para el Seguimiento de Expedientes (FESE).* Issued by the Judicial Council and published at the Diario Oficial de la Federación on July 3, 2007.

[28] Speech delivered by Chief Justice Guillermo Ortiz in the Inauguration of 2009 Judicial Calendar Year, January 2009.

[29] Speech delivered by Chief Justice Guillermo Ortiz at the inauguration of 2010 Judicial Calendar Year, January 2010.

decision-making process by launching a rights consciousness campaign. The primary purpose of this campaign was to reach out to civil society and interest groups to invite them to collaborate with the Supreme Court in cases with social implications for the country. In the past, civil society had minimal opportunity to influence political or judicial decision-making processes (Blake 1996). Further, distrust in the judiciary discouraged human rights advocates from seeing the Supreme Court as a forum to challenge state actions. In 2007, the Supreme Court took various steps to end those authoritarian legacies and establish a judicial arena in which civil society, litigants, and activists could seek political reform.

As part of this rights consciousness campaign, Justice Cossío Díaz suggested new channels through which academic and scientific institutions could influence the Court's decision-making process, such as amicus curiae briefs,[30] public-interest litigation (Hernández Arcos 2009), and public hearings. For instance, in a lecture on "Science, Technology and Law," Justice Cossío Díaz underscored how the filing of amicus curiae briefs helped bring about social change in the United States. He also invited the scientific community, nongovernmental organizations, and human rights activists to work together with the Supreme Court in the construction of Mexico's constitutional theory.[31] In similar forums, Justice Cossío Díaz discussed the importance of providing law students with training in social justice through Public Interest Clinics and emphasized the driving force this type of litigation could represent in fomenting societal change. Successful litigation outcomes in the newly established Public Interest Clinics at two top academic institutions, Centro de Investigación y Docencia Económicas and Instituto Tecnológico Autónomo de México reflect the positive response of the academic and scientific communities.

THE NEW SUPREME COURT AS AN ARENA FOR POLITICAL CONTESTATION

Beginning in 2007, the Mexican Supreme Court emerged as a critical arena for political contestation. From that time, individuals and groups have used the Court as a forum to generate attention over particular issues, and the Court has been asked to decide technical cases with enormous social implications including challenges involving unlawful monopolistic practices (*Ley Televisa*, 2007),[32] the definition of abortion,[33] gross violations of indigenous people's human rights (*El caso Acteal*,

---

[30] Cossío Díaz, José Ramón. "La figura del Amicus Curiae en la Jurisdicción Constitutional," speech delivered at the Seminar "Science, Technology and Law," the Mexican Supreme Court and the Mexican Academy of Science, May 26, 2008.

[31] For example, Centro de Investigación y Docencia Económica (CIDE), in collaboration with the Prevention and Control Center for HIV/AIDS (Centro de Prevención y Control del VIH/SIDA), filed an amicus curiae brief on cases that challenged the constitutionality of the Social Security Legislation of the Mexican Forces.

[32] "Con expertos revisará la Corte la Ley Televisa," *Diario Milenio*, December 1, 2008.

[33] Elsa Conde, "La Suprema Corte ante la Interrupción Voluntaria del Embarazo," *La Jornada*, June 27, 2008; Marta Lamas, "Justicia y Aborto en México," *El País*, September 9, 2008.

2009),[34] and even the recognition of same-sex marriages and its legal implications.[35] In all of these cases, the Supreme Court saw an opportunity to open new channels for societal participation: Justices welcomed amicus curiae briefs and the expertise of renowned scientists from the Universidad Nacional Autónoma de México and the National Polytechnic Institute. The Court also began holding public hearings (*audiencias públicas*) in landmark cases.[36] This new decision-making process distinguishes the Mexican Court from other high courts around the world, and constitutes an open invitation to different sectors of society such as NGOs, political party leaders, members of the church, and the public in general to participate in the consolidation of democratic principles.

As a result, since 2007, the Court has received societal opinions about public interest issues, and requested scientific guidance on scientific technicalities embedded in the language of the law. To give just one example, in 2007 the Supreme Court debated landmark amparo cases involving the withdrawal of army members because of their HIV-positive condition, unleashing harsh debate between the liberal and ultraconservative wings at the Court. This case represented an opportunity for Justice Cossío Díaz to reach out to civil society and interest groups and solicit their participation in the judicial decision-making process. Acknowledging publicly that there are cases that exceed the legal knowledge of judges, for the first time in the history of the Supreme Court, Justice Cossío Díaz sought scientific guidance on technicalities embedded in the language of the law. Further, he formulated a questionnaire with his concerns about HIV and the seropositivity condition and elicited responses from prestigious scientists and experts of the Mexican Academy of Science. After reading the answers to his questions, Justice Cossío Díaz concluded that the seropositivity condition did not prevent individuals from conducting normal activities.[37] This decision established an important precedent of societal change, and further opened the door to broader participation in future judicial debates on government policies.

The Court's openness to society also triggered forceful public-interest litigation from newly established clinics in prestigious academic institutions across the country. The positive effects of this new societal participation motivated Justice Cossío Díaz to advocate for the signing of various collaboration covenants with prestigious institutions and organizations such as the Mexican Academy of Science,[38]

---

[34] Laura Poy Solano, "El Fallo de la Corte sobre Acteal no descarta el crimen de Estado: CIDE," *La Jornada*, August 29, 2009.

[35] "Solicita Ministro Valls Apoyo Técnico a la UNAM sobre Matrimonios del mismo Sexo," The Supreme Court Press Release, April 2010; Fabiola Cancino, "La Suprema Corte acepta el derecho de adopción a matrimonios gay," *CNN*, August 16, 2010.

[36] *Reglas Operativas para el Desahogo de las Audiencias Públicas en relación con la acción de inconstitucionalidad 146/2007 y su acumulada.*

[37] Carlos Avilés, "Divide opiniones en la Corte el caso con militares con SIDA," *El Universal*, February 20, 2007.

[38] "Asesora la Academia Mexicana de Ciencias a la Suprema Corte," The Mexican Academy of Science Press Release, November 2006.

the National Medical Academy of Mexico,[39] the National Commission of Medical Arbitration, the Autonomous Metropolitan University,[40] the National Polytechnic Institute,[41] the Justice Studies Center of the Americas,[42] Mexican Transparency,[43] and the National Women's Institute, among many others.[44] Further, as part of its new role, the Court also placed gender issues on the judicial agenda, creating new opportunities for women to participate in the decision-making process. For instance, in September 2009, Justice Olga Sánchez and Justice Cossío Díaz – both members of the newly created Supreme Court Gender Commission – presented the "Diagnostic on Gender Equality at the Mexican Supreme Court," and initiated a new gender project in the Court.[45] From that time, the Court has actively emphasized gender roles in the judicial decision-making process and signed covenants with women's organizations such as the National Women's Institute,[46] and the National Council to Prevent Discrimination in an effort to incorporate gender perspectives into judicial activity.

The active role of Justice Cossío Díaz and a series of institutional changes implemented under his leadership transformed the Mexican Supreme Court into a space for political activism and contestation. Since 2007, when the Court institutionalized this arena, it has sought to create and capitalize on societal support structures, providing them with various legal channels and remedies to influence the judicial outcomes such as filing amicus curiae briefs and engaging in public-interest litigation. All of these changes have allowed the Court to hand down landmark fundamental-rights decisions. By 2010, its rulings had begun to receive considerable attention from the academia, civil society, interest groups, and media. In a positive cycle, media dissemination has had a positive impact on public opinion, fomenting further participation in the Court's initiatives by multiple societal sectors, the executive, and the legislature.

CONCLUSION

Since the mid-1990s, Mexico has experienced a rights revolution. This chapter argued that legal reform in 1994 and the new competitive party system contributed to, but do not completely explain, the shift in judicial attitudes toward the protection of fundamental rights. In order to explain this outcome, we must closely examine

---

[39] Urbano Barrera, "Suscribe SCJN Convenio con la Academia Nacional de Medicina," *Ovaciones*, February 3, 2009.

[40] Signed May 2007, *Portal de Transparencia, Suprema Corte de Justicia de la Nación.*

[41] Signed May 2007, *Portal de Transparencia, Suprema Corte de Justicia de la Nación.*

[42] Signed December 2007, *Portal de Transparencia, Suprema Corte de Justicia de la Nación.*

[43] Signed November 2007, *Portal de Transparencia, Suprema Corte de Justicia de la Nación.*

[44] "Firman Convenio de Colaboración la Suprema Corte de Justicia de la Nación y el CONAPRED," *Consejo nacional para prevenir la discriminación,* Supreme Court Press Release, April 2010.

[45] "Presentan Micrositio con temas de equidad y genero en el PJF," *Compromiso: The Judicial Power of the Federation,* October 2009, pp. 26–29.

[46] Signed May 2010, *Portal de Transparencia, Suprema Corte de Justicia de la Nación.*

the actions of the progressive justices who made possible the Mexican Supreme Court's new role as a forum for political activism and contestation. In Mexico, significant societal transformation occurred as part of political campaigns advocated by progressive justices promoting a new judicial agenda, pushing for judicial independence, and inspiring political action. To develop this new role – and a fundamental-rights agenda in Mexico – justices promoted new interactions and interdependence between the Court and the other branches of government, civil society, the legal profession, and interest groups. Doing so helped the Court initiate unprecedented constitutional interpretation of fundamental rights and freedoms such as freedom of expression, religious creeds, reproductive rights, gender equality, and criminal justice.

This research thus depicts a new model of rights revolutions. Whereas Charles Epp attributes the transformation of courts into guardians of individual rights to pressure from below, especially deliberate, strategic, organized effort by rights advocates, the development of the Mexican Supreme Court from 1995 to 2010 tells a different story. The Supreme Court effectively became a guardian of fundamental rights only after progressive justices reached out to new audiences and provided them with new tools and legal channels (amicus curiae briefs, public hearings, judicial remedies, and public-interest litigation) to influence the Court's decisions. These institutional changes implemented by progressive justices are central to understanding how the Mexican Supreme Court became an arena for political contestation: it was only in the last seven years – when the executive, Congress, media, civil society, and interest groups acted in tandem with the Supreme Court – that the number of fundamental-rights decisions increased considerably.

The contribution of Justice Juventino Castro y Castro was particularly crucial in setting the judicial agenda of the Supreme Court in its four post-PRI terms. Justice Genaro Góngora Pimentel was central in dismantling former PRI legacies, and emancipating the Court from the Executive's and Congress's influence. Góngora Pimentel did so by proposing three key constitutional reforms, including the Amparo Law (ultimately passed in October 2011), which will facilitate use of that mechanism to challenge fundamental-rights violations. Justice José Ramón Cossío Díaz advocated for a more liberal reading of the constitutional text, greater media coverage of Supreme Court decisions, and more participation by civil society, the scientific community, the legal profession, and interests groups in the judicial decision-making process. In short, all these justices' leadership proved pivotal in creating a new role for the Court – as an arena for political contestation.

REFERENCES

Aguinaco Alemán, José Vicente. 1997. *La Suprema Corte de Justicia de la Nación protagonista del cambio en la consolidación del Estado de Derecho*. Mexico City: Suprema Corte de Justicia de la Nación.
Blake, Joanne. 1996. *The Unmasking of Civil Society in Mexico: The EZLN Discourse on Democratic Development*. British Columbia: Simon Fraser University.

Castillejos Aragón, Mónica. 2005. *La Suprema Corte de Justicia de la Nación y el Control Previo de los Tratados Internacionales en México*. Mexico City: Porrúa.

Castro y Castro, Juventino. 2003. "Dos Cumbres Profesionales," in *Dr. Juventino Castro y Castro*, Mexico City: Suprema Corte de Justicia de la Nación.

Castro y Castro, Juventino. 2004. *La Descomposición Cultural en México: Estrategia para una cruzada contra la corrupción*. Mexico City: Grupo Enlace.

Cossío Díaz, José Ramón. 2001. *La Teoría Constitucional de la Suprema Corte*. Mexico City: Doctrina Jurídica Contemporánea.

Cossío Díaz, José Ramón. 2005a. *Génesis y* "Evolución del Acceso a la Información en el Poder Judicial de la Federación," in *A un año de la expedición del Reglamento de la Suprema Corte de Justicia de la Nación y del Consejo de la Judicatura e en materia de Transparencia y Acceso a la Información*. Mexico City: Supreme Court of Mexico.

Cossío Díaz, José Ramón. 2005b. *Constitucionalismo Iberoamericano y migración de criterios*, 10 años de la Novena Época, Discursos, Mexico City, Suprema Corte de Justicia de la Nación.

Cossío Díaz, José Ramón. 2006. "Los Abogados y la necesidad de una teoría de la Constitución en México," *Este País* 184.

De Bell, Leendertand Pansters Wil. 2001. "Winners and Losers: Preliminary Reflections on the 2000 Presidential Elections in Mexico," *European Review of Latin American and Caribbean Studies* 70, April, p. 79.

Domingo, Pilar. 2004. "Judicialization of Politics or Politicization of the Judiciary? Recent Trends in Latin America." *Democratization*, 11(1): 104–126.

Epp, Charles. 1998. *The Rights Revolution. Lawyers, Activists and Supreme Courts in Comparative Perspective*. Chicago: The University of Chicago University Press.

Ferejohn, John. 2002. "Constitutional Review in the Global Context," *6 N.Y.U. J. LEGIS. & PUB. POL'Y*, 49: 51–52.

Finkel, Jodi. 2000. "Judicial Independence: The Politics of the Supreme Court in Mexico," *Journal of Latin American Studies*, 32(3): 705–735.

Finkel, Jodi. 2003. "The Supreme Court Decisions on Electoral Rules after Mexico's 1994 Judicial Reform: An Empowered Court," *Journal of Latin American Studies*, 35: 777–799.

Finkel, Jodi. 2008. "Judicial Reform as Insurance Policy: Mexico in the 1990s," *Latino American Politics and Sociology*, 46(4): 87.

Fix Fierro, Héctor. 1981. "The Writ of Amparo in Latin America," *Lawyer of the Americas*, 13(3): 361–391.

Fix Fierro, Héctor. 2003. "Judicial Reform in Mexico: What's Next?" in *Beyond the Common Knowledge: Empirical Approaches to the Rule of Law*, Eric G. Jensen and Thomas Heller (eds.), Stanford: Stanford University Press.

Fix Fierro, Héctor. 2007. "The Role of Lawyers in the Mexican Justice System in Reforming the Administration of Justice in Mexico," Wayne A. Cornelius and David A. Shirk (eds.), South Bend: University of Notre Dame Press.

Fix Zamudio, Héctor. 1993. "La Suprema Corte de Justicia de México como Tribunal Constitucional," *Revista Jurídica de Petróleos Mexicanos*, No. 59–60.

Galanter, Marc. 1974. "Why the Haves Come Out Ahead: Speculations on the Limits of Legal Change," *Law & Society Review*, 9: 95.

Góngora Pimentel, Genaro. 2000. "Sin Independencia no somos nada," Mexico City: Suprema Corte de Justicia de la Nación.

Góngora Pimentel, Genaro. 2000. "El Estado de Derecho como promotor del Desarrollo Económico Nacional, Suprema Corte de Justicia," Mexico City: Suprema Corte.

Góngora Pimentel, Genaro. 2005. "La Suprema Corte de Justicia de la Nación como árbitro nacional, a diez años de la reforma constitucional," *Lex*, 118.

Gudiño Pelayo, José de Jesús. 2005. "La participación de la Suprema Corte de Justicia de la Nación en la construcción del modelo democrático mexicano," *Lex*, Volume 116.

Halliday, Terrence, Lucien Karpik, and Malcolm M. Feeley (Eds.). 2007. *Fighting for Political Freedom: Comparative Studies of the Legal Complex for Political Change*. Oxford: Hart Publishing.

Hernández Arcos, Raúl. 2009. "Clínicas de Interés Social y Litigios de Interés Público, para bienestar con garantías universales," *Compromiso: Revista del Poder Judicial de la Federación*, October.

Inclán Oseguera, Silvia. 2009. "Judicial Reform in Mexico: Political Insurance or the Search for Political Legitimacy?" *Political Research Quarterly*, 62(4): 753–766.

Jiménez Remus, Gabriel. 1996. "La Suprema Corte como Tribunal Constitucional," Estudios Parlamentarios del Congreso, September–October, pp. 72–77.

Kagan, Robert A. 2001. *Adversarial Legalism*, Cambridge, MA: Harvard University Press.

Kahn Zemans, Frances. 1980. "The Neglected Role of Law in the Political System," Paper presented at the Annual Meeting of the American Political Science Association, Philadelphia.

Kessler, Mark. 1990. "Legal Mobilization for Social Reform: Power and Politics of Agenda Setting," *Law & Society Review*, 24(1): 121–143.

Lasser, Mitchel. 2009. *Judicial Deliberations: A Comparative Analysis of Judicial Transparency and Legitimacy*, Oxford: Oxford University Press.

Magaloni, Beatriz. 2003. "Authoritarianism, Democracy and the Supreme Court: Horizontal Exchange and the Rule of Law in Mexico" in *Democratic Accountability in Latin America*, Scott Mainwaring and Christopher Welna (eds.), New York: Oxford University Press.

Magaloni, Beatriz and Arianna Sánchez. 2006. "An Authoritarian Enclave? The Supreme Court in Mexico's Emerging Democracy." Paper presented at the 2006 Annual Meeting of the American Political Science Association, Philadelphia, PA, September.

Magaloni, Ana Laura and Arturo Zaldívar. 2006. "El Ciudadano Olvidado," 24 (*Nexos*), No. 342, June.

Mahoney Barry. 1988. *Changing Times in Trial Courts*, Williamsburg, VA: National Center for State Courts.

Moustafa, Tamir. 2007. *The Struggle for Constitutional Power*. Cambridge: Cambridge University Press.

Moustafa, Tamir. 2008. "The Political Origins of 'Rule-by-Law' Regimes," Prepared for presentation at Yale University Workshop on the Rule of Law, March 28–29.

Raphael, Ricardo. 2006. "Justicia de baja intensidad," *Nexos*, May, Volume 342.

Redding, Andrew. 1995. "Mexico: Democracy and Human Rights," Hemispheric World Policy Institute, July, p. 69.

Ríos-Figueroa, Julio. 2007. "Fragmentation of Power and the Emergence of an Effective Judiciary in Mexico," *1994–2002 Latin American Politics & Society*, 49(1): 31–57.

Rosenberg, Gerald, 1991. *The Hollow Hope: Can Court Bring about Social Change?* Chicago: The University of Chicago Press.

Schatz, Sara. 2000. "The Political Context: Nullifying the Punitive of the Court's Legal Formal Rulings and the Attempt to Continue the Reign of Informal, Case-by-Case Justice." In *Elites, Masses, and the Struggle for Democracy in Mexico: A Culturalist Approach*. Boston: Praeger, 2–4.

Scheingold, Stuart. 1974. *The Politics of Rights: Lawyers, Public Policy and Political Change.* New Haven: Yale University Press.

Shapiro, Martin. 1981. *Courts. A Comparative and Political Analysis,* Chicago: The University of Chicago.

———. 1992. "The Giving Reasons Requirement," *U. CHI. LEGAL F.,* 179: 182.

———. 1994. "The Judicialization of Politics." *International Political Science Review,* 15(2): 101–112.

Shapiro, Martin and Alec Stone Sweet. 2002. *On Law, Politics and Judicialization,* New York: Oxford University Press.

Staton, Jeffery. 2003. "Lobbying for Judicial Reform: The Role of the Mexican Supreme Court in Institutional Selection," Center for U.S.-Mexican Studies, University of California at San Diego.

———. 2008. "Cabildeo por una Reforma Judicial: El papel de la Suprema Corte Mexicana en la selección institucional," in *La Reforma de la Justicia en México,* México City: El Colegio de México-Centro de Estudios Sociológicos. pp. 267–297.

———. 2010. *Judicial Power and Strategic Communication in Mexico,* New York: Cambridge University Press.

Wice, Paul. 1995. *Court Reform and Judicial Leadership: Judges George Nicola and the New Jersey Justice System.* Boston: Praeger.

Zamora, Stephen et al. 2004. *Mexican Law.* New York: Oxford University Press.

PART II

Expanding Judicial Roles in Established Democracies

6

Courts Enforcing Political Accountability
The Role of Criminal Justice in Italy

*Carlo Guarnieri**

On October 6, 2009, the Italian Constitutional Court quashed the so-called *lodo Alfano*, a statute hastily passed by the right-wing parliamentary majority in July 2008, just after winning the parliamentary elections. The statute had the effect of freezing all criminal proceedings against the highest state officials: the president of the Republic, the presidents of the two chambers of Parliament, and the prime minister. In fact, the actual goal of the statute was to suspend all the criminal charges brought against Berlusconi. The reaction of Berlusconi and his allies to the decision has been to denounce the court's leftist propensities and call for radical reforms of the judicial system. Without doubt, the court's decision was by no means favourable to Berlusconi, as it is likely that in the near future he will have to confront several criminal proceedings.[1] However, in the recent past it was a criminal investigation that opened the way for the return to power of the Italian tycoon.

In January 2008, the justice minister of the center-left Prodi government, Clemente Mastella – together with his wife and twenty-three members of his small party – was put under investigation. The charges were several, ranging from extortion against the chief executive of the Campania region to various administrative illegalities. As a consequence, the minister resigned, denouncing the investigation as a "persecution." After some days, the weak twelve-party government led by Romano Prodi collapsed, opening the way to new elections. Thus, in April, the center-right coalition – led by Silvio Berlusconi – which had ruled 2001–2006, was returned to power – with a stronger majority. Although the Prodi government was far from stable, the judicial intervention was the trigger of the crisis.

* Department of Political Science, University of Bologna (Italy). An earlier version of this paper was presented at the Sawyer seminar, Centre for the Study of Law and Society, University of California, Berkeley, November 7th, 2008. The paper has been supported by the program "New Forms of Democracy" financed by the University of Bologna and the Italian Ministry of Higher Education (D.M. 8.5.2001), coordinated by Giorgio Freddi, University of Bologna.

[1] Among them, one regarding the corruption of a witness (the British lawyer David Mills) and another related to fraud in his company's budget.

As these two recent incidents illustrate, especially in the last twenty years, criminal justice has consistently and significantly impacted the political process in Italy. In some circumstances, public prosecutors have performed not only the institutional role of enforcing the criminal law but have also taken on a new political role in Italian governance: assuring a sort of political accountability of public officials (Kapiszewski and Taylor 2008: 751). On the whole, courts have supported the trend. In fact, the Italian judicialization of politics cannot be understood without considering the way the judicial system has been transformed beginning in the middle of the last century.

THE TRANSFORMATION OF THE ITALIAN JUDICIAL SYSTEM

Traditionally, Italian judges were part of a hierarchical organization, controlled by high-ranking judges, with the Ministry of Justice at the top. Following the French Napoleonic tradition, judges and prosecutors belonged to the same corps: both were – and still are – defined as magistrates. During their professional life, they could – and still can – switch from one function to another and vice versa. Also in Italy, as in most continental European countries, the judicial function was largely defined in passive terms: the judge was considered to be the "mouth of the law," faithfully applying the will of the legislator (Bell 2006). The Court of Cassation – the traditional apex of the judicial pyramid – exerted its control on inferior courts; formally through its review powers, informally also through its influence on promotions and discipline. Therefore, even without considering the Fascist period – when civil and political rights were severely restricted – courts played a subordinate role in the Italian political system. On the other hand, their minor role assured a relative insulation from political pressure. Italian judges – and also prosecutors – could pursue their career without significant political interferences. Only the top of the judicial hierarchy was appointed by the government, although even in this case professional qualifications mattered.

The Constitution of 1948 introduced significant changes in this setting. Its most relevant innovations were constitutional review of legislation and a strong increase in judicial independence. Constitutional review was assigned to a special court – organized according to the teaching of Hans Kelsen – allowing access to separation-of-powers questions and more importantly, to any court having doubts on the constitutionality of a statute it had to apply in a concrete case. Judicial independence was to be guaranteed by entrusting all decisions regarding the status of judges and prosecutors to a body – the Higher Council of the Judiciary –two-thirds of which was composed of magistrates elected by their colleagues, the rest lawyers elected by Parliament.

Why were the judges so empowered? After the experience of the Fascist regime, the need to assure better protection of political and civil rights was deeply felt. The major political parties in the Constituent Assembly – Christian Democrats, Socialists, and Communists – did not trust each other. However, no party alone could muster a majority to pass a Constitution its leaders preferred. With the development of the Cold War and Stalinization of Eastern Europe, however, Christian Democrats – and the other small centrist parties – were fearful of a possible communist-dominated Executive. For its part, the left became increasingly worried about being isolated in the opposition and perhaps subjected to legal restrictions. Moreover, uncertainty about which party would govern in the future was high. At the end, all major parties agreed on the Constitution, which provided an impressive array of guarantees against possible Executive and Legislative abuses.

The Italian case fits the "insurance" model of judicial power proposed by Tom Ginsburg (2003) well. Constitutional review and judicial independence were designed as a way to check the political branches by political actors uncertain about their future power and divided by a low level of trust. An additional confirmation is provided by what happened after the Christian Democrats triumphed at the first parliamentary elections in 1948. Whereas the parties of the left began to reconsider their traditional distrust for courts and advocate a strengthening of judicial power,[2] Christian Democrats' enthusiasm for judicial checks cooled down. Giving up the traditional instruments of executive influence on the judiciary seemed a gratuitous gift to the Communist opposition. Moreover, notwithstanding its initial monarchist sympathies, the Court of Cassation had quickly aligned itself with the new political order. It seemed to welcome the Christian Democrats electoral victory, for example, by interpreting the amnesty laws in a way hostile to the left – and lenient toward old Fascists – and having its former president run as a successful CD candidate for the Senate and fill the justice portfolio for a time.

Only after the 1953 elections, when Christian Democrats' hold on the legislative process began to weaken, was the implementation of the Constitution resumed, leading to the institution of the Constitutional Court in 1956 and the Higher Council of the Judiciary in 1959. The new Constitutional Court began to vigorously cleanse the remains of Fascist legislation from the legal system, a role substantially welcomed by most political parties (Pederzoli 2008). The only significant opposition came from the Court of Cassation. In the 1960s, the two courts collided concerning the final power of interpreting statutes. The Court of Cassation – more ideologically conservative – was jealous of the fact that the Constitutional Court impinged on its prerogative of deciding the "exact" interpretation of the law.[3] In the end, a sort of alliance was forged between lower-ranking judges – happy to free themselves from the control of the Cassation – and the Constitutional Court – which, with the support of the academic doctrine, was able to report a victory in the fight. In this political interpretive struggle, the growing independence of lower-court

---

[2] As the Israeli case also shows (Reichman, Ch. 9 in this volume), political forces out of power are quick to discover the virtues of constitutionalism.

[3] According to Art. 65 of the Judicial Organization Act of 1941 (still in force), the Court of Cassation "assures the exact compliance and uniform interpretation of the law and the unity of the national objective legal system."

judges – who increasingly sided with the Constitutional Court – played a significant part.

The composition of the Higher Council of the Judiciary was another subject of conflict. The initial decision that the judicial members would be drawn, above all, from the higher ranks was strongly contested by the rest of the judiciary. In consequence, between the late 1960s and the early 1970s the power of the judicial hierarchy was destroyed. Promotions were entrusted to the Higher Council, which was now elected according to the principle "one magistrate, one vote." The result was that the independence of judges and prosecutors was strengthened in both its dimensions: externally from political power, and internally from higher ranks.[4] In addition, the judiciary was able to develop a significant capacity to exert political pressure, as most of the changes in judicial governance came about thanks to legislation advocated and supported by the judicial unions. In fact, since the end of the 1950s, magistrates had organized themselves into various, ideologically different groups. These groups played a crucial role in the reform process by forging connections with political parties and winning the support of public opinion (Guarnieri 2003; Vauchez 2004).

As a consequence of all these changes, Italian courts began to accumulate power. The institution of the Higher Council and its "democratization" increased guarantees of judicial independence in Italy to the highest level prevailing in continental Europe (Guarnieri and Pederzoli 2002). The Constitutional Court contributed to the decline of the influence of the Court of Cassation. The practice of judicial review began to diffuse itself among ordinary courts. Because they had to make a first appraisal of the constitutionality of a statute in order to decide whether or not to send a case to the Constitutional Court, lower-court judges thus became accustomed to critically evaluating legislation, a practice foreign to the traditional "judge as mouth of the law" approach to legal interpretation. In addition, through its so-called interpretive judgments, the Constitutional Court maintained that a statute was – or was not – constitutional, depending on the way it was interpreted. Thus, the court invited ordinary judges to interpret existing statutes in such a way as to make them compatible with the Constitution, in this way justifying a sort of judicial lawmaking (Pederzoli 2008). The result was a decline of the traditional stereotype of the judge as mere executor of the law, and hence an increase in judicial creativity and the development of new, more activist conceptions of the judicial – and also prosecutorial – role.

Changes in the structure of public prosecution were even more significant. Especially after the institution of the Higher Council in 1959, the powers of the minister of justice over prosecution were progressively erased. The Constitution's principle

---

4 In practice, today, judicial salaries are related to career seniority; specific positions are allocated through a variable consideration of seniority and party and judicial union politics. This fact has contributed to the decline of the Court of Cassation's influence in the judicial system. For an analogous development in the Netherlands, see Huls (Ch. 7 in this volume).

of mandatory prosecution increasingly came to be interpreted as sparing prosecutors from any kind of supervision coming from outside the judicial system, thereby expanding their discretion.[5] Also, the powers of the higher ranks of the prosecutoriat were gradually reduced. The long season of political violence in the 1970s and, later, the still unfinished fight against organized crime had important effects on the judicial system. A new drive toward increasing coordination between judicial offices developed, but traditional systems of coordination, on the basis of hierarchy, proved themselves to be slow and ineffective. New, direct, face-to-face relationships developed between prosecutors and instructing judges[6] of different offices, overcoming old, bureaucratic channels. These developments enhanced the coordinating role of the Higher Council, with its powers over the career and discipline of magistrates.

Another important change was the growing influence of the judiciary on police forces. Traditionally, prosecutors and instructing judges did not interfere with police investigations: they just waited for the police to provide them with the evidence for starting a prosecution in court. However, some initial police failings in the fight against terrorism and organized crime pushed the judiciary to take a more proactive stance; for example, by taking on the task of directly leading the investigations (Di Federico 2004: 485–489; Vogliotti 2004). In this way, magistrates were able to improve their investigative skills and exert a growing influence on police forces. The reform of the code of criminal procedure in 1989 abolished the instructing judge and entrusted the investigation to the prosecutor, ratifying this situation (Grande 2000). Prosecutors – many of whom had been instructing judges before 1989 – were able to employ their powers and skills, as well as their good relationships with the police, to broaden the range of their investigations and later, as we will see, strongly pursue cases of political corruption.

All of these developments were supported by the increasing fragmentation that characterized Italian politics after the end of the 1950s, with weak multiparty coalitions and factionalized governing parties (Cotta and Verzichelli 2008). The decision to systematically dismantle the old judicial structure has to be understood in light of the fact that the political environment was receptive to judicial demands. Once the traditional alliance between the Executive and senior judiciary had been weakened, new and increasingly important relationships developed between political parties and representatives of magistrates' associations. The parties permanently in opposition (such as the Communists) or those slowly moving from opposition to government (such as the Socialists in the 1960s) were interested in developing contacts with a strategic body such as the judiciary and strengthening the judiciary's independence from an Executive branch they did not expect to control. The party traditionally in government – the Christian Democrats – was confronted with new

---

[5] See the discussion by influential magistrates and academic lawyers in Conso (1979).
[6] Until 1989, Italian criminal justice was organized along the traditional French-style semi-inquisitorial model, in which the investigation of significant cases was entrusted to an instructing judge (Damaska 1986).

and powerful rivals. Moreover, competition among the various factions within the
governing party meant the judiciary found allies even there. This new relationship between the judiciary and Italian political parties, together with the growth of
Socialist and Communist influence on parliamentary decision making, resulted in
the reforms that satisfied magistrates' demands: the dismantling of the traditional
career and the increasing role of the Higher Council, where judicial groups began
to play a crucial part. Therefore, in the 1970s, the judiciary was able to expand its
roles, thanks also to the part played in the fight against terrorism. The following
decade was characterized by a relative stability in which the judiciary settled into its
new assertive prosecutorial role, dismantling the remaining terrorist networks and
beginning to develop large-scale investigations on organized crime, a fact more or
less tacitly accepted by a large part of the political class. However, the new roles of
courts were put somewhat in question by the Socialist party, which was resenting
the real or supposed influence of Communists and Christian Democrats on large
segments of the judicial corps.

THE POLITICAL CRISIS OF THE 1990S AND THE FURTHER EXPANSION OF JUDICIAL POWER

The political crisis of the early 1990s gave courts a significant chance to assert
the power already accumulated in new ways. The fall of the Berlin wall – that
is, the breakdown of socialist regimes in Central and East Europe and Russia –
had a deep influence on Italian politics. The failure of the communist experiment
fueled internal conflict and seriously reduced the electoral appeal of the Italian
Communists. The dissolving of the "red threat" had a corresponding effect on the
main anticommunist party, the Christian Democrats, which began to lose votes
dramatically. Meanwhile, European constraints made it more difficult to pursue the
policy of deficit spending that had supported the clientelistic practices of governing
parties: the governments had to cut expenses and raise taxes, with the result of further
increasing popular dissatisfaction. This state of public opinion made itself known in
the elections of April 1992: the centrist governing coalition (the *pentapartito*) fell to
less than 50 percent of votes and only received a thin majority of seats in Parliament.
A serious political crisis followed, and only after three months a new, weak cabinet
was formed.

The political landscape was ready for the so-called Clean Hands movement to
erupt. The weakening of the governing parties radically undermined the traditional ways in which they were able to contain judicial power to combat political
malfeasance.[7] After the 1992 elections, the investigations undertaken by prosecutors
in Milan – and later in other cities – increasingly involved prominent politicians

7 In the Higher Council, especially before 1992, political party representatives were able to profit from
the competition between different judicial groups, for instance by supporting the appointment of
non-overzealous chief prosecutors (Guarnieri 2003). Moreover, Parliament often declined to waive
immunity from prosecution for its members, and conflicts of jurisdiction obstructed the development

of the governing coalition – as well as managers of state and private companies – facing charges of corruption and other related crimes. According to one of the leading prosecutors of the Clean Hands investigations (Colombo 2006: 520), they ultimately involved more than 5,000 people: among them, 4 prime ministers, various cabinet ministers, and about 200 members of Parliament.[8]

The Clean Hands investigations focused on bribery of or extortion by public officials and on other crimes related to the performance of public functions. Already in the 1980s, some important investigations had involved the political class. Although these initiatives led to the conviction of some local politicians, their impact on national politics was minor. The changed political environment of the early 1990s, however, allowed judicial investigations to develop all their capacity and jolt the political system with maximum impact. Prosecutors were able to exploit the resources accumulated in the past in the fight against terrorism and organized crime. Their more proactive stance, thanks in part to their influence on the police, facilitated the development of investigations in search of crimes, in contrast to the prosecutor's traditional attitude of acting only after receipt of a report of a crime. The accused were induced to collaborate by offers of more lenient treatment in exchange for giving evidence. The structural disparity in resources between prosecution and defence during the investigation and the proximity between prosecutors and judges made it more likely for the prosecution to get arrest warrants and authorization of pre-trial detention (Di Federico and Sapignoli 2002).

Another important element supporting the development of judicial investigations was the role played by media. Especially between 1992 and 1994, the media were overwhelmingly supportive of the investigations, often leaking their results, and in any case siding with the judiciary and against the political class.[9] Only after 1994 did part of the media – especially those under the direct or indirect influence of the new leader of the right, Berlusconi – begin to take a more critical stance, leading to a sort of division between those for and against the tycoon. As a consequence, the impact of the "judicial-mediatic circus" (Soulez-Larivière, 1993), extremely strong at the beginning, began to wane; today, right-wing electors seem to have been somewhat "immunized" from its effect, which can still be felt among those on the left.[10]

---

of investigations. Above all, defendants were not ready to collaborate with the investigators; for instance, by acting as a prosecution witness.

[8] All leaders of traditional governing parties were convicted, sometimes of minor crimes. While there are no complete data on final convictions and acquittals, according to the Milan prosecution office, 5,000 people were investigated, and of these, 413 were acquitted at trial, 1,233 were convicted in different forms, and the cases of the rest were likely dropped prior to trial.

[9] The reasons behind this propensity are many: see, for example, Giglioli (1996), who emphasizes the growing independence of the news from political influence, thanks to the commercialization of the media.

[10] See, for example, the opinion surveys published in "La Repubblica," October 14, 2009, after the aforementioned Constitutional Court's decision on the *lodo Alfano*. Although 84 percent of those identified with the left were in favor, 70 percent of those on the right were against.

However, at least for a time, the favorable attitude by the media supported the strong impact of judicial investigations on the political system. The charges on which most investigations were based – illegal financing and bribery – were represented as the principal causes of waste of public money and maladministration. In this way, the high tax pressure felt by Italian citizens was related to political corruption. Indeed, the popularity of Clean Hands was also because of the fact that a network of illegalities was uncovered at the same time the ordinary citizen had to pay more taxes in order to balance the state budget, whose deficit could be portrayed as being the consequence of corruption.

It must also be emphasized that prosecutors were able to interpret crimes in a rather broad way. For example, illegal financing of parties – a less serious crime, but easier to prove – was often considered as implying bribery, even where there was no clear indication of the administrative decisions the money was supposed to buy. The judges initially supported this interpretation, and in any case, few opinion makers or academic lawyers objected. In fact, it has been argued that the roots of Italian judicialization lie in the high degree of corruption of the Italian political class. According to this view, judicial investigations have to be understood as a reaction to a situation of widespread political corruption. Thus, the magnitude of Italian judicialization has to be related to a political class unable or unwilling to successfully fight corruption (Della Porta and Vannucci 2007).[11]

Judicial initiatives also came to be represented as a way to enforce a form of accountability on an unmovable political class. At a general level, Pizzorno (1998) maintains that judicialization is related to long-term changes in democratic political systems. The traditional "programmatic" politics – in which parties compete with different policy programs – has given way to a kind of "moralistic" politics – in which personal attributes of candidates play a major part. In this new situation, the check on candidates' moral qualities – the so-called *controllo di virtù* (virtue check) – cannot any longer be performed by the opposition that – at least in Italy – has been inserted in a web of transactions with the governing parties. Under these circumstances, courts can play a significant part in the political process, serving as a mechanism of political accountability in a situation in which traditional forms no longer function in a satisfactory way.

BACKLASH? COURTS AND POLITICS IN ITALY: A COMPLEX RELATIONSHIP

As we have noted, thanks to the fragmentation of political forces at the Constituent Assembly, the original constitutional design supported a strong judicial power, with

---

[11] Several indicators point to Italy as a relatively corrupt country, at least in Europe. See, for instance, the 2011 Corruption Perception Index prepared by Transparency International. In any case, the argument by Della Porta and Vannucci does not seem to disprove the diffusion hypothesis: whatever the level of corruption, it is political fragmentation that has made it easier for courts to intervene.

significant prerogatives in the criminal field. Although the Constitution began to be implemented in the mid-1950s, for a long time judicial initiatives were kept somewhat in check by the political system. Only in the early 1990s, when the party system began to crumble, could the judiciary fully exploit its prerogatives. The governing parties were paralyzed by the electoral setback of 1992, and the opposition parties – both on the left and right – were keen to profit from the situation, supporting courts in their crusade against corruption. A good example of the prevailing trend was the enactment in the fall of 1993 of a constitutional amendment radically reducing the range of parliamentarians' immunity from judicial investigations. In the past, as mentioned earlier, refusal to waive the immunity had helped political parties keep judicial investigations under control. Since 1993, however, investigations against parliamentarians have been able to develop without previous authorization by Parliament, facilitating the prosecution of political figures.

The high degree of involvement of courts in the political process prompted different reactions from the political class. Following the election of March 1994, which was conducted under a new semi-majoritarian electoral law, a new right coalition led by Silvio Berlusconi rose to governmental power. Meanwhile, just before the elections Berlusconi had come to the attention of Milan prosecutors. In November 1994, when he was attending a UN conference in Naples on the fight against crime, he was publicly notified of being under investigation – a development that contributed to the fall of his first cabinet. Since the middle of the 1990s the Milan investigations have focused on Berlusconi, bringing him to trial on charges of fraud, tax evasion, and corruption.[12] It goes without saying that the right – and especially Forza Italia, Berlusconi's party – has been critical of these developments. For example, in the period 2001–2006, when again in power, the right coalition tried in different ways to reduce judicial power. This attitude resurfaced again in 2008. Sympathy for courts remains widespread in the left, although we must distinguish between the so-called *giustizialisti* – staunch supporters of judicial power – and the much more tepid attitude of the rest, worried that judicialization could eventually hit their parties (as to some extent it did).

Meanwhile, the evolution of the party system was not without consequences for judicial power. Since 1996, as a direct result of the new electoral system, Italy has been governed by two coalitions. In 2001, for the first time in Italian electoral history, an incumbent – the left – was replaced by the opposition – the right. This shift was repeated in 2006, although in a more fragmented contest, and again in 2008 when the right was returned to power with a strong parliamentary majority. This trend

---

[12] There are no exact figures, but the number of judicial investigations of Berlusconi seems to be rather high. He claims to have been investigated more than 90 times and to have spent at least 168 million euro in legal fees. In the last twenty years he has been the defendant in at least ten criminal trials. So far, he has always escaped a final conviction, sometimes because of the statute of limitations or of changes in the law brought about by his parliamentary majority.

toward a decrease of political fragmentation, although not linear, threatened greater political capacity to control judicial power.

One example concerns the powers of prosecutors. As we have seen, the 1989 code of criminal procedure abolished the instructing judge and shifted the task of preparing the case to the public prosecutor. However, although the code had foreseen many limitations to the powers of the prosecutor, understood to be only one of the parties to the case, in the context of some dramatic mafia killings[13] and under the pressure of the judiciary, a series of Constitutional Court decisions brought about a strong reinforcement of prosecutorial prerogatives (Pederzoli 2008). Building on the newly discovered principle of the need of "economizing the means of evidence" – in practice a variation of the old truth-seeking function of the trial of the civil law tradition – the Court restored to the prosecutor many of the traditional powers of the instructing judge. This made it easier for the prosecution's dossier to be taken into consideration as evidence at the trial, although it contained proofs obtained *inaudita altera parte* and therefore in violation of the adversary principle. A long confrontation followed between the Parliament, trying to strengthen the individual rights of the defendant, and the Constitutional Court, with its emphasis on the primacy of the search of truth at trial. In 1999, a constitutional amendment inserted into the Constitution the principle of the accusatorial trial –the first time in Italian constitutional history the Court was overruled. The amendment was voted by a wide majority composed of the right and large part of the left – irritated by the Constitutional Court's persistently negative attitude toward its legislation – with only a small group of giustizialisti against. The mistake of the Court was its inability to realize that the party system was slowly recovering from the crisis of 1992–1996 and that most parties, even on the left, were willing to somewhat contain the expansion of judicial power. This can be explained by the weakening of the Court's political component[14] – a consequence of the breakdown of the old parties – and the corresponding increase of the role of career judges (Pederzoli 2008).

After 2001, with the right in power, the conflict between courts and politics rose to new heights. Berlusconi, already the target of several investigations, began a systematic policy to reduce the threat of judicial investigations and circumscribe the independence of judges and prosecutors. An example of the first has been the reform of the crime of "fraud in accounting," introducing a sort of tolerance area in which differences between the official financial statement of a company and the reality, as ascertained by the court, is no longer to be considered a crime. The new

---

[13] Similar to those in 1992, against two prominent anti-mafia magistrates: Falcone and Borsellino. After the attacks, the government increased the powers of prosecution in organized crime cases. As pointed out in the text, the Constitutional Court further enlarged these powers.

[14] One-third of the fifteen constitutional judges are elected by Parliament, one-third appointed by the President of the Republic, and one-third elected by the highest ordinary courts. Normally, parliamentary judges have a political background, whereas presidential appointees tend to be academics, and courts elect fellow judges.

law – which had the effect of dismantling some of the cases against Berlusconi – provoked a reaction by Milan prosecutors. They appealed first to the European Court of Justice – claiming that the law did not meet the European standards of protection of companies' accounts – and later to the Constitutional Court, but in both cases without success. It should be underlined that the Italian Court showed a remarkable caution in addressing the case: this time, it seemed worried about directly confronting the Legislative majority (Pederzoli 2008).

Second, the political right conflicted with the judiciary concerning the governance of judicial careers and discipline of judges – with the left opposition siding with the judiciary. In 2005, a conservative reform aiming at somewhat restoring the old hierarchical structure was passed, but it was not implemented because, after the election of 2006, the new left majority quickly watered down much of its content. As we have seen, in 2008, the right – again in power – immediately passed a law freezing all criminal prosecutions against the prime minister. However, under the pressure of lower courts, the new statute has been voided by the Constitutional Court, again raising the tensions between courts and the political majority.

We should not overvalue the majoritarian turn of the 1996–2008 period, as the decline of political fragmentation may only be temporary.[15] It is clear, however, that stronger political majorities had the consequence of increasing the level of conflict between the judiciary and political branches trying to contain criminal judicialization.

FRANCE AND SPAIN AS CONTROL CASES

The significance of political fragmentation for the expansion of judicial roles is confirmed by a comparison of Italy with France and Spain.[16] Both of these countries belong to the civil law tradition, with a judicial system similar to the Italian (Merryman and Perdomo 2007). France and Italy share a judicial corps composed of magistrates performing judicial and prosecutorial functions. Spanish *fiscales*, although belonging to a separate organization, share the same channel of recruitment with the judges. In addition, both French and Spanish criminal procedures – as the Italian before 1989 – are centered on the role of the instructing judge. Therefore, although in these countries – unlike Italy – prosecutors are, at least in principle, under Executive influence, the investigation of more important cases is entrusted to an independent judge.

[15]   The effective number of parties – calculated according to the Laasko and Taagepera index – in the Parliaments of the First Republic oscillated between 2.9 in 1948 and 4.1 in 1987. It rose to 7.3 in 1994. It declined to: 6.2 in 1996; 5.2 in 2001; 5.1 in 2006; and 3.1 in 2008 (Cotta and Verzichelli 2008).

[16]   Generally speaking, judicial roles – at least in the criminal field – seem more restricted in most central and northern countries (e.g., Germany and Sweden), where political fragmentation is rather low and the judicial system is organized in a way somewhat different from Latin Europe. On the contrary, Belgium – a case characterized by high political fragmentation and a French-style judiciary – seems to confirm the argument put forward in the text.

France and Spain have also been reforming the traditional setting of the judiciary, reinforcing its independence. In Spain after the fall of Franquismo, the Constitution of 1978 followed the Italian model by instituting a Judicial Council (Consejo General del Poder Judicial) entrusted with the task of appointments and promotions and presided over by the chief of the Supreme Court. A 1980 statute stipulated that the Council be made up of twelve judges directly elected by their peers and eight other members appointed by Parliament. In France, the Higher Council of the Judiciary was instituted in 1946, although its role was severely circumscribed with the accession of the Fifth Republic. A constitutional reform in 1993 enlarged the powers of the Council and prescribed that six out of its twelve members would be elected by their judicial colleagues, although with a system allowing greater weight to higher ranks.[17] To sum up, in both France and Spain during the postwar period, judicial independence has been strengthened, although in a more limited way than in Italy.

Since the 1980s in both France and Spain, judicial investigations have repeatedly been launched against political corruption and other crimes related to the performance of public functions (Pujat and Rodhes 1999; Guarnieri and Pederzoli 2002). Some important politicians were involved and some political careers truncated (Maravall 2003; Adut 2004). For example, in France, the SIDA case – involving negligence on the part of the administration in allowing the circulation of blood contaminated with the AIDS virus – led to the trial of three ministers and the conviction of one, with a sort of criminalization of political responsibility (Beaud 1999). Prosecution of public figures has become a permanent trait of the French political landscape; for example, former President Chirac has recently been convicted for diverting public funds and abusing public confidence.[18] In all of these cases the media played a major part; actually, the term "mediatic-judicial circus" was coined with reference to France (Soulez-Larivière 1993). As a consequence, the tension between the judiciary and political branches increased. However, there was no political breakdown, as in Italy. A stronger party system and stronger political institutions were able to withstand the judicial offensive and strike back, at least to some extent. For instance, in France a 2008 constitutional reform has altered the composition of the High Council in a way less favourable to the judicial corps. In Spain, the autonomy of the Judicial Council was reduced by insisting on parliamentary appointment of the Council's judicial component.[19] This emphasizes the significance of the fact that

[17] The 1993 reform was passed by a declining Socialist majority fearing defeat in the approaching elections, a fact confirming the insurance function of institutional reforms aimed at strengthening judicial power.
[18] See "French ex-president Jacques Chirac guilty of corruption," *BBC News*, December 15, 2011. The charge concerned illegal activities before 1995 by Chirac, when he was mayor of Paris. The trial was suspended during the twelve-year term of Chirac as president of the Republic. Other significant cases are: Strauss-Kahn (1999–2001), resigning from the Treasury but later cleared; and Dumas (1998–2000), resigning from the presidency of the Constitutional Council and later convicted.
[19] In fact, the Socialist Party, strongly entrenched in power, realized the risks of judicialization, when dealing with the negative attitudes many conservative judges had toward the agrarian reform, one of the main policies of the party.

Spain and, especially, France present a much less fragmented political setting than Italy (Lijphart 1999).

OVERVIEW: ROLES, STRATEGIES AND CONDITIONS OF JUDICIALIZATION IN ITALY

The high political significance of criminal justice in Italy reflects this chapter's focus on lower courts and prosecutors. Although high courts – the Court of Cassation and the Constitutional Court – also played a role, lower courts and, above all, public prosecutors have been the main protagonists. It also reflects the special nature of Italian – although not only Italian – public prosecutors: as we have seen, they are magistrates, and their status has been largely assimilated to that of judges. Therefore, in Italy – but not only in Italy – judicial activism often means prosecutorial activism (Shapiro 2005). Without taking the role of public prosecution into account, the analysis of Italian judicialization would be seriously incomplete.

In the first decades of the republican period, Italian courts mainly performed the traditional roles of legitimating and enforcing dominant policies. For example, immediately after the war, the Court of Cassation quickly aligned itself with the moderate, centrist majority led by the Christian Democrats. The activism of the Constitutional Court – which, after 1956, declared a great deal of fascist legislation unconstitutional – was also actually welcomed by most parties, as the Court was doing a useful job for them. Moreover, especially in the 1960s, with the new governing coalition on the basis of the alliance between the Christian Democrats and Socialists, a liberal mood was prevailing in Italian politics and public opinion. Thus, the Constitutional Court's rulings on defendants' rights found an almost total consensus.

In the 1970s, with the expansion of Communist influence on the political process and the rise of terrorism and, later, organized crime, ordinary courts – especially instructing judges and prosecutors – began to play an increasingly significant role. Fighting crime became the task of the judicial system, a process tolerated and often supported by the political class. The governing parties were willing to shift responsibility to an unelected corps, whereas others – especially the Communists – trusted courts more than police.[20] In the 1990s, prosecutorial activism ended with courts trying to assure a sort of accountability of the political class through the criminal process. The *controllo di virtù*, focused on the "morality" of the rulers, has been the main role courts have played since 1992 (Pizzorno 1998: 56). During these years, prosecutorial initiatives and the increasing reference to morality as the main criterion of political accountability have gone hand in hand. Although first-instance courts – and prosecution offices – have played the dominant role, high courts have substantially supported the trend, sustaining the broadening of prosecutorial powers even at the expense of the rights of defendants. Indeed, in a particularly telling

---

[20] Police were often considered to have extreme right sympathies. In any case, it has been under Christian Democrat control since the end of the war.

episode, the Constitutional Court was for the first time in its history overruled via a constitutional amendment.

The strategies followed by courts in their interventions have depended, above all, on their role in the judicial system. High courts in Italy have obviously resorted to judicial creativity. They could do so because civil law courts also – similar to common-law courts – enjoy discretion in the process of rule interpretation and application (Shapiro 1981). In the course of its fifty years of activity, the Constitutional Court has developed all sorts of instruments of judicial lawmaking (Pederzoli 2008). Its role has been strongly enhanced by its collaboration with lower courts. Here, a sort of exchange seems to have taken place: lower courts have opened the gates of constitutional review, sending all sorts of cases to the Court, often leapfrogging the Cassation. The Constitutional Court on its part has supported the expansion of judicial creativity at the lower level, by justifying the practice of interpreting ordinary laws according to the values and principles of the Constitution. The strong relations between the Constitutional Court and lower courts have been behind the liberal decisions of the 1960s but also those supporting inquisitorial traits of criminal justice in the 1990s.

The significance of criminal justice has been supported and encouraged by specific judicial strategies. The principle of compulsory prosecution has been successfully employed by the judiciary to argue for the dismantling of any form of political control on prosecutors' decisions – and often the reduction of any form of control – with the consequence of increasing de facto prosecutorial discretion. The redefinition in active terms of the role of the prosecutor – and, when in force, the instructing judge – has been another important step in the process of strengthening the capacity of criminal courts. We should keep in mind that the inquisitorial structure of the criminal process entrusts judicial officials with considerable powers (Damaska 1986). The slow but steady erosion of traditional controls – for instance, political influence over prosecution and hierarchical controls on lower courts – cannot but magnify these powers. As we have pointed out, their effectiveness has been tested in the fight against terrorism and organized crime, but also against the political class.

If we pause to consider the when and why of judicial interventions, several elements have to be taken into account. Without doubt, as the short analysis of France and Spain has confirmed a contrario, political fragmentation has been the main general condition enabling judicialization in Italy.[21] The design of the Italian Constitution was deeply influenced by the legacy of the Fascist past, which led to an emphasis on guarantees against possible Executive and Legislative abuses, and also by the fragmented and polarized state of political forces in the postwar period. Thus, in the Constitution, courts were entrusted with significant power and autonomy: constitutional review was introduced and judicial guarantees of independence strengthened. The implementation of the constitutional design was temporarily

---

[21] See Ferejohn (Ch. 14 in this volume). The argument is also supported by several cases analyzed in this volume; see especially the chapters on the United States (Kagan, Ch. 8 in this volume), Israel (Reichman, Ch. 9 in this volume) and India (Mate, Ch. 10 in this volume).

frozen thanks to the extraordinary electoral success of Christian Democrats in 1948, but it was slowly but steadily implemented later, when the electoral fortunes of that party began to decline and a weaker governing coalition had to be formed. At the end of the 1980s, Italian courts were able to muster a considerable amount of resources: the practice of constitutional interpretation had diffused itself in all sectors of the judicial system, enlarging judicial lawmaking power; and the judiciary enjoyed an extremely high level of independence, a condition shared by public prosecutors, who had already been completely autonomous from the Executive and able to exert considerable influence on the police.

The reforms implemented after 1959, besides reinforcing judicial independence, had a deep impact on the judicial organization. The dismantling of the hierarchical structure gradually shifted the reference group to which judges and public prosecutors attended from the higher ranks of the judiciary to the leaders of judicial unions and party politicians (i.e., those in control of the decisional process of the Higher Council). Top judicial positions, on whose appointment the Executive no longer had any significant influence, were increasingly filled by personnel enjoying the support of judicial unions (Vauchez 2004). The influence of traditional academic doctrine was also circumscribed, in part because of its declining homogeneity, in part because legal competence was no longer the main criterion for a successful career in the judiciary. As we have pointed out, the media have also become a significant point of reference for the judiciary: in the last twenty years, a sort of alliance between activist judges and prosecutors and progressive media has emerged. Judicial initiatives can provide the media with important news, and at the same time, media support magnifies the impact of judicial investigations. All of these developments have encouraged judicial activism: lower-ranking judges and prosecutors no longer have to fear hierarchical controls. On the contrary, their initiatives can bring them popularity and in some cases also a brilliant career, promotions having been entrusted to a body such as the Higher Council where – since the 1970s – the influence of the judicial and political left has been significant (Guarnieri 2003).

As we have seen, after the expansion of the 1970s in the 1980s, judicial roles to some extent stabilized, but the context was ready for judicial initiatives to further develop and impact the political system. Political fragmentation had supported the growth of judicial power and the reforms in the organization of the judiciary had altered the motivations of the judicial actors in activist directions. Moreover, the legitimacy of the political class had consistently declined, at least in comparison with that of the judiciary. The political crisis of the early 1990s provided the final trigger: the political vacuum created by the weakness of the governing parties – especially Christian Democrats and Socialists – opened a space quickly filled by the judiciary. Judicial investigations accelerated the crisis of the traditional parties, giving way to a sort of virtuous – or, from another point of view, vicious – circle. Judicial roles began to expand again. Only after 1996 did the party system begin to show signs of recovery. However, only in 2001 – and again in 2008 – did a political majority willing to rein in the judiciary emerge, although so far a new phase of stabilization has not been reached.

As for the effects of courts' initiatives, the ascendance of judicial power contributed to the already fragmented nature of the Italian political system (Kapiszewski and Taylor 2008: 756). Especially in the 1970s and 1980s, in parallel with the expansion of parliamentary prerogatives, the significant role played by prosecutors and judges in the fight against terrorism and organized crime contributed to the progressive circumscription of the power of the Executive. After 1992, with the breaking down of the party system, courts increasingly acted as a check on political power. However, the judiciary's impact on politics has been mixed. Generally speaking, their actions have supported the left, for instance by focusing on Berlusconi's misbehaviour. However, in 2008 a judicial initiative precipitated the fall of the Prodi government, opening the way for Berlusconi's triumph in the following elections – a fact reflecting the decentralized and uncoordinated nature of the lower judicial and prosecutorial system.

The growing significance of criminal justice has sometimes been carried out at the expense of the rights of the defendants, especially in terrorist and organized crime cases. However, in recent years the criminal bar has been able to react and rebalance the system. In fact, Italian counterterrorist activities cannot be judged as particularly intrusive. More complex have been the effects on political and legal values. As it has been pointed out (Nelken 1996), Clean Hands investigations strongly emphasized the need to restore legality. However, the relatively nontransparent nature of prosecutorial choices – a by-product of the formalistic implementation of the principle of compulsory prosecution – has made it easier to raise charges of prosecutorial partisanship. These charges have been supported by the prosecutors' frequent resort to the media. That practice – designed to elicit the support of public opinion – has actually exposed prosecutorial activism, as it runs counter to the civil law's traditional image of the prosecutor as an impartial magistrate whose role tends to be defined in terms similar to those of the judge. Popular concern about prosecutors' exploitation of the media is exacerbated because it occurs in a context in which trust in the judicial system, as in all political institutions, tends to be low (Guarnieri 2003: 163). This fact has been exploited by those under investigation – for instance, Berlusconi – in denouncing the "partisanship" of prosecutors and by the right in its attempts at significantly curbing judicial power. However, the right coalition has been increasingly hit by internal conflict, a fact that – together with the worsening of the financial crisis – led at the end of 2011 to the demise of the Berlusconi government, although it is still too early to see if this change will lead to a more stable equilibrium.

CONCLUSION

This chapter has described and sought to explain the expansion of the judiciary's role in Italian governance. It has examined how the implementation of the 1948

Constitution and the increasing level of political fragmentation created new modes of governance in the Italian judiciary. Judicial and prosecutorial independence was progressively strengthened and the traditional influence of the higher ranks practically dismantled, whereas the need to fight terrorism and organized crime was providing courts with more effective investigative weapons. This development, together with a growing popular dissatisfaction with the performance of the political system and increasing support of the media for judicial initiatives, generated new incentives for prosecutorial activism. Therefore, in the aftermath of the fall of the Berlin Wall – which weakened communist and anticommunist parties alike – prosecutors were able to launch a series of investigations that destroyed the traditional political class.

Certain more-recent political changes, particularly the emergence of a stronger political majority under the leadership of the much-discussed tycoon Silvio Berlusconi, have brought the prosecutors' and lower-court judges' corruption-attacking roles under political attack. However, that underscores a basic point this chapter highlights: greater fragmentation of political power both in the national government and in the judiciary itself creates conditions under which judicial roles in governance can expand; whereas the reassertion of hierarchical political control can constrict the judicial system's roles in governance. On the other hand, the criticism of the judges – featuring charges of political bias – suggests that when judges do play new, more-assertive roles in governance they become more vulnerable to charges of politically motivated misuse of power and counterattack. Much depends, therefore, on the political skills of the judges themselves: the extent to which they are able to exploit the divisions inside the political class and at the same time continue to enjoy the support of public opinion.

REFERENCES

Adut, Ari 2004. "Scandal as Norm Entrepreneurship Strategy: Corruption and the French Investigating Magistrates," *Theory and Society* 33: 529–578.
Beaud, Olivier 1999. *Le sang contaminé: Essai critique sur la criminalisation de la responsabilité des gouvernants*. Paris: Presses Universitaires de France.
Bell, John 2006. *Judiciaries within Europe: A Comparative Review*. Cambridge: Cambridge University Press.
Colombo, Gherardo 2006. "Investigating and Prosecuting Large-Scale Corruption," *Journal of International Criminal Justice* 4: 510–521.
Conso, Giovanni (ed.) 1979. *Pubblico ministero e accusa penale*. Bologna: Zanichelli.
Cotta, Maurizio and Luca Verzichelli 2008. *Political Institutions in Italy*. Oxford: Oxford University Press.
Damaska, Mirjan R. 1986. *The Faces of Justice and State Authority*. New Haven: Yale University Press.
Della Porta, Donatella and Alberto Vannucci 2007. "Corruption and Anti–Corruption: The Political Defeat of 'Clean Hands' in Italy," *West European Politics* 30: 830–853.
Di Federico, Giuseppe 2004. *Manuale di ordinamento giudiziario*. Padova: Cedam.

Di Federico, Giuseppe and Michele Sapignoli 2002. *Processo penale e diritti della difesa.* Roma: Carocci.

Giglioli, Pier Paolo 1996. "Political Corruption and the Media: the Tangentopoli Affair," *International Social Science Journal* 48: 381–394.

Ginsburg, Tom 2003. *Judicial Review in New Democracies.* Cambridge: Cambridge University Press.

Grande, Elisabetta 2000. "Italian Criminal Justice: Borrowing and Resistance," *American Journal of Comparative Law* 48: 227–259.

Guarnieri, Carlo 2003. *Giustizia e politica. I nodi della Seconda Repubblica.* Bologna: Il Mulino.

Guarnieri, Carlo and Patrizia Pederzoli 2002. *The Power of Judges.* Oxford: Oxford University Press.

Kapiszewski, Diana and Matthew M. Taylor 2008. "Doing Courts Justice? Studying Judicial Politics in Latin America," *Perspectives on Politics* 6: 741–767.

Lijphart, Arendt 1999. *Patterns of Democracy.* New Haven: Yale University Press.

Maravall, José Maria 2003. The Rule of Law as a Political Weapon, in José Maria Maravall and Adam Przeworski (eds.). *Democracy and the Rule of Law.* Cambridge: Cambridge University Press, pp. 261–301.

Merryman, John H. and Rogelio Perdomo 2007. *The Civil Law Tradition* Stanford: Stanford University Press.

Nelken, David 1996. "The Judges and Political Corruption in Italy," *Journal of Law and Society* 23: 95–112.

Pederzoli, Patrizia 2008. *La corte costituzionale.* Bologna: Il Mulino.

Pizzorno, Alessandro 1998. *Il potere dei giudici.* Bari: Laterza.

Pujat, Veronique and Martin Rodhes 1999. Party Finance and Political Scandals in Italy, Spain and France, *West European Politics* 22: 41–63.

Rayner, Hervé 2005. *Les scandales politiques.L'opération "Main propres" en Italie.* Paris: Michel Houdiard Editeur.

Shapiro, Martin 1981. *Courts: A Comparative and Political Analysis.* Chicago: The University of Chicago Press.

Shapiro, Martin 2005. "Law, Courts and Politics," in Robert Kagan and Tom Ginsburg (eds.). *Institutions and Public Law: Comparative Approaches.* New York: Peter Lang, pp. 275–297.

Soulez-Larivière, Daniel 1993. *Du cirque médiatico-judiciaire et des moyens d'en sortir.* Paris: Seuil.

Vauchez, Antoine 2004. *L'institution judiciaire remotivée.* Paris:Livrairie General de Droit et Jurisprudence.

Vogliotti, Massimo 2004. "Les relations police-parquet en Italie: un équilibre menacé?" *Droit et Societé* 58: 453–504.

7

The Dutch Hoge Raad
Judicial Roles Played, Lost, and Not Played

*Nick Huls**

The expansion of high courts' roles in governance, this book asserts, has become a prominent feature of modern democracy. This chapter, focusing on the Hoge Raad, the High Court of Cassation of the Netherlands, illustrates that trend. However, the story of the Hoge Raad in the last four decades also shows that shifts in judicial roles are not always permanent. For lack of internal leadership, over time the Hoge Raad passively retreated from some activist roles in governance, and other political, administrative, and judicial bodies – hungry for influence – partially shouldered it aside. In recent years, however, the Court has shown signs of resurgence. This chapter demonstrates that the analysis of judicial roles in governance must be attentive to the place of courts in the broader political landscape, to the important roles that courts fail to play – to the ebb and flow of judicial power – as well as to the effect that societal and political changes can have on judges' roles in governance.

The Kingdom of the Netherlands is a small country that does not have a tradition of visible courts. Article 120 of the Constitution forbids judicial review. For a long time it was deemed unthinkable that Dutch politicians would enact laws that did not comply with the Constitution; this assumption reflects the general trust in authorities that was so characteristic of the Netherlands (Koopmans 2003: 76–77; Hofstede 1991). Thus, for a long period of time the Dutch people were accepting of their ruling national elites (Buruma 2006). The country is governed by coalition governments with varying political combinations. This solid tradition reflects a submissive electorate that until the end of the 1960s was organized and disciplined in four separate socioreligious, vertically organized groupings known as pillars (*Lijphart*). The Netherlands has a queen as head of state, which makes my country an odd case for a positive theory of democracy. Moreover, Dutch political culture has been labeled as a consensus democracy, as opposed to majoritarian democracies such as the United States and

---

* Vice Rector Academic Affairs and Research, Institute for Legal Practice and Development (ILPD), Nyanza, Rwanda, on leave as professor of socio-legal studies of Erasmus School of Law, Rotterdam and Leiden Law School.

the United Kingdom. Ten Kate and Van Koppen have described the "hands-off"
relationship between elected politicians and appointed Hoge Raad Justices. They
predicted in 1995 that the time had come for judicial review in the Netherlands (ten
Kate & van Koppen 1995, van Koppen 1990). However, some plans are still pending,
and unlike recent changes in Belgium and France, the Netherlands do not yet have
a direct form of judicial review.

THE DEFINING CONSTITUTIONAL MOMENT: 1953

In 1949, the Netherlands lost their political power over Indonesia, the big colony
in Asia that had contributed so much to the wealth of its motherland over several
centuries. Because of this loss, the small kingdom in the northwestern part of Europe
had to rewrite the parts of its Constitution that regulated its relations to the international world. By 1953, there was a wide consensus among Dutch political and legal
leaders that becoming part of a united Europe would constitute the best basis for the
economic and moral future of the country. The implied loss of national sovereignty
was simply not a contested issue in Dutch politics at that time. The ruling elite –
the *Regenten* as they were called – agreed that internationalization at the political,
economic, and legal level was in the best interest of the Netherlands.

After a rather complicated process (Claes & de Witte 1998: 171), two new articles
were included in the Constitution of 1953. Article 93: Treaties are directly binding
for the national authorities and courts; and Article 94: International law is higher
law than national Dutch law, the so-called supremacy clause. These changes were
presented as technical amendments, and were readily accepted by both chambers of
Parliament. Since 1953 the Constitution has allowed Dutch courts to review national
laws and acts of government when they violated international treaties, but denied
the courts the same power when a law was violating the Constitution!

Two treaties became pivotal in the decades after World War II, and the Netherlands's accession to the two treaties fit perfectly in the long-held idea that in the
Dutch soul there is a permanent dialogue between the merchant and the vicar.
First, a single market for Coal and Steel (the European Coal and Steel Community, 1953) was created as a first startup of the European Union (the merchant). In
the 1950s and 1960s, Dutch legal doctrine was prominent in the opinions of the
European Court of Justice (ECJ). Moreover, the Netherlands were regarded as "the
least problematic country" (Claes & de Witte 1998: 181) in the construction of a
European legal order in its infant years. Because the Dutch economy is very dependent on exports, the creation of one single market was a prerequisite for economic
growth. Second was the European Convention of Human Rights (ECHR, 1948)
(a "never again" to Nazi laws, the vicar). In that period, it was deemed axiomatic
that the Dutch legal order was both decent and ethical, in which violations of
human rights did not occur. Unlike Germany, Italy, or Spain, the Netherlands

had not experienced homegrown dictatorship. The Convention was written for others, not for the Netherlands, which viewed itself as an ethically impeccable country.

Submission to European institutions was also not considered an unwanted breach of sovereignty. There were no fundamental debates about the meaning of Europe for Dutch democracy, as might be expected of the pragmatic Dutch legal culture (Blankenburg & Bruinsma 1994). The Dutch Constitution incorporated a European space for the ECJ in Luxemburg and the European Court of Human Rights (ECtHR) in Strasbourg. Dutch judges were actively engaged in developing a European legal order. There was no split of opinions between the legal and political Dutch elite that Europe was a good thing for our small country.

Some of the Dutch top judges participated in European Courts; they became silent and subtle ambassadors of both treaties. In the ECJ, A.M. Donner and T. Koopmans (for eleven years) were strong representatives. G.J. Wiarda and S.K. Martens, both president of the Dutch Cassation Court, were judges in the ECtHR, which was then a part-time job. Initially, this creation of a European legal order remained invisible to the Dutch public.

A CHARACTERIZATION OF THE DUTCH POLITICAL SYSTEM: ACCOMMODATION AND PRAGMATISM

The System of the 1950s

The Netherlands have the political form of a constitutional monarchy. The state is headed by a queen without executive power. The Netherlands live under a system of parliamentary supremacy: the majority of the elected Second Chamber has the power to dismiss the governing coalition.

The system of coalition cabinets that evolved implies that there is no strict separation of the Legislative and Executive branches. The Netherlands do not have a tradition of fascism or large-scale corruption of political representatives. Unlike France, Holland is not ruled by an aristocratic political elite.

Lijphart has described the Dutch system as a form of "politics of accommodation" (Lijphart 1969). In the 1950s, Dutch society consisted of four hierarchical pillars – Catholics, Protestants, Socialists, Liberals – each of which included a political party, schools, trade unions, newspapers, broadcast stations, sports, and so forth. There were strong cultural and social cleavages between the people in different pillars, but at the top the elites from each pillar worked together smoothly. In the Dutch consensus democracy, majorities are not the result of elections; they must be created via negotiations of political leaders who want to participate in a power-sharing coalition government. The Dutch elections are decided by a system of proportional representation, with no real thresholds for new political parties. This led to so-called pacification politics: thorny problems were solved practically by the elites via secret political deals. The Dutch political elite also used several avoidance tactics, such as referring the problem to a prestigious committee, redefining the problem in such a way that the government was not the only responsible agent anymore, or depoliticizing the issue by making it "technical" or "procedural" (Andeweg & Irwin 1999). This was accepted by a quite passive electorate in a taken-for-granted atmosphere of tolerance.

In economic affairs, the consensus was created in several corporatist–interest-group structures. In the Social and Economic Council (SER), the economic policies of the country were largely determined in tripartite negotiations between the government, labor unions, and organized employers. Furthermore, big multinational companies such as Shell, Philips, AKZO-Nobel, and others exercised informal power in economic policies. In sum, there were some ideological nuances, but in the first decades after World War II Dutch politicians managed to forge a wide societal consensus about the building of a generous welfare state for all.

The Events of 1968

In the same period that Lijphart's book was published, the Dutch pillars began to crumble. Four changes can be highlighted here: democratization and participation, cultural liberalization, prosperity, and the reform of the welfare state. First, beginning in 1968 a broad protest movement arose against the authoritarian and top-down structures in universities, companies, and politics. Students, workers, and citizens asked for more democracy, which led to student and workers' councils, but not to forms of direct democracy (referenda and elected mayors).

Second, under the influence of Provo and other contestant groups, a lot of cultural emancipation took place in the cultural sphere. New freedom was reached in the use of drugs, euthanasia, and sexual liberties. The institutions of the pillars lost their grip on their members, churches became empty, voters became more volatile, and the pillared traditional broadcasting system was challenged by commercial companies from abroad.

Third, when a huge gas bubble was discovered in Dutch soil, the revenues were invested quite intelligently. Dutch exports grew steadily with the growth of the European market. The Netherlands became one of the richest countries per capita of the world, with a rather fair distribution of income. Finally, the welfare state was built on a combination of high taxes and collective organized solidarity. Under the leadership of two strong prime ministers – Ruud Lubbers (Christian Democrat, a millionaire [1982–1994]) and Wim Kok (Social Democrat, union leader [1994–2002]) – the welfare state was transformed. The Dutch Polder model became a role model for the Third Way of Tony Blair and Bill Clinton (Giddens 1998): deregulation and privatization proved to be acceptable for the population (and was necessary to qualify for the Euro).

After 2002

This rosy picture of Dutch politics was disturbed by Pim Fortuyn, whose populist approach blew away the consensus of "old politics." He was murdered May 6, 2002, but other new populist politicians and parties have arisen and adhere to Fortuyn's creed: "I say what I think, and I do what I say." He did so especially in relation to the integration of foreigners of Turkish and Moroccan background in Dutch society, a topic the existing political parties did not dare to address adequately.

Another blow to the consensus democracy that the Dutch political elite liked to cherish was the completely unexpected "No" by the Dutch population to the referendum regarding a European Constitution on June 1, 2005. It was more proof of the general distrust in the way the existing political parties represented the popular will. Since 2008, Geert Wilders has been the flamboyant and influential representative of Dutch populist politics, with a strong and antagonistic anti-Islam program.

THE POSITION OF DUTCH COURTS

The Netherlands have two highest courts: (1) since 1848, the Hoge Raad, a Cassation Court; and (2) since 1976, the judicial branch of the Council of State. The Netherlands does not have one single guardian of the Constitution and its values.

Hoge Raad

Unlike other countries, the Netherlands does not have a Constitutional Court on top of the judiciary. The Dutch court system follows French lines: historically, the Hoge Raad has been considered the highest court of the land, responsible for legal unity among lower courts in civil, criminal, and tax matters. A cassation system is on the basis of the separation of law and facts, the Hoge Raad being competent only in the field of the law. The study and interpretation of Hoge Raad rulings are an important part of the legal education at the law schools. In terms of prestige among the legal community, the Hoge Raad is definitely on top.

The Hoge Raad does not have a certiorari system in which access is granted only by leave of the courts; but in practice, a specialized cassation bar operates as a kind of filtering mechanism. The Court delivers its opinions in a composite version. No dissenting opinions are expressed, although the advice of the advocate general – and to a certain extent the authoritative note of the annotator – may be viewed as a part of the decision. This reflects the "bifurcated discourse" thesis elaborated by Mitchel Lasser's analysis of French courts (Ch. 11 in this volume).

The political elite has always seen the Hoge Raad as an apolitical body, and Parliament showed no real interest in appointing members along party lines, although there has been some evidence that in former days some Catholic seats were reserved on the Raad (van Koppen 1990: 770). The Hoge Raad selects its new members itself, on the basis of internal considerations of legal expertise and prestige (co-optation). Approximately half of its thirty-five members are recruited from the lower courts, the other half from the bar and legal academia. With respect to the latter, the Leiden Law School has dominated (although that is now diminishing). Formally, the list of new proposed members is presented as advice to Parliament, but number one on the list has always been appointed without debate. Until recently, the presidency of the Hoge Raad was held by the most senior judge, promoted whenever the vacancy is open.

The Hoge Raad became intellectually and politically more prominent in the 1980s and 1990s. The civil chamber especially was seen as a kind of innovative Dutch Warren-court, praised by legal academics because of its progressiveness and responsiveness. From 1984 on, it was acknowledged that the Hoge Raad was not only applying existing laws. If, in a concrete case, application of the rules would lead to an unjust result, the Hoge Raad would decide on the basis of open or vague norms and equity (*redelijkheid en billijkheid*) (Wiarda 1993). This opened the discussion toward lawmaking by the Hoge Raad, which placed it in a more visible position. The examples provided demonstrate how this court expanded its role.

Cooperation of Powers: Precooking of Political Hot Potatoes

From the late 1970s, the Hoge Raad led the way in policy fields where deadlocked political parties were unable to produce legislation. A good example is the handling of a strike in labor law by the Court. In a series of cases,[1] the Hoge Raad developed procedural and material rules that the trade unions should follow in order to ensure that a strike would not be judged as an illegal breach of the labor contract. Crucial procedural criteria are that the strike has been announced in a timely way, and the preceding negotiations have been exhaustive (strike as *ultimum remedium*). Another material criterion is that there is a proportionality between means and goals of the strike. In the private sector, this test is not a big barrier for the unions, but in the public sector the Hoge Raad puts more emphasis on the position of third parties and comes up with creative solutions; for instance, no strike is allowed during rush hours. This case law was so authoritative and practical that until today no legislation on strikes has been passed in the Netherlands.

Other examples of leadership of the Hoge Raad are to be found in the religiously sensitive areas of abortion and euthanasia. Legislation was blocked on ethical grounds by the Christian Democrats, who were for a long time always part of the governmental coalition. In 1985, the Hoge Raad decided for the first time in a euthanasia case that a medical doctor who complies with the requirements of due care can successfully invoke the justification of necessity. Criteria were: a voluntary and well-considered

---

[1] Panhonlibco, HR January, 15, 1960, 84 was a forerunner; the leading case is HR May 30, 1986, NJ 1986, 688 (National Railways Services); and later HR November 11, 1994, NJ 1995, 152 and HR March 21, 1997, JAR 1997/70 en HR January 28, 2000, JAR 2000/63.

request from the patient; a situation of "unacceptable" suffering; and the consultation of a second doctor (Griffiths, Weyers, & Adams 2008: 30–31). Here, the Hoge Raad acted as a kind of *deputy legislator*, or scout, for the legislator. In the late 1990s, the legislator finally closed the political debate by incorporating the Court's case law into new legislation. The development of that law may be interpreted as a form of cooperation of powers, in contrast to the classical imagery of unproductive separation of powers. Indeed, when the Hoge Raad decided the euthanasia cases, there was no perceived countermajoritarian difficulty. Rather, it was the other way around; the Court made law that had been blocked by a (powerful) Legislative minority.

Domain Expansion: Human Rights

Other sources of support for the leading role of the Hoge Raad were the previously mentioned ECHR and the UN Treaty on Civil and Political Rights. In the first thirty years, the ECHR was hardly ever invoked by advocates before Dutch Courts. However, in 1979 in the *Winterwerp* case,[2] the Strasbourg Court ruled that Dutch treatment of mentally ill patients violated the Convention on Human Rights, because the prosecutor and not an independent judge decided the prolongation and release of patients in mental hospitals. Through *Winterwerp*, for the first time the Dutch public became aware that violations of human rights did occur in their country, and that the Convention was of practical importance for the Netherlands.

Consequently, a combination of ambitious advocates, receptive Hoge Raad judges, and some enthusiastic academics (a Dutch "legal complex" – see Ch. 13 in this volume) drew on the European and UN treaties to infuse the legal system with a very liberal set of ethical values. Not only was the Hoge Raad willing to overturn its own case law when the Strasbourg court had ruled otherwise, the court also created a body of case law in which the recently revised Dutch legislation in the field of family law was tested against the ECHR. In response, the government had to review and change the recently adopted Book I of the Civil Code on Family Law. For example, a broad interpretation of family life in Article 8 ECRM led to a revision of the statutes regarding the descent of children, joint custody if parents are not married, equal rights of homosexuals, and more.

Soon, lower courts followed. Today, the ECHR is invoked and applied very often in Dutch practice, not only in civil but also criminal law. In the field of labor and social law, European equal treatment of men and women became a big issue for the courts. The progressive application of European law led to an incremental broadening of the judicial domain: the courts created more power for themselves vis-à-vis the legislator.

By the same token, however, the Hoge Raad subordinated itself willingly to higher European courts, which meant less power for the Raad itself. The Dutch Hoge Raad

---

[2] ECtHR, decision of October 24, 1979, Case 6301/73.

viewed itself as a kind of loyal state court in a federal Europe. Sometimes national courts are required to refer to so-called prejudicial questions (preliminary rulings) to the ECJ before deciding a case (s. 234 EU Treaty).

A Hoge Raad Judge Rewrites the Civil Code

In the 1980s, a vice president of the civil chambers of the Hoge Raad as well as a member of the Court – Wouter Snijders – wrote large parts of the new Civil Code. As Regeringscommissaris (General Counsel to the Minister), he was the first draftsman of the hard core of civil law, property and obligations, consumer protection, and so forth. Snijders held consultations with interest groups and appeared in Parliament to answer questions. No one advanced the argument that there might be a problem with separation of powers. The intricacies of the Civil Code were deemed to be too complex for ordinary politicians, who listened obediently to this judge. Such a high-court judge does not need strong judicial review of a statute. He can write the law himself.

Facing Resistance

In 1989, the Hoge Raad was in the position to exercise a kind of judicial review in a piece of retroactive legislation regarding educational student loans. At this *moment suprème*, the Hoge Raad appraised the law critically but did not dare to invalidate it. The Hoge Raad indicated that such a decision would trespass the existing borders between the judicial and Legislative branches. Thus, a direct political confrontation with the Minister of Education was avoided (Koopmans 2003: 83). This can be considered either a missed opportunity for a constitutional moment (Ackerman 1991) or a strategic withdrawal on a politically controversial issue (Epstein, Knight & Shetsova 2001) in order to preserve the Court's legitimacy and institutional prerogatives.

DEVELOPMENTS SINCE THE EARLY 1990S

Beginning in the early 1990s, the blind admiration by the legal community of the Court's progressive law-creating role was gradually replaced by a more detached and critical attitude. In 1992, Barendrecht opened the first intellectual attack on the Court's casuistic legal decision-making method on the basis of vague norms, whereby ultimately the application of rules succumbs to an ex post moral equity-based judgment. He argued that this approach led to unpredictability for practising lawyers and legal uncertainty for their clients (Barendrecht 1992). In a follow-up study, he went a few steps further in his criticism, demonstrating how the Hoge Raad engaged in a considerable number of trivial issues. He called for the Hoge Raad to exercise leadership, that is, give guidance to the lower courts and focus on important legal issues (Barendrecht 1998).

The formalities and technicalities of the cassation system have also led to criticism, both from within the legal profession and the forensic science community. After a number of miscarriages of justice in criminal cases, psychology of law scholars – who fundamentally criticized the way in which lawyers collect and verify facts – argued for a Criminal Cases Review Board outside the judiciary such as the United Kingdom model (Wagenaar, Israel, & van Koppen 2009). The public at large also questioned the legitimacy of the Court after these highly publicized miscarriages of justice (*Putten, Schiedam*). In addition to these academic critics, two rival institutions appeared on the stage who challenged the superior position of the Hoge Raad.

Council of State (Raad van State)

Traditionally, the Council of State has been cast as the highest advisor of the crown. Historically, it has been a refuge for ex-politicians. The queen is the chair, and the vice chairman of the Raad van State is one of her principal advisors. Members are directly appointed by the Cabinet along political party lines. The Council is very close to politics. It is not a critical countervailing power, but part of the inner circle of the ruling elites. Members of the Council of State sometimes act as troubleshooters when nasty political or difficult societal problems arise. For instance, the Council of State assisted the Dutch government in the political neutralization of the no against a European Constitution by the Dutch population in the 2005 referendum.

Members are often "wise men" or power brokers. Two former ministers of justice were members of the Raad van State. The Council of State also exerts the function of judicial preview. That is, it tests all proposed statutes with regard to their accordance with the Constitution, international laws, and other legal aspects before the cabinet can send a draft law to Parliament. The Council has only an advisory role, however; the Cabinet may pursue its intentions, even if the Council objects.

Since 1976, a new branch of the Council of State was created as the Highest Court in administrative cases, with exclusive and supreme supervision in the field of administrative actions of the government. Several Councils of State in European member states have fallen under criticism from the ECtHR in Strasbourg. In the 1995 *Procola* decision, the issue was raised that the combination of an administrative judicial role and an advisory role in legislative affairs might jeopardize the independence of the Councils of State[3].

The Dutch Council of State has been criticized on material grounds, as well. Academics argued that the Council's strict interpretation of immigration laws always led to the denial of the claims of asylum seekers. Indeed, in 2007 it was decided that an asylum seeker from Somalia was not obliged to exhaust Dutch national remedies because according to the ECtHR, he did not have a fair chance in the procedures before the Dutch Council of State.[4]

[3] Decision of September 28, 1995, Reports A326 (Procola) (application 14570/89).
[4] ECtHR, decision of January 11, 2007, Salah Sheekh v. the Netherlands (application 1948/04).

From the standpoint of separation of powers, the combination of providing advice on legislation and acting as an administrative court is difficult to defend. Moreover, the Council of State is partly made up of former politicians and administrators, some of whom could not be appointed as judges as part of the regular judiciary. In some respects, the Council of State is too close to the government to be viewed as an independent court.

Rivalry between Highest Courts

The supremacy of the Cassation Courts is limited because the Council of State, as part of its administrative jurisdiction, has been given competence in proceedings against the government. Thus, in administrative law (with the exception of tax law), the Dutch Hoge Raad is not the highest court.

A certain rivalry exists between these two high courts. Traditionally, the Hoge Raad has always enjoyed the most prestige in the legal world, and its rulings dominate the legal curriculum. Unlike the Council of State, the Hoge Raad also has the institution of Advocate General, who provides authoritative opinions before the Hoge Raad decides cases. On the other hand, the Council of State has at its disposal an extensive legal staff, which prepares the decisions. The case law of the Council of State's Judicial Division receives comments from annotators, as well.

The jurisdictional battle between the two high courts plays out at the national level, but also obtains an international dimension, because they both must apply and interpret European law. I take an example of a recent gambling law case. One of the political hot potatoes in that field is whether Europe has the authority to regulate. At the level of the European Council, only the UK and Malta advocate one single gambling market. All the other member states are in favor of restrictive national legislation. Gambling was explicitly excluded from the Service Directive, but nonetheless there was a constant threat of infringement procedures by then-European Commissioner McCreevy.[5]

The ECJ introduced a hypocrisy test in its *Gambelli* ruling of 2003[6]: national courts have to decide whether restrictive gambling legislation is really serving legitimate goals such as preventing addiction and criminal activities, rather than protection of national suppliers. On May 14, 2008, the Judicial Division of the Council of State had submitted the following questions in the *Betfair* case to the ECJ (the phrasing is my own):

- Does Article 49 EC Treaty mean that the Dutch authorities cannot prohibit an English license holder (Betfair) from offering games online if Betfair is permitted to do so in the United Kingdom? (mutual recognition)

---

[5] They were not continued by his French successor, Michel Barnier.
[6] Case C-243/01, Criminal Proceedings against P. Gambelli and Others [2003] ECR I-13031.

- Is the case law of the ECJ in concession cases (C-458 /03, C-507/03 C-231/03) also applicable if only one license is issued?
- When renewing a license to a monopolist (de Lotto), must other parties also be given the chance to seek a license?

On June 13, 2008, the Hoge Raad submitted the following questions in the *Ladbrokes* case to the ECJ (submitting the first question to the Council of State, as well):

- Can a gaming policy still be referred to as restrictive when the monopolist is allowed to advertise and present itself as an attractive alternative to the illegal offering of games of chance?
- In this case, does it make any difference if in enforcing the gaming regulations a Dutch license holder (thus not the state) acts against a foreign competitor (Ladbrokes)?

In its decisions of June 3, 2010, the ECJ (C 258/08 *Ladbrokes* and C203/08 *Betfair*) answered all of two Dutch top courts' questions. Advocate General Y. Bots had written a conclusion in which he treated both cases jointly. The ECJ, which after its *Gambelli* decision had chosen to avoid an open conflict with the European Commission and the majority of the member states in gambling matters – rendered a rather predictable decision; that is, that national courts are in the best position to judge the content and value of the national gambling policies. Commentators rightly concluded that the preliminary references had not been necessary.

Apparently, in this case the Hoge Raad referred the case rather than deciding it directly because it was wary of stepping on the toes of the Council of State, which had made preliminary references before. Consequently, the two courts were involved in a game of running and dodging: neither of them dared to make a final decision. I consider the attitude of the Hoge Raad as a form of timid judicial retreat, which created not only a policy deadlock (nothing can be done by the legislator while the gambling law is sub Judice) but also opened the gate for a lawyer's paradise. With its hands-off attitude, the Hoge Raad has created a lame-duck position for itself. Its leading role in interpreting the gambling act was beyond dispute, but because it did not dare to decide the *Ladbroke* case (in which it had decided already in an earlier procedure!), it failed to hold the position of the leading court. Unlike the Council of State, which is also the legal adviser of the government in gambling legislation, the Hoge Raad is much better positioned to give an independent ad impartial judgment about the compatibility of the Dutch gambling act with European law. This comparative advantage has been given up voluntarily by asking questions instead of rendering a decision. Put another way, the Hoge Raad decided to retreat from the role of authoritative interpreter of the impact of EU law on Dutch law and governance.

The Council of the Judiciary: Management of the Court System

The issue of judicial leadership entails not just the substantive guidance provided by the courts. Zuckermann concludes that the proper administration of justice requires a trade-off between rectitude of decision, costs, and time (Zuckermann 1999). Courts throughout the world are faced with the task of managing their caseloads, accelerating the completion time for cases, and controlling costs (Fix-Fierro 2003). In this way, new public management is making its entry into the judiciary, both within the court structure (case management) and the form of new administrative institutions; to wit, Councils for the Judiciary. These councils have far-reaching power in the area of financing, management, and encouragement of innovations within the judiciary, and have a strong influence on the adjudication practice. Formally, the working processes are independent of the substantive decisions, but the continuous emphasis on efficiency affects the substantive work of courts The councils meet each other in the European Network of Councils for the Judiciary (ENCI).

The Hoge Raad and Raad van State have not seen any role for themselves with regard to these administrative and management activities. They merely provide substantive guidance, by answering legal questions in individual cases. Occasionally, there are some grumblings from the top that the quality of the lower echelons is deteriorating because of the workload, but that is the extent of it. In reality, a new player has appeared on the stage: the Council for the Judiciary (Bell 2006).

Two examples may demonstrate how the Hoge Raad has lost its grip on the lower courts, if they do not participate in new forms of case management. The Hoge Raad does not regard judicial guidelines – written by mandated experts groups of lower-court judges (e.g., in the field of alimony and consumer bankruptcy) – as legally relevant. The Hoge Raad ignores these guidelines and decides the individual case according to its own wisdom. As a consequence, the Highest Court does not give guidance to the lower courts, and the lower courts ignore the few opinions of the Hoge Raad as exceptions to their own rules.

The Hoge Raad also failed to act as a leading court in the mass tort class-action claim (400,000 cases) against the Dexia Bank. After a long period of individual proceedings, a collective settlement was reached by the Amsterdam Court of Appeal. The Hoge Raad, however, decided in later individual cases that it was not bound by the collective solution of the lower court. This disjunction between the work of lower and highest courts, of course, is detrimental to an efficient handling of so-called bulk cases.

In sum, the Netherlands likes to present The Hague as the legal capital of the world, because a lot of prestigious international courts have their residence there. The Netherlands was a legal avant-garde in 1953, when the country opened itself to the emerging European and world legal order. Top judges played a pivotal role in the interplay of Dutch national laws and EU and ECHR law. They acted as ambassadors of the EU and the Council of Europe.

Furthermore, the Dutch legal system is cognitively open to the surrounding world. At all levels, the judges do their best to faithfully apply European rules in Dutch case law. These international inroads into the national system make the task of judging very complex in legal terms, but also draws judges into a lawmaking role, making it more complex politically, as well. So far, the third branch has maintained a good relationship with the political elite. The Dutch judiciary is well funded, and unlike Italy and France, the Netherlands did not experience bitter legal and political fights about corrupt politicians defending themselves in court.

However, the question arises whether the Dutch system fits well with the European polity. The typical Dutch approach of getting things done via silent diplomacy works within a small country where everybody knows everybody else, but the lack of transparency and openness poses serious questions about the legitimacy of the Dutch system in terms of the standards articulated by the ECJ and ECtHR. Moreover, the three captains on the ship of the judiciary (Hoge Raad, Raad van State, Judicial Council) point in different directions, and that makes the effective management and maintenance of the integrity of the system very hard. The democratic deficit of Europe and the Euro crisis may have contributed further to the decline of the superior position of the Hoge Raad.

JUDICIAL LEADERSHIP AND JUDICIAL ROLES IN GOVERNANCE

I believe it is worthwhile to analyze shifts in the position and governance roles of the Hoge Raad courts in terms of leadership, a concept that is currently receiving much attention from both political scientists and business administration scholars, but which as yet has hardly been applied to the judicial organization. The analysis of high courts can profit from discussions on leadership within comparable (so-called non majoritarian) institutions that have an autonomous position vis-à-vis the politicians, and which are crucial to the functioning of a democratic society (Kane, Parapan, & 't Hart 2009).

For example, in the Netherlands a few years ago, the General Accounting Office (Algemene Rekenkamer) shook off its role as timid bookkeeper and demanded a full-fledged role for itself in the political debate. Comparisons with the leadership of Central Banks – for example, during times of financial crises – can also produce useful suggestions for leadership by the Highest Courts. Understanding the shifts in roles of high courts can be advanced by analyzing the past, present, and potential governance roles of the Dutch Hoge Raad – paying attention to what its leadership does not do as well as what it does do well.

The Hoge Raad and Organizational Leadership: Roles Not Played

In terms of its lawmaking and law-coordinating roles, the Hoge Raad's leadership faces a challenge concerning the internal coherence of its own case law. In many respects, the three chambers of the Hoge Raad lead a life of their own. At least as important, however, is that the Hoge Raad must demonstrate leadership to the lower judiciary, particularly by playing a guiding role with regard to judicial substance. Here, the Hoge Raad and the Procureur Generaal could play a much more active role, among other things by teaching courses and participating in innovative forms of judicial collaboration.

Moreover, in terms of its lawmaking role, the Hoge Raad is currently too distanced from the working processes within the lower instances. The vertical control mechanism within the judicial power must be properly coordinated to the practical work of the judges in the first and second (appellate) line. Further, I believe it is desirable that the Hoge Raad line up with the Council for the Judiciary. A legal system is unable to function properly with three directors conducting the judicial orchestra. As regards leadership, the Hoge Raad is better qualified than the Judicial Division of the Council of State. I would suggest it is desirable that the job of president of the Hoge Raad and chairman of the Council for the Judiciary be combined.

THE HOGE RAAD AND INSTITUTIONAL LEADERSHIP

The judiciary is not only a functional organization that has to perform its tasks efficiently and effectively but also an institution within which specific values are central, as Philip Selznick pointed out many years ago (Selznick 1957). It is the leadership's task to support the core values of the institution and ensure society is aware of these values. The following three values are dominant in the judiciary.

Independence and Disinterestedness. The Hoge Raad scores highly here. In comparison with the Council of State, its distance from politics is great – an advantage from the point of view of independence and disinterestedness. Moreover, the Hoge Raad complies better with the norms laid down in the ECHR. The Hoge Raad is loyal when the Strasbourg jurisprudence demands this, however, the independent, law-elaborating function of the Hoge Raad in this regard is not currently disputed.

Craftsmanship. The governance roles of high courts are also linked in many ways to the legal skills of the judges. However, there are almost no discussions regarding the judicial craftsmanship of the Hoge Raad. Unlike the state councillors, the justices write the (drafts of) their rulings themselves. Members of the Hoge Raad are part of the judicial community. The embedding of the Hoge Raad's work in a network constituted by a specialized bar, highly qualified advocates general, and annotators creates an entirely individual and strongly based legitimacy (Huls, Adams, & Bomhoff 2009).

In comparison with other courts of appeal in Europe, the Hoge Raad does not do badly with regard to the quality of its reasoning and power of persuasion. For example, in terms of social acceptability, the Dutch *Baby Kelly* ruling in a wrongful birth case was much more convincing and effective than the *Peruche* case of the French Cour de Cassation (Loth 2009). The Hoge Raad was able to depoliticize the debate by framing the wrongful birth as an ordinary tort case. Furthermore, the

Hoge Raad has always loyally performed the coordinating function between the national legal order and Europe.

Autonomy vis-à-vis other disciplines. The Hoge Raad has a special responsibility in safeguarding the autonomy of the legal system in the face of criticism from hard sciences. In the plans announced with respect to the review of miscarriages of justice – a very sensitive political issue – the procureur general at the Hoge Raad has been given the leading part. He can engage the assistance of experts.

CHANGING JUDICIAL ROLES

The Dutch Hoge Raad derives its legitimacy and broad role in governance from the democratic system of which it is a part. From the 1970s until the 1990s, the Dutch Cassation Court formulated provisional answers to questions politicians did not wish to burn their fingers on. The Court thus played the role of scout for the politicians and explored controversial territory as a kind of advance observer. Parliament sometimes came up with a different answer later if the court decision was not accepted by society, but it often codified the high court's answer into law. Co-optation, rather than separation, of powers occupied center stage.

In the 1990s, the Hoge Raad actively played an additional role – as an influential ambassador of the ECHR and EU treaties in the Netherlands. By applying ECHR precedents and EU law in domestic court cases, the Hoge Raad helped transform the Dutch legal order from a traditional and paternalistic legal bulwark to a more liberal and rights-based system.

However, the growing salience of the European legal order, which the Hoge Raad encouraged, has also imposed limits on the role of the court. After *Procola*, it is unlikely that Hoge Raad judges may act as legal drafters in the style of Wouter Snijders in the 1980s. Furthermore, the Hoge Raad's exclusive ambassador role has been challenged by the Raad van State, and the Hoge Raad has given in, instead of acting as a truly supreme court.

In a context of expanding supranational and international law, many observers regard it as important for cassation courts to play another important role: safeguarding the unity of the national legal system. With changes rapidly following one another in criminal law, for example, the coordination of various laws with each other is difficult. It is then up to the highest court to specify the interrelationship between laws and find a balance between the competing interests. Moreover, because of the denationalization of major legal fields brought about by the European Union, coordination of the national and international legal order is a new and complicated judicial task. The signals given by the ECJ and ECtHR are not always clear or explicit enough, adding impetus to the need for national judicial legal coordination.

The Cassation Court can play a major role in safeguarding the integrity of the legal system, including coordinating the relationship between private and public law (Canivet 2009: 125). In their role of guardians of the coherence of the national judicial system, cassation courts can become important legal political actors. However, to provide that kind of leadership, the Hoge Raad probably needs more political and legal space than the present cassation system allows. To do so, the Hoge Raad must get more control of its agenda. In January 2008, the Hoge Raad made some proposals to get a better grip on its caseload. In a law that came into force in 2011, three Selection Chambers are proposed as a first step toward a "leave system," giving the judges more case-selecting discretion. Furthermore, the procureur general is encouraged to bring more interesting cases to the Hoge Raad. Finally, the lower courts are given the authority to refer prejudicial questions (preliminary rulings) to the Hoge Raad.

In a time in which the Court needs leadership, the president of the Court has become more visible. Former President Willibrord Davids was the chairman of the committee that investigated the Dutch government's involvement in the war in Iraq. The new President Geert Corstens was elected by his fellow judges in 2008 in deviance from the seniority rule. Corstens was an outspoken criminal law professor who both before and after his appointment at the Hoge Raad has not been afraid to express his opinions in public. These changes might indicate that the Hoge Raad wants to regain some of the prominence that it had been losing to rival institutions (i.e., the Council of State and Council of the Judiciary).

The many rapid changes in Dutch society, politics, and the legal order have not left the position of the top of the judiciary unaffected. The Hoge Raad has lost some of its leading role in social policy making and governing the judicial system. The days of the brave scout and sovereign ambassador seem to be over. The role of a robust guardian of national legal coherence in a turbulent European legal order might well be an attractive new role.

REFERENCES

Ackerman, Bruce A. 1991. *We the people: Foundations.* Cambridge, MA: Harvard University Press.

Andeweg, Rudy B. & Galen A. Irwin. 1999. *Governance and politics of the Netherlands.* Houndmills/New York: Palgrave McMillan.

Barendrecht, Maurits. 1992. *Recht als model van rechtvaardigheid: Beschouwingen over scherpe en vage normen, over binding aan het recht en over rechtsvorming.* Deventer: Kluwer.

Barendrecht, Maurits. 1998. *De Hoge Raad op de hei.* Deventer: Tjeenk Willink.

Bell, John 2006. *Judiciaries within Europe. A comparative review.* Cambridge: Cambridge University Press.

Blankenburg, Erhard and Fred Bruinsma. 1994. *Dutch legal culture,* second edition. Deventer: Kluwer.

Buruma, Ian. 2006. *Murder in Amsterdam, liberal Europe, Islam and the limits of tolerance.* New York: Penguin.

Canivet, Guy. 2009. "Formal and informal determinative factors in the legitimacy of judicial decisions: The point of view of the French Cour de Cassation," in Nick Huls, Maurice Adams, and Jacco Bomhoff (eds.), *The legitimacy of Highest Courts rulings: "Judicial deliberations" and beyond,* The Hague: T.M.C. Asser Press, pp. 125–143.

Claes, Monica and Bruno de Witte. 1998. "Report on the Netherlands," in Anne-Marie Slaughter, Alec Stone Sweet, & J.H.H. Weiler (eds.), *The European court and national courts: Doctrine and jurisprudence, legal change in its social context*, Oxford: Hart Publishing, pp. 171–194.

Epstein, Lee, Jack Knight, & Olga Shvetsova. 2001. "The role of constitutional courts in the establishment and maintenance of democratic systems of government," *Law & Society Rev.* 35: 117–164.

Fix-Fierro, H. 2003. *Courts, justice and efficiency. A socio-legal study of economic rationality in adjudication*. Oxford: Hart.

Giddens, Anthony. 1998. *The Third Way: The renewal of social democracy*. Cambridge: Polity Press.

Griffiths, John, Heleen Weyers, and Maurice Adams. 2008. *Euthansisa and law in Europe*. Oxford and Portland, OR: Hart Publishers.

Halliday, Terence H., L. Karpik, & M.M. Feeley (eds.). 2007. *Fighting for political freedom: Comparative studies of the legal complex and political liberalism*. Onati Series of Law and Society, Oxford: Hart Publishing.

Hofstede, Geert. 1991. *Cultures and organizations: Software of the mind*. London: McGraw Hill.

Huls, Nick, Maurice Adams, and Jacco Bomhoff (eds.). 2009. *The legitimacy of Highest Courts rulings: "Judicial deliberations" and beyond*. The Hague: T.M.C. Asser Press.

Kane, John, Haig Parapan, & Paul 't Hart. 2009. *Dispersed democratic leadership: Origins, dynamics and implications*. Oxford: Oxford University Press.

Kate, Jan ten & Peter van Koppen. 1995. *The Netherlands: Toward a form of judicial review*, in C.N. Tate and T. Vallinder (eds.), *The global expansion of judicial power*, New York: New York University Press, pp. 369–380.

Koopmans, Tim. 2003. *Courts and political institutions: A comparative view*. Cambridge: Cambridge University Press.

Koppen, Peter van. 1990. "The Dutch Hoge Raad and Parliament: Political decisionmaking versus nonpolitical appointments," *Law & Society Review* 24(3): 741.

Lasser, Mitchel. 2004. *Judicial Deliberations. A comparative analysis of judicial transparency and legitimacy*. Oxford: Oxford University Press.

Loth, Marc. 2009. "Courts in quest of legitimacy: A comparative approach," in Nick Huls, Maurice Adams, and Jacco Bomhoff (eds.), *The legitimacy of Highest Courts rulings: "Judicial deliberations" and beyond*. The Hague: T.M.C. Asser Press, pp. 267–288.

Lijphart, Arend. 1969. *The politics of accommodation, pluralism and democracy in the Netherlands*. Berkeley: University of California Press.

Selznick, Philip. 1957. *Leadership in administration: A sociological interpretation*. Berkeley: University of California Press.

Wagenaar, Willem, H. Israëls, & P.J. van Koppen. 2009. *De slapende rechter* [The sleeping judge]. *Waarom het veroordelen van burgers niet alleen aan de rechter kan worden overgelaten*, Amsterdam: Bert Bakker.

Wiarda, G.J. 1999. *Drie typen van rechtsvinding*. Bewerkt en van een nabeschouwing voorzien door T. Koopmans. Deventer: W.E.J. Tjeenk Willink.

Zuckermann, A.A. (ed.). 1999. *Civil justice in Crisis: Comparative perspectives in civil procedures*. Oxford: Oxford University Press.

COURT CASES

European Court of Human Rights
Decision of October 24, 1979, Case 6301/73 (*Winterwerp*).

Decision of September 28, 1995, Reports A326 (*Procola*) (application 14570/89).
Decision of January 11, 2007, *Salah Sheekh v. the Netherlands* (application 1948/04).

European Court of Justice
Case C-243/01, Criminal Proceedings against P. Gambelli and Others [2003] ECR I-13031.
Case 258/08 Ladbrokes and C 203/08 (*Betfair*) June 3, 2010.

Hoge Raad
HR January 15, 1960, NJ 1960, 84 (*Pahonlibco*).
HR May 30, 1986, NJ 1986, 688 (*National Railways Services*).
HR November 11, 1994, NJ 1995, 152.
HR March 21, 1997, JAR 1997/70.
HR January 28, 2000, JAR 2000/63.

8

A Consequential Court

The U.S. Supreme Court in the Twentieth Century

*Robert A. Kagan**

To say that a constitutional court has played a significant role in governance of a nation implies that the court's decisions are *consequential* – that they make a difference, have an independent effect on politics, public policy, and power relationships, or on social or economic life, the treatment of minorities, criminal suspects, political or religious dissidents. This essay, accordingly, discusses the roles played by the U.S. Supreme Court in the twentieth century, asking to what extent and in what ways the Court was a consequential political actor.

Lawyers and legal scholars take it for granted that the U.S. Supreme Court, which has exercised the power of constitutional judicial review for more than 200 years, has been a politically consequential court. To many political scientists, however, the Court's actual influence is an unsettled empirical and theoretical question. Scholars often referred to as regime theorists argue that constitutional courts only rarely, if ever, have a powerful independent effect on government and society (Dahl, 1957; Rosenberg, 1991; Peretti, 1999; Pickerell & Clayton, 2004; Whittington, 2008). Regime theorists see high courts not primarily as politically powerful principals but as agents whose decisions in politically significant cases generally reflect the preferences of the political leaders who appointed them. Even if judges are personally inclined to make bold, politically unpopular rulings, it is argued, prudence usually impels them to act strategically, avoiding decisions that important political leaders are likely not only to denounce but to resist, reverse, or retaliate against (Epstein, Knight, & Shvetsova, 2001). In this view, therefore, when judicial decisions do have broad social or political consequences, it is because powerful political leaders or parties approve of (or at least accept) those decisions and – just as importantly – are willing to implement them. In regime theory, the judges may appear to be the engineer driving the legal or constitutional train, but political leaders have built the track and selected the engineers, thus deciding what direction they want the train to go.

* Department of Political Science and School of Law, University of California, Berkeley.

Even within the ambit of regime theory, however, there is room for courts to independently influence the course of law and governance (Keck, 2007). To return to the railroad train metaphor, sometimes political leaders need the courts to release the brakes and pull the throttle. That is, by "reinterpreting" a nation's constitution or statutory law, the court can take legal or policy initiatives that political leaders support but find politically difficult or legally impossible to launch on their own because of existing legal precedents or political constraints (Silverstein, 2009; Graber, 1993).

Moreover, political leaders are often divided on salient issues or wish to avoid them for political reasons or have no clear ideas at all about issues that come before the Court. This means, first, that a high court often has the opportunity or even necessity to act independently and in ways not entirely predictable in terms of regime theory (Tushnet, 2006; Silverstein, 2003). Second, division and indecision among political leaders reduces the likelihood that they will successfully strive to reverse a high-court decision they disagree with, post hoc; that in turn gives the judges some freedom to pursue an independent course. Those kinds of openings for judicial independence and assertiveness occur with some frequency in highly competitive democratic polities, particularly those with unstable ruling coalitions or relatively weak political-party unity and discipline. During the twentieth century, the U.S. Supreme Court, using just such openings, took on new political roles and had a significant independent influence on American government and governance.

It is commonly observed that the power-fragmenting features of the American governmental system – federalism, separation of powers, weak political-party discipline – tend to impede the national government's efforts to enact and implement nationwide policies and legal norms. In the three decades beginning in the mid-1930s, however, the U.S. Supreme Court played a major role in helping the federal government overcome those impediments. By radically reinterpreting the Constitution, the Court granted legal legitimacy to new nationwide governmental programs and created new federally protected legal rights – programs and rights that previously had been precluded by existing constitutional norms and political divisions (some of which the Court's prior decisions had fostered). More specifically, this chapter, summarizing material that is familiar to scholars of American constitutional history and law, will focus on three particularly consequential "constitutional moments"[1]:

(1) A series of judicial decisions in the late 1930s that reinterpreted the Constitution to authorize construction of a much larger national administrative and regulatory state, followed by a series of decisions in the 1960s that created a new body of administrative law that helped further legitimate administrative government;

---

[1] My account of these three constitutional moments makes no claims to originality. It draws on existing scholarship, although my interpretation of that material may sometimes diverge from that of the authors. My use of the term "constitutional moments" is borrowed from Ackerman (1991), although I use it here in a more general way.

(2) A series of judicial decisions in the 1960s that extended most provisions of the federal Constitution's Bill of Rights to bind state and local levels of government, thereby enabling federal courts to help regulate unprofessional or repressive local criminal justice systems, particularly but not exclusively in southern states;

(3) A series of judicial decisions in the 1950s and 1960s, both constitutional and statutory, that contributed significantly to the extension of civil rights and equal opportunity to African Americans.

In terms of the discussion of judicial roles in the Introduction to this volume, although the U.S. Supreme Court had long played an important role in adjudicating conflicts concerning federalism, in the decisions discussed in this chapter the Court decisively shifted the way it played that role. First, it affirmed and enhanced the authority and influence of the central government vis-à-vis state and local governments. Second, through those and other decisions, the post–World War II Court also assumed a much larger role in influencing political, social, and economic relations in civil society. More specifically, the Supreme Court and related federal court rulings expanded opportunities for civil-society actors to influence government policy and performance through litigation, thereby contributing to enhanced regulatory protections, more civil treatment of criminal suspects and prisoners, and lower levels of racially discriminatory treatment. As regime theory would suggest, the Supreme Court did none of these things alone, without substantial political support and collaboration. However, the Supreme Court did enable them to happen, or to happen sooner and in somewhat different ways than would have been the case if the Court had not acted as it did.

This story of judicial potency has another face, however. As with other governmental bodies that make law, a court that exercises substantial lawmaking power may not be able foresee all of the social effects that flow from its rulings – including effects the judges neither intended nor subsequently approved of. Unlike a legislature or rule-making administrative agency, a constitutional court preparing to make a consequential ruling does not first hold hearings that invite a wide array of groups to inform the decision maker about the intensity of the opposition its ruling will generate, or about adverse impacts the elite decision makers may not have imagined.[2]

Judicial decisions, moreover, produce losers as well as winners. A constitutional court's most consequential decisions rebalance the competing values that had been embodied in the pre-decision legal status quo. A court decision that increases equality may reduce liberty and redistribute power or wealth, triggering efforts to reverse or limit that decision. A court decision that increases liberty may erode some valued forms of order and stability, provoking fierce opposition. A constitutional ruling

---

[2] In the most salient U.S. Supreme Court cases, the information-about-consequence deficit sometimes is partly (but I suspect only partly) filled by amicus curiae briefs filed by a variety of interested institutions and advocacy groups.

that is endorsed by national political elites may nevertheless inspire social groups who strongly disagree with it to evade or circumvent the rule implicit in the court's decision or organize a political movement that seeks to reverse or restrict it. Finally, consequential court rulings, even if complied with, may change incentives in unanticipated ways, triggering new patterns of political or social activity that in turn generate new social or political problems.

In short, like other powerful political actors, an active and consequential high court operates on politically risky, not altogether calculable, terrain. Its rulings often have a range of consequences; some intended, some not. To illustrate that point, the last section of this chapter will provide a brief catalogue of some unintended but consequential social and political changes caused at least in part by heralded decisions of the U.S. Supreme Court in the 1950s, 1960s, and 1970s.

THE SUPREME COURT: NOT OMNIPOTENT, BUT POTENT

As suggested, the U.S. Supreme Court, despite its imposing name, does not rule supreme, in splendid isolation, its rulings sweeping all resistance aside. Court decisions that conflict with majority public opinion have rarely influenced majorities to change their attitudes (Persily, Citrin, & Egan, 2008). After the Court decided that mandatory prayer and Bible readings in public schools violated the First Amendment's strictures against governmental establishment of religion,[3] the majority of Americans surveyed continued to favor prayer in public schools, as they do to this day (Gash & Gonzales, 2008). Hundreds of school districts in the South refused to comply (Dolbeare & Hammond, 1971). In the South, but elsewhere as well, thousands of families abandoned the public schools for religiously oriented private schools – which may have been one of the most far-reaching social consequences of the Court's decision.

Nevertheless, most school districts did comply with the Court's school prayer decisions; some promptly, some eventually. Compliance with the rulings was abetted by two of the Court's assets: the coercive power of litigation and the political-legal legitimacy of the Court itself. As William K. Muir Jr. (1973) put it, the Court's school prayer rulings lent "adventitious strength" to the civil liberties lawyers who – except in the homogenously religious communities of the Bible Belt – could threaten noncompliant school districts with lawsuits in lower federal courts, which could be counted on, by and large, to enforce the rulings' principles. School board lawyers explained the risk of litigation to local school superintendents and elected boards; some persuaded school boards that the Court's opinions made constitutional and educational sense (Muir, 1973). Put more generally, the Court's opinions, when disseminated and summarized effectively by lawyers and journalists, have persuasive weight; not always, and not with every audience, but often, and with many.

[3] *Engel v Vitale* (1962); *Abingdon School District v Schempp* (1964).

Another reason school boards complied was that neither the U.S. president nor his successors denounced the Court's rulings or urged resistance. Moreover, Congress declined to enact proposed constitutional amendments that would have explicitly authorized prayer in the schools (Gash & Gonzales, 2008). The national political leaders' acquiescence or implicit support mattered greatly. Because Court decisions are not self-enforcing, and the Supreme Court does not have a large law-enforcement bureaucracy to deploy, its decisions have the intended consequences only to the extent that the Court has potent allies – committed interest groups and lawyers, or powerful politicians and influential opinion leaders – as well as a willingness, among opponents of the Courts' decisions, to accede rather than fight back.

Of course, the same is roughly true for the president and congressional lawmakers. No political actor succeeds by playing solos; they succeed only if they can help mobilize and lead the whole orchestra, or most of it, to play the same tune.[4] Changes in politics, policy, culture, and law usually have multiple causal drivers, each interacting with the others. The sensible question is not whether the Court – or the president or a congressional policy entrepreneur – has brought about change single-handed, but whether its actions and writings significantly helped shift or nudge law, policy, and practice in a particular direction.

This discussion, it is important to note, presupposes that the Court's potential to have systemic consequences arises primarily from rulings of unconstitutionality, instructing governments what they can no longer do (e.g., conduct morning school prayers, assign children to school on the basis of their race, criminalize first trimester abortions) or telling governments what they must do, affirmatively (e.g., provide free defense counsel for indigent criminal defendants, make sure that electoral district lines are drawn to ensure "one man, one vote," inform arrested criminal suspects of their right to remain silent). However, such assertive commands are only one mode of judicial influence. Courts can also be influential when they uphold and endorse controversial governmental laws and decisions. A president acts consequentially not only when he vetoes legislation but also when he signs a congressional statute he is not entirely happy about. So, too, the Supreme Court may act consequentially when it declines a petition to hold a controversial statute or governmental decision or practice unconstitutional. In some circumstances, an endorsing decision by a high court – at least if it is a reasonably independent, respected court – lends legitimacy to a governmental policy or practice.

Judicial endorsement decisions can be especially consequential if the decisions are *activist*, in the sense of departing from long-standing precedent or understandings of the constitutional text. That is, by implicitly amending the constitution, the Court can open the door – for good or for ill – to governmental laws and practices that had previously been held forbidden. Such was the nature of most of the key Supreme Court decisions in the late 1930s concerning the growth and legal character of the national regulatory and administrative state.

---

4 Thanks to Mark Graber for this metaphor.

One last preliminary point: If the Court is only one actor, one factor, in bringing about any particular change, it is not easy to determine what the Court's "value added" has actually been. Such a determination depends, at bottom, on generating a persuasive speculative counterfactual story: How would things have been different had the Court declined to decide the case, or had decided to the contrary? Generating persuasive counterfactuals is more like writing "social science fiction" than producing rigorous proofs (Polsby, 1983). However, that speculative effort, I hope this chapter's readers will agree, can be stimulating and enlightening.

LEGITIMATING A *NATIONAL* ADMINISTRATIVE AND REGULATORY STATE

In 1937, in *National Labor Relations Board v Jones & Laughlin Steel Corporation*, the Supreme Court – by a bitterly contested 5:4 vote – upheld the constitutionality of the National Labor Relations Act (NLRA), which established rights to organize labor unions and strike, imposing cognate obligations on all businesses "affecting commerce" between the states. The statute was to be enforced not through courts but via a new federal government agency – the National Labor Relations Board (NLRB) – which was to adjudicate disputes over the fairness of workplace elections and punish "unfair labor practices." In upholding the NRLA, the Court veered away from precedents in which it had drawn a wavering line between: (a) interstate commerce (which, according to the Court's interpretation, the Constitution authorized Congress to regulate); and (b) manufacturing, mining, labor relations, and retail sales (which the Court had defined as beyond the reach of national regulatory authority). However, in *Jones & Laughlin*, the power to regulate "commerce between the states," the majority opinion stated, authorized Congress to enact regulatory laws designed to remove "burdens and obstructions" to interstate commerce – such as labor unrest and strikes – "springing from other sources" – including intrastate labor relations.

To understand the import of the *Jones & Laughlin* opinion, note that just two years earlier, in *Schechter Poultry Corp v United States* (1935), the Court had struck down the National Industrial Recovery Act (NIRA), the keynote regulatory program of President Franklin D. Roosevelt's New Deal.[5] The Court held that the local prices and labor relations that NIRA and its implementing agency (the NRA) sought to control were intrastate rather than interstate commerce. The Court also held that the Act violated the Fifth Amendment's due process clause, as Congress had delegated extensive price- and wage-setting powers to unelected NRA officials and private-sector

---

[5] Designed to stop the downward spiral of prices, profits, and wages that had left a third of the workforce unemployed, the NIRA granted sweeping nationwide regulatory powers to the National Recovery Administration (NRA), which in turn created industry-by-industry panels to establish nationwide minimum prices and wages. The NIRA also granted employees the right to strike, form unions, and – via the NRA panels – negotiate the industry-wide wage levels.

advisory-panel members without establishing any precise statutory standard by which they could be held legally accountable.

Congress responded to the *Schechter* decision by enacting the NLRA.[6] President Roosevelt, reelected in 1936 by a huge majority, forcefully denounced the *Schechter* decision, along with several other 1935–1936 Supreme Court decisions that had struck down New Deal statutes. Further, the President announced a plan to expand the Court, allowing him to appoint new, more progressive judges. While Congress was considering the controversial Court-packing plan in early 1937, a 5:4 Supreme Court majority – the product of Justice Owen Roberts's alleged "switch in time that saved nine"[7] – issued surprising decisions in the *West Coast Hotel v Parrish* and *Jones & Laughlin* cases. In its opinions, the Court discarded earlier judicial precedents, endorsed the Roosevelt administration's arguments, and thereby helped launch a new era in American government. In the words of John Fabian Witt (2007: 276):

> The courts, it seemed, would no longer rigorously police the constitutional limits on the power of the federal government and the states to replace the common law with comprehensive regulatory systems. Nor, it seemed, would courts reject (as they once had) the delegation of broad powers by Congress to administrative agencies such as the NLRB. The administrative state, in short, seemed poised to replace . . . what political scientist Stephen Skowronek has influentially called the "state of courts and parties" that the United States had inherited from the nineteenth century.

The Court's dramatic doctrinal shift in the 1937 decisions was soon cemented and extended when elderly conservative justices began to resign and Roosevelt appointed justices who were sympathetic to the New Deal agenda. Between 1937 and 1942, the Court essentially rewrote the Constitution. It transformed Congress from a body of limited powers to one of virtually unlimited powers in the realm of economic regulation, and it granted constitutional legitimacy to a massive expansion of federal administrative policymaking and implementation. Four lines of decisions were important in this regard:

Interstate Commerce as All Commerce. In *Wickard v Filburn* (1942),[8] the Court indicated that Congress could regulate even local businesses in any category of

---

[6] The NLRA called for workplace-by-workplace elections, policed by the NLRB, rather than the mandatory industry-wide wage setting (and price setting) mandated by the now-defunct NIRA.

[7] It isn't entirely clear why Justice Roberts apparently "switched sides" in those cases, abandoning the four conservative justices who continued to insist on constitutional restrictions on government regulation and federal governmental powers. Many legal historians have pointed to evidence suggesting that Roberts' motivation was not purely strategic, designed to blunt Roosevelt's attack on the Court (Cushman, 1998). However, recent analyses of voting patterns indicate that after a brief period of more centrist or liberal votes in 1936, Roberts returned to his conservative voting pattern (Ho & Quinn, 2010) – indicating that Roberts did act in a politically strategic manner.

[8] Through the Agriculture Adjustment Act of 1938, Congress sought to stabilize farm prices and income by empowering the secretary of agriculture to set a nationwide quota for wheat production and assign allotments to individual farmers. Filburn, an Ohio dairy farmer who raised small amounts of wheat for cattle feed, selling any excess, was fined for exceeding his quota. The Court rejected Filburn's

economic behavior that cumulatively affects interstate commerce. The Supreme
Court thus endorsed a radical shift in the nature of American federalism, laying the
constitutional foundation for the subsequent expansion of congressionally authorized administrative regulation of matters previously deemed the province of state
government, from racial discrimination in workplaces and restaurants to leakage
from municipal waste disposal sites, education of handicapped children, and air
pollution from virtually any source.

The Abandonment of Substantive Review of Regulatory Policy. In *Nebbia v New
York* (1934) and more decisively in *West Coast Hotel v Parrish* (1937), the Supreme
Court sharply rejected the so-called substantive due process doctrine, which it had
earlier often invoked to review the economic rationality of state regulatory enact-
ments and limit state regulation of labor relations. "So far as the requirement of due
process is concerned," the Court said in *Nebbia*, "a state is free to adopt whatever
economic policy may reasonably be deemed to promote public welfare" and "it does
not lie with the courts to determine that the rule is unwise." In *West Coast Hotel v
Parrish* (1937), the Court explicitly rejected the concept of "liberty of contract" that
it had previously used in striking down labor legislation. "Even if the wisdom of the
policy be regarded as debatable and its effects uncertain," the Court added, "the
legislature is entitled to its judgment." The Court thereby abandoned its previous
role of policing the "reasonableness" of regulatory policy, endorsing state-level reg-
ulators' constitutional capacity to fulfill the New Deal vision of active governmental
control of the externalities and inequalities engendered by market forces.

Endorsing Administrative Lawmaking. The 1789 U.S. Constitution vested legislative power in Congress. However, to deal with the complex details of regulating
a complex, diverse twentieth-century economy, Congress often enacted generally
worded regulatory legislation, delegating the task of filling in the legal details to specialized administrative agencies. To many Americans, the rise of this administrative
"fourth branch of government" presented both constitutional problems and deep
concerns about administrative bias and accountability. The Supreme Court's 1935
Schechter Poultry decision reflected these concerns when it insisted that Congress
had to provide more detailed legislative standards – a task that could paralyze a
busy legislature, slowing its response to urgently sought regulatory protections. However, in 1940, the Court (now with a solid majority of Roosevelt appointees) upheld
the Bituminous Coal Act of 1937, which like the NIRA granted broad price-setting
powers to a federal administrative agency and panels of company representatives –
although the law provided scarcely more specific legislative guidance than NIRA
had included.[9] The *Schecter Poultry* "non-delegation doctrine" henceforth virtually

claim that the law far exceeded Congress's power to regulate interstate commerce. Even if Filburn's
contribution to nationwide demand for wheat "may be trivial by itself," the Court said, the effect of
his behavior "taken together with that of many others similarly situated is far from trivial." For an
excellent account of *Wickard v Filburn* and its consequences, see Chen (2006).
[9] *Sunshine Anthracite Coal v Adkins* (1940). See also *Yakus v United States* (1944).

disappeared from constitutional jurisprudence, opening a clear path for the growth, legal reach, and policymaking authority of the federal administrative state.

Unleashing the Federal Government's Taxing and Spending Power. In an effort to halt the disastrous collapse of farm income, the federal Agricultural Adjustment Act of 1933 imposed a tax on processors of farm products such as cotton and wheat. The proceeds were to be used to subsidize farmers who agreed to restrict their production. However, in *United States v Butler* (1936), the conservative majority on the Supreme Court held that the statutory plan sought to "regulate and control agricultural production, a matter beyond the powers delegated to the federal government." The Court rejected the government's argument that the tax fell within Article II's grant to Congress of the power "to lay and collect Taxes . . . to pay the debts and provide for the common Defence and general Welfare of the United States." That general welfare clause, the Court's majority said, was not an open-ended power to tax and spend on activities such as agricultural production that were not specifically delegated to Congress by Article II, and hence implicitly reserved to the state governments.

A year later, however, in the wake of the 1936 election and the Roosevelt Administration's Court-packing plan, the Court reversed course. In *Steward Machine v Davis* (1937), a 5:4 majority upheld the constitutionality of another fundamental New Deal initiative, a federal law establishing a nationwide unemployment compensation system. The Court's opinion rejected the dissenters' argument that a federal tax mandated by law was unconstitutional because it was used to shape state employment and tax policy, matters far beyond the powers delegated to the federal government by Article II. The federal government, the Court now indicated, could employ its powers to tax and spend to advance the general welfare as Congress saw it. On the same day, the Court upheld the Social Security Act, which imposed federal payroll taxes on employers and employees to fund retirement pensions.[10] The constitutional pathway was open for the massive expansion of the federal welfare state (e.g., to fund nationwide disability programs and medical insurance for the elderly and poor through later amendments to the Social Security Act). The pathway was also now open for federal funding of state and local infrastructure projects, hospitals, and education systems through grants on which detailed regulatory conditions were imposed. As the Court abandoned constitutional scrutiny of the purposes for which federal funds could be spent, and of the conditions the federal government could impose on grantees, there was little that the federal government could not now influence and regulate.

How Much Did the Supreme Court Matter? In the 1990s, conservatives on the U.S. Supreme Court – abetted by a growing cadre of conservative legal scholars and lawyers (Teles, 2008; Hollis-Brusky, 2011) – launched a counterattack on the New Deal Court's reversal of the constitutional power relations between states and the federal regulatory and administrative state (Pickerell & Clayton, 2004). The Court

---

[10] *Helvering v Davis*, 301 U.S. 619 (1937).

held that some federal regulations (e.g., of local wetlands and gun possession in school yards) were too unrelated to interstate commerce to fall within Congress's regulatory power, and the Court proclaimed some limits on direct federal regulation of state and local governments' obligations as employers. In 2012, conservative lawyers and justices posed a more serious challenge in litigation involving the 2010 Affordable Health Care Act . Thus far, however, the conservative legal movement has done relatively little to shift meaningful amounts of constitutional power away from the federal government and back to the states.[11] One reason is that the New Deal Court's constitutional revision has remained politically acceptable to political majorities and national political elites. Since the 1930s, the electorate and the political establishment have grown accustomed to looking to Washington for financial aid and policy solutions. When crisis strikes – as in the financial implosion of 2008 – those demands intensify, for only the federal government, as constitutionally empowered by the Court in the 1930s, has the taxing and spending powers and regulatory reach to take meaningful action.

In light of the political demand for national leadership, one might argue that the Supreme Court's interpretive revision of the Constitution in the late 1930s was inevitable, and hence not very consequential. Suppose, however, that in 1937 the conservative justices had remained unified and rejected the government's arguments in *West Coast Hotel, Jones & Laughlin,* and *Steward Machine.* Suppose further that the elderly conservative bloc, buoyed by its success, had a new burst of energy – no retirements or deaths for three or five more years – and had continued to strike down state regulatory laws, national regulatory and welfare statutes, and restricted congressional delegations of authority to government agencies. Then perhaps Roosevelt might have revived his Court-packing plan, this time with strong support from an infuriated Democratic Congress. Or perhaps Congress would have passed legislation restricting federal court jurisdiction over regulatory legislation or proposed a constitutional amendment overriding the Court's conservative interpretation of the Commerce Clause, Due Process Clause, and so forth. Or perhaps those efforts would have failed, so that it would have taken a decade or more before new Supreme Court justices finally extended the regulatory authority of the federal government. In any of those scenarios, the transition endorsed by the Court in the late 1930s

---

[11] In 2012, a conservative Supreme Court majority did strike down an important component of the 2010 federal health care law, holding that it exceeded Congress's powers under the Spending Clause in attempting to coerce state governments to participate in the federal plan to expand medical coverage under the Medicaid program. Moreover, although the Court upheld the Act's 'individual mandate" on other grounds, that majority held that the Commerce Clause did not empower Congress to compel individuals to purchase health insurance – a decision that departed from long-standing precedents requiring judicial deference to Congressional judgments about implementation mechanisms. How great a limitation on federal power that decision will lead to is far from clear. But the fact remains that the late New Deal Supreme Court decisions have remained solid precedents for seventy years, and probably more, creating a constitutional umbrella over a huge expansion of the federal regulatory and administrative state.

probably would have occurred, but less smoothly, with more damage to the Court's legitimacy, and much delay in the construction of national regulatory and social security programs that have been at the heart of the nation's public law.

Regime theory holds that continued judicial resistance to powerful political pressures is unlikely to last indefinitely. Assuming that is so, our counterfactual story reminds us that the *timing* and *character* of the Supreme Court's adjustment to new political winds can vary, depending on how many justices placed on the Court by earlier political winds dig in their heels and for how long. The counterfactual suggests, too, that the Supreme Court's cooperation with the Roosevelt administration's agenda was critical to the expansion of the national regulatory and administrative state in the 1930s. By doing so relatively quickly, without resort to congressional Court-curbing measures, the Supreme Court in the late 1930s provided a consequential endorsement of a large constitutional change in American federalism and governance, curtailing what could have been a wrenching, drawn-out constitutional crisis. In terms of this volume's analysis of judicial roles, the Court – by reinterpreting the Constitution – served as an enabler or facilitator of a politically popular shift concerning the role of government in the economic life of the nation.

Legitimating Administrative Lawmaking through Federal Administrative Law. Although the New Deal Supreme Court reshaped constitutional law to endorse enhanced congressional power and federal administrative policymaking, the legitimation of a larger administrative state was not fully complete. In the post–World War II years, regulated business firms distrusted the competence and judgment of presidentially appointed administrators whom they viewed as unsympathetic or even hostile to the legitimate concerns of capitalist enterprise. Political liberals, conversely, complained that regulatory agencies were often "captured" by deep-pocketed regulated enterprises. In response, in the 1960s and 1970s, the Supreme Court and lower federal courts engaged in what Richard Stewart (1975) famously labeled "The Reformation of American Administrative Law," imposing a thick layer of legal and judicial accountability on the "unaccountable fourth branch of government." The purpose and (to a considerable degree) the consequence of these new judge-made doctrines was to increase the transparency, pluralistic responsiveness, and rationality of administrative policymaking (Croley, 2008) – which has arguably helped bolster the legitimacy of far-reaching administrative governance.

One important line of decisions expanded citizens' standing to challenge agency decisions in court. In 1965, for example, the 2nd Circuit U.S. Court of Appeals allowed an environmental group to seek judicial review of a Federal Power Commission decision permitting the construction of an electric power plant on a beautiful stretch of the Hudson River, although the group and its members did not have an individualized economic stake in the outcome.[12] Henceforth, prudent agencies had to be more responsive to environmentalists' concerns (Silverstein, 2009). Other

---

[12] *Scenic Hudson Preservation Conference v Federal Power Commission* (1965).

fateful court decisions involved expansive judicial interpretations of the 1946 Administrative Procedure Act (APA). In *Citizens to Preserve Overton Park v Volpe* (1971), a citizens group argued that the U.S. Department of Transportation's decision to fund a highway that cut through a park in Memphis violated the APA because the decision was "arbitrary, capricious, and an abuse of discretion." To meet that statutory standard, the Supreme Court announced, the agency must provide a written record of its deliberations and facts considered, so that the justices could determine whether the decision was reasonable. The Court's opinion meant that controversial government agency decisions that had previously reflected a mix of technical, economic, environmental, and political factors henceforth would have to meet standards of rational public policy, as determined, at least to some significant degree, by reviewing judges (Strauss, 2006; Shapiro, 1988).

The federal Courts of Appeal applied that standard to rulemaking decisions by federal regulatory agencies, requiring agency officials to provide detailed written reasons for their policy choices, including reasoned responses to all serious objections to a proposed rule. Endorsing those precedents, the Supreme Court later decided that the incoming administrator of the National Highway Traffic Safety Agency (NHTSA) appointed by President Ronald Reagan in 1981 could not simply suspend a controversial mandatory automotive airbag regulation that had been promulgated (but not yet implemented) by the outgoing Carter Administration. NHTSA, the Court held, would first have to conduct notice-and-comment rulemaking procedures and provide reasons – backed by new scientific data – that would rationally support its decision to withdraw or suspend the earlier regulation.[13] In that decision, administrative law scholar Jerry Mashaw (2006: 336) noted, the Court "demanded that administrative legitimacy be premised on the transparent demonstration that power is being exercised on the basis of knowledge."

As regime theorists would expect, the federal courts' intensification of judicial review of administrative decision making was not accomplished in defiance of the national political leadership. In the 1960s and 1970s, both political parties responded to public demands for further expansion of the administrative state, but each party feared that discretionary administrative power would be misused by their political adversaries. Congress therefore began to enact much more detailed regulatory statutes, which facilitated checks on agency discretion by litigants and judges (Kagan, 2001; McCubbins, Noll, & Weingast, 1989). However, the courts themselves often led the thrust for administrative accountability through litigation. It was judges who relaxed constitutional restrictions on standing to sue, discovered implied private rights to enforce the National Environmental Protection Act via lawsuits, and read an entire procedural code of participatory, science–and–reason-based administrative decision making into the spare language of the APA. Subsequently, Congress and the president have not pushed the courts back out of the administrative oversight

[13] *Motor Vehicle Mfrs Ass'n of the US v State Farm Mutual Automobile Ins Co* (1983).

business, as both Democrats and Republicans, both liberal advocacy groups and conservative business groups, see the courts as insurance against the day when their political adversaries gain control of the presidency and appoint agency heads (Kagan, 2001: 249–250). In providing that insurance and expanding legal checks on administrative bias, the Supreme Court and federal courts of appeals have played an independent role in legitimating an expanded administrative state whose construction they first authorized in the late 1930s.

The result has not been a total victory for administrative rationality, of course. Politics continues to matter greatly in shaping administrative policymaking priorities and goals (Mashaw, 2006). However, the new administrative law compels the administrative policymaking process to be more science based and attentive to policy alternatives, economic costs, and social benefits (Croley, 2008). More negatively, fear of judicial reversal makes many agencies exceedingly cautious, delaying badly needed new rules until they can justify their policy choices with detailed (but costly and necessarily slow) studies of all relevant risks, costs, and benefits (Mendeloff, 1987; Dwyer, 1990; Mashaw & Harfst, 1991). It is also clear that the searching, procedurally formal style of judicial review developed by American federal courts makes American administrative policymaking much more transparent, legalistic, and adversarial than parallel processes in other economically advanced democracies (Badaracco, 1985; Kagan, 2001, 2007).

THE WARREN'S COURT'S CRIMINAL DUE PROCESS REVOLUTION

Partly because of the claims to democratic virtue engendered by the battle against totalitarianism in World War II and the Cold War, American national political elites became increasingly sensitive to the contradiction between the egalitarian "American creed" and ugly reality of Southern apartheid (Dudziak, 1988). Nazi and Soviet propagandists had been quick to broadcast news of lynchings of black men accused of crimes in Southern states (Klarman, 2007: 131). By 1960 and 1961, the Civil Rights Movement was filling national television screens with images of Southern sheriffs beating civil rights marchers. For years, civil rights activists had claimed – and researchers had confirmed – police practices in the black ghettos of Northern cities were not much better than in Southern counties (Epp, 2009). National political, journalistic, and legal elites came to believe that something should be done to rein in racist, brutal, and unjust practices in state and local criminal law enforcement, adjudication, jails, and prisons.

The U.S. Constitution, however, did not give Congress or the president clear constitutional authority to act. Neither the president nor his attorney general could fire a racist sheriff in Birmingham, Alabama, a South Carolina judge who denied black defendants a fair trial, or a locally elected district attorney in Mississippi who failed to prosecute white vigilantes' crimes against black citizens. Congress had no constitutional power to amend state criminal laws, procedural rules, modes of adjudication, or penal practices. Moreover, the threat of filibuster by Southern senators had long impeded congressional enactment of anti-lynching and civil rights laws that federal prosecutors could invoke against local criminal justice officials in federal courts.

Many proponents of criminal justice reform, therefore, looked to the Constitution – as interpreted by federal courts – as a way of projecting federal power into local criminal justice systems. The post–Civil War Fourteenth Amendment, by forbidding state governments from depriving persons of life, liberty, or property "without due process of law," ostensibly authorized federal courts to impose uniform constitutional standards on local police, prosecutors, and courts. The obstacles in that reform pathway, however, were long-standing judicial precedents. In the early nineteenth century, the Supreme Court had held that the Bill of Rights in the U.S. Constitution, which included various protections against arbitrary criminal processes, was intended to constrain the federal government, not state or local governments.[14] The due process clause of the Fourteenth Amendment (1868), as interpreted by a conservative post–Civil War Supreme Court, did not incorporate the Bill of Rights or make its provisions binding on state and local criminal justice systems.

In the 1920s and 1930s, the Supreme Court took some steps away from that position in widely publicized cases involving egregious prosecutions and trials in Southern states. In the case of the "Scottsboro Boys" – young black defendants who had summarily been convicted of murder in Alabama – the Court held that in capital punishment cases, due process requires the state to provide meaningful defense counsel.[15] In *Palko v Connecticut* (1937), however, even the New Deal Supreme Court rejected pleas to incorporate the federal Bill of Rights into the Fourteenth Amendment; the Court instead opted for case-by-case consideration of whether a state or local practice violated fundamental rights. Although this approach yielded some reversals of individual state criminal convictions based on shocking evidence gathering or adjudicative practices, it did not promise wholesale reform.

As described by Epp (2009): "The NAACP, the American Civil Liberties Union, and the National Lawyers Guild began broad campaigns against police brutality during the war years and ratcheted up their efforts in the late 1940s and 1950s." The Supreme Court, accordingly, was confronted with more appeals that described blatantly unfair practices not only by Southern police, courts, and prosecutors but by their counterparts in many Northern cities, as well. In the early 1960s, under the leadership of Chief Justice Earl Warren – who earlier had been a reform-minded county prosecutor in California – the Supreme Court dramatically expanded the reach of the Fourteenth Amendment, incorporating provision after provision of the Bill of Rights into the Due Process Clause. Incorporation made those provisions, as interpreted by previous federal court decisions, constitutionally binding on state and local

---

[14] *Barron v Baltimore* (1833).
[15] *Powell v Alabama* (1932).

jurisdictions. New interpretations of Bill of Rights provisions by the Warren Court also steadily increased the level of protections provided. In this case-by-case manner, the Court elaborated detailed nationwide rules concerning pretrial detention,[16] interrogation of suspects,[17] police searches for evidence,[18] double jeopardy,[19] access to trial by jury,[20] and rights to confront adverse witnesses.[21]

Just as importantly, the Supreme Court made those broader constitutional rights more readily enforceable through adversarial legal advocacy. In *Mapp v Ohio* (1961), the Court held that state courts could not use or base convictions on illegally obtained evidence – a rule that gave defense lawyers a club for enforcing a growing body of judge-created rules concerning search warrants, "unreasonable" searches for evidence, and coercive interrogation. In *Gideon v Wainwright* (1963), the Court held the Sixth Amendment's right to counsel was binding on states in all criminal cases, and that states must provide indigent defendants free defense lawyers in all felony cases. *Gideon* led to the establishment of governmentally funded "public defender" offices (or governmentally paid private attorneys) throughout states that had not yet established parallel rights to counsel. The Court thus raised a new army of lawyers who could protest and appeal violations of the court-elaborated web of criminal defendants rights. The Court extended that right to counsel to misdemeanor cases,[22] juvenile court proceedings,[23] and the police station house – requiring state and local law enforcement officials to inform arrested suspects of their right to silence and a lawyer before interrogating them (*Miranda v Arizona*, 1966). The Court expanded opportunities for defendants convicted by state courts to seek collateral review in federal courts,[24] opened the door for federal reprosecution of racist law enforcement officers who had been acquitted by juries in state courts, and reinterpreted a long-moribund provision of the post–Civil War Klu Klux Klan Act to enable individuals to bring lawsuits for damages against individual local law enforcement officers who had aggressively violated their constitutional rights.[25]

Because these new policies and procedures were cast as constitutional rules, they were largely insulated from reversal or amendment by legislatures or police administrators, state or federal. Defense lawyers' motions to suppress illegally obtained evidence and confessions became a routine practice in local criminal prosecutions. The appellate courts, not state legislatures or Congress, laid down the principles for

---

[16]   In *re Gault* (1967).
[17]   *Miranda v Arizona* (1966).
[18]   *Aguilar v Texas* (1964); *Chimel v California* (1969).
[19]   *Benton v Maryland*, 395 U.S. 784 (1969).
[20]   *Duncan v Louisiana* (1968).
[21]   *Pointer v Texas* (1965).
[22]   *Argersinger v Hamlin* (1972).
[23]   In *re Gault* (1967).
[24]   *Faye v Noia* (1963).
[25]   *Monroe v Pape* (1961).

determining when cops need a warrant, when they can search a suspect's car trunk, and so on (Walker, 1993; Bradley, 1993).

In extending the Bill of Rights to the states and constructing a more demanding judge-made code of criminal procedure, the Supreme Court did not act entirely alone. The Department of Justice often filed amicus briefs in support of the American Civil Liberties Union's or National Association for the Advancement of Colored People's arguments for expanded due process protections (Epp, 1998; Clayton, 1992). Through most of the 1960s, although law enforcement officers' associations railed against the Court for "handcuffing" their efforts to stanch a rapidly growing crime rate, Democratic presidents and congressional leaders did not attack the Court. Rather, they saw the Court's due process revolution as a complement to or extension of the landmark federal Civil Rights Act enacted in 1964. The devastating 1965 and 1967 ghetto riots in Los Angeles, Detroit, and Newark, New Jersey, made racially insensitive, sometimes brutal police practices in the inner city a matter of urgent national political concern. The National Advisory Commission on Civil Disorders, appointed by President Johnson to investigate the causes of the riots, cited African-American resentment of police harassment and abuse as a very significant factor (Epp, 2009: 46–47). In 1966, Congress enacted a statute that codified Supreme Court cases expanding state prisoners' rights to obtain habeas corpus review in federal courts.[26]

On another front, in the mid-1960s and early 1970s, civil rights activism and expanded habeas corpus review made national legal and political elites more attentive to the inhumane treatment, overcrowding, grossly inadequate medical care, and extremely harsh disciplinary measures that characterized many state prisons, particularly in Southern states. Again, in the decentralized American constitutional order, there was no congressional law governing state correctional systems, no national official charged with supervising state prisons or county jails. Moreover, for years, federal judges had turned away complaints about unbearable prison conditions (Friedman, 1993: 309–13). Two Warren Court decisions, however, provided precedents for more aggressive prison-reform initiatives by the lower federal courts. In 1958, in *Trop v Dulles*, the Court suggested that the Eighth Amendment ban on "cruel and inhuman punishments" included not only those specific punishments abhorrent to the constitutional framers in 1789 but also those condemned by "evolving standards of decency that mark the progress of a maturing society." In 1962, in *California v Robinson*, the Court held that the Eighth Amendment is included in the Fourteenth Amendment's insistence on due process of law, hence binding on state governments. In the 1960s, pressed by lawyers who drew on both precedents, lower federal courts – first in Arkansas and then in Alabama – held that inhumane prison conditions constituted cruel and unusual punishment and violated the Due Process Clause, and issued detailed reform orders to state officials. These precedents led to scores

---

[26] 28 U.S.C. 2244, 2254.

of detailed judicial reform orders against prisons and county jails throughout the country, fashioning what Feeley & Rubin (1998: 14) called a "comprehensive set of judicially enforceable rules for the governance of American prison." Moreover, echoing the theme that courts can sometimes implement policies that national political elites endorse but find politically or constitutionally hard to enact, in 1980 Congress enacted a statute that endorsed this court-stimulated revolution in oversight and reform of state penal practices by requiring states to meet Federal Bureau of Prisons standards, and made those standards enforceable by the Department of Justice[27] (Feeley & Rubin, 1998: 167–168).

By 1968, popular concern about rising crime had become a salient political issue. Richard Nixon was elected president after condemning the Warren Court for being "soft on crime." Gradually, his more conservative appointees to the Supreme Court, joined by Republican justices appointed by President Ronald Reagan in the 1980s, carved out exceptions to or otherwise weakened some Warren Court due process doctrines. Police became adept at persuading (or tricking) criminal suspects to waive their Miranda rights to silence and a lawyer and then to confess (Leo, 2008). Beginning in the 1980s, harsher sentencing laws led to enormous increases in prison populations, further increasing the harshness of American criminal law and practice as compared to other economically advanced democracies (Whitman, 2005; Kagan, 2001, 2007).

Nevertheless, the basic institutional building blocks mandated by the Warren Court, particularly the system of public defenders, remained in place. Those offices are often inadequately funded, but the greater frequency with which defense counsel appear and make legal objections compelled prosecutors' offices to become more professional. Police academies drill recruits in the details of the Supreme Court's search and seizure jurisprudence. To a considerable extent, urban police officers respect those rules (Orfield, 1987). A 1978 Supreme Court decision[28] that authorized lawsuits for damages against city governments (not merely individual officers) for egregious violations of individual suspects' rights led to a major increase in those kinds of cases and the size of damage awards. Police reformers successfully used the resulting fear of litigation to prod police departments to enact and enforce regulations and training programs that have significantly constrained police use of force in many cities and commanded more respectful treatment of citizens and criminal suspects (Epp, 2009).

The Supreme Court's deep involvement – and hence that of the lower federal courts – in developing rules of criminal procedure and regulating local law enforcement and adjudication is a distinctively American phenomenon. Western European democracies rely on hierarchically organized nationwide bureaucracies to train, supervise, and discipline judges, police, and prosecutors – a more direct

[27] 42 U.S. Code, sec 1997a–j.
[28] *Monell v Social Service Department* (1978).

method (and many would say a more effective method) than the American reliance
on litigation and courts. The enhanced defendants' rights mandated by the Court
have helped make criminal litigation more complex and costly in the United States
than in other rich countries, helping make it ever more likely that cases will be
resolved by low-visibility plea bargaining than adjudication (Kagan, 2001). However,
few would deny that important aspects of criminal justice in the United States today
have improved markedly as compared to the period before the Warren Court's
due process revolution, or that the Supreme Court's actions were consequential in
helping bring those changes about. The persistence of "law and order" politics and
penal policies in the previous few decades (Simon, 2007; Garland, 2001) suggests
that absent the Supreme Court's leadership, those improvements would have been
far less extensive.

RACE

During the nineteenth century, the U.S. Supreme Court played a significant role
in entrenching white supremacy and black subordination. Before the Civil War,
the Court affirmed the rights of slaveholders to demand the return of fugitive slaves
from "free states" (Cover 1975). In *Dred Scott v Sandford* (1857), the Court held
that Congress lacked the constitutional authority to bar slavery from the Western
Territories, adding that in terms of the Constitution as written, blacks were "so far
inferior, that they have no rights that the white man was bound to respect." After the
war, the Court limited the reach of the Fourteenth Amendment[29] and congressional
statutes designed to combat white vigilantism and protect the civil rights of former
slaves.[30] In *Plessy v Ferguson* (1896), the Court's pinched interpretation of the Fourteenth Amendment's equal protection clause provided Constitutional legitimacy for
Southern state "Jim Crow" laws that mandated segregation in transportation, public
facilities, and education.

Had the Supreme Court decided each of those cases to the contrary, it almost
certainly would not have prevented the Civil War, the collapse of post-War Reconstruction, or racial apartheid in the South; larger political and cultural forces were at
work. However, if the Court had decided those cases otherwise, thereby denying legal
support to fierce opponents of racial equality, it is not implausible to speculate that
the timing and course of the War and the resurgence of Southern racial apartheid
would have been affected to some degree, perhaps substantially. Conversely, because
the Court in fact provided judicial support for the white supremacists' position, its
decisions lent them "adventitious strength," fortifying their beliefs and sense of
righteousness.

---

[29] The *Slaughterhouse Cases*, 83 U.S. 36 (1873).
[30] *U.S. v Cruikshank* (1875); *U.S. v Harris*, 106 U.S. 629 (1882); *Civil Rights Cases* (1883).

So, too, the positive developments in racial legal equality in the second half of the twentieth century owe far more to broader cultural and political movements than to *Brown v Board of Education* and other U.S. Supreme Court decisions that finally sought to redeem the Fourteenth Amendment's promise of equal protection of the laws for black Americans. However, as in the case of the nineteenth-century decisions, the Supreme Court's decisions were not inconsequential. The twentieth-century Supreme Court denied legal legitimacy to officially mandated white supremacy and Southern resistance to the Civil Rights Movement. By boldly reinterpreting the Constitution and the 1964 Civil Rights Act, the Court mandated important equality-promoting policies that the Democratic Party's national leadership (and some Republicans) favored or accepted, but were politically unable to legislate and implement. It is hard to believe that gains and shortfalls in the struggle for racial equality in the United States would have been quite the same, in timing and degree, if the Court had *not* made the decisions that it did in the 1950–1980 period.

Brown v Board of Education. The Supreme Court's famous 1954 decision was consistent with the premises of regime theory. Fifteen years earlier, as Kevin McMahon (2000) has shown, President Franklin Roosevelt, stymied by Southern Senators in Congress, sought to advance the cause of racial equality by staffing the Department of Justice and federal courts (including the Supreme Court) with lawyers and judges who tended to share those values and goals. In the 1939–1945 period, the Department of Justice's Civil Liberties Unit (subsequently relabeled the Civil Rights Division) launched high-profile prosecutions against the perpetrators of lynchings and racially oriented police brutality (McMahon, 2000: 39–44). The Supreme Court, by then dominated by Roosevelt appointees, ruled that racially exclusionary "white primaries" conducted by the Democratic Party in Southern states violated the Fourteenth and Fifteenth Amendments (*Smith v Allwright*, 1944). Thereafter, black voter registration began to increase substantially (Klarman, 2007: 136).

Public attitudes and government policies began to change, as well. The U.S. battle against Nazi Germany during World War II and the participation of black soldiers in combat stimulated more intense white discomfort with racial segregation and more black activism (Ibid.; McMahon, 2000). In 1941, threatened by a black march on Washington organized by the Sleeping Car Porters union, President Roosevelt ordered an end to race discrimination in federal governmental agencies and companies awarded defense contracts. In 1946 President Truman appointed a Civil Rights Committee, and in 1948, following its recommendations, issued executive orders demanding racial integration in the armed services and federal civil service system (Klarman, 2007; McMahon, 2000). In the decade following the War, many Northern states passed civil rights laws. Professional sports teams became racially integrated. Nevertheless, Democratic Senators from Southern states were still in a position to block federal civil rights legislation attacking segregation.

President Truman's endorsement of a federal civil rights law led to a schism in the Democratic Party, with Southern "Dixiecrats" running their own candidate in the 1948 presidential election.

For Northern and Western Democratic party leaders, therefore – as well as advocacy groups seeking racial equality – the courts remained the most hopeful mechanism for projecting federal authority into Southern states. In a 1950 case challenging Interstate Commerce Commission regulations that mandated racial segregation in interstate railroad trains, President Truman's Department of Justice urged the Supreme Court to overrule *Plessy v Ferguson* (Pacelle, 2003: 70). The Department made a related argument in *Brown v Board of Education* when it first reached the Court in late 1952 (Id. at 72), as did President Eisenhower's Department of Justice when the Court reheard the case in 1953 (Ibid.; Clayton, 1992). Thus, when the Supreme Court in effect overruled *Plessy* in *Brown v Board* (1954) and declared official racial segregation in public schools unconstitutional, the justices were reflecting a moral conviction that a great many national political leaders shared but were still unable to implement through congressional legislation.[31] Strong majorities of non-Southern whites approved of the decision (Murakami, 2008: 23). A contrary decision, or even a nondecision, could well have been extremely damaging to the Court's reputation.

Of course, as Gerald Rosenberg (1991) has emphasized, the Supreme Court's 1954 decision in *Brown v Board* did not bring an end to racial segregation. Despite the Court's gradualist pronouncement about enforcement of *Brown*,[32] Southern white opposition was bitter, intense, and persistent. By 1963, in the eleven states of the former Confederacy, only 1 percent of black students attended school with whites (Rosenberg, 1991: 50, 345–47). Because it has no army of enforcement officials to deploy, the Supreme Court was incapable of bringing about social changes that were so passionately opposed by so many and their local political leaders. Significant integration did not occur in those states until the latter half the 1960s, after Congress – responding to the vivid grassroots Civil Rights Movement – enacted civil rights legislation, mandated withdrawal of federal education funds from recalcitrant school districts, and authorized further aid for districts that cooperated.

Nevertheless, it can be argued that the Supreme Court's decision was in fact consequential. *Brown v Board* prompted many school officials in border states to dismantle segregation, particularly in large cities such as Baltimore, Washington, DC, and St. Louis – albeit with only moderate immediate results in terms of classroom

[31] Michael Klarman (2004: 450) writes that despite doubts that the decision was compelled by the text and history of the Fourteenth Amendment, "By 1954, segregation seemed like such an egregious evil to the nation's cultural elite that the justices simply could not make themselves sustain it."

[32] Fearing Southern resistance, the Court's remedial order opted for gradualism: compliance should be accomplished "with all deliberate speed" under the supervision of lower federal courts – which meant "if and when lawyers can be found brave enough to sue each local southern school district in those courts and if the southern-born white judges are inclined to issue strong desegregation orders" (Klarman, 2004)."

integration (Tushnet, 1994: 175). *Brown v Board* prompted civil rights groups in the North and Midwest to pressure and sue school districts to remedy "de facto" segregation stemming from residential segregation (Sugrue, 2008: 450–463). By the early 1960s, *Brown v Board* – a centerpiece in law school casebooks – was thought by many to have inspired hundreds of law students to embark on careers dedicated to the use of litigation to pursue policy goals. It certainly provided a template for subsequent successful rights claims in the courts by women, ethnic minorities, handicapped people, and gays and lesbians.

There is considerable debate about whether the Court's decision in *Brown* directly inspired Southern blacks to mount the now-famous public protests against racial segregation in the late 1950s and early 1960s (Rosenberg, 1994; Garrow, 1994; Klarman, 1994; Tushnet, 1994). However, the conclusion that I draw from that literature is that *Brown* did contribute to the Civil Rights Movement. Klarman (2004: 403) writes that the Court's ruling "furthered the hope and the conviction that fundamental racial change was possible." The hope and justification provided by *Brown* was prominent in the minds of the leaders of the 1956–1957 Montgomery, Alabama, bus boycott, which is widely regarded as having inspired the mass black protests that constituted the Civil Rights Movement.[33] *Brown* also provided the precedent for a 1956 U.S. District Court decision (affirmed by the Supreme Court) that held state and local bus segregation laws unconstitutional[34] – a court decision, Coleman, Nee, and Rubinowitz (2005: 683–684) demonstrate, that provided crucial legal and moral support for the boycott leaders and participants.

Moreover, Klarman (2007) argues, *Brown* played a significant role by inspiring the fierce and violent Southern white backlash that in turn stimulated national television coverage, ever-larger civil rights demonstrations, and shifts in public attitudes that finally inspired Congress to enact the landmark Civil Rights Act of 1964 and Voting Rights Act of 1965.[35] The causal link, to be sure, is not uncontested, as it was the non-violent public demonstrations by civil rights activists that were the immediate trigger for the ascendance of openly defiant white supremacist politicians and police and vigilante violence (Rosenberg, 1994). However, U.S, District Court school desegregation orders implementing *Brown* played a role in stimulating the hostile white backlash. They deeply threatened Southern white supremacy and prompted political leaders in many Southern counties and state capitals to openly defy the federal courts and rally further antagonism to integration.

---

[33] Garrow (1994) cites contemporaneous remarks by Martin Luther King Jr. and subsequent interviews with Rosa Parks and other black leaders to that effect.

[34] *Browder v Gale* (1956).

[35] Klarman (2007: 176) reports, "The percentage of Americans who deemed civil rights to be the nation's most urgent issue rose from 4 percent before Birmingham [where in 1963 news cameras filmed law enforcement officials unleashing police dogs and fire hoses on non-violent demonstrators] to 52 percent afterward." (For detailed supporting data, see Rosenberg, 1991: 130.) Soon thereafter, President Kennedy announced much more stringent civil rights proposals.

Busing for Balance. Another fateful backlash was stimulated by the Supreme Court's decisions in the 1970s, which authorized and encouraged federal district courts not only in the South but in many Northern and Western cities to order citywide busing programs to offset neighborhood de facto segregation and promote racial balance in public schools.[36] Although far from being the sole cause of "white flight" to suburban and private schools, these extremely controversial busing orders were undoubtedly a significant contributing force (Armor, 1978, 1980; Rossell & Armor, 1996). White flight crushed the dream of racially integrated education for huge numbers of poor inner city black children. Lacking the power to create new metropolitan school governance and finance systems that would eliminate the economically stratified city-suburb divide, in 1974 the Court acquiesced in that divide by rejecting mandatory city-suburb busing remedies.[37] For in launching the busing-for-balance remedy phase, the Court lacked the widespread popular and political support that had bolstered the legitimacy of the *Brown* ruling. Therefore, those decisions were consequential, but not in the ways the justices had intended.

Griggs v Duke Power. The epochal U.S. Civil Rights Act of 1964 forbade employers from discriminating on the basis of race in employment decisions. Facing stiff opposition, however, Congress built into the statute protections for existing seniority plans and merit-based employment decisions. Moreover, instead of creating a powerful enforcement agency, Congress left enforcement of the Act primarily to private lawsuits; at first, this limited the law's power, as it is often very difficult for a black worker to prove in court that an employer's decision not to hire, promote, or retain him was based on a negative racial judgment rather than a legitimate qualitative assessment of his ability. For example, a group of black laborers at a Duke Power Company facility in North Carolina claimed in court that they had been precluded from a transfer to more desirable positions because of their race. The real reason, the company responded, was that those workers lacked a high school diploma or had failed a written test, both long-standing criteria for the positions sought. The U.S. District Court rejected the plaintiffs' claim, noting that there was no proof that the company had adopted its educational and testing criteria for racial reasons. The Civil Rights Act, the Court noted, explicitly authorizes use of "any professionally developed ability test" that is not "designed, intended or used to discriminate because of race."

Nevertheless, the U.S. Supreme Court, as encouraged by the Nixon Administration Department of Justice (Pacelle, 2003: 120), reversed the lower-court judgment. In *Griggs v Duke Power* (1971), the Court interpreted the Civil Rights Act to proscribe

---

[36] *Swann v Charlotte-Mecklenberg Bd. of Education* (1971); *Keyes v Denver School District* (1973).
[37] *Milliken v Bradley* (1974). Had *Milliken v. Bradley* been decided otherwise, it could quickly have led to city-suburb busing orders in many metropolitan areas, which could well have instigated an even more intense political backlash that ended up curtailing the power of the Court itself (Kagan, 1983).

"not only overt discrimination but also practices that are fair in form, but discriminatory in operation. The touchstone is business necessity. If an employment practice which operates to exclude Negroes cannot be shown to be related to job performance, the practice is prohibited." Moreover, if a test or criterion produces racially disparate outcomes in the employer's workforce, the Court indicated, the burden falls on the employer to produce data proving that the test is in fact "job related." The Court's requirement that the employer validate the test with data comes from guidelines promulgated by the Equal Employment Opportunity Commission, which – the Court said – require great deference from the judiciary. (The Court repeatedly used this technique – endorsing, and hence giving judicially enforceable weight to, expansive administrative interpretations of the Civil Rights Act – in various areas of civil rights policy) (Melnick, 2010).

The Court's innovative reading of the Civil Rights Act in *Griggs v Duke Power* gave that statute more potency than the language its drafters managed to get through the Senate in 1964. The *Griggs* precedent enabled civil rights lawyers to launch powerful class-action lawsuits based on proof of "racially disparate outcomes" rather than elusive proof of discriminatory intent. For many large employers, uncertain they could actually prove that a test or job criterion accurately predicted job performance, *Griggs* created incentives to institute affirmative action programs that guaranteed a proportionate share of promotions for black employees. More generally, the *Griggs* doctrine gave large corporations strong incentives to formally specify hiring and promotion criteria along with a more formal approach to rating job performance (so that employers could test the relationship between test scores, for example, and job performance).

A contrary decision in *Griggs* could have hobbled the civil rights employment litigation industry in its temporal infancy and slowed black employees' access to more desirable positions. By the early 1980s, when a more conservative Court began to shift the burden of proof in disparate impact cases back to plaintiffs, that civil rights litigation industry was well-established, and politically influential. In 1991, a Democratic Congress amended the Civil Rights Act to restore the *Griggs* interpretation, returning the burden of proof of "job necessity" to the employer in disparate racial-impact cases.

Affirmative Action. The Court's expansive reading of the Civil Rights Act in *Weber v Kaiser Aluminum & Chemical Co* (1979) was equally consequential. Brian Weber, a white employee, was denied access to an apprenticeship program. His employer and his factory's labor union, seeking to improve racial balance, had instituted a policy of alternating acceptances to the apprenticeship program from separate white and black seniority lists. In consequence, the opening Weber sought was filled by a black employee with less seniority. The U.S. District Court and the U.S. Court of Appeals decided in Weber's favor, holding that the legislative history of the Civil Rights Act, as well as its basic textual command, precluded employment criteria that explicitly disfavored whites as well as those that discriminated against blacks.

The Supreme Court, however, reversed – again, as urged by the Department of Justice. Justice Brennan's majority opinion held that, "Title VII's prohibition in § 703(a) and (d) against racial discrimination does not condemn all private, voluntary, race-conscious affirmative action plans."[38]

The Court's decision in *Weber* reinforced the federal Office of Contract Compliance's (OFCC) guidelines, which required recipients of federal contracts and grants to institute affirmative action programs that set specific targets and timetables for increasing minority representation in all sectors of the grantee's or contractee's workforce. A contrary decision in *Weber* would have undermined or hampered the OFCC's program, through which affirmative action programs spread into most major corporations and universities as well as many local governments.

The *Weber* case turned on competing interpretations of the Civil Right Acts. More famous, however, were the *constitutional* challenges to government affirmative action programs brought by white men. The Court was divided; its initial decisions were wavering or inconclusive.[39] In *Regents of the University of California v Bakke* (1978), with eight justices evenly split 4:4, Justice Powell wrote an opinion holding that a medical school's preferential admissions policy that included numerical race-based quotas violated the equal protection clause of the Fourteenth Amendment. On the other hand, Powell said, universities could take race into account on a case-by-case basis in order to produce more diverse student bodies. Powell's opinion enabled state universities to continue to employ racial preferences as long as they were subtle about it; that is, eschewed obvious quotas and did not publicize how much extra weight they accorded minority applicants in the competition for scarce slots.

In the 1980s, continuing its ambivalence, the Court upheld some racially preferential employment policies in public schools and agencies, but struck down others.[40] The overall effect, like that of the *Bakke* decision, was to leave the many existing affirmative action programs in the public sector undisturbed. At the end of the 1980s and in the 1990s, with more Reagan appointees on the Court, a majority announced a very strict standard of review for affirmative action cases.[41] However, this apparently

---

[38] Justice Rehnquist's dissent in *Weber* notes that, "In the opening speech of the formal Senate debate on the bill, Senator Humphrey [the chief sponsor of the Act] addressed the main concern of Title VII's opponents, advising that not only does Title VII not require use of racial quotas, *it does not permit their use.*" Rehnquist also cited the bill's Senate floor captains Clark and Case's statements that any employer who sought to correct a history of racial discrimination "would not be obliged – *or indeed permitted* – to fire whites in order to hire Negroes, *or to prefer Negroes for future vacancies, or, once Negroes are hired, to give them special seniority rights at the expense of the white workers hired earlier.*"

[39] In *DeFunis v Odegaard* (1974), the Court declined to rule on a white law school applicant's claim that the University of Washington's admissions criteria unconstitutionally discriminated against white applicants.

[40] *Local 28 of Sheet Metal Workers v EEOC*, 478 U.S. 421 (1986); *Local 93 International Association of Firefighters v City of Cleveland*, 478 U.S. 501 (1986); *United States v Paradise*, 480 U.S. 149 (1987); *Johnson v Transportation Agency*, Santa Clara, California, 480 U.S. 616 (1987); *Wygant v Jackson Bd of Ed.*, 476 U.S. 267 (1986).

[41] *City of Richmond v Croson* (1989); *Adarand Constructors v Pena* (1995).

clear line was blurred in 2003 in two 5:4 decisions involving preferential minority admissions to the University of Michigan, whereby the Court struck down a preferential program for undergraduate applicants[42] but upheld a more individualized program for law school admissions.[43] Then in 2007, again by a bare majority, the Court forbade two local public school districts from using racial identity to assign students to schools in order to increase racial balance – although Justice Kennedy's concurring opinion suggested that seeking racial balance was important and that some uses of race as a criterion might be constitutionally acceptable.[44]

Overall, then, although casting doubt on the constitutionality of governmental programs that favor racial minorities, nobody can be sure the Court's closely divided rulings have firmly and finally closed that door. The Court's ongoing inconsistency and ambivalence reflects the sharp difference of opinion among political elites and the inability of either political party to establish sufficient dominance to appoint a supermajority of justices favoring either position. In *Bakke*, a shift of one vote on the Court could have dealt affirmative action a constitutional deathblow. Instead, the Court created an atmosphere of legal uncertainty that enabled affirmative action programs to persist in substantial swaths of higher education, public employment, and governmental contracting with minority firms. Affirmative action plans, nowadays changed by an emphasis on "diversity" stimulated by Justice Powell's opinion in *Bakke*, have disappointed many of their initial proponents. They have done little for the large numbers of young blacks who drop out of high school and acquire prison records (Pager, 2005). However, affirmative action policies have given thousands of minority students access to elite universities and graduate schools (Bowen & Bok, 1998) and helped make public employment a major pathway for integration and upward mobility for hundreds of thousands of minority men and women. The Court's ambivalence, therefore, has in itself been consequential.

UNINTENDED CONSEQUENCES

As stated in the introduction to this chapter, an active and consequential high court operates on politically unpredictable and hence risky terrain. Its decisions may trigger surprising levels of anger and resistance. The consequences of important decisions may ripple out in directions far from those intended or desired by the judges who issued the rulings. Rather than playing a steadying or healing role by "settling" controversial issues, a high court may end up playing the role of exacerbating political and social cleavages. We have already touched on some of these unintended[45] consequences.

---

[42] *Gratz v Bollinger* (2003).

[43] *Grutter v. Bollinger*, 539 U.S. 306 (2003).

[44] *Parents Involved in Community Schools v Seattle School District No. 1* (2007).

[45] In labeling some consequences "unintended," I cannot be positive, of course, what the justices who voted for a decision actually predicted or intended. I simply infer that intent from the justifications

For example, the U.S. Supreme Court's 1962 and 1963 decisions banning mandatory Bible reading and prayers in public schools, by thrusting the Court into the role of mediating between religious and secular tensions, led millions of families to abandon the public schools for religiously oriented private schools – intensifying for many children the parochialism that the Supreme Court's majority had sought to reduce. As also noted previously, one of *Brown v Board of Education*'s most important consequences was the fierce political and social backlash it helped stimulate in Southern states, intensifying white supremacist positions in politics and hence the violence of their resistance to civil rights activists. Although that intransigence swung national sentiment and congressional majorities toward support for civil rights legislation, it also cost lives and inflicted much pain on millions of Southern black families. We also noted how court-ordered busing-for-racial-balance plans in many cities contributed greatly to white flight to suburban and private schools (Armor, 1978, 1980; Rossell & Armor, 1996), thus frustrating hopes that *Brown* would lead to universal racial integration of public schools. Consider in addition three briefly stated examples of the unintended consequences of major decisions of the U.S. Supreme Court in the 1960s and 1970s.[46]

Abortion. The Supreme Court's famous *Roe v Wade* (1973) ruling was intended to free women's difficult decisions about abortion from political control, at least in the first trimester of pregnancy. The decision was very consequential. It made safe abortion services available to millions of women, often changing their lives profoundly. But the decision – as is well known – also stimulated a passionate and occasionally violent political backlash. In consequence, many state legislatures restricted access to and funding for abortions. Several years after the Court's decision, virtually no abortion services were available in many states, counties, and hospitals (Rosenberg, 1991: 189–195), and that remains true today (Finley, 2004: 404). Moreover, *Roe v Wade* enveloped the Supreme Court in a populist political storm that has not subsided after thirty-nine years. It was responsible, above all other factors, for the intense politicization of the Supreme Court appointment process, as "pro-life" and "pro-choice" advocacy groups have sought to appoint or block the appointment of justices who are likely to overturn or restrict *Roe v Wade*. Thus, *Roe v Wade* has also contributed enormously to the politicization of the Court's popular image.

Legislative Redistricting. The Supreme Court's pathbreaking one man-one vote decisions in the 1960s[47] thrust the Court into a new role in governance, regulating

---

offered in the majority opinions. I should add that unintended is not always the same thing as unforeseeable. Legal advocates for the losing side may well have warned the Court about the possibility of negative reactions, but in rejecting those negative scenarios, the Court's majority presumably assigned them a lower probability than did those legal advocates. What is often unintended therefore is that the probability of a full-blown negative scenario turned out to be much higher than the majority justices expected.

[46] Thanks to Martin Shapiro for his comments on this topic.

[47] *Baker v Carr*, 369 U.S. 186 (1962); *Gray v Sanders*, 372 U.S. 368 (1963); *Wesbury v Sanders*, 376 U.S. 1 (1964); *Reynolds v Sims*, 377 U.S. 533 (1964).

an important aspect of the electoral process – a role continued in its subsequent decisions on political campaign finance. The 1960s "reapportionment decisions" in effect required redrawing of legislative districts for elections to both state legislatures and Congress after each decennial census. The Court's goal, of course, was to correct severe malapportionment in many states, ensuring that each citizen's vote, regardless of district, counted roughly equally. Relatedly, the Supreme Court's interpretations of the 1965 Voting Rights Act compelled governments to draw electoral district lines that did not restrict racial or ethnic minorities' chances of electing candidates of their race or ethnicity (Thernstrom, 1987).

Taken together, both lines of decisions, although succeeding in achieving their immediate reapportionment goals, stimulated the development of sophisticated computerized technologies for electoral line drawing. Political party leaders in state legislatures have employed those techniques for repeated partisan gerrymandering, carefully reshaping districts to include strong majorities of their party members, thereby creating "safe seats" for their incumbent legislators. The consequence – contrary to the values underlying the Supreme Court reapportionment decisions – has been the *erosion* of governmental representativeness, as minority party voters in a large number of congressional and state legislative districts are effectively disenfran- chised. Further, the proliferation of essentially one-party districts has enhanced the importance of the dominant party's primary elections, which in turn has fostered the election of less centrist candidates and produced much more politically polarized and dysfunctional legislatures.

When Chief Justice Earl Warren said he thought *Baker v Carr* was the most important decision the Court had made under his leadership (Powe, 2000: 200), he may have been right, but he probably would not have been happy with the unforeseen ways in which the redistricting processes he stimulated have worked out. Ironically, some of the most consequential Supreme Court decisions of the last decade have been those in which the Court declined to interpret the Equal Protection Clause to impose meaningful restrictions on politically partisan gerrymandering.[48]

The "Culture Wars." In addition to *Roe v Wade*, a number of other Supreme Court decisions have made the Court a fulcrum in the so-called culture wars between lib- eral elites and religious conservatives that have been a salient feature of American politics for the last thirty years. Consider in this regard the Courts' decisions not only forbidding prayer in public schools but also striking down an Alabama statute autho- rizing a moment of silence for meditation and voluntary prayer;[49] its decisions cre- ating substantial First Amendment protection for the pornography that has flooded American society (*Roth v U.S.*, 1966; *Miller v California*, 1973); and more recently, in ruling that the Constitution protects homosexual adults rights to engage in inti- mate sexual relations (*Lawrence v Texas*, 2003). In the minds of many conservatives,

[48] *Vieth v Jubilirer* (2004).
[49] *Wallace v Jaffree* (1985). Thanks to Sandy Levinson for reminding me of this case and its significance.

those decisions helped make the Court a negative symbol of a national political and cultural elite hostile to Christian religion and values. In response, Christian law schools and legal advocacy organizations have been established. Conservative politicians regularly denounce "judicial activism" (at least by politically liberal judges), and dramatic political battles surround each Supreme Court nomination.

As in our earlier discussion of the administrative regulatory state, criminal justice, and civil rights, Supreme Court decisions were not the sole cause of the unintended consequences summarized in this section. The political and cultural conflicts mentioned probably would have occurred anyway. However, the Court and its decisions were in fact salient factors in all of these developments. The important lesson is that a powerful court cannot easily control or even foresee the manifold responses to its consequential decisions. For some commentators, the lesson is that judges should be wary of making sweeping constitutional rulings, using their opinions to limit the precedential meaning of their rulings to a limited range of situations (Sunstein, 1999). Over time, however, as regime theory teaches, political leaders and ideological activists will invite or even compel the Court to make decisions on important and controversial issues. Often the Court will do so, with both intended and unintended consequences.

CONCLUSION

In the three broad areas of law discussed, the Supreme Court's decisions wrought enormous changes in the constitutional ground rules of American federalism. The Warren Court's decisions on race, Malcolm Feeley (2007) wrote, "transformed a constitutional structure that had been anchored in deference to the states into one that imposed a single national norm for the equal protection of the laws."[50] One could say that the Court did the same with respect to the due process clause as applied to state and local criminal justice systems. The late New Deal Court did the same with respect to congressional authority to enact nationwide regulatory norms and social benefit programs, as elaborated and implemented by national administrative agencies.

Consistently with the arguments of regime theorists, these judicial revisions of the Constitution were not achieved without instigation or support from national political leaders, the legal profession, and civil society organizations. However, the Court's cooperation with those political sponsors and legal allies, and in some cases the Court's leadership, were vitally important. Moreover, its decisions were not entirely foreordained by political forces, and in that sense the Court was an independent

---

[50] That is not to say that the single national norm is wholly static, clear, or uniform, as interpretations or applications of it vary and change as a result of both legislation and court decisions. Feeley's point is that the Supreme Court's rulings and endorsement of congressional civil rights laws establish the primacy of the Court interpretations of the Fourteenth Amendment and Congressional civil rights law; primacy, that is, in constraining and influencing state and local law regarding race relations.

partner, not merely an agent. In that sense, the Court was in itself a consequential participant in legal change and national governance.

The Court's decisions also resonated in the domains of economic and social life. By reallocating power from states and localities to the federal government, the Court cleared away constitutional impediments that had theretofore limited or inhibited governmental social benefit programs, labor rights, and regulatory restrictions on the harmful externalities of market processes. Similarly, the Court's criminal due process decisions reallocated power from state and local police, prosecutors, and penal institutions to the federal courts – all of which had effects on the ground, enhancing the rights of criminal suspects in their interactions with police and local criminal justice systems. The Court's decisions on race, statutory as well as constitutional, both limited the discretion of employers and contributed to amelioration of particularly blatant and degrading aspects of racial inequality.

Viewed in terms of comparative and theoretical inquiry concerning the political consequence of judicial power, the U.S. Supreme Court decisions discussed here exemplify two additional kinds of roles high courts can play in national political systems. The Court's late New Deal decisions indicate that high courts can adapt older constitutions to help governments meet the imperatives of managing more complex, interconnected, and dynamic economic systems. The Court's criminal due process and race-relations decisions indicate how high courts can help national political elites impose more progressive norms on conservative regions or segments of the polity.

On the other hand, as we have seen, such consequential judicial decisions can have unintended and often negative consequences, as well. When judges rule on fundamental conflicts that political leaders have been reluctant to take on directly, they may encounter resistance, evasion, or political backlash from the very social or political groups the political leaders had not wanted to antagonize. The broader the range of roles high courts assume in the governing process, the more they confront the same dilemmas and risks that confront other powerful political actors – and the more they are likely to learn (or should learn) to consider the politician's prudential values along with the judge's traditional legal values.

REFERENCES

Ackerman, Bruce (1991) *We the People, Volume I: Foundations.* Cambridge, MA: Harvard University Press.

Armor, David J. (1980) "White Flight and the Future of School Desegregation," in Walter Stephan & Joseph Feagan, eds., *School Desegregation: Past, Present and Future.* New York: Plenum Books, pp. 187–226.

———. (1978) *White Flight, Demographic Transition and the Future of School Integration.* Santa Monica. Santa Barbara: RAND Institute Paper Series.

Badaracco, Joseph L. (1985) *Loading The Dice: A Five Country Study of Vinyl Chloride Regulation.* Boston: Harvard Business School Press.

Bowen, William & Derek Bok (1998) *The Shape of the River: Long Term Consequences of Considering Race in College and University Admissions.* Princeton: Princeton University Press.

Bradley, Craig (1993) *The Failure of the Criminal Procedure Revolution.* Philadelphia: Pennsylvania University Press.

Chen, Jim (2006) "The Story of *Wickard v Filburn*," in M. Dorf, ed., *Constitutional Law Stories.* New York: Foundation Press, pp. 69–118.

Clayton, Cornell W. (1992) *The Politics of Justice: The Attorney General and the Making of Legal Policy.* Armonk, NY: M. E. Sharpe.

Coleman, C., L. Nee, & L. Rubinowitz (2005) "Social Movements and Social-Change Litigation: Synergy in the Montgomery Bus Protest," *Law & Soc. Inquiry* 30(4): 663–701.

Coleman, James et al. (1975) *Trends in School Integration, 1968–1973.* U.S. Department of Health, Education & Welfare.

Cover, Robert (1975) *Justice Accused: Antislavery & The Judicial Process.* New Haven: Yale University Press.

Croley, Steven (2008) *Regulation and Public Interests: The Possibility of Good Regulatory Government.* Princeton: Princeton University Press.

Cushman, Barry (1998). *Rethinking the New Deal Court: The Structure of a Constitutional Revolution.* New York: Oxford University Press.

Dahl, Robert A. (1957) "Decision-Making in a Democracy: The Supreme Court as a National Policy-Maker," *Journal of Public Law* 6: 279.

Dolbeare, Kenneth & Philip Hammond (1971) *The School Prayer Decisions: From Court Policy to Local Practice.* Chicago: University of Chicago Press.

Dudziak, Mary (1988) "Desegregation as a Cold War Imperative," *Stanford L. Rev.* 41: 61.

Dwyer, John (1990) "The Pathology of Symbolic Legislation," *Ecology Law Quarterly* 17: 233.

Epp, Charles R. (2009) *Making Rights Real: Activists, Bureaucrats, and the Creation of the Legalistic State.* Chicago: University of Chicago Press.

———. (1998) *The Rights Revolution: Lawyers, Activists, and Supreme Courts in Comparative Perspective.* Chicago: University of Chicago Press.

Epstein, Lee Jack Knight & Olga Shvetsova (2001) "The Role of Constitutional Courts in the Establishment and Maintenance of Democratic Systems of Government," *Law & Society Rev.* 35: 117–164.

Feeley, Malcolm M. (2007) "The Black Basis of Constitutional Development," in Harry N. Scheiber, ed., *Earl Warren and the Warren Court.* Lanham: Lexington Books.

Feeley, Malcolm M. & Edward Rubin (1998) *Judicial Policy Making and the Modern State: How the Courts Reformed America's Prisons.* New York: Cambridge University Press.

Friedman, Lawrence M. (1993) *Crime and Punishment in American History.* New York: Basic Books.

Finley, Lucinda (2004) "The Story of *Roe v. Wade*," in Michael Dorf, ed., *Constitutional Law Stories.* New York, NY: Foundation Press, pp. 359–406.

Garland, David (2001) *The Culture of Control: Crime and Social Order in Contemporary Society.* New York: Oxford University Press.

Garrow, David J. (1994) "Hopelessly Hollow History: Revisionist Devaluing of Brown v. Board of Education," *Virginia Law Review* 80: 151–160.

Gash, Alison & Angelo Gonzales (2008) "School Prayer," in N. Persily, J. Citrin, & P. Egan, eds., *Public Opinion and Constitutional Controversy.* New York: Oxford University Press, pp. 62–79.

Graber, Mark (1993) "The Nonmajoritarian Difficulty: Legislative Deference to the Judiciary," *Studies in Amer. Pol. Dev.* 7: XX.

Ho, Daniel & Kevin Quinn (2010) "Did a Switch in Time Save Nine?" *J. of Legal Analysis* 2: 1–44.

Hollis-Brusky, Amanda (2011) "Support Structures and Constitutional Change: Teles, Southworth, and the Conservative Legal Movement," *Law & Social Inquiry* 35: 516–36.

Kagan, Robert A. (2007) "Globalization and Legal Change: The 'Americanization' of European Law?" *Regulation & Governance* 1: 99.

———. (2001) *Adversarial Legalism: The American Way of Law.* Cambridge, MA: Harvard University Press.

———. (1983) "What if Abe Fortas Had Been More Discreet?" in Nelson Polsby, ed., *What If? Explorations in Social Science Fiction.* Albany, GA: Lewis Publishing.

Keck, Thomas M. (2007) "Party, Policy, or Duty: Why Does the Supreme Court Invalidate Federal Statutes?" *American Political Science Review* 101: 321–38.

Klarman, Michael (2007) *Unfinished Business: Racial Equality in American History.* New York: Oxford University Press.

———. (2004) *From Jim Crow to Civil Rights: The Supreme Court and the Struggle for Racial Equality.* New York: Oxford University Press.

Leo, Richard (2008) *Police Interrogation and American Justice.* Cambridge, MA: Harvard University Press.

Mashaw, Jerry (2006) "*Motor Vehicle Mfgrs. Assn v. State Farm Mutual Auto Insurance*," in P. Strauss, ed., *Administrative Law Stories.* New York: Foundation Press, pp. 334–397.

Mashaw, Jerry L. & Daniel Harfst (1991) *The Struggle for Auto Safety.* Cambridge, MA: Harvard University Press.

McCubbins, Matthew, Roger Noll, & Barry Weingast (1989) "Structure and Process; Politics and Policy: Administrative Arrangements and the Political Control of Agencies," *Virginia Law Review* 75: 431.

McMahon, Kevin (2000) "Constitutional Vision and Supreme Court Decisions: Roosevelt on Race," *Studies in American Political Development* 14: 20.

Melnick, R. Shep (2010) "The Great Debate over the Civil Rights State," paper prepared for delivery at the Western Political Science Association Meeting, San Francisco, April 1, 2010.

Mendeloff, John (1987) *The Dilemma of Rulemaking for Toxic Substances.* Cambridge, MA: MIT Press.

Muir, W. K., Jr. (1973) *Law and Attitude Change.* Chicago: University of Chicago Press.

Murakami, Michael (2008) "Desegregation," in N. Persily, J. Citrin, & P. Egan, eds., *Public Opinion and Constitutional Controversy.* New York: Oxford University Press, pp. 18–40.

Pacelle, Richard L., Jr. (2003) *Between Law & Politics: The Solicitor General and the Structuring of Race, Gender, and Reproductive Rights Litigation.* College Station, TX: Texas A & M University Press.

Pager, Devah (2005) "Double Jeopardy: Race, Crime and Getting a Job," *Wisconsin L Rev* 2005(1): 617–662.

Peretti, Terry Jennings (1999) *In Defense of a Political Court.* Princeton: Princeton University Press.

Persily, Nathaniel, Jack Citrin, & Patrick Egan, eds. (2008) *Public Opinion and Constitutional Controversy.* New York: Oxford University Press.

Pickerill, J. Mitchell & Cornell Clayton (2004) "The Rehnquist Court and the Political Dynamics of Federalism," *Perspectives on Politics* 2: 233–48.

Polsby, Nelson, ed. (1983) *What If? Explorations in Social Science Fiction.* Albany, GA: Lewis Publishing.

Powe, Lucas A., Jr. (2000) *The Warren Court and American Politics.* Cambridge, MA: Belknap Press of Harvard University Press.

Orfield, Myron, Jr. (1987) "The Exclusionary Rule and Deterrence: An Empirical Study of Chicago Narcotics Officers," *U. Chicago Law Rev.* 54: 1016.

Rosenberg, Gerald (1994) "Brown is Dead! Long Live Brown!: The Endless Attempt to Canonize a Case," *Virginia Law Review* 80:161.

_____. (1991) *The Hollow Hope: Can Courts Bring about Social Change?* Chicago: University of Chicago Press.

Rossell, Christine & David Armor (1996) "The Effectiveness of School Desegregation Plans, 1968–1991," *American Politics Research* 24: 267–302.

Shapiro, Martin (1988) *Who Guards the Guardians? Judicial Control of Administration.* Athens, GA: University of Georgia Press.

Silverstein, Gordon (2009) *Law's Allure: How Law Shapes, Constrains, Saves, and Kills Politics.* New York: Cambridge University Press.

_____. (2003) "Globalization and the Rule of Law: A Machine that Runs of Itself?" *International Journal of Constitutional Law* 1: 427–45.

Simon, Jonathan (2007) *Governing Through Crime: How the War on Crime Transformed American Democracy and Created a Culture of Fear.* New York: Oxford University Press.

Stewart, Richard (1975) "The Reformation of American Administrative Law," *Harvard Law Review* 88: 1669.

Strauss, Peter (2006) *"Citizens to Preserve Overton Park v Volpe* – of Politics and Law, Young Lawyers and the Highway Goliath," in Peter Strauss, ed., *Administrative Law Stories.* New York: Foundation Press, pp. 258–332.

Sugrue, Thomas J. (2008) *Sweet Land of Liberty: The Forgotten Struggle for Civil Rights in the North.* New York: Random House.

Sunstein, Cass (1999) *One Case at a Time: Judicial Minimalism on the Supreme Court.* Cambridge: Harvard University Press.

Teles, Steven M. (2008) *The Rise of the Conservative Legal Movement.* Princeton: Princeton University Press.

Thernstrom, Abigail (1987) *Whose Votes Count? Affirmative Action and Minority Voting Rights.* Cambridge, MA: Harvard University Press.

Tushnet, Mark (2006)"The Supreme Court and the National Political Order: Collaboration and Confrontation," in Ronald Kahn & Ken Kersch, eds, *The Supreme Court and American Political Development,* Kansas U Press, pp. 117–138.

Walker, Samuel (1993) *Taming the System: The Control of Discretion in Criminal Justice, 1950–1990.* New York: Oxford University Press.

Whittington, Keith (2008) *Political Foundations of Judicial Supremacy: The Presidency, the Supreme Court, and Constitutional Leadership in U.S. History* (Princeton University Press).

Whitman, James (2005) *Harsh Justice: Criminal Punishment and the Widening Divide between America and Europe.* Oxford University Press.

Witt, John Fabian (2007) *Patriots and Cosmopolitans: Hidden Histories of American Law.* Harvard University Press.

COURT CASES

Adarand Constructors v Pena, 515 U.S. 200 (1995)

Abingdon School District v Schempp, 374 U.S. 203 (1964)

Aguilar v Texas. 378 U.S. 108 (1964)

Argersinger v Hamlin, 407 U.S. 25 (1972)

Barron v Baltimore, 32 U.S. 243 (1833)

Benton v. Maryland, 395 U.S. 794 (1969)

Browder v. Gale, 142 F. Supp. 707 (1956), affirmed, Gayle v. Browder, 352 U.S. 903 (1956)

Brown v Board of Education of Topeka, Kansas, 347 U.S. 483 (1954)

Brown v. Board of Education (Brown II), 349 U.S. 294 (1955)

California v. Robinson, 370 U.S. 660 (1962)

Chimel v California, 395 U.S. 752 (1969)

Citizens to Preserve Overton Park v Volpe

City of Richmond v. Croson, 488 U.S. 469 (1989)

Civil Rights Cases, 109 U.S. 3 (1883)

DeFunis v Odegaard, 416 U.S. 312 (1974)

Duncan v. Louisiana, 391 U.S. 145 (1968)

Engel v Vitale, 370 U.S. 421 (1962)

Fay v. Noia 372 U.S. 391 (1963)

Gideon v. Wainwright, 372 U.S. 335 (1963)

Gratz v Bollinger, 539 U.S. 244 (2003)

Griggs v Duke Power Co. 401 U.S. 424 (1971)

Grutter v. Bollinger, 539 U.S. 306 (2003)

Helvering v. Davis, 301 U.S. 619 (1937)

In re Gault, 387 U.S. 1428 (1967)

Keyes v Denver School District 413 U.S. 189 (1973)

Lawrence v. Texas, 539 U.S. 558 (2003)

Mapp v Ohio, 367 U.S. 643 (1961)

Miller v California, 413 U.S. 15 (1973)

Milliken v Bradley, 418 U.S. 717 (1974)

Miranda v. Arizona, 384 U.S. 436 (1966)

Monell v. Department of Social Services, 436 U.S. 658 (1978)

Monroe v. Pape 365 U.S. 167 (1961)

Motor Vehicle Mfrs Ass'n of the US v State Farm Mutual Automobile Ins, Co, 463 U.S. 29 (1983)

Nebbia v. New York, 291 U.S. 502 (1934)

N.L.R.B. v. Jones & Laughlin Steel Corp, 301 U.S. 1 (1937)

Palko v. Connecticut 302 U.S. 319 (1937)

Parents Involved in Community Schools v Seattle School District No. 1, 551 U.S. __ (2007)

Plessy v Ferguson, 163 U.S. 537 (1896)

Pointer v Texas (1965) 380 U.S. 400 (1965)

Powell v. Alabama, 287 U.S. 45 (1932)

Regents of the University of California v Bakke, 438 U.S. 265 (1978)

Roe v Wade, 410 U.S. 113 (1973)

Roth v. United States, 354 U.S. 476 (1957)

Scenic Hudson Preservation Council et al v Federal Power Commission, 354 F. 2d. 608 (2nd Cir., 1965)

Schechter Poultry Corp v U.S., 295 U.S. 495 (1935)

The Slaughterhouse Cases, 83 U.S. 36 (1873)

Smith v. Allwright, 321 U.S. 469 (1944)

Steward Machine Co. v. Davis 301 U.S. 548 (1937)

Sunshine Anthracite Coal Co. v. Adkins, 310 U.S. 381 (1940)

Swann v Charlotte-Mecklenberg Bd. of Ed., 402 U.S. 1 (1971)

Trop v Dulles 356 U.S. 86 (1958)

United Steelworkers of America v. Weber 443 U.S. 193 (1979)

U.S. v Cruikshank, 92 U.S. 542 (1885)
U.S. v Harris, 106 U.S. 629 (1882)
U.S. v. Butler, 297 U.S. 1 (1936)
Vieth v Jubilirer (2004) 541 U.S. 267
Wallace v Jaffree, 472 U.S. 38 (1985)
West Coast Hotel Co. v. Parrish, 300 U.S. 379 (1937)
Wickard v. Filburn, 317 U.S. 111 (1942)
Wygant v Jackson Bd. of Ed, 476 U.S. 267 (1986)
Yakus v. United States, 321 U.S. 414 (1944)

9

Judicial Constitution Making in a Divided Society
The Israeli Case

Amnon Reichman[*]

During the mid-1990's, Israel experienced a legal and political transformation known as "the constitutional revolution" (Gavison 1997: 27; Hirschl 1997: 136; Salzberger & Voigt 2002: 490; Edrey 2005: 78; Sapir 2008: 4). In essence, this "revolution" entailed the empowerment of the judiciary to exercise constitutional judicial review over primary legislation when such legislation does not comply with the requirements set forth in Israel's Basic Laws. This revolution, although on the basis of two Basic Laws enacted by the Knesset in 1992 (and amended in 1994), was nonetheless Court driven in the sense that the Justices of the Supreme Court in the *Bank Hamizrachi United v. Migdal Communal Village* (1995) significantly expanded the rather modest mandate given in these two Basic Laws (Gavison 1997: 95). The Supreme Court elevated the status of all Basic Laws to the constitutional sphere and denied the power of the Knesset to exempt a statute from judicial review unless it explicitly amends the Basic Laws themselves.

In this chapter, I will provide the historical background in a nutshell and then briefly sketch the legal contours of the revolution (i.e., what happened), analyze the judicial moves that brought this change about (i.e., how it happened), and hypothesize on the forces that brought this change about (i.e., why it happened the way it happened). I will then examine in brief some of the possible ramifications of the revolution for the political and legal landscape in Israel. Throughout the chapter, I will point to some general lessons that may be gleaned from the Israeli story and highlight the importance of a number of specific dynamics including the relationship between the judiciary and the legal academy; the relative prestige bestowed by the media on justices and the Supreme Court compared to the treatment of the legislature and politicians; the fragmentation of the political system; particular aspects of Israel's political economy; and of course, the attitudes and leadership of the political and legal leaders. All of these are variables worthy of examination in

[*] Faculty of Law, University of Haifa.

233

any country undergoing a constitutional transformation that is not a consequence of an acute crisis (such as the foundation of a state or the conclusion of a serious civil struggle).

The expansion of judicial power in Israel was rather remarkable in view of the original understanding of the role of the High Court in Israeli government. From the time of its establishment, the Israeli Court saw itself – and was seen by the other branches of government – as lacking the power to exercise constitutional judicial review over primary legislation (*Ziv v. Gubernick* 1948; *Bazul v. Minister of Interior* 1963). The general understanding among jurists, politicians, bureaucrats, and the media was that because Israel was still working on its Constitution (by way of enacting one Basic Law at a time), the Court was not (yet) empowered to treat these Basic Laws (or other potential sources, such as the Declaration of Independence) as supreme to ordinary statutes (*id.*). The governing legal and social norm was that as the legal sovereign, the statutes passed by the Knesset were immune from judicial review (Sapir 2008: 14). In fact, the prevailing view was that parliamentary supremacy was a foundational constitutional principle, on par with other democratic principles (such as separation of powers and commitments to basic human rights) (*"Negev" Automobile Services Station Ltd. v. State of Israel* 1983; Hofnung 1996: 595).

Lacking the constitutional power to review primary legislation, the Court's constitutional role was nonetheless far from trivial. The Court took on itself to ensure that, as applied, the Knesset statutes conformed to the unwritten (read: judge-made) constitutional principles of Israel as a Jewish and Democratic state (*Kol Ha'am Co. Ltd. v. Minister of Interior* 1953). This was achieved by two judicially developed interpretative presumptions. The first was that the Knesset did not intend its statutes to infringe basic rights unless the statute specifically empowered the relevant state agency to act in a manner infringing those rights. The second was that if and when the achievement of an important state interest by a state agency required the infringing of a basic human right, the Knesset, in empowering that state agency, would be understood to have intended that the agency exercise its assigned powers in a manner that infringed the right no more than necessary to achieve the legislative goal (*Poraz v. State of Israel* 1990). Although basic rights – with but a few exceptions[1] – were not written into law, the Israeli Court in fact created a judicial bill of rights that applied to all local and national state agencies (the administration) and limited the exercise of their powers. Consequently, despite a lack of formal constitutional judicial review, the Court has played a major role in protecting rights through administrative judicial review (Edrey 2005: 82).[2] Nevertheless, where the Knesset was clear and explicit, its statutes were beyond the purview of judges. Thus, if human rights were violated as

---

[1] A notable exception is The Law of Equal Rights for Women, 1951, and, some would say, Israel's public education system and social security scheme, which were taken in the 1950's are providing basic rights.

[2] As early as 1949, the Court has insisted that violating (some fundamental civil and political) basic rights is ultra vires the relevant state agency, unless such violation is specifically authorized by statute (*Bajerano v. Minister of Police* 1949).

a result of the explicit words of the enabling statute, the Court would not examine or challenge the constitutionality of this statute (Hofnung 1996: 590).

WHY ISRAEL HAD NO FOUNDING WRITTEN CONSTITUTION

Several factors led the State of Israel to refrain from adopting a formal constitution with strong judicial review over primary legislation: (a) political fragmentation; (b) the lack – given the particular timing of the drafting process – of an overarching incentive to ensure against a winner-takes-all; (c) the structure of the (socialist) economy; (d) the high esteem enjoyed by politicians; and (e) having more urgent matters on the political agenda.

Political Fragmentation

First and foremost, the Israeli political system was too fragmented to reach a deal on the basic values of the state (Rackman 1955: 171). Perhaps the only shared understanding regarding the Constitution was that as a constitution for the Jewish state it should be agreed on (at least tacitly) by most, if not all, of the political movements associated with the Jewish people. However, because the stakes were particularly high – a long-lasting Constitution (for a people who measure "long-lasting" by hundreds if not thousands of years) – no faction was willing to agree to a compromise (Sapir 2008: 4). Beyond the ideological conflicts, there was great uncertainty about the operation of key state institutions such as the legislature or the courts. With little modern experience to rely on (the last time the Jewish nation enjoyed territorial sovereignty was some 2,000 years earlier), different factions were unsure about the risks entailed in various compromises. Agreeing to move forward with an unwritten constitution may well have been the only viable way to move forward (Lerner, 2011: 51–108).[3]

---

[3] The first Knesset – elected in 1949 specifically to enact a written constitution – was unable to do so as no compromise could be reached on whether to include religious references (the Zionist religious parties insisted on including them (Segev 2007: 416); the United Workers Party (Mapam), one of the two strong socialist parties, categorically refused to agree to do so. Mapam, in turn, insisted on a robust set of labor rights in the constitution with a representative constitutional court. This approach was a hard sell for the small but influential (at least within the legal milieu) liberal segment, which favored the protection of classic individual rights, accompanied by U.S.-style judicial review (Freudenheim 1973: 32–37). However, efforts to protect classic individual rights in any constitution met resistance from many in Israeli security establishments – well represented among leading figures in the Workers of Israel's Party (Mapai) – who viewed Israeli Arabs with suspicion and insisted on retaining emergency powers that had been put in place by the British, at least until more peaceful times might arrive (Bechor 1996: 40).

   If we add to that the non-Zionist segments (such as the Ultra-Orthodox faction that believed the people of Israel already have a constitution – the Bible) and the non-Jewish segments (who were unable or unwilling at that time to participate in the political game of negotiation and compromise at all), it becomes clear that agreement on a binding single constitution would require far more time and energy than the leaders of the various parties were willing to invest (Hofnung 1996: 588).

Political Timing: The Evaporation of the "Internal Insurance" Incentive and the External Commitment to the UN

As unbridgeable as these disagreements might have seemed in 1949, headway might have been possible (and perhaps even likely) for a brief period between the time when it became clear that the British would leave but before the first elections were held. In that period (between November 1947 and January 1949) a committee of legal experts was able to complete about 70 percent of the articles of a future constitution (Freudenheim 1973: 25–32). There were two primary incentives. First, Israel had undertaken before the United Nations to establish a constitutional democracy (Edrey 2005: 90; Freudenheim 1953: 19–21). Second, at that point in time, it was unclear what the relative power of the various parties would be in a future legislature; under such circumstances, it made logical sense to agree on a set of rules before the elections to the Constitutional Assembly, which would serve as an "insurance" against future capture by any political faction (Ginsburg 2003: 22–23; Ramseyer 1994: 722; Salzberger & Voigt 2002: 23). However, this unique window of political opportunity soon closed because of both internal and external developments. Externally, the UN failed to intervene when Israel was attacked (in May 1948). Consequently, Israeli leaders felt the commitment to the UN lost much of its weight (Freudenheim 1973: 21–25).

Internally, the committee did not finish its job before the elections to the Constitutional Assembly. Once these elections were held, the chips had fallen, and the window of political willingness to compromise closed. With the urgency to reach a constitutional deal gone, more immediate concerns took over: there was a nation to secure and a state to build. The people elected to the first Knesset (notwithstanding that they were elected to serve on a Constitutional Assembly, not a legislature) saw it as their job to legislate, rather than to deliberate on a future constitution. As legislators, they now had an institutional incentive not to limit the powers of the legislature; as members of various political parties, they had little incentive to agree to constitutional rules that would, at least in the short run, favor one party over another.[4]

A Socialist Political Economy

Israel's political economy in 1948 was such that there was little demand by investors and businesses – domestic or foreign – to protect against overtaxation by instituting judicial review. On establishment, Israel had not expected to attract foreign investment interested solely in profit. There was little reason to believe Israel could, in 1948, offer a better return compared to other nations recovering from World War II.

---

[4] The most vocal voices for a constitution came from the margins: on the left, Israel's Communist party and on the right Herut, Begin's revisionist party, strongly urged the Knesset to adopt a constitution that would protect minority rights. Both ends of the spectrum were worried about the unchecked power of the state.

Moreover, the dominant thinking at that time was that this form of capitalism (or economic colonialism) was not something the state should encourage. More importantly, in the Zionist movement's experience, wealthy Jews invested in Israel mostly for ideological reasons. Thus, there was little need to convince them to invest by securing their investment from local politics via the institution of strong judicial review (as may have been the case in the United States when it was created) (Farber 2002: 86–95). If at all, the direct access the investors enjoyed to the heads of government was a much better assurance.

Domestically, the nascent Israeli economy was not only state dominated, but party dominated. Each political party established a mini-economy: it had settlements that followed its ideology (and therefore lands and agriculture or industrial plants), companies, newspapers, sports clubs, representation in labor unions, and so on. The state, when established, was dismally poor. Later on, when it became evident that the state had benefits to allocate, it was still not the case that economic interests called for judicial protection: given Israel's proportional representation, it was actually easier and more effective to use the political machinery to secure economic interests. It should also be noted that somewhat paradoxically, the socialist organizations (which were also committed to progressive taxation) were the ones with the greatest assets.

Attitudes Toward Judges and the Judicial Process

It is obvious from the historical record that Prime Minister David Ben Gurion did not particularly trust judges (Goldberg 1993: 45). He thought of them as representing the bourgeois, and their decisions as favoring capital over labor. For him, judges were antiprogressive, and more than once he referred to the U.S. case of *Lochner v. New York*, in which the U.S. Supreme Court struck down state legislation that imposed maximum hour limits for bakery employees, as an example. Moreover, he thought that the judicial institution had to first gain public confidence before it could tackle the value-laden questions prevalent in Israeli politics. If judges were thrust into the ideological thicket – as they must if they were to be entrusted with constitutional judicial review – the judiciary would be perceived quite soon as political (i.e., as aligned with one political party or another), and thus would never be able to achieve the necessary "neutral" place in Israeli society (Gavison 1997: 77).

Interestingly, this notion was shared by the early Israeli justices, who did not think it would necessarily be a good idea to be empowered to strike down legislation as unconstitutional. This was not only because they were raised, professionally, under the British system, but also because many of them felt that the Court wasn't ready yet, or that the conditions of the Israeli society were not yet ripe for such a judicial role (Landau 1980: 199).

Moreover, it seems that the social and political logic undergirding judicial review requires a certain degree of distrust of the government (and the politicians). Otherwise, why do we need unelected judges to strike down the will of the representatives of the people? In Israel's inception, such distrust was the province of very few. Many, including the first two attorneys general, trusted politicians more than they trusted judges. After all, these politicians were able to deliver: they created a state and thus fulfilled dreams harbored for 2,000 years. Why should we, the citizens of Israel, distrust the very power we fought to establish?

The Nature of the National Political Agenda

Judicial review, by its nature, is a form of brake: it "checks" the power of the legislation by stopping the machinery of government from running, or at least it may force it to pause and alter course. When Israel was created, the challenges were great: a nation had to be built; immigration from all over the globe had to be absorbed; a state had to be settled and its infrastructure – roads, water, electricity, cities – upgraded; an economy had to be developed; a culture had to be revived and updated (Goldberg 1993: 38). These collective endeavors not only did not sit well with the individuality presupposed by human rights, but were also seen as antithetical to judicial review precisely because judicial review stands in the way of the collective achieving its objectives quickly. The last thing Ben Gurion needed was judges striking down the coalition's measures and thus delaying the realization of the Zionist project (Yannay 1990: 25). So the Israeli story is not only a story of the majority not wishing to limit its powers (why would it?) or a conscientious Ben Gurion worrying that it is undemocratic to impose the values of one generation on future generations (Kedar 2012: Ch. 5). It is also a story of a ruling coalition and large segments of the opposition that shared an understanding that now is not the time: bigger fish need to be fried, and judicial review could spoil the dish (Yannay 1990: 29; Goldberg 1993: 45).

PIECEMEAL CONSTITUTIONAL CONSTRUCTION

This is not to say that the Israeli political system had fully withdrawn from the quest for a constitution. Rather, it embarked on a piecemeal approach: addressing the various chapters of a future constitution by enacting one Basic Law at a time. Indeed, by 1990, the Knesset had enacted nine Basic Laws, using the same procedure that governs the passage of any other legislation, save for the fact that the bill must past through the Knesset's Constitution Committee. Each of these Basic Laws covered a chapter in a future constitution: the powers of the various branches of government and state institutions;[5] structural elements of the Israeli regime (i.e., the land regime and the state economy);[6] and some symbolic matters (such as Basic Law Jerusalem).[7]

---

[5] Basic Law: The Knesset, 1958 S. H. 69; Basic Law: The Government, 1992 S. H. 14; Basic Law: The Judiciary, 1984 S. H. 78; Basic Law: the Army, 1976 S. H. 154; Basic Law: State comptroller, 1988 S. H. 30; Basic Law: The President, 1964 S. H. 118.

[6] Basic Law: Israeli Lands, 1960 S. H. 56.

[7] Basic Law: Jerusalem, 1980 S. H. 186.

As of the 1990's, three main issues remained unresolved: the borders of the state (including the question whether the territory of the state should be part of the future constitution at all); human rights (including a bill of political and civil rights, social rights, and due-process rights in legal proceedings, as well as the relation of rights to the character of the State as a Jewish Democracy); and the matter of legislation and judicial review. The latter included the primacy of Basic Laws, the procedure for amending them, and the power of the court to exercise judicial review when ordinary statutes clash with Basic Laws. The Knesset considered various bills on all these matters, but did not legislate any into law.[8] Given this state of affairs, the Court did not treat Basic Laws differently than any other statutes, and did not exercise judicial review when a legal conflict arose between ordinary statutes and a Basic Law. As mentioned, some justices questioned the wisdom of constitutional judicial review given the deep ideological divisions within the Israeli society. Even for justices who favored constitutional judicial review as a form to maintain the separation of powers and protect human rights, it was clear that without explicit authorization (either in the form of a basic law, or in the form of a comprehensive constitution), Knesset statutes were beyond judicial reach, save for by way of interpretation.

The 1969 Bergman Exception: Weak-Form Review of Election Laws

A sort of exception to the rule against judicial review of primary legislation was crafted in 1969 in a very limited set of cases dealing with election laws. In this narrow context, the Court (first in the *Bergman* case and later in others) accepted an invitation from petitioners, with a nod of approval from the attorney general, to declare whether a statute allocating funds (and later, state-funded broadcasting time) to political parties in a differential manner violated Section 4 of Basic-Law: Knesset,[9] which stipulated that national elections will be conducted in an equal manner. Ordinarily, statutory amendments require only the majority of Knesset members present in the three readings. However, for amending Section 4 of Basic Law: Knesset a majority of all Knesset members is needed (61 out of the 120 members). In the *Bergman* case, the Court was willing to examine whether a statute that provided funds only for parties already represented in the Knesset conformed to the standard of equal elections. The Court found that Section 4 had indeed been violated, and sent the matter back to the Knesset in order to decide whether to amend it so it would not violate Section 4 or reenact the offending statute with the support of at least sixty-one Knesset members for it to have legal force.

---

[8] For example, draft bill The Legislation, regarding the powers of the Knesset as a legislature and constitutional assembly (which, firstly, included explicit reference to judicial review) has been pending since the 1970s. For a more recent draft bill of Basic Law: The Legislation see http://www.knesset.gov.il/privatelaw/data/18/317.rtf.

[9] Basic Law: The Knesset, 1958, S. H. 244.

Under the *Bergman* exception, then, the Court could review the statute but the Knesset retained the power to respond to the exercise of judicial review (or immunize its statute from review in the first place) by enacting the piece of legislation with a Knesset majority (sixty-one members). Indeed, on the four occasions the Court ruled the statute in question contradicted Section 4, the Knesset responded by reenacting the statute with the necessary majority (*id.*; *Agudat Derech Eretz v. The Broadcasting Authority* 1981; *Laor Movement v. Chair of the Knesset* 1989; *Rubinstein v. Chairman of the Knesset* 1982).

The Knesset's response to the *Bergman* decision was subsequently challenged under the theory that the Knesset should have amended the Basic Law itself (rather than reenact the offensive legislation with the required majority), because Basic Laws are supreme and can only be amended by other Basic Laws. The judicial response to this argument was swift and clear: the Court stated that the phrase "Basic Law" was a matter of semantics only and there was no reason to assume such superiority; the judicial role ended if a statute met the procedural entrenchment requirements (i.e., was enacted with the necessary majority) (*Ressler v. Chairman of Elections Committee* 1977; *Kaniel v. Minister of Justice* 1973). The Court thus left open the theoretical question of the hierarchy of norms in the Israeli system. In practice, however, the rules were clear: if the Knesset chose to bind itself by way of requiring a special majority for amending a certain provision, the Court would play its role by examining whether a subsequent statute, if not enacted with the required majority, has indeed violated the entrenched provision.

It is beyond the ambit of this chapter to fully analyze the conditions that pushed for (or enabled) this mode of "mild" or "soft" judicial review. Suffice it to say that this exception, which could not have developed without the express consent of the attorney general, was met with applause by the various media outlets, and did not evoke any serious contention from the political system. The main reason was that at issue was a clear case of an agency problem – cats (i.e., Knesset members) guarding the cream (i.e., public funding for their own election). Moreover, the Court was acting on a rather solid base when all it was doing was enforcing the Knesset's own demand that if equality in election is breached, the breaching statute should require the majority of sixty-one MKs, thus insisting that the Knesset should respect its own self-binding.[10]

During this period – and in fact until the early 1990s – the Court solidified its stature as a serious institution mindful of protecting human rights vis-à-vis the administration and protecting equal elections vis-à-vis the Knesset. The Court was

[10] Some argue that this design allowed the Knesset to harness the legitimacy provided by judicial rulings: in complying with the judicial demand to enact a problematic statute with the special majority, the Knesset could claim that it was following the rules laid down and at the same time in essence breaching the duty to run equal elections. However, this depiction is somewhat misleading because under this design, the Knesset remained responsible (and accountable) for its decision to enact a certain provision with a special majority, and thus could not fully avoid public criticism by relying on judicial pronouncements.

careful not to align itself with any political party. The media treated judicial rulings with relative reverence (Bassok 2003). Judges, the prevalent perception was, were wise people working in order to secure Israeli democracy and the rule of law, to the best of their ability under the law.

The Basic Laws of 1992 – Constitutional Politics in the Early 1990s

There was a more dramatic shift in 1992. For the first time, the Knesset enacted two Basic Laws dealing with human rights: Basic-Law: Human Dignity and Liberty and Basic-Law: Freedom of Vocation.[11] These Basic Laws were distinct legally and politically. Legally, they included three unique clauses. First, a limitation clause, stipulating that rights protected in the Basic Laws may not be infringed unless the infringement is by a statute that meets certain conditions. This implies that somebody – judges? – ought to check subsequent legislation for conformity with these conditions. Although the Basic Laws did not say so explicitly, it would seem that if subsequent legislation is found as failing to meet the conditions set forth in the limitation clause, the infringing provisions lack legal force. This would imply that these Basic Laws are supreme in a sense over other legislation.

The second legal oddity was the statement that all branches of government must comply with the provisions of the Basic Laws. This is odd because it would be somewhat bizarre to assume some governmental branches – the legislature? – are above the law, or exempt from complying with any law. After all, the rule of law itself implies that all are subject to the law. So why mention it explicitly in the Basic Laws? A reasonable conclusion might be that these Basic Laws were meant to convey the message that the Knesset itself must respect these Basic Laws when enacting subsequent legislation, and hence another indication for the supremacy of these two Basic Laws.[12]

Thirdly, these two Basic Laws contained a grandfather clause, stipulating that all laws enacted prior to the enactment of the Basic Laws would remain in force.[13] The presence of such a clause could lead to the interpretative conclusion that without such a clause "old" statutes could have been subject to review for conformity with these Basic Laws. Furthermore, the presence of this clause could also mean that laws that would be enacted after these Basic Laws were enacted and would fail to meet the requirement set forth in these Basic Laws would not be exempt from review. Legally speaking, it was rather obvious that the new Basic Laws were different not

---

[11] Basic Law: Human Dignity and Liberty, 1992, S. H. 1391; Basic Law: Freedom of Occupation, 1992, S. H. 1387.

[12] Chief Justice Barak in *Bank Hamizrachi* case.

[13] In Basic Law: Freedom of Occupation, the grandfather clause had a time limit after which it would expire. This was done in order to allow the Knesset some time to review its statutes and ensure conformity with the right to pursue an occupation. The grandfather clause of Basic Law: Human Dignity and Liberty contained no expiration date, and was intended to shield all past legislation, primarily legislation that incorporated religious law into the Israeli system.

only in content – namely the direct protection of human rights – but also in design. Their application called for some form of judicial review. The Court, for the first time, had thus been put in a place where it was expected to exercise some form of substantive judicial review in matters directly related to human rights. Interestingly, however, the two Basic Laws only allude to such review – they did not specifically mention it, nor did they touch on the issue of supremacy.

Politically, the two new Basic Laws were a result of a long and winding compromise. Basic rights such as equality and freedom of expression were deliberately omitted from the Basic Laws, in order to secure the passive acquiescence of the religious parties and segments of the right-wing parties. The matter of judicial review was specifically left vague, and the sponsors of the bill stated that these Basic Laws were not intended to create a court empowered with novel constitutional powers. In order to ease any misgivings MKs might have regarding the relinquishment of the supremacy of the Israeli parliament, Basic-Law: Human Dignity and Liberty was not procedurally entrenched, as the clause demanding special majority for its amendment was dropped in the advanced reading of the bill.[14]

Underlying the political compromise were three major developments. First, for the first time Israel had seriously shifted toward a market-based economy. Private capital and foreign investment were gaining prominence, and thus the issue of protecting economic rights (property, freedom of vocation) from the vicissitudes of politics became an issue for the economic elite (Hirschl 1997: 142) in an endeavor to preserve its hegemony (Hirschl 2004: 11–16, 42–48, 97–99; Hirschl 2009, 481–487).[15]

Second, the political fragmentation for which Israel has been renowned infiltrated a level deeper, to the level of candidate selection. Traditionally, Israeli political parties had strong central committees that selected candidates. The new candidates' selection schemes adopted by the major parties, including primary elections, drove candidates to appeal more strongly to the deeply committed members of their parties, who rejected politicians who engaged in brokering deals and seeking consensus building. Instead, populist demands rose for more decisive (read: extreme) positions. Moderate politicians became increasingly anxious, and some saw the Court as a possible ally: the Court and judicial review might provide political cover, a way to step back from the extreme measures demanded by the party base. Rather than oppose these extreme positions, a more moderate politician could claim that a bill demanded by the party base would simply not pass judicial muster. This in turn provided an incentive for the moderate politicians of the leading parties to coalesce and support at least a weak form of judicial oversight. We see, then, that fragmentation may act not only to forestall judicial review, as was the case early on in Israeli history. Fragmentation – this time internal fragmentation within political

---

[14] Divrey HaKnesset (Minutes of the Knesset), March 17, 1992. Retrieved from. http://www.knesset.gov .il/Tql/knesset/Knesset12/html/19920317@19920317008@008.html.

[15] In this context, the reluctance of the Court to protect the claims of the have-nots under the right to human dignity is apparent. See *Manor v. Minister of Treasure* (2002).

parties – can also push toward the judicialization of politics and empowerment of courts to exercise judicial review (Ginsburg 2009: 7; Kagan 2001: 37).

Fragmentation also led one of the staunch opponents of judicial review to reconsider. The Israeli multiparty system requires coalition building, and the one constant in these coalitions has been the presence of the National Religious Party (NRP) as part of the coalition. The NRP was the quintessential tiebreaker party sought out by both the Likud and Labor party as a coalition partner. The NRP had long opposed judicial review for ideological reasons, because the Court has been a secular institution and the rights it saw as fundamental clashed with some religious legislation.[16] Equally, if not more importantly, as a tiebreaker party the NRP would fare much better in politics than the judicial process. So, the NRP had been a key factor in Israel's reluctance to speed up the Basic Laws project.

The late 1980s, however, saw the emergence of a heretofore underrepresented force in Israeli politics – the Mizhrachi Jews, spearheaded by the Shas party.[17] Shas emerged as an alternative to the NRP as the ultimate tiebreaker without which no government can form a stable majority. No longer confident that the political process could protect its interests, the NRP finally acquiesced to the relentless pressure from the liberal forces and allowed the enactment of the Basic Laws, with the understanding that Israeli constitutional jurisprudence, being at greater odds with Shas' ideology than NRP's worldview, would ultimately derail Shas' quest for dominance. The further fragmentation of the median parties thus allowed the liberal forces in the Knesset to move ahead and further empower the Court.

These political incentives added to the economic incentives discussed previously. Shas saw legislative power as a pathway to achieve for the Mizrachi Jews what Mapai, the leading party in the 1950s, had been able to secure from the state for their members when the state was established. As noted, current economic elites were less than enthusiastic. As their power was not in numbers, they, too, saw a rising incentive to turn to the courts for the protection of their economic rights against primary legislation (Hirschl 2004: 60–71; Mandel 1999).

On a deeper level, 1992 saw the Israeli media and some segments of the political system tire of political hyper-fragmentation. During most of the 1980s, neither the left nor the right was able to form a coalition on its own. National-unity governments or other very broad coalitions were established, leading to political stagnation. The main parties were occupied largely in trying to steal an MK from the opposite bloc in order to establish a razor-thin majority (Hofnung 1996: 595; Bechor 1996: 127).

[16] For instance, religious marriage laws do not recognize no-fault divorce and technically, only the husband may divorce the wife. Rabbinic Courts Jurisdiction (Marriage and Divorce), 1953; Rabbinic Courts (Enforcement of Rulings of Divorce), 1995.
[17] Shas was founded as a religious party not fully committed to Zionism in the sense that it preferred a Hallachic (religious) state over a democracy; the NRP held the opposite view. Furthermore, NRP encourages its followers to serve in the army (or enlist in community service); Shas supports the mass waver for orthodox Jews. Whereas the NRP's ideology limited state support only to those in dire need, Shas called for increasing state support for large families regardless of the ability to earn income.

Political deals were broken at any opportunity, and some deals were signed just for show; the real deals were kept from the public (*Zarzevsky v. Prime Minister of Israel* 1991). There was a sense that the long-term national interest was lost in the very short-term pork-and-barrel politics of each faction to itself. In that atmosphere, the idea of a constitution with judicial review seemed a way to save politics from itself, by putting some public goods out of the reach of daily logrolling and pushing forward with the nation-building process (Bechor 1996: 143).

However, although the idea of constitutionalization enjoyed a renaissance of sorts, the best that could be politically achieved were the two Basic Laws described above – a stripped-down version of a human-rights act. In any event, there was no political agreement on constitutionalizing all Basic Laws, nor was there a political agreement on elevating the Basic Laws enacted in 1992 to the constitutional level. At best, there was a tacit agreement to allow a weak form of judicial review, without undermining the ability of the Knesset to work around limits set by the Court, much the same as its ability to respond according to the 1969 precedent discussed earlier.

THE "REVOLUTION": JUDICIAL ASSERTION OF THE SUPREMACY OF BASIC LAWS VIA SCHOLARLY WRITINGS

When the new Basic Laws were enacted, there was very little buzz. Judging by attendance at the vote and the speeches on the floor, as well as by media coverage, it is almost impossible to seriously claim that the political system or the media saw this move as anything but a modest step forward. Two more Basic Laws en route to a constitution are an important development but definitely not a revolution. The political attention was directed instead at the coming elections (Sapir 2008: 16, 21).

The legal academy, on the other hand, realized something important had happened. A leading constitutional scholar lamented in an evening paper that a constitutional revolution has happened, and nobody noticed. Justice Barak, a former professor himself, seized on the expression, and launched a scholarly campaign aimed to establish that indeed the Court was granted "unconventional" powers to strike down legislation infringing basic human rights as well as establish a common understanding of how these new provisions could and should be interpreted. Justice Barak gave lectures, published papers, and wrote a hefty and wide-ranging book (all published in a single year!), in which he analyzed in detail the operative sections in the new Basic-Law: Human Dignity and Liberty and offered what he considered the appropriate interpretation (Barak 1992/3, 1993, 1994. See later Barak 2000a, 2000b). The legal community – judges, lawyers, and academics – was put on notice. An invitation for petitions had been delivered, complete with a comprehensive manual.

The first judicial interaction with the Basic Laws of 1992 predated Barak's publications, and was somewhat unfortunate. The Court was considering a petition, filed several years earlier, challenging the government's policy denying import licenses for nonkosher meat (*Meatrael Ltd. v. The Prime Minster* 1992; Barak-Erez 2007:

81, 2010: 430). The Court found that the government lacked legal authorization to infringe on the importer's freedom to pursue his vocation.[18] Thus, the policy was found ultra vires. However, in an obiter dictum, Justice Or stated that should the Knesset decide to empower the government to prohibit the import of nonkosher meat, the enabling legislation could only be enacted through a supermajority vote. The Court's obiter was legally erroneous, because, as mentioned, Basic-Law: Freedom of Vocation contains a limitation clause, which empowers the government to infringe the protected right provided the conditions enumerated in that clause are met. Consequently, if a new authorizing statute that infringed the protected right met the conditions set forth in the limitation clause, there would be no need to enact the statute with a supermajority.[19]

The political system reacted sharply. The NRP, which had pushed for the nonkosher meat import policy, felt cheated. Shas saw it as yet another indication that the Supreme Court was undermining Israel's Jewish heritage.[20] These parties swiftly capitalized on their political power to introduce an amendment to Basic-Law: Freedom of Vocation that allowed the Knesset to legislate notwithstanding the fact that the legislation infringes a right protected in the Basic Law, even if the legislation in question failed to meet the requirements of the limitation clause. On the other hand, Israel's chronic political fragmentation prevented an all-out repeal of the Basic Law. This time around – in 1994 – there was a very lively debate in the Knesset regarding the status of the Basic Laws, because the views of Shas and the NRP were at odds with Barak's widely influential book. Some might argue that the Knesset retroactively accepted Barak's position (by not denouncing it), but others asserted that the Knesset had proactively asserted a "zone of tolerance" (Hamilton & Braden 1941: 322), demarcating the zone beyond which it would respond to what it perceives as "judicial trespass." By amending the Basic Law pursuant to a judicial obiter (that indicated what the Court would do in case future legislation is enacted), the Knesset signaled that it will not accept such judicial intervention, and for that purpose it devised a legal mechanism that enabled such future legislation to stand notwithstanding a judicially proclaimed conflict with the right protected in the Basic Law.

The first time a justice in Israel invalidated a statute for contradicting the new Basic Laws was in a minority opinion dealing with a rather convoluted economic issue. Justice Levin, in the *Clal* case (*Clal Insurance Company Ltd. v. Minister of*

---

[18] The doctrine was pronounced by the Court in the *Bajerano* case (1949).

[19] Justice Or assumed the infringement of the right in the specific case would not meet the requirements set in the clause. In that case, the Knesset would have had to amend the Basic Law itself.

[20] It could be argued that these reactions affirm the contention that MKs were not fully aware of the revolution created by enacting the Basic Laws in 1992. For example, the Chair of the Constitution Committee MK Lin affirmed as part of the debate that the enactment of the two Basic Laws (Freedom of Vocation and Human Dignity and Liberty) was not about changing the basic balance of power between the judicial and the Knesset. http://www.knesset.gov.il/Tql/knesset/Knesset12/html/19920317@19920317008@008.html.

treasury 1994), found that a temporary measure the Knesset enacted that froze the allocation of special bonds to pension funds violated the freedom of vocation of investment funds seeking to be included in the program. *Clal* was a small case: only three justices were on the panel, and not necessarily the big names; the issue was complicated and the infringement of a right, if there was one, was only temporary and therefore proportional; and the case involved freedom of vocation – an entrenched Basic Law, the same as Section 4 of Basic Law: Knesset. The political system was still waiting for the "big" case – one dealing with Basic Law: Human Dignity and Liberty, which contained the more central rights and did not require any special majority for its amendment.

From that perspective, *Bank Hamizrachi United v. Migdal Communal Village* 1995 – arguably Israel's *Marbury vs. Madison* – was far from an ideal case. It was a civil case, in which the constitutional question arose only incidentally. It had percolated its way up the civil system after rather peculiar decisions of lower courts. The evidentiary basis was murky, and as the court papers reveal, both parties were not ready to mount a full and vigorous examination of the constitutional issues. From the standpoint of strategically minded High Court justices, however, the case was appealing because the issue – which dealt with a slight expansion of a previous statutory scheme – was unlikely to evoke any major political reaction. Moreover, the matter was a technical one, although its relation to protected rights – the right of property – was straightforward.

More specifically, the case dealt with an expansion of the powers of a special office established to deal with nearly bankrupt rural settlements. Because this office had powers to forgive some debt, the creditors (including Bank Hamizrachi) claimed that expanding its powers violated their right to property. Although arguably the case arose too soon – the system had barely registered the enactment of the two Basic Laws – the window of opportunity the case provided was really unique. Chief Justice Shamgar was retiring, after a long and distinguished career, and the case gave him a chance to ensure a long-lasting legacy by giving the Israeli legal system the gift (so to speak) of judicial review. As justice Barak was taking the helm, this would probably be the only constitutional case the two would be sitting together as the outgoing chief justice and the newly appointed chief justice.

On appeal, the Supreme Court faced the Tel Aviv district court's unprecedented decision to nullify the law. The district court judge relied heavily on Barak's book and its operative conclusions, and found that the state had brought forth no evidence to support the argument that the infringement to the property right of the creditors was narrowly tailored. In fact, the state brought forth no evidence that it had considered other means and found them ineffective. The Supreme Court assigned the case to a very strong panel consisting of seven justices, including the retiring Chief Justice Shamgar and the new Chief Justice Barak. Without delving into the intricacies of the concurring opinions, the Court found that all Basic Laws had now become supreme over ordinary legislation. This meant that Israel, without a clear decision by the Knesset, had in fact become a regime with a written constitution.[21] It also meant that the Court was now empowered to exercise judicial review not only with respect to the two new Basic Laws, but with respect to all Basic Laws. The old Basic Laws suddenly gained teeth.

These holdings were not the only possible legal conclusions. It would have been a legally plausible interpretation to decide that the Court was indeed called on to exercise judicial review with respect to the two new Basic Laws, but the status of these Basic Laws, and all other Basic Laws, has not changed. Practically, that would mean that the Knesset may, in subsequent legislation, exempt itself from the requirements of the Basic Laws (and from judicial review) by explicitly stating so. That would be a much weaker form of judicial review, but it appears more in keeping with the political choices underlying the enactment of the two Basic Laws.[22] The path chosen by the Court precluded this option.[23] The Court, in effect, enacted Basic-Law: Legislation, declaring the supremacy of the Basic Laws and establishing full-scale constitutional judicial review. This would have been the final piece the Knesset was to enact, after completing all other substantive matters.

As for the resolution of the actual case, however, the Court overturned the district court's decision of unconstitutionality, after finding that the infringement of the right of property was proportionate and thus in conformity with the conditions set forth in the Basic Law's limitation clause. Chief Justice Barak stated that although the district court judge correctly applied his book, the state should be given some leeway, as this was the first time the issue was seriously litigated.[24] At the end of the day, the case then produced no operative remedy. The issue itself, as noted, was of little concern politically because at stake was a slight expansion of a previously enacted scheme. The reasoning of the Court spun over an indigestible 350 pages. The opinion was published immediately after the assassination of Prime Minister Rabin, when the attention of the media was devoted to the national trauma and its aftermath. Consequently, there was nearly no political response to *Bank Hamizrachi*.

[21] Justice Heshin, dissenting, attacked both Shamgar's and Barak's analysis of the Court's constitutional power as derived from the Basic Laws. He disagreed with the conclusion that Israel now has a constitution.

[22] See Sapir: 2010. However, when the two basic laws were later amended, it could be argued that many in the Knesset were aware of the possible legal and political ramifications of these basic laws. For example, Mk David Tzuker, Divrey HaKnesset, retrieved from http://www.knesset.gov.il/Tql/knesset/Knesset13/html/19940309@19940309035@035.html.

[23] The Court's decision left the Knesset with the option of directly amending the Basic Laws to exclude this or that statute from the reach of the Court. Although technically amending most Basic Laws does not require a special majority, the amendment process carries a rather heavy political price, as the Basic Laws are considered the building blocks of a future constitution, and thus the Knesset has traditionally not been too keen on amending them frequently.

[24] Some scholars have claimed that *Bank Hamizrachi* is but an obiter, because the disposition of the case would have been the same even if the Basic Laws were not supreme. Others have stressed that among the seven justices, there was little agreement on the reasoning regarding the supremacy of the Basic Laws, and as the various ways of reasoning contradicted each other, the result was a rather confusing seminar on Israel's constitutional law (Salzberger 1996; Gavizon 1997).

The Court waited a couple of years before actually declaring a law lacking force or effect, and when it did so, the section in question was so inconsequential that the case raised doubts regarding the relationship between human rights and judicial review. The section dealt with the requirements those already providing financial investment services would have to meet under a novel system of certification and registration legislated by the Knesset (*Investment Managers' Committee v. Minister of Treasury* 1997). The statute grandfathered all those in business for more than seven years by exempting them from most, but not all, of the newly legislated requirements. The statute failed, however, to sufficiently distinguish between those in practice for one or two years and those in practice for five or six years in terms of the exams they would have to pass in order to continue their practice. The Court found that this section violated the freedom of vocation provision in the Basic Law, and sent it back to the Knesset to devise a more narrowly tailored transition. This case did not resonate with the justification for judicial review offered by some justices in *Bank Hamizrachi* – that judicial review over primary legislation is needed in order to protect against grave violations of fundamental rights. Needless to say, the politicians did not react to the invalidation of the transitional section, as the matter was seen as a technical issue (Salzberger & Kedar 1998: 507).

The next case also followed the same technique of splitting the legal and political importance of the case. The first time a section of a statute was actually struck down on account of its violation of a right protected under Basic-Law: Human Dignity and Liberty, occurred in 1999. The Court struck down a section of the military code – technically a statute of the Knesset but in essence a legislative piece at the level of secondary legislation – allowing the detention of soldiers for up to ninety-six hours before they could see a military judge, whereas civilians were guaranteed (at that time) to see a judge after forty-eight hours (*Tzemach v. Minister of Defence* 1999). The state claimed the only reason for the differential statutory timeframes was fiscal: the military needed a budget raise in order to ensure that a soldier could be brought to a military judge sooner; it had no other objection to equalizing the terms. The sums in question were relatively minute. Consequently, the judicial intervention again met no opposition concerning the particular issue. Even the treasury department did not understand what the fuss was about, for detailed plans were already in the making for equating the two regimes in the coming fiscal year (Sapir 2010: 101).

By that time, *Bank Hamizrachi* and two cases actually implementing its obiter meant judicial review had become a fact, and the proposition that all Basic Laws are supreme to ordinary legislation had become accepted. As apparent from the previous description, without Barak's intellectual prowess and leadership, this transition almost surely would not have come about. Barak's ability to lead the legal community – judges, lawyers, and academics – via his scholarly writings was central to the success of the revolution. Also central was the Court's ability to control the timing of publishing its decisions and its craftsmanship in splitting the political importance from the legal significance of the cases, which allowed the Court to ensure the cases on which the transition was founded were of low political visibility. The Court progressed from an obiter to an actual exercise of power in a series of issues on which there were no strongly held beliefs or disagreements within Israel's divided society. By the time the cases were decided by the Court, precedents could be cited. Judicial review has now become a widely accepted element of the Israeli system. High school books in civics were changed accordingly, and so has the public discourse.

The Knesset was slow to react. By 2001, a new speaker and head of the constitution committee were elected, and they saw the constitutional revolution as a power grab by the justices. For the first time in Israeli history, the rhetoric in the Knesset by leading members became adversarial toward the Court (Avraham 2006). Although the political fragmentation prevented a legislative overruling of *Bank Hamizrachi*, the threatening position of the Knesset had quite an effect on judicial steps, which exists to this day.

THE REVOLUTION: WHY DID IT HAPPEN THE WAY IT DID?

Having touched on what has happened and how it happened, it is time to offer conjectures regarding why it happened the way it did. As mentioned, in *Bank Hamizrachi* the Court adopted an expansive interpretation of the Basic Laws enacted in 1992. Although most scholars agreed that the development that took place in 1995 was positive in terms of providing greater protection for human rights in Israel, the unease regarding the jurisprudential underpinning of the case was palpable. No single opinion resonated with the Court's established jurisprudence or its practice of careful, meticulous legal analysis restricted to the facts and legal question before it. No single justice wrote what would have probably been the legally correct decision: (a) that whether the Knesset is or is not empowered to enact a constitution, it has not done so by enacting the two new Basic Laws; and (b) that all the Knesset had done was empower the Court, albeit implicitly, to examine statutes vis-à-vis the substantive requirements set forth in these two Basic Laws, and at the same time retaining the power to exempt future legislation from judicial review by explicitly stating so in the legislation itself. That would have been no major revolution, only a modest, if important, step forward.[25]

Although legally speaking it is somewhat pointless to speculate why the rather obvious course of action was not followed by the Court, it is nonetheless worthwhile

---

[25] This modest evolution would have allowed the Knesset to test the waters and operate under conditions of judicial review with respect to the rights it chose to protect and still retain the power to make the modifications and adjustments before it moved to elevating all Basic Laws to the constitutional sphere and empowering the Court to exercise judicial review across the board. As mentioned, however, the Court took the extra step and declared all Basic Laws as constitutional and at the same time rejected the power of the Knesset to specifically exempt statutes from judicial review unless it does so in the Basic Law itself. As previously explained, the Court basically pushed the legal regime in Israel from a regime of parliamentary sovereignty (with modest exceptions) to a constitutional regime with an incomplete constitution.

academically, as the Israeli Supreme Court justices were clearly well aware of the options before them. It seems three forces pushed the justices toward the expansive course chosen. First – they could. A legal opportunity emerged, and the Court seized it. In so doing, the justices must have realized that the fragmentation of the political system would allow the Court to push farther than the initial ground given to it (Ginsburg 2009: 7). Furthermore, unlike the previous generation, the justices sitting in the 1990s felt that the Court's standing in society was strong enough and its social capital would allow it to withstand the heat associated with the assertion of judicial review. The Court enjoyed considerably greater public support than the Knesset or the government. The intellectual leadership of Professor Barak and his ability to marshal the legal academy cannot be overemphasized. Also, although Shamgar was not the entrepreneurial justice seeking to innovate and reform that Barak was, his standing as a pillar of "responsible judgemanship" provided the Court with the necessary credibility. So a legal opportunity, professional leadership, and a relative advantage over the political system provided the Court with the "could."

Second – the Court felt it should. The justices of the 1990s – as well as most of the academic and cultural elites – had become fully committed to the idea that judicial protection of human rights is a core element of democracy (Hirschl: 2009, 479). The strong influence of the U.S. system – where Justice Barak and most of contemporary legal academics study – eclipsed the traditional British approach.[26] The new constitutions emerging in the 1980s (including the Canadian Charter of Rights, the South African Constitution, and the constitutions of the states of the former Soviet Union) have all shared a similar ethos, which resonated in Israel: the lessons from oppressive regimes are that popular democracy must be checked, and that it is the role of judges to ensure commitment to foundational values, primarily human rights. The Israeli justices not only felt that Israel belonged to this club of modern democracies, they felt that its political system was either unable or unwilling to complete a constitution on its own, and therefore a little push was necessary. In this context, the Court was also responding to signals from academic and human rights activists' critique – the Court's "support structure" (Epp: 1998; Hirschl: 2009, 469) – that in the past the Court had missed opportunities to treat the values enshrined in the Declaration of Independence as constitutional.[27] So as an opportunity had arisen, a more modest approach that would not have fully realized the potential of establishing a constitution for the state of Israel, it seems, would have amounted to yet another opportunity missed – and perhaps the last in the foreseeable future. In

---

[26] In 1980, Israel officially severed its legal ties with the United Kingdom by enacting the Foundations of Laws Act, which stipulates that in case no answer is found in existing law the court should turn to principles of liberty, justice, equity, and piece of the Jewish heritage, rather than to the principles of British equity and common law that served as the residuary source of law until that point.

[27] As noted, the Court refused to treat the Declaration of Independence as grounds for constitutional judicial review (*Ziv v. Gubernick*). For a critical review see Bendor, (2000). For a general review of the question see Rubinstein and Medina (2005).

that sense, the pull to secure personal legacies, already mentioned, was interwoven with the pull to secure the Court's institutional legacy.

The "could" and the "should" converged with one more factor – the "now is the time" presented by the larger political context of the early 1990s. Israel of 1995 was a state with a dramatically different economic structure than it had in 1948–1953. Some scholars have claimed that the empowerment of the Court was part of a campaign by the economic elite aiming to protect their assets and secure the dominance of their capitalistic outlook (Hirschl 1997: 142; Hirschl 2004; Hirschl 2009: 484–485; Salzberger & Kedar 1998: 504, 516). Although some justices were indeed pro-market, there does not appear to be much support for the proposition that the Court constitutionalized all of Israel's Basic Laws in order to protect the property of Israel's private sector vis-à-vis the state. At that time the private sector enjoyed cozy enough relationships with the politicians. There was little sense in pushing the Court a step further than necessary when it was much easier to enact economic protections via ordinary political channels.

The reaching out of the Israeli Supreme Court may be explained more convincingly in relation to the overall position of Israel in 1992–1995. Recall that the two Basic Laws were legislated as the Knesset was winding its business down. The elections held a couple of months later saw Rabin and the Labor party taking control. By 1995, the Oslo accords were signed and the general sentiment was that the historical conflict with the Arab world may soon be over, and Israel would evolve into a "normal" democracy. The one remaining brick necessary to complete the foundation of a democratic state was a constitution. By providing the extra push the Court took it on itself to move the Jewish people closer to this Promised Land (Jacobsohn 2000: 140) at a time when political attention was focused on the debate with the Palestinians. Once this debate was settled (and again, the sense then was that this would be just a matter of time), the focus of the political system would turn inward, and – as the lessons of the failed attempt to reach a compromise in 1948–1950 suggest – the positions of the various factions in Israel's divided society were likely to harden, driving the parties apart and further delaying the enactment of a comprehensive constitution.

By altering the landscape, the Court ensured that any future political debate on the last remaining major item on the agenda of the Zionist movement would start from a position that Israel already had a Constitution, albeit an incomplete one, and judicial review was part of it. The factions would still need to wrestle with completing the task, but they would be doing so within an existing framework. Should this political process of completing the Constitution drag on longer, the Court may in the meantime interpret the existing rights and develop their meaning one case at a time, thus closing the remaining gaps on its own.[28]

---

[28] Whether this process was successful or not is arguable; One thing is sure though, that the court did use that opportunity to set up numerous interpretive assumptions regarding the rights enumerated in the two Basic Laws, thus enlarging the scope of these rights. A good example could be the *Ganimat*

CONSTITUTIONAL JUDICIAL REVIEW IN THE 2000S: DID IT MAKE A DIFFERENCE?

During the early 2000s, the Court has demonstrated that it could exercise its powers not only in cases without much political salience, but also in matters of concern to political parties. In a famous case, the Court struck down a statute that granted broadcasting licenses to radio stations that had been broadcasting without a license (i.e., illegally) for a period of at least five years (*MK Oron v. Chairman of the Knesset* 2002). The legislative scheme was designed to legalize one radio station – Channel 7 – catering to the right-wing settlers. Facing criminal charges for operating an unlicensed station, the broadcasters turned to the Knesset for retroactive legalization, but the Court found that the statute infringed the freedom of vocation of all other potential broadcasters who obeyed the law and stated that a proportional way to proceed would be through a public tender, not by way of preferring those who systematically ignored the law in the past. That ruling was met with opposition by the right-wing religious parties, but the attorney general himself sided with the petitioners, and it was generally understood that the Court was acting against the rent-seeking power of these parties.

In another case, which led to considerable public debate, the Court was asked to strike down the Disengagement Act – the statute according to which Israeli settlements in the Gaza Strip (and three in the West Bank) would be evacuated (or "uprooted") and remedies would be given to the settlers. The Court refused to interfere with the evacuation itself, noting that indeed it violated the property rights and human dignity of the settlers, but it was proportional. However, the Court did strike down the compensation plan, finding the infringement of the settlers' property rights disproportional. The practical implication of this ruling was that the Court granted legal legitimacy to the disengagement plan, but the price of the plan rose by roughly a couple of hundred million dollars (*Regional Municipality Gaza Beach v. Knesset* 2005).

The last statute that was struck down during Barak's term as president was even more politically contentious. Barak found unconstitutional the amendment to the Civil Torts Act that granted immunity to the state for damages claimed by Palestinians for negligent action by the Israeli military for actions in the West Bank unrelated to actual combat. The amendment changed the legal test for state immunity from whether the action was combat related (in which case there was immunity) to whether the action was in a zone declared by the minister of defense as combat zone (*Adallah v. Minister of Defense* 2006). The Court found that shift was too broad, noting that the minister of defense had declared much of the West Bank as combat zones. The Knesset introduced the legislation again with cosmetic changes only, stating that the Court has misdirected its review: it should have reviewed the decision of the minister of defense (under administrative law) to declare a certain

---

affair, in which the court ruled that statutes enacted prior to Basic Law: Human Dignity and Liberty would be interpreted "in its spirit" (despite the grandfather clause) (*Ganimat v. State of Israel* 1995).

area as a combat zone, rather than the constitutionality of the empowering statute. Because there was little military action in the West Bank in recent years, the issue has remained on the back burner.

By 2010, the Court had struck down three other statutes. The first instituted a private prison in Israel. The second allowed courts to conduct a detention hearing in military offenses without the presence of the accused. The third provided preferential treatment financially for Yeshiva students over other students. In the first case, the Court dealt a blow to the privatization policy of the Israeli Prisons Service (and the Treasury Department), finding the notion of incarceration by a private entity that was empowered to make decisions on the daily lives of prisoners as a violation of their liberty. The case received considerable attention in the press, as it raised the question regarding the constitutional limits of privatization (*Academic Center of Law and Business v. Minister of Finance* 2009). In the second case, the Court stood for the due process of the accused, and noted that there were alternatives to the scheme adopted by the legislature in case the security concerns were so grave as to warrant restrictions on the right to be present at court (*Anonymous v. The State of Israel* 2010). That case was perceived as within the mandate of the Court because it dealt with matters directly related to the criminal procedure. In the third case, the section of the budget law that gave the preferential treatment was struck down, but it was not clear whether the basis of the decision was the relationship between the budget law and the framework legislation governing budget legislation, or the conflict with Basic-Law: Human Dignity and Liberty. The matter received considerable public attention but the actual remedy was suspended by the Court, so the matter is still under parliamentary consideration (*The Movement for Quality Government in Israel v. The Knesset* 2006).

These cases reveal that the judicial role in Israeli society has expanded to include protection of rights vis-à-vis the legislature. such policies enacted into legislation are now subject to judicial review, and at the very least that means that opponents may challenge social legislation in Court. There is evidence that the presence of constitutional judicial review has influenced the legislative process, as legislatures now have to consider whether the proposed statutes will likely pass judicial muster.[29] In Hirchl's terminology, legislative politics – mega politics – has been judicialized (Hirschl 2004, 2009). However, it would be wrong to assume that the Court was able to truly tackle divisive issues head-on, even when human rights were involved. In a famous case dealing with a statute that prevented family unifications of Israeli citizens and residents of the West Bank, all the court was able to do was declare

---

[29] There is an ongoing debate whether the presence of judicial review increases or decreases accountability. Although it is obvious that most politicians would refrain from having the statutes they support being struck down as unconstitutional, the presence of judicial review can be handled strategically. In the case of Channel 7, for example, the presence of the Court allowed some Likud and Labor members to abstain (so as not to cross the religious parties), stating that they had full faith in the Court to strike down the legislation. Politicians may also present more radical bills, knowing the legal advisors would most likely tame these bills. The politicians would then be able to blame the lawyers for the inability to deal decisively with the crisis at hand (whatever that crisis may be).

that human rights were violated, and send the matter back to the Knesset for further consideration (without invalidating the operative legal scheme, but with a warning that if the scheme stays as it is the Court is likely to strike it down) (*Adallah v. Minister of Interior* 2006). When the Knesset reenacted the statute with only minimal modifications, the Court, in a 6:5 vote and after several years of contemplations, left the statute intact (*Galon v. Attorney General* 2012). In another famous case, the court was unwilling to declare that an economic plan (enacted by the Knesset), which cut welfare support to those without any other means of income by 30 percent, violated their right to human dignity. In an uncharacteristic move, the Court, through an opinion by President Barak (with Justice Levi dissenting), insisted that the issue be litigated as applied, namely per each individual who may be harmed by the statute, rather than via abstract review, where the Court is willing to rely on aggregated evidence (*Commitment to Peace and Social Justice v. Minister of Finance* 2005).

THE AFTERMATH

It is of course too soon to assess the full impact of the constitutional revolution on the Israeli legal and political systems. The few observations sketched here should thus be read as a snapshot of the situation as these lines are written; over time, patterns may of course emerge or subside and the assessment of the revolution in the future may be different.

The first observation is that the Court was indeed able to change national perceptions with respect to Israel's Basic Laws and effectively establish a written constitution where none had existed before. The Basic Laws are now understood as constitutional provisions by the legal system, political system, media, and bureaucracy (including the education system). Earlier judicial rulings that described the term "Basic Law" as a mere matter of semantics have been relegated to near obscurity. The phenomenon of judicial review has indeed become a fact.

However, that gain came at a price. First, it is safe to say that the legal academy, which previously had been the leading bastion of support for the Court, is now considerably more critical. Perhaps it is the role of scholars to be critical, but prior to the revolution the critique was rather tame and it focused, in constitutional matters, on the missed opportunities of the past. It is now substantially more vocal, and it questions both the role of the Court in the revolution and, as mentioned, the Court's reasoning in *Bank Hamizrachi* (and subsequent cases). Whereas in the past the Court could rely on the support of the legal academy in its quest to protect rights, today such support would be more tentative or divided (Gasizon 1997: 25; Sapir 2008: 20).

The political system now views the Court with significantly greater suspicion. The perception that the Court has taken more than was given to it is shared by many politicians, and thus the confidence the Court previously enjoyed has been shaken. Whereas crude attempts at stripping the Court from its constitutional jurisdiction or otherwise limiting its powers have thus far failed, the very fact that these bills were presented – some even by the justice minister himself – has put the Court on notice.[30] In some public debates, the Court had to draw on the support of retired justices to thwart reforms, a move which led the justice minister to question the ethics of political action by retired judges (Shalita 2007).

Moreover, the Knesset did amend the procedure for selecting judges by giving the ruling parties a de facto veto power. Beyond the signaling effect embedded in such a change – a warning signal – the move would allow politicians to ensure that no "overly activist" candidates (to the left or right) would be nominated to the Supreme Court (or that if a so-called activist to one side is nominated, a deal would have to be struck to appoint an activist to the other side). Beyond this statutory amendment, it is interesting to note that for the first time in history (other than, of course, on the constitution of the Court) Israel has appointed two lawyers straight from private practice to the Supreme Court (Stoil 2007).

After *Bank Hamizrachi*, all attempts to continue with the process of enacting Basic Laws have been blocked. The Knesset invested a great deal of time in trying to draft a comprehensive Constitution, in part in order to rein the Court in, but that process has also reached a dead end, in part because politicians were wary of empowering the Court any further. As these lines are written, there is little chance of enacting any new Basic Laws unless some reconciliation between the judiciary and the Knesset is reached (or until the passage of time and change of personnel alters the dynamics). One such possible mode of reconciliation may come in the form of Basic-Law: Legislation, by which the Knesset will grant itself the explicit power to override, with a supermajority, judicial invalidation of a statute. However, the precise contours of such a design are unclear.

It would be erroneous to assert that the decline in the Court's standing is solely attributable to its role in the constitutional revolution; far from it. In the early 1990s, some segments of the administration itself, which had traditionally accepted judicial review as a necessary check on executive power, became critical of the expansion of justiciability and lowering of standing requirements (Lapid 2007), as well as the development of new causes of action (such as doctrines that allow the Court to examine whether a state action is grossly unreasonable).[31] These developments – which took place prior to and independent of the constitutional developments described – increased the friction between the Court and Executive branch. This tension is likely to intensify even further as the expansion of judicial review to the constitutional domain would limit the ability of the administration to respond to judicial decisions by asking the Knesset to amend the enabling legislation.

The media also changed its attitude toward the Court, and began to treat it as a political institution. Again, this cannot be attributed to the constitutional revolution

---

[30] Some believe that putting the Court on notice reduces protection of basic human rights, as fear from political backlash makes the Court more cautious when considering whether to strike down statutes for infringing constitutional norms. Others, including many MKs, say putting the Court on notice is essential because of the "activism" performed by the Court.

[31] For Supreme Court rulings on the matter as well as the doctrines used, see *Dapey Zahav Ltd. v. Broadcasting Authority* 1980; *Hess v. Deputy Chief of Staff* 2005; *Eduardo v. Minister of Defense* 2007.

alone: the high visibility of the clashes between the administration and Court mentioned, the orchestrated public-relations campaigns by those seeking to tarnish the
image of the Court, as well as the rise of a commercial TV channel seeking to
increase its ratings have all fostered the type of journalism that reports on public
law matters primarily in terms of winners and losers – the Court (and the individual
justices) being among the players (e.g., Asherie 2005). However, the change in the
judicial role at the center of the revolution certainly contributed to the change of
the Court's image as portrayed by the media. The exercise of constitutional judicial
review by definition carries with it political consequences, and the constitutional
language is almost by definition value laden. As the language of the Court became
the language of the fundamental values of the state of Israel as a Jewish democracy,
the media responded by treating the Court as "ideological." This was translated by
general readers and viewers as aligning the Court with a certain political agenda,
rather than with "the law."[32]

Moreover, the bar, previously the guardian of the judiciary against such attacks,
was less willing to stand strongly and decisively by the Court given its own misgivings
about the overall judicial performance in private law and criminal law matters.
Furthermore, segments of the Bar that disagreed with jurisprudence of the Court on
human rights or with Chief Justice Barak's approach to the role of a (supreme court)
judge as a guardian of fundamental principles (and the consequential expansion of
standing, the lowering of the justiciability bar and the development of the doctrine
of unreasonableness and proportionality in administrative matters), couched their
reservations in terminology related to mismanagement of scarce judicial resources.
How come, they claimed, the Court is spending so much time on these public
law matters, when it should be adjudicating torts claims, disputes over contracts or
criminal matters?

Perhaps the most important question is: "Are human rights better protected in
Israel as a result of the constitutional revolution?" The answer would be a qualified
"Yes". On one level, because statutes are now subjected to judicial review, the Court
protects against violations of rights not only with respect to administrative acts but
also with respect to the enabling statute itself. Whereas at first the Court exercised
its powers with respect to rather inconsequential matters, cases that came before the
Court in the first decade of the twenty-first century demonstrated the Court's ability
to exercise its constitutional powers on broadly significant issues.[33]

Moreover, the mere presence of judicial review cast its shadow over the legislative
process, taming down offensive bills likely to attract judicial review. "Proportionality"
has become the new buzz word in the Legislative chambers and corridors of the

---

[32] The case dealing with Israel's disengagement from Gaza is a good example: judges were by-and-large
held as pro-disengagement (except for dissenting Justice Levy), although the sole question in that case
was legal (whether the Knesset can legally perform such an act) and not moral (should the Knesset
adopt such an act) (*Regional Municipality Hof Aza v. Knesset of Israel* 2005).

[33] It should be stressed that the Court has acted judiciously and invalidated statutes only very rarely,
contradicting the claims that the Israeli Court is a power-hungry activist institution.

Knesset and Justice Ministry. The legal advisors to the various state-agencies are now expected to examine whether an act of the Knesset (or a section thereof), or secondary legislation enacted by a minister or by a local authority, is constitutional (i.e., will pass judicial muster).

On the other hand, a close examination of the cases brought before the Court reveals that in several cases decided in the last decade, the Court backtracked from applying some of the doctrines it developed in the earlier cases that established the contours of the "revolution" and refrained from invalidating statutes that appeared to contradict the Basic Laws.[34] Perhaps the Court wished to preserve its institutional capital for more important cases or for cases that would not get the Court entangled in subsequent litigation if the Knesset managed to amend the offensive law. In some cases, it is safe to say that the Court failed to provide a remedy because it has reached its political limits (*Adallah v. Minister of Interior* 2006). The reaction of the relevant political forces (primarily the security establishment, the treasury department, or the religious sector) would have been too severe for the Court to withstand, given the shaky ground on which it stood when exercising judicial review. The lack of specific authorization in law to exercise such review, the perception that the Court took more than given, and the lack of procedural protections against amending the jurisdiction of the Court have placed the Court on precarious grounds. So although the Court has technically become stronger than ever – with its legal arsenal extending to the review of primary legislation – its ability to use these powers remains limited. The promise embedded in *Bank Hamizrachi*, for a new Israel where human rights are fully protected, has thus not been fully fulfilled.

More broadly, if the past fifteen years tell us anything, it is that the Israeli Court, its rhetoric notwithstanding, does not stray too far away from the position of the majority on value-laden issues even when the infringement of human rights may be at stake. As judicial behavior in 2010–2012 reveals, the Court is much more likely to strike down legislation when it is clear the majority of the public does not support the legislation and the Knesset itself would have amended it if it weren't constrained by coalition agreements that favored tiebreaker parties or afraid to upset an economic balance orchestrated by the powerful finance ministry. For example, the Court finally struck down the statute exempting Haredi men and women from military service (of course, suspending the decision in order to allow the Knesset to find an alternative arrangement) when it was evident all of the leading parties in the Knesset, save for the ultrareligious parties, were trying to do just that (*Rubinstein v. Minister of Defense* 1998; *Ressler v. The Knesset* 2012). Similarly, following a summer of mass civil protests under the slogan "The People Demand Social Justice", the Court, after considering the case for some seven years, finally struck down a statutory provision that established an irrefutable presumption deeming a person owning a car (regardless of its value or usage) as above the minimum threshold for receiving

---

[34] An example for that could be the Stipends affair, where despite serious harm inflicted on petitioners, the Court refused recognizing the budget law as unconstitutional.

low-income state support (*Hassan v. National Insurance Institute* 2012). This decision, although resting on due process logic, attempts to portray the Court as a
defender of social rights, despite its peppered record on that point.

The result is that Israeli constitutional jurisprudence has become less consistent.
The application of the doctrine often varies wildly, although the words used by the
Court remain the same (Mautner 2008: 124). The lack of consistency strains public
confidence in the Court and the principle of the rule of law itself. One sector after
another sought the protection of the Court when it appeared the rights of members
of that sector were violated. As the Court delivered only what it could – trying to act
responsibly and in some cases defensively given the heightened critique its rulings
would bring about – the hope of each sector became somewhat hollow (see, for
example, *Shoharey Gilat Association v. Minister of Education and Culture* 1995).

Furthermore, the Court's constitutional powers have affected the old administrative powers it has had since its inception. The old doctrine used by the Court
in most cases applied a strict level of scrutiny, requiring the administration to show
explicit authorization in law as well as near likelihood that a grave harm would
be inflicted on the public interest if a right is not infringed by the exercise of
administrative power. Now, as mentioned, the word is "proportionality." This term
allows for greater flexibility. The Court now cuts the administration greater slack:
several cases decided under the new Basic Laws' proportionality doctrine, which
upheld the infringement of rights, are quite difficult to reconcile with yesteryear's
administrative law (*Hamifkad Haleumi Ltd. v. Attorney General* 2008).

Fifteen years is of course too short a time to assess with any degree of credibility
the long-term effects of the constitutional revolution. It may very well be that after a
period of readjustment the Court will be able to proceed and cash the promissory note
embedded in *Bank Hamizrachi* in terms of providing full protection for human rights
in Israel. After all, it took decades for the United States Supreme Court to exercise
rights-based judicial review vis-à-vis Congress. One can only hope that the Knesset
will complete its undertaking and enact the remaining Basic Laws that would explicitly empower the Court to exercise judicial review for the protection of enumerated
rights, and which would also include appropriate mechanisms to allow the political
system to respond to such review by assuming responsibility and further developing
channels for political participation and effective checks on the bureaucracy.

REFERENCES

Asherie, Ehud 2005. "When Roni Daniel is Angry," *Haaretz,* October 9, viewed December
  27, 2011, retrieved from http://www.haaretz.co.il/opinions/1.1049291.
Avraham, Ruty 2006. "Shneler: H.C.J is Harming the Core of Democracy," *Arutz* 7, December
  12, viewed December 27, 2011, retrieved from www.inn.co.il/News/News.aspx/157246.
Barak, Aharon 1992/3. "The Constitutional Revolution: Protected Human Rights," *Mishpat
  Umimshal* 1: 9.
Barak, Aharon 1993. "The Supreme Court and Basic-Law: Human Dignity and Liberty,"
  Hamishpat 2: 15–21.

Barak, Aharon 1994. *Interpretation in Law Volume III Constitutional Interpretation*. Jerusalem: Nevo Publishing.

Barak, Aharon 2000a. "Human Dignity as a Constitutional Right," in Cohn, Haim H. and Zamir, Itzhak (eds.), *Aharon Barak Selected Essays*, Vol. A. Jerusalem: Nevo Publishing, pp. 417–445.

Barak, Aharon 2000b. "The Constitutional Revolution," in Cohn, Haim H. and Zamir, Itzhak (eds.), *Aharon Barak Selected Essays*, Vol. A. Jerusalem: Nevo Publishing, pp. 349–355.

Barak-Erez, Daphne 2007. *Outlawed Pigs*. Madison: University of Wisconsin Press.

Barak-Erez, Daphne 2010. "Symbolic Constitutionalism: On Sacred Cows and Abominable Pigs," *Law, Culture and The Humanities* 6: 420–435.

Bassok, Or 2003. "A Decade after the Constitutional Revolution – A View on the Constitutional Process in Israel Thru a Comparative Historic Prism," *Mishpat U'Mimshal* 6(2): 495–509.

Bechor, Guy 1996. *Constitution for Israel*. Jerusalem: Keterpress.

Bendor, Ariel 2000. "The Legal Status of the Basic Laws" in Barak, Aharon and Berenson Haim (eds.), *Berenson Book*, Vol. 2, Jerusalem: Nevo Publishing, pp. 119–181.

Divrei HaKnesset, *Protocols of the 13th Knesset, 17 March 1992*, viewed November 10, 2012, retrieved from http://www.knesset.gov.il/Tql/knesset/Knesset12/html/19920317@19920317008@008.html.

Divrei HaKnesset, *Protocols of the 13th Knesset, 9 March 1994*, viewed November 10, 2012, retrieved from http://www.knesset.gov.il/Tql/knesset/Knesset13/html/19940309@19940309035@035.html.

Edrey, Yoseph M. 2005. "The Israeli Constitutional Revolution/Evolution, Models of Constitutions, and a Lesson from Mistakes and Achievements," *The American Journal of Comparative Law* 53: 77–123.

Epp, Charles 1998. *The Rights Revolution: Lawyers, Activists and Supreme Courts in Comparative Perspective*. Chicago: University of Chicago Press.

Farber, Dan 2002. "Rights as Signals," *J. Legal Stud.* 31: 83–100.

Freudenheim, Yeoshua 1973. *Government in Israel*. Jerusalem: Rubin mas Press.

Gavison, Ruth 1997. "The Constitutional Revolution: A Reality or a Self-Fulfilling Prophecy?" *Mishpatim* 28: 21–147.

Ginsburg, Tom 2003. *Judicial Review in New Democracies: Constitutional Courts in Asian Cases*. New York: Cambridge University Press.

Ginsburg, Tom 2009. "The Judicialization of Administrative Governance," in Ginsburg, Tom & Chen, Albert H. Y. (eds.), *Administrative Law and Governance in Asia*, New York: Routledge, pp. 1–20.

Goldberg, Giora 1993. "You don't Need a Constitution to Plant Trees: On State-Building and Constitution Framing," *State, Government and International Relation* 38: 29–48.

Hamilton, Walton H. & George D. Braden 1941. "The Special Competence of the Supreme Court," *Yale Law Journal* 50: 1319–1375.

Hirschl, Ran 1997. "The 'Constitutional Revolution' and the Emergence of a New Economic Order in Israel," *Israel Studies* 2: 136–155.

Hirschl, Ran 2004. *Towards Juristocracy: The Origins and Consequences of the New Constitutionalism*. Cambridge: Harvard University Press.

Hirschl, Ran 2009. "The Socio-Political Origins of Israel's Juristocracy," *Constellations* 16(3): 476–492.

Hofnung, Menachem 1996. "The Unintended Consequences of Unplanned Constitutional Reform: Constitutional Politics in Israel," *The American Journal of Comparative Law* 44(4): 584–604.

Jacobsohn, Gary 2000. "After the Revolution," *Israeli Law Review* 34: 139–169.

Kagan, Robert A. 2001. *Adversarial Legalism*. Cambridge: Harvard University Press.

Karp, Yehudit 1990. "The Legislative Council: The Beginning of the Legislative Tale," in Barak, Aharon and Shepnitz, Tena (eds.), *Ori Yadin Book*, Vol. B. Jerusalem: Bursi Publishing Co., pp. 209–255.

Kedar, Nir *Ben-Gurion and the Constitution: on Constitutionalism, Democracy and Law in David Ben-Gurion's Policy* (forthcoming, 2012), chapter 5.

Kidder, Nir 2009. *Mamlakhtiut David Ben-Gurion Civic Thought*. Jerusalem: Yad Yitzhak Ben-Zvi and Ben-Gurion University.

Landau. Moshe 1980. "The Power of the Court and its Limits," *Mishpatim* 10: 196–202.

Lapid, Tommy 2007. "Because of the Standing Requirements," *nrg*, July 25, viewed December 27, 2011, retrieved from www.nrg.co.il/online/1/ART1/613/328.html.

Lerner, Hanna 2011. *Making Constitutions in Deeply Divided Societies*. New York: Cambridge University Press.

Mandel, Michael 1999. "Democracy and New Constitutionalism in Israel," *Israel Law Review* 33(2): 259.

Mautner, Menachem 2008. *Law and Culture in Israel at the Threshold of the Twenty First Century*. Tel Aviv: Am Oved.

Rackman, Emanuel 1955. *Israel's Emerging Constitution 1948–51*, New York: Columbia University Press.

Ramseyer, J. Mark 1994. "The Puzzling (in)Dependence of Courts: A Comparative Approach," *The Journal of Legal Studies* 23(2): 721–747.

Rubinstein, Amnon and Barak Medina 2005. *The Constitutional Law of the State of Israel*. Tel Aviv and Jerusalem: Nevo.

Salzberger, Eli M. 1996. "The Constitutional Authority in Israel," *Mishpat U'Mimshal* 3: 679–696.

Salzberger, Eli M. & Alexander (Sandy) Kedar 1998. "The Quiet Revolution: More on Judicial Review in Accordance to the New Basic Laws," *Mishpat U'Mimshal* 4: 489–520.

Salzberger, Eli M. & Stefan Voigt 2002. "On Constitutional Processes and the Delegation of Power, with Special Emphasis on Israel and Central and Eastern Europe," *Theoretical Inquiries in Law* 3(1): 1–57.

Sapir, Gideon 2008. "The Israeli Constitutional Revolution – How did it Happen?" viewed December 27, 2011, retrieved from http://works.bepress.com/gidon_sapir/1.

Sapir, Gideon 2010. *Constitutional Revolution in Israel*. Tel Aviv: Miskal & Bar-Ilan University & University of Haifa Press.

Segev, Joshua 2007. "Who Needs a Constitution? In Defense of the Non-decision Constitution-Making Tactic in Israel," *Alb. L. Rev.* 70: 409–491.

Shalita, Chen 2007. "Beinish has some 'soldiers' in the Battle Against Daniel Friedman – but Most Won't Sacrifice Themselves for Her," *Globes*, December 30, viewed December 27, 2011, retrieved from www.globes.co.il/news/article.aspx?did=1000290776.

Stoil, Anna 2007. "Danziger Appointed to High Court of Justice," *The Jerusalem Post*, July 30, viewed December 27, 2011, retrieved from www.jpost.com/Israel/Article.aspx?id=70367.

Yannay, Natan 1990. "The Transition to a State of Israel: Politics and Establishment of a Constitution," in Pilowski, Varda (ed.), *Transition from "Yishuv" to State 1947–1949: Continuity and Change*, Haifa: University of Haifa Press, pp. 23–37.

COURT CASES

H.C. 2605/05, *Academic Center of Law and Business v. Minister of Finance*, (Nevo) (2009).

H.C. 7052/03, *Adallah the Legal Center for the Rights of the Arab Minority v. Minister of Interior*, P.D. 51(2) 202 (2006).

H.C. 8276/05, *Adallah the Legal Center for the Rights of the Arab Minority v. Minister of Defence*, (Nevo) (2006).

H.C. 246/81, *Agudat Derech Eretz v. The Broadcasting Authority*, P.D. 35(4) 1 (1981).
Cr.A. 8823/07, *Anonymous v. The State of Israel*, (Nevo) (2010).
H.C. 1/49, *Bajerano v. Minister of Police*, P.D. 2 80 (1949).
C.A. 6821/93, *Bank Hamizrachi united v. Migdal Communal Village*, P.D. 49(4) 221 (1995).
H.C. 188/63, *Bazul v. Minister of Interior*, P.D. 19(1) 337 (1963).
H.C. 98/69, *Bergman v. Minister of Finance*, P.D. 23(1) 693 (1969).
H.C. 726/94, *Clal Insurance Company Ltd. v. Minister of treasury*, P.D. 48(5) 441 (1994).
H.C. 366/03, *Commitment to Peace and Social Justice v. Minister of Finance*, IsrLR 355 (2005).
H.C. 389/80, *Dapey Zahav Ltd. v. Broadcasting Authority*, P.D 35(1) 421 (1980).
H.C. 8397/06, *Eduardo v. Minister of Defense*, (Nevo) (2007).
H.C. 466/07, *Galon v. Attorney General* (Nevo) (2012).
H.C. 10203/03, *Hamifkad Haleumi Ltd. v. Attorney General*, (Nevo) (2008).
H.C. 5757/04, *Hess v. Deputy Chief of Staff*, P.D. 59(6) 97 (2005).
H.C. 10662/04, *Hassan v. National Insurance Institute* (Nevo, decided Feb. 28, 2012).
H.C. 1715/97, *Investment Managers' Committee v. Minister of Treasury*, P.D. 51(4) 367 (1997).
H.C. 148/73, *Kaniel v. Minister of Justice*, P.D. 27(1) 794 (1973).
H.C. 73/53, *Kol Ha'am Co. Ltd. v. Minister of Interior*, P.D. 7 871 (1953).
H.C. 142/89, *Laor Movement v Chair of the Knesset*, P.D. 44(3) 529 (1990).
H.C. 5578/02, *Manor v. Minister of Finance*, P.D. 59(1) 729 (2004).
H.C. 3872/93, *Meatrael Ltd. v. The Prime Minster*, P.D. 47(5) 485 (1992).
H.C. 6427/02, *The Movement for Quality Government in Israel v. The Knesset*, (2)Tak-SC 1559 (2006).
Cr.A. 107/73, *"Negev" Automobile Services Station Ltd. v. State of Israel*, P.D. 28(1) 640 (1983).
H.C. 1030/99, *MK Oron v. Chairman of the Knesset*, P.D. 56(3) 640 (2002).
H.C. 2994/90, *Poraz v. State of Israel*, P.D. 44(3) 317 (1990).
H.C. 1661/05, *Regional Municipality Hof Aza v. Knesset of Israel*, P.D. 59(2) 481 (2005).
H.C. 60/77, *Ressler v. Chairman of Elections Committee*, P.D. 31(2) 556 (1977).
H.C. 6298/07, *Ressler v. The Knesset* (Nevo, decided Feb.21, 2012).
H.C. 141/82, *Rubinstein v. Chairman of the Knesset*, P.D. 37(3) 141 (1982).
H.C. 3267/97, *Rubinstein v. Minister of Defense*, P.D. 52(5) 481 (1998).
H.C. 1554/95, *Shoharey Gila"t Association v. Minister of Education and Culture*, P.D. 50(3) 2 (1995).
H.C. 6055/95, *Tzemach v. Minister of Defence*, P.D. 33(5) 241 (1999).
H.C. 1635/90, *ZarZevsky v. Prime Minister of Israel*, P.D. 45(1) 749 (1991).
H.C. 10/48, *Ziv v. Gubernick*, P.D. 1 85 (1948).

BASIC LAWS (INCLUDING DRAFTS)

The Law of Equal Rights for Women, 1951, S.H. 248.
Basic-Law: The Government, 1992, S.H. 14.
Basic-Law: Haknesset, 1958, S.H. 69.
Draft Bill of Basic Law: The Legislation, 2009. Viewed December 27, 2011, retrieved from http://www.knesset.gov.il/privatelaw/data/18/317.rtf.

STATUTES

Law of Rabbinic Courts Judging (Marriage and Divorce), 1953, S.H. 165.
Law of Rabbinic Courts (Enforcement of Rulings of Divorce), 1995, S.H. 139.
The Law of Transition, 1949, S.H. 1.

10

Public Interest Litigation and the Transformation of the Supreme Court of India

Manoj Mate*

The Supreme Court of India today is arguably one of the most powerful constitutional courts in the world. The Court has taken on an active and central role in the governance of the Indian polity through its activity in public interest litigation cases, and in some cases, has virtually taken over functions that were once the domain of Parliament and the Executive. Within the past two decades, the Indian Court wrested control over judicial appointments from the Executive,[1] and assumed a leading role in policymaking in the areas of affirmative action, environmental policy, education, and development. The Court has generally exerted a great deal of authority in securing compliance with decisions in which it has asserted expanded power. However, during the first two decades after India's independence, the Court played a relatively limited role in governance. How can one explain the expansion of the Court's role in Indian politics today?

This chapter examines a critical "moment"[2] in the expansion of judicial power in India: the development of the Public Interest Litigation (PIL) regime in the post–Emergency Indian Court. Following the end of Indira Gandhi's Emergency

---

* Assistant Professor, Whittier Law School. An earlier version of this chapter were presented at the Mellon Sawyer Seminar "The Dilemmas of Judicial Power in Comparative Perspective," at the Center for the Study of Law and Society in Berkeley, January 30, 2008. I am grateful to Martin Shapiro, Robert A. Kagan, David Caron, Christopher Edley, Jonathan Simon, Terence Halliday, Malcolm Feeley, Gordon Silverstein, and Gary Jacobsohn for their comments, suggestions, and insights.

[1] *See Supreme Court Advocates-on-Record Ass'n v. Union of India*, (1993) 4 S.C.C. 441 [hereinafter *Second Judges' Case*].

[2] I use the term "moment" here to describe a different concept than Bruce Ackerman's well-known idea of a "constitutional moment." Ackerman's conception of a constitutional moment describes episodes of constitutional change and transition through "higher lawmaking" outside the constitutionally prescribed methods and rules of amendment. In contrast, I define moment more narrowly, as a set of legal-constitutional changes or developments, including judicial decisions, that have a significant impact on the power of high courts, although this conception of a moment may not be mutually exclusive from Ackerman's conception (*see* Ackerman 1991).

regime (1975–1977) and the election of the Janata party government in 1977, the Supreme Court of India expanded popular access to the Court and broadened its own power and jurisdiction through PIL cases involving repression of human rights and malgovernance. Through PIL, the Indian Court asserted itself as a "champion" of the rule of law and responsible governance in the 1980s, although the Court avoided direct challenges to the policies and actions of the Executive and Parliament in this period. As India transitioned from an era of one-party rule under the Congress party to an era of multiparty politics and coalition governments in the early 1990s, the Court became more assertive in challenging the central government, particularly in key governance domains including judicial appointments, corruption and accountability, and environmental policy.

What makes the expansion of judicial power in India so remarkable is that the Indian Court has overcome important political and structural constraints. The Indian Supreme Court was armed by the Indian Constitution with the power of judicial review, appellate jurisdiction over the state High Courts, advisory jurisdiction through presidential reference of issues, and original jurisdiction on the basis of Article 32, which allows for direct suits in the Supreme Court to enforce the Fundamental Rights provisions[3] and empowers the Court to issue writs to enforce these rights.[4] However, three key aspects of India's political structure and historical legacy limited the Court's development early on. First, the Constituent Assembly intended the Court to serve as a weaker, subservient institution to Parliament. The Constitution conferred on Parliament the power to easily override the Court's decisions through a constitutional amendment process that required majorities in both houses of Parliament. Second, the Constituent Assembly placed provisos and limitations on many of the fundamental rights provisions. The Assembly also eliminated a due process clause from the final draft of Article 21 to prevent the Court from reviewing the socialist Congress regime's redistributive, collectivist, and economic policies as well as reviewing the government's provisions for preventive detention (see Austin 1966).[5] Third, the British legacy of Austinian positivism (many of India's early jurists were educated or trained in England or Indian law schools versed in

---

[3] *See* India Constitution, Articles 13–31.

[4] India Constitution, Article 32, §§ 1, 2:

> Remedies for enforcement of rights conferred by this Part. – (1) The right to move the Supreme Court by appropriate proceedings for the enforcement of the rights conferred by this Part is guaranteed. (2) The Supreme Court shall have power to issue directions or orders or writs, including writs in the nature of *habeas corpus, mandamus*, prohibition, *quo warranto* and *certiorari*, whichever may be appropriate, for the enforcement of any of the rights conferred by this Part.

[5] For an analysis of the Indian Supreme Court's jurisprudence in the area of preventive detention laws and personal liberty, *see* Manoj Mate (2010). "The Origins of Due Process in India: The Role of Borrowing in Personal Liberty and Preventive Detention Cases", *Berkeley J. Int'l L.* 28: 216.

British traditions) meant that India's early jurisprudence would be limited by more formalist modes of constitutional interpretation.[6]

As this chapter will show, the origins of the Supreme Court of India's departure from that tradition and its development of PIL in the post–Emergency era (1977–2007) can be traced to the epic battles between the government of Indira Gandhi and the Court during the late 1960s and 1970s. During the 1960s and 1970s, the Court shifted toward a new activism in a series of decisions involving the constitutionality of government land reform laws and the right to property (see Sathe 1989; Ramachandran 2000). In these decisions, the Court for the first time asserted limits on Parliament's power of constitutional amendment through the development of the basic structure doctrine. These battles drove the Gandhi regime to attack the Court in two ways – by packing the Court with judges who shared her social-egalitarian populism, and curbing the Court's power through the the the enactment of amendments curbing judicial power and declaration of Emergency rule in 1975. The Court acquiesced and upheld the suspension of constitutional rights and liberties during the Emergency. Following the defeat of the Emergency regime by the Janata party coalition in 1977, however, the Court turned in an activist direction that was qualitatively different from the Court's pre–Emergency activism. It dramatically expanded the scope of fundamental rights, and expanded popular access to the Court by inviting PIL claims involving direct human rights violations and governance failures by government agencies. Over the next three decades, the Court significantly expanded its role in the governance of the Indian polity in areas including judicial administration, corruption and government accountability, and environmental policy.

How can one account for and explain this extraordinary shift in the Court's role and power? Drawing on existing scholarship, field research interviews, and analysis of judicial decisions, this chapter illustrates how the development of PIL was directly shaped by both institutional motives and the sincere policy values of senior justices of the Indian Supreme Court. PIL was driven in part by several leading justices' desire to rehabilitate and bolster the institutional legitimacy of a Court that had been tarnished by its acquiescence to Gandhi's Emergency rule regime (see Baxi 1980). In addition, the justices' activism and assertiveness in early PIL cases reflected the social-egalitarian policy values and worldviews of senior Supreme Court justices who had been appointed by Gandhi during the 1970s (interviews with Justice Bhagwati, Justice V.R. Krishna Iyer, Senior Advocate Rajeev Dhavan). By inviting a vast array of new PIL claims in the 1980s, the Court served both motives.

On the other hand, in the 1980s the Court largely avoided direct challenges to the policies and actions of the central government of Indira Gandhi in politically salient areas, such as judicial appointments, economic policy, and national security. The Court "trimmed its sails" and dampened its assertiveness because of an inhospitable

---

[6] According to Arthur Von Mehren, the emphasis on formalism in early Indian judicial decisions inevitably resulted in a "static conception of the law" (*see* Mark Galanter 1984: 484, citing Von Mehren 1965).

political opportunity structure. Following Gandhi's return to power in 1980, she continued to exert pressure on the Court. In contrast to the pre–Emergency era, however, the Court was able to gradually build popular support and power, by avoiding challenges to the central government that could trigger backlash and attacks and diminish the Court's authority. PIL was thus effectively deployed by the Court as a strategy for protecting, consolidating, and ultimately expanding the Court's institutional strength and power.

In the post–1990 era, the policy values of justices continued to reflect broader elite frustrations with increasing levels of corruption, malgovernance, bureaucratic ineffectiveness, and the lack of accountability and transparency in government (see Andhyarujina 1992; Verma 1997). A significant change in the political environment also provided a more hospitable opportunity structure for the exercise of power. In the 1990s, India's political system shifted to an era of rule by weaker, fragmented coalition governments at the center (see Manor 1990; Yadav 1999; Chhibber 2001). A weaker Executive (prime minister and Council of Ministers) and Parliament had diminished ability to attack and override the Indian Court. Thus, the Supreme Court judges acted to displace the Executive in several policy and governance domains where the government was deemed to have failed to perform its functions. Where the court in the 1980s sought to build power by serving as an agent of the central government in enforcing and implementing laws in the areas of human rights and environmental policy, the Court in the 1990s wielded enhanced power against elected party regimes that themselves had failed to secure the rule of law.

The first part of this chapter examines the historical context of PIL, by briefly examining the Court's activism and assertiveness in basic structure decisions in the pre–Emergency era. The chapter's second section analyzes the development and expansion of PIL. The third part seeks to provide an explanatory account of the expansion of the Court's role.

THE BATTLE OVER THE BASIC STRUCTURE DOCTRINE AND THE EMERGENCY

Following India's independence and the drafting and ratification of the Indian Constitution in 1950, *zamindars* (landholders/landlords) challenged state-level land reform laws that sought to redistribute land through abolition of the Zamindari regime that had developed under British colonial rule (see Merillat 1970). In *Kameshwar Singh v. State of Bihar* (1951), the Patna High Court invalidated one such law – the Bihar Land Reforms Act – as invalid under Article 14 (equality). The High Court held that the Bihar Act, "by providing a graduated scale of compensation that was related to the size of the landholdings, set up an unreasonably discriminatory classification."

In response, the Nehru-led Congress Government enacted the First Amendment to the Indian Constitution, which sought to place limits on the right to compensation for property acquired by government takings (as set forth in Article 31). The amendment added Articles 31A and 31B and a Ninth Schedule to the Constitution (the Constitution originally contained eight schedules that set forth lists of the various states, languages, and various categories of government and bureaucratic structure and powers) (see Merillat 1970). Article 31 originally provided that no person could be deprived of property except by authority of law, and that no property could be acquired by the government for public purposes without compensation.[7] Article 31A, however, barred the Courts from reviewing the constitutionality of all laws enacted for the taking of estates or rights in them for compliance with the Fundamental Rights section; Article 31B specifically insulated any laws placed in the Ninth Schedule of the Constitution from judicial review (Austin 1999: 85; Sathe 1989: 4). The Ninth Schedule expanded the scope of Article 31 by creating a separate schedule containing thirteen specific laws that would be "certified by the President and deemed valid retrospectively and prospectively notwithstanding anything in the Constitution" (Austin 1999: 85). Over the next decades, the government added additional laws to this schedule through the enactment of subsequent constitutional amendments.

In 1950, in *Sankari Prasad v. Union of India*,[8] petitioners argued that the First Amendment violated Article 13(2) – which prohibited the government from passing any law that infringed on the fundamental rights provisions – and that an amendment was included in the definition of law. However, the Court rejected this argument, holding that "there was a clear distinction between ordinary law made in exercise of legislative power, and constitutional law made in exercise of constituent power" (Ramachandran 2000: 109).[9]

Soon thereafter, however, the Court adopted a new activist approach that led to a period of prolonged conflict between the government and the judiciary. In a series of decisions in 1954, the Supreme Court ruled that economic regulations that caused restrictions on property rights constituted an abridgment of the property right, and thus triggered the compensation requirement.[10] In these decisions, the Court interpreted the term "compensation" in Article 31 as requiring fair and adequate compensation.[11,12] In response, the government enacted the Seventeenth Amendment, which sought to expand the term "state" in Article 31 to encompass a broader

[7] Article 31 was subsequently repealed in 1978 by the Janata government.
[8] 1952 S.C.R 89; A.I.R. 1951 S.C. 458 (1951).
[9] Similarly, in *Sajjan Singh v. State of Rajasthan*, 1 S.C.R. 933 (1965); A.I.R. 1965 SC 845, the Court adjudicated a challenge to the constitutionality of the Seventeenth Amendment. In upholding the amendment, the Court reaffirmed its earlier decision in *Shankari Prasad*.
[10] *See State of West Bengal v. Bela Banerjee* (1954) SCR 558; *State of West Bengal v. Subodh Gopal* A.I.R. 1954 S.C. 92; *Dwarkadas Srinivas v. Sholapur Spinning & Weaving Co.*, A.I.R. 1954 SC 119 (1954).
[11] Raju Ramachandran, "The Supreme Court and the Basic Structure Doctrine," in B.N. Kirpal et al., eds. 2000. *Supreme but not Infallible: Essays in Honour of the Supreme Court of India*. New Delhi: Oxford University Press: 110.
[12] The Supreme Court invalidated the Kerala Agrarian Relations Act of 1961 and the Madras Land Reforms Act of 1961 on the grounds that the state governments had defined the term "estate" as

array of land units, and also added an additional forty-four laws into the Ninth Schedule to immunize them from judicial review. The battle between the judiciary and the government over property rights ultimately culminated in two landmark decisions – *Golak Nath v. State of Punjab*[13] in 1967, and *Kesavananda Bharati v. State of Kerala*[14] 1973.

Golak Nath v. Union of India (1967)

In a 6-5 ruling, the Court in *Golak Nath* overruled its earlier decision in *Sankari Prasad* and *Sajjan Singh*, ruling that under Article 368, Parliament could not enact constitutional amendments that violate the fundamental rights provisions of the constitution. Writing for the majority, Chief Justice K. Subba Rao held that Article 368 did not actually confer the power to amend the Constitution, but rather set forth the procedures for amendment, and that amendments enacted under Article 368 were ordinary laws and thus could be subject to judicial review. The Court also ruled that it was within Parliament's power to convene a new Constituent Assembly for the purposes of amending the Constitution. Nevertheless, in a strategic move, the Court invoked the doctrine of *prospective overruling*, which meant that the ruling would only apply to future amendments (and that the First, Fourth, and Seventeenth Amendments enacted by Congress, although deemed to be unconstitutional, would remain in effect) (Sathe 1989: 17).

Although *Golak Nath* did not invalidate the three amendments, the Court did seek to mitigate the effect of the Fourth Amendment, which stipulated that the adequacy of compensation in takings would be nonjusticiable, and added seven additional laws to the Ninth Schedule. In *R.C. Cooper v. Union of India* (1970),[15] the Court invalidated the Bank Nationalization Act passed by Indira Gandhi's Congress government, on the grounds that the act provided only illusory compensation and constituted hostile discrimination by imposing restrictions on only certain banks (Sathe 1989: 18). The Court also asserted that it could hold that regulations were not reasonable under Article 31(2) of the Constitution where those regulations failed to provide adequate compensation. In another challenge to the Gandhi government, the Court in *Madhav Rao Scindia v. India* (1970)[16] invalidated the Gandhi government's efforts to abolish the titles, privileges, and privy purses of the former rulers of the princely states.

In response to these rulings, Indira Gandhi dissolved the Lok Sabha early, called for new elections, and openly campaigned against the Court, promising to make

excluding "ryotwari estates," the subject of the local land reform regulations. See *Karimbil Kunhikonam v. Kerala*, A.I.R. 1962 S.C. 723; *Krishnaswami v. Madras*, A.I.R. 1964 S.C. 1515.

[13]   2 SCR 762 (1967); A.I.R. 1967 S.C. 1643.

[14]   A.I.R. 1973 S.C. 1461.

[15]   A.I.R. 1970 S.C. 564.

[16]   A.I.R. 1971 S.C. 530.

basic changes in the Constitution to provide for social equality and poverty allevi-
ation (Sathe 1989). Following a landslide win, Gandhi's government enacted the
Twenty-Fourth Amendment, which sought to overrule *Golak Nath* by reasserting
Parliament's unlimited power to amend the Constitution, including the Fundamental Rights provisions under Article 368, and declared that such amendments were
not ordinary laws under Article 13, and immune from judicial review.[17] The government also sought to override the *R.C. Cooper* decision by enacting the Twenty-Fifth
Amendment, which made compensation associated with land acquisition laws nonjusticiable; accorded primacy to the Directive Principles in Article 39 over the
Fundamental Rights provisions in Articles 14, 19, and 31; and stipulated that laws
enacted to give effect to the aforementioned Directive Principles could not be challenged in Court. Finally, the government enacted the Twenty-Ninth Amendment,
which added two Kerala land reform laws to the Ninth Schedule.

Kesavananda Bharati v. State of Kerala (1973)

In *Kesavananda*,[18] the Court heard a series of challenges to the Twenty-Fourth,
Twenty-Fifth, and Twenty-Ninth Amendments. In a 1,002-page decision consisting
of 11 separate opinions, the a closely divided 7-6 Court overruled its earlier decision in *Golak Nath*. It held that Parliament could amend the fundamental rights
provisions (Ramachandran 2000: 114) but that under Article 368, Parliament could
not enact constitutional amendments that altered the "basic structure" of the Indian
Constitution.[19] Again, as in *Golak Nath*, the Court's ruling was prospective: the
Court avoided a direct challenge to Gandhi's political priorities by upholding the
validity of the existing amendments, asserting that the Court had the power to review
future amendments, including additions to the Ninth Schedule.

The justices offered differing views of what might comprise the basic structure of
the Constitution. Chief Justice Sikri held that the basic structure included:

(i) Supremacy of the Constitution, (ii) Republican and democratic form of government, (iii) Secular character of the Constitution, (iv) Separation of powers between
the legislature, the executive and the judiciary, (v) Federal character of the Constitution. The above structure is built on the basic foundation, i.e. the dignity and
freedom of the individual. This is of supreme importance. This cannot by any form
of amendment be destroyed.[20]

[17] *Id.*
[18] A.I.R. 1973 S.C. 1461.
[19] At the time of the decision, there was a great deal of confusion regarding the actual "ratio" or
rationale underlying the majority decision in *Kesavananda*, as only six justices held that the power
of constitutional amendment was not unlimited, given that there were implied limitations on it. Six
other justices held that the power of amendment was unlimited (Andhyarujina 1992). The end of the
opinion, however, contained a summary of the "view of the majority" that was signed by nine of the
twelve justices that asserted that Parliament could not alter the basic structure through the amending
power under Article 368 (*Id.*, citing Kesavananda, A.I.R. 1973 S.C. 1461; *see* Seervai 1973).
[20] *Kesavananda*, A.I.R. 1973 S.C. 1461 at 1535 (Sikri, C.J.).

In addition to the foregoing features, Justice Shelat believed "the unity and integrity of the nation" and "the mandate given to the state in the directive principles of state policy" were also basic features of the Constitution.[21]

The *Kesavananda* decision represented a direct political challenge by the Court to the electoral mandate of Gandhi's Congress party regime, which had won 350 out of 545 seats in the 1971 elections In its manifesto, Gandhi's Congress party had sought a mandate "for the reassertion of Parliamentary Supremacy in the matter of amendment of fundamental rights," a direct reference to the Court's decision in *Golak Nath* (Baxi 1980: 22). However, in its decision, the Court went so far as to question the electoral mandate of the Congress party, noting that, "Two-thirds of the members of the two Houses of Parliament need not represent even the majority of the people in this country. Our electoral system is such that even a minority of voters can elect more than two-thirds of the members of either House of Parliament."[22] Most scholars of Indian constitutional law today have noted the significance of this moment in India's political and constitutional history (see e.g., Baxi 1974; Ramachandran 2000).

The immediate reaction to the decision, however, was more hostile. The controversial *Kesavananda* decision did not sit well with Indira Gandhi. She selected A.N. Ray to be the next chief justice, superseding (or passing over) the three next senior justices in the *Kesavananda* majority. The three superseded judges resigned. Gandhi then packed the Court with judges who shared her social-egalitarian vision.

The Emergency Rule Period: The Indian Judiciary Under Attack, the Supreme Court Retreats

In 1975, the Allahabad High Court set aside Indira Gandhi's election to Parliament on the grounds that her campaign had committed a "corrupt practice" (Ramachandran 2000: 15). In response, Gandhi declared an Emergency on June 25, 1975 and appealed the High Court's decision to the Supreme Court.[23] However, her government also enacted the Thirty-Ninth Amendment, which retroactively validated Gandhi's election, superseding the applicability of all previous election laws and immunizing all elections involving the prime minister or speaker of the Lok Sabha from judicial review (Ramachandran 2000: 116). The government also enacted the Fortieth, Forty-First, and Forty-Second Amendments, which further curbed judicial power, imposed new draconian laws allowing the regime to preventively detain political opponents, suspended fundamental rights and habeas corpus, and consolidated Executive power.

The Court acquiesced to Emergency rule and did not challenge key provisions of the Maintenance of Internal Security Act and other emergency laws. In the *Shiv*

---

[21] *Kesavananda*, A.I.R. 1973 S.C. 1461 at 1603 (Shelat, J.).
[22] *Kesavananda* at 481.
[23] Other factors cited by Gandhi in declaring an internal Emergency included widespread national agitation and unrest and labor strikes nationwide.

Kant Shukla decision, the Supreme Court upheld the Gandhi regime's suspension of access to the courts by political detainees (through habeas petitions), and thus overturned the actions of several high courts[24] that had agreed to hear several habeas petitions of detainees, notwithstanding the declaration of Emergency rule. In the *Bhanudas* decision, the Court refused to challenge the legality or conditions of preventive detention by the Emergency regime (Dua 1983).[25]

PUBLIC INTEREST LITIGATION AND THE EXPANSION OF JUDICIAL ROLES

Following Congress Prime Minister Indira Gandhi's dissolution of the *Lok Sabha* and sudden call for elections on January 18, 1977, a broad-based coalition of opposition parties united to form the Janata Party coalition to challenge Indira Gandhi's Congress party in the March 1977 elections. Janata's campaign manifesto called for an end to Emergency rule, the repeal of restrictions on the media, repeal of the draconian preventive detention laws allowing for preventive detention, warrantless search and seizure, wiretapping, and rescinding the antidemocratic Forty-Second Amendment (Limaye 1994: 153–157, 205–215, 295). Janata's victory marked the first time that a party other than Congress took control of the Government. During the tenure of the Janata government (1977–1979), the Supreme Court of India adopted a new activist approach to constitutional interpretation, particularly in establishing the PIL regime.

A group of senior activist justices expansively interpreted Article 32[26] to widen standing to sue (locus standi), thereby expanding access to the Court to third-party advocates and public-interest groups. The Court expanded access to public interest litigants by relaxing formal pleading and evidentiary requirements. The Court also expanded its equitable and remedial powers, enabling it to assert an enhanced monitoring and oversight function in PIL cases (see Cunningham 1987). At the same time, increased media attention on state repression of human rights and governance failures led to a surge in public-interest claims challenging these governance failures in court (see Baxi 1985). National newspapers such as the *Indian Express* published investigative reports on the excesses of the Emergency period and also highlighted atrocities committed by state and local police, the abhorrent condition of prisons, and abuses in the systems of protective custody, such as mental homes for women

---

[24] *A.D.M Jabalpur v. Shivakant Shukla* (1976) 2 S.C.C. 521.

[25] *Union of India v. Bhanudas Krishna Gawde* (1977) 1977 A.I.R. 1027.

[26] India Constitution, Article 32, §§ 1,2:

> Remedies for enforcement of rights conferred by this Part. – (1) The right to move the Supreme Court by appropriate proceedings for the enforcement of the rights conferred by this Part is guaranteed. (2) The Supreme Court shall have power to issue directions or orders or writs, including writs in the nature of *habeas corpus, mandamus*, prohibition, *quo warranto* and *certiorari*, whichever may be appropriate, for the enforcement of any of the rights conferred by this Part.

and children. This shift in media attention "enabled social action groups to elevate what were regarded as petty instances of injustices and tyranny at the local level into national issues, calling attention to the pathology of public and dominant group power" (Baxi 1985: 37). In commenting on the importance of the media in bolstering PIL, Baxi observed, "All this enhanced the visibility of the court and generated new types of claims for accountability for wielding of judicial power and this deepened the tendency towards judicial populism. Justices of the Supreme Court, notably Justices Krishna Iyer and Bhagwati, began converting much of constitutional litigation into SAL, through a variety of techniques or juristic activism" (Baxi 1985: 37–38).

During the Janata years, the Court – led by Justices P.N. Bhagwati and V.R. Krishna Iyer (both appointees of Prime Minister Indira Gandhi) – also pioneered a new activist jurisprudential regime in the area of fundamental rights, providing the substantive doctrinal foundation for the Court's expanded role in governance. In *Maneka Gandhi v. Union of India* (1978), the Court dramatically expanded the right to life and liberty in Article 21[27] by effectively reading the concept of due process into that provision, and broadened rights-based scrutiny of government actions under Article 14 ("Equality before the law")[28] and Article 19 (providing for protection of fundamental rightsincluding the right to freedom of speech).[29] The Court in *Maneka Gandhi* also created a new doctrine of non-arbitrariness review based on this reinterpretation of Articles 14 and 21 (see Mate 2010b).

Interestingly, PIL was an extension of the legal aid movement that had been launched during the Emergency by Indira Gandhi – a significant component of her social-egalitarian Twenty-Point Programme.[30] Justices Krishna Iyer and Bhagwati had both been leading advocates in the Government for policies and programs expanding legal aid[31] and access to justice, having pushed for the organization of

[27] India Constitution, Article 21 provides as follows: Protection of Life and Personal Liberty – "No person shall be deprived of life or personal liberty except according to procedure established by law."

[28] India Constitution, Article 14 reads as follows: "Equality before law. The State shall not deny to any person equality before the law or the equal protection of the laws within the territory of India."

[29] India Constitution, Article 19 provides as follows: "Protection of certain rights regarding freedom of speech, etc. –

(1) All citizens shall have the right:
    (a) to freedom of speech and expression;
    (b) to assembly peaceable and without arms;
    (c) to form associations or unions;
    (d) to move freely throughout the territory of India;
    (e) to reside and settle in any part of the territory of India; and
    (f) *to acquire, hold, and dispose of private property* [repealed by 44th Amendment];
    (g) to practice any profession, or to carry on any occupation, trade or business.

[30] Gandhi's Twenty Point Programme largely focused on economic policies, and included proposals for provision of land reforms, rural housing, the abolition of bonded labor, fighting tax evasion and smuggling, expanding worker participation in the industrial sector, and combating rural indebtedness. *See* Klieman 1981: 241, 251.

[31] As Chief Justice of the Gujarat High Court, Bhagwati chaired the state legal aid committee of that state, which issued recommendations for broadening legal aid and access to justice. Government of Gujarat, Report of the Legal Aid Committee (1971). Similarly, Justice Krishna Iyer chaired a Central

legal aid camps in villages, encouraged high court justices to adjudicate grievances in villages, and established people's courts (*lokadalats*).

The Judges Case (1981): An Activist but Strategic Court

The landmark decision on expanded locus standi was *S.P. Gupta v. Union of India* (the *Judges' Case*),[32] in which the Court adjudicated a challenge to the central government's control over judicial transfers and appointments in the High. Senior advocates in several states had filed suits challenging the Union Law Minister's assertion of power to transfer state high court judges to other jurisdictions, bypassing the normal consultation procedures. The government argued that the petitioners lacked standing because they did not suffer a legal harm or injury as a result of the transfers, and that only the judges themselves could bring claims. The Court rejected the government's standing objections, ruling that the advocates, as officers of the court, had a strong interest in maintaining the independence of the judiciary, and that the challenged transfers impacted the independence of the judiciary, which, the justices asserted, is part of the basic structure of the Constitution.

The majority of the Court, in ruling on the merits of the claims, held that, although the term "consultation" under Article 124(2) and Article 222(1) required that the Executive consult with at least one justice of the Supreme Court and of the High Court in addition to the Chief Justice of India, it did not mean that the Executive was required to follow the opinion or advice of these judges (Baxi 1985).[33] The Court's decision in the *Judges' Case* was thus a classic *Marbury* move: the Court expanded its own jurisdiction by endorsing standing for PIL, but gave the government what it wanted by deferring to the supremacy of the Executive in transfers and appointments. Upendra Baxi notes that the Court's decision appeared to be more strategic than motivated by doctrine, fashioning "a strategy of 'something for everybody'" by giving both the bar and the government victories (Baxi 1980: 39). However, the Court did assert the doctrine of expanded standing in a matter of high national salience, when it had been previously invoked only in matters of lesser importance. In so doing, the Court explicitly redefined the role of courts as a mechanism by which individuals could challenge failures of government in terms of statutory nonenforcement, violations of the Constitution, or breach of public duty. As Bhagwati noted in his opinion:

> We would hold therefore, hold that any member of the public having sufficient interest can maintain an action for judicial redress for public injury arising from breach of public duty or from violation of some provision of the Constitution

Government panel that called for restructuring the legal system. Government of India, Ministry of Law, Justice and Company Affairs, Report of the Expert Committee on Legal Aid: Processual Justice to the People (1973).

[32] *S.P. Gupta v. Union of India* (1981) Supp SCC 87.

[33] *S.P. Gupta*, (1981) Supp S.C.C. 87.

or the law and seek enforcement of such public duty and observance of such constitutional or legal provision. This is absolutely essential for maintaining the rule of law, furthering the cause of justice and accelerating the pace of realization of the constitutional objectives.[34]

The Supreme Court thereby assumed a new oversight and accountability function through which it could review the actions of national and state government entities. Justice V.R. Krishna Iyer describes this new function succinctly in his opinion in another early PIL decision, *Fertilizer Corp. Kamgar Union v. Union of India*,[35] observing that law "is a social auditor and this audit function can be put into action only when someone with real public interest ignites this jurisdiction."[36]

The Growth of PIL in the 1980s

From 1977 through the 1980s, the Court dramatically expanded the scope of its equitable and remedial powers in PIL cases, taking on challenges to government illegality and state repression of human rights For example, in one of the first PILs, *Hussainara Khatoon v. State of Bihar* (1979),[37] the Court developed the procedural innovation of "continuing mandamus." In *Hussainara*, the Court responded to a writ petition filed by advocate Kapila Hingorani, on the basis of a series of articles in the *Indian Express* about the problem of "undertrial prisoners" in Bihar and other states. Undertrial prisoners had served extensive pretrial detention terms in jail because they were unable to afford bail. In many cases, these prisoners had been in jail longer than the sentence that would have accompanied a conviction for the crime they were accused of committing. First, the Court allowed Hingorani to bring the habeas petition on behalf of the undertrial prisoners, effectively relaxing the standing requirement. Second, without issuing a dispositive judgment, the Court issued relief in the form of interim orders and directives, thus retaining jurisdiction pending a final ruling. This enabled the Court to monitor the reform process in the course of the litigation. In addition, the Court expanded the case, taking on several other human rights cases involving prisoners' rights, prison reform, bonded labor, and the rights of children and the mentally ill.

In a series of orders, *Hussainara I–VI*, the Court laid down new guidelines reforming the administration of bail, requiring the government to inform all undertrial prisoners of their entitlement to bail, and to release undertrial prisoners if their period of incarceration exceeded the maximum possible sentence for the offences for which they had been charged. The Court also ordered the release of the undertrial prisoners

---

[34] *S.P. Gupta*, (1981) Supp S.C.C. 87.
[35] *Fertilizer Corp. Kamgar Union v. Union of India*, (1981) 1 S.C.C. 568.
[36] *S.P. Gupta*, (1981) Supp S.C.C. 87. at 218 (citing *Fertilizer Corp.*, [1981] 1 S.C.C. 568 at 585).
[37] 1980 1 S.C.C. 81.

that had been mentioned and identified in the news article. The Court thus helped end the practice of "protective custody", mandating the release of thousands of prisoners in Bihar. Through the innovation of continuing mandamus, the Supreme Court could indefinitely retain jurisdiction over PIL matters by issuing orders and directives without issuing final dispositive judgments. Clark Cunningham referred to this procedural innovation, which was invoked in subsequent governance cases, as 'remedies without rights'" (Cunningham 1987: 511–515). According to Cunningham, "*Hussainara* thus set a pattern which the Supreme Court has followed in many public-interest cases: immediate and significant interim relief prompted by urgent need expressed in the writ petition, together with a long deferral of final decision as to factual issues and legal liability" (*Id.*).

In the late 1970s and early 1980s, the Court also relaxed standing requirements by treating letters from individuals, journalists, or third parties as legal petitions under Article 32,[38] initiating what Upendra Baxi has termed, "epistolary jurisdiction" (see Baxi 1985: 32, 41). For example, in *Bandhua Mukti Morcha v. Union of India*[39] (*BMM*), a three-justice bench of the Court initiated a PIL in response to a letter petition filed by Bandhua Mukti Morcha, a social reform group committed to ending the practice of bonded labor in India. Justice Bhagwati's opinion in BMM described the justifications and rationale for the relaxation of procedural requirements in PIL as follows:

> Where the weaker sections of the community are concerned . . . this Court will not insist on a regular writ petition to be filed by the public-spirited individual espousing their cause and seeking relief for them. This Court will readily respond even to a letter addressed by such individual acting pro bono publico. It is true that there are rules made by this Court prescribing the procedure for moving this Court for relief under Article 32 and they require various formalities to be gone through by a person seeking to approach this Court. But it must not be forgotten that *procedure is but a handmaiden of justice* and the cause of justice can never be allowed to be thwarted by any procedural technicalities. . . . Today a vast revolution is taking place in the judicial process; the theatre of the law is fast changing and the problems of the poor are coming to the forefront.[40]

---

[38] Article 32 of the Indian Constitution reads:

Remedies for enforcement of rights conferred by this Part. –

(1) The right to move the Supreme Court by appropriate proceedings for the enforcement of the rights conferred by this Part is guaranteed. (2) The Supreme Court shall have power to issue directions or orders or writs, including writs in the nature of *habeas corpus*, *mandamus*, prohibition, *quo warranto* and *certiorari*, whichever may be appropriate, for the enforcement of any of the rights conferred by this Part.

[39] *Bandhua Mukti Morcha v. Union of India*, (1984) 3 S.C.C. 161.

[40] *Id.* at 210–211.

Environmental Policy Cases

Beginning in the mid-1980s, through PIL cases, the Court took on a major role in enforcement and monitoring of statutory compliance with environmental policy. Public-interest lawyers, including M.C. Mehta (who has been described by some experts as a "One Person Enviro-Legal Brigade"), brought numerous PILs involving toxic gas leaks and air and river pollution, including the Shiram Fertilizer case, the Delhi pollution case,[41] and the Taj Mahal Pollution case.[42] In these cases, and others that were not as politically significant, the Court was doctrinally activist, developing a new doctrine of tort law and expanding equitable powers to enforce existing environmental laws.

An Activist, But Selectively Assertive Court

During the 1980s, although the Court gradually expanded its power in human rights and malgovernance cases, it was not a uniformly assertive Court. In high salience areas, the Court continued to avoid directly challenging the central government's policies and actions. This strategy, illustrated by the Court's decision in the *First Judges' Case*, also extended to economic policy. In the 1980s the Court upheld and/or endorsed most of the Congress governments' socialist-statist policies. For example, in *R.K. Garg v. Union of India* (1980), the Court upheld the Gandhi government's Special Bearer Bonds (Immunities and Exemptions) Ordinance Act, which granted immunity from prosecution under the Income Tax Act to individuals who purchased these bonds with "black money" (money that had been earned without being officially reported for tax purposes), and forbid any investigation into the source of this money. The petitioner, R.K. Garg, challenged the Act on the grounds that the separate treatment of black money investors in the act was arbitrary and violated Article 14 (equality). The Court ruled that the Act's separate treatment of black money investors did not violate the Article 14 ban on arbitrariness, holding that the classification had a rational basis – the government's effort to channel black money back into the productive sector to promote economic growth. The Court ruled that it could not question the morality of particular legislation on the basis of Article 14, and stressed the need for a deferential, rational-basis mode of review when examining government economic policies.[43]

In the early 1990s, as India adopted economic liberalization reforms, the Court continued to defer to government economic policies. The Congress regime of P.V. Narasimha Rao sought to move India from a socialist to an open, market-based economy, relaxing government controls and regulations on the private sector, liberalizing licensing regimes across various industries, and promoting privatization

---

[41] *M.C. Mehta v. Union of India* (1996) 4 S.C.C. 750.
[42] *M.C. Mehta v. Union of India* (1996) 4 S.C.C. 351; (1996) 4 S.C.C. 750.
[43] *R.K. Garg* at 705–706.

of state-owned industries and enterprises (Denoon 1998). Several aspects of these policies were challenged in the Supreme Court. In almost all of these cases, the Court upheld and endorsed the governments' policies, reiterating the mild rational basis review it had applied in *R.K. Garg* (see Bhushan 2004).

The Expansion of PIL in the Post-1990 Era: The Court Takes on the Central Government

The Court's PIL jurisprudence in the 1980s was typical of what one would expect from a "regime" Court. It performed the role of an agent of the central government, reigning in lawlessness and the arbitrariness of state and local governments and the bureaucracy, such as state repression in human rights cases, and state and local noncompliance with environmental laws. The Court avoided challenges to the central government's policies directly (Baxi 1985). In the post-1990 era, however, the Indian Supreme Court dramatically expanded its role in governance, becoming more assertive in challenging the power of the central government. The Court was able to do so because it faced a significantly more hospitable political environment characterized by weaker coalition governments in Delhi. Although the Court continued to defer to the central government in fundamental rights cases that involved challenges to economic and national security policy, it became highly assertive in cases involving governance in three key areas : (1) judicial appointments; (2) corruption and accountability; and (3) environmental policy. At the same time, the Court also expanded its role as a policymaker and problem solver in other areas including education, human rights, affirmative action, and development policy (see Dhavan 2000).

Judicial Appointments: The Second and Third Judges' Cases

In 1993, in *Supreme Court Advocates-on-Record Ass'n v. Union of India*[44] (hereafter the *Second Judges' Case*) the Court revisited the *First Judges Case*, which held that the Executive had primacy and final authority in appointing judges to the Supreme Court and High Courts. The petitioners' in the *Second Judges' Case* alleged that the Executive had failed to properly discharge its duties in filling judicial appointments in the High Courts in a timely manner, and in failing to select the most qualified judges. These failures had detrimentally affected the High Courts' ability to function efficiently and effectively. The Court overturned the *First Judges' Case*, holding that the Chief Justice of India (in consultation with a collegium of two senior justices), not the Executive, had primacy and the final say in judicial appointments and transfers.

In doing so, the Court rejected the rationale in *S.P. Gupta* that the Executive should have primacy because it is more accountable to the people.[45] That, wrote

---

[44] *Second Judges' Case* (1993) 4 S.C.C. 441.
[45] *Second Judges' Case* (1993) 4 S.C.C. 441 at 694.

Justice Verma, "is an easily exploded myth, a bubble which vanishes on a mere touch" because the Executive does not discuss appointments with Parliament and political parties do not make judicial appointments a key issue in their election manifestos.[46] "On the other hand," Justice Verma claimed, "in actual practice, the Chief Justice of India and the Chief Justice of the High Court, being responsible for the functioning of the courts, have to face the consequence of any unsuitable appointment which gives rise to criticism leveled by the ever vigilant Bar. That controversy is raised primarily in the courts."[47] According to Justice Verma's opinion, preserving judicial independence, integrity, and the professional excellence of the judiciary were all essential for protecting the rule of law and good governance, and allowing the chief justice to have primacy in appointments would advance these goals.[48]

A second rationale for the Court's holding was on the basis of the Executive's recent practice of deferring to the chief justices of the Supreme Court and High Court in judicial appointments and transfers. The Court thus transformed actual practice into doctrine, "locking in" judicial independence through a bold and unprecedented assertion of judicial independence. Five years later, in the *Third Judges' Case* (1998), the Court laid out more detailed procedures for the appointment process, and expanded the collegium[49] that the chief justice must confer with from two to four judges. Moreover, through PIL, the Court has continued to assert its independence and control over judicial administration in a series of decisions dealing with state-level appointments and administration.[50]

Corruption and Accountability: Vineet Narain (1998) and the RTI Cases (2002–2003)

The Court in the mid-1990s also became more assertive in corruption cases involving high-level government officials. In *Vineet Narain*,[51] for example, the Court asserted its power over the Central Bureau of Investigation (CBI) on the basis of the agency's failure to investigate and prosecute several prominent politicians implicated in the "Jain Hawala" bribery scandal. The Court took over monitoring

---

[46] *Id.*

[47] *Id.*

[48] *Id.*

[49] In *In re Special Reference No. 1 of 1998*, (1998) 7 S.C.C. 739 (hereafter the *Third Judges' Case*), the Court revisited its decision in the *Second Judges' Case* and ruled that the chief justice must consult with a collegium of the four (instead of two) most senior justices on the Court (see Desai and Muralidhar 2000 at 188, n. 31).

[50] *See All India Judges Association v. Union of India* (1994) 4 S.C.C. 288 (prescribing minimum qualifications for appointment in state courts); *All India Judges Association v. Union of India* (1994) 4 S.C.C. 727 (issuing directions dealing with the provision of residential accommodation to all judicial officers, libraries, vehicles, and recommending the establishment of an All India Judicial Service); *All India Judges Association v. Union of India* (2002) 4 S.C.C. 247 (issuing directions regarding pay scales of High Court judges and subordinate judiciary).

[51] *Vineet Narain v. Union of India* (1998) 1 SCC 226.

and control of the CBI's investigation, and observed that "The continuing inertia of the agencies to even commence a proper investigation could not be tolerated any longer," and that "merely issuance of a mandamus directing the agencies to perform their task would be futile."[52] The Court issued directives and guidelines that delinked the CBI from political control to ensure it more autonomy, and invoked the novel equitable power of continuing mandamus to dramatically reorganize the structure of the CBI and the Enforcement Directorate, ordering them to directly report to the Court. In fact, the Court established a new oversight body – the Central Vigilance Commission – to monitor the CBI. Finally, the Court, in a bold move, invalidated the single directive protocol, which required that the CBI receive prior authorization from the Executive branch before proceeding with an investigation against high-ranking government officials. The Court's intervention led not only to the filing of "34 chargesheets against 54 persons," including leading cabinet ministers and other government officials, but also led to critical media coverage and public backlash that helped contribute to the defeat of Prime Minister Rao's Congress government in the elections of May 1996. Since Vineet Narain, the Court has continued to play a key role in policing government corruption, as evidenced by the Court's recent decision in the 2G Scam decision, in which the Court cancelled 122 telecommunications licenses that were issued in an arbitrary manner by the government.[53]

In response to increasing levels of criminality in politics in the 1990s and 2000s, the Court also ordered the adoption of significant electoral reforms in the Right to Information (RTI) cases. In *Association for Democratic Reforms v. Union of India* (2002),[54] the Court held that voters had a right to information under the Indian Constitution and ordered the Election Commission to promulgate regulations requiring candidates for Parliament and State Legislative Assemblies to disclose candidates' prior criminal records, and records of financial assets. Parliament attempted to override this decision through the enactment of a new law in August 2002, but the Court subsequently invalidated this law as violating the right to information and reasserted disclosure requirements for legislative candidates in *P.U.C.L. v. Union of India* (2003).[55]

Environmental Policy

In the post-1990 era, building on its activism in the 1980s, the Court continued to expand its role in environmental policy, further encroaching on central government power. The Court has often assumed the role of a quasi-administrative agency

---

[52] *See* S. Muralidhar, *India: Public Interest Litigation, Survey 1997–1998*, 33–34 ANNUAL SURVEY of INDIAN LAW 525 at 533 (1997–1998), citing *Vineet Narain* at 237.
[53] *Dr. Subramanian Swamy v. Dr. Manmohan Singh* (2012) 3 SCC 64.
[54] *Ass'n For Democratic Reforms v. Union of India* (2002) 5 SCC 294.
[55] *People's Union for Civil Liberties v. Union of India* (2003) 4 SCC 399.

through the designation of special investigatory or monitoring committees.[56] As T.R. Andhyarujina has observed, the courts in India today "not only correct unreasonable conduct of the State but lay down norms of reasonable conduct for the State. These rules of conduct and schemes are akin to those made by administrative agencies themselves" (Andhyarujina 1992: 34). In dealing with the issue of deforestation, for example, the Supreme Court in the *Godavarman*[57] cases (1996–present) designated a High-Powered Committee to serve as an investigative, fact-finding arm of the Court and oversee the implementation of the Court's orders. Since *Godavarman*, the Court and Committee, according to one leading scholar, have "virtually become the Ministry of Forests" (Dhavan 2007; see Rosencrantz and Lele 2008).

Policy-making in Other Areas: Education, Human Rights, and Affirmative Action

Through the post-1990 period, the Court has assumed an interstitial policy-making role to address governance failures not only in environmental policy but in areas such as human rights law, police custodial violence, and police reform – areas in which the central government has failed to legislate or set guidelines; for example, in *Vishaka v. State of Rajasthan* (1997).[58] In *Vishaka*, the Court held that sexual harassment violated the rights of gender equality and the right to life and liberty under Articles 14, 15, and 21 of the Constitution, and that until Parliament adopted a law implementing the Convention on the Elimination of All Forms of Discrimination Against Women (to which India was a signatory), the Court would adopt the guidelines of the Convention and thereby make them enforceable (Desai and Muralidhar 2000: 178).

The Court has also taken a leading role in the area of development and poverty. In *P.U.C.L. v. Union of India* (2007), the Court recognized the right to food as part of the right to life in Article 21 and therefore justiciable, going on to rule that the government had a positive duty to help prevent malnutrition and starvation.[59] In 2007, the Court ordered the Indian government to pay 1.4 million rupees to help combat starvation and malnutrition through implementation of the Integrated Child Development Services plan.[60]

The Court has also assumed a key policy-making role concerning police reform. In response to a series of PILs documenting widespread cases of custodial violence and killing by police nationwide, the Court in the *D.K. Basu* cases (1997–2003) established national guidelines governing how police take suspects into custody

---

[56] The Court asserted its power to engage in investigative fact finding and appointed commissions for this purpose in the bonded labor case. See Bandhua Mukti Morcha (1984) 3 S.C.C. 161.

[57] *T.N. Godavarman v. Union of India*, at 642.

[58] *Vishaka v. State of Rajasthan* (1997) 6 S.C.C. 241.

[59] *People's Union for Civil Liberties v. Union of India* (2007) 1 S.C.C. 728 (ordering state governments and union territories to implement the Integrated Child Development Scheme).

[60] *People's Union for Civil Liberties v. Union of India* (2007) 1 S.C.C. 719.

and interrogate suspects. In the *Prakash Singh* decision (2006), the Court issued guidelines for national police reform, and ordered the creation of a National Police Commission to oversee the implementation of these guidelines. However, in this and other areas, the government failed to fully implement or effectuate Court orders.

In other policy areas, the Court has played an important role in proactively supporting the central government's agenda. In the *In Re Interlinking Rivers Case* (2002), the Court helped initiate the interlinking of rivers project that had been advocated by the president in a speech (Bhushan 2004). The Court issued interim orders that directed the central government to set up a high-level task force to consider the modalities of interlinking the major rivers of India within ten years and develop a consensus among states on the feasibility of the proposed 560–trillion-rupees (roughly $14 trillion U.S. dollars) project. The central government promptly responded by setting up a task force charged with preparing an action plan and feasibility studies.

EXPLAINING THE DEVELOPMENT AND EXPANSION OF PIL

Understanding the Motives That Drove PIL

How can one explain the development and expansion of PIL in the Indian Supreme Court in light of existing theories of judicial power? Proponents of the dominant regime-theory (or regime-politics) approach suggest that judges and courts seek to advance the political or policy agenda of the governing coalition in power and/or the party regime that appointed and/or promoted judges on High Courts (see Dahl 1957; Shapiro 1964; Peretti 1999). However, regime theory does not provide a complete account of the expansion of the power of the Supreme Court of India in PIL decisions.[61] In addition, one must also examine both the justices' own policy values and institutional motives within the broader context of the elite institutional environment and intellectual atmosphere of the Court to fully understand what drove the Court's activism, and shift to greater assertiveness and authority in the post-1989 era (see Mate 2010a).

The Indian Supreme Court's initial activism in developing PIL was driven by the social-egalitarian policy values of senior justices of the Indian Supreme Court, as confirmed by my interviews with Justices Bhagwati and Krishna Iyer. Justice

---

[61] Following the Court's decisions in *Golak Nath* and *Kesavananda*, Indira Gandhi's government appointed Justices A.N. Ray, P.N. Bhagwati, V.R. Krishna Iyer, and other judges to the Court who shared the Gandhi government's social-egalitarian reform agenda. However, it should be noted that the Gandhi government's consideration of judges' political attitudes and values in the appointment process was exceptional and marked a departure from earlier (and later) conventions of appointments (Gadbois 2011). Nehru's government, and governments in the post-*Second Judges Case*-era (1993) usually deferred to the chief justice's (and senior Supreme Court justices') recommendations for appointments, and these recommendations were mainly on the basis of assessment of judges' professional merit, regional representation, religion, and caste (see Dhavan and Jacob 1978; Gadbois 2011, 190–196). This suggests that the regime-politics approach may be limited in its application to the Indian case.

Bhagwati stated that he was motivated by a sincere desire to uplift the poor by activating the public-interest jurisdiction of the Court. He had done so, he said, after witnessing the extreme poverty of individuals who came to the Gujarat district court during his tenure as chief justice of the Gujarat High Court in the 1960s.[62] As a justice of the Supreme Court, Bhagwati toured the country and held several open meetings, noting:

> I saw stark naked poverty, and the utter helplessness of the people, they came and attended their meetings and looked upon me with awe, but they never tasted the fruits of this whole system of justice – justice was far[,] far removed from them – then I realized that justice I was administering in the courts was hollow justices – never reached the large masses of my own people . . . I realized I needed to address the three As which prevent them from accessing justice – the lack of awareness, lack of availability of machinery, and the lack of assertiveness. . . . So I said I must evolve a method by which they can come to court and what was preventing them was our whole doctrine of locus standi or standing. Because any NGO or other person could not bring a litigation on their behalf under the system as it then prevailed.[63]

In an interview with the author, Justice Krishna Iyer also recounted his own past experience as a young lawyer who was thrown into jail (under the existing preventive detention laws) for defending Communists and other dissident groups in the 1950s. Iyer thus had firsthand experience as a prisoner, and later, as the home minister and minister for law, power, prisons, irrigation, and social welfare in the Communist state government of Kerala. Iyer also spearheaded prison reform as one of his main goals as a minister and Supreme Court justice.[64]

PIL and the Opportunity Structure for Judicial Power: A Path to Legitimation?

In the pre–Emergency era, the Court's support of the basic structure doctrine reflected a growing consensus on the Court and among professional and intellectual elites about the need to impose limits on the Gandhi regime's power to amend the Constitution, and to preserve and protect constitutional rights from further erosion. In asserting and supporting the basic structure doctrine, the justices acted on their own institutionalist motivations and values. According to the *institutionalist model*, institutional norms, jurisprudential traditions, and other institutional factors help motivate and drive judicial behavior.[65]

---

[62] *Id.*

[63] Interview with Justice P.N. Bhagwati, January 2007, New Delhi, India.

[64] *Id.*

[65] Proponents of the institutional model argue that judges are motivated not only by their own policy views and understanding of existing doctrine, but also by their concern for maintaining or strengthening the legitimacy and solidity of courts as institutions. As Gillman suggests, judges "may view themselves as stewards of particular institutional missions, and . . . this sense of identity [may] generate motivations of duty and professional responsibility which sometimes pull against their policy preferences and partisan commitments" (Gillman 1993: 79–80).

In supporting limits on the amending power, and later the basic structure doctrine, Supreme Court justices sought to bolster the institutional solidity of the court, and to maintain its role of the Court as guardian of the constitution, the rule of law, and fundamental rights. As Austin observed, the "court mollified the government by over-ruling *Golak Nath* and upholding the three amendments – in effect, nearly returning to the *Sankari Prasad* case position – while preserving, indeed strengthening, its own power of judicial review" (Austin 1999: 276). In discussing the motivations that drove the majority in *Kesavananda*, Madhu Limaye, a leading scholar and thinker within the Janata party, observed: "What weighed with them was both apprehension about the future of liberty as well as their own desire to save and protect their own power and jurisdiction" (Limaye 1994: 57). As we have seen, however, the Court did not enjoy a high degree of authority within the broader political environment. Parliament overturned some of the Court's decisions through constitutional amendments, and the Gandhi regime directly attacked the Court through the appointment process and curbing the Court's power and jurisdiction. During the Emergency, the Court acquiesced – and lost a great deal of support, both in elite circles and among the broader public.

The Court's activism and assertiveness in early PIL cases was driven not only by the social-egalitarian values of the leading justices on the Court, but also by institutionalist motives, including the justices' desire to increase support for the judiciary (see Baxi 1980; Sathe 2002) The Court sought to atone for its acquiescence to the Gandhi regime during the Emergency-rule period in the *Shiv Kant Shukla* decision (Baxi 1985; Sathe 2002).[66] Baxi suggested that the Court's activism in PIL was partly "an attempt to refurbish the image of the Court tarnished by a few Emergency decisions and also an attempt to seek new, historical bases of legitimation of judicial power" (Baxi 1985: 36). Baxi observed that during the late 1970s and early 1980s, the Court was "seeking legitimacy from the people and in that sense (loosely) there are elements of populism in what it is now doing" (Baxi 1980: 126).

The institutional model or approach may also provide insight into the Court's activism and assertiveness in the *Second* and *Third Judges' Cases*, in which the Court asserted control over judicial appointments and transfers. These decisions were moti-vated by the justices' concerns regarding continued interference and politicization of the process by the government in the decade following the Court's decision in the *First Judges' Case*, and the adverse impact of that politicized process on judicial independence, the integrity of judges, and the functional efficiency of high courts.[67]

Similar to the Second Russian Constitutional Court in the 1990s (Epstein, Knight, and Shvetsova 2003), in the immediate post–Emergency era the Indian Court heeded

---

[66] In *Shiv Kant Shukla*, the Court upheld the regime's suspension of access to the courts by political detainees (through habeas petitions), and overturned the actions of several high courts (see Neuborne 2003: 482). These high courts had decided to hear several habeas petitions of detainees, notwithstanding the declaration of Emergency rule.

[67] See *Second Judges' Case*, (1993) 4 S.C.C. 441 at 497 (Verma, J.).

the "strategic caution" message that it learned from its earlier confrontations and clashes with the government. The election of the Janata government in 1977 signaled a change in the broader political environment that enabled judges to act more assertively, and in ways that bolstered the institutional solidity of the Court as an institution. A combination of the justices' institutionalist motives and sincere policy values (which still included a strong flavor of social-egalitarian reform) drove the Court to launch a new phase of activism and assertiveness via PIL. However, the assertiveness was selective. The post–Emergency Court was well aware of the need to rehabilitate its legitimacy and cultivate popular support, without further imperiling the Court's legitimacy by challenging the central government's policies and actions in high salience areas. Baxi thus argued that the activism of the post–Emergency Supreme Court in developing PIL regime was motivated by the Justices' desire to regain legitimacy lost during the Emergency "by widening the scope of judicial power in quite a socially visible manner" (Baxi 1980: 124).

Although the Court was highly deferential to the central government in the 1980s, the rise of weaker coalition governments beginning in 1989 created a more hospitable political opportunity structure for the exercise of judicial power. Justices in the post-1990 era were able to expand their role as a force for political reform and accountability through intervening in and monitoring the prosecution of the famous Jain Hawala scandal in the *Vineet Narain* case (1996–1998), in taking over management of India's forests in the *Godavarman* litigation (1996–present), and in many other human rights cases including the *Vishaka* case (1996) (regulating sexual harassment), the *D.K. Basu* case (1997) (promulgating standards for curbing police custodial violence), and the *Prakash Singh* case (2006) (ordering the government to establish a National Commission on Police Reform and implement a series of police reform measures).

I suggest that the justices' own policy values embodied in those decisions and remedies generally reflected the broader outlook and sensibilities of professional and intellectual elites within the Indian media, NGOs, academia, the bar, and in some cases, national public opinion (see Mate 2010a).[68] Similar to many professional and intellectual elites, judges had become increasingly frustrated by increasing levels of corruption and graft, the lack of transparency and accountability, and weak or ineffective governance in the Executive branches (see Dhavan 2000). The justices felt the need to act and intervene to save the rule of law and preserve good governance, because of the perceived failures of the Executive and Legislative branches to uphold such norms (see Andhyarujina 1992; Verma 1997; Dhavan 2000). Moreover, broad support for those judicial initiatives from other national elites – in politics, law, journalism, and academia – gave the justices some assurance that their assertiveness would not elicit governmental retaliation (see Mate 2010a).

---

[68] It is worth noting that some advocates and experts have argued that in key PIL decisions, the Court in the post-1990 era became less sensitive to the causes of the poor and underprivileged, and has expressed support for the government's policies of economic liberalization (see e.g. Bhushan 2004).

Without question, the PIL strategy entailed some risk of governmental retaliation when the Court intervened in politically sensitive matters. In fact, in April of 2007, Prime Minister Manmohan Singh was highly critical of the Court in his remarks at a conference of chief ministers and High Court chief justices, noting that the Court has been overreaching into the domain of the other branches.[69] However, the PIL strategy also allowed the Court to act strategically in expanding its role in governance and policy making through the gradual and incremental process of case-by-case dispute resolution, by occasionally accommodating the political interests or agenda of political elites, simultaneously broadening jurisdiction and their own remedial powers. Additionally, the PIL movement has had the added advantage of broadening the Court's base of support beyond its earlier base of elite claimants. Furthermore, the PIL line of cases engendered an inertial path dependency whereby the Court became embedded in many aspects of governance and problem solving, making the Court indispensable to ruling elites and elites dependent on the Court.

CONCLUSION: PUBLIC INTEREST LITIGATION AND THE JUDICIALIZATION OF GOVERNANCE

PIL has been aggressively utilized by the Supreme Court of India to reign in government agencies or bodies that violate or tolerate the violation of constitutional rights provisions or fail to enforce and implement both statutory and constitutionally mandated policies. The Court has thus gradually gained power as it has become increasingly involved in monitoring, overseeing, and even directing government activity in matters of environmental policy, land planning, development, education, affirmative action, health care, and other areas.

The Court's power and role in governance has dramatically increased over time through an iterative process in which an increasing number of public-interest groups, and public-minded individuals and advocates, have taken advantage of loosened standing to challenge governance failures across a wide range of policy domains. In this sense, PIL has enabled the Court to gradually accrete power in a cyclical, path-dependent "chakra" that is similar to Stone Sweet's analysis of the empowerment of the French Constitutional Council from 1974 onward (Stone Sweet 2002: 184–207).

---

[69] Prime Minister Manmohan Singh, "Administration of Justice on Fast Track" (2007) 4 S.C.C. J-9, speech delivered at the Conference of Chief Ministers of States and Chief Justices of High Courts, April 8, 2007. In his remarks, the Prime Minister observed:

> At the same time, the dividing line between judicial activism and judicial overreach is a thin one. As an example, compelling action by authorities of the State through the power of mandamus is an inherent power vested in the judiciary. However, substituting mandamus with a takeover of the functions of another organ may, at times, become a case of overreach . . . So is the case with PIL. PILs have great utility in initiating corrective action. At the same time, PILs cannot become vehicles for settling political or other scores. We need standards and benchmarks for screening PILs so that only genuine PILs with a justiciable cause of action on the basis of judicially manageable standards are taken up.

In fact, as Stone Sweet illustrates, the judicialization of governance in France was facilitated by complementary constitutional entrenchment and judicialization of governance moments. In 1971, the Council effectively entrenched and incorporated a new bill of rights in invalidating, for the first time, a piece of legislation. In 1974, the Constitution was amended to enable any sixty senators or deputies to refer a piece of proposed legislation to the Council. As a result, the Council's caseload dramatically increased and consisted mostly of opposition references challenging the majority government. Stone Sweet argues that the entrenchment of rights and expansion of standing created a steady stream of referrals that "produced a self-sustaining process of judicialization." These referrals facilitated the construction of a new body of constitutional law "to justify annulment in terms of an authoritative interpretation of constitutional rules," which in turn "provoked more referrals" from opposition parties (Stone Sweet 2002: 184–207).

Likewise in India, the Supreme Court's expansion of standing helped facilitate a similar process of judicialization, although the Indian Court's role expansion was largely driven by the government's failures to enforce existing statutory law and other severe governance failures. By broadening standing doctrine to invite a broad array of public-interest governance claims in the late 1970s and early 1980s, the Indian Court was able to transform itself from an institution that adjudicated the claims of landed and upper-class elites to one that dealt with a much broader array of claims from new public-interest groups and actors who challenged the government and private actors across a wide array of policy and issue domains. This phenomenon was aided by the lack of responsible government and corruption and bureaucratic failures that further increased the demand for judicial intervention and oversight of administrative bodies (see Kagan 2001). Over time, the Court's expanded role in adjudicating these claims resulted in the creation of a new corpus of constitutional rights and equitable remedies that ultimately solidified the Court's own power, and enabled it to assert limits on the government's power in controversial areas such as affirmative action.

In enhancing accountability and expanded opportunities for participation in governance, the Indian experience suggests that judicial "good governance" moments, such as the development of PIL, can provide a strong mechanism for bolstering the legitimacy of courts. Judicialization allows courts to act strategically in expanding their role in governance and policy making through the gradual and incremental process of case-by-case dispute resolution. The Court can occasionally accommodate the political interests or agenda of political elites, simultaneously broadening jurisdiction and its own remedial powers. Additionally, as the Indian case demonstrates, the judicialization of governance can broaden a Court's base of support. Through an iterative process, judicialization produces a path-dependency effect whereby the Court becomes embedded in many aspects of governance and problem solving, making the Court indispensable to ruling elites, and elites dependent on the Court. As a result, the Court also builds popular support nationally as it enhances its credibility as an institution. It thus becomes increasingly difficult to attack a Court that has become a significant institution of governance, and one that secures accountability from the Executive and Administrative branches.

REFERENCES

Ackerman, Bruce. 1991. *We the People, Volume I: Foundations*. Cambridge, MA: Harvard University Press.

Andhyarujina, T.R. 1992. *Judicial Activism and Constitutional Democracy in India*. Bombay: N.M. Tripathi.

Austin, Granville. 1966. *The Indian Constitution: Cornerstone of a Nation*. Oxford: Clarendon Press.

Austin, Granville. 1999. *Working a Democratic Constitution: A History of the Indian Experience*. New Delhi: Oxford University Press.

Baxi, Upendra. 1974. "The Constitutional Quicksands of Kesavananda Bharati and the Twenty-Fifth Amendment," *SCC* 1: 45.

Baxi, Upendra. 1978. "Some Reflections on the Nature of Constituent Power," in Alice Jacob et al (eds.) *Indian Constitution, Trends and Issues*. Bombay: N.M. Tripathi.

Baxi, Upendra. 1980. *The Indian Supreme Court and Politics*. Delhi: Eastern Book Company.

Baxi, Upendra. 1984. *Courage, Craft and Contention: The Indian Supreme Court in the Eighties*. Bombay: N.M. Tripathi.

Baxi, Upendra. 1985. "Taking Suffering Seriously – Social Action Litigation in the Supreme Court of India." in R. Dhavan et al. (eds.) *Judges and the Judicial Power: Essays in Honor of Justice V.R. Krishna Iyer* (London: Sweet and Maxwell; Bombay: N.M. Tripathi).

Bhushan, Prashant 2004. "Supreme Court and PIL: Changing Perspectives Under Liberalisation." *Economic and Political Weekly* 39(18): 1770–1774.

Chhibber, Pradeep K. 2001. Democracy Without Associations: Transformation of the Party System and Social Cleavages in India. Ann Arbor: University of Michigan Press.

Cunningham, Clark D. 1987. "Public Interest Litigation in the Indian Supreme Court: A Study in the Light of American Experience." *Journal of Indian Law Institute* 29: 494.

Dahl, Robert A. 1957. "Decision-Making in a Democracy: The Supreme Court as a National Policy-Maker," *Journal of Public Law* 6: 279.

Desai, Ashok, and S. Muralidhar. 2000. "Public Interest Litigation: Potential and Problems," in B.N. Kirpal et al., eds., *Supreme But Not Infallible: Essays in Honour of the Supreme Court of India*. New Delhi: Oxford University Press: 163.

Denoon, David. 1998. "Cycles in Indian Economic Liberalization," *Comparative Politics* 31(1): 43–60.

Dhavan, Rajeev. 1994. "Law as Struggle: Public Interest Law in India," *Journal of the Indian Law Institute* 36: 302–328.

Dhavan, Rajeev. 2000. "Judges and Indian Democracy: the lesser evil?," in Francine Frankel et al., eds. *Transforming India*. Delhi: Oxford University Press, p. 322.

Dhavan, Rajeev. 2007. "It is too Late in the Day to Put a Lid on PIL," *Mail Today*.

Dhavan, Rajeev and Alice Jacob. 1978. *Selection and Appointment of Supreme Court Judges: A Case Study*. Bombay: N.M. Tripathi.

Divan, Shyam and Armen Rosencrantz, eds. 2001. *Environmental Law and Policy in India: Cases, Materials and Statutes*. New Delhi: Oxford University Press.

Dua, Bhagwan, D. 1983. "A Study in Executive-Judicial Conflict," *Asian Survey* 23(4): 463–483.

Epstein Lee, Jack Knight, and Olga Shvetsova. 2001. "The Role of Constitutional Courts in the Establishment and Maintenance of Democratic Systems of Government," *Law & Society Review* 35(1): 117–164.

Gadbois, George. 2011. *Judges of the Supreme Court of India: 1950–1989*. New Delhi: Oxford University Press.

Galanter, Mark. 1984. *Competing Equalities: Law and the Backward Classes in India*. Berkeley: University of California Press.

Galanter, Mark. 1989. *Law and Society in Modern India*. Oxford: Oxford University Press.

Gillman, Howard. 1993. *The Constitution Besieged: The Rise and Demise of Lochner Era Police Powers Jurisprudence*. Durham: Duke University Press.

Iyer, V.R. Krishna and P.N. Bhagwati. 1977. *Report on National Juridicare: Equal Justice-Social Justice*. Government of India, Ministry of Law, Justice and Company Affairs.

Jacobsohn, Gary. 2003. *The Wheel of Law*. Princeton: Princeton University Press.

Kagan, Robert A. 2001. *Adversarial Legalism: The American Way of Law*. Cambridge. Harvard University Press.

Klieman, Aaron. 1981. "Indira's India: Democracy and Crisis Government," *Political Science Quarterly* 96(2): 251.

Limaye, Madhu. 1994. *Janata Party Experiment: An Insider's Account of Opposition Politics: 1975–1977*, 2 vols. New Delhi: B.R. Publishing.

Manor, James. 1990. "Parties and the Party System," in Atul Kohli (ed.), *India's Democracy: An Analysis of Changing State Society Relations*. Princeton: Princeton University Press.

Mate, Manoj. 2010a. *The Variable Power of Courts: The Expansion of the Power of the Supreme Court of India in Fundamental Rights and Governance Decisions*. PhD Dissertation, Political Science, University of California, Berkeley.

Mate, Manoj. 2010b. "The Origins of Due Process in India: The Role of Borrowing in Personal Liberty and Preventive Detention Cases," *Berkeley Journal of International Law* 28: 216.

Merillat, H.C.L. 1970. *Land and the Constitution in India*. New York: Columbia University Press.

McCloskey, Robert. 1962. "Economic Due Process and the Supreme Court: An Exhumation and Reburial, Supreme Court Review." *The Supreme Court Review* 34–62.

Muralidhar, S. 1998. "India: Public Interest Litigation Survey 1997–1998," *Annual Survey of Indian Law* 525: 33–34.

Neuborne, Burt. 2003. "The Supreme Court of India." *International Journal of Constitutional Law* 1(3): 476–510.

Noorani, A.G. 2001. "Behind the Basic Structure Doctrine," *Frontline* 18(9).

Peretti, Terri Jennings. 1999. *In Defense of a Political Court*. Princeton: Princeton University Press.

Ramachandran, Raju. 2000. "The Supreme Court and the Basic Structure Doctrine," in B.N. Kirpal et al., eds., *Supreme But Not Infallible: Essays in Honour of the Supreme Court of India*. New Delhi: Oxford University Press, p. 107.

Rosencranz, Armin and Michael Jackson. 2003. "The Delhi Pollution Case: The Supreme Court of India and the Limits of Judicial Power." *Columbia Journal of Environmental Law* 28: 223.

Rosencrantz, Armin and Sharachchandra Lele. 2008. "Supreme Court and India's Forests." *Economic and Political Weekly*, Feb. 2, 2008: 11.

Sathe, S.P. 1989. *Constitutional Amendments 1950-1988: Law and Politics*. Bombay: N.M. Tripathi.

Sathe, S.P. 2002. *Judicial Activism in India: Transgressing Borders and Enforcing Limits*. New Delhi: Oxford University Press.

Seervai, H.M. 1973. "The Fundamental Rights Case at the Crossroads." *Bombay Law Reporter* LXXV: 47.

Seervai, H.M. 1991. *Constitutional Law of India: A Critical Commentary*, Vol. 2 (3rd ed.). Bombay: N.M. Tripathi.

Shapiro, Martin. 1964. "Political Jurisprudence," *Kentucky Law Journal* 52: 294.

Shapiro, Martin. 1981. *Courts: A Comparative and Political Analysis*. Chicago: University of Chicago Press.

Shapiro, Martin. 2002. "The Success of Judicial Review and Democracy," in Martin Shapiro and Alec Stone Sweet, eds., *On Law, Politics, & Judicialization*. London: Oxford University Press, p. 149.

Verma, Justice J.S. 1997. "The Constitutional Obligation of the Judiciary – R.C. Ghiya Memorial Lecture," *Supreme Court Cases* 7: 1.

Von Mehren, Arthur Taylor. 1965. "Law and Legal Education in India: Some Observations," *Harv. L. Rev.* 78: 1180.

Yadav, Yogendra. 1999. "Electoral Politics in the Time of Change: India's Third Electoral System: 1989–99," *Economic and Political Weekly* 34: 2393–99.

11

The Judicial Dynamics of the French and European Fundamental Rights Revolution

*Mitchel de S.-O.-l'E. Lasser**

This chapter analyzes an important and complex development that is currently playing out at the intersection of the French and European judicial systems: a whole series of courts (and court-like institutions) that had little or nothing to do with "judicial review" are now in the midst of a mad scramble to master and direct the development of fundamental rights jurisprudence. This chapter traces this development and explains how the advent of the European Court of Justice and the European Court of Human Rights has led to an intense interinstitutional competition between the French and European High Courts, a competition in which fundamental rights have served both as the opportunity that triggered this competition and the preferred means to engage in it.

Part of the story of the dramatic rise of fundamental rights is undoubtedly social and intellectual in nature. At the domestic level, France has been increasingly fragmenting along pluralistic lines. This fragmentation has posed ever greater challenges to French republicanism, which has traditionally stressed the unitary nature of both "the general will" and "general interest." The result has been a marked rise in individual- and group-oriented pluralism increasingly expressed in fundamental rights terms.

This trajectory functions at the supranational or transnational level, as well. As political communities have become increasingly complicated cross-nationally as well as intranationally, fundamental rights have risen dramatically in importance. Fundamental rights have served in effect as a lingua franca across jurisdictions: they operate as a common legal denominator and pool of common legal terms transferable within and across the European polities. By focusing on individuals (including firms) and their fundamental rights, courts have found a cross-culturally operative technique for resolving disputes that ostensibly steers clear of bigger aggregation/polis-building enterprises.

* Jack G. Clarke Professor of Law, Director of Graduate Studies, Cornell Law School.

This common social and intellectual momentum has likely been reinforced by the fall of the Berlin Wall and incorporation of ex-Soviet bloc and/or ex–totalitarian states into the Western European legal order. This liberalizing and anticommunist reaction has taken legal form not only via the constitutional process within these states, but also by their adherence to such symbolically charged rights-based institutions as the Council of Europe and the European Court of Human Rights.[1] In short, both the internal fragmentation and the external aggregation of political communities have contributed to the stunningly rapid rise of the fundamental rights idiom throughout Europe.

However, that is not the entire story. The fundamental rights revolution is also a matter of the complex – and often competitive – interinstitutional dynamics that increasingly define the judicial arena in our ever more globalized legal space. These judicial dynamics are particularly visible and pressing in contemporary Europe for two reasons. First, the European judicial arena possesses two layers of powerfully operational courts: the domestic and the European judiciaries. Second, almost all national judiciaries in Europe belong to the Civil Law tradition; as a result, they typically possess multiple and often quite distinct judicial hierarchies, each headed by its own "supreme court." In fact, even the European judiciary is led by two different courts: the European Court of Justice (ECJ) and the European Court of Human Rights (ECHR).

The European domestic and supranational judicial orders therefore possess a distinctive structural feature: they deploy a plethora of high courts that operate in an overlapping and richly interactive judicial environment. As a result, all of these high courts are now scrambling to master and direct the high ground offered by the emergent fundamental rights regime. Some are better positioned to do so than others.

This multiplicity of high courts leads to a group dynamic that reinforces the recourse to the fundamental rights idiom and contributes to its increasing dominance. Almost every European judicial player now faces powerful pressures to jump on the fundamental rights bandwagon or be left intellectually and institutionally behind. Each judicial institution must accordingly deploy and seek to control this rising idiom, even if doing so threatens to refashion or even replace that institution's traditional role definition. This has prompted a frantic race to the "top" of an increasingly unitary doctrinal, procedural, jurisdictional, and intellectual scheme: the evermore powerful and ubiquitous fundamental-rights framework.

This chapter offers a case study of the dramatic circulation of fundamental rights pressures between the numerous high courts in play at the intersection of the domestic and supranational European judiciaries. It examines the ongoing "fair trial" litigation (conducted under Article 6-1 of the European Convention on Human

---

[1] Of course, some of the motives for such adherence are deeply practical: candidate countries for the EU must effectively sign onto the ECHR fundamental rights regime. See the "Copenhagen Criteria" for accession to the EU, Bulletin of the European Community 6/1993, at I.13.

Rights) challenging the decision–making procedures used by the numerous high courts designed on the French judicial model.

This analysis, which summarizes the conclusions of my recent book (2009), focuses on the French and European high courts. It explains that what appears at first blush to be a simple case of external European (and, in particular, ECHR) pressures on the French judiciary to modify its traditional decision-making procedures actually represents a far more complex and highly charged set of interactions between multiple French and multiple European courts. This examination could easily and fruitfully be expanded to include other national high courts, ranging from those directly involved in the "fair trial" litigation (such as the Belgian, Dutch, and Portuguese Supreme Courts) to others particularly prominent in the rise of fundamental rights (such as the Bundesverfassungsgericht, the German Federal Constitutional Court). As will soon become apparent, however, the multifaceted interaction between the French and European courts is more than sufficient to suggest the key structural dynamics currently driving the European fundamental-rights revolution.

For heuristic purposes (and heuristic purposes only), I adopt a four-part analysis that examines the four basic types of judicial pressures that operate between and within the European and French courts: European pressures on the French courts (Part II); French pressures on the French courts (Part III); French pressures on the European courts (Part IV); and European pressures on the European courts (Part V). This highly structured approach offers two advantages. First, it organizes an otherwise confusing morass of interactions between a wide range of domestic and international courts. Second, working systematically through this simplified analytic structure eventually demonstrates that the French and European judicial orders are increasingly difficult to disentangle, both theoretically and practically: interventions at every level constitute interventions at all others.

This chapter comes to several conclusions. I state them straightforwardly right now in order to help the reader work through the institutional complexities that follow. First, the current interinstitutional dynamics are prompting a group convergence of all domestic and European High Courts on the fundamental-rights idiom, however disruptive this may be to the particular courts in question. As the French and European example demonstrates quite clearly, there appears to be no effective opt-out of the fundamental-rights framework for any of these courts.

Second, this all-but-obligatory convergence has forced these courts to translate their prior procedural, doctrinal, and conceptual schemes into fundamental-rights terms. This translation process has proven to be not only deeply competitive, but often quite creative as well: numerous individual, group, and institutional interests are in play; the stakes are patently major; and the results are not preordained. This has led to widely divergent interpretations of how to construct and implement the emerging fundamental-rights framework.

Third, the struggle to master and direct these legal developments has further reinforced the rising fundamental-rights regime. The domestic and supranational

European judiciaries function in an interinstitutional context whose group dynamics have created a strong incentive regarding fundamental rights. The most empowering strategy for any given court is not to attempt to evade the often disruptive fundamental-rights regime; not only does such a refusal appear retrograde, it leaves the institution at the interpretive, doctrinal, and institutional mercy of those who have taken the opposite tack. The more effective strategy is to embrace and even seek to lead the emerging regime by aggressively developing expansive fundamental-rights positions. This "maximalist" approach is the most effective means to disable and trump troublesome interpretations by legal competitors, maintain control over one's own institution, and exercise institutional and intellectual leadership of the emerging judicial order.

Fourth, these developments have prompted major constitutive developments in both the French and European judicial systems. The former is turning itself ever-more completely and explicitly into a fundamental-rights-based system, in stark contrast to its traditional republican approach, which focused on a (supposedly) unitary general will. The latter is following suit by: 1) reproducing the intra-domestic tensions between the ordinary-administrative and fundamental-rights high courts; and 2) replicating these domestic courts' solutions to such tensions. This suggests that the European high courts are increasingly organizing themselves into an integrated judicial order along recognizable domestic lines. The chapter concludes with some methodological warnings.

THE TRADITIONAL FRENCH JUDICIAL MODEL: THE PREEXISTING EQUILIBRIUM

The French legal system has traditionally been defined – procedurally, doctrinally, institutionally, structurally, and intellectually – by its distinctive brand of republicanism. The classic French package has consisted of four fundamental and interlocking features: 1) a unitary conception of the general will and general interest; 2) the supremacy of the legislature as the voice of the general will; 3) a strict separation of the judiciary from the political branches of government; and 4) a commitment to elite and expert institutional decision making. These features have traditionally been understood to entail several more, including: 5) the refusal of judicial review; 6) the establishment of separate administrative and constitutional tribunals; 7) a doctrine of the "sources of the law" that refuses to grant the ordinary judiciary lawmaking powers; 8) the theory of *la loi écran* (i.e., the "legislative screen" that shields legislation from administrative review regarding its compatibility with the Constitution or international obligations); 9) legality based – as opposed to fundamental-rights based – administrative review; and 10) institutionally oriented – as opposed to individually oriented – judicial decision-making procedures.

Article 6 of the 1789 Declaration of the Rights of Man and of the Citizen declares: "*La loi est l'expression de la volonté générale*" ("Legislation is the expression of the general will"). This statement of principle establishes the core of the traditional French understanding of law. Political will is, in good Rousseauian fashion, general; it is not divisible into subgroups, never mind into the conflicting rights and interests of individuals (Suleiman 1974: 24–29, 297–323; Hazareesingh 1994: 155–171; Rousseau 2002: 164–182, 193–196, 214, 227–30).[2]

The supremacy of general legislation requires a strict separation of the judiciary from the political branches of government. The Revolutionaries established this strict separation as early as August 1790, when they passed the Law on Judicial Organization: judges were explicitly forbidden to interfere with legislative and administrative decisions (French *Code de l'organisation judiciaire* tit. II, arts. 10, 13, Aug. 16–14, 1790). Far from adopting a system of checks and balances, this approach unambiguously rejects judicial review.

That said, the French system has long been far more flexible and nuanced than has traditionally been portrayed. Although judicial review of the acts of the political branches has been anathema, the French established a series of specialized administrative tribunals within the Executive branch to perform quasi-judicial review of the executive. Furthermore, although the ordinary judiciary was explicitly denied lawmaking powers (French Civil Code Articles 5 and 1351), the Courts have neither been, nor were they intended to be, passive actors in the French legal order. Portalis, the Civil Code's primary author, made the point expressly: codified legislation could only establish the general outlines of the law; judges (and academics) would necessarily have to work out the specifics and adapt the law to the demands of a society in constant change (Portalis 1799).

Institutional and professional structures were designed to ensure the accountability and representativeness of French judges. These judges spend their entire careers within a unified and hierarchical judicial institution (Lasser 2005: 182–185). Because they have tested into the system by formal state examinations, have been trained for their office by state educational institutions, and been promoted by state-defined and managed meritocratic means, the judiciary as a whole bears the imprimatur of elite republican representation (Lasser 2005: 331–334).

Having gone to such effort to select, train, and organize its judges, the French system then gives them the necessary procedural and institutional means to manage the application and development of la loi's broad provisions. The judicial decision-making process of the French High Courts is accordingly dominated by the Courts themselves: in some important sense, it is the Court, not the litigants, who are understood to be appropriately representative of the state and citizenry at large.

Once the parties have submitted their written pleadings, it is therefore the judicial panel that effectively takes responsibility for the case. Partisan oral argument by the parties all but withers away, as elaborate and multistage internal discussions

---

[2] In fact, Article 3 of the 1958 Constitution goes to the bother of spelling out that, "No portion of the people may arrogate to itself, nor may any individual arrogate to himself, the exercise [of national sovereignty]."

between key judicial magistrates – such as the advocate general and the judicial rapporteur – take center stage (Garapon and Papadopoulos 2004: 110–112). Shielded from public view, judicial debates unfold in absolute candor and without fear of political retribution.

This sequestering approach also produces an important secondary effect: it greatly diminishes the argumentative and doctrinal control that these judges can exert through their cryptic, collegial, single-sentence, and syllogistic judgments. The syllogism also stands as a powerful reminder: only legislation constitutes the true expression of the general will.

This supremacy of the general will has traditionally meant that the ordinary judiciary – or, for that matter, the quasi-judicial administrative tribunals – cannot call la loi into question, whether on domestic (constitutional) or international (treaty/convention) grounds. Even when the administrative tribunals review Executive branch actions at the behest of disgruntled citizens, they traditionally do so not so much in order to vindicate the rights of the individual, but rather to ensure that the state has acted according to its own standards of appropriate behavior. This review has therefore traditionally been focused not on the *individual*'s fundamental constitutional *rights*, but on the *legality* of the *state*'s actions.

Finally, the Fifth Republic's treatment of constitutional review reflects almost all of these traditional assumptions. It therefore adjusted, rather than subverted, the traditional equilibrium between the ordinary courts, administrative tribunals, and political branches. First, constitutional review was established to police the division between the Legislature and Executive branches, not to protect fundamental rights from legislative or governmental encroachment. Second, individuals could not trigger such review; only a small set of major state actors could file constitutional complaints. Third, the newly created Constitutional Council was established outside of the judiciary. Finally, the Council could only perform review a priori (i.e., while the challenged legislative act was still a pending bill). Once the bill had been passed into law, and had thus become the formal expression of the general will, it was no longer subject to challenge.

EUROPEAN PRESSURES ON THE FRENCH JUDICIAL SYSTEM: THE DOMESTIC ORDER THROWN INTO FLUX

General External Pressures

The traditional model just described has certainly not been the product of a static legal or judicial history. Slowly developed and deeply entrenched over the course of the last two centuries, the model had nonetheless reached a recognizable – if undoubtedly complex and somewhat malleable – state of equilibrium. In the last few decades, however, it has been undergoing a stunningly rapid and sweeping transformation.

The first important pressures for the current transformation emerged from the European legal plane. In 1964, the ECJ began insisting on the supremacy or "precedence" of European law over conflicting national law.[3] This doctrine called on national courts to refuse to apply national laws inconsistent with European law; in effect, it required judicial review, albeit in the name of European law.

Given the traditional model described in Part II, it should come as no surprise that the French legal system did not exactly rush to adopt this jarring new doctrine. Indeed, it was not until 1975 that the Cour de cassation took the step demanded by the ECJ in 1964. It is a testament to the lasting power of the classic French approach, however, that the Conseil d'Etat and the Constitutional Council refused to follow suit for almost fifteen more years: it was not until 1989 that the Conseil d'Etat finally buckled under by overturning its own jurisprudence.[4] This shift represented an important moment in the acceptance of European law; but it was a truly monumental event in the internal history of French law. The theory of the loi écran had finally fallen, and with it the primacy of legislation and the general will, if only in the context of European law.

This development threw the French legal order into a state of disequilibrium. The new role adopted by the French courts meant that individuals could now seize the ordinary and administrative courts to block the operation of French legislation in the name of *European* rights (including fundamental rights) of EU or ECHR origin. However, these same individuals could *not* do so in the name of domestic *French* rights, even of constitutional status.

This discrepancy had a dual effect. First, the sudden availability of justiciable European rights constituted a bonanza for individuals and firms searching for a basis to challenge unfavorable legal outcomes at the national level. Second, this new turn to superior European norms not only empowered the national judiciary vis-à-vis the political branches, but also disrupted the traditional French mode for reviewing the acts of the Executive branch. Quasi-judicial review of the executive had been an integral part of the French legal order since at least 1799, when Napoleon established the Conseil d'Etat (Brown and Bell 1998: 46–48). Over the ensuing 200 years, the Conseil developed a sophisticated jurisprudence for challenging executive rules and acts, which has been applied throughout the country by a large administrative court hierarchy.

European rights jurisprudence accordingly challenges French administrative jurisprudence rather directly. Elaborated by the ECHR and the ECJ, this jurisprudence undermines the institutional leadership of the Conseil d'Etat, which traditionally elaborated the bases for reviewing state acts. This institutional shift also challenges the conceptual structure and very ethos of French administrative jurisprudence. Review had been steeped in French republican notions. It was grounded in a

---

[3] *Costa v. E.N.E.L.*, Case 6.64 (1964) CMLR 425.
[4] *See* Judgment of the Conseil d'Etat of 20 October 1989 (*Nicolo*), (1989) Rec. Lebon 190.

series of "legality" doctrines traditionally oriented toward the state: the key issue was whether the state had behaved according to proper administrative morality.[5] The increasingly dominant European approach, however, offers a more liberal perspective: its key question is whether the rights – including the fundamental rights – of the individual have been violated.[6]

Targeted External Pressures

Plaintiffs have now successfully wielded these newly justiciable European rights to overturn a whole series of specific French legal rules, ranging from the nonrecognition of sex changes to the calculation of VAT taxes.[7] Amazingly, plaintiffs have even leveraged their European rights to target the decision-making procedures traditionally deployed by all of the French High Courts. This "procedural" litigation has proven to be immensely disruptive: it subjects the ethos and practices of these proud "Supreme Courts" to the critical appraisal of foreign courts on the basis of an unfamiliar fundamental-rights logic.

In a major and ongoing line of decisions handed down over the last ten years, the ECHR has struck repeatedly at the decision-making procedures of the high courts designed on the French model.[8] In doing so, it has condemned precisely those practices and institutional structures that reflect the classic French republican understanding of the judicial role: stressing the importance of permitting the individual litigant to take an active role in litigation, it has criticized the French high courts' characteristically closed and institutionally oriented decision-making procedures.

These French procedures were traditionally designed to permit two key judicial figures – the rapporteur and an advising magistrate (known as the advocate general at the Cour de Cassation or the commissaire de gouvernement at the Conseil d'Etat) – to lead the judicial panel in intensive and candid debates about how to decide cases in such a manner as to promote the general interest and public good. As a result, the litigants would almost always wave their nominal right to engage in oral arguments: once they had submitted their written pleadings, their role in the decision-making process was effectively over.

---

[5] I owe the elegant term "administrative morality" to Brown and Bell (1998: 216).

[6] These two approaches could of course be fused: the violation of an individual's rights could, for example, be treated as a violation of state morality.

[7] *See, e.g.,* Court of Cassation judgments of Dec. 11, 1992, JCP, *jurisprudence* no. 21991, p. 41 (conclusions Jéol); Joined cases C–177/99 and C–181/99 *Ampafrance v. Directeur des services fiscaux de Maine-et-Loire* (2000) ECR I–7013.

[8] The ECHR cases specifically condemning the French Supreme Courts only date back to 1998, but the first ECHR decision to condemn the French model of judicial decision making dates to 1991, when the ECHR censured similar procedures utilized by the Belgian Cour de Cassation. *See Borgers v. Belgium,* 214 Eur. Ct. H.R. (Ser. A) 22 (1191); *Reinhardt and Slimane-Kaïd v. France,* 1998-II Eur. Ct. H.R. 640; *Kress v. France,* 2001-VI Eur. Ct. H.R. 1; *Martinie v. France,* case no. 58675/00, (April 12, 2006). Retrieved from http://www.menschenrechte.ac.at/orig/06_2/Martinie.pdf.

Elaborating a fundamental-rights perspective that stresses the right of individuals to take an active role in litigation, the ECHR has found much to fault in the traditional French procedures. In particular, it has insisted that individual litigants be granted access and response rights with respect to the key internal documents generated within the French preparatory judicial debates. First, because the judicial advisor might put forward damaging arguments, the litigant must be allowed to receive the advisor's conclusions in advance in order to respond to them as necessary at oral arguments. Second, the judicial advisor must not be put in a privileged position by gaining access to the otherwise unavailable report and draft judgments of the rapporteur. Finally, the advisor must also be removed from the judicial panel's final deliberations, lest he be perceived (accurately or not) to be gaining an argumentative advantage.

The ECHR's Article 6-1 "fair trial" jurisprudence could hardly have done a more thorough job of pitting its individual fundamental-rights perspective against the French judicial system's republican self-understanding. Reducing the prototypically republican figure of the judicial advisor to little more than a potential opponent of the individual litigant undermines the governing logic of the French system; namely, that it is the judicial institution – rather than the individual and self-interested litigant – that best represents the general interest and public good. The ECHR instead placed the individual litigant in a privileged position: by dint of his fundamental procedural and substantive rights, he had to be empowered to play an analytically and procedurally central role, even at the expense of the French courts' traditional structure, ethos, and practices.

FRENCH PRESSURES ON THE FRENCH JUDICIAL SYSTEM: INTERNAL MOTIVATIONS

The French legal order has thus been subjected to tremendous pressures from the European rights-based approach in general and the ECHR's fair trial jurisprudence in particular. However, it has also been exerting major pressures on itself at the same time. These internal motivations and dynamics are caused in large measure by the broad and enduring structural design of the French courts.

As is the case in most Civil Law systems, the French "judiciary" is organized into several distinct hierarchies. The "ordinary" "judicial" courts, headed by the Cour de Cassation, handle civil and criminal litigation. The "administrative" tribunals, headed by the Conseil d'Etat, are instead housed within the Executive branch. This distinction is not merely formal. Ordinary French judges receive their educational and vocational training at the Ecole Nationale de la Magistrature, the national judge school. Administrative judges, however, receive theirs at the particularly prestigious Ecole Nationale de l'Administration, which trains all high-ranking Executive-branch civil servants. They are therefore prepared above all not to be judges, but to manage state affairs. For its part, the Constitutional Council is a free-standing (and largely political) institution, distinct from both the ordinary and administrative tribunals.[9]

This division of judicial turf into subparts has prompted somewhat competitive interinstitutional motivations and dynamics. On the sociological front, the high Executive judges look upon their civil/criminal counterparts with a certain disdain. The former are the cream of the elite management team that composes the "State nobility" (to use the term coined by Bourdieu 1996); the latter are mere judges. On the institutional front, the Constitutional Council has come to play an increasingly prominent role in defining the proper structure and operation of the state, a field previously dominated by the Conseil d'Etat. Finally, on the doctrinal front, the partitioning of the "judiciary" has fostered interpretive complexities: even if the jurisdictional field is divided between the three hierarchies, the three institutions periodically elaborate doctrines in related and even overlapping fields.[10]

The addition of a strong European presence on the French legal scene has greatly multiplied the number and stakes of such competitive judicial interactions; this has added another layer of internal motivation for the assorted French courts' institutional responses. First, European law represents a whole new field of action on which French judicial institutions can compete. Second, to conquer the European legal terrain is to occupy the high ground for French domestic law purposes: European law is, by both its own definition and French constitutional standards, superior to French law. Third, European law cuts across the key jurisdictional and doctrinal divisions that we have been describing: corporate, environmental, or other European regulation can generate litigation in any of the domestic judicial hierarchies. These factors have in essence thrown the French courts into an ongoing negotiation regarding their respective roles, domains, and powers.

The fundamental rights doctrines of the ECHR offer the clearest example of the collapsing of domestic divisions and distinctions. ECHR law is superior law; it must be applied by all state actors (including the courts); and it therefore operates across the board in disputes litigated in any and all of the judicial hierarchies. This alters the nature and intensity of the competition between the three major "judicial" institutions. Now that European law bridges the substantive and jurisdictional divisions between the three major institutions, the classic partitioning of the French "judicial" field blurs: all three must increasingly interpret and apply the same (superior) fundamental-rights principles.

The internal motivations and dynamics of the French judiciary were already apparent decades ago when the ECJ insisted that the precedence (i.e., superiority)

---

9 Unlike the ordinary and administrative judges, the members of the Constitutional Council serve for limited terms (nine years) and are directly politically appointed by the heads of the political branches (the President of the Republic and the Presidents of the two legislative houses).

10 For example, "tort" doctrines are elaborated in both the ordinary courts (for private injuries) and the administrative tribunals (for public ones). Similarly, procedural rights of "defendants" have been elaborated in the ordinary, administrative, and constitutional courts, albeit in somewhat different contexts.

of European law required domestic courts to refuse to apply conflicting national norms. Deeply attached (professionally, institutionally, and intellectually) to the French republican tradition, the Conseil d'Etat was dead set against recognizing the precedence of European law and violating the doctrine of la loi écran by exercising review over French legislation. Composed primarily of major French political figures similarly attached to existing national traditions and power structures, the Constitutional Council was not much more enthusiastic. Indeed, having recently granted itself the power to review legislation for substantive violations of fundamental rights incorporated into the 1958 French Constitution, the Council was in no rush either to adopt another deeply controversial position or subjugate the authority of its constitutional mission to routine European legal norms. The Cour de Cassation, however, had excellent motivations for staking out a different (and pro-European) position: not only could it drastically empower itself relative to the legislative branch,[11] but it could also greatly increase its standing relative to the Conseil d'Etat and Constitutional Council. By dutifully following the ECJ's demands, not only would it adopt the mantle of the open-minded, progressive, and commercially sensitive institution, it could suddenly wield legal materials superior to those handled by its sister institutions. The results followed suit: in 1975, the Cour was the first French Supreme Court to set aside a loi that conflicted with a European norm; the Constitutional Council began to waver noticeably in the mid-1980s; and the Conseil d'Etat finally caved in 1989.[12]

Similar French interinstitutional motivations and dynamics have been unleashed repeatedly in the face of European legal pressures. The ongoing Article 6-1 "fair trial" litigation offers a particularly clear and telling example. The Conseil d'Etat has steadfastly resisted the ECHR's "fair trial" jurisprudence. Advancing arguments so tenuous as to border on the disingenuous, it has done all in its power to maintain its traditional understanding of republican procedures. It has refused to remove its judicial advisor (the Commissaire de gouvernement) from its internal deliberations; and it has offered litigants as little as possible in the way of information and response rights (Lasser 2009: 93–94).[13]

The Cour de Cassation, however, has jumped on the opportunity presented by the ECHR's jurisprudence to institute a major overhaul of its decision-making procedure. These reforms significantly increase the capacity of individuals, firms, and interested parties to intervene aggressively in the decision-making process. In all important cases, the rapporteur must now disclose her report's legal analysis not only to the parties well in advance of oral argument, but also to the public at large:

---

[11] This is the so–called empowerment thesis (Weiler 1981, 1994).

[12] *See* Cass. mixte, Judgment of May 24, 1975, D. 1975, p. 497 (*Jacques Vabre*); Judgment of the Constitutional Council 86–116 of Sep. 3, 1986, (1986) Recueil des decisions du Conseil Constitutionnel 135; *Nicolo.*

[13] Even the Conseil d'Etat's recent reforms changing the title of the judicial advisor from the Commissaire de gouvernement to the Rapporteur public are designed to resist the ECHR's jurisprudence. See Art. R 733 of the Code de justice administrative.

it is to be published alongside the final judgment in the Cour's official reports. As a result, the judicial advisor (the advocate general) no longer obtains privileged access to internal judicial information. Not only can he only receive the same "objective report" as the litigants, but he has been banished altogether from the Cour's pre– and post–oral-argument deliberations. Finally, the litigants can respond either orally or in writing to the advisor's conclusions to the court. In short, the Cour has chosen to shift the balance of procedural power noticeably in the direction of private parties at the expense of the advocates general. The Article 6-1 "fair trial" litigation has thus triggered a schism between the Conseil d'Etat and the Cour de Cassation, which again reveals the latent structural and intellectual tensions between these two domestic high courts.

This window into the internal diversity of the French judiciary holds great analytic importance for the examination of the French judicial system, European judicial system, and interaction between the two. On the French side of the equation, the tensions between the Cour and the Conseil demonstrate that the institutional and intellectual threat (or promise) posed by the rise of the European courts and fundamental rights idiom affects different institutional players quite differently. Put simply, their motivations differ.

Furthermore, the institutional schism between these two high courts hardly exhausts the wide range of domestic responses. Even within the Cour de Cassation, which has taken a pro-European law and fundamental–rights-friendly approach, there is endless disagreement about what such stances actually require. All of the fundamental-rights norms need to be interpreted, and the range of possible interpretations is obviously quite large. Some factions wish to interpret these fundamental rights in a dignitarian fashion that empowers disadvantaged groups relative to the state and powerful private interests. Others seek, to the contrary, to interpret them in such a fashion as to protect vested economic and property rights from the disruptions threatened by such a dignitarian approach. The key is to recognize that, despite their disagreements, all of these French institutions and factions have converged on fundamental rights as the appropriate mode of legal analysis, as each jockeys to control the development of supremely powerful fundamental rights within the domestic legal order.

Moreover, the institutional competition on the fundamental-rights front has developed simultaneously with regard to French constitutional norms. The reasons for this are both structural and doctrinal. First and foremost, the Constitutional Council has traditionally been limited to abstract a priori review of legislation. As a result, it only got one crack at reviewing a given piece of legislation. Once it had given the law its blessing, the ordinary and administrative courts took over that law's interpretative development. Although these courts could not formally review the law and declare it unconstitutional, they could – and necessarily often did – apply it in light of their own interpretations of constitutional norms.

The Constitutional Council has had only very weak means to control such ongoing constitutional interpretation of both legislative and constitutional norms.[14] Individuals could neither petition the Council directly nor refer concrete judicial interpretations to the Council for further constitutional review. The Council therefore had only the first say in constitutional interpretation;[15] the ordinary and administrative courts would then elaborate their own interpretations in a relatively decentralized fashion.[16]

The absence of an important "state action doctrine" compounds this interpretive decentralization. Almost any litigant in any private controversy can put forward arguments couched in fundamental-rights terms, thereby triggering further constitutional interpretations. In this manner, contract clauses have been challenged on the grounds that they violate the right to exercise a profession, malpractice liability has been imposed in the name of the dignitarian right to bodily integrity, and the like.[17]

The combination of external pressures, internal motivations, and institutional structures has thus led fundamental rights (of both European and French origin) increasingly to dominate the French legal terrain in almost all domains. The advent of fundamental rights thus challenges the structural, institutional, and doctrinal divisions that have traditionally partitioned the French judicial order into relatively distinct subparts. As we shall soon see, it challenges the division between the French and European judicial orders, as well.

FRENCH PRESSURES ON THE EUROPEAN JUDICIAL SYSTEM: EXTERNAL PRESSURES IN REVERSE

The pressures exerted between the European and French judicial orders are not a one-way street. The institutional roots of the returning pressures can be inferred from the internal tensions and motivations described above: the multiplicity of domestic high courts. The European courts are negotiating their relationship with a multifaceted and fractured set of French judicial institutions whose own interinstitutional motivations function as strongly on the domestic level as on the European one. The

---

[14] Perhaps the most important of these powers is the capacity to condition its approval of legislation on interpretive reservations (Bell 1992, 2001). This approach seeks to control the potential meaning and application of the challenged legislation over time. However, there exist no formal policing mechanisms for enforcing such reservations.

[15] Even this power is debatable: the Conseil d'Etat actually has the first say, as it gives advice to the government about the constitutionality of proposed legislation (Bell 1992).

[16] The recent amendment of the French Constitution has changed this state of affairs, although it is not yet clear how significantly. The addition of Article 61-1 now allows references to be made to the Council in concrete cases. Although this opens the door for a posteriori review of legislation (undoubtedly a major development), it establishes the Cour de Cassation and the Conseil d'Etat as the gatekeepers to the Conseil. This effectively maintains the partial autonomy of these high courts' interpretive powers in the constitutional realm (Lasser 2009).

[17] *See, e.g.*, Cass. Soc., July 10, 2002, D. 2002, 2491, note Serra; Cass. 1re civ., Oct. 9, 2001, D. 2001, 3470, rapport P. Sargos, note D. Thouvenin.

judicial chess match is therefore being played on at least two levels at once, with moves on either level affecting the relationships on the other.

This reality presents strong opportunities for the European judiciary. Because European law qualifies as superior (if only by ECJ doctrine), it is relatively easy for European legal institutions to enlist the support of tactically insightful domestic counterparts, who now function as agents for European legal progress in the national legal order. Internal French judicial motivations thus offer welcoming points of entry for European fundamental-rights pressures.

However, this state of affairs also imposes significant costs. The multiplicity of domestic high courts, when combined with the interpretive leeway of fundamental-rights norms, leaves the development of European law vulnerable to the interpretive decisions taken by self-interested domestic legal institutions. The Article 6-1 fair trial litigation provides an excellent example of this dynamic.

When the ECHR started condemning French High Court decision-making procedure some ten years ago, the French courts had some tough decisions to make about how to respond. The range of possibilities was quite large. For example, the 1998 *Reinhardt* decision condemned the unequal ("imbalanced") access given to the reporting judge's work product in Cour de Cassation cases (the judicial advisor received all of this preparatory material prior to oral arguments; the litigants received none).[18] Furthermore, the 2001 *Kress* judgment held that the judicial advisor at the Conseil d'Etat (the commissaire de gouvernement) could not legitimately retire with the sitting judicial panel to participate in post–oral-argument judicial deliberations, lest the appearance be given that he might press his arguments in a prejudicial fashion.[19] The French Supreme Courts could have legitimately adopted a wide range of potential responses, each premised on more or less expansive or restrictive interpretations of the ECHR's jurisprudence.[20] For example, the requirement that the litigants receive the same access as the advisor to the judicial materials prepared in advance of oral arguments does not settle how much access should be given to what kind of information.

As we have seen, the Conseil d'Etat and the Cour de Cassation adopted fundamentally different tacks in the face of the ECHR's decisions. The Conseil stonewalled as best it could by refusing to remove the judicial advisor from its final deliberations (it merely required him to remain silent). The Cour de Cassation, however, removed him not only from the final deliberations (as apparently required by the ECHR's *Kress* judgment), but also from the preparatory ones that take place before oral argument. Indeed, the Cour used the ECHR's jurisprudence as a springboard to rework its decision-making procedures in a manner that significantly increased the procedural rights of litigants, interested parties, and the public at large.

---

[18] *See Reinhardt*, 1998–II Eur. Ct. H.R. at 666.

[19] *Kress* at para. 70–72.

[20] Nick Huls (Ch. 7 in this volume) underlines this interpretive agency in his insightful analysis of the Dutch Hoge Raad's expansive interpretations of EU law and jurisprudence.

We can learn a great deal from this type of interchange. First, even in instances in which a European court has settled an issue in a seemingly straightforward fashion, there nonetheless remains more than enough room for ongoing interpretive effort at the domestic level. Second, expansive domestic interpretations of European law in effect become European law, if only for domestic purposes. That is, the Cour's expansive interpretation of what was required by the ECHR's jurisprudence functions as the meaning of European law in France. The Cour's procedural modifications were made in the name of European law, and the ECHR has few viable means of policing, never mind overriding, this interpretation. On the practical level, the ECHR can only effectively oversee a tiny percentage of the cases that raise fundamental-rights issues arising from the Convention: there are limits to how many cases an institution composed of only one judge per country can possibly handle. As a prudential matter, things are not much better. Faced with the recalcitrance of the Conseil d'Etat, could the ECHR really object to the exuberance of the Cour de Cassation, thereby jeopardizing the Cour's ongoing support of the ECHR project? As a legal matter, furthermore, on what basis could the ECHR criticize the Cour? The Convention and its ECHR interpretation set minimum fundamental-rights standards, not maximum ones. Beyond this minimum level, domestic legal actors are free to read the Convention as liberally as they like.

These factors demonstrate that expansive domestic interpretations of European law exert strong pressures not only within a given domestic level order, but also on the European one, to the point that they effectively become European law. Within the national legal order, they specify what European law requires. At the European level, the ECHR has excellent prudential reasons to adopt such interpretations as its own. In fact, these expansive domestic interpretations even operate between different domestic orders: expansive positions taken by the Belgian courts, supported (almost by necessity) by the European ones, exert pressures on their French counterparts (Lasser 2009).

This cycle of pressures reveals an essential attribute of the ongoing fundamental-rights explosion. Domestic legal actors have powerful incentives to frame their interpretations in expansive fundamental-rights terms. To adopt a contrary tack is to invite sanction, but to take an expansive approach is deeply empowering. When artfully done, it helps insulate the domestic court from effective European intervention (Caruso 2004), at the same time permitting it to exercise intellectual, institutional, jurisdictional, and doctrinal leadership on both the national and supranational levels.

This dynamic has helped fuel the fundamental-rights revolution. Every major domestic judicial institution has good reason to engage in the increasingly frantic "race to the top" of the fundamental-rights regime, in which the courts seek to recast their preexisting doctrinal and intellectual frames in fundamental-rights terms. This dynamic exerts tremendous pressures back on the European judicial order, as it fosters a decentralized fundamental-rights one-upmanship that the European courts cannot effectively control. The internal motivations of the French courts thus manifest as external pressures imposed on the European courts.

EUROPEAN PRESSURES ON THE EUROPEAN JUDICIAL SYSTEM

The European courts are by no means immune to these fundamental-rights pressures. As suggested above, the domestic courts can back the European ones into something of a corner: by casting their domestic judgments as expansive interpretations of European fundamental-rights norms, they can pressure the European courts to ratify and even adopt these interpretations. That is not all. The European judiciary is no more unified than its domestic counterparts: it is headed by two preeminent courts, the ECJ and the ECHR, who have strong internal motivations of their own to pressure each other quite strongly on the fundamental-rights front.[21] It should not be surprising, therefore, to see that the European courts reproduce many of the same interinstitutional dynamics that characterize the domestic judicial terrain.

As in the domestic arena, the European courts are situated differently with regard to fundamental rights. The ECHR is on its home turf when elaborating fundamental-rights doctrines. Such work represents its jurisdictional, institutional, and doctrinal raison d'être. The ECJ, however, is in a very different situation. It has long exercised review over actions taken by the EU institutions. But such review was based not on fundamental rights, but on the four "legality" grounds listed in Article 263 (ex 230) of the EC Treaty: "lack of competence, infringement of an essential procedural requirement, infringement of [the] Treaty or of any rule relating to its application, or misuse of powers." As knowledgeable readers will recognize, this legality framework faithfully reproduces the state-oriented good-governance approach deployed domestically by the Conseil d'Etat: the four traditional grounds for reviewing the legality of French administrative actions are none other than *incompétence, vice de forme, violation de la loi*, and *détournement de pouvoir* (Brown and Bell 1998: 239).

The explosion of fundamental-rights doctrines accordingly challenges the conceptual and doctrinal framework of the ECJ, which was derived directly from the Conseil d'Etat. As might be expected, the ECJ has met this challenge with some resistance: it only accepted to develop a fundamental-rights jurisprudence when faced with mounting institutional threats. These pressures came from at least two directions. Classic EU analyses stress the first: pressure exerted by domestic constitutional courts, especially the German Federal Constitutional Court (FCC). The FCC threatened to protect the fundamental rights of German citizens against encroachment by the acts of the community institutions unless the community (and the ECJ in particular) took on this task in a manner substantially similar to German

---

[21] The struggle for institutional, intellectual, and doctrinal leadership of the European high courts is on the verge of entering a new and potentially explosive phase: when the EU accedes to the European Convention system, the ECJ will suddenly become directly subject to the ECHR's jurisdiction. *See infra* Note 27 and accompanying text.

constitutional protections.[22] Our analysis highlights a second, European motivation that complements this domestic pressure: the ECJ was also increasingly threatened by the ECHR, whose evermore bold and influential fundamental rights analyses of governmental action challenged its own legality-based approach.[23]

Pushed from both directions, the ECJ had little tactical choice but to hop onto the fundamental-rights bandwagon, regardless of how unsettling this may have been to its traditional prism. Tellingly, however, it did so in a manner that faithfully reproduced the Conseil d'Etat's approach: it started to develop its own fundamental-rights jurisprudence under the rubric of "general principles of [European] Community law."[24] This solution – since enshrined in Article 6-2 of the Treaty of Amsterdam – parrots the Conseil d'Etat's creative elaboration of such "general principles of law" under the rubric of the cardinal French administrative notion of legality.[25] It also offers the same basic tactical advantage: it allows the ECJ to partake of, be responsive to, and influence the existing fundamental-rights regimes (both domestic and European), while also establishing the legal independence of the ECJ and its fundamental-rights doctrines.

These startlingly vivid institutional, conceptual, and doctrinal parallels between the ECJ and the Conseil d'Etat support several conclusions. At the most general, systemic level, the European courts are gradually organizing themselves as a complexly integrated judicial order, and they are doing so along recognizable domestic lines. Not only do they replicate the basic institutional division between fundamental-rights-oriented "constitutional" courts (the ECHR playing the role of the Constitutional Council) and legality-oriented "administrative" courts (the ECJ playing the role of the Conseil d'Etat), but they are reproducing the tensions, motivations, and solutions that characterize these domestic judicial orders. This confirms our analysis of the fundamental-rights dynamics that have been operating at the national level; justifies its transposition to the supranational level; and illustrates its relevance to

---

[22] When the ECJ did so, the FCC suspended its own review. *Re Wünsche Handelsgesellschaft* (*Solange II*), Judgment of Oct. 22, 1986, (1987) 3 CMLR 225, 265. *See also Brunner v. European Union Treaty*, (1994) 1 CMLR 57, 89 BverfGE 155.

[23] The centrality of the ECHR and its rights-based analyses has since been formalized in the EU legal order. The Charter of Fundamental Rights of the European Union, which took effect in 2000, established that the EU's institutions (including the ECJ) would respect fundamental rights "as they result," inter alia, from the European Convention on Human Rights and "the case-law of the [ECHR]." It even specified that insofar as it "contains rights which correspond to rights guaranteed by the [European Convention], the meaning and scope of those rights shall be the same as those laid down by the said Convention." Charter of Fundamental Rights of the European Union, Article 52(3).

[24] These general principles were to be inspired by the "constitutional traditions common to the Member States" and the European Convention on Human Rights. *See, e.g., Hauer v. Land Rheinland-Pfalz*, Case 44/79, December 13, 1979, (1979) ECR 3727.

[25] Developed most aggressively and expansively in the post–War years, these general principles have permitted the Conseil to crystallize a set of overarching principles of legality that ground the French state and its actions. *See* conclusions of CDG Fournier in *Syndicat général des ingénieurs-conseils*, June 26, 1959, Rec. Lebon 364; Conseil d'État 5 mai 1944 *Dame Trompier-Gravier* and CE 26.10.1945, *Aramu*, Leb. 213.

the increasingly porous and interactive environment at the intersection of these two domains.

The Article 6-1 fair trial litigation reveals quite clearly the operation of these dynamics. In theory, this litigation should not have been a bone of contention between the ECJ and ECHR: the former is not subject to the latter's jurisdiction.[26] The litigation has nonetheless spilled over into the Euro-European realm, because the decision-making process of the ECJ is so clearly patterned on the French model.[27] Litigants have therefore sought to challenge unfavorable ECJ judgments on the grounds that they were the product of similarly flawed judicial procedures. In fact, this procedural link between the ECJ and the French high courts has been stressed by almost all parties involved as a means to exert leverage on one another.

These Euro-European Article 6-1 debates have played out in multiple venues. First, the ECHR has explicitly and repeatedly addressed the ECJ's judicial decision-making processes in litigation concerning similar practices employed by the French and Belgian Supreme Courts. ECHR majority decisions have worked hard to distinguish ECJ from national Supreme Court decision-making practices: it would be highly impolitic for the ECHR to condemn the practices deployed by its august European colleague.[28] Dissenting ECHR judges have, to the contrary, stressed Franco-ECJ parallels as a means to critique the majority's developing jurisprudence in a (largely unsuccessful) attempt to shield French-style supreme courts from ECHR condemnation.[29] Indeed, the national high courts under review have done the same, both in domestic litigation and when defending themselves before the ECHR.[30]

Second, the Article 6-1 litigation has also surfaced before the ECJ itself. In effect, the ECHR's 6-1 jurisprudence has all but forced the ECJ to defend its traditional judicial decision-making procedures against the claim that they violate the fundamental right to a fair trial in a manner comparable to those of the French, Dutch, Belgian, and Portuguese Supreme Courts. In *Emesa Sugar v. Aruba*, the ECJ took matters in hand by issuing an order that held explicitly that its procedures do not run afoul of fair trial guarantees.[31]

---

[26] The EU has not yet acceded to the European Convention on Human Rights, as the ECJ ruled in 1996 that accession was outside the scope of EU's competences. *See* Accession by the Communities to the European Convention for the Protection of Human Rights and Fundamental Freedoms, Opinion 2/94, 1996 E.C.R. I-1759, at para. 35. Accession has been further delayed by the failure to ratify the proposed Constitutional Treaty. The Lisbon Reform Treaty calls for such accession. *See* Article 6 TEU.

[27] For more on these procedural parallels and their limits, *see* Lasser (2009: Chapters 4 and 7).

[28] *See, e.g., Delcourt v. Belgium*, 11 Eur. Ct. H.R. (Ser. A) 1 (1970), para. 30; *Kress* at para. 52, 86.

[29] *See* dissenting opinions of Judge Van Compernolle and Judges Gölcüklü, Matscher, and Pettiti in *Vermeulen v. Belgium*, 1996-I Eur. Ct. H.R. 224 (1996); *Reinhardt*, Dissenting Opinion of Judge De Meyer, at No. 13; Partly dissenting opinion of Judges Wildhaber, Costa, Pastor Ridruejo, Kūris, Bîrsan, Botoucharova, and Ugrekhelidze in *Kress*, at para. 11.

[30] *See, e.g., Kress* at para. 62.

[31] *See* Order of the Court in Case 17/98, *Emesa Sugar (Free Zone) NV v. Aruba*, 2000 E.R.C. I-665.

This exchange demonstrates a number of key points. First, the ECHR has been exerting significant pressure on the ECJ through the development of its fundamental-rights doctrines, although it does not formally exercise jurisdiction over its sister court. Second, the ECJ has understood that it has no choice but to meet this challenge directly on its own fundamental-rights terms: it must make an effort to seize control of the fundamental-rights analysis insofar as possible, lest it be at the mercy of less favorable interpretations. Third, the ECJ is nonetheless in a disadvantageous position in these exchanges. Fundamental-rights analysis is not the traditional source of its jurisdictional or doctrinal power. Worse, the ECJ finds itself in a defensive posture, as it must fend off the suggestion that its own decision-making procedures violate the fundamental right to a fair trial. This puts the ECJ in the awkward and seemingly retrograde position of fighting a rearguard action against fundamental-rights protections.

The ECJ has nonetheless held firm, claiming the authority to make its own fundamental-rights determinations. Relying on its self-availed – and treaty- and charter-ratified – power to interpret fundamental-rights norms as "general principles of law," it has even taken the dramatic tack of challenging the ECHR overtly: by explicitly refusing to follow the Strasbourg Court's Article 6-1 fair trial jurisprudence, the ECJ is in effect challenging the ECHR's leadership in the fundamental-rights arena.

Tellingly, the ECJ could hardly have picked less congenial ground on which to make its stand. It was the very institution charged with having violated the fundamental-rights norms in question; its analysis was therefore inescapably self-interested, if not self-serving. Worse, the ECJ was effectively forced to frame its self-defense as a restrictive, rather than an expansive, fundamental-rights interpretation: the ECJ had to conclude that the litigants' fair trial rights did not extend to the decision-making procedures at issue. The ECJ's very willingness to stand its ground under such unfavorable circumstances demonstrates the severity of the threat posed by the ECHR's Article 6-1 jurisprudence: backed against the wall, the ECJ had to claim fundamental-rights authority more forcefully, lest the ECHR dominate the field completely.

Equally telling, the ECJ defended its decision-making procedures in terms that unabashedly reproduced those put forward two years earlier by the French Conseil d'Etat.[32] By closing ranks in this manner, the ECJ presented the ECHR with a threateningly unified front against its developing jurisprudence. In so doing, the ECJ effectively recognized that it and the Conseil d'Etat are structurally, intellectually, doctrinally, and procedurally kindred institutions; the rise of the fundamental-rights idiom and fundamental-rights courts subjects both courts to deeply analogous pressures. These structural parallels confirm that the European courts are indeed

---

[32] *See Id.*, drawing heavily from *Esclatine*, Conseil d'Etat, July 29, 1998, D. 1999, at Jur. 85, concl. Chauvaux, at 89.

organizing themselves into an integrated judicial order along recognizable domestic lines.

SUBSTANTIVE CONCLUSIONS AND METHODOLOGICAL CAVEATS

The French and European judiciaries are both in the midst of a major constitutive moment. On its side, the French judicial system is rapidly turning itself evermore completely and explicitly into a fundamental–rights-based regime. This has triggered a major realignment of French judicial doctrines, procedures, jurisdictions, and ideologies. All French courts now interpret constitutional rights when handling litigation, even if formal constitutional review has traditionally been vested solely in the Constitutional Council. When combined with the establishment of fundamental-rights review of European derivation, the French judicial order has shifted ever further from its traditional package of republican-inspired attributes.

The French constitutional amendments of July 2008 offer the latest and clearest indication of this transformation. The addition of Article 61-1 opens the door for a posteriori concrete review of legislation on behalf of individuals: it allows references to be made by the Cour de Cassation and Conseil d'Etat to the Constitutional Council in ongoing litigation. This means, by definition, that all judicial (and/or quasi-judicial) branches of the French legal order are suddenly and explicitly important players in triggering judicial review of legislative norms on constitutional fundamental-rights grounds. One can only assume that this represents the death knell of the general will as classically defined.

On its side, the European courts are replicating ever-more faithfully the structure and logic of domestic legal orders such as the French. The ECJ and ECHR, although rooted in different treaty regimes and doctrinal logics, are gradually organizing themselves into an integrated judicial order. They have not only reproduced the institutional ethos and conceptual framework of the Conseil d'Etat and the Constitutional Council, respectively, but also the tensions between them. Indeed, they have even gone so far as to elaborate the same doctrinal mechanism for bridging between their legality and fundamental-rights perspectives: general principles of law. The full extent of these emerging parallels is only underlined by the ECJ's defense of its decision-making procedures in terms that explicitly parrot those authored by the Conseil d'Etat. What remains to be seen, however, is whether the EU's ratification of the Lisbon Reform Treaty, which should bring the ECJ under the fundamental-rights jurisdiction of the ECHR, will significantly alter this familiar institutional balance.

The complex and ongoing transformations occurring at the intersection of the French and European judicial systems therefore pose an analytic conundrum. Are the French and European judicial systems in the process of moving toward a unified fundamental-rights regime, led most likely by the key fundamental-rights court at the European level, the ECHR? Or do their complex and shifting interinstitutional dynamics actually represent a decentralized form of equilibrium in its own right, one that allows the plethora of domestic and supranational courts to govern their respective domains as they all converge on – and compete over – an increasingly common fundamental-rights idiom? This problem of historical perspective is compounded by what might be termed a problem of systemic perspective. The interrelated convergence of all of these domestic and European courts on the fundamental-rights idiom has made it increasingly difficult to treat the domestic and supranational judicial orders as truly external to each other.

The Article 6-1 fair trial litigation demonstrates this phenomenon quite elegantly. When the Cour de Cassation interpreted the ECHR's jurisprudence so expansively as to require a large-scale reconstruction of its own decision-making processes, it all but forced the ECHR to adopt this interpretation of European law and impose it on the Conseil d'Etat. It is not at all clear whether this cycle of French and European judicial interaction is best understood as an example of: 1) external European (ECHR) pressure on the French courts; 2) internal (Cour de Cassation) motivations regarding its relations to the Conseil d'Etat; or 3) reverse (Cour de Cassation) pressure on the ECHR. My own inclination is to understand it as an example of all three at once, not only because the pressures and motivations operate simultaneously on all fronts, but also because the more one knows what one is looking at, the less and less clear it becomes whether, for example, the Cour de Cassation can best be described in such instances as a French or European legal actor. This suggests a fourth interpretation; namely, that the Cour de Cassation was internally motivated – as one European court – to exert interpretive pressure on another – the ECHR. In this complex and shifting legal environment, domestic institutions such as the Cour de Cassation act as both the subjects and objects of European law, constructing Europe and realizing European law even as they reformulate French legal traditions and rework French legal institutions (Lasser 2009).

The dramatic emergence of fundamental rights manifests this complexly interactive and fluid state of affairs. Fundamental-rights analysis crossed traditional jurisdictional boundaries, linking together a series of courts that had previously operated in relatively distinct legal and political spheres. This doctrinal linkage not only provided the opportunity for interinstitutional communication in common terms, but also triggered intense and ongoing interinstitutional competition: each of the high domestic and European courts was – and still is – deeply invested in mastering the high ground of fundamental rights. Finally, as the highest ranking and most readily applicable norms in the emerging legal regime, fundamental rights have become the privileged and ubiquitous medium for engaging in these charged interinstitutional struggles.

REFERENCES

Bell, John 1992. *French Constitutional Law*. Oxford: Clarendon Press.
Bell, John 2001. *French Legal Cultures*. London: Butterworths.
Bourdieu, Pierre (Clough, trans.) 1996. *The State Nobility: Elite Schools in the Field of Power*. Stanford: Stanford University Press.

Brown, L. Neville and John Bell 1998. *French Administrative Law*. Oxford: Clarendon Press.

Caruso, Daniela 2004. "Private Law and Public Stakes in European Integration: The Case of Property," *European Law Journal* 6: 751.

Garapon, Antoine and Ioannis Papadopoulos 2004. *Juger en Amerique et en France: Culture juridique française et common law*. Paris: Odile Jacob.

Hazareesingh, Sudhir 1994. *Political Traditions in Modern France*. New York, Oxford: Oxford University Press.

Kahn-Freund, Claudine Levy, and Bernard Rudden 1991. *A Source-Book on French Law*. Oxford: Clarendon Press.

Lasser, Mitchel 2005. *Judicial Deliberations: A Comparative Analysis of Judicial Transparency and Legitimacy*. Oxford: Oxford University Press.

Lasser, Mitchel 2009. *Judicial Transformations: The Rights Revolution in the Courts of France and Europe*. Oxford: Oxford University Press.

Portalis, Jean-Etienne-Marie 1799. "Discours préliminaire, prononcé le 24 thermidor an VIII," translated and reprinted in Kahn-Freund, et al. 1991, pp. 233–235.

Rousseau, Jean-Jacques (Dunne, trans.) 2002. *The Social Contract and the First and Second Discourses*. New Haven and London: Yale University Press.

Suleiman, Ezra 1974. *Politics, Power, and Bureaucracy in France: The Administrative Elite*. Princeton: Princeton University Press.

Weiler, Joseph 1981. "The Community System: The Dual Character of Supranationalism," *Yearbook of European Law* 1: 268.

Weiler, Joseph 1994. "A Quiet Revolution: The European Court and its Interlocutors," *Comparative Political Studies* 26: 510.

12

Constitutional Courts as Bulwarks of Secularism

Ran Hirschl*

One of the fascinating but seldom-explored phenomena in comparative constitutional law is the growing reliance on constitutional courts in the non-secular world to block the spread of religiosity or advance a relatively universalist interpretation of sacred texts. The American constitutional system has successfully maintained a stable secular order in one of the most religious societies in the West. Although the specter of religiosity is haunting Europe once again, European national high courts, from Germany to Britain to France, assumed the role of guardians of secularism against the perceived threat to the concept of a religiously neutral public sphere.[1] Likewise, Turkey's adherence to a strict separation of religion and state (at least until the recent constitutional amendments) has allowed the Turkish Constitutional Court to exclude religious practices, parties, and policies from the purview of Turkey's political sphere. The Supreme Court of India has drawn on the "basic structure" doctrine to maintain and advocate a secularist vision of the Indian Constitution amid a markedly religious setting and increased political presence of Hindu and Muslim religiosity.[2] Its jurisprudence on personal-status law has sounded a clear voice for uniformity and standardization in that domain. In short, despite the many pertinent differences, the constitutional jurisprudence of countries that adhere to a strict separation of religion and state reveals a clear secularist tendency and vision of religion as confined to the private sphere.

A notably harder challenge to the constitutional containment of religion is posed by constitutional orders that defy the Franco-American ideal of separating religion

---

* Canada Research Chair, Professor of Political Science & Law, University of Toronto. An earlier draft was presented at the Sawyer Seminar Plenary Conference, held at the University of California, Berkeley in November 2008. I thank the volume editors and participants for their helpful comments and suggestions.
[1] National high courts in Germany (e.g., the *Ludin* case, 2003), Britain (*Shabina Begum*, 2006), and France (the Conseil d'État ruling in the *Faiza M* case, 2008) have addressed the hotly contested question of differentiated citizenship and wearing of religious attire in the public education system.
[2] See, e.g., *S. R. Bommai v. Union of India*, A.I.R. 1994 S.C. 1918.

and state along private-public lines. At least 1 billion people now live in polities or
subnational units that not only designate a single religion as the "state religion" but
also enshrine that religion and its interlocutor as "a" or "the" source of legislation
(meaning that legislation must comply with principles of that religion), incorporate
religious precepts in law, grant religious tribunals jurisdiction over important aspects
of life, public and private, in addition to the tremendous symbolic weight religious
edicts often carry. At the same time, religion and its institutions and interpretive
hierarchy are expected to comply with overarching constitutional norms and are
subject to review by constitutional courts and judges.

Examples of such mixed legal regimes are many. In the past four decades, at
least 30 of the world's predominantly Muslim polities, from Mauritania to Oman to
Pakistan, declared Shari'a (Islamic law) "a" or "the" source of legislation (meaning
that legislation must comply with principles of that religion). The new Constitutions
of Afghanistan (2004) and Iraq (2005), as well as the Constitutional Declaration of
Libya (2011) reflect a dual commitment to principles of Shari'a as "state religion"
and "source of legislation" alongside commitment to general principles of constitutional law, human rights and popular sovereignty. Although few of these polities'
constitutions were adopted in an authentic bottom-up, "we-the-people" fashion,
Islamization does reflect a set of values that a large portion of the population in these
countries seems to support. Early post–"Arab Spring" election results in Tunisia and
Egypt, to pick two examples, show considerable increase in the influence of Islamic
parties. In several other countries, precepts of Islam have been incorporated into the
constitution, penal code, and personal-status laws of subnational units, most notably
in twelve Nigerian states, Pakistan's North-West Frontier Province, and Indonesia's
Aceh, to varying degrees in two Malaysian states, and to an increasing extent in
Russia's Chechnya and Dagestan. Granted, Malaysia and Tunisia are a world apart
from Iran or the Vatican in how lax or rigid the actual translation of religious principles into public life is. However, in virtually all these countries religion not only
plays a key collective-identity role but is also granted a formal constitutional status,
serves as a source of legislation – whether symbolically or practically – and, more
important, enjoys jurisdictional autonomy in matters extending from education and
personal-status law to essential omnipresence in every aspect of life, law, and politics.

In this chapter, I explore the scope and nature of religion-and-state jurisprudence
in such hybrid settings. To that end, I look at various modes of interpretive ingenuity
(and to some extent strategic judicial behavior) developed by constitutional courts
in several non-secular polities – most notably Egypt, Kuwait, Pakistan, Malaysia,
and Israel – in order to contain, tame, and mitigate the resurgence of sacred law in
their respective polities. These countries differ in their formal recognition of, and
commitment to, religious values. Accordingly, there are considerable differences in
the interpretive approaches and practical solutions adopted by the seven countries'
respective high courts in dealing with core questions of religion and state. Despite
these dissimilarities, however, a close look at actual constitutional jurisprudence

of religion in these countries reveals some striking parallels in the way in which the constitutional courts in these and some other similarly situated countries have positioned themselves as important religion-taming within their respective societies despite intense scrutiny from the more religious segments of the public. Each of these countries illustrates the remarkably creative interpretive techniques adopted by judges confronted with concrete legal disputes that reflect and encapsulate the greater issues emerging from the tension between constitutionalism and religion. This may suggest that the existential fear of the constitutional domain from alternative interpretive hierarchies, most notably religion and its interlocutors, is a universal phenomenon that manifests itself even in the least likely ("most difficult") of settings.

I conclude by drawing some general lessons concerning the embedded religion-taming inclination of the constitutional domain, and the role of constitutional courts in "domesticating" or disarming religion of its potentially radical edge. In virtually all religion-laden polities, constitutional courts have emerged as pragmatic, moderate agents relative to the context within which they operate. Even in the least likely settings, constitutional courts are agnostic towards religion's alternative cosmology, interpretive hierarchy, and its non-statist vision of the political order. The demand for taking on that religion-taming role emanates from moderate political leaders, statist elites, secularist elements of civil society (more often than not, the urban intelligentsia), and powerful economic stakeholders who share a deep resentment of radical religion. It is given added impetus by the internal motivations of constitutional courts and judges, most notably their veneration for the rule of (state) law and embedded antipathy toward competing interpretive hierarchies, as well as the judges' own educational background and belief systems. Although the courts' interpretive creativity often enables them to push the religion-taming agenda further than one might have expected, the intensity and strength of the religious tide imposes strategic limits on how the courts play their secularizing role. Taken as a whole, however, turning to constitutional law and courts to bring religiosity under check or defuse its potentially radical edge may be a rational choice of action by secularists and moderates. Despite occasional and inevitable setbacks, it is a prudent, judicious gamble.

CONTAINING RELIGION THROUGH CONSTITUTIONAL JURISPRUDENCE

Regimes throughout the non-secularist world have been struggling with questions of a profoundly foundational nature and have been forced to navigate between cosmopolitanism and parochialism, modern and traditional meta-narratives, constitutional principles and religious injunctions, contemporary governance and ancient texts, and judicial and pious interpretation. More often than not, the clash between these conflicting visions results in fierce struggles over the nature of the body politic and its organizing principles. These tensions are evident in virtually every aspect of public life, from court hearings to university lectures, crowded soccer stadiums to secluded board meetings, and casual conversations in markets and street eateries to manoeuvres in the upper echelons of politics. Consequently, throughout the world of constitutional theocracies – be they soft or rigid, formal or informal – fascinating, largely unexplored jurisprudential landscapes form, reflecting uneasy amalgams of universal aspirations and domestic realities and constitutional principles and religious directives (Hirschl 2010). Let us consider several examples.

Restricting anti-establishment religious movements may be done by outright delegitimation of radical religion; Islamic parties are outlawed even in countries that enshrine Islam as their state religion. Algeria is merely one example. Alternatively, religion may be disarmed by co-optation; until recently, Tunisia's 1988 Law on Mosques, for example, provided that only personnel appointed by the government may lead activities in mosques, and stipulates that mosques must remain closed except during prayer times and other authorized religious ceremonies, such as marriages or funerals. The 1961 formal nationalization by President Gamal Abdel Nasser of al-Azhar university in Cairo (the main center of religious learning for nearly a billion Sunni Muslims) has allowed the government to monitor religious activism at will over the last half-century. In Saudi Arabia, Wahhabi discourse is channeled through the *ulama* (learned Muslim high clergy), largely state appointed and historically loyal to the royal family. This type of co-optation seems to echo Adam Smith's astute observation that the official establishment of a religion, alongside government support and privileges, is likely to discourage the monopoly clergy from engaging in any type of dissident social activism (Smith 1994).

In other countries – Tajikistan, Turkmenistan and Uzbekistan are only three examples – Muslim followers of non-state-approved religious organizations may be arrested for holding "unsanctioned gatherings" or labeled "extremists" by state courts and leaders of registered religious organizations. In 2007, for example, the Supreme Court of Tajikistan declared a dozen such unregistered organizations, including the Islamic Movement of Turkestan, extremist. The practice is by no means confined to predominantly Muslim countries. Most Vietnamese, for example, follow Mahayana Buddhism. Driven by anti-American suspicions, Vietnamese law requires that religious groups register with the government. Those groups that do not join one of the officially authorized religious organizations, the governing boards of which are under government control, are considered illegal. This has led to effective infringement on religious freedom of various Christian and non–state-controlled Buddhist sects.

Meanwhile, the Indonesian Constitutional Court has reinforced the government monopoly over the definition of official religion. Two recent landmark rulings illustrate this approach. The Indonesian Religious Courts Law lists a number of areas (e.g., marriage, divorce, inheritance, trusts, gifts, and Islamic finance) over which Shari'a tribunals have jurisdiction. In the *Religious Court Law Case* (2008), the Constitutional Court unanimously rejected a claim made by a religious student who argued that the state-imposed limitation of the jurisdiction of religious courts to particular civil matters is unconstitutional because it prevents his full observance of Islam.[3] The Court held that expanding the list of subject matters falling within the jurisdiction of religious courts is within the exclusive prerogative of the federal government, and is not something the Court can do (Butt 2010, 297).

In 2010, the Indonesian Constitutional Court upheld (8:1) the legality of the country's controversial 1965 Blasphemy Law.[4] The law officially acknowledges six religions – Buddhism, Catholicism, Confucianism, Hinduism, Islam, and Protestantism – and prohibits "religious based activities" that "resemble the religious activities of the religion in question, where such interpretation and activities are in deviation of the basic teachings of the religion." This amounts to a prohibition on alternative teachings and has been used to clump down on "unofficial" Islamic voices ranging from the Ahmadiyya sect to militant Wahhabism. Proponents of Western-style rights argued that the law in its current form infringes on basic religious freedoms as well as group rights, and violates the International Covenant on Civil and Political Rights. Drawing on a "war on terror" impulse (Bali and other parts of Indonesia have been targets of bombings tied to Islamic militants), the government countered that the law must be upheld to avoid interpretation-at-will of Islam and Shari'a. Upholding the law, the government argued, would "maintain social harmony and prevent an explosion of new religions." The Court agreed. Repealing the Blasphemy Law, it ruled, could bring "misuses and contempt of religion and trigger conflicts in society." By upholding the law, the Court has thus aided authorities in preventing "runaway" radical Islamization by keeping the process of religious interpretation under official check. However, religion-limiting constitutional interpretation can get considerably more innovative. Let us consider a few examples.

Egypt and Kuwait

How Egyptian state-and-religion relations shape up following the so-called Arab Spring and the overturning of the Mubarak regime is still too early to tell. Early signs indicate an ever-stronger popular support for further Islamization of law and policy. The charged relations between constitutional law and religion in Egypt is not new, however. In 1980, Egypt amended Article 2 of its Constitution (originally adopted in 1971) to introduce Shari'a as "the" (instead of "a") primary source of legislation. (This provision was reproduced in the new 2012 Constitution with the addition of Article 219, which uses technical terms from Islamic legal tradition to define what is actually meant by "the principles of the Islamic Shari'a," as stated by Article 2, most likely in direct reaction to the modernist jurisprudential trend described in the following pages). For more than thirty years now, Egypt's courts have been grappling with the contested status and role of Shari'a as a potentially determinative source of authority. To address this question in a moderate way, Egypt's Supreme

[3] Indonesian Constitutional Court Decision No 19/PUU-VI/2008.
[4] Indonesian Constitutional Court Decision No 140/PUU-VII/2009.

Constitutional Court (SCC) developed an innovative interpretive matrix of religious directives – the first of its kind by a nonreligious tribunal. As Nathan Brown and Clark Lombardi explain, the Court distinguishes between undisputed, universally binding principles of Shari'a and flexible applications of those principles (Brown 1999; Lombardi 1998, 2006). Legislation that contravenes a strict, unalterable principle recognized as such by all interpretive schools is declared unconstitutional and void; at the same time, *ijtihad* (contemplation or external interpretation) is permitted in cases of textual lacunae, or where the pertinent rules are vague, open-ended, or subject to various acceptable interpretations. Although certain laws may not be in line with classical Islam, they do not necessarily contravene Egypt's overall commitment to Islamic values. Furthermore, as Brown and Lombardi indicate, the SCC has given the government broad legislative discretion in policy areas where Shari'a is found to provide unclear or multiple answers, provided that the legislative outcome does not contravene the general spirit of Shari'a.

Perhaps most interestingly, in a few landmark judgments concerning issues ranging from women's rights to the scope of Islamic banking, and the place of religious attire in the public school system to liberalizing reforms to family law, the SCC engaged in a substantive interpretation of both the Qur'an and evidence available in Sunna. In developing this somewhat elastic interpretive device, the Court relied on the fact that the classical Islamic jurists and the different schools of jurisprudence vary in their interpretations and applications of the texts. This interpretive flexibility offers the chance to implement Shari'a in different social environments and allow jurists, including constitutional court judges who wish to invoke religious law, to choose which school of interpretation they deem applicable in a given instance. In so doing, this interpretive approach provides one of the clearest concrete illustrations currently on offer of the argument that Islamic law is not inherently incompatible with interpretive pluralism or democracy.[5]

Either way, the Egyptian SCC's two-tier hierarchy of Shari'a norms has allowed it (as well as the Supreme Administrative Court) to issue moderate or liberalizing rulings on contested matters such as the wearing of religious attire in the public school system, the scope of Islamic banking restrictions, Islamic divorce procedures, and the banning of female genital mutilation. On the basis of a similar rationale, Muhammad Sayyid Tantawi, the moderate grand imam of al-Azhar Mosque and grand sheikh of al-Azhar University – one of the highest spiritual authorities for nearly a billion Sunni Muslims – asserted that there is no categorical text in the Qur'an and Sunna forbidding women to assume the post of judge. So, the first female judge was

---

[5] Interestingly, conceptually similar distinctions exist in other religion-infused jurisprudential settings. Simon Butt (2010) reports that in its ruling in the *Polygamy Case* (2007), the Indonesian Constitutional Court endorsed a distinction between acts of devotion or worship of God (*ibadah*) and relations between humans (*mu'amalah*) – unlike the former realm, the second may be subject to government regulation (i.e., polygamous marriage may be banned by state law although many hard-line clerics in Indonesia maintain it should be allowed).

appointed to the SCC in 2003. In a major follow-up move in 2007, Egypt's Supreme Judicial Council selected thirty-one female judges to serve on courts throughout the country. These candidates were later appointed by a presidential decree in a move that angered conservatives. In 2010, the Supreme Judicial Council overturned the Council of State's (an administrative body) vote to bar women from judicial positions. The matter reached the SCC on referral by the government. The Court took an inclusive approach and stressed that the law grants both men and women equal rights to assume judicial positions in administrative courts. The pertinent legislation stipulates that members of the Council of State must be "Egyptian," a word which in Arabic is specific to the male gender. However, the Supreme Constitutional Court ruled that in this context the word means "citizen," which includes both genders. In short, through a development of an innovative jurisprudential matrix, the SCC has been playing an important role in the containment of radical religion.It remains to be seen how this role evolves given the direction in which Egyptian political and constitutional order are currently heading. For now, suffice it to say that a clear indication of the Court's religion-taming legacy is the express efforts by the drafters of the 2012 Constitution to introduce concrete, constitutionally-entrenched Shari'a-based guidelines for interpreting Article 2 (e.g. Article 219) as well as a guarantee (via Article 4) that al-Azhar scholars are consulted in matters of Islamic law, so as to reverse what the Freedom and Justice Party (founded by the Muslim Brotherhood) regards as a continuous "watering down" of that key constitutional provision through creative judicial interpretation.

A brief excursion to Kuwait is quite telling here. Similar to its Egyptian counterpart, Kuwait's Constitutional Court has emerged as an advocate of a moderate, relatively progressive agenda – given the context of an Islamic state and morality – and it has done so within a constitutional framework that resembles that of Egypt. The Kuwaiti Constitution (1962) states that, "Islam is the religion of the state," and that Shari'a is "a main surce of legislation." This phrasing is considered the source of the 1971 Egyptian Constitution's definition of the status of Shari'a as "a" source of legislation until the 1980 amendment changed that to "the" source of legislation. The Egyptian rulings discussed earlier fed recent Kuwaiti Constitutional Court rulings on similar issues. Let us consider two recent illustrations of this trend, both of which follow the Egyptian trail.

In 2005, Kuwait adopted a law that for the first time in its history allowed women to vote and hold political office. The law also stipulated that women voters and candidates must comply with Shari'a law. On the basis of that law, four women were elected to the Kuwaiti Parliament in May 2009 – a historic breakthrough, no doubt. However, a few months later a religious edict was published by the Ministry of Islamic Affairs' fatwa department (on request by an ultraconservative MP) stating that any woman who wants to take part in politics must dress in accordance with Shari'a law norms – with her head covered and "a long robe that hides all parts of the body and which is not so tight so that it would give prominence to any curves." Conservative opponents of women's rights cited that edict, alongside the requirement for compliance with Shari'a law stipulated in the 2005 law and the preamble to the Constitution, to argue that women who refuse to wear the *hijab* may not serve in Parliament.

This claim was a direct attack on two of the explicitly modernist women elected to the Parliament. The struggle over women's dress code found its way to Kuwait's Constitutional Court, which had to decide on a much more substantive question than the way women MPs are clothed: what is the meaning of the clause in the 2005 law that requires compliance with Shari'a law? More generally, what is the scope of the provision "Islam is a main source of legislation" in the Constitution? In October 2009, Kuwait's Constitutional Court ruled that women lawmakers do not have to wear the hijab when in Parliament. The clause in the 2005 legislation was deemed too broad or vague and failed to specify what concrete norms women voters and candidates must comply with. Because the clause was generic, and because Shari'a law is not unified in its approach to the headscarf, one cannot arrive at the conclusion that wearing the hijab is the only possible interpretation of the clause in the 2005 law. What is more, wearing the hijab, the court ruled, is a matter of personal preference, not of state policy.

This ruling came on the heels of another progressive ruling released by the Kuwaiti Constitutional Court only a week earlier. In that ruling, the court held that a provision of the Personal Status Law requiring a woman's husband, parents, or male guardian to grant her permission to obtain a passport (and hence denying her the freedom to travel abroad without permission) violated guarantees of personal freedom and gender equality inherent in the Kuwaiti Constitution. Any way one looks at them, these are secularizing rulings, made all the more important when they come from a court that operates within a constitutional framework that designates Islam as the state religion and enshrines its principles as a main source of legislation.

Pakistan

A different illustration of religion-containing interpretive ingenuity comes from Pakistan. The process of the "Islamization" of Pakistani law goes back to 1973, and has known many twists and turns. It's pinnacles have been the 1978–1980 establishment of a Shari'at court system at the provincial and federal levels, as well as the Shari'at Appellate Bench (SAB) at the Supreme Court; and the introduction in 1985 of a set of amendments to the Constitution, effectively stipulating that "[a]ll existing laws shall be brought in conformity with the Injunctions of Islam as laid down in the Holy Qur'an and Sunna, in this Part referred to as the Injunctions of Islam, and no law shall be enacted which is repugnant to such Injunctions." In theory, this means that legislation must be in full compliance with principles of Shari'a. The Supreme Court of Pakistan (SCP), however, has begged to differ.

In response to the possible conclusiveness of the Islamization reforms, the Court developed its "harmonization doctrine," according to which no specific provision of the Constitution stands above any other provision. In a landmark ruling in 1992, the SCP held that the "Islamization amendment" shall not prevail over the other articles of the Constitution, as the amendment possessed the same weight and status as the other articles of the Constitution and therefore "could not be placed on a higher pedestal or treated as a *grund norm*."[6] The Court's subsequent judgments of this key issue have firmly precluded and strongly warned against an interpretation of the Islamization amendments that would "raise it to the point of being a litmus test for gauging, evaluating, and potentially justifying the judiciary to strike down any other constitutional provisions" (Siddique and Hayat 2008, 368). Any reading of the amendments as elevated "special clauses" would undermine the entire Constitution. The Constitution as a whole must be interpreted in a harmonious fashion so that specific provisions are read as an integral part of the entire Constitution, not as standing above it. In the words of the Court: "It may be observed that the principles for interpreting constitutional documents as laid down by this Court are that all provisions should be read together and harmonious construction should be placed on such provisions so that no provision is rendered nugatory."[7]

To be sure, although it has shown some liberalizing tendencies, the SCP, similar to its counterparts elsewhere, does not operate in a political or ideological vacuum. To some extent, it may be considered an extension of the executive branch rather than a fully autonomous organ. It is hardly surprising that in several rulings it sided with the Islamist face of the Constitution. A notable example is the Court's approval in 1993 of part of the 1984 blasphemy laws that made members of the Ahmadiyya community liable to prosecution for engaging in activities associated with Islam. Likewise, in the politically charged area of personal-status and family-law matters, the equality provisions of the Constitution are seldom invoked by the Court. Indeed, the constitutional status of women in Pakistan is a far cry from any Western liberal standards. Women's groups pushing for greater gender equality face intense opposition. As Sadia Saeed notes, the initial containment of religious zeal via constitutionalization may have the effect of subsequent entrenchment of more moderate, but nonetheless illiberal, rights discourses. That said, the SCP has managed to block calls for major Islamic-based family-law overhaul.

In addition to its refusal to accept the Islamization amendments as a supra-constitutional norm, the Court has retained its overarching jurisdictional authority, including its de facto appellate capacity over the Shari'at Appellate Bench at the Supreme Court. This has proved time and again to be a safety valve for secular interests. In 2002, for example, the Supreme Court ordered the SAB to reconsider its 1999 ruling that interest or usury (*riba*) in any form contravened Shari'a principles

---

[6] *Hakim Khan v. Government of Pakistan*, P.L.D. 1992 S.C. 595.
[7] *Qazi Hussain Ahmed et al. v. General Pervez Musharraf*, P.L.D. 2002 S.C. 853.

and was therefore impermissible.[8] The Supreme Court accepted the government's argument that the transition to a riba-free economy, as it had been defined by the SAB, was effectively infeasible. It noted concerns about the economic stability of Pakistan should the reforms occur and stated that they were simply impractical. The Court also accepted the government's claim that the reasoning employed by the SAB misinterpreted both the Qur'an and Sunna, had invoked only one conception of riba, and thus lacked the objectivity needed to render an adequate verdict in the case. The court thus ordered the SAB to "to conduct thorough and elaborate research, and comparative study of the financial systems which are prevalent in the contemporary Muslim countries of the world."[9]

In 2003, to give another example, the Pakistani Supreme Court ruled that the Hudood Ordinances (adopted in 1979 to introduce harsh penalties for offenses described in the Qur'an) had been drafted hastily, had many gaps, were defective, and were the source of many challenges to the establishment of human rights in the country. The enforcement of the ordinances, stated the Court, was not in line with the justice-seeking purpose of enforcing Islamic law. In 2004, the SCP went on to curtail the Federal Shari'at Court's competence to overturn any legislation judged to be inconsistent with the tenets of Islam. The Court held that any Shari'a-related jurisprudence that involves significant constitutional law aspects must take a cohesive view of Pakistan's constitutional law, as well as the supremacy of federal legislation over provincial legislation.[10]

Principles of federalism have also aided the court in its mission to contain radical religion. In July 2005 and again in December 2006, for example, the SCP blocked attempts to enact laws to enforce Islamic morality in the North-West Frontier Province (NWFP), which has been governed by an alliance of religious parties sympathetic to the Taliban since 2003. Specifically, the NWFP Islamization bill (also known as the Hisba [Accountability] Act, 2005) aimed at implementing greater Islamic regulation in the NWFP by establishing a government agency headed by a special cleric given the title of *mohtasib* (ombudsman). This agency was responsible for overseeing the Islamization of everyday life in the province, including many aspects of private life. To that end, the act created an enforcement force – essentially a religious police squad – that would help ensure the moral and virtuous conduct of Muslims in the province. President Musharraf, whose administration supported an enlightened, moderate form of Islam, denounced the bill as a fundamental breach of human rights that would, accordingly, violate federal legislation and constitutional rights. On Musharraf's request and on these grounds, Pakistan's attorney general challenged the constitutionality of the proposed Islamization bill, using the constitutional reference procedure that allows the Executive branch to refer constitutional

---

[8] *United Bank Ltd. v. M/S Farooq Brothers*, P.L.D. 2002 S.C. 800.
[9] *Id.*, 815–816.
[10] *Muhammad Siddique et al. v. Government of Pakistan* (decision released on Nov. 5, 2004).

questions to the Supreme Court in its advisory jurisdiction (Section 186 of the Constitution). The main question the Court was asked to address was "whether the Hisba Bill or any of its provisions would be constitutionally invalid if enacted."[11]

The SCP unanimously agreed and ordered the NWFP governor not to sign the Hisba Bill into law: "The Governor of the North-West Frontier Province may not assent to Hisba Bill in its present form as its various Sections . . . have been declared *ultra vires* the Constitution of the Islamic Republic of Pakistan, 1973."[12] The Court ruled that "Islamic jurists are unanimous on the point that except for *sallat* [prayer] and *zakat* [alms] no other religious obligation stipulated by Islam can be enforced by the state."[13] In other words, much like its Egyptian counterpart, the Court suggested that even within Islamic jurisprudence there is no agreement that state enforcement of religious values is warranted. The decision again contained a conflation of Islamic and secular constitutional law, suggesting that the functions of the mohtasib would interfere in the citizens' "personal life, freedom of assembly, liberty, dignity, and privacy which is strictly prohibited in Islam."[14] The bill was sent back to the NWFP Assembly for redrafting and was subsequently passed in a diluted version, which the Supreme Court struck down again in December 2006. In short, although falling short of advancing a truly progressive human rights agenda by Western standards, the Supreme Court has nonetheless served as a bastion of relative cosmopolitanism in an otherwise increasingly religious Pakistan. It has thus allowed moderately religious politicians to talk the talk of strong commitment to religion, at the same time transferring the costs of not implementing that talk to the courts.

Malaysia

Malaysia provides another captivating although seldom explored illustration of the subtle religion-taming function of constitutional jurisprudence. Malaysia, despite its vast socioeconomic disparity, is one of Asia's economic tigers and a major tourist destination. Its capital, Kuala Lumpur, is one of Asia's most bustling business centers – home of the landmark Petronas Twin Towers, as well as the Menara Kuala Lumpur, currently the world's fifth-tallest telecommunications tower. Putrajaya, Malaysia's new administrative capital next to Kuala Lumpur, features a fully electronic government, matching with its neighboring planned city Cyberjaya, in accordance with former Prime Minister Mahathir bin Mohamad's vision of Malaysia as the "Japan of the Islamic world" (Bakar 2008, 84). At the same time, however, the Malaysian political sphere, at both the state and federal levels, has undergone substantial Islamization over the last three decades. The Pan-Malaysian Islamic Party (Parti Islam Se-Malaysia [PAS]) has been gaining political support and clout since

---

[11] Reference 2/2005 *In Re: NWFP Hisba Bill*, P.L.D. 2005 S.C. 873.
[12] *Id.*
[13] *Id.*
[14] *Id.*

the 1980s.[15] It has positioned itself as a party that aims to establish Malaysia as a country on the basis of Islamic legal theory derived from the primary sources of Islam, the Qur'an, Sunna, and Hadiths. In contrast, the National Front (Barisan Nasional [BN]) coalition led by the historically hegemonic United Malay National Organization (UNMO) adopts the more mainstream Islam Hadhari doctrine (a moderate or "civilizational" Islam), which PAS sees as on the basis of a watered-down, compromised, secularized understanding of Islam. This has brought to the fore the constitutional status of Islam as Malaysia's state religion and marker of Malay collective identity.

The Constitution of 1963 establishes Malaysia as a unique form of Islamic state where "Islam is the religion of the Federation; but other religions may be practiced in peace and harmony in any part of the Federation" (Article 3), and where "every person has the right to profess and practice his religion and to propagate it" (Article 11.1). Further, "every religious group has the right to manage its own religious affairs" (Article 11.3), and state law (and, in the Federal Territories of Kuala Lumpur and Labuan, federal law) "may control or restrict the propagation of any religious doctrine or belief among persons professing the religion of Islam" (Article 11.4). To add further complication, Malaysian law draws on religious ascriptions to establish what has been termed "ethnic democracy," where, despite the existence of some ethnic power-sharing mechanisms and an accompanying façade of interracial harmony, Malay political dominance is ensured. Core elements of the political system are organized so as to benefit members of the Malay ethnic group to the detriment of others, and members of minority ethnic groups are not granted proportional access to power. Although Islam is constitutionally enshrined as Malaysia's state religion, more than one-third of Malaysia's population consists of members of other denominations, mainly Buddhists, Hindus, and Christians. However, ethnic Malays (Bumiputra or "sons of the soil"), generally Muslim, are granted constitutionally entrenched preferential treatment in various aspects of public life over members of other ethnic groups (Article 153 of the Constitution). Malay citizens who convert out of Islam are no longer considered Malay under the law and hence forfeit the Bumiputra privileges afforded to Malays under Article 153.

In the face of the growing Islamization, Malaysia's constitutional division of powers between the federal and state governments has been used to effectively block religious–parties-led governments in the states of Kelantan and Terengganu from instituting Qur'an- and Sunna-based *hudood* and *qisas* (retaliation) law as the basis for their criminal code. Although the Kelantan State Assembly passed the Syariah (Malay for "Shari'a") Criminal Enactment in 1993, it has yet to be implemented,

[15] In the March 2008 general elections, for example, a coalition of PAS and its allies (the Pakatan Rakyat coalition), won 82 of the 222 seats; the establishment BN coalition won only 140 seats. The difference in actual votes was very slim: approximately 4.1 million votes for the BN coalition (or 50.1 percent) and 3.8 million votes for the Pakatan Rakyat coalition (46.4 percent).

mainly because criminal law is in federal hands. According to the Federal Constitution, Syariah courts do not have jurisdiction over offenses "except in so far as conferred by federal law"; state authorities can only legislate for Islamic offenses "except in regard to matters included in the Federal List" (e.g., criminal law and procedure). What is more, Article 75 provides: "If any State law is inconsistent with a federal law, the federal law shall prevail and the State law shall, to the extent of the inconsistency, be void." Finally, item 4(k) in the list of matters falling under federal jurisdiction provides that "[a]scertainment of Islamic Law and other personal laws for purposes of federal law" is a federal matter.

Although the power to create and punish offenses against the precepts of Islam has been assigned by the Constitution to the states, Syariah courts have jurisdiction only over persons professing the religion of Islam. Further, the enactment of hudood as state law runs counter to Article 11 (freedom of religion), which has been interpreted to protect individuals against prosecution on the basis of choice of religion. What is more, Article 8 provides that every citizen is equal before the law, hence rendering the blanket application of hudood laws arguably unconstitutional because they discriminate against non-Muslims and women. Finally, as the Malaysian Federal Court – the country's supreme court since 1985 – has observed on numerous occasions, Malaysian public law is secular, and unless the Federal Constitution is amended to reflect the Syariah law as the supreme or basic law, this remains the case. The Federal Constitution has not been amended to reflect that position. Article 4(1) still declares that the Federal Constitution is the supreme law.

The religious-secular duality embedded in the Malaysian legal system is further reflected in the changing jurisdictional interrelation between the civil and Syariah courts. Muslims (and non-Muslims who marry Muslims) are obliged to follow the decisions of Syariah courts in matters concerning their religion, most notably marriage, inheritance, apostasy, conversion, and custody. Historically, the civil and Syariah courts existed side by side in a dual court structure established at the time of Malaysia's independence, with the prevalent understanding that Syariah courts were subordinate to the civil courts and the common law was superior to other laws. In the landmark ruling in 1984, the Federal Court, then known as the Supreme Court of Malaysia, held that the common law had not been ousted or otherwise affected by the introduction of the Federal Constitution, and that it would allow secular courts to resolve legal issues even where the parties to the case were Muslims.[16] However, in 1988 an amendment to the constitution, Article 121(1A), was introduced; it provided that civil courts "shall have no jurisdiction in respect of any matter within the jurisdiction of the Syariah Courts."

Even after the 1988 amendment the civil court system continued to view Syariah courts as subordinates and, at any rate, subject to general principles of administrative and constitutional law. The civil courts consistently interpreted the jurisdictional

---

[16] *Che Omar bin Che Soh v. Public Prosecutor* (1984) 1 MLJ 113.

boundaries between the two court systems to prevent the expansion of the Syariah court system. Likewise, the Malaysian Bar Council has continued to argue that Article 121(1A) does not exclude the supervisory review power of the Federal Court. However, because Islam has become a major political force in Malaysia, taking an anti-Islamist stand on the question of jurisdictional boundaries is no longer a feasible option for the court. It has opted instead for a strategy of mixed messages and vagueness. Several recent rulings illustrate this trend.

The *Lina Joy* case (2007) raised the question of Syariah courts' jurisdictional authority over apostasy in a case of conversion out of Islam.[17] Ms. Lina Joy, who was born Azalina Jailani, claimed to have converted from Islam to Christianity and argued that conversion was protected by the right to freedom of religion under Article 11 of the Constitution, and that she had the right to convert to Christianity without being designated as apostate. However, the National Registration Department refused to change her name or her religious status as they appeared on her identity card on the grounds that the Syariah Court had not granted permission for her to renounce Islam. In other words, Lina Joy questioned the hierarchy of three core tenets of Malaysian constitutional order: Shari'a court jurisdiction over conversion, individual religious freedoms, and the ethnic issue (conversion out of Islam questions one's Bumiputra status).

Following a long legal battle, the case reached the Federal Court of Malaysia, which ruled (by a 2:1 vote) in May 2007 that approvals of conversions out of Islam fall under the exclusive jurisdiction of the Syariah court system. In other words, the court refused to limit the jurisdictional boundaries of Syariah courts in Malaysia, even at the cost of infringing on general principles of freedom of religion or formal gender equality.

However, only two months later the Federal Court sent a somewhat different message in the *Latifa Mat Zin* case (2007), an inheritance dispute that raised the question whether the applicable law was the Islamic law of gifts *(hibah)* or the federal law of banking or contract.[18] Although the court sided with the claimant, holding that Islamic law should apply in the particular situation under dispute, it also stated clearly that "[i]n case an application to the syariah court is resisted on the ground that the syariah court has no jurisdiction in the matter, let me answer that question right now. Interpretation of the Federal Constitution is a matter for this court, not the syariah court. [If] this court says that the syariah court has jurisdiction, [then] it has."[19]

The Court's cautious navigation through this politically charged jurisdictional quagmire continued in the *Subashini* case (2007).[20] The originally Hindu husband

---

[17] *Lina Joy v. Majlis Agama Islam Wilayah Persekutuan* (2007) 4 MLJ 585.
[18] *Latifa Mat Zin v. Rosmawati Binti Sharibun* (2007) 5 MLJ 101.
[19] *Id.*
[20] *Subashini v. Saravanan and other* (2008) 2 MLJ 147.

of a Hindu woman converted to Islam in 2006 and went on to convert their elder son, as well. The husband then applied to the Syariah Court to dissolve the couple's civil marriage and obtain custody of both their sons. The Federal Court – in another 2:1 equivocal ruling – held that the civil court has jurisdiction over marriage and divorce, as well as over custody of children in a civil marriage, even when one spouse has converted to Islam, because the original marriage took place when both parties were Hindus. At the same time, the court held that the consent of only one parent was sufficient for a conversion of the children to be lawful. To support its ruling, as well as to increase the legitimacy of this and several other contested decisions, the Court cited several solicited opinions of respected religious scholars. These opinions and their authors' academic credentials (including their postsecondary degrees and institutions of higher learning they attended, and their main publications), were cited in great detail by the court, presumably in order to signal the court's respect for sacred law. At any rate, the Court granted a partial victory to each side of the dispute, compounding the jurisprudential ambiguity. Or, to be more colloquial, it threw each side a chewy bone, and jurisprudential wishy-washiness reigned. What better way to maintain the court's legitimacy, at the same time avoiding the possible wrath of influential stakeholders from both sides?

In the same year both *Lina Joy* and *Subashini* were decided, a Catholic newspaper in Malaysia used the word "Allah" to refer to God in its Malay-language edition. A controversy arose regarding who may use the word "Allah," whether it is an exclusively Muslim word (as some Muslim leaders in Malaysia suggest) or a neutral term referring to One God that may be used by all regardless of their religion, as the newspaper argued. A law was enacted in the 1980s to ban the use of the term in reference to God by non-Muslims, but had seldom been enforced prior to 2007. In December 31, 2009, the High Court in Kuala Lumpur ruled that the ban on non-Muslims using the word "Allah" to refer to God was unconstitutional as it infringed on freedom of expression and freedom of religion principles. The court went on to state that the word "Allah" is the correct word for "God" in various Malay translations of the Bible, and that it has been used for centuries by Christians and Muslims alike in Arabic-speaking countries. This ruling was viewed by radical Islamists as a legitimation of deceitful attempts to convert Muslims to Christianity. Riots and church burning pursued. The government appealed the High Court ruling, and the implementation of the decision has been suspended until the appeal is heard before the Federal Court.

The blurred jurisdictional matrix in Malaysia has given rise to a jurisdictional "war of courts." Aided by increased public support, Syariah courts in several states have begun to suggest that they are authorized to interpret relevant aspects of the Constitution itself (i.e., to go beyond the interpretation and application of Shari'a law). In its judgment in the *Abdul Kahar bin Ahmad* case (2008), the Federal Court dismissed, in an atypically decisive tone, an argument that the 1988 amendment – and

in particular, Article 121(1A) – conferred jurisdiction on Syariah courts to interpret
the Constitution in matters falling under the jurisdiction of such courts. The Federal
Court stated:

> Before the jurisdiction of this court is excluded it must be shown that the Syariah
> Court has jurisdiction over the matter first. That is not the case here.... The
> constitutionality of any law, whether a law made by Parliament or by the Legislature
> of a State ... is a matter for this court to decide, not the Syariah High Court."[21]

The Majlis Agam Islam of Selangor – that state's Islamic council – argued that
Article 121(1A) granted full and exclusive jurisdiction to the Syariah Court to decide
whether a practice falls within the precepts of Islam regardless of its constitutionality.
In other words, the Syariah Court suggested that the matter of jurisdiction itself
should be decided under Shari'a law. The Federal Court countered by ruling that
"nowhere in the Constitution is there a provision that the determination of Islamic
Law for the purpose of interpreting the Federal Constitution is a matter for the
State Legislature."[22] The Court held that Article 121(1A) was not inserted "to oust the
jurisdiction of this court in matters that rightly belong to it."[23] The entire realm of
the constitutionality of state law, however Shari'a based it may be, can be decided
only by the Federal Court.

In short, the Malaysian Federal Court has used constitutionally enshrined principles of federalism to block attempts to expand the ambit of Shari'a law. Operating
within an increasingly Islamic political environment, it has been wrestling with the
harmonization of constitutional and Shari'a law on a case-by-case basis. Although
it has been sending mixed messages with regard to the scope and nature of the
1988 constitutional amendment that established the exclusive jurisdiction of Syariah
courts in personal-status matters, it has also asserted its authority vis-à-vis the religious
establishment as the sole and ultimate interpreter of Malaysia's Federal Constitution.

Akin to other charged political settings discussed in this chapter, the close ties
between the statist-nationalist elite and the Malaysian judiciary are easily discerned.
In 1988, Malaysian Lord President Tun Salleh Abas and a number of Supreme
Court judges were suspended and later dismissed in reaction to the Court's antigovernment position in an electoral crisis in 1987. The Constitution was amended to
remove direct reference to judicial power. The Malaysian judiciary has been under
close political control ever since. Consider, for example, the professional biography
of Zaki Tun Azmi, who served as the Chief Justice of Malaysia's Federal Court (the
highest court of the country) from 2008 to 2011. His father, Tun Azmi Mohamed,
was also Chief Justice (then Lord President) from 1966 to 1974. Like father, like
son: Zaki received an elite legal education in both English and Malay. For years he
served as legal adviser to the ruling UNMO – the main political force advocating

---

[21] *Abdul Kahar bin Ahmad v. Kerajaan Negeri Selangor Darul Ehsan* (2008) 4 CLJ 309.
[22] *Id.*
[23] *Id.*

a moderate, inclusive version of Islam – before becoming the first lawyer directly appointed a judge of the Federal Court in September 2007. Three months later, Zaki Tun Azmi was appointed president of the Court of Appeal, and in October 2008 – following the end of Datuk Abdul Hamid Mohamed's term because of mandatory retirement – Zaki was appointed Chief Justice. At a time when the very essence of Malaysia as an Islamic state is hotly contested in the political sphere, the UNMO and supporters of its moderate "civilizational" Islam vision know that the likelihood of the Federal Court and its Chief Justice adopting a notably more conservative position on state-and-religion matters is very slim.

Israel

As already mentioned, such existential constitutional tensions and unique jurispru-dential formations are not confined to the Islamic world. Israel is arguably one of the world's capitals of embedded, near-oxymoronic contradictions of that nature. The very title of the utopian novel *Altneuland* (The Old New Land, 1902) by Theodor Herzl, the founder of political Zionism, captures some of these existential paradoxes. Israel defines itself as a Jewish and democratic state. Much has been written about this duality, how logically plausible it may be, given the fact that non-Jews make up approximately one-fifth of Israel's citizenry, and how these two foundational tenets may be translated into a fairly coherent set of guidelines for public life. Even within the Jewish population itself the exact meaning of Israel as a "Jewish" state has been highly contested. Nevertheless, for a host of historical and political reasons, the Orthodox stream of the Jewish religion has long enjoyed the status of being the sole branch of Judaism formally recognized by the state. This exclusive status has enabled the Orthodox community to establish a near monopoly over the supply of public religious services and impose rigid standards on the process of determin-ing who is a Jew – a question that has crucial symbolic and practical implications because – according to Israel's Law of Return – Jews who immigrate to Israel are entitled to a variety of benefits, including the right to immediate full citizenship. All of this has taken place despite the fact that more than two-thirds of the world's Jews – on whom Israel relies for essential symbolic, material, and strategic sup-port – continue to live outside Israel and do not subscribe to the Orthodox stream of Judaism.

To add further complication, over the last three decades there has been a con-tinuous decline in the political power and representation of Israel's historically hegemonic and largely secular Ashkenazi constituencies (mostly Jews of European descent), with a corresponding rise of the previously marginalized and distinctly more religious groups, some of which are strong advocates of Halakha (the entire body of Jewish law, biblical, rabbinical, and customary) playing a pivotal role and providing the basis for the operation of the state and its identity. The collapse of the once-hegemonic Labor Party and impressive rise of religious parties, most notably the Shas Party (representing Orthodox religious Mizrahi residents of development towns and poor urban neighborhoods), is merely one illustration of this broad trend.

Over the last few decades, the Supreme Court of Israel (SCI) has become a bastion of "reason" and "sanity" for Israel's "enlightened public" – a criterion frequently used by the SCI throughout the 1990s to determine the "reasonableness" of specific acts. This Court-constructed public closely conforms to the characteristics of the old Ashkenazi establishment at the center of the Zionist consensus, and shares its worldviews and policy preferences. Since the late 1980s, the Court has pursued a distinctly liberalizing agenda in core matters of religion and state, ranging from the curtailment of the exclusive jurisdiction of the rabbinical courts in matters of personal status and the erosion of the Orthodox monopoly over the provision of religious services to the liberalization of rules pertaining to commercial activity on the Jewish Sabbath, the solemnization of marriage, *kashrut* (kosher) and *shmita* (land sabbatical) laws. In an important case involving blatant ethnic segregation policy by an ultra-Orthodox girl school (the segregation was justified by school authorities as addressing the distinct needs of two separate religious streams), the Court ruled (2009) that although the right to cultural pluralism in education is recognized by Israeli law, religious affiliation as a basis for autonomous schooling is not an absolute right when it collides with the overarching right to equality.[24] In 2011, the Court held in another landmark case that gender segregation in public buses operating in several ultra-Orthodox towns was unlawful.[25] Bus companies offering services in religious neighborhoods were ordered to carry anti-segregation signs indicating that all passengers were allowed to choose any seat, except seats designated to the disabled.

Proponents of secular policies have also scored victories with the Court's relatively progressive treatment of the issue of non-Orthodox conversion to Judaism and the related question "Who is a Jew?" In one of its recent landmark rulings on the subject (2005), the Court agreed (7:4) to recognize non-Orthodox "bypass" conversions to Judaism performed de jure abroad but de facto in Israel.[26] It held that a person who came to Israel as a non-Jew and, during a period of lawful residence there, underwent conversion in a recognized Jewish community abroad would be considered Jewish. In its judgment the Court stated that:

> The Jewish nation is one. . . . It is dispersed around the world, in communities. Whoever converted to Judaism in one of these communities overseas has joined the Jewish nation by so doing, and is to be seen as a "Jew" under the Law of Return. This can encourage immigration to Israel and maintain the unity of the Jewish nation in the Diaspora and in Israel.

---

[24] HCJ 1067/08 *Noar Ke'Halacha v. Ministry of Education* (decision released on Aug. 6, 2009). Curiously, the newly established United Kingdom Supreme Court has drawn on the same general logic in a case involving a selective, some say discriminatory, admission policy by a North London Jewish school. See *R(E) v Governing Body of JFS* (2009) UKSC 15.

[25] HCJ 746/07 *Ragen v Ministry of Transport* (decision released on January 5, 2011).

[26] HCJ 2597/99 *Thais-Rodriguez Tushbaim v. Minister of Interior*, 59(6) P.D. (2005).

Few would articulate the non-Orthodox view of Judaism in present-day Israel more potently. So it is hardly surprising that in May 2009 the Court (in a decision written by then Chief Justice Dorit Beinisch) went on to order the government to fund non-Orthodox conversion study programs just as it has been funding Orthodox conversion programs. In an important decision in 2012, the Court confirmed the validity of thousands of conversions to Judaism that had been previously annulled by the Orthodox-controlled rabbinical court system for being allegedly too lenient or insincere. These conversions, mainly by immigrants from the former Soviet Union, were initially validated by special conversion courts established by the government to circumvent the rabbinical courts' stringent requirements that were seen as deterring immigrants from converting.

A pinnacle of the SCI's liberalizing jurisprudence in matters of religion and state is its subjection of the religious courts' jurisprudential autonomy in matters of personal status to the general principles of administrative and constitutional law, most notably due process and gender equality. This has had far-reaching implications in areas as diverse as family and personal-status law, representation in statutory religious bodies, and gender equality in the religious labor market. In Israel, no unified civil law applies to all citizens in matters of marriage and divorce. Instead, for various political and historical reasons (the roots of contemporary Israeli family law go back as far as the Ottoman Empire's premodern *millet* system), the courts of the different religious communities hold exclusive jurisdiction over marriage, divorce, and directly associated personal-status matters. A number of other personal-status matters may be adjudicated through the rabbinical court system (controlled by Orthodox Judaism) if the involved parties consent to such extended jurisdiction. Muslim, Christian, and Druze courts also have exclusive jurisdiction over the personal-status affairs of their respective communities.

Since the mid-1990s, the SCI has gradually been attempting to limit the authority exercised by religious courts. The most important SCI judgment regarding these matters was rendered in 1995 in the *Bavli* case.[27] In several earlier decisions, the SCI ruled that religious tribunals must comply with provisions of concrete laws pertinent to their operation and jurisdictional boundaries. In its ruling in *Bavli*, the SCI considerably expanded its overarching review of religious tribunals' jurisprudence by holding that all religious tribunals, including the Great Rabbinical Court, are statutory bodies established by law and funded by the state; in principle, all aspects of their judgments are thus subject to review by the Supreme Court. Although the SCI recognized the special jurisdictional mandate awarded to Jewish, Muslim, Christian, and Druze courts by the legislature, it nevertheless asserted its power to impose fundamental constitutional norms on their exercise of authority. Rabbinical Court officials have responded by publicly asserting their resistance to the idea that the Supreme Court, as a secular entity, possesses the authority to review their

---

[27] HCJ 1000/92 *Bavli v. The Great Rabbinical Court*, 48(2) P.D. 6 (1995). On Shari'a Court jurisdiction, see C.A. 3077/90 *Plonit (Jane Doe) v. Ploni (John Doe)*, 49(2) P.D. 578 (1996).

adjudication, which rests on religious law. Some have gone so far as to declare their intention to ignore the court's ruling in *Bavli*, which they perceive as an illegitimate intrusion into their exclusive jurisdictional sphere. The Supreme Court was not impressed. On the basis of its landmark decision in *Bavli*, it went on to overturn at least two dozen other Rabbinical Court and Shari'a Court rulings for not conforming with general principles of Israel's constitutional and administrative law, including gender equality, reasonableness, proportionality, natural justice, and procedural fairness.

A fascinating recent illustration of this trend is the Court's ruling in *Plonit (Jane Doe) v. The Great Rabbinical Court* (2008).[28] Section 5 of the Property Relations between Spouses Law (*Hok Yahasei Mammon bein Bnei Zug* 1973, amended in 1995) states that in case of divorce, the couple's assets will be split evenly between the two spouses regardless of the formal registration status of these assets. However, Section 8 of that law grants courts the authority to determine "special circumstances" in which an uneven split may be justified. A woman who married her husband in 1985 had an extramarital affair in 2003 that eventually brought about the breakup of her marriage. The Great Rabbinical Court ruled that the wife's unfaithful behavior constituted special circumstances, and that the husband was entitled to more than half of the couple's assets, in this case, pension monies owed to him.

On appeal, the SCI used its reasoning in *Bavli* to overturn the ruling. It accepted the wife's argument that the Great Rabbinical Court ruling did not comply with earlier SCI decisions on the matter; namely, that adulterous behavior may justify neither a departure from the presumption of an even split nor a retroactive negation of the adulterous spouse's rights to accumulated property in the years before his or her extramarital affair. Even more important, the SCI rejected the husband's claim that the law assigned to either the Rabbinical Court or the general court dealing with the matter the authority to decide what special circumstances were in this context. The SCI stated decisively that the two systems are not parallel, but unitary. Rulings of the rabbinical court system, including rulings of the Great Rabbinical Court, are subject to review by the Supreme Court and must comply with pertinent jurisprudential principles established by the SCI over the years. One can hardly think of a greater blow to the rabbinical court system's jurisdictional autonomy. It is little wonder that religious parties led by Shas vow to pass laws that expand the jurisdiction of the rabbinical court system and exempt it from the Supreme Court's scrutiny.

CONCLUSION

Universalists and modernists increasingly turn to constitutional jurisprudence to block, delay, or mitigate the impact of religion in public life, and they know why.

---

[28] HCJ 8928/06 *Plonit (Jane Doe) v. The Great Rabbinical Court* (decision released on Oct. 8, 2008).

A comparative examination of religion-and-state constitutional jurisprudence of the highest courts in religion-laden settings demonstrates how the courts have become key religion-limiting agents, skilfully delivering the goods for anti-religious stakeholders despite intense scrutiny from the more religious segments of the public who are gaining more sway through electoral processes. Each of these examples illustrates the remarkably creative interpretive techniques adopted by judges confronted with concrete legal disputes that reflect and encapsulate the greater issues emerging from constitutional theocracy.

Bound by Article 2 of the Egyptian Constitution, Egypt's Supreme Constitutional Court has developed its own moderate "interpretation from within" of religious rules and norms. The Kuwait Supreme Court followed suit. The Supreme Court of Pakistan has been able to advance a holistic view of the Constitution that emphasizes the interdependence and harmony of its various sections, so that no specific provision (including the Islamization amendments) enjoys an elevated status vis-à-vis any other provision. At the same time, the Court has been able to counterbalance the pro-religious jurisprudence of the SAB. This has proved to be a safety net for moderate interests. The Federal Court of Malaysia has used constitutional principles of federalism to block the implementation of religious legislation at the state level, and although making concessions with regard to civil/religious court jurisdictional boundaries, it has effectively asserted its exclusive authority as the ultimate interpreter of the Constitution. The Supreme Court of Israel has meanwhile responded to the increased tension between Israel's dual commitment to cosmopolitan and particularistic values by subjecting the jurisprudence of religious courts to the general principles of administrative and constitutional law.

To remain relevant and maintain their public legitimacy, national high courts in polities that have witnessed increasing popular support for theocratic governance do occasionally side with religious authorities and tribunals, mainly those formally recognized and funded by the state. The Malaysian Federal Court's controversial ruling in the *Lina Joy* case (2007) is an illustration of this kind of reactive conservatism. When the political stakes are high, and the costs of an anti-religious ruling seem too high – as illustrated in the Pakistani Supreme Court's ruling on the Ahmadiyya apostasy, or the Malaysian Federal Court's something-for-everyone approach in *Subashini* (2007) – the courts find creative ways to minimize the risk for themselves and avoid swimming against the stream.[29]

However, these notably religion-infused rulings are the exception. Although courts in religion-laden polities operate within different constitutional traditions, frameworks, and constraints, they have been able to advance secularizing responses to fundamental religion-and-state questions. In so doing, they have been able to impose effective limitations on the accommodation of religious values in public life. Given

---

[29] For similar trends of selectively strategic judicial behavior in other polities, *see, e.g.,* Trochev (Ch. 2 in this volume), as well as Helmke (2002) and Kapiszewski (2011).

this jurisprudential record, it is hardly surprising that against the strictures of an increasingly conservative interpretation of Shari'a, even in Middle Eastern polities that lack established traditions of judicial activism (e.g., Iran, Afghanistan, and Saudi Arabia), judicial reform has been instigated in order to create and empower state-controlled courts in an attempt to counterbalance the spread of religious fundamentalism. The jurisdiction of constitutional courts in such settings, even if formally religious in some sense, will inevitably reflect a less militant view of religious identity.

The fact that the constitutional domain sports a near-universal tendency toward curbing religion regardless of the sociopolitical context within which it operates, suggests that there may be deeper reasons for why constitutional law and courts are so appealing to a-religious or anti-religious social forces in polities that face divisions along secular/religious lines. Granted, instrumentalist factors are many. Effective political control over, as well as better access to, the constitutional arena makes it attractive to political power holders who seek to keep religious authority under check. If we look at the composition of constitutional courts in the Near and Middle East, as well as in North Africa, many judges have received general legal education and are familiar with Western law's basic principles and methods of reasoning. This is certainly true in places such as India, Israel, Malaysia, Egypt, and Pakistan. More often than not, the judge's educational background, cultural propensities, and social milieu are closer to those of the urban intelligentsia and top state bureaucrats than those of any other social group. Constitutional courts are established and funded by the state, and their judges are appointed by state authorities, often with the approval of political leaders. Consequently, a judge's record of adjudication is well known at the time of his or her appointment.

However, there seem to be embedded structural and epistemological reasons for the religion-taming tilt of constitutional jurisprudence. Constitutional courts, even in the most diversity-accommodating jurisdictions, let alone in stricter ones, are inherently unsympathetic toward alternative hierarchies of authority and adjudication, which they constantly strive to bring under check (Hirschl and Shachar 2009). There is a certain "seeing like a state" tilt to their outlook (Scott 1999). The very logic of constitutional law, with its reasoned set of core tenets, prevalent modes of interpretation, and embedded emphasis on overarching state authority, makes it an attractive enterprise to those who wish to contain religiosity and assert state or civil-society authority over religious texts, worldviews, and interpretive hierarchies. Ironically, many of the jurisdictional, enforcement, and co-optation advantages that gave religious legal regimes an edge in the premodern era are now aiding the modern state and its laws in its effort to contain religion. The important role of rights provisions and jurisprudence in contemporary constitutional discourse alongside the ever-increasing cross-jurisdictional fertilization in that area and formation of a transnational epistemic community of jurists add to constitutional law's secularist appeal. The combination of anti-religious propensities and interests, alongside creative interpretation that leads to religion-limiting jurisprudence, may explain why constitutional law and courts have become a secularist shrine in the post-secularist age.

REFERENCES

Bakar, Osman. 2008. "Malaysian Islam in the Twenty-First Century," in John Esposito et al., eds., *Asian Islam in the 21st Century*. New York: Oxford University Press, pp. 81–108.

Brown, Nathan. 1999. "Islamic Constitutionalism in Theory and Practice," in Eugene Cotran and Adel Omar Sherif, eds., *Democracy, the Rule of Law and Islam*. New York: Springer.

Butt, Simon. 2010. "Islam, the state and the Constitutional Court in Indonesia," *Pacific Rim Law & Policy Journal* 19: 279–301.

Helmke, Gretchen. 2002. "The Logic of Strategic Defection: Court-Executive Relations in Argentina under Dictatorship and Democracy," *American Political Science Review* 96: 291–303.

Hirschl, Ran. 2010. *Constitutional Theocracy*. Cambridge, MA: Harvard University Press.

Hirschl, Ran and Ayelet Shachar. 2009. "The New Wall of Separation: Permitting Diversity, Restricting Competition," *Cardozo Law Review* 30: 2535–2560.

Kapiszewski, Diana. 2011. "Tactical Balancing: High Court Decision Making on Politically Crucial Cases," *Law and Society Review* 45: 471–506.

Lombardi, Clark. 1998. "Islamic Law as a Source of Constitutional Law in Egypt: The Constitutionalization of the Sharia in a Modern Arab State," *Columbia Journal of Transnational Law* 37: 81–123.

_____. 2006. *State Law as Islamic Law in Modern Egypt: The Incorporation of the Shari'a into Egyptian Constitutional Law*. Leiden: E.J. Brill.

Scott, James C. 1999. *Seeing like a State*. New Haven, CT: Yale University Press.

Siddique, Osama and Zahra Hayat. 2008. "Unholy Speech and Holy Laws: Blasphemy Laws in Pakistan – Controversial Origins, Design Defects, and Free Speech Implication," *Minnesota Journal of International Law* 17: 303–385.

Smith, Adam. 1994. *The Wealth of Nations*. New York: Random House.

PART III

Four "Provocations"

13

Why the Legal Complex is Integral to Theories of Consequential Courts

*Terence C. Halliday**

A puzzle lies at the heart of the excellent treatments of courts in this volume. With important exceptions, it is the absence of a certain kind of politics. In these pages there are the distal politics of parties and dictators, insurgencies and militaries, civil society and religions, unions and the media. Mostly absent, however, are the most proximate politics to courts – the legal occupations which embed, enable, draft, litigate, implement, oppose, critique, and ally with judges and courts, a configuration of occupations captured by the concept of "the legal complex" (Halliday and Karpik 2011).

There has been a tendency in scholarship on courts in general to permit its hermetic segregation from scholarship on other legal occupations – most notably the legal profession, but also legal academics and practicing lawyers within the state or corporations (Feeley 2012). This detachment from courts in their most immediate institutional context contributes to a hollow core theory of judicial politics, a lacuna which does not properly reflect the practices of such politics either in history or in contemporaneous headlines.

I will offer a view of the conditions under which courts are consequential that is a variant of the introductory essay. I argue that the relative power of courts across the multiplicity of their roles cannot be explained without theoretically privileging the proximate singularity of the legal complex. The proximate and embedding politics of

* Research Professor, American Bar Foundation; Co-Director, Center on Law and Globalization, American Bar Foundation and University of Illinois College of Law; Adjunct Professor of Sociology, Northwestern University; Adjunct Professor, School of Regulation, Justice and Diplomacy, Australian National University. I am grateful to the editors of this volume and its contributors for the opportunity to participate in conversations around the power of courts, to Malcolm Feeley for his insights and encouragement on this paper, and for Lucien Karpik and Malcolm Feeley for their continuing expansion and refinement of the ideas that have emerged from our common endeavor on the legal complex. I appreciate Martin Shapiro's re-affirmation for the logic of this argument, which he anticipated long ago.

the legal complex are singular in two respects. First, they are not just another configuration of interest groups. Everything judicial is refracted through the legal complex
in one manner or another. Second, their politics is distinctively legal; that is, it con-
verts any other kind of interest – economic, social, material – into legal concepts,
forms, representation, and ideology with all of their strengths and weaknesses.

Consequently, this essay proposes that the prominence and power of courts cannot
be understood without the empirical investigation and theoretical integration of
judicial studies within the legal complex. It will show how that concept emerged
precisely because treatment of legal occupations as empirical "silos" cannot be
sustained, particularly in epochal shifts toward or away from political liberalism and
constitutionalism of various sorts. Taking as an example four moments in the lives
of constitutional courts, this essay will demonstrate where empirical chapters in this
book point to the significance of the legal complex and explanations implicitly call
for a missing politics of the legal complex.

This chapter's discussion of how the legal complex refracts judicial power reflects
ideas expressed in several volumes focusing on political liberalism that I have
coedited with Lucien Karpik and Malcolm Feeley.[1] As our latest collection (2012)
treats countries also discussed in *Consequential Courts*, the essay draws on that collection to offer examples of the politics of the legal complex that reveal it to be
inseparable from the consequentiality of courts.

THE LEGAL COMPLEX

Lawyers have been deeply implicated in the fight for political liberalism. From
eighteenth-century France to nineteenth-century Germany to twentieth-century
United States, Korea, and Brazil to twenty-first-century Egypt, Pakistan, Malaysia,
Zambia, and China, a lawyers' politics of liberalism cannot be severed from judicial
politics. Indeed, at the heart of the legal complex lies a potent potential alliance or
destructive potential inhibition of collective action on behalf of political liberalism.
Repeatedly, it is the alliance of an organized bar and bold judiciary that energizes
and enables the defense of basic legal freedoms; and, repeatedly, it is the division or
conflict between the bench and bar that inhibits the emergence of political liberalism
or permits a slide back from liberal to illiberal politics. The recurrence of a judicial
politics in harness with a politics of the legal profession has led historians and
anthropologists, political scientists and sociologists to a more systematic approach
to the cluster of legal occupations whose actions are frequently intertwined in the
constitution of the state, civil society, and individual rights. The concept of the legal

---

[1] Since the early 1990s, Lucien Karpik (Ecoles des Mines, Paris, and L'Ecole des Hautes Etudes en
Sciences Sociales/EHESS), Malcolm Feeley (University of California, Berkeley), and I have been
leading a project that seeks to discover the origins of Western political liberalism (Halliday and Karpik
1997a) and subsequently the fates of political liberalism across the world (Halliday, Karpik, and Feeley
2007a, 2012).

complex therefore emerged in relation to a specific issue – political liberalism – and insistent empirical recurrences.

The legal complex comprises all those legal occupations that exist within the legal and judicial institutions of a society. In addition to private lawyers and judges, it will include legal academics, civil servants practicing law, lawyers in corporations or unions, military lawyers or judges, and even private prosecutors, as in some Latin American countries. It is action oriented: it denotes actors engaged in legal activity, whether drafting or writing law, teaching or commenting on law, prosecuting or defending clients, advising or judging. Further, action by these legal occupations is issue specific. For methodological and theoretical reasons, it makes little sense to talk about the legal complex as a political actor unless those politics are oriented to a specific issue, whether political liberalism, the defense of secular constitutionalism, the writing of commercial law, or the creation of global legal conventions. The legal complex is also a structural concept, much less concerned with varieties of actions by individuals and much more focused on collective action and structural relationships among the various legal occupations. Finally, it is dynamic and mutable. Its proclivities to action shift over time and across circumstances. Methodologically, therefore, it is imperative to study it both over the *longue durée*, where long arcs of political orientations and actions can be observed, and in *événements*, particular events which enable an intricate disentangling of relationships and processes.

Hints, and sometimes more than hints, of the legal complex are evident in many chapters in this volume. When we begin to search for indications that stories of courts are about more than courts, when we apply the analytical tools developed to excavate evidence of the legal complex (Karpik and Halliday 2011), we discover that a more nuanced politics is in play. Judges, of course, are everywhere in this volume, but they are not alone. Lawyers appear, sometimes as "ambitious civil advocates" eager to expand the powers of the Dutch Hoge Raad court (Huls, Ch. 7 on the Netherlands in this volume); in one or another place as critics of courts (Klug, Ch. 3 on South Africa in this volume; Reichman, Ch. 9 on Israel in this volume); occasionally as recruits to a nation's highest court (South Africa; Israel); on occasion as creations of a court (Kagan, Ch. 8 on the United States in this volume); frequently as litigators bringing cases to courts (Mate, Ch. 10 on India in this volume; Kagan, Ch. 8 in this volume); and on notable occasions as collective defenders of particular judges and entire courts (Ginsburg, Ch. 1 on Pakistan in this volume).

Legal academics, too, appear in various guises. It is a scholar who provides the powerful jurisprudential ideas that are seized on by the Indian Supreme Court in its assertion of constitutional ascendancy (Mate, Ch. 10 on India in this volume). "Enthusiastic academics . . . infused the legal system with an ethical and very liberal set of values" in the Netherlands (Huls, Ch. 6 in this volume). Scholars observed both the "missed opportunities" of Israel's potential moments of constitutional construction and recognized swiftly that the new Basic Laws of 1992 had far-reaching consequences for constitutionalism and the power of courts (Reichman, Ch. 9 in this volume). Lasser (Ch. 11 in this volume) observes how French judges are compelled to express themselves in "relatively cryptic, collegial, and single-sentence syllogisms" that both precludes their dominance and "empowers other legal players, such as legal academics" to participate meaningfully in "interpretive authority."

With the exception of Guarnieri's discussion of Italian prosecutors (Ch. 6 in this volume), other putative elements of the legal complex – prosecutors and civil servants – scarcely appear, although Chile's Controller General Office (Scribner, Ch. 4 in this volume) and France's new advocate general (Lasser, Ch. 11 in this volume) point to the necessity of an expanded matrix of legal occupations to explain the changing roles of courts.

It is one thing to observe a trace here and there of another legal occupation in the evolution or devolution of courts; it is another to discover: (a) the collective politics within each legal occupation; (b) the structural relationships among elements; and (c) the dynamics that order those relationships. A theory of the legal complex requires such investigations. Here again some chapters tantalize the reader with traces of legal complex politics.

The expansive assertion of power by India's Supreme Court has been shown by Mate (Ch. 10 in this volume; see also Mate 2012) to be a mutually constructive, albeit sometimes fraught, set of relationships amongst academics, leading barristers, and Supreme Court judges. Over decades they came to forge a national consensus of the legal complex around the basic structure doctrine where academics provided intellectual leadership, the bar solidified as an order of "priests in the temple of justice," and high court benches of India rested on the assurance of broad coalitions of support from other elements of the legal complex. As we shall indicate, relations of reciprocity and support among legal occupations are noted in The Netherlands, France, Pakistan, and Chile.

In short, the chapters provide examples, and sometimes only hints, that within each legal occupation or institution there are a proximate politics that inhibit or facilitate collective action or institutional solidarity: there may be internal divides (*Hoge Raad v. Council of State*; *Conseil d'Etat v. Constitutional Council v. Cour de Cassation*); internal cohesion (Pakistan's lawyers in 2007–2009); or failure to find common ground. Amongst the elements of the legal complex, we find active coalitions (lawyers with judges; judges with lawyers with academics; judges with civil servant lawyers), cleavages (lawyers against courts), isolated institutions (courts alone), and crosscutting cleavages (one set of lawyers and judges opposed to another set).

These structural ties or cleavages are institutionalized sometimes through active cooperation or relations of reciprocity (Ghias 2012), sometimes through persisting disengagement (in numbers of civil law regimes), and sometimes from periodic or persistent opposition (e.g., lawyers critical of courts) (Gould 2012; VonDoepp 2012).

FOUR MOMENTS IN THE LIVES OF CONSTITUTIONAL COURTS

As a concept, the legal complex emerged in relation to a specific theoretical problem – how to explain the emergence of or retreat from political liberalism. Because the concept obtains theoretical bite when it is directed to specific issues, and indeed the configurations, processes, and repertoires of the legal complex vary across issues, let me turn to examine the actualities and possibilities of this theoretical approach in relation to the substantive issue that recurs most often in *Consequential Courts* – the rise (and fall) of constitutional courts.

There are four moments where constitutional politics of judiciaries might play themselves out within the embedding structures of the legal complex. Ginsburg (Ch. 1 in this volume) anticipates this approach with his distinction between the role of courts during democratic transition and consolidation. This useful distinction can be amplified into four moments: (1) agitating for constitutionalism; (2) instituting constitutional courts[2] or courts with liberal constitutional responsibilities; (3) consolidating (and expanding) the authority and power of courts; and (4) defending constitutional courts. How do the politics of courts in each of these moments play themselves out as a contextualized politics of the legal complex?

Agitation for Constitutionalism

This phrase refers to situations in a non-liberal regime where legal actors mobilize for a shift toward constitutional regimes, signified here by the establishment of constitutional courts. Ginsburg (Ch. 1 in this volume) alludes to these with the notion of "upstream triggers." In his earlier work, Ginsburg shows that alongside social disquiet, student activism, and mobilization of Korean civil society in the 1980s, there was the development of a capacity to channel these grievances through legal functionaries and into legal institutions (Ginsburg 2007). Activist lawyers secretly, then openly, formed an association in the 1980s that drew in hundreds of lawyers willing and able to represent political prisoners, agitate for a responsive rule of law, and put themselves at the vanguard of litigation as a strategic mechanism for liberalization. Thus, the founding of the Constitutional Court in 1987, and its subsequent impact, turned substantially on the capacity of a substantial bar able to channel civil society grievances into the courts. Indeed, the transformations in the bar appeared to be a necessary condition for expanding judicial power. In this effort, private lawyers were aided and abetted by prosecutors who sought to rehabilitate their tarnished status as handmaidens of an authoritarian state by rooting out corruption in government. The story of the Korean Constitutional Court thus becomes the story of the politics of the Korean legal complex.

---

[2] For convenience, I use "constitutional courts" and "courts with constitutional responsibilities" as synonymous.

It is this kind of politics that would have given texture and contingency to Scribner's (Ch. 4 in this volume) account of Chilean courts from 1980 to 1989. Although valuable in its own right, the Chilean case implicitly calls for a multifaceted treatment of lawyers and prosecutors, professors and legal officials – the cast of characters integral to Couso's explanation of Chile's capitulation to Pinochet and the path out of that legal darkness (Couso 2007). Put another way, if Chile's descent into repression can be explained in part by the apolitical isolation of its courts, not least from the bar (Hilbink 2007), can its slow reassertion of constitutional values be attributed to any mobilization of lawyers or legal scholars, prosecutors, or lawyers in the Controller General's Office?

Instituting a Constitutional Court

A second moment occurs at the points of constitutional politics where there is the establishment of a judiciary with powers to moderate Executive and Legislature power and uphold basic legal freedoms. Here Klug (Ch. 3 in this volume) rightly comments that "the [South African] judiciary, and constitutional courts in particular, are empowered or constrained by a number of specific conditions." Comparative research has shown that lawyers and judges acting to protect fundamental rights in the waning days of illiberal regimes (De 2012; VonDoepp 2012) enter a new constitutional order with heightened legitimacy (Halliday and Karpik 2012). Although it is not clear how far a legal complex began to cohere for constitutionalism before the end of apartheid, Klug does suggest that the "extraordinary degree of legitimacy" accorded the new Constitutional Court derived in part by a microcosm of the legal complex – lawyers, judges, and legal academics – who "had gained high stature during the struggle against apartheid." Moreover, opinions of the bar mattered when the new Constitutional Court confronted the Constitutional Assembly over certification of the new Constitution. How did those opinions matter? (Were they skeptical, supportive, stiffening of the court? Did bar leaders issue statements or seek to move publics? Did the bar and academy swing in behind the Court's bold opinion not to certify in full in order to buttress its authority?) Did those opinions express the consensus of the bar? Did individual lawyers speak on behalf of an assenting bar? Did bar associations speak with one voice? We don't know, but Klug provocatively implies that the transitional period of the Court's founding and reinforcing of its legitimacy requires an explanation that embraces other legal occupations.

The constitutional significance of Israel's 1992 new Basic Laws also seems to occur in a wider legal matrix. Although others may not have recognized that a "constitutional revolution" had just happened, "the legal academy," at least in the person of one "leading constitutional lawyer," did realize something had happened. When Justice Barak (not incidentally a former law professor) sought to inform the public that indeed a revolution had occurred, "the legal community – judges, lawyers, and academics – was put on notice" (Reichman, Ch. 8 in this volume).

More generally, it must be asked whether it is conceivable for a "constitutional revolution" to take place without a cluster of judges, lawyers, and legal academics to be in alliance. The most dramatic moment in recent headlines must surely be Pakistan's struggle from 2007 to 2009. Although it is clear there was a line of increasingly expansive decisions leading up to the momentous events that caused Chief Justice Chaudhry's dismissal, it is inconceivable that the assertion of the Court's authority at the decisive moment of Chaudhry's manhandling by the police could have been sustained without the vocal, nationwide, public leadership of a united bar (Ghias 2012; Munir 2012). The public drama in this moment of Pakistan's turn in the "evolution" of the courts is very probably paralleled less publicly and dramatically in other nations and historical moments. They will not be observed, however, if courts are treated as soloists, not members of the legal orchestra.

Consolidating and Adapting Constitutional Courts

Although the notion of consolidation itself is not unproblematic, for my purposes here it stands loosely for an enhancement of court power, an assertion of greater court autonomy, and adaptations to situate courts more efficaciously in changing domestic and international circumstances. The analytic orientation of the legal complex compels scholars to systematically examine the politics of legal occupations that surround courts and judges in these moments.

The rich texture of the legal complex appears manifestly in Mate's account of India's Supreme Court (Ch. 10 in this volume; see also Mate 2012), which drew on new legal concepts imported from a German legal scholar, and built on a succession of cases brought by distinguished barristers, so that over decades an initially timid bench and fractious bar came to reach a broad consensus with Indian legal scholars that the basic structure doctrine gave India's highest courts a power of legislative review and expansive constitutional reach unimaginable at the moment of independence. Arguably, the power progressively seized by India's highest courts could not have emerged or endured without the underwriting of the court's legitimacy by India's most prominent lawyers and ultimately its bar writ large, not least during its stand under the Emergency (Epp 2012).

The embedded politics of high courts also emerge in Huls's (Ch. 7 in this volume) account of a Dutch legal complex that becomes integral to the internecine struggles of the Hoge Raad against the Council of the State and Council of the Judiciary. Huls suggests that the assertion of a professional politics against the conventional politics of the Council of State required an alliance of judges, lawyers, and legal academics to bolster the authority of law and courts vis-à-vis conventional politics. In his book, Lasser (Lasser 2004), too, points to struggles among the highest French courts and the two European courts (European Court of Justice, European Court of Human Rights), a competition that surely draws into its struggle the bar and legal academy as allies in interinstitutional rivalries. Moreover, Lasser implies that the powerful turn to interests and litigants in a new rights-based jurisprudence in France and Europe must also be a politics of the legal complex.

In the orchestration of his thesis on the expanding consequentiality of the U.S. Supreme Court, Kagan (Ch. 8 in this volume) points incidentally to processes that tie the potency of the court to its embedding occupations. Kagan shows, first, that courts can help constitute other elements of the legal complex, as the U.S. Supreme Court, by essentially creating a "new army of lawyers" through "establishment of governmentally funded 'public defender' offices." Second, this had an iterative impact on expansion of constitutional rights that could now be litigated through expanded "adversarial legal advocacy." In short, the Court created and empowered a bar that in recursive cycles would enlarge the terrain on which the Court could act. In sharply different circumstances, Ghias (2012) shows how Pakistan's highest court intervened in bar elections to ensure victory for activist bar leaders who would later return the favor through defense of the Court when it was attacked by Musharraf. Third, more consequential courts could then add "adventitious strength" to non-governmental organizations (NGOs) with assertive legal strategies, such as the American Civil Liberties Union (ACLU), and lawyers advising school boards and other constituencies on how to comply with court rulings. Fourth, government lawyers in the Department of Justice lent their weight to the ACLU and National Association for the Advanced of Colored People lawyers by filing supported amicus briefs. In short, a recursive and reciprocal relationship among three elements of the legal complex concomitantly enlarged the reach of the Supreme Court as it was also leveraged by their "persuasive weight." This intricate account of three événements in all but name only points to an embedded politics of the courts and the legal complex.

In like vein but a radically different situation, Moustafa's work on the Egyptian Constitutional Court (Moustafa 2007a, 2007b) demonstrates how the muscular emergence of the Court as the center of resistance to Mubarak in the 1990s and early 2000s depended on a mutuality of purpose and division of labor within the legal complex. A circularity of enhancement enabled the courts to protect and embolden lawyers, just as the activist bar became a principal constituency for the courts, both inciting the courts to bolder decisions and protecting them when under assault from a wounded regime. Here the resources of the legal complex mattered a great deal. Judges used their city and national associations, journals, and annual conference to forge a cohesive stance. Lawyers mobilized bar associations, used professional journals, conferences, and legal aid organizations to mobilize on behalf of basic legal freedoms. The Ministry of Justice, prosecutors, and international lawyers' organizations, although not academics, also become part of the mix.

Defending Courts

The Egyptian case elides into the fourth moment – the defense of judicial autonomy and power when under direct attack by executives and legislatures. India during the

Emergency is one case in point (Mate 2012). Klug (Ch. 3 in this volume) tantalizes his readers with this question when the South African Constitutional Court came under attack. A theory of the legal complex would immediately ask: did the bar offer support through news releases or speeches or reports on the importance of judicial independence? Did the bar seek to shield or fortify the Constitutional Court? Did lawyer-led NGOs do likewise? Reichman (Ch. 9 in this volume) hints that the bar had been "guardian of the [Israeli] judiciary" against attacks in the past. When the bar began to divide over whether the Supreme Court was becoming too political, as it drifted from criminal and civil matters into public law, again we observe circumstances that may be limiting for the organized bar everywhere – the more it moves away from the "idiom of legalism" the more it risks fracturing along party-political lines; hence, the less capacity it has to mount a purely legal and constitutional defense of courts (Harding and Whiting 2012). However, it takes a theory of the legal complex to reach this limiting condition of courts' abilities to defend themselves.

Two parallel readings of the Malaysian courts on religious issues reinforce the salience of the legal complex in defending constitutional courts, or a particular orientation for those courts. Hirschl (Ch. 12 in this volume) sketches growing tensions in Malaysia over its constitutional conundrum: although Malaysia identifies itself constitutionally as an Islamic state, and recognizes separate civil and Islamic jurisdictions, a pressing insistence for the expansion of Islamic law and courts confronts the professed secularism of the Malaysian Federal Court. Controversial cases over the last several years have potentially compromised the legitimacy of its highest court, which nonetheless has succeeded so far in using "constitutionally enshrined principles of federalism to block attempts to expand the ambit of Shari'a law." In their empirical study of the legal complex of Malaysia around these same cases, however, Harding and Whiting (2012) show that the politics of a vocal and publicly visible bar are intricately interwoven with the actions and legitimacy of the Court. On matters of religious jurisdiction, identity, conversion, and the status of minors, the Malaysia Bar Council has fought publicly with government ministers over constitutional supremacy of Islam, spearheaded campaigns for "the supremacy of the secular constitution," forged civil society coalitions (InterFaith Commission), publicly "chided the secular courts for deferring to the jurisdiction of the *syariah* court," authorized leading lawyers to maintain a "watching brief" in the *Lina Joy* case, lent public support to the dissenting opinion in that case, and sought to lead the public in open forums and travelling "road shows" to explain the meaning of supremacy of the secular Constitution. After decades defending the secular Constitution, the bar itself began to show rifts on some of these matters. In short, the story of the courts must be about more than the courts. There is an embedding politics that reveals why courts could withstand powerful political and religious currents that threatened to drive them off course and how they were able to maintain their legitimacy.

CONCLUSION

I conclude with three observations. First, a politics of courts, their roles, and power can no longer be justified in splendid isolation from a broader politics of the legal complex. Kapiszewski, Silverstein, and Kagan's nautical metaphor for changing judicial roles (Introduction in this volume) presupposes the contextual and contingent politics of the legal complex. Each of the four moments in the lives of constitutional courts, I have shown, implicitly or explicitly imagines a politics that is seldom revealed but integral to the constitutional roles and orientations and capacities of the courts.

Second, Kapiszewski, Silverstein, and Kagan rightly maintain that judicial roles will vary across political and social domains. The legal complex mobilizes most cohesively and broadly when the issues are able to be construed narrowly as those peculiarly within the professional remit of legal occupations, that is to say, core legal and civil rights, legal procedure, independence of the judiciary, and rule of law writ small. The more that issues for lawyers press into social, economic, and political rights writ large, the more probable it is that elements of the legal complex will fracture internally on party-political rather than legal-professional grounds (Karpik 2007). If the theory of the legal complex on political liberalism holds true in other domains, it should follow that the legal complex will be of more service to the legitimacy and power of courts when their remit is construed narrowly rather than broadly. It is almost always the genius of the legal complex to convert a broader policy issue into a narrower technical/legal issue (Halliday 1985).

Third, research across time and space shows that the legal complex is integral to broader social science explanations of four out of the five "conflict arenas" identified in the introductory chapter (Kapiszewski, Silverstein, and Kagan, in this volume). Even the possible exception – cultural and religious cleavages – can be a terrain on which the "idiom of legalism" championed in the politics of lawyers may be decisive for judicial confidence and creative solutions to seemingly intractable cultural conflicts (Harding and Whiting 2012).

In sum, as this volume richly demonstrates, a political jurisprudence or the politics of the courts qua courts has produced a sophisticated and complex body of knowledge over the past decades. In part, this has been possible because it has adopted a methodological and theoretical parsimony that has excluded parallel intellectual enterprises on other legal occupations. That shorthand can lead to disciplinary isolation, empirical constrictions, and theoretical distortion. It amplifies the power and autonomy of courts, at the same time concomitantly muting their contingency. Is it too much to say that a politics of consequential courts in the absence of its embedding, singular, and most proximate politics of the legal complex is comparable to a politics of legislatures without political parties, executive agencies without lobbyists, global lawmaking without lawyers?

REFERENCES

Couso, Javier A. 2007. "The Role of Chile's Legal Complex in the Configuration of a Moderate State." Pp. 315–344 in *The Legal Complex and Struggles for Political Liberalism*, edited by Terence C. Halliday, Lucien Karpik, and Malcolm M. Feeley. Oxford: Hart Publishing.

De, Rohit. 2012. "Emasculating the Executive: The Federal Court and Civil Liberties in Late Colonial India: 1942–1944." Pp. 59–90 in *Fates of Political Liberalism in the British Post-Colony: The Politics of the Legal Complex*, edited by Terence C. Halliday, Lucien Karpik, and Malcolm M. Feeley. New York: Cambridge University Press.

Epp, Charles R. 2012. "The Legal Complex in the Struggle to Control Police Brutality in India." Pp. 91–111 in *Fates of Political Liberalism in the British Post-Colony: The Politics of the Legal Complex*, edited by Terence C. Halliday, Lucien Karpik, and Malcolm M. Feeley. New York: Cambridge University Press.

Feeley, Malcolm M. 2012. "Judge and Company: Courts, Constitutionalism and the Legal Complex." Pp. 493–522 in *Fates of Political Liberalism in the British Post-Colony: The Politics of the Legal Complex*, edited by Terence C. Halliday, Lucien Karpik, and Malcolm M. Feeley. New York: Cambridge University Press.

Ghias, Shoaib A. 2012. "Miscarriage of Chief Justice: Lawyers, Media, and the Struggle for Judicial Independence in Pakistan." Pp. 340–377 in *Fates of Political Liberalism in the British Post-Colony: The Politics of the Legal Complex*, edited by Terence C. Halliday, Lucien Karpik, and Malcolm M. Feeley. New York: Cambridge University Press.

Ginsburg, Tom. 2007. "Law and the Liberal Transformation of the Northeast Asian Legal Complex in Korea and Taiwan." Pp. 43–63 in *The Legal Complex and Struggles for Political Liberalism*, edited by Lucien Karpik, Terence C. Halliday, and Malcolm M. Feeley. Oxford: Hart Publishing.

Gould, Jeremy. 2012. "Postcolonial Liberalism and the Legal Complex in Zambia: Elegy or Triumph?" Pp. 412–454 in *Fates of Political Liberalism in the British Post-Colony: The Politics of the Legal Complex*, edited by Terence C. Halliday, Lucien Karpik, and Malcolm M. Feeley. New York: Cambridge University Press.

Halliday, Terence C. 1985. "Knowledge Mandates: Collective Influence by Scientific, Normative and Syncretic Professions." *British Journal of Sociology* XXXVI: 421–447.

Halliday, Terence C. 2010. "The Fight for Basic Legal Freedoms: Mobilization by the Legal Complex." Pp. 210–240 in *Global Perspectives on the Rule of Law*, edited by James J. Heckman, Robert L. Nelson, and Lee Cabatingan. London: Routledge-Cavendish.

Halliday, Terence C., and Lucien Karpik (Eds.). 1997a. *Lawyers and the Rise of Western Political Liberalism: Europe and North American from the Eighteenth to Twentieth Centuries*. Oxford: Clarendon Press.

Halliday, Terence C., and Lucien Karpik. 1997b. "Politics Matter: A Comparative Theory of Lawyers in the Making of Political Liberalism." Pp. 15–64 in *Lawyers and the Rise of Western Political Liberalism: Europe and North American from the Eighteenth to Twentieth Centuries*, edited by Terence C. Halliday and Lucien Karpik. Oxford: Clarendon Press.

Halliday, Terence C., and Lucien Karpik. 2012. "Political Liberalism in the British Post-Colony: A Theme with Three Variations." Pp. 3–58 in *Fates of Political Liberalism in the British Post-Colony: The Politics of the Legal Complex*, edited by Terence C. Halliday, Lucien Karpik, and Malcolm M. Feeley. New York: Cambridge University Press.

Halliday, Terence C., Lucien Karpik, and Malcolm M. Feeley (Eds.). 2007a. *Fighting for Political Freedom: Comparative Studies of the Legal Complex for Political Change*. Oxford: Hart Publishing.

Halliday, Terence C., Lucien Karpik, and Malcolm M. Feeley. 2007b. "The Legal Complex and Struggles for Political Liberalism." Pp. 1–42 in *Fighting for Political Freedom: Comparative Studies of the Legal Complex for Political Change*, edited by Terence C. Halliday, Lucien Karpik, and Malcolm M. Feeley. Oxford Hart Publishing.

Halliday, Terence C., Lucien Karpik, and Malcolm M. Feeley (Eds.). 2012. *Fates of Political Liberalism in the British Post-Colony: The Politics of the Legal Complex*. New York: Cambridge University Press.

Harding, Andrew, and Amanda Whiting. 2012. "'Custodian of Civil Liberties and Justice in Malaysia': The Malaysian Bar and the Moderate State." Pp. 247–304 in *Fates of Political Liberalism in the British Post-Colony: The Politics of the Legal Complex*, edited by Terence C. Halliday, Lucien Karpik, and Malcolm M. Feeley. New York: Cambridge University Press.

Hilbink, Lisa. 2007. *Judges beyond Politics in Democracy and Dictatorship: Lessons from Chile*. New York: Cambridge University Press.

Karpik, Lucien. 2007. "Postscript: Political Lawyering." Pp. 463–494 in *The Legal Complex and Struggles for Political Liberalism*, edited by Terence C. Halliday, Lucien Karpik, and Malcolm M. Feeley. Oxford: Hart Publishing.

Karpik, Lucien, and Terence C. Halliday. 2011. "The Legal Complex." *Annual Review of Law and Social Science* 7: 217–236.

Lasser, Mitchel de S.-O.-l'E. 2004. *Judicial Transformations: The Rights Revolution in the Courts of France and Europe*. Oxford: Oxford University Press.

Mate, Manoj. 2012. "'Priests in the Temple of Justice': The Indian Legal Complex and the Basic Structure Doctrine." Pp. 112–148 in *Fates of Political Liberalism in the British Post-Colony: The Politics of the Legal Complex*, edited by Terence C. Halliday, Lucien Karpik, and Malcolm M. Feeley. New York: Cambridge University Press.

Moustafa, Tamir. 2007a. "Mobilising the Law in an Authoritarian State: The Legal Complex in Contemporary Egypt." Pp. 193–281 in *The Legal Complex and Struggles for Political Liberalism*, edited by Terence C. Halliday, Lucien Karpik, and Malcolm M. Feeley. Oxford: Hart Publishing.

Moustafa, Tamir. 2007b. *The Struggle for Constitutional Power: Law, Politics, and Economic Development in Egypt*. New York: Cambridge University Press.

Munir, Daud. 2012. "From Judicial Autonomy to Regime Transformation: The Role of the Lawyers' Movement in Pakistan." Pp. 378–411 in *Fates of Political Liberalism in the British Post-Colony: The Politics of the Legal Complex*, edited by Terence C. Halliday, Lucien Karpik, and Malcolm M. Feeley. New York: Cambridge University Press.

Perdomo, Rogelio Perez. 2007. "Lawyers and Political Liberalism in Venezuela." Pp. 345–360 in *The Legal Complex and Struggles for Political Liberalism*, edited by Terence C. Halliday, Lucien Karpik, and Malcolm M. Feeley. Oxford: Hart Publishing.

VonDoepp, Peter. 2012. "Legal Complexes and the Fight for Political Liberalism in New African Democracies: Comparative Insights from Malawi, Zambia and Namibia." Pp. 455–490 in *Fates of Political Liberalism in the British Post-Colony: The Politics of the Legal Complex*, edited by Terence C. Halliday, Lucien Karpik, and Malcolm M. Feeley. New York: Cambridge University Press.

14

Judicial Power
Getting it and Keeping it

John Ferejohn *

One could think that the move from authoritarian rule to parliamentary democracy would be generally favorable to legality. There are certainly many cases of authoritarian rulers who have seen courts and legal processes as threats to their powers and insisted on subservient judges, willing to permit lawless actions as required. However, not every authoritarian regime has been hostile to legality and independent legal institutions. Indeed, Steven Holmes has argued that law and independent judges are often in the interest of authoritarian as well as democratic rulers because they permit the upward flow of information valuable to maintaining stable rule.

Whether that is so or not, it seems clear that the transition away from an authoritarian regime, insofar as it entails a break in the old legal order, can undermine the establishment of genuinely legal institutions. Many of the laws might be either new or, if old, of questionable pedigree. There may have been special deals or pacts – necessary to disband the old authoritarian system – aimed at protecting certain traditional elites from legal rules that apply to others. Moreover, judges might well have continued or at least been trained under the previous regime, so they may not have earned or deserved a high level of trust. One could hope, however, that as democratic or liberal institutions become more established, these conflicts would fade away. Perhaps; but the chapters in this volume provide reason to think that there remains a significant tension between law and democratic rule and judges are sometimes placed in a position where they must negotiate these difficult issues.

Legality requires that legal norms be available to resolve most disputes, those who are to resolve disputes have interpretive control over the relevant norms, legal institutions are capable of reaching decisions efficiently, and the application of legal norms is relatively uniform and coherent. Institutions capable of resolving

* The Samuel Tilden Professor of Law, New York University School of Law.

legal disputes in this way must be more or less hierarchical, in the sense that there must be a way to get a final legal answer to any dispute. When courts finally decide a case, and when rights of appeal are exhausted, that is supposed to end the conflict and permit the parties to get on with other business. A judicial resolution brings something new into the situation: one party is told that, according to the "accepted" legal norms, she is entitled to the disputed object and the other party's claim is rejected on the basis of those prior norms. The loser is told in effect that if you don't like the result, you should have persuaded a judge (or jury) that she somehow misunderstood the norms or facts in the dispute, or else try to persuade us (the polity) to change the rules governing future disputes. Obviously, this notion of finality is limited in the sense that the losing party can always appeal the verdict to a higher court (if there is one) or try to get the law changed. However, new or amended laws typically govern future conduct rather than disputes that arose in the past.

Democratic rule requires a set of institutions that enable some kind of collective self-government or at least some degree of popular control over political leaders who will exercise governmental powers. From the time of the Athenians, many different institutional structures have appeared suited to democratic demands, ranging from direct popular rule in a popular assembly (such as the Athenian ekklesia; the Roman comitia; or the Swiss cantonal governments) to parliamentary governments made up of elected representatives that temporarily act as political sovereigns in between elections (as in the UK and Third Republic France; see Manin, 1997). Another tradition of indirect rule resists the notion of an institutional "sovereign" and delegates governmental powers to a complex institutional scheme including representative assemblies and separate executive and judicial departments, and possibly to regional entities, as well. Such complex divisions of sovereign powers require some kind of constitutionalism, whether written down or not, that can arbitrate disputes among empowered institutions.

Each of these political arrangements is itself enormously complex organizationally, as it has to be if it is to govern effectively and be seen as a plausible form of self-rule. Intellectual guidance is needed to recognize threats to stability, and to criticize and reform existing practices in a more democratic direction. At the same time, energy and decisiveness are necessary for effective performance of governmental functions even as disagreements about policy remained only partly resolved. For that reason, democratic institutions are generally accompanied and supported by democratic ideologies that seek in some ways to justify particular institutions and practices as constituting a genuine form of self-government (appearances to the contrary notwithstanding). Of course, these ideologies differ across the various institutional implementations of democracy. Different democratic ideologies also see the position of the judge in quite different ways. In what might be called "sovereigntist" traditions, parliamentary government is the prominent example, law amounts to sovereign (legislative) command and the duty of the judge is to apply the law as an "honest agent" of the sovereign.[1] In constitutional democracy, judges are to be agents of the legislature only when those commands are themselves consistent with the constitution. This stipulation requires (as Hamilton said in *Federalist* 78) the judge herself to make the determination that the legislature's command is lawful. Evidently, therefore, there is more of a political burden placed on judges in constitutional democracies than in parliamentary systems. Even where parliament is assumed to be fully sovereign (as in the UK or France during the Third and Fourth Republics), however, judges are sometimes forced or tempted to make political judgments as to the validity or scope of a statute.

In principle, the tensions between politics and law might be no less strong in a democratic than authoritarian or even transitional regime. Conflicts between the legislature and courts are as old as democracy itself. They cut in both directions: democratic legislatures can justifiably see the judiciary as limiting the reach of its own legitimate efforts. After the end of the Peloponnesian wars, for example, the Athenians deployed (popular) courts to check and regulate the activities of the ekklesia or legislative assembly. The various devices of statutory construction of the eighteenth-century British judiciary to restrain and limit the reach and impact of laws made by Parliament are legendary (i.e., See David Lieberman's *The Province of Legislation Determined*, Cambridge University Press, 1989 or Blackstone's famous legal treatise) and are widely employed everywhere. At the same time, judges, lacking powers of enforcement and self-funding, can easily be threatened by elected officials even when performing their lawful function of applying the laws.

Indeed, insofar as elected political leaders enjoy an extra advantage in legitimacy, democracy could be more threatening to legality than more weakly legitimated authoritarian rule. However, there are countervailing forces in democracy. For one thing, organizing political force in a democratic regime is more difficult (so many cooks want to add to the recipe) than in an authoritarian regime. Moreover, democracies (almost by definition) generally employ elections to institutionalize a new and characteristic kind of instability, making positions of leadership temporary and contestable, and policies changeable. For that reason, sustaining a political coalition in a democracy is usually difficult. Although nothing is ever really settled in human life, in democracies the absence of political finality is a defining feature of democratic rule.

All things considered, judges in democratic regimes have reason to hope that threats to legality will be hard to mobilize and difficult to sustain. This is because everyone in society has a general interest in legality – as long as they are not

---

[1] This model is traceable to Bentham and John Austin. See H.L.A. Hart, *The Concept of Law*, Oxford Press (1961), for summaries and critiques of these views. As Hart showed, this model needs some tweaking to include implicit delegations of others to issue commands in the name of, and with the sufferance of, the legislature. So Parliament can be understood as implicitly delegating the authority to make common law, or the authority of private parties to make contracts, and so forth. However, the point remains: the sovereign is free to step in and alter any rule produced in court or contract.

themselves embroiled in a legal dispute. Such politically motivated threats as do appear might naturally tend to peter out by themselves, as coalitions fragment and impatient minds are diverted. Ordinarily, it might be thought, it would be good judicial strategy to narrow the legal stakes to the contending parties and avoid direct confrontations with broad political coalitions, if possible, and wait for times to get better. This advice seems sensible in many democratic circumstances, but the appearance of disciplined political parties may mitigate its force as several of the Sawyer essays suggest. Where a political party is able to maintain a large and stable majority sufficient to control constitutional institutions for a long period of time (as in India until recently, South Africa at the present time, Japan since the last world war, and many other places), the democratic threat to legality can force judges into subservient positions despite what is said in a written constitution.

Indeed, the tension between legality and notions of political sovereignty reached a new level with the collapse of the authoritarian systems after the Second World War, which discredited the "command theory" version of legal positivism in favor of a system of substantive human or natural rights (embedded in a written constitution or in international law), which are to restrain governments within a legal framework. The postwar period has thus been marked simultaneously by the growth of constitutionalism on the one hand and democracy on the other. These two trends are especially pronounced in postauthoritarian regimes whose new constitutions have subjected the legislature to legal controls, typically by a specialized court. However, even in the older democracies (such as the UK or Netherlands, Canada, and New Zealand) there has been widespread acceptance of the idea that the legislature ought to be bound somehow by legal norms. Most of the remaining dispute has to do with how much power judges should have to enforce those norms.[2]

There are, in this sense, more or less permanent structural tensions between the ideals of democracy and legality, and this is carried over into the specific institutionalizations of these ideals. Although the tension may be inevitable in some sense (we value both things after all), the appearance of particular conflicts is episodic. In a particular conflict there may be opportunities for judges to act strategically in ways that honor and preserve one or both values at the same time they are deciding (or not deciding) a particular dispute. Sometimes strategic action has the whiff of lawlessness or lack of principle. One can suppose that sometimes this charge is deserved. However, underlying ideals are central to the self-understanding of many of the peoples of the world. That may warrant a little strategizing in a particular case.

THIS VOLUME'S EMPIRICAL STUDIES

Many of the studies appearing in this volume focus on critical historical moments: circumstances in which a decisive turn in the development of legal and political

---

[2] This issue is discussed in Mark Tushnet, *Weak Courts, Strong Rights: JudicialReview and Social Welfare Rights in Comparative Constitutional Law* (Princeton: Princeton University Press, 2008).

institutions and practices might or might not take place. In each of these studies we are offered careful descriptions of circumstances in which the actions taken or not taken by legal officials mattered crucially for what happened to the political and legal systems.[3] In some of the chapters, the critical moment marks a decisive and successful transition in the direction of a more genuine or consolidated democracy, or to a sudden increase in judicial power or independence. By contrast, other studies illustrate similarly decisive failures either by judges or other officials, where judicial powers were shrunk or authoritarian rule persisted despite courts' attempts to end or ameliorate it. Sometimes these failures might have been a miscalculation by a legal actor, an overly optimistic judicial confidence that orders that might be given would be obeyed by the government. Some cases, however, have an additional "tragic" aspect: a judge or judges were placed in a situation where legality demanded a particular action but where the logic of political power demanded its rejection.

In this respect, the political/constitutional regime itself is depicted as being some-how on a precipice where things could go one way or another. Sometimes it is a court, often a high or constitutional court, that is in the position to take an impor-tant decision that will push events one way or another. Such circumstances call for political judgment and strategy if the regime is not to be forced to a crisis. It is, of course, controversial among lawyers to describe courts as "political" or "strategic" in this sense. However, such an attribution is sometimes unavoidable and it is there that many of the Sawyer essays train their focus. The typical event in many of the chapters included here can be described as a "Marbury" moment, wherein a high court asserts new jurisdiction or claims powers to control elected officials but does so in a subtle or strategic way that makes it hard for politicians to reject it. Moreover, this innovation tends, for some reason, to "stick" and mark a decisive and more or less permanent turn in the legal/constitutional order. That's why, in retrospect, we can see the Marbury-like character of these decisions.

Ordinarily, in a complex political system, politicians are not able to marshal power single-mindedly to oppose the courts. There is simply too much disagreement within the political classes to agree on such a project, and courts (and legality) are often quite valuable to various elements in the ruling classes. Moreover, courts are normally sufficiently deferential to political authority to avoid direct confrontation. Besides, when a court claims some new jurisdiction or authority, politicians of all persuasions can often make use of these new options in their political struggles. This may not happen immediately of course, as it did not following *Marbury*; it was half a century before the Supreme Court struck down another federal statute. However, even when it was not deployed by courts, the assertion of the power of judicial

---

[3] The perspective is radically different than the one that Adam Przeworski has taken in several works where transitions of the kind described, or their absence, here might be largely (although not com-pletely) explained by material factors – especially the level of per capita income in the society. I think that Przeworski is probably right and that material factors do make a difference in making democratic or constitutional rule more or less likely, but that the role these factors play is not very visible in the (mostly) single country studies here.

review immediately opened the door to courts to hear other challenges, providing an avenue for opponents of federal or state laws to complain and seek redress in courts. Given some amount of alternation in power, and the complex nature of the federal system, this option could be valuable to almost anyone from time to time.

Opponents of a strong central government surely found the Marbury precedent valuable in 1819 when, in *McCulloch v Maryland* they asked the Court to invalidate the act establishing the Second Bank of the United States. The opponents lost of course, but they had the chance to make their case. They could reargue it in the future in many other settings, too. Those who favored strong central institutions could also find new judicial powers valuable in their own causes, as when they were able to preempt state jurisdiction in *Gibbons*. In any event, as long as the Court did not let its own claims to power become a political issue, politicians would tend to pick their fights with each other rather than with judges. It was a lesson not fully learned by the Supreme Court (viz. *Dred Scott* and *Schecter Poultry* or other pre-1937 cases where the Court struck down New Deal legislation).

Marbury Moments

The chapters in this volume lay out an impressive list of Marbury moments, of which I will survey a few. Reichman (Ch. 9 in this volume), for example, labels the *Bank Hamizrachi* case, where the Supreme Court announced that the Basic Laws were supreme over ordinary legislation, Israel's *Marbury v Madison*. Similar to Marbury, the opinion left the statute standing and made the supremacy assertion in the context of insisting that the Court had judicial review powers (this took 350 pages), so it could strike down the statute. A stranger case is reported by Ginsburg (Ch. 1 in this volume), but one which nevertheless fits the Marbury pattern – where a court exercises judicial review but refuses to order anyone to do anything. It is the ruling of the Korean Constitutional Court in the impeachment of President Roh Moo-hyun. After conceding that Roh had indeed violated the election law, it decided that the (technical) offenses were not aimed at undermining the democracy and therefore were not serious enough to warrant his removal from office. The complication here is that Roh and his allies did not control the National Assembly, which had impeached him. So the refusal to remove the president would have frustrated that powerful body.

Two more complex stories are told by Ginsburg of the Constitutional Court's role in refusing to overturn tainted elections in Thailand. Ginsburg separates these events, saying of the first that the Court deferred to a popular democratic president (Thaksin). In the second it deferred instead to those who perpetrated an antidemocratic coup. However, each seems to have Marbury aspects, as the Court recognized the legal defects in the choices made by political leaders, but then refused to order anyone in power (the president or coup leaders) to do anything as a result of their legal findings.

Robert Kagan's (Ch. 8 in this volume) masterful retelling of Supreme Court jurisprudence contains numerous candidates for Marbury-ish moments, but the most famous is the Court's ruling in the two *Brown* decisions, the first of which overturned *Plessey* but did not issue concrete orders to desegregate the nation's schools. Once again, jurisdiction and judicial power had been asserted but not actually exercised. One could also cite the peculiar circumstance of the nondelegation doctrine announced in *Schecter* but never subsequently enforced against any congressional delegation of authority, no matter how suspect under the *Schecter* standard.

A more dramatic series of events can be discovered in Mate's study of the Indian Supreme Court (Ch. 10 in this volume). In 1967, the Court blocked a series of governmental attempts to confiscate property from wealthy landholders and resisted attempts by Gandhi's government to limit their jurisdiction over such cases. Similar to what FDR had done thirty years earlier, Mrs. Gandhi responded by campaigning against the Court and, following her electoral victory, got Parliament to enact an amendment conferring unlimited authority to Parliament to amend the Constitution, and limit the jurisdiction of the Court to review the land-confiscation cases. When faced with these new limiting amendments, in *Kesavananda* the Court effectively retreated on all fronts (a bit like a "switch" but not quite in time), insisting that Parliament could not alter the "basic structure" of the Constitution. However, as in *Marbury*, when faced with a popular and powerful government it limited the effect of its defiance by making its ruling prospective, in effect conceding every legal claim the Gandhi government had actually made. Thus, the Court had made a legal assertion – that the Constitution had a firm and unamendable basic structure – but made no claim on the sovereign to do anything in consequence. The opinion itself was long (more than 1,000 pages) and fractured, indicating that the judges themselves could not really agree as to what precisely the basic structure was. Still, the justices left their mark on the legal terrain where it could be picked up later when political circumstances were not so adverse. Even this was too much for Gandhi, however, and she promptly packed the Court with more amenable justices. A few years later when new amendments were enacted during the second "Emergency" – aimed directly at suppressing dissenters and preventing judicial regulation of elections – the Court, once again, meekly acquiesced in all of them.

That was not the end of the story, however. As momentous as these confrontations were, Mate's main focus is on legal events after the end of the Emergency. He discusses, for example, the *Judge's Case*, where the Court agreed to widen standing doctrine relying in part on the basic structure doctrine introduced earlier. "The Court's decision in the *Judges Cases* was thus a classic *Marbury* move: the Court expanded its own jurisdiction . . . but gave the government what it wanted by deferring to the supremacy of the Executive" (Ch. 10 in this volume). This was not the final use of this strategy by the Indian Supreme Court: "[D]uring the 1980s, while the Court gradually expanded its power in human rights and malgovernance cases, it was not a uniformly assertive Court. In high salience areas the Court continued to avoid directly challenging the Central Government's policies and actions" (Ch. 10 in this volume).

Lasser (Ch. 11 in this volume) provides a fascinating description of a long-running conflict between the European Court for Human Rights and the French Conseil d'Etat, which may be described in Marbury-like terms. Unlike the other examples I have described, this is not a case of a domestic or national Court seeking to expand its powers in the face of a hostile and powerful sovereign. Rather, what we see in this dispute is the effort of the fledgling European Court for Human Rights (ECHR) seeking to develop a more or less uniform rights jurisprudence in a complex federation, each member of which had its own legal traditions and powerful legal institutions. In France, both of the supreme courts (the Cour de Cassation and the Conseil d'Etat) have traditionally employed procedures permitting a unique institutional role for a government spokesman, the advocat general, within their internal proceedings. This official traditionally enjoyed procedural privileges denied to ordinary litigants (reading the report of the rapporteur, for example, and actually sitting in the meeting with the judges as the case is discussed). The ECHR began challenging this practice in 1991 on the grounds that it violated its own "fair trial" jurisprudence.

Interestingly, the reactions of the two French supreme courts have been very different: according to Lasser, the Cour avidly followed the recommendations of the ECHR and removed the avocat from any privileged procedural role (without actually being ordered to do so); the Conseil has essentially stonewalled the European Court by refusing any procedural reform. It is not clear that the ECHR has forced any kind of a showdown with the Conseil; more likely this is a continuing dispute in which the ECHR has taken a *Marbury* posture of announcing new fair trial doctrine but then not actually enforcing it against an offending institution for fear of what it or its defenders might actually do. This is probably because the success of the ECHR jurisprudence depends on its acceptability to the national judicial and political institutions, so confrontation – at least with one of the major European powers – seems unpromising as an effective strategy. (By contrast, the ECHR has been much more aggressive in challenging Belgian procedures, which were essentially identical to the French.)

Klug's (Ch. 3 in this volume) discussion of South Africa introduces yet another example of a *Marbury* moment, but he also makes an important distinction – which will be useful later in this essay – between rights-protecting and power-allocating decisions. Famously, the South African Constitutional Court (CC) ruled that the death penalty was unconstitutional despite widespread popular support for it. Klug finds this ruling (and other rulings upholding equal protection claims) to have been much less difficult for the Court than direct challenges to powerful governmental institutions that arise when it is asked to maintain constitutionally separated powers. Specifically, he discusses the *Western Cape* case: the provincial government of the Western Cape challenged a Mandela decree establishing local constituency

boundaries. The Court overturned the decree by declaring that Parliament's delegation to Mandela was unconstitutional but then, rather than voiding the decree, the
Court simply gave the Parliament time to remedy the legal situation, which eventually permitted the central government to have what it wanted (i.e., it permitted the
government to regulate the restructuring of local government during the transition).
Again, a classic *Marbury* maneuver but executed in a dangerous separation-of-powers
case.

Finally, Scribner (Ch. 4 in this volume) tells how the Chilean Constitutional
Tribunal accomplished a similar pirouette in declaring President Lagos's decree
in *Restricción a Catalíticos* (2001) unconstitutional (by means of devising a new
nonoriginalist interpretive approach to constitutional interpretation), which then
permitted the decree's restriction on automobile use to stand temporarily until
a legislative remedy could be devised. Again, the Court announced a significant
expansion in its jurisdiction and powers but then did not order the government to
do very much in consequence.

FAILURES

The examples discussed in the previous section largely focus on successful cases –
where legality or judicial independence or constitutional democracy prevailed. However, *Marbury* moments do not always succeed. Mate's (Ch. 10 in this volume)
discussion of the *Kesavananda* decision has already provided a stark cautionary
tale. When the court attempted in *Kesavananda* to craft a new and more modest
doctrine that would allow the Court to retain some power to review constitutional
amendments, the Gandhi government was able to ignore it and pack the Court with
subservient justices. In retrospect, we can see that the Court's preferred position has
eventually prevailed, but that result seems due as much to the electoral rejection of
Congress Party hegemony as to any doctrinal sticking power of *Kesavananda* itself.

Students of the U.S. courts can provide lots of evidence of *Marbury* failures:
unsuccessful assertions of judicial power either because the other branches ignored
the Court's decision (as in *Worcester v Georgia*) or stripped the Court's jurisdiction
(in *ex Parte MacArdle*) or forced the Court to change its approach to the Constitution
altogether (in the switch in time and subsequent appointment of justices by FDR).[4]
Each of these confrontations took place in roughly similar political conditions: a
large political majority that was disposed to push a certain policy was confronted
by a Court that expressed doubts as to the constitutionality of new legislation.

---

[4] I should say that the interpretation of each of these events is controversial. *Worcester* was, in form,
very similar to *Marbury*, as the Court did not actually order the president to do anything. Whereas
MacArdle stripped the Court's jurisdiction over MacArdle himself, the Court understood the jurisdiction stripping act in a very narrow way, permitting it to continue supervising Reconstruction; and
the switch in time remains a subject of academic debate, as well. My view is that although one can
quibble over the technicalities, each of these events was understood generally as a setback for the
Court and was understood that way by everyone at the time and by most thereafter.

In other words, the political circumstances were similar to those in *Marbury*. In such a situation the Court should be cautious about issuing an order and, at most, give a lecture or a limited ruling that asserts a claim but does not require explicit compliance. In any case, this way of thinking probably undercounts failures because there could have been countless times the Supreme Court could have attempted to enlarge its jurisdiction but refrained out of worry about adverse political reactions.

The cases discussed in the previous section can read as suggesting more conditions under which judges might successfully assert the power of courts and legality. These conditions can be described in terms of three variables: the nature of the society (and particularly how deeply divided it is), structural features of the political/legal regime, and the leadership ability of leading judges (and possibly other political leaders). What these variables permit us to see is that in certain circumstances judges have capacities, if they choose to use them strategically, that can help transform political conflicts into legal questions and resolve them in ways that further the development of new legal or constitutional norms in ways acceptable to elected officials. The key to political acceptance is that the dispute is decided according to accepted legal norms, by more or less impartial judges rather than by contending parties, and that powerful political officials are not actually required to sacrifice vital political projects by accepting new legal norms. These common features make courts and judges generically useful to other social actors in a very wide range of social circumstances (which is why they are found everywhere): courts can help political leaders impose demands on others and settle conflicts that are otherwise difficult to resolve (without incurring great costs).

At the same time, however, the very capacity of legal actors to resolve disputes, and to persuasively characterize such settlements as legal, makes courts and judges potentially dangerous competitors for political power. Some of the chapters show that political leaders are aware of these dangers and try to prevent them. Thus, we can see evidence in some of the chapters that the relationship between politics and law is intrinsically unstable in certain circumstances and that things don't always work out in the way described in the previous section. This instability would appear to be greatest in absolutist regimes where there is a single ruler (or a well-disciplined hierarchical ruling structure) from whom a court may or may not withhold something she wants. It is from such situations that dramatic (and sometimes apocryphal) tales of conflicts between judges and rulers have arisen. The alleged confrontation between Edward Coke and James I is one example: Coke, so the story goes, told the king that he was incompetent to decide cases at law; not something the king wanted to hear. Although Coke's story may have been an exaggeration, more is known of the repeated conflicts between Louis XIV and Louis XV and their Parlements, which sometimes refused to register royal edicts if they thought them legally defective. One suspects that confrontations with absolute monarchs must have been exceptional, as judges would already have known their likely outcome and would have been unwilling to risk life and career on a fight. Not every judge is an Edward Coke.

The most direct story of failure is given in Trochev's description of the rise and fall of judicial power in Georgia (Ch. 2 in this volume). He argues that one of the conditions for judges to establish their court as a real power in a transitional regime is in exercisingjurisdiction over electoral disputes. I think he may be wrong about that. Such a jurisdiction is extremely dangerous for courts because it places them in a position where they may be compelled, legally, to take actions against powerful political actors that they have no means of enforcing. Unless the courts are very well institutionalized and their legitimacy well accepted by the elites, this seems a recipe for humiliating retreat or disaster. The Georgian experience seems direct evidence of that danger. In any event, the story is one where the Supreme Court essentially asserted such a jurisdiction in 2003 following allegations of widespread corruption, canceled some elections, and in effect triggered what became known as the Rose Revolution. The reaction of the new government was essentially to completely marginalize existing judicial institutions and certainly to limit the capacity of judges to review elections.

What could the Georgian Supreme Court have done? As I read Trochev's contribution, it need not have asserted jurisdiction here at all. Trochev argues that the Court's claim was in fact novel or even extra-constitutional. However, even if it could not have ducked the issue, ways might have been found to limit its rulings to a few well-chosen contests where evidence was particularly strong; it need not have attempted to issue any broader order to the government. Such efforts might have been unsatisfying from the standpoint of strict legality, if that was really was at stake, but not nearly as unsatisfying as the rout of the judiciary that followed.

STICKINESS

The chapters of this volume do not explicitly address the issue of when or why new assertions of judicial authority tend to stick, but seem to assume that somehow decisive judicial victories will automatically persist. This could be wrong; maybe some judicial assertions stick and others do not, and the ones that do are picked out after the fact as having special significance. Could this really be known in advance? Or should we see the *Marbury* moments as those that for some reason stuck and gained post hoc significance, rather like *Marbury* itself? On the other side, if those opposed to expanded judicial powers had reason to think that a judicial assertion would not last, they may not have thought it worthwhile to oppose it. So it seems important, for these studies, to try to understand when and why judicial decisions stick.

In any case, the chapters implicitly suggest that stickiness cuts across legal regimes – it is not unique to common–law based legal systems but is found in civil-law systems, as well. Maybe this is true. If so, perhaps this is because constitutional courts, or at least courts with constitutional jurisdiction in whatever legal system they are found, tend to engage in something like common-law methodology (crafting new legal rules in the context of reaching decisions, and following earlier rulings). Or it may be that stickiness is an emergent political phenomenon – brought about, in effect, by other actors and the public generally who come to take advantage of new legal opportunities and, over time, increasingly rely on them. Perhaps increases in judicial power or independence expand the set of rights held by citizens and, once people get a new right or the opportunity to defend an old one, they might fight hard to keep that new legal advantage – harder than they would have fought to get it in the first place. So courts may rapidly acquire new allies, after the fact, in their assertion of jurisdiction or independence.

My view is that any successful explanation for stickiness must also take account of the political characteristics of pivotal moments themselves, and such things could be known at the time of the dispute itself. The political circumstances in which a court's decision could create a powerful new right or jurisdiction are likely to be pretty uncommon. The *Marbury* decision may be a useful guide: in *Marbury* a powerful and unified (and newly elected) political class confronted a judiciary that stood in its way. This situation was brought about by what has been called the "revolution of 1800," when the Jefferson Democrats drove their Federalist opponents from every national institution except the Supreme Court. The new political majority was sufficiently large and unified that it was capable of ignoring or suppressing judicial claims or even removing judges and abolishing federal courts. The Democrats did impeach two judges, removing one from the bench. In that political situation, the idea of directly confronting the president must have seemed very unpromising. Indeed, at the time *Marbury* was decided the Court actually conceded authority of the president to eliminate the jobs of life-protected federal judges by abolishing their Courts. It is indeed hard to imagine a more supine judicial holding than the Court's ruling in *Stuart v Laird*.[5]

In this political context, judicial powers and independence were under a great deal of threat and might have been impossible to assert in a direct confrontation. So, if it hoped to assert a power to review federal statutes, Marshall's court had to rely on an indirect tactic, hoping to assert its powers in a way that the political majority could not easily resist. It is a fine question whether the Court asserted a new power or simply protected an old one; we cannot address that question here. Judges and lawyers often take the first view; many historians seem to think the second more likely (i.e., that the power of judicial review of federal laws was implicit in the constitutional scheme as Hamilton had argued in the *Federalist*). The point is that the moment *Marbury* was decided was politically dangerous, as the Court faced a unified and large political majority that was suspicious of judges and judicial powers. However, as students of American politics now appreciate, such political circumstances are rare, and once things return to normal (which normally happens fairly quickly, as it did following *Marbury*) the Court is free to stick to (and even

---

[5] *Stuart v Laird*, 1 Cranch (5 U.S.) 299 (1803).

build on) its asserted power without reason to fear a political intervention. Of course, John Marshall could not have been sure that is the way things would actually go in the new republic. So, probably, when *Marbury* was announced, he could not have been sure that it would stick politically (he would have been more confident in legal stickiness, at least as long as the justices were not removed or intimidated).

DEMOCRACY, CONSTITUTIONALISM AND POLITICAL FRAGMENTATION

Most of the empirical contributions to this volume deal with critical moments either in more or less democratic polities or in circumstances of transition away from an authoritarian past of some sort or another. Most of these transitional stories are incomplete in the sense that one cannot know how they will actually turn out. Some have gone well, so far, others not so well; however, the overall thrust of the chapters is optimistic with respect to the correlated development of democracy and independent and powerful legal institutions. Whatever contradictions or tensions there may be between legality and democracy, there is a message in these chapters that both normative systems can develop and thrive simultaneously. Whether they do or not depends (at least partly) on courts being able and willing to negotiate dangerous political circumstances successfully – by refraining from forceful assertions of legal powers in dangerous political circumstances – and this capacity has varied over the cases and time.

Some other contributions deal with more gradual developments that I cannot discuss in any detail in this brief piece. I believe, however, that the Dutch and Italian cases (Chs. 7 and 6 in this volume) fit with the general model that I have developed here; political power in both nations has been fairly fragmented among political parties throughout the postwar periods (and therefore not dangerous to courts), which permits judges to decide cases without much fear of political intervention. So it was possible for Dutch High Court judges to take the lead in experimenting with expanded forms of judicial review (see Huls, Ch. 7 in this volume). However, these developments are complex, as they are situated within a framework of European law that permits a separate and novel form of judicial review in the European courts. It is not clear that these postwar political conditions will persist as new issues arise.

In Italy, too, the fragmentation of the political elite and institutional developments within the judicial system weakened the control of the Cassation Court and political officials could exercise over ordinary judges. According to Gaurnieri (Ch. 6 in this volume), one effects of the changes was to shift the self-conception of judges (who could now refer questions directly to the Constitutional Court), who could now see themselves as partners with the Constitutional Court in deepening legal and constitutional norms. These developments allowed prosecuting judges to develop a closer relationship to the police and employ investigatory techniques developed in the fights against terrorism and organized crime, to investigate and prosecute corruption of public officials. The Berlusconi government reacted sharply to these initiatives, introducing jurisdictionstripping legislation, but the Constitutional Court has struck those down. It remains unclear whether there will be some kind of successful backlash against the judges; Guarnieri argues that politicians on the left as well as the right may be willing to act together to limit judicial powers. If so, the Italian courts may face a Marbury moment of their own.

We can see from these chapters that the project of reconciling democracy and legality remains unfinished in many places. It is always possible that political forces can come suddenly into alignment in ways that threaten judicial powers, and when that happens, much depends on the capacity of courts to negotiate the dangers and limit their assertions of authority to what they can actually accomplish. Doing this takes no small element of judicial wisdom and patience and no small amount of legal craftsmanship. Courts, even in dangerous times, must make their strategic moves appear principled and legal lest they lose or tarnish the aura that makes them useful to society and its ruling classes.

15

Constitutional Politics in the Active Voice

Mark A. Graber*

The passive voice is preferred by many students of comparative judicial politics during the prologue to their tales of judicial power. Constitutions are framed and ratified. Legal and constitutional rules and standards are announced. The precise meaning of these rules and standards is debated. Courts are established. Judges are appointed. Jurisdiction is conferred. Legal and constitutional disputes are placed on the agenda of these courts. Legal and constitutional arguments are made. Agency is absent from both sentences and analysis.

Constitutional politics shifts sharply to the active voice between oral argument and disposition. Judges make decisions. Many elected officials oppose those judicial rulings. Executives refuse to implement court orders. Legislators propose contrary constitutional amendments. Political activists demand that elected officials replace the offending judges by legal or extralegal means. Supporters who mobilize to defend the judicial decision wax eloquent on the virtues of an independent judiciary.

Ginsburg documents this linguistic transition in the second paragraph of his contribution to this volume (Ch. 1). "The election case is sent to the courts to resolve, along with constitutional disputes about the investigative committees," he writes. Who, if anyone, sent the case to the courts is left to the imagination. Suddenly, agency appears. Ginsburg declares: "The court held that the election was valid, the investigation constitutional, and the leader takes power." In sharp contrast to the previous sentence, readers are informed who held the election to be valid and do not have to speculate about unknown entities or magical processes. Courts made the decision in question. Courts matter, most contributors to this volume concur, because judicial decisions change the course of constitutional politics.

---

* Associate Dean for Research and Faculty Development and Professor of Law, University of Maryland Francis King Carey School of Law.

Contrary to the syntax in many papers,[1] all of constitutional politics takes place in the active voice. Human beings frame and ratify constitutions. Constitutional framers announce legal and constitutional rules and standards. Governing officials establish courts, appoint judges, and confer jurisdiction. Political entrepreneurs raise constitutional issues and find the means to place those issues on the judicial agenda. Human beings perform all these actions for reasons. Politicians who empower courts may be providing insurance against electoral failures,[2] imposing national policy in the hinterlands,[3] entrenching their supporters,[4] foisting responsibility for hot political issues on to a different branch of government,[5] or securing other political and legal ends.[6] Much constitutional politics consists of struggles over which institutions should resolve various political disputes and partisan efforts to staff with political allies those institutions that are resolving or likely to resolve particular political disputes. Scholars risk missing and misunderstanding much political action when they impute agency only when and after courts make decisions.

This essay details four common habits that inhibit perception of agency in both the essays in this volume and in other studies of constitutional politics. Scholars deny all human agency when they overuse the passive voice or attribute agency to such nonhuman entities as a national constitution. They deny judicial agency when they adopt the very strong "regime politics" theory that treats judges as mere minions of more powerful governing officials or coalitions. Commentators deny legislative agency when they claim that political fragmentation prevents all major parties from influencing the course of judicial decision making. Finally, and most important, studies of constitutional politics unduly limit political agency when, by attributing agency primarily to institutions, they overlook how individual judges, legislators, and political activists frequently act as participants in a common (liberal) cause.

That the essays in an anthology entitled *Consequential Courts: Judicial Roles in Global Perspective* might unduly deny human agency seems perverse and probably wrong. Both accusations are correct. Each contributor does a wonderful job detailing the constitutional politics underlying constitutional developments in the regimes they studied. My complaints about the passive voice often go to style rather than substance. The authors are frequently guilty of nothing more than focusing on some

[1] Or the draft papers before copyediting. In some cases, the authors abandoned the passive voice during the final editing process. When that occurred, I have relied on the original drafts I was expected to comment on.
[2] Tom Ginsburg, *Judicial Review in New Democracies: Constitutional Courts in Asian Cases* (Cambridge University Press: New York, 2003), p. 18.
[3] See Martin Shapiro, *Courts: A Comparative and Political Analysis* (University of Chicago Press: Chicago, 1981), p. viii.
[4] See Jack M. Balkin and Sanford Levinson, "Understanding the Constitutional Revolution," *Virginia Law Review* 87(1045): 1066–83 (2001).
[5] Mark A. Graber, "The Non-Majoritarian Difficulty: Legislative Deference to the Judiciary," *Studies in American Political Development* 7: 35 (1993).
[6] See generally, Mark A. Graber, "James Buchanan as Savior? Judicial Power, Political Fragmentation, and the Failed 1831 Repeal of Section 25," 88 *Oregon Law Review* 95, 95–98 (2009).

dimension of constitutional politics at the expense of others. Nevertheless, the essays read as a whole suggest that students of comparative courts and constitutionalism are developing bad habits that lead them to overlook or discount human agency at crucial moments in constitutional politics. By identifying these habits and detailing their consequences, this essay hopes to offer a fuller spectrum of the ways in which judges, elected officials, political activists, and other human beings influence the course of constitutional development.

Scholars who break the habits that obscure agency in constitutional politics may notice that the previous essays are as concerned with liberal constitutionalism as with the roles of constitutional courts. During much of the twentieth and early twenty-first centuries, various political movements, elected officials, and what Terence Halliday (Ch. 13 in this volume) calls the "legal complex" sought to secure liberal conceptions of fundamental human rights. Virtually all of the participants in this transnational endeavor assigned constitutional courts major responsibilities for advancing a liberal policy agenda and a liberal constitutional vision. The essays in this volume discuss how well constitutional courts served liberal purposes, whether those purposes be promoting secularism (Hirschl, Ch. 12 in this volume), ensuring fair elections (Trochev, Ch. 2 in this volume) or achieving compliance with international law (Huls, Ch. 7 in this volume; Lasser, Ch. 11 in this volume). The lessons these essays teach, therefore, are about judicial capacity to play distinctive liberal roles, and not about how courts and judges committed to a very different policy agenda and constitutional vision might function in very different times and places.

The close connection between contemporary judicial policymaking and liberal constitutionalism suggests a research agenda devoted to the following questions. What roles do liberals assign to constitutional courts, and under what conditions, if any, do courts play those roles well? How does liberal constitutionalism influence how courts function in both theory and practice? How does the extensive reliance liberalism places on courts influence the theory and practice of liberal constitutionalism?

Readers should be forewarned that I am one of those ugly Americans who knows little about constitutional systems outside the United States (and, therefore, arguably knows little about the American constitutional regime). The editors as a practical joke might have included essays that discuss fictional events, judicial decisions, judges, and perhaps even countries. Given my commitment to a historical institutionalism that relies on thick description, readers should take with more than a grain of salt any criticisms I make of the wonderful essays that preceded this polemic.

THE PASSIVE VOICE AND MISSING AGENTS

The essays in this volume combine remarkable erudition with a remarkable number of sentences in the passive voice. Diana Kapiszewski, Gordon Silverstein, and Robert

Kagan set an early tone in the second paragraph of the Introduction when they assert, "Courts in more established democracies . . . have been given . . . more power to protect individual rights and invalidate government policies." Shortly thereafter they assert, "Several chapters in this book illustrate ways in which courts have been called on to play, and have played, this new judicial role." Carlo Guarnieri in the introduction to his essay (Ch. 6 in this volume) asserts, "Judicial and prosecutorial independence was progressively strengthened and the traditional influence of the higher ranks practically dismantled." Not to be outdone, Druscilla Scribner's first paragraph states, "Over the next fifteen years, the TC [Tribunal Constitucional] was called on to interpret and rearticulate the power relationships set out by the authoritarian regime" (Ch. 4 in this volume). The introduction to Ran Hirschl's essay (Ch. 12) chimes in with, "Religion and its institutions and interpretive hierarchy are expected to comply with overarching constitutional norms." Similar sentences, all without agents, litter the essays. Courts and judges are consistently called on to play, empowered to play, or expected to play various roles by unknown beings and mysterious processes.

My concern with these passive constructions partly reflects my parochial language training. Persons trained in the United States and persons trained in other countries write differently.[7] Whereas Americans are more comfortable declaring, "Moderate political leaders, statist elites, secularist elements of civil society and powerful economic stakeholders demand courts take on a religion taming role," Hirschl's original draft declared "The demand for taking on that religion-taming emanates from moderate political leaders . . . " (Ch. 12). In both instances, the author has identified the human agents making the demands. Frequently, a contributor, after penning a passive-voice sentence of the form, "Constitutional protections for labor were demanded," later in the paragraph or in the next paragraph, flags the human agents demanding those same constitutional protections for labor. In short, we seem to have questions of style rather than substance.

Nevertheless, the circumstances under which many contributors employ the passive voice suggests something more serious than a debate between American and foreign English teachers. In too many cases, the contributors never specify the human agents or they do not specify the agents until much later in the essay. As important, almost all the passive constructions appear when the contributors discuss the prequel to the judicial decisions. Constitutions are ratified, but judges hand down decisions. Issues are placed on the judicial agenda, but political activists proposed constitutional amendments reversing offensive judicial edicts. Consider Kapiszewski, Silverstein, and Kagan's sentence from the Introduction, previously noted: "Several chapters in this book illustrate ways in which courts have been called on to play, and have played, this new judicial role." The sentence does not

---

[7] My colleague, Michael Van Alstine, informs me that lawyers trained in Germany frequently use the passive voice.

specify who has called on courts to play this new judicial role, but asserts in the active voice that courts are playing this new role. Human agency in this paragraph and many others in this volume begins only when justices issue rulings.

Several contributors have other common habits that obscure human agency in the constitutional politics that takes place before judges decide cases, even when the authors use the active voice. Too often, the specified agent is not human. Scholars attribute agency to texts and institutions, rather than to government officials or political activists. Manoj Mate's rough draft tells us that the "Indian Supreme Court was armed by the Indian Constitution with the power of judicial review," and that "the Constituent Assembly intended the Court to serve as a weaker, subservient institution" (Ch. 10 in this volume). We do not learn whether participants in the Constituent Assembly contested judicial review or the role of courts, the nature of those contests, the relevant partisan divisions, and how the structure of the Indian judiciary reflects the outcome of those contests. The Constitution and constitutional provisions on the judiciary just happened. In other instances, important events take place without any cause, human or otherwise. Reichman (Ch. 9 in this volume) begins his discussion of constitutional politics in Israel with a wonderful analysis of the political forces that prevented that nation from developing a constitution with robust judicial review. He then discusses the politics responsible for two Basic Laws and the campaign, led by Justice Aharon Barak, to use these laws as a means to bring robust judicial review to Israel. Several pages later, Reichman notes, almost in passing, that Barak became the chief justice of Israel. That appointment, apparently, just happened. Readers learn nothing about the process by which Barack became chief justice, about the persons who supported that appointment, or the opposition, if any, to Barak's elevation. This silence is remarkable given the obvious significance of the human decision to promote to chief justice the most prominent champion of robust constitutional review in the nation.

Students of constitutional politics should write in ways that recognize how human agency occurs whenever constitutions are framed and ratified, judges are appointed and promoted, and issues are placed on the judicial agenda. Breaking such common habits as using the passive voice and attributing agency to texts is the first step in this endeavor. Sometimes commentators need only pen sentences that remind readers that crucial features of constitutional politics do not just happen. The assertion, "The French legislature, by a party-line vote, conferred jurisdiction on the Cours de Cassation" better highlights the constitutional politics of jurisdiction than, "French law conferred jurisdiction" or "Jurisdiction was conferred," even if the author is uninterested in the constitutional politics of jurisdiction. Often, the reminder that constitutional politics always takes place in the active voice may help scholars look for human agency they might otherwise miss. I suspect there is an important story about how Aharon Barak became chief justice in Israel, one that will reveal a good deal about why Israeli courts became more powerful during the 1990s.

REGIME POLITICS

Proponents of the regime politics school of thought in political science self-consciously deny judicial agency. The strongest versions of regime politics theory insist that constitutional courts have little independent influence on constitutional politics. Robert Kagan (Ch. 8 in this volume) asserts, "Regime theorists see high courts not primarily as politically powerful 'principals' but as 'agents' whose decisions...generally reflect the preferences of the political leaders who appointed them." "In regime theory," he continues, "the judges may appear to be the engineer driving the legal or constitutional train, but political leaders have built the track...deciding what direction they want the train to go."[8] Tom Keck bluntly describes proponents of regime politics as asserting "that governing coalitions dictate the results of the Court's decisions."[9] This powerful version of regime politics is most often articulated by critics of that approach to constitutional politics.[10] Nevertheless, some prominent proponents of regime politics make only slightly weaker claims. Bradley Joondeph writes, "Those forces that currently dominate American politics typically construct the Court's power and substantive views. As a result, the Court tends to function more as a policy-making partner of the ascendant political majority – or at least an influential segment of that majority – than as an independent check on the political process."[11] Terri Peretti endorses a regimes politics approach that "focus(es) on the incentives and power of politicians to construct courts in particular ways that would benefit the ruling regime."[12] "Rather than a check on majority power," Cornell Clayton and Mitchell Pickerill declare, "the federal courts often function as arenas for extending, legitimizing, harmonizing, or protecting the policy agenda of political elites or groups within the dominant governing coalition."[13] Mate (Ch. 10 in this volume) asserts that the Indian judiciary in the 1980s acted as a "'regime' Court" when "it performed the role of an 'agent' of the central government, reigning in lawlessness and the arbitrariness of state and local governments and the bureaucracy."[14]

This strong, perhaps straw man, version of regime politics conceives of government as an ant colony where all units have identical values. A dominant national coalition

---

[8] Robert A. Kagan, "A Consequential Court: The U.S. Supreme Court in the 20th Century," pp. 219–220.

[9] Thomas M. Keck, "Party Politics or Judicial Independence? The Regime Politics Literature Hits the Law Schools," *Law and Social Inquiry* 32: 511, 517 (2007).

[10] See Amanda Hollis-Brusky, "Support Structures and Constitutional Change: Teles, Southworth, and the Conservative Legal Movement," *Law and Social Inquiry* 36: 516, 518 (2011).

[11] Bradley W. Joondeph, "Judging and Self-Presentation: Toward a More Realistic Conception of the Human (Judicial) Animal," *Santa Clara Law Review* 48: 523, 553 (2008).

[12] Terri Peretti, "Constructing the State Action Doctrine, 1940–990," *Law & Social Inquiry* 35: 273, 275 (2010).

[13] Cornell W. Clayton and J. Mitchell Pickerill, "The Politics of Criminal Justice: How the New Right Regime Shaped the Rehnquist Court's Criminal Justice Jurisprudence," *Georgetown Law Journal* 94: 1385, 1391 (2006).

[14] See also Tom Ginsburg and Tamir Moustafa, *Rule by Law: The Politics of Courts in Authoritarian Regimes* (Cambridge University Press: New York, 2008), p. 4.

controls every governing institution. All government officials either endorse in full the political agenda and constitutional vision of the dominant coalition or believe that their job description requires them to act as agents of the dominant coalition. Persons employed by the Department of Defense (ants 327,047–368,031) and the national judiciary (ants 437,911–476,201) agree on such matters as the proper distribution of power between the national executive and legislature, the vices and virtues of capital punishment, and the merits of assassination attempts on known terrorist leaders. Courts and other institutions are consequential in this political universe only because of the division of labor – the ants that staff various institutions develop specialized skills for achieving shared regime goals. Navy SEALS and federal judges may agree on the virtue of hunting down Osama bin Laden, but the former are likely more able to perform the job successfully than the latter. A dominant national coalition whose members unanimously agree that murderers and only murderers should be executed may think that the persons who staff the legal system have special capacities to identify those murderers who ought to be executed.[15]

One problem with this strong version of regime politics is that dominant national coalitions are never composed of identical worker ants. Power is frequently divided among more than one political party. Political parties may share power or alternate in power so frequently that they share power for all practical purposes. In presidential systems, control over the national executive and legislature may be divided. In federal systems, control over national and state institutions may be divided. Even when one party controls all government institutions, party members are likely to have different policy agendas and constitutional visions. The Democratic Party that won landslide victories in all American elections held between 1932 and 1944 housed both the leading proponents and opponents of racial segregation in the United States. Recent controversies over the staffing of the Constitutional Court of South Africa highlight sharp rifts within the dominant African National Congress. Trochev (Ch. 2 in this volume) details how justices may defect from a former dominant national coalition when events weaken the authority of a previous political elite or splinter the political coalition in power.

The balance of power in the national judiciary when no monolithic, dominant national coalition exists is unlikely to mirror the balance of power in other governing institutions or the national government as a whole. The judicial selection process in many countries privileges appointees whose opinions cannot be fully ascertained on the issues that divide the governing elite. National courts, therefore, are often staffed by judges whose precise policy commitments and constitutional visions cannot be precisely determined in advance of crucial rulings. Persons hoping to gain an appointment to the Supreme Court of the United States are well advised not to reveal whether they believe bans on abortion or same-sex marriage constitutional.

---

[15] Courts may also be consequential in the ant colony regime if the public regards judicial decisions as more legitimate than decisions handed down by other institutions. Why the public in the ant colony regime would make this institutional distinction, however, is not clear.

If a particular government institution exercises disproportionate control over the staffing of judicial institutions, the courts will more likely reflect the balance of power in that institution than in the government as a whole. Klug (Ch. 3 in this volume) details how President Mandela used the judicial appointment process to buttress his distinctive constitutional vision for South Africa. Justices are almost always selected from the legal elite of the country. The more the legal elite influence the judicial selection process, the more likely the justices will reflect the sensibilities of whatever legal complex exists in that society. In Chile, Scribner details how "a judicial culture of legalism and institutional and ideological conservatism" braked judicial tendencies to accept invitations to make wide-ranging constitutional rulings (Ch. 4 in this volume). Mitchel Lasser notes that in Europe, a developing legal culture committed to protect fundamental human rights is influencing both national judiciaries and the European Court of Justice (Ch. 11 in this volume). Ran Hirschl (Ch. 12 in this volume) notes how justices in Islamic constitutional theocracies share the secular commitments of most legal elites in those polities.

Specialized judicial education and training provide further reasons why courts are not likely to mirror other governing institutions. Judges and lawyers view problems, at least in part, using distinctive legal lenses. Klug notes how liberal justices in South Africa perceive legal barriers to judicial decisions implementing social rights that do not seem as pressing to some liberal social workers. Justices have distinctive experiences as justices that shape their policy and constitutional commitments. A judge who hears numerous appeals from decisions imposing capital punishment may become more or less opposed to the death penalty, as well as develop greater expertise in identifying murderers.

Regime politics theory deviates from the original purpose of scholarship demonstrating that judicial review is politically constructed.[16] That literature detailed how politics structured and constrained opportunities for justices to exercise agency. The basic idea was that if the dominant coalition consisted of members of factions A, B, and C, then justices were usually free to pursue policies preferred by most members of any of these factions. What justices could not do was pursue a policy preferred by members of faction D that was not preferred by any sizeable number of members

---

[16] The classics include Ran Hirschl, *Toward Juristocracy: The Origins and Consequences of the New Constitutionalism* (Cambridge, MA: Harvard University Press, 2004); George I. Lovell, *Legislative Deferrals: Statutory Ambiguity, Judicial Power, and American Democracy* (New York: Cambridge University Press, 2003); Kevin J. McMahon, *Reconsidering Roosevelt on Race: How the Presidency Paved the Road to Brown* (Chicago: University of Chicago Press, 2004); Keith Whittington, *Political Foundations of Judiciary Supremacy: The Presidency, the Supreme Court, and Constitutional Leadership in U.S. History* (Princeton: Princeton University Press, 2007); Paul Frymer, "Acting When Elected Officials Won't: Federal Courts and Civil Rights Enforcement in U.S. Labor Unions, 1935–85," *American Political Science Review* 97: 483 (2003); Howard Gillman, "How Political Parties Can Use the Courts to Advance their Agendas: Federal Courts in the United States, 1875–1891," *American Political Science Review* 96: 511 (2002); Mark A. Graber, "The Nonmajoritarian Difficulty: Legislative Deference to the Judiciary," *Studies in American Political Development* 7: 35 (1993). For one summary of this literature, see Mark A. Graber, "Constructing Judicial Review," *Annual Reviews in Political Science* 8: 425 (2005).

of factions A, B, or C. This is the meaning of Robert Dahl's famous claim, "The policy views dominant on the Court are never for long out of line with the policy vies dominant among the lawmaking majorities of the United States."[17]

In sharp contrast to regime politics theory, scholars who maintain judicial review is politically constructed recognize that the numerous occasions on which the political elite are divided provide substantial opportunities for judicial agency. At times, the dominant coalition is so united that judicial decisions could be predicted from the structure of that coalition. More often, in ways that are sometimes predictable and sometimes surprising, judicial decisions help some governing elites achieve their policy agenda and constitutional visions, at the same time placing obstacles in the path of alternative policy agendas and constitutional visions championed by other governing elites. When allocating power between the national executive and national legislature, for example, the Tribunal Constitucional in Chile was choosing which government institution to support to what degree, and was neither an agent of other governing elites nor a check on the power of the government as a whole.

Courts are simultaneously exceptional and normal institutions. Courts are exceptional because the process for staffing the judiciary differs from the process for staffing other government institutions, most justices think of themselves as members of a distinctive profession, and justices must use distinctively legal logics when justifying their judicial decisions. Courts are normal institutions because slightly edited versions of the last sentence describe many government agencies. The persons who staff the Farm Bureau or central national bank are probably selected in ways that differ from the selection process used for staffing other government institutions; many think of themselves as members of a distinctive profession and they often rely on distinctive professional logics when justifying decisions. These common differences between governing institutions suggest that few, if any, will be mere agents for the dominant national coalition and few, if any, will consistently hand down decisions that challenge all other governing elites. Rather, courts and other governing decisions are consequential because their decisions promote the policy agendas and constitutional visions of some governing elites at the expense of those championed by other governing elites. Courts differ from other governing institutions because, given methods of judicial selection and judicial socialization as lawyers, judges are likely to privilege a different set of governing elites than, say, the persons who staff the Farm Bureau or national bank.

FRAGMENTATION AND GRIDLOCK

Many essays in this volume attach powerful casual significance to political fragmentation. In the volume's Introduction, Kapiszewski, Silverstein, and Kagan note that

---

[17] Robert Dahl, "Decisionmaking in a Democracy: The Supreme Court as a National Policy-Maker," *Journal of Public Law* 6: 285 (1957).

"the degree to which political authority and power are concentrated or fragmented" is one of the "relatively enduring features of the institutional and political structure within which courts operate" that "often influence[s] the roles they play." Scribner agrees that "political fragmentation affords judges greater room for maneuvering" (Ch. 4 in this volume). Several contributors suggest that political fragmentation empowers judges by paralyzing political coalitions and other governing institutions. Scribner notes that one consequence of political fragmentation during the period when Chile became a democracy was that "neither the government nor the opposition could mount a politically credible threat against" the national judiciary. Mónica Castillejos-Aragón (Ch. 5 in this volume) reaches a similar conclusion when she asserts, "when there are multiple competing parties, those parties are less likely to override judicial decisions through legislation or reshape the courts through changing personnel, allowing courts to become powerful and act as an autonomous branch of government. Thus, the greater the fragmentation in the Executive and Legislative branches, the more likely it is that courts will rule against the government and engage in policy-making." John Ferejohn (Ch. 14 in this volume) concludes that the Dutch and Italian cases discussed in this volume fit with his general model: "Political power in both nations has been fairly fragmented among political parties throughout the postwar periods ... which permits judges to decide cases without much fear of political intervention."

Fragmentation theory reverses the political universe imaged by strong regime politics theorists. Strong regime politics theorist limits agency to political actors. Elected officials, in this view, dictate results to courts. Fragmentation theorists limit agency to courts. When politics is fragmented and gridlocked, they write, courts are free to make whatever decision the justices think best. Elected officials, in these circumstances, exercise little or no influence over the course of constitutional politics. When "Indian politics and elections shifted to an era of rule by weaker, fragmented coalition governments ... a weaker Executive (prime minister and Council of Ministers) and Parliament had diminished ability to attack and override the Indian Court" (Mate, Ch. 10 in this volume).

This common rendering of fragmentation treats constitutional politics as a wrestling match between powerful political coalitions over a Wagnerian magic ring that gives the possessor the power to make important policy or constitutional decisions. When control over electoral institutions is badly divided, all the contestants in the wrestling match can do is prevent the others from gaining power. Although the contestants immobilize each other, some bystander, in this case a court, takes the magic ring without much opposition. Each participant in the electoral wrestling match, standing alone, is strong enough to prevent the court from advancing a distinctive legal or constitutional agenda. The problem is that each wrestler is so immobilized by the other wrestlers that none has the capacity to prevent a third party from possessing the precious object of desire.

This vision of electoral politics as a deadlocked wrestling match wrongly assumes the sole goal of all political coalitions in legislative politics is to defeat their rivals. Until some political coalition gains a decisive electoral victory, commentary sometimes treats policy as in a state of suspended animation where nothing happens or changes. Chief Justice Harlan Fiske Stone of the United States Supreme Court noted one problem with this notion that politics stands still in his famous *Miller v. Schoene* opinion. The issue in that case was whether Virginia could cut down cedar trees that contained a fungus deadly to nearby apple trees. When sustaining the Virginia decision, Stone asserted:

> On the evidence we may accept the conclusion of the Supreme Court of Appeals that the state was under the necessity of making a choice between the preservation of one class of property and that of the other wherever both existed in dangerous proximity. It would have been none the less a choice if, instead of enacting the present statute, the state, by doing nothing, had permitted serious injury to the apple orchards within its borders to go on unchecked.[18]

The politics of legislative inaction, Stone recognized, has consequences. Had Virginia officials been unable to reach any decision, the apple trees would have died. The persons who owned cedar trees in Virginia, aware of this natural consequence, did not need to defeat the persons who owned apple trees in hand-to-hand electoral combat. Political inaction favored their interests as much as favorable legislation.

National legislative deadlocks often empower other governing institutions with decided proclivities. The congressional inability to pass antilynching legislation left Southern states free to determine how to police that behavior. Prominent white supremacists in the Senate were content to filibuster civil rights legislation because they understood that national legislative paralysis ensured that persons committed to Jim Crow made civil rights policies in the former slave states. Courts, as the literature on fragmentation repeatedly notes, thrive when legislative politics is paralyzed. For this reason, political coalitions that believe they are likely to obtain favorable judicial rules have strong incentives to stalemate legislatures. As long as a pro-choice majority sits on the Supreme Court of the United States, proponents of legal abortion can deploy resources to prevent legislative defeats rather than focus exclusively on gaining legislative victories.

This analysis of the politics of deadlock suggests that the better metaphor is a wrestling match between two schools, rather than between two individuals. Just as participants in legislative struggles may be aware that a judicial decision is likely to favor particular interests, so the individuals who wrestle in the early matches recognize that one team is heavily favored to win the later matches. This knowledge influences practice. One side must go all out for victories or pins in the legislative

[18] *Miller v. Schoene*, 276 U.S. 272, 279 (1928).

contests or early matches. The other may be content to just not lose, knowing that a deadlock in the legislature or early matches will likely give their side the ultimate victory. What appears to the outsider as a deadlock or tie, in these circumstances, is often a victory for the party favored in the downstream contests.

Ran Hirschl's hegemonic preservation thesis offers an account of political agency, even when legislatures are seemingly paralyzed. "[W]hen their policy preferences have been, or are likely to be, increasingly challenged in majoritarian decision-making arenas," his account of constitutional politics maintains, "elites that possess disproportionate access to, and influence over, the legal arena may initiate a constitutional entrenchment of rights and judicial review in order to transfer power to supreme courts."[19] Hegemonic preservation initially requires conventional political victories. A party in relative control of the national government must, through a combination of constitutional reform, legislation, and judicial appointments, empower courts to resolve certain disputes, ensure that persons sympathetic to their policy agenda and constitutional vision staff the national judiciary, and create a series of legislative veto points that make politically difficult legislative attacks on judicial rulings. The second phase of hegemonic preservation requires the successful coalition to maintain a legislative deadlock, so that no political coalition is able to undo that coalition's initial victories. During this time period, the previously dominant faction will be more interested in preventing rivals from passing legislation than in taking any positive action. Fighting under the banner of judicial independence, the formerly dominant elite power may prefer stalemating politics, confident that (just as) good policy will be made in the national legislature. The more veto points the originally powerful coalition built into constitutional politics in the initial phase, the less power that declining coalition needs in the second phase to exercise substantial control over constitutional development.

The papers in this volume, although not exploring as fully as I might like the agency inherent in much legislative gridlock, nevertheless provide evidence that such agency frequently takes place. Trochev notes, "Fragmentation in [former Soviet] regimes allows judges to shield the judiciary's informal system of promoting and sanctioning judges from interference by authoritarian rulers, and defect from the ruling regime when they sense that the incumbents are too weak to punish them and incoming leaders are strong enough to protect them" (Ch. 2 in this volume). The opposition leaders need not be strong enough on their own to subdue the authoritarians. They need only the political strength necessary to prevent executive and legislative attacks on the courts. Mate begins his essay on constitutional politics in India by suggesting that fragmentation prevents all politicians from passing legislation that influences the path of the law. Readers soon learn that many prominent Indians have little interest in such legislation. The Janata Party and many prominent

---

[19] Ran Hirschl, *Toward Juristocracy: The Origins and Consequences of the New Constitutionalism* (Cambridge, MA: Harvard University Press, 2004), p. 12.

elites have been steadfast supporters of the course of judicial politics in India (Ch. 10 in this volume). What appears to the uninformed eye to be legislative paralysis may be a successful effort on the part of the political actors and coalitions that support judicial power to prevent rival coalitions from altering the balance of power in the Indian judiciary or transferring power from Indian judiciary to an institution likely to pursue a contrary policy agenda and constitutional vision. At the very least, the examples of India, the former Soviet Republic, and many of Hirschl's case studies suggest scholars of constitutional politics should consider that fragmented politics is the goal of some political movements and not only a condition that prevents any political movement from realizing distinctive constitutional visions.

COURTS AND JUDGES

Courts are the unsurprising subject of *Consequential Courts*. The contributors to the volume are interested in whether courts are consequential, how courts are consequential, and the conditions under which courts are consequential. When they discuss judicial action, they use the active voice. The Introduction to this volume declares, "When courts play these new roles in ways that depart from political leaders' preferences, they can exert a significant, independent, and distinctively judicial influence on broad realms of public policy, redistributing political authority." Kagan (Ch. 8 in this volume) concludes that the Supreme Court of the United States "was in itself a consequential participant in legal change and national governance." Many essays consistently attribute agency to national judiciaries. Reichman (Ch. 9 in this volume) states, "The Court ensured that any future political debate on the last remaining major item on the agenda of the Zionist movement would start from a position that Israel already had a Constitution, albeit an incomplete one, and judicial review is part of it." Mate (Ch. 10 in this volume) declares, "The Indian Court wrested control over judicial appointments from the Executive."

Perhaps because of the volume title and ambitions, the previous essays rarely attribute agency to individual judges. Contributors discuss Court decisions, not judicial votes or opinions. Readers can be excused for thinking the vast majority of cases the authors discuss were decided unanimously or that divisions within a court are unimportant for political science analysis. Kagan takes the most common position in the volume when he baldly asserts, "The Court extended that right to counsel to misdemeanor cases, juvenile court proceedings, and the police station house – requiring state and local law enforcement officials to inform arrested suspects of their right to silence and a lawyer before interrogating them," not pointing out that all these cases were decided by a divided court. Mate notes in passing that the Supreme Court of India decided *Golak Nath v. Union of India* 6:5 (Ch. 10 in this volume), and that each of the eleven justices in *Kesavanada Bharati v. State of Kerula* (1973) issued an opinion. These divisions, however, play no role in his discussion of the function of the Indian judiciary. We do not learn whether the divisions on the Supreme Court of India or another national tribunal are similar or different than divisions in the rest of the political system. The focus is on the agency courts exercise as a monolithic institution, not on the agency exercised by the persons who staff judicial institutions.

Judges exercise agency in ways that courts cannot. Justices vote and write opinions. Chief Justice Hughes wrote a letter to the Senate Judiciary Committee, refuting President Franklin Roosevelt's claim that the Supreme Court was overworked. Chief Justice Aharon Barak gave speeches and wrote articles defending an independent judiciary with the power of constitutional review. Courts cannot perform any of these actions. Most important, individual justices often have or form relationships with some political actors in other governing institutions, relationships that may not be fully appreciated by scholarship that attributes agency primarily to courts.

Judges in the modern world rarely think of themselves politically only as judges. They may identify with political parties, even if they do not retain membership. They may support a variety of political causes. As such, they may form alliances or part- nerships with other political actors in other institutions who support those parties or causes. Sometimes, these are true partnerships, where judges and other government officials work together to draw up joint plans of action. Supreme Court Justice Joseph Story regularly drafted legislation for political supporters in the national legislature to introduce in Congress. More often, persons who share a similar policy agenda and constitutional vision work to strengthen their supporters in other institutions, even if they do not actually meet to jointly prepare a strategy. Justices may decide voting-rights cases in ways likely to bring more supporters of their preferred political party to the polls. Once elected, those party members may augment the number of their supporters in the federal judiciary.

These observations suggest that a number of essays in this volume might have focused as much on political movements as courts. Consider how Robert Kagan's essay (Ch. 8 in this volume) might have been recast as a study of a certain strand of American liberalism. Kagan might have begun by noting that the liberal coali- tion that came to power in 1932 was united in the belief that the national govern- ment ought to have the power to resolve all national economic crises. This goal could be achieved by a combination of passing appropriate legislation, threatening the court, and then staffing all judicial openings with persons known to favor the liberal understanding of federal power. Liberals were, however, divided on such matters as racial segregation and free speech. One divide was over policy: Roosevelt Democrats disputed the merits of desegregation and restrictions on anti-Communist speech. On race, for a long time these disputes meant that the national government would do little for persons of color. Nevertheless, many racial liberals were able to do an end-run around Congress to the federal judiciary.[20] They were able to

---

[20] See Gordon Silverstein, *Law's Allure: How Law Shapes, Constrains, Saves, and Kills Politics* (New York: Cambridge University Press, 2009) pp. 17–21.

do so in part because the presidential wing of both parties was more committed to racial liberalism than the legislative wing of either party, at least before 1960, and in part because the American legal complex by 1940 was increasingly committed to abolishing Jim Crow and providing greater protection for speech rights. The result was a federal judiciary that was far more sympathetic to racial liberalism and progressive free-speech rights than any other national institution. A second divide over law soon emerged. Some racial liberals on the Supreme Court, most notably Justice William O. Douglas, were committed to using judicial power to advance many causes associated with progressive liberalism. Others, whose policy commitments did not differ substantially – most notable Justice Felix Frankfurter – insisted that liberal justices should defer to illiberal decisions made by elected officials. At this point, the narrative would detail the variety of political and legal decisions that resulted in a liberalism that by 1960 was committed to racial equality, free speech, and the use of judicial power to protect those rights.

Many of the other papers in this volume might be similarly recast. The Klug essay on South Africa (Ch. 3 in this volume) and the Lasser essay on fundamental rights in France and the European Union (Ch. 11 in this volume) seem particularly good candidates for this treatment. Heinz Klug declares that his purpose is to "provide insight into the way in which courts and judges have entered into national political life, and what difference their participation has made in the construction of constitutional democracy in South Africa." My proposed alternative would begin with the persons who constructed constitutional democracy in South Africa, to examine the role of the legal complex in that founding, to see how these founders sought to empower the court, explore how the court sought to realize their mutual vision, and determine the extent to which that vision was influenced by the decision to vest so much power in a court. Rather than talk about judicial functions in the abstract, we would talk about a shared vision of the judicial function, who shared that vision, how those political actors attempted to implement that vision, and the extent to which they succeeded. The Lasser chapter is similarly about the fundamental-rights revolution in Europe, rather than an essay about judicial functions. Again, that essay might be recast along the same dimensions as the Kagan (Ch. 8 in this volume) and Klug essays. Who was in the coalition that sought to introduce greater protections for certain fundamental rights in both France and Europe? How did the presence of lawyers in the coalition influence the policy agenda and constitutional vision of that coalition? To what extent did existing understandings of judicial functions influence the role of courts in that coalition, and to what extent did that coalition seek to fashion new judicial roles? What explains the various successes and failures of that coalition?

Judges, these essays suggest, may be best understood as participants in liberal political and constitutional movements. Judges throughout the world have led, followed, supported, and built on various liberal efforts. "Participant" seems more accurate than "partner" because justices often do not collaborate or engage in concerted action with liberals in other governing institutions. Indeed, Kagan notes that liberal judicial decisions sometimes create backlash or otherwise have consequences that adversely influence liberal political movements outside of the courts (Ch. 8 in this volume).

Judges better capture agency than do courts. To begin with, many judges have identified with constitutional and political liberalism. Courts as institutions do not identify in such a way (although others may identify a court as a "liberal" or "conservative" one). More important, the emphasis on individuals highlights how most of the time the majority of institutions are fragmented, and that the divisions within judicial institutions bear a family resemblance to divisions within other governing institutions. For this reason, we might suspect that some judicial roles should be the consequence of judges behaving as judges and some judicial roles the consequence of judges behaving as liberals. Better yet, as students of intersectionality point out with respect to race and gender,[21] a liberal judge is no more a combination of discrete liberal and judge elements than a lesbian black woman is simply an amalgam of lesbian, black, and woman.

OF JUDGES AND LIBERALS

Military and political strategists recognize that where a battle is fought is often more important than how the battle is fought. Victory is won by the general who places the right number of soldiers and weapons at the point of the attack, not the commander with the most men and weapons. Political and constitutional victories are similarly often gained before the actual fighting takes place. Much of politics involves maneuvering over which institution will make decisions, efforts to control those institutions most likely to make decisions, and efforts to preserve the autonomy of those institutions that one does control.

One purpose of this essay is to identify the techniques and concepts that obscure this dimension of constitutional politics so we can better assess the nature of judicial agency. In particular, these pages urge authors to emphasize agency, to stop thinking of all-powerful courts or all-powerful elected officials, and to look at the relationships that form between persons in different institutions who share a similar policy agenda and constitutional vision. A liberal judge is different than a liberal legislator. We lose the distinctiveness of courts when we lump all liberals together into an amorphous blob. We nevertheless miss a good deal of what judges do when we write as if they always act as judges and never as liberals or, better yet, liberal judges.

The other purpose of this essay is to turn the spotlight on liberal courts rather than generic courts. Virtually all of the contributors in this volume discuss the efforts of liberals to empower courts or of judges to implement a liberal constitutional vision.

---

[21] See Kimberle Crenshaw, "Demarginalizing the Intersection of Race and Sex," *University of Chicago Legal Forum* 139 (1989).

In order to implement their vision, liberals to some degree had to change judicial functions. Courts in the United States that had previously been considered a bulwark for property rights suddenly developed special capacities to listen to voices from the margins. This reliance on courts may also have changed liberalism. One senses notions of fundamental rights changing so that these rights become the sort of entities that can be implemented by a judiciary. These observations suggest that even if Martin Shapiro is right in concluding that we are far from developing a general theory of judicial power, these essays bring us a good deal closer to developing a theory of liberal judges.

16

The Mighty Problem Continues

*Martin Shapiro**

In 1979, Mauro Cappelletti entitled a pioneering comparative study "The Mighty Problem" of constitutional judicial review. Since then, review has become even mightier and even more problematic in a number of ways, as noted in the Introduction to this volume and its subsequent chapters. Initially, the problem was largely seen as a normative one about the compatibility between majoritarian democracy and a judicial veto power over legislation. Put somewhat differently, a strong measure of judicial independence might be a prerequisite to judicial review as an instrument for limiting government and protecting rights. Such review necessarily involved some judicial lawmaking. In a democracy, lawmakers should be accountable to the electorate. How could judicial independence and accountability for lawmaking be accommodated to one another? At a more rough-and-ready empirical level, when, where, and why did the powers that be – whoever they might be – allow a handful of judges without purse or sword to get away with making major policy decisions? For as this volume insists, judicial review courts are often consequential.

Let us suppose that we wished to construct a causal model or theory for relatively long-term, successful judicial review. By success, I mean a reviewing court with some decisions entailing substantial changes in public policy that are obeyed by other policy makers and implementers. Although this volume seems to yearn for a developmental model, suppose instead we attempted a more static model to state in a parsimonious way the necessary and/or sufficient conditions under which relatively long-term, successful judicial review would, or at least could, flourish.

At the time of World War II, three countries had successful constitutional judicial review, or something close to it: the United States, Canada, and Australia. (British statutes served as surrogates for constitutions in the two dominions.) Thus, the number of possible necessary and/or sufficient preconditions for review appeared to be few: democracy, the common law tradition, a written constitution (with or

* James W. and Isabel Coffroth Professor of Law (Emeritus), Berkeley Law, UC Berkeley.

without a Bill of Rights), and federalism. Given that Switzerland also had a form of review, federalism seemed the most prominent candidate for both necessary and sufficient condition.

Subsequent to World War II, the number of polities, both natural and transnational, that adopted judicial review multiplied dramatically. As the multiplication occurred, the set of candidates for necessary and/or sufficient preconditions for review also multiplied dramatically. At first, federalism seemed to hold up pretty well even as a necessary condition. The postwar German and Italian Constitutions contained strong federal elements and provided for review. Specifically, free–trade-enforcing judicial review occurred in the new European Economic Communities (now European Union [EU]) institutions and World Trade Organization and North American Free Trade Agreement judicial panels. Alas, we have also learned that formal federalism alone does not assure successful judicial review as the new experience of the Russian federation and even the new Canadian constitutional experience has shown, and the Mexican experience has long indicated. (Quebec fairly often negates review on language questions.) Only federalisms to which all members are strongly committed may be sufficient causes of successful review. More importantly, a number of unitary states such as France have introduced review. So federalism does not appear to be a necessary condition for review.

As to the other early identified preconditions, the whole message of this volume is that as the numbers of review polities increases, the necessity and sufficiency of each suggested independent variable fades away. At least one state without a written constitution, Israel, has judicial review. The UK, famously without a written constitution, has accepted European Court of Justice and European Court of Human Rights Review. This volume, as Ginsburg's contribution (Ch. 1 in this volume) immediately points out, presents review in both democratic and democratizing countries. In some of them at least judicial review may be as much or more a cause as an effect of democracy – South Africa being perhaps the best example (Klug, Ch. 3 in this volume). Other contributions to the volume remind us that effective judicial review, in an arguably perverted form, can even exist in very shaky democracies and nondemocratic regimes.

When German and Italian review came along, they could be attributed to federalism, but such an attribution would, even then, have seemed deliberately blind to the historical experience out of which they came. Surely judicial developments in those countries were more motivated by a concern for protecting individual or human rights than free-trade federalism. The new Canadian Constitution, whose adoption was debated largely in terms of federalism, nevertheless contained rights provisions that have subsequently generated a lot of review. Similarly, the new French Constitution was centrally about the division of powers between the presidency and prime minister – Cabinet and Parliament. It did not even contain a Bill of Rights, but eventually the French Constitutional Council so felt the need of one for judicial review purposes that it invented one and stuck it in the Constitution.

The now-global religion of human rights, with or without written bills of rights, now surely takes center stage among the putative causes of review.

Similar to federalism, constitutional division of powers among branches or institutions of central government at first glance seems a promising candidate – or at least one of an assortment of alternative necessary conditions – for successful review. Indeed, the recent tendency toward the constituting of quasi-presidential systems in which lawmaking power is divided between legislature and president, à la Francais, might seem to necessitate a reviewing court to police the problematic dividing line. However, active policing by the judiciary of the boundary between legislative and executive branches would repeatedly pit the reviewing court against one or the other of the two very–much-more powerful institutions of the central government, and often against the major political party or coalition of parties that controlled it.

The relatively low profile of the U.S. Supreme Court in reviewing a conventional division of powers Executive-Legislature format and the Chilean Court in the quasi-presidential format tends to sap our confidence in division of powers as a condition of successful review. The Argentine experience might also be cited. However, to the extent that separation of powers often leads to divided government that cannot easily pass legislation or take other action to "correct" a decision of the constitutional court, separation of powers may facilitate review by undercutting the retaliatory capacity of the so called political branches.

So, more and more constitutional judicial review shows up in more and more places. For scholars, the result is that more and more variables in more and more combinations suggest themselves as causes or preconditions or independent variables generating review. This volume was inspired by and contributes to the difficulty of arriving at a parsimonious theory of the origins and maintenance of successful constitutional judicial review. Indeed, it seeks to complicate the question by subdividing "judicial activism" into a variety of different roles in governance.

The origins of or motivations for the establishment of constitutions and review is much debated. That debate remains of great historical interest. In the contemporary world, however, every new country must have a constitution, just as it must have a flag and a national anthem. Today, the origin of constitutions, similar to the pockets on jeans, is a matter of mere fashion. A few years ago, the same thing might be said of the origins of Bills of Rights within constitutions. Today, that fashion is being rivaled in some parts of the world by the constitutional insertion of Islam – which may or may not be antithetical to rights. So the question now is much less why do polities proclaim constitutions and bills of rights, and much more why, when, where, and how over time some constitutions actually limit government and protect rights. It may well be – as some contributors to this volume and others have argued – that constitutions, cum bills of rights, cum judicial review, were instituted in some politics because then-dominant political elites saw a constitution as a means of insuring their own future political and economic interests. In other polities, however, they have been instituted simply as declarations of nationhood. In both varieties, the crucial question is under what conditions the constitutions, cum rights, cum review actually work to preserve interests by limiting government. The examples in which they don't work are myriad and dissolve into the broadest questions of when democratization works or doesn't work. Indeed, even where democratization works, constitutions, cum rights, cum review may not serve the interests they were intended to serve. For instance, the Chilean constitutional protections of private property may not have achieved the capitalist glories intended by the Chicago boys, and whether the South African Constitution will protect white agricultural property remains touch and go.

THE COSTS AND BENEFITS OF REVIEW

Nearly every contribution to this volume addresses a central question of constitutional judicial review; sometimes directly, sometimes by implication. No matter what its origins in a particular polity or the intentions of its originators, why are so many people in so many countries willing to allow major policy decisions to be made by a handful of (usually lawyer) judges?

The answer for authoritarian states is relatively easy and rests on well-developed theories of complex organizations. Large, multi-task organizations such as governments depend on hierarchy and specialization. Judiciaries are specialized hierarchies designed to provide a social service that the ruled want – conflict resolution – but to provide that service in a way that communicates and enforces central government policies at grassroots levels and communicates grassroots concerns to the central government. Courts are particularly good instruments for central regime control over its localities not only because they provide a desired service to the governed but because a whole mythology of courts and judges disguises their control functions from those being controlled.

The cost to authoritarian regimes of exercising this kind of control, however, is that, in order to maintain the myth, the regime must actually grant a certain degree of independent authority to the courts. A crucial question for future research is: when can and will judges exploit the appearance of independence granted them by authoritarian regimes to actually place limits on those regimes, limits that the regimes may feel obliged to obey in order to keep up the appearance of judicial independence that remains useful to them, for instance in their attempts to attract foreign investment?

Whether a democratic, democratizing, or nondemocratic regime, the initiation and continuing support of an active constitutional judicial review court entails both benefits and costs – what I have referred to elsewhere as the "junkyard dog" phenomenon. Such a court may provide fierce long-term protection of whatever interests (rights, free trade, and divisions of power) it is set to guard, but at the cost of sometimes biting the very interests that set it loose. Presumably those interests will let it run free, so long as they deem its guard functions worth the bites. Thus, one surely necessary condition for successful constitutional judicial review is that the court itself must have sufficient strategic sense to fashion its decisions in such a way that in sum and over time their benefits exceed their costs for the political regime in which the court is imbedded. This key variable is so difficult to measure and itself so variable over time for any given court that it becomes nearly impossible to propose a relatively specific, predictive model of the conditions necessary for successful review. Indeed, such efforts tend to become circular, with successful courts said to have exercised good strategies and unsuccessful ones not having done so.

SUPPLYING AND DEMANDING REVIEW

Even if we could achieve a table or more likely a spreadsheet of exterior conditions conducive to constitutional judicial review, we would not be able to accurately predict when such review would occur. A constitutional court capable of review must still choose to exercise review for it to occur. So a number of studies presented here pay attention to the background, training, ideologies, and career patterns of judges that may then lead to judicial activism. Of course, there is a fairly long U.S. tradition of studies linking party affiliation to judicial voting, but one not easily applied to those many nations in which judicial voting is not revealed.

More recent, and clearly present in this volume, is concern for judicial "leadership." Whether active judicial review occurs at any given time for any given court may depend in considerable part on whether one or more members of the court – not necessarily its chief – marshals the court into judicial action and displays sufficient strategic sense to get away with it.

So the question is not only what can a given court get away with at a given time, but what does it want to get away with. Obviously, part of the answer to the "want to" question lies in such internal factors as judicial ideology and leadership. Just as obviously, part of what a court wants to do must be determined by what it is asked to do. It is only recently that we have learned to pay great attention not only to the judge but to the judge and company. Governments respond to lobbying. Courts are lobbied by litigation. Litigation markets, the multiple, sometimes coordinated, sometimes not, decisions of many persons to demand litigation, as well as the supply of litigation opportunities provided by the courts, determines to some degree what the courts produce. To some extent, supply will seek equilibrium with demand. Courts capable of acting will to some degree act as they are asked to act.

Thus, as the Halliday contribution (Ch. 13 in this volume) reminds us, we have learned that both the levels and directions of judicial intervention are determined to some degree by the lawyers who are the traders in this market bringing together the buyers and sellers of judicial product. We rather assume that the big institutional players' – member states in constitutional federalisms, branches of government in constitutionally divided "checks and balances" governments – will have adequate representation. Insofar as constitutional review is, or could be, rights review, those concerned with judicial review have become more and more concerned with the size, shape, and relative vigor of a rights bar in the polity under study. Such a bar will not only influence what a court wants to do, it may also provide or orchestrate a level of support that enables a court to get away with what it wants to do.

THE NORMATIVE QUESTION: REVIEW AND DEMOCRACY

This volume is an empirical one. Its contributors address themselves primarily to questions of what conditions – particularly those external to the courts, but also internal ones – determine when, where, and whether successful constitutional judicial review will occur. However, it is impossible for either its writers or readers to entirely avoid normative questions, particularly because democracy, typically defined by the presence of effective party electoral competition, so often appears to be a key variable in successful review equations. In a democracy, the laws are supposed to be made by the people or their elected representatives. We know, of course, that in reality a great deal of law even in democracies is made by nonelected administrators. At least in theory, however, these administrators are under the control of elected political executives and legislatures. To the extent that "independent" nonelected judges make law, a normative problem for democracy arises. Constitutional judicial review is about the most dramatic and undeniable – although frequently denied – form of lawmaking in which courts engage. At this point, we need hardly go through the argument showing that constitutional review entails judicial vetoing of legislation and vetoing laws is as much an act of lawmaking as passing laws. It is now commonplace in the United States for 5 judicial votes to sometimes outweigh 269 Congressional ones.

In the United States, hardly a year goes by without some new book on the compatibility of constitutional judicial review with democracy. In spite of endless, ingenious, and sometime ingenuous attempts to achieve compatibility, it just can't be done. If it could, the endless succession of books would stop. Comparative studies such as those in this volume certainly enrich the discussion, but surely will not bring it to an end. Indeed, the studies presented here underline an as-yet–under-considered problem of review and democracy.

PROACTIVE AND REACTIVE REVIEW

One of many assorted responses to the democracy-review problem has been the argument that courts do not proactively seek lawmaking opportunities. They can only act when cases are brought to them, when lawmaking is thrust on them. Of course, the argument is somewhat disingenuous. By their present decisions, courts frequently signal what cases they are willing to hear next and/or that certain policy-freighted legal positions have enough chance of winning next to justify the cost of litigation. Judicial hints of what they may be willing to supply will certainly influence what is demanded; that is what is litigated.

Beyond particular supply offers, in many of the polities considered in this volume courts have at least some control over the rules of standing that govern access to the courts. In some systems, too, the courts may use "political questions," "national security," forum non conveniens, or other doctrines to exercise discretion over what they will and will not hear.

In some polities, constitutional provisions and political arrangements interact in such a way – or interest groups are so various, energetic, and well-funded – that nearly all currently relevant political issues will somehow be litigated. For instance, in France, the constitutional provision that any sixty members of the Assembly may challenge any newly enacted statute in the Constitutional Council, combined with a multiparty system that practically assures there will be at least sixty votes against any new law, results in nearly comprehensive and continuous surveillance of the whole legislative agenda by the Constitutional Council. In many industrialized, prosperous states, the array of active interest groups is so great and the bar so prolific that nearly every government initiative is litigated. The courts may only do what they are asked to do, but in some polities they are asked to do nearly everything.

This volume and other recent studies teach us, however, that there are polities where constitutional courts do not even have to wait to be asked or in practice are always asked about everything. Some constitutions provide that any citizen may bring a constitutional claim to court about any action of government. Given human nature, such provisions really mean that every policy issue will come to court and the courts must of necessity pick and choose among the endless flood. Finally, in some nations, constitutional courts are authorized *sua sponte* to take up any constitutional issue they choose to identify. Quite obviously, provisions of these sorts are designed to assure active judicial guardianship of the constitutional rights of those without the resources to mount their own challenges to invasions of their rights. In the process, however, they undercut the argument that in constitutional democracies, courts only make law when they are forced to do so in order to resolve cases thrust on them.

DECLARING THE CONSTITUTION UNCONSTITUTIONAL

Constitutional review is a peculiarly unlimited kind of judicial lawmaking, and thus peculiarly difficult to reconcile with democracy. Courts are courts of law. Their decisions are supposed to implement the law; that is, the statutes enacted by the legislature. It is impossible, however, to implement any legal text without some degree of interpretation of that text by the implementer, and thus some degree of discretionary choice by the implementer as to what the text shall actually mean in practice. So, judicial statutory interpretation inevitably and inescapably involves judicial lawmaking. Such lawmaking, however, is not a great threat to democracy because a democratically elected legislature can always amend a statute to "correct" judicial errors of statutory interpretation. Constitutional interpretation by judges is quite a different matter. Most of the world's constitutions are quite difficult to amend. Indeed, if they were very easy to amend they would lose most of their virtue, which is, after all, to limit government. So, unlike statutory interpretation, most judicial constitutional interpretation – that is, lawmaking – is final, "uncorrectable" by the elected or the electors, correctable only by further discretionary judicial action.

The comparative method employed in this volume even further complicates this problem of constitutional judicial review and democracy. At first glance it might seem oxymoronic to claim that a court may declare a constitutional amendment unconstitutional. Nevertheless, most constitutional courts can declare an amendment unconstitutional on procedural grounds; that is, that it was not enacted according to the rules for enacting amendments laid down in the constitution itself. Notable in this regard are the decisions of U.S. state supreme courts where state constitutions contain a "single subject" provision. Those courts have fairly often ruled an amendment invalid on the grounds that it treated more than one subject. Because constitutional provisions are supposed to be rather general in character, nearly any amendment might be considered to treat of more than one subject. Judicial single subject decisions are likely to be highly discretionary.

Beyond the judicial capacity for procedural review of amendments, comparative studies reveal instances of far greater judicial powers. Most notably in India (Mate, Ch. 10 in this volume) and Germany, constitutional courts have declared that certain constitutional provisions are so basic or fundamental that they may not be altered by amendment. Such decisions rest either on judicial discernment of the intent of the framers or arguments that some constitutional provisions are so inherent in or vital to the constitution that altering them would destroy the very nature of the constitution as a constitution. Indeed, the California State Constitution contains an explicit provision forbidding amendments to its "fundamental" guarantees, but with no list of what those guarantees are.

So we now encounter some constitutional courts that can even block "corrections" to their constitutional lawmaking by more or less democratic amending processes. (By the way, this is an appropriate place to point out that this volume reflects a new scholarly vogue in comparative constitutional studies and thus a healthy corrective to the previous nearly exclusive treatments of review in a U.S. context. This volume, however, also reflects an overcorrection, that is the new studies have largely ignored the rich comparative opportunities provided by the fifty U.S. state Supreme Courts. State constitutional studies have largely been undertaken not by comparativists but by liberal U.S. constitutional lawyers looking for havens from the new conservative U.S. Supreme Court.)

JUDICIAL INDEPENDENCE

These phenomena of proactive constitutional courts and unconstitutional constitutional amendments are only extreme examples of the central normative problem

inherent in and often touched on in most of the comparative empirical studies in
this volume. That is the problem of review and democracy.

The standard solution to this problem, or at least the solution most often offered
by defenders of review, lies along a route of "judicial independence" and rule of law.
Under the flags of democracy, democratization, international human rights, nation
building, and/or economic development, judicial independence is touted around
the world by governments, international organizations, and nongovernmental organizations (NGOs). Everyone is for it, for everyone. Surely constitutional judicial
review must be a sham without it.

Alas, things are not as simple as they seem. Courts make law. Constitutional courts
often make big law, and the law they make is not easily invalidated by others. In
a democracy, the people or its elected representatives are supposed to make law.
If courts are truly independent, then they are lawmakers who are not politically
accountable to the demos. Try flying that flag.

Put another way, courts are courts of law. Their job is to implement law. So they
are agents of principals. One such principal – a very prominent one – is the statute
maker; that is, the legislature. An agent is supposed to be accountable to his/her
principal. Courts are supposed to be accountable to legislatures – in a democracy to
an elected, representative legislature. If courts are truly independent, they are not
accountable to democratic legislatures. Same flag, same problem.

So obviously we must not mean judicial independence when we say judicial
independence. Or we mean both judicial independence and judicial accountability
for judicial lawmaking. It may be quite logical to say we can't have both. The reality
of building politically viable and effective judicial institutions is that we want and
must have both. Unless courts are seen to be independent, they cannot effectively
perform any useful tasks, at least in democratic polities. This is merely the old and
true cliché that courts have neither the purse nor the sword. They depend heavily
on consent, and that consent depends in large part on the perception that they are
independent. On the other hand, in a democracy, no matter what adjectives such as
constitutional or deliberative or pluralist we add, no amount of lawyer talk is going
to persuade the demos that important lawmakers are not supposed to be accountable
to it.

Faced with this dilemma, we adopt one or more of a range of self-contradictory
but pragmatic compromises. They range from the partisan election of judges for
relatively short terms to life term appointments by political executives or by panels
whose membership represents a range of interests. Every possible mix and match of
a dozen different judicial selection methods is found somewhere in the world and in
this volume. Each of them represents some compromise between independence and
accountability. Even authoritarian states provide some masquerade of independence
because without it courts lose all institutional utility. Only a judiciary that was entirely
self-selecting by co-option with entirely independent funding would be without any
accountability. None such are reported in this volume.

If we concentrate on successful constitutional judicial review courts – that is, courts whose vetoes of laws or other government actions are actually obeyed – it is clear that this perceived independence from dictation by others is essential to their success. However, in working through this volume, is it possible to discover any successful constitutional review court in any more or less democratic society that is accountable to no one? Is it possible to find any democratic polity in which constitutional judicial review has not at some time or another been rendered problematic by the tensions between independence and democratic accountability? For Americans, of course, the bizarre ritual of Senate confirmation hearings provide a periodic theater of the independence-accountability paradox, with nominees asked to show that they will independently paddle in the mainstream.

Most of the contributions to this volume touch in one way or another on the strategic sense or leadership skills of constitutional courts or individual members of those courts. A constant refrain is the limits or boundaries of maneuver imposed on high courts by the constellations of political, economic, and social forces in which they operate. The mightiest of the problems of constitutional judicial review is the problem of achieving a successful balance between judicial assertions of independence and demonstrations of accountability.

PRESENT AND FUTURE: ADMINISTRATIVE REVIEW

In a number of respects, this volume represents the currently most advanced stage of judicial review studies. It is interdisciplinary and comparative. Moreover, it is comparative not only in the sense of juxtaposing a variety of single country studies all asking roughly the same questions, but comparative in the sense that some contributions actually compare. Obviously, it moves beyond variations in the formal textual provisions for review and beyond the courts themselves to the whole political matrix in which they are imbedded. Not unnaturally, most studies of judicial review, both United States and otherwise, have concentrated on the constitutional law that constitutional judicial review courts have established. Thus, the concentration was on legal doctrine. Indeed, in the normal course of law school and undergraduate political science teaching, analysis of judicial review was a kind of addendum to surveys of the substance of constitutional-law doctrines. If the question put is (as it is here) not what did the court say, but how, where, when, and why courts get away with saying it and achieving compliance with what they say, then doctrine recedes and politics comes to the fore. So this volume remains centered on courts, but courts in the matrix politics. In two interrelated respects, however, this volume only hints at where judicial review studies may go next. Throughout my discussion here, I have fairly steadily employed the expression "constitutional judicial review." This is a good point at which to view judicial review more broadly.

One of the contributors to this volume, John Ferejohn, along with his coauthor Bill Eskridge, has recently published a book entitled *A Republic of Statutes: The*

New American Constitution.[1] Its main argument is that in the United States, a series of super-statutes has been enacted by Congress that provide a set of basic, general, pervasive, and superior legal rules that are equivalent to constitutional provisions in generating judicial decisions of great political, economic, and social impact. Obvious examples are the Civil Rights Acts, the voting rights statutes, the Sherman Act, and the Administrative Procedures Act.

To those who have spent many years teaching U.S. constitutional law, what the book has to say is obvious and has long been part of their everyday life as teachers. (Most important books state what is obvious once the book has stated it.) If one began teaching constitutional law in the 1960s or 1970s, that law was proliferating at such a rate that it could barely be squeezed into a yearlong course. The half-year devoted to civil rights and liberties particularly became a rat race. Then it got worse. Increasingly over time, no relatively complete picture of civil rights and liberties, and certainly none that would prepare young lawyers for practice, could be presented without getting into the various antidiscrimination, voting, and campaign-financing statutes. More and more litigation entangled constitutional and statutory rights and remedies. There just wasn't time. The law school result is new courses in employment discrimination and the like to follow the basic constitutional law course.

Teachers of administrative law have had a comparable experience. In the 1960s and 1970s, the administrative law rules guiding judicial review of agency "informal" rule making multiplied enormously. The course must have had five times as much necessary content by 1990 as it had in 1950. Then agencies learned how to jump over all the new procedural hurdles that the judges (seconded by Congress) had put in their rule-making way. So now if you want to challenge an agency rule, often the best bet is to challenge it not on procedural but substantive grounds. The rule is alleged to be unlawful because it is not in accord with the statute that authorized such a rule to be made. Thus, the typically one-semester administrative law course, already overflowing with procedural nitpicking, needed to turn into a course on statutory interpretation because so many cases turned on whether an agency rule was or was not in accord with the text of the statute. Again, there just isn't enough room and time to add a statutory interpretation course to the administrative law course.

In calling this congeries of statutes a new constitution, Eskridge and Ferejohn quite obviously are engaging in a marketing ploy. Constitution law is the queen of the law school curriculum, with all those former Supreme Court clerks lined up to teach it. It is typically the sole course on American law in the undergraduate political science curriculum. If you can get all this statutory (and thus traditionally less glamorous) law promoted into constitutional law then you can get it the attention

---

[1] William N. Eskridge Jr. and John Ferejohn, *A Republic of Statues: The New American Constitution* (New Haven: Yale University Press, 2010).

it deserves. It is really not worth fighting over whether the super-statutes are really "constitutional" or constitution like or just important. A major portion of the law of most modern states lies in rules enacted by administrative agencies under lawmaking powers granted to them by statute. In most legal systems courts are given review powers to determine whether the rule was in accord with the delegating statute. In polities such as the United States, EU, and Israel the highest court is both a constitutional and administrative court, and when the court strikes down a rule it makes little difference whether if did so on constitutional or statutory grounds. In polities such as the United States and EU, where the constitutional text itself contains norms for proper agency action, it may not even be clear whether the agency action has been struck down on statutory or constitutional grounds.

As noted earlier, constitutional and statutory review may be in quite a different position politically because judicial interpretation of statutes can relatively easily be overturned by further legislative action; judicial constitutional interpretations can only be overturned by the difficult process of constitutional amendment. In practice, however – in many legislatures – a given statute is enacted through the coming together of a fragile coalition of the moment, which is very unlikely to be capable of reforming much later to correct a judicial "misinterpretation" of what it had wanted. Indeed, many countries have legislatures in which passing or amending laws is so difficult that most real lawmaking is done by agencies. In those countries, administrative judicial review may be far more politically empowering than constitutional review both because it is exercised more frequently and it is little subject to correction by the legislature. In some nations, administrative review may be a decisive substitute for formal constitutional review, as, for instance, in UK courts employing such notions as "natural justice." If we are concerned with constitutional judicial review because it arms courts with considerable policy or lawmaking powers, and often relatively independent ones, then we probably ought to take as our subject of study "judicial review" not constitutional judicial review.

There is another, and quite pragmatic, reason to conflate constitutional and administrative review, particularly for those basically concerned with review as an instrument for furthering human rights. When a court protects rights by striking down a statute or other government action as unconstitutional, it puts itself in the position of directly opposing powerful political actors, of thwarting the will of the people's representatives or of the authoritarian ruler(s). Such a position is at best uncomfortable for the court and at worst suicidal. Where a court strikes down an administrative decision on the grounds not that it is unconstitutional but merely that it is unlawful, the court presents itself not as an opponent of the lawmaking regime but as its loyal enforcement agent.

For most citizens of most countries, protection in their daily lives from arbitrary actions by local officials is far more important than protection of their grand rights of freedom of speech, voting, and so on. Getting a license to sell vegetables in the market or getting a housing assignment may be far more important than being able to make a speech or cast a meaningful vote. So particularly in democratizing or authoritarian regimes, administrative review can provide very important judicial protections for individuals without dangerous judicial challenges to the powers that be. Indeed, as in contemporary China, a central authoritarian regime may welcome judicial assistance in maintaining discipline over local officials.

There is, however, more to be said. In the contemporary world, even in the world of Asian and African dictatorships, there is much conflation of law and rights. The romance of rights is frequently expressed in the language of the rule of law or due process of law. An administrative review court constantly waving the banner of rule of law is in a position to slip at least a little – and maybe a lot – of rights proclamation – and even real rights protection – into decisions that on their face only compel local officials to do the bidding of their lawmaking masters. Administrative review as well as constitutional review courts may become rights protectors. Constitutional review courts must exercise some strategic sense if they are to be successful. One strategic mode is to caste decisions asserting and protecting individual rights as based in administrative law rather than constitutional law. Constitutional law decisions invalidating government action are seen as ultimate and final short of constitutional amendment. Administrative law decisions are more or less based in statutory law that legislatures may change at will and are caste as judicial enforcement of the law made by the legislature not as independent assertions of judicial constitutional powers. Administrative law based judicial assertions of rights are little, humble judicial review rather than big defiant review.

Europeans have long been in a good position to look at constitutional and administrative review together because the civil law tradition clumps administrative law and constitutional law together as public law. American political science could have done the same thing because it employed the same public law rubric, but its long-held constitutional fetish kept it from paying much attention to any other kind of law. U.S. law professors typically teach two areas of law, but until recently the pairings were often arbitrary. Starting roughly two academic generations ago, however, a substantial number of law professors began to couple constitutional and administrative law. At about the same time, political scientists began to pay more attention to law other than constitutional.

So perhaps now is the time to begin defining scholarly specializations and constructing courses in terms of judicial review rather than sticking constitutional review in one place and administrative law review in another. Such a combination would be good for rights and would respond to the need to spotlight super-statutes that are largely judicially implemented by review of agency decision making. If we are concerned fundamentally with how the judges "get away with it," we might want to pay much more attention to the practices through which it is easiest for them to get away with it.

Indeed conditions on the ground are beginning to compel comparativists to a merged study of constitutional, other higher law and statutory review. European national courts are now implementing a wide range of the mandates of the European Convention on Human Rights and the EU. This national court action is sometimes seen as constitutional judicial review because international treaty law is directly incorporated into the national constitution. Sometimes it is statutory review of administrative action because the national legislature has enacted European norms as national statutes. Often it is treated as review on the basis of European Conventions or Union *higher law*, a law treated as subordinate to the national constitution but superior to national statutes.

At the same time that this European law in national context is seen as higher or constitutional law, in the context of the EU itself it may be merely statutory law, that is norms contained in directives or regulations enacted through the EU legislative process rather than derived directly from the language of the treaties that are the EU Constitution. The several EU antidiscrimination directives are the kind of super-statutes that Eskridge and Ferejohn talk about. In some EU member states, they are constitutional mandates.

This European law is now implemented by regular, administrative, and constitutional member-states courts. It is implemented by highest courts in the regular and administrative court hierarchies as well as the typically sole constitutional court. Increasingly, it is implemented by lower as well as higher courts and by courts whose standing rules severely limit access to some and give others the broadest possible access. Thus, the Kelsenian model of constitutional judicial review calling for a single constitutional review court of very limited access, with judges appointed on the basis of political considerations rather than pure professional merit and exclusive jurisdiction over constitutional issues and no jurisdiction over purely statutory matters – which was supposed to the continental model – is now in continental shambles.

Certainly these momentous changes in review can be seen as driven by the popular religion of human rights.[2] On the other hand, they may be seen as a U.S.-like story of the European Court of Justice first achieving successful free-trade federalist review supporting powerful economic actors, then the legitimacy recruited in those endeavors being transferred to its rights review, that of the European Court of Human Rights and even that of the courts of member states that had not previously exercised much or any rights review.

All of the current member states of the EU are democracies. Most but not all of the signatory states of the European Conventions on Human Rights are democracies, and it may be that higher law review is not really successful in those that are not. The EU and Convention are indeed highly fragmented in terms of political power. The member states, even excluding the nondemocratic members of the Convention, range from very fragmented to relatively unfragmented – unless you count all

---

[2] See Alec Stone Sweet, *A Europe of Rights* (Oxford: Oxford University Press, 2009).

democracies as fragmented. What is surely more fragmented is judicial review itself as now exercised by many courts embedded in multiple judicial hierarchies.

"Insurance" concerns are obviously at play, but of a number of different sorts. The EU was formed in large part to ensure future peace among the states of Western Europe. Both it and especially the Convention were formed to ensure against any return of Nazi-Fascist national regimes. A major motive of many Eastern European states bent on joining the Convention and EU has been to ensure their newfound independence from the successor to their former Soviet dominator. Neither the Convention nor EU seems initially to have been a response of one political party in a particular member state to the dangers posed by the succession to office of a rival party, but such considerations may have been at play among Eastern European states with still-active Communist parties. Overall, the new European Convention and EU generated judicial review, but surely this does not make the mighty problem less mighty but does make reviewing judiciaries far mightier.

Indeed, a number of instances provided in this volume show the desirability, indeed the inevitability, of treating administrative and constitutional review together even when separate administrative and constitutional courts exist. As the chapter on France clearly shows (Lasser, Ch. 11 in this volume), the new French constitutional law – that is the incursion of EU and European Convention on Human Rights law – has been implemented not only by the Constitutional Council but by the administrative court system and even the regular court system through judgments not of the unconstitutionality but merely of the unlawfulness of government administrative acts. In Chile, the question of whether the president has exceeded the legislative power granted him by the Constitution is determined by whether the power to legislate on a particular matter has been delegated to him by a statute enacted by the legislature (see Scribner, Ch. 4 in this volume). Thus, the constitutional question is a question of statutory interpretation identical to that raised throughout the world in administrative courts (or courts of general jurisdiction) reviewing whether an administrative agency rule or regulation is in accord with some statute purportedly delegating rule-making authority to that agency. I leave it to the reader to note the number of instances in this volume in which administrative review pops up in one guise or another before being resubmerged in the volume's concern for constitutional review.

OF DEMOCRACY, FRAGMENTATION, TAUTOLOGY, CIRCULARITY, TRAFFIC COPS AND CHICKENS

On the basis of this volume, "fragmentation" should be one of the favorite nominees for conditions underlying successful judicial review. Democracy may well be another, although a certain sort of successful review sometimes may appear in authoritarian states. A number of perhaps insurmountable problems arise. First of all, are fragmentation and democracy different things or the same thing? Nearly any definition of democracy includes competitive elections. Competitive elections almost necessarily demand two or more political parties, each with some chance of winning something. They must be parties offering voters some real political choices. If there are two or more relatively effective and relatively differing political parties, isn't that in and of itself fragmentation? What if you have a two-party, competitive electoral system in which, over time, each party controls all or at least a blocking part of the government part of the time? What if both parties share the same basic political, social, and economic values, differing only on a relatively narrow range of means to those ends? Are you fragmented or not? If, as a number of contributors suggest, successful review depends on judges seizing opportunities presented by fragmentation, is that different than saying democracy is a prerequisite of judicial review? Are there unfragmented democracies that could be examined to test the proposition: "no fragmentation – no successful judicial review." Or is there a single democracy that was fragmented at some times and unfragmented at others, and in which judicial review followed the same periodization?

Moreover, it is possible we are dealing with two kinds of fragmentation. In one, parliament is sovereign but internally so fragmented that it cannot exercise its supposedly exclusive lawmaking powers, so reviewing courts exercise those powers by "interpreting" stagnant statutory texts. In each particular polity a nonjudicial concern for rights may have led to successful review. Or successful review, either on rights or federalism or division of powers issues, or at least a hint or a promise of such review to come, may have engendered a rights movement which in turn engendered initial or continuing successful rights review. In some instances review may have engendered public urges to protect rights. In others public urges to protect rights may have engendered review. Or, the Legislature – Executive at any given moment is sufficiently unfragmented as to be productive, but the polity is sufficiently fragmented that one party or coalition controls the government at some times and the other at other times. Then the "insurance principals" kicks in, with each of the parties agreeing to judicial review to protect it when the other gains control in the future. Here again, however, fragmentation and democracy are hard to separate.

Division of powers raises some comparable problems. Unless there is a separate and relatively independent judiciary, there cannot be successful judicial review. If there is a separate judiciary, there is division of powers. Thus, wherever you find successful review you will find a division of powers, but this is a matter of definition, not causality. We will not have shown that division of powers necessarily or sufficiently causes review. Indeed, sometimes we may be encountering the traffic jam–traffic cop problem. It may not have been that division of powers caused judicial review but that courts established a division of lawmaking powers between themselves and other parts of government by the successful exercise of judicial review. Moreover, they may even end such a division of powers by passively accepting all the law that other branches make. Should we count as having division of powers only those polities that have separate legislative and executive branches?

Rights-creating or -enhancing review threatens similar causation problems high-lighted by Halliday's reminder that we should pay attention to lawyers (Ch. 13 in this volume). In some places at some times courts may be responding to rights concerns among domestic elites or political classes; in others, to international-rights move-ments. In some times and places, the judges' own decisions may encourage or even engender cause lawyering that then moves courts to be more active about rights. In each particular polity has a non-judicial concern for rights led to successful review or has successful review, either on rights or federalism or divisions of powers issues, or at least a hint and a promise of such review to come, engendered a rights movement which in turn engendered successful rights review. Perhaps this is a chicken-and-egg rather than a traffic cop problem.

In this volume, there is general global agreement that courts have become more dangerous but remain the least dangerous branch. A number of our contributors refer to a notion of a "zone of tolerance," and many tell stories of judicial overreaching followed by devastating reprisals. However, zone of tolerance comes down to "judges can get away with what they can get away with." Such an approach is not only tautological but does not distinguish judges in any way. All political actors can get away with what they can get away with given the constellation of other political forces of the given time and place. Zone of tolerance is simply, "Welcome to the Club."

If, of course, we could arrive at a relatively precise map of boundaries to the zone – boundaries that were relatively fixed over time and across polities – the zone could contribute to a causal model of successful review. The contributors to this volume, however, depict a rather large atlas of zone boundaries as they have existed at different times and places. So here we have a very fruitful set of overlays, but have yet to construct the basic map. As a purely pragmatic matter, however, it is undoubtedly a good idea to tell activist judges that their real powers may not be as great as their formal powers and passive judges that their real powers may actually sometimes be greater than their formal powers.

However various the boundaries, the zones seem to exist universally and suggest one resolution, or at least amelioration of the tension between democracy and review; that is, lawmaking by nonelected nonrepresentatives. Judicial review may not be self-limiting, but appears to be auto-limited. Actual review – that is, review that seeks to initiate policy or institutional change – seems to nearly always generate opposition. Reviewing courts always appear to be sufficiently weak that their opposition will become successful if the courts move too far and/or too fast. They are subject not only to the checks and balances of other branches, but as many of the contributions to this volume show, to the checks and balances of public sentiment. The dependence on the purse and sword of others, the need to recruit more or less voluntary agreement to judicial decrees, may mean that ultimately the benefits of the judicial review that is actually carried out always exceeds the costs to democracy, because otherwise it will be successfully reversed. (An interesting question is whether this auto-limitation rule would apply in an Islamic state with democratically elected legislature – executive but with courts constitutionally empowered to follow the Shari'a as the supreme law of the land.)

This volume takes very long steps toward a comparative anatomy of judicial review. It may even take some steps toward a kind of evolutionary biology of the stages of judicial review, its speciation, and its sometimes extinction. For me at least, it presents a truly daunting body of data on which to build a physiology of judicial review – an account of what causes what. As the number of observed cases multiply, it becomes harder and harder to come up with a single, or a list of single, necessary and sufficient causes of review. The list of variables that in some combination will cause review lengthens, and the number and complexity of possible winning combinations or sequences of causes increases. No double helix appears to be on the horizon. Path dependence rears its ugly head. We are able to tell more and more increasingly sophisticated stories of the rise and fall, unrise, refall, and rerise of successful judicial review in various places. A parsimonious causal model of judicial review from which all of these developments could be deduced logically is still beyond our grasp.

Conclusion

Of Judicial Ships and Winds of Change

Diana Kapiszewski, Gordon Silverstein, and Robert A. Kagan[*]

CHANGES IN JUDICIAL ROLES: THE ELUSIVENESS OF SIMPLE EXPLANATORY MODELS

In his chapter in this volume, Martin Shapiro observes that "'The mighty problem' of constitutional judicial review" raises a major empirical challenge: "when, where, and why do the powers that be . . . allow a handful of judges without purse or sword to get away with making major policy decisions?" (Ch. 16 in this volume, p. 380). In recent decades, the salience of these questions has increased. More political regimes have established constitutional courts. More courts have overruled legislation and executive orders. Thus, more judges have played important roles in politics, policy, and governance. However, in some countries, courts have been cautious about engaging in judicial review or, when they have done so, have been politically attacked and driven to retreat. In other regimes, political authorities have preempted or limited the exercise of judicial review, preventing an expansion of judicial roles in governance.

Faced with this variation, scholars interested in the political roots of judicial power have focused on three related aspects of Shapiro's when, where, and why questions. Under what conditions are courts granted (or do they themselves adopt) judicial review powers and significant remedial authority? Under what conditions do courts exercise those powers assertively? Under what conditions can courts exercise those powers both assertively and successfully (i.e., achieving compliance with their rulings)?

Precise and parsimonious answers to these questions have become increasingly elusive, Shapiro notes. A primary reason is that the number of likely causal variables has multiplied rapidly. Since the end of World War II, constitutional courts with

---

[*] Respectively, Assistant Professor of Political Science, University of California, Irvine; Assistant Dean, Yale Law School; Professor Emeritus of Political Science and Law, University of California, Berkeley.

varying degrees of power have followed many different political pathways – in countries with civil law as well as common law traditions, in unitary states such as France as well as in federal systems such as Germany, in well-established democracies such as Israel and Canada as well as in countries more recently transitioned to democracy such as Brazil, Hungary, and Korea.

Consequently, rather than addressing the three under-what-conditions questions head on, this volume emphasizes a related although different query: if courts are in fact gaining power in a growing number of countries, what exactly are judges doing with that power? In what domains of politics and aspects of policy, and in what ways do courts assert their authority successfully? What roles in governance do politically consequential courts now play? Those essentially descriptive questions inspired and permeate the twelve empirical chapters that comprise the bulk of this book. Of course, as will be discussed, this focus and the great variety of roles to which the chapters point only complicate the search for a parsimonious explanatory model. We believe, however, that before such a model will come within our collective grasp, we must develop a more complete and detailed mapping of the types of roles in politics and governance that courts are now undertaking.

Our introductory chapter categorizes the authors' answers to our descriptive questions in terms of a set of arenas of political conflict in which critical court cases and judicial decisions can and (in our empirical studies) did arise. To summarize our findings briefly, in many countries, courts have decided crucial legal issues arising from disputes between political incumbents and challengers (including determining winners and losers in critical elections). Courts have also resolved constitutional disputes between units of government about decision-making procedures and the allocation of governing authority. They have addressed legal conflicts arising from clashes between secular and religious beliefs. They have responded to popular outcry about government corruption, deadlock, or stasis. They have helped define the scope of individual and minority rights. In sum, this volume suggests that courts – at various judicial levels, in every world region, in countries with varying legal traditions and histories of judicial independence – rule on important disputes in multiple arenas of political conflict and play consequential roles in governance.

These findings and the categorization we propose suggest that judicial power should not be considered as a monolithic dependent variable, but rather as a *set* of variables, implying that the relevant question should be, "In which domains of governance do courts exercise power and play significant roles (and in which do they not)?" However, as the number of dependent variables grows, the number of independent variables – the factors and forces whose presence or absence influence or explain the growth and restriction of judicial roles in governance – potentially grows as well. In our Introduction, we grouped those factors into three broad categories – (1) *structural factors* (for example, the degree to which political authority and power are fragmented rather than consolidated in a single, disciplined ruling party; the duration of traditions of judicial independence and judicial review);

(2) *proximate political dynamics* (e.g., demands for courts to play new roles and resistance to them doing so stemming from wars, political crises, economic crises, and political movements that thrust important controversies onto court dockets and – as Halliday's chapter persuasively argues – the degree to which a national "legal complex" has mobilized for or against particular judicial roles in governance [Ch. 13 in this volume]); and (3) *intra-court factors* that affect judicial willingness or ability to play new roles (e.g., shifts in the judicial or political philosophies of judges on the court, and the rise and fall of forceful, charismatic judicial leaders).[1]

In sum, the expanding array of judicial roles in governance and the correspondingly large number of causal factors that might affect those roles make the under-what-conditions questions raised still more difficult to answer. Indeed, because the factors that influence judicial roles often develop simultaneously and interact, it is very difficult to assign a relative causal weight to any one factor – even with regard to a single example of judicial role change, much less in a general theory of judicial power. Nonetheless, we hope that our mapping of judicial roles and our proposed analytic framework will help scholars begin to understand how the three sets of causal factors we have identified – political-structural conditions, short-term shifts in national politics, and intra-court variables – act and interact to induce change in judicial roles.

In our Introduction, we suggested that it is useful to envision the development of judicial power not as linear but in terms of ships sailing on a stormy sea. The ships are propelled by variable "winds of demand" – requests that courts decide cases that would draw them into expanded roles in governance – as well as variable "winds of resistance" – opposition or attacks that impede their ability to play their current or additional roles. These winds thus reflect (and vary in strength in accordance with) short-term political dynamics. The resistant winds grow stronger, for example, when the ship starts to venture beyond the "tolerance intervals" (Epstein, Knight, and Shvetsova 2001) of powerful political leaders, risking political backlash. The winds of demand accelerate when civil society calls for more judicial intervention in key issues, as when litigation campaigns emerge from social movements, and political leaders look to the courts as a means of advancing politically costly policy objectives. When the court considers a case involving a highly controversial political issue, both winds often blow strongly and the seas may become dangerously turbulent.

The roughness of the ocean, in this metaphor, also reflects political-structural conditions far beneath the surface. Ships constructed in politically stable, competitive constitutional democracies with long-standing traditions of judicial independence more often face calmer waters and fewer headwinds, facilitating their safe passage. By

---

[1] These categories are, of course, not completely mutually exclusive; for instance, one might include enduring aspects of the legal complex (such as the size and cohesiveness of the organized bar, or the visions of the proper judicial role perpetuated by law faculties and judges) within the category of structural factors.

contrast, those ships built in fragile democracies, with less-institutionalized party systems and greater political instability, likely have fewer resources and less dependable support – and thus face rougher, more challenging seas. Courts from authoritarian states sail in perhaps the most turbulent waters, which can easily curtail their power and the roles they can play. Moreover, forces emanating from the international environment can shape the topography below the waves.

Nevertheless, the oceanic metaphor also reminds us – and the chapters in this book attest – that squalls and worse can arise without warning, turning even the most reliable sea lanes turbulent and dangerous. Like a ship's captain and officer corps, high court justices must constantly consider how they will react to unexpected political storms. Even the most skilled captains (and chief justices) must contend with the worries, fears, aspirations, and conflicting views of their officers (and fellow justices). Strategic timing and skilled crafting of rulings can sometimes make it possible to navigate the judicial ship through threatening seas, emerging with a powerful grip on new roles, powers, and responsibilities. Good examples of this are the "*Marbury* moments" emphasized by Ferejohn in his contribution (Ch. 14 in this volume), and described in several empirical chapters, in which judges follow the pattern of Chief Justice John Marshall in *Marbury v. Madison*. That is, in such moments, the judges combined an assertion of a court-empowering legal principle with a decision in the instant case that did not directly challenge elected leaders, thus maneuvering them to accept the general principle the judges asserted and thereby strengthen the assertion of a new judicial role.

Even with clever strategic maneuvering, however, judicial captains cannot always anticipate and navigate the storms of political backlash unleashed by their rulings, as we see in this book's contributions on the United States (Kagan, Ch. 8 in this volume), India (Mate, Ch. 10 in this volume), Thailand (Ginsburg, Ch. 1 in this volume), and Georgia (Trochev, Ch. 2 in this volume). These cases remind us that the more roles in governance a court takes on, the more likely it is that it will have to confront politically controversial cases.[2] However, it is difficult to anticipate precisely how intense the political backlash will be when courts confront and decide such cases – just as it is difficult to anticipate how much legitimacy they may gain when they do so (enhancing their immunity from subsequent political resistance and attack). One can picture our metaphorical judicial ships emerging from a storm with torn sails and a trail of jettisoned cargo (judicial roles) scattered behind – or cutting through the waves, sails billowing, having added the ballast of increased legitimacy, enabling them to carry even more cargo in the future, taking on more and greater roles in governance. However, precisely because these political challenges and their consequences are so unpredictable, it is tremendously difficult to determine the

---

[2] These cases are also a sobering reminder that courts are, at base, reliant on other actors and institutions for their power: without control of the purse or the sword, as Alexander Hamilton made clear in *Federalist* 78, they "must ultimately depend upon the aid of the Executive arm even for the efficacy of [their] judgments."

"stickiness" of expansive judicial roles – that is, to predict whether a ship will tack one way or another, let alone whether it will press forward or retreat into a safe harbor.

On balance, however, we believe that a focus on the risk of judicial miscalculation and political backlash can lead students of judicial politics to overemphasize the fragility of judicial power. That is the subject of our concluding section, in which we step back from the detailed and dramatic narratives offered in our empirical studies and reflect more broadly – and more speculatively – on longer-term trends in political structure and culture that in many places seem to have strengthened the winds of demand for judicial action and weakened the winds of resistance, enhancing the prospects for political legitimacy and stability of expanded judicial roles in governance.

SAILING BETWEEN FRAGILITY AND STABILITY

Images of the fragility of judicial power rest on the assumption that strong political leaders can and will successfully denounce and resist court decisions that fall outside their "tolerance intervals" (Epstein et al., 2001). The offended politicians sometimes replace or punish the offending judges, or reduce the court's jurisdiction and powers. On the other hand, Epstein et al. also assert that constitutional courts can build up "reservoirs of public support that legislators and executives are loathe (though not unwilling) to challenge" (*Id.* at 155), even when courts issue rulings those political leaders bitterly dislike.

For instance, one may think of U.S. President Richard Nixon complying with the Supreme Court's 1974 mandate that he surrender to a lower court (and ultimately to a special prosecutor) tapes of secret conversations whose revelation would seal his political fate. Or one may think of U.S. Vice President Albert Gore's reaction to a Supreme Court decision that stopped the counting of disputed Florida ballots in the 2000 presidential election and ended his bid for the White House. The next day, Gore stepped to a podium in the Old Executive Office Building and announced that, "While I strongly disagree with the Court's decision, I accept it. I accept the finality of this outcome." One might object that neither President Nixon nor Vice President Gore was an overwhelmingly popular figure at these pivotal moments, which may have tipped the institutional legitimacy scales toward the Court. However, during his showdown with the Court in 1937, President Franklin Roosevelt had just been reelected the previous year in a stunning landslide (losing just two of the then–forty-eight states). Further, he had a huge Democratic Party majority in both houses of Congress. Furious that a conservative majority on the Supreme Court had struck down statutes that were pillars of his New Deal agenda to combat the Great Depression, Roosevelt pressed Congress to empower him to add new justices to the Court who could outvote his opponents there. Congress refused – in great part because, despite the President's popularity and political power, the public was unwilling to see the Court restructured for political and policy purposes.[3] As a result, the Court's authority and structure were left intact, and an enduring aura of judicial invulnerability was generated.

Political leaders' deference to judicial authority is often attributed to a court's *legitimacy* – the widespread sense in a society that certain decision makers (such as duly appointed judges) ought to be obeyed. In modern societies, Max Weber argued, legitimacy stems from "a belief in . . . the right of those elevated to authority under [settled legal] rules to issue commands" (Weber 1978: 215).[4] Gibson et al. (2011) – quoting David Easton (1965) – suggest that an institution's legitimacy can be equated with its "diffuse support" – the "reservoir of favorable attitudes or good will that helps [people] to accept or tolerate [institutional] outputs to which they are opposed or the effects of which they see as damaging to their wants" (Easton 1965: 273). "Diffuse support," Gibson et al. clarify, is "not contingent on satisfaction with the immediate outputs of the institution" (or, indeed, with the judicial ship's current captain and officer corps), but simply captures the notion that people "have confidence in institutions to make, in the long run, desirable public policy." Institutions without a reservoir of goodwill, they suggest, may be limited in their ability to defy the preferences of the majority (Gibson et al. 2011, 546). Increasing judicial legitimacy, then, represents a form of institutional development that can embolden courts to make more assertive decisions, confident that they will not be attacked or ignored.

How does a court's reservoir of goodwill grow over time? Courts themselves, of course, can act in ways that enhance their legitimacy. The classic technique is to display the trappings of judicial neutrality, reinforcing the idea that they are merely mouthpieces of the law by justifying decisions in terms of specific constitutional provisions and judicial precedents. Courts can also exercise power "judiciously." For instance, they may decide politically critical legal disputes in ways that favor new majorities rather than incumbents (Ginsburg, Ch. 1 in this volume; Trochev, Ch. 2 in this volume) or, as in the South African case, rule on some cases in ways that protect minority (white citizens') constitutional rights and others in ways that validate majority (black citizens') demands (Klug, Ch. 3 in this volume). Courts can also reach out for support, as Mate (Ch. 10 in this volume) suggests the Indian Court did by authorizing public interest litigation and making assertive, reform-oriented decisions that were likely to meet with popular approval; as Castillejos-Aragón (Ch. 5 in this volume) shows the Mexican Court did by reaching out to various civil society actors; or as Klug (Ch. 3 in this volume) shows the South African Court did by

[3] The Court's apparent softening of its opposition to the expansion of federal regulatory power in a case decided just as Congress was considering Roosevelt's demand may be another reason Congress refused to go along, stripping the Supreme Court reform proposals from the final version of the Judicial Procedures Reform Bill that Roosevelt ultimately signed on August 26, 1937 (Kagan, Ch. 8 in this volume; Shesol 2010).

[4] Weber called this "legal rational authority" as opposed to other modes of legitimate power, which he labeled "traditional authority" and "charismatic authority."

choosing to operate out of the Old Fort, symbolically transforming a symbol of apartheid repression into a symbol of a racially evenhanded constitutional rule of law.

However, judicial legitimacy can also grow as high courts make controversial decisions that support popular political leaders – who in turn denounce critics of the court and extol the sacred importance of judicial supremacy (Whittington 2007). Further, judicial legitimacy is built as political authorities comply with court rulings that do *not* favor their interests; the more they do so, the less politically acceptable it becomes for successive leaders to defy the court or strive to reduce its powers. Overall, the more courts successfully resolve important disputes, the more useful or essential they are considered to be by more elements of society, and the more legal claims they thus attract, a virtuous cycle emerges through which judicial power – and, we suggest, judicial roles in governance – expand (Stone Sweet 1999). Most broadly, then, judicial legitimacy grows as politicians and the general public come to value the courts' contributions to constitutionalism and the rule of law – as they are perceived as an anchor of stability in what Ferejohn (Ch. 14 in this volume) aptly describes as the "institutionalized instability" of democratic politics.

There is nothing inevitable about this legitimacy-expanding scenario, of course. It is a frequently observed pattern (Stone Sweet 1999), but far from an iron law. In countries in which democratic consolidation has stalled, courts may simply lack opportunities to begin to build legitimacy, as they remain heavily manipulated. Further, judicial captains can make tactical errors that sap – or prevent their court from developing – legitimacy; the Hungarian Constitutional Court's behavior through the decade of the 1990s might be an example. Alternatively, courts dealing with extraordinarily sensitive issues can make decisions that are easily characterized as irresponsible, allowing political leaders to partially or fully disregard the court in the name of political necessity or national stability; the U.S. Supreme Court's rulings on Native American land claims may be a case in point. Very popular transformative political leaders (perhaps especially in illiberal democracies with a weaker tradition of rule of law) may defy or reconstitute assertive courts – even those that have begun to build legitimacy – without extensive fallout; one example might be Venezuelan President Hugo Chávez's manipulation of the Supreme Court shortly after assuming office in 1999.

Nevertheless, as previously suggested, one can point to several long-term global trends in political structure and legal culture that seem to have strengthened the winds of demand and weakened the winds of resistance to judicial action, gradually if not always consistently enhancing the legitimacy and stability of expanded judicial roles in governance.[5]

---

[5] We are, of course, not the first to notice the substantive political arenas in which courts are becoming increasingly involved, or the large structural trends that helped spark and may help perpetuate their involvement; see, among others, Hirschl 2008.

The Spread of Constitutional Democracy

Since the 1970s, in many parts of the world – Iberia, Latin America, Eastern Europe, South Africa, and East Asia (e.g., Taiwan, Korea, Thailand, Indonesia) – authoritarian regimes have been replaced, at least in form but often in practice, by constitutional democracies. Both the constitutional and regime aspects of this political trend encourage judicial legitimacy and expanded judicial roles in governance.

Post-authoritarian constitutions, such as those promulgated in the wake of World War II, reflect what Ginsburg (2003: 1–3) has called the "decline of parliamentary sovereignty." That ideal has been weakened by its association with illiberal and oppressive regimes, which too easily became dominated by a single authoritarian party. Instead, the new constitutions embody an alternative foundation of limited government, in which elected political leaders are constrained by constitutionally prescribed checks on their authority and constitutionally enumerated rights – civil and political, but often social and economic, as well. The ideal of constitutional (rather than parliamentary) supremacy means that elected leaders should be constrained by national charters and judicial authority to interpret and apply them, reversing legislation, executive orders, and bureaucratic decisions that conflict with constitutional provisions. In many cases (for instance, in South Africa, Chile, and many post-Communist polities), brand-new constitutional courts untainted by association with the previous regime have been created for this task. In such contexts, support for constitutional supremacy (and, thus, courts) is often understood as support for the rule of law over naked political power.

The actual institutionalization and stabilization of liberal, law-constrained constitutional democracy, to be sure, has been a halting and irregular process, successful in some places, much less so or not at all in others. However, foundations matter. The official establishment (or resuscitation) of courts with explicit powers of review and remediation at the very least creates the possibility that courts will play a significant role in governance. Where democratic transition entails the fragmentation of political power into two or more parties or coalitions with reasonable chances of electoral success, the resulting political uncertainty, Ginsburg (2003) and Ferejohn (Ch. 14 in this volume) argue, gives competing political factions incentives to endorse the creation and continuity of strong, independent courts that can enforce the "constitutional bargain" (in particular, provisions that protect the interests and values of minority political factions). In this way, politicians and publics begin to view courts not as contrary to the ideal of democracy (as the "countermajoritarian difficulty" suggests) but rather as an integral aspect of an evolving ideal of democratic constitutionalism.

Analogous dynamics emerge in contexts in which democratization has been strongly or even moderately institutionalized, so that power is divided among competing parties or coalitions. Where the constitution provides for abstract powers of judicial review, parties out of power have incentives not only to rely on constitutional courts to maintain a level political playing field, but also to advance those parties' political and policy goals by petitioning constitutional tribunals to reject or limit pending (or enacted) legislation on constitutional grounds (see, for instance, Tate and Vallinder 1995 generally; Stone Sweet 2000 on France; and Kommers 2012 on Germany). In such contexts, political division also generates political space for judges to expand their roles without generating unified opposition – space that can be secured and extended when courts have politically potent allies in the elected branches who can stymie any attempts to target courts. Democratic leaders may also find that strong courts can serve as useful partners in governance (Nunes 2010), or at the least as mechanisms for blame avoidance. That is, judicial endorsements can help legitimate controversial policy decisions. Further, courts can be called on to consider policies that elected officials find too politically costly to support (or to resist) – they can be tossed political "hot potatoes" (to use the image Huls [Ch. 7 in this volume] suggests). Indeed, in such cases, constitutional courts may be seen by the public as more democratically responsive than the elected branches of government (see Scheppele 2003–2004). As these types of scenarios appear and repeat around the world, political leaders increasingly accept and even embrace a strong role for constitutional courts.

Globalization and Economic Liberalism

Another set of structural changes that favor the expansion of judicial roles has been stimulated in the last few decades by the increasing advocacy and acceptance of economic liberalism and the acceleration of globalization. Competitive pressures (and opportunities) have led many nations to liberalize economic governance, opening their economies to foreign trade and investment. State-controlled monopolies or cartels have given way to more competitive markets. These changes have generated more risks of opportunistic behavior, and hence – following Steven Vogel's dictum "freer markets, more rules" (Vogel 1996) – more elaborate regulatory law, competition law, corporate law, intellectual property law, labor law, and more. The upshot is more legal conflict among businesses, between business and labor, and between business and governments concerning economic issues. In particular, firms and business associations, as well as political advocacy groups aligned with big business or property owners, more often challenge statutes and government agencies in court. In order for their countries to emerge as (or remain) desirable trading partners and attract foreign investment, national leaders have increasingly felt compelled to adhere to this ever-expanding set of rules, and pledge (and abide by) contracts and property protections. To accentuate their nation's "legal reliability," leaders have empowered and granted independence to the courts (including constitutional courts) that will adjudicate the expanding legal conflict (North and Weingast 1989; Farber 2002; Silverstein 2003, 2008). Again, then, structural conditions have placed leaders and courts on the same side of the playing field and drawn courts into new roles, this time in economic governance.

Activist States and Evolving Legal Culture

One striking impression generated by the empirical studies in this book is how eagerly judges in some countries have seized the opportunity to make bold rulings, thrusting their courts into new judicial roles. Courts have helped popular political challengers win electoral victories in new democracies (Ginsburg, Ch.1 in this volume; Trochev, Ch. 2 in this volume), shifted the balance of power between executives and legislatures (Scribner, Ch. 4 in this volume), battled governmental corruption and failure (Mate, Ch. 10 in this volume; Guarneri, Ch. 6 in this volume), expanded judicial influence on substantive and constitutional law (Lasser, Ch. 11 in this volume; Huls, Ch. 7 in this volume; Reichman, Ch. 9 in this volume), and used constitutional principle to check even popular presidents and parties (Klug, Ch. 3 in this volume). These new judicial roles, we submit, reflect a fundamental transformation in litigants' and potential litigants' attitudes. Decades ago (at least in older democracies), judges who effectively prevented the state from infringing on citizens' and business firms' legally established civil and political rights were seen as effectively playing their understood roles – defending individual liberties and providing legal stability. Today, by contrast, many political and societal actors seem to want courts to play an independent and creative role in the political process. Courts, in short, increasingly seem to be envisioned as agents of governance and even agents of change, not just legal dispute resolvers.

In view of the famously formal nature of legal education and the historic irrelevance of courts to politics in many countries, it is somewhat unexpected that sociopolitical actors would increasingly turn to courts to resolve political conflicts over public policy – and equally surprising that judges would feel highly motivated to do so. As we have suggested, we can only speculate about the deeper changes in society, politics, and legal culture that have led political actors, interest groups, and individuals to expect more from courts; pushed courts to provide litigants with an avenue to protect and extend their interests and policy preferences; and led judges to adopt a more expansive view of their own authority and responsibility.

In addition to the two factors already mentioned, this apparent reinterpretation of judicial power can be viewed as springing from a broader evolution in the role of the state and law in both developed and developing societies. In *Total Justice* (1985), legal historian Lawrence Friedman argues that since the early twentieth century, a fundamental change has occurred, most often but not exclusively in economically advanced countries, in how people view the state and law and what they want from both. Scientific, technological, and organizational developments, Friedman writes, have led to steady increases in economic growth and facilitated governmental and corporate capacities to transform society – to bridge distances with telephones, motorways, motor vehicles, and airplanes; to bring about major improvements in sanitation and medicine; to provide systems of both private and public insurance; to bring electricity, literacy, and education to whole societies. Correspondingly, attitudes of political and social fatalism have declined. Increasingly, educated citizenries have begun to imagine that many sources of danger and oppression, previously borne with stoicism, can in fact be eliminated, and that extreme forms of human misery and social injustice can be ameliorated. If people in democratic societies believe such changes can be made, Friedman claims, it is but a short step for them to believe that such changes *should* be made. Hence, citizens have come to demand more active and responsive governments – governments that enact laws that help realize citizens' hopes for greater economic security, equal treatment, and respect for human dignity and human rights. Law, in consequence, has come to be viewed not only as a means of maintaining order but as a mechanism for addressing social problems and advancing justice.

Even as democratic governments have sought to respond to such citizen desires, they have been plagued by institutional failure, inadequate funding, bureaucratic ossification, corruption, and dysfunctional politics. Citizens, in turn, have increasingly turned to courts to compel their elected leaders to comply with their own statutory and constitutional promises and check bureaucratic arbitrariness or heedlessness. Of course, public will and the ability to use courts in this way are not automatic in either the developed or developing world, as Epp (1998) rightly cautions. Indeed, in many countries, it has been the development of a more politically engaged legal complex (Halliday, Karpik, and Feeley 2007) that has facilitated and strengthened these calls, as activist law professors advocate new constitutional interpretations and doctrines, and lawyers seek to advance policy goals through the courts rather than only through governmental bodies and political parties.

Sociologists Philippe Nonet and Philip Selznick (2001) sought to capture these changing conceptions of law and legal governance in terms of a partial shift away from the long-standing ideal of "autonomous law" and toward a more inchoate ideal of "responsive law." In the autonomous-law ideal, the legitimacy of laws is evaluated in terms of the process followed to enact them (whether they were passed by duly elected legislatures and legitimated via procedural constitutionalism) rather than in terms of their substantive fairness or wisdom. Judges are insulated from the world of politics and policymaking: their institutional task is to faithfully and accurately apply statutes and precedents to individual cases, not to make law. The responsive-law ideal has ascended, Nonet and Selznick suggest, as legal elites, politicians, and the educated public have begun to regard law as legitimate only when it exhibits the proper procedural pedigree *and* is responsive to human needs and conceptions of fairness. Law, in other words, is viewed as a mechanism of social problem solving and a way to address social needs. Courts, in this ideal, are concerned not merely with correct law application but with how their decisions affect individual litigants and society more broadly.

Facilitating this broad shift toward responsive law has been an ongoing evolution in legal education and training around the world – a move away from a tendency to study only the institutions and rules of one's own jurisdiction and toward the examination of cases, doctrine, and judicial behavior in other countries and even transnationally. As part of this shift, judges are increasingly exposed to the jurisprudence of other jurisdictions, and increasing numbers attend formal seminars and even earn advanced degrees in countries other than their own. Judges are not only more willing to deploy tools and techniques developed elsewhere, but have the skills to do so. This is reinforced by the increasingly transnational nature of the legal complex itself (Halliday, Ch. 13 in this volume; Epp 1998, 2010).

Through one pathway or another, responsive-law ideals have penetrated legal scholarship and teaching, legal advocacy, and the courts themselves, encouraging the dynamics at the heart of this inquiry. Judges, particularly high court judges with judicial review authority, have been more inclined to wield their powers as tools of governance, alert to political and social imperatives, willing to craft new doctrines and remedies. Social and political actors, for their part, request, aid, and abet their efforts. This form of law is abundantly illustrated in many decisions of the Warren Court in the United States (Kagan, Ch. 8 in this volume), the Indian Supreme Court's development and extension of public interest litigation (Mate, Ch. 10 in this volume), and the anticorruption prosecutions by Italian Magistrates (Guarnieri, Ch. 6 in this volume), to refer to just a few examples.

In many "third wave" democracies, similar shifts in constitutional design, legal thought, and judicial self-conceptions have developed – but have done so rapidly and unevenly, rather than gradually and steadily. As countries in Southern and Eastern Europe, Latin America, and parts of Asia and Africa transitioned from autocratic rule, citizens who had experienced tyranny called on courts to check any tendency new democratic leaders might exhibit toward reverting to the authoritarian or totalitarian habits of the past. However, weakly institutionalized judiciaries – which often had been marginalized or ignored for years or decades and had little experience challenging governments – often struggled to do so. Likewise, many countries in these regions transitioned to democracy amidst dramatic economic turmoil, meaning that from the very start the state was significantly handicapped in developing public policy and providing public goods. Citizens who turned to courts to push for greater government effectiveness in these areas (often by requesting that they vindicate social and economic rights) were thus often disappointed. In short, in new democracies, citizens turned to courts and judges – institutions uniquely unequipped to help them – to limit leaders and push for positive change and substantive public policy simultaneously. To be sure, some courts in such countries have tried to carry out these roles – but how many courts have done so, how they have done so, and how effectively they have done so are all open empirical questions. We hope they will be the topic of many additional studies.

WINDS OF CHANGE

In sum, amidst global political and constitutional change, judicial self-perceptions as well as popular conceptions of judges and what it is reasonable to ask of them have begun to change. Judicial roles and judicial politics have changed along with them. Now more than ever before, in some contexts (although certainly not all), courts are seen as, and have begun to act as, quasi-independent elements of government. As a result, courts are becoming increasingly consequential.

To emphasize a point that we hope is by now clear, by our definition, courts do not need to clash with elected leaders to be consequential, nor do they need to make things "better" or "right" (undeniably subjective notions in any context). Courts have emerged as policy makers, dispute resolvers, legitimacy generators, political insurance providers, and social healers – as well as catalysts of retrenchment, foci for political opposition, and countermajoritarian in the best and worst senses of that term. In calling courts consequential, we simply mean to suggest that they make a difference in politics, policy, and social life. We hope this volume has demonstrated that this is increasingly the case: in more and more polities, with regard to an increasing variety of issues, politics would play out differently but for courts.

Judicial consequentiality, we have suggested, does not develop linearly. Rather, courts develop new roles much as ships ply stormy seas – following varying routes, some direct, some indirect, and some that end in tragedy. Which judicial roles develop and how they do so is influenced by the ideology and skills of judicial captains and officers, the resources with which the ships have been provisioned, and how the former manage the latter. However, captains and officers are not the sole masters of their destiny. They must deftly react when changes in weather (which can be sudden and violent) lead to shifts in the prevailing winds (from demand for new roles to resistance thereto, for instance). Structural factors – large waves of regime instability or socioeconomic downturn – may also impinge on judicial role expansion, just as contingent factors – unseasonable icebergs or barely submerged sand bars – may unexpectedly come into view. Different captains, commanding different ships at different times, will react to these factors differently.

Nonetheless and despite all of the inherent uncertainty, this volume and the Andrew W. Mellon Sawyer Seminar series at UC Berkeley from which it grew, suggest that the overall trend is toward the continuing elaboration of judicial roles in governance. That trend recommends that we collectively rethink our approach to the study of courts. Our categorization of judicial roles, causal framework, and nautical metaphor represent initial efforts at organizing our thoughts and observations about these critical changes in the roles and consequentiality of courts. All three have significant limitations, of course, among them a lack of precision and an unquestioning acceptance of multicausality. In this sense, Martin Shapiro is right: the mighty problem continues. However, we hope this volume will facilitate further steps toward identifying the variety of politically crucial tasks courts around the world have taken on, and toward a better understanding of the wide array of forces that impinge on their assumption of those new roles in governance.

REFERENCES

Bickel, Alexander. 1986. *The Least Dangerous Branch: The Supreme Court at the Bar of Politics*. New Haven: Yale University Press.

Easton, David. 1965. *A Systems Analysis of Political Life*. New York: John Wiley and Sons.

Epp, Charles. 1998. *The Rights Revolution: Lawyers, Activists and Supreme Courts in Comparative Perspective*. Chicago: University of Chicago Press.

Epp, Charles. 2010. *Making Rights Real: Activists, Bureaucrats, and the Creation of the Legalistic State*. Chicago: University of Chicago Press.

Epstein, Lee, Jack Knight, and Olga Shvetsova. 2001. "The Role of Constitutional Courts in the Establishment and Maintenance of Democratic Systems of Government," *Law & Society Review* 35: 117–164.

Farber, Daniel. 2002. "Rights as Signals." *The Journal of Legal Studies* 31(1): 83–98.

Gibson, James, Jeffrey Gottfried, Michael Delli Carpini, and Kathleen Hall Jamieson. 2011. "The Effects of Judicial Campaign Activity on the Legitimacy of Courts: A Survey Based Experiment." 64 *Political Research Quarterly* 64(3): 545–558.

Ginsburg, Tom. 2003. *Judicial Review in New Democracies: Constitutional Courts in Asian Cases*. New York: Cambridge University Press.

Graber, Mark. 2008. "The Countermajoritarian Difficulty: From Courts to Congress to Constitutional Order." *Annual Review of Law & Social Science* 4: 361–84.

Graber, Mark. 1993. "The Non-Majoritarian Problem: Legislative Deference to the Judiciary," *Studies in American Political Development* 7: 35.

Halliday, Terry, Lucien Karpik, and Malcolm Feeley, eds. 2007. *Fighting for Political Freedom: Comparative Studies of the Legal Complex and Political Change*. Portland: Hart Publishing.

Hirschl, Ran. 2008. "The Judicialization of Politics." In *The Oxford Handbook of Law and Politics*. Keith E. Whittington, R. Daniel Kelemen, and Gregory A. Caldeira, eds. New York: Oxford University Press, pp. 119–141.

Kommers, Donald. 2012. *The Constitutional Jurisprudence of the Federal Republic of Germany, Third Edition*. Durham: Duke University Press.

Moustafa, Tamir. 2009. *The Struggle for Constitutional Power: Law, Politics, and Economic Development in Europe*. New York: Cambridge University Press.

Nonet, Philippe and Philip Selznick. 2001. *Law and Society in Transition: Toward Responsive Law*. New Brunswick: Transaction Publishers.

North, Douglass C. and Barry Weingast. 1989. "Constitutions and Commitment: The Evolution of Institutions Governing Public Choice in Seventeenth-Century England." *Journal of Economic History* 49: 803–832.

Nunes, Rodrigo. 2010. "Politics Without Insurance: Democratic Competition and Judicial Reform in Brazil." *Comparative Politics* 42(3): 313–331.

Scheppele, Kim Lane. 1999. "New Hungarian Constitutional Court," *Eastern European Constitutional Review* 8(4): 81–87.

Scheppele, Kim Lane. 2003/2004. "A Realpolitik Defense of Social Rights." *Texas Law Review* 82(7): 1921–1961.

Scheppele, Kim Lane. 2011. Published in Paul Krugman, "Hungary's Constitutional Revolution." Retrieved from http://krugman.blogs.nytimes.com/2011/12/19/hungarys-constitutional-revolution/.

Shapiro, Martin. 1981. *Courts: A Comparative and Political Analysis*. Chicago: University of Chicago Press.

Shesol, Jeff. 2010. *Supreme Power: Franklin Roosevelt vs. the Supreme Court*. NY: WW Norton.

Silverstein, Gordon. 2003. "Globalization and the Rule of Law: A Machine that Runs of Itself?" *International Journal of Constitutional Law* 1: 427–45.

Silverstein, Gordon. 2008. "The Exception That Proves Rules Matter." Tom Ginsburg and Tamir Moustafa (eds). *Rule by Law: The Politics of Courts in Authoritarian Regimes*. New York: Cambridge University Press, pp. 72–102.

Stone Sweet, Alec. 2000. *Governing with Judges: Constitutional Politics in Europe*. Oxford: Oxford University Press.

Stone Sweet, Alec. 1999. "Judicialization and the Construction of Governance,' *Comparative Political Studies* 32: 147–184, reprinted version from Martin Shapiro and Alec Stone Sweet. 2002. *On Law, Politics and Judicialization*. New York: Oxford University Press, pp. 55–89.

Tate, C. Neal and Torbjörn Vallinder, eds. 1995. *The Global Expansion of Judicial Power*. New York: New York University Press.

Vogel, Steven K. 1996. *Freer Markets, More Rules: Regulatory Reform in Advanced Industrial Countries*. Ithaca: Cornell University Press.

Weber, Max. 1978. *Economy and Society: An Outline of Interpretive Sociology*, Vol. 1. Guenther Roth and Claus Wittich, eds. Berkeley: University of California Press.

Whittington, Keith. 2007. *Political Foundations of Judicial Supremacy: The Presidency, the Supreme Court, and Constitutional Leadership in U.S. History*. Princeton: Princeton University Press.

Index

430 *Index*

The Movement for Quality Government in Israel v. The Knesset, Israeli Supreme Court, 253
Musharraf, Pervez, 60–62

national administrative and regulatory state, U.S., 204–211
  abandonment of substantive review of regulatory policy, 206
  endorsing administrative law-making, 206–207
  federal government's taxing and spending power, 207
  importance of Supreme Court, 207–209
  interstate commerce as all commerce, 205–206
  legitimating administrative lawmaking through federal administrative law, 209–211
  overview, 204–205
National Front (Barisan Nasional, BN) coalition, Malaysia, 322
National Highway Traffic Safety Agency (NHTSA), U.S., 210
National Industrial Recovery Act, U.S., 204–205
national judicial system, Dutch Hoge Raad as guardian of coherence of, 195–196
National Labor Relations Act (NLRA), U.S., 204
National Labor Relations Board v Jones & Laughlin Steel Corporation, U.S. Supreme Court, 204
national political agenda, and lack of founding written constitution in Israel, 238
National Religious Party (NRP), Israel, 243
national-subnational government conflict over allocation of governing power, 13
nautical metaphor, to explain change in judicial roles, 19–22, 400–402
Nebbia v New York, U.S. Supreme Court, 206
neoconstitutionalism, 128
Netherlands. *See* Dutch Hoge Raad
"New Amparo Law Project", Mexican Supreme Court, 148
New Deal Supreme Court, U.S., 205–209
new democracies. *See also* colored revolutions; Constitutional Tribunal, Chile; Mexican Supreme Court; politics of courts in democratization; South African Constitutional Court
  and changing judicial roles, 409
  disputes between political incumbents and challengers in, 8–10
NHTSA (National Highway Traffic Safety Agency), U.S., 210
Ninth Schedule, Indian Constitution, 266
Nixon, Richard, 402
NLRA (National Labor Relations Act), U.S., 204

non-democratic regimes. *See* authoritarian regimes; semi-authoritarian regimes, colored revolutions in
Nonet, Philippe, 408
non-Orthodox conversion to Judaism, Supreme Court of Israel rulings on, 328–329
non-secular polities, constitutional courts in. *See* religion-taming function of constitutional jurisprudence
non-state-approved religious organizations, 314–315
normal institutions, courts as, 371
North-West Frontier Province (NWFP), Pakistan, 320–321
NRP (National Religious Party), Israel, 243
NWFP Islamization bill (Hisba Bill), Pakistan, 320–321

oceanic metaphor, to explain change in judicial roles, 19–22, 400–402
Office of Contract Compliance, U.S., 222
Old Fort, South African Constitutional Court, 100–101
"one man-one vote" decisions, U.S. Supreme Court, 224–225
opposition
  criticism of Supreme Court by after Georgia's Rose Revolution, 77–78
  delivery of benefits to by judges, in cases of contested elections, 73–74
Orange Revolution, Ukraine
  conditions enabling anti-government decisions, 68–73
  courts as upstream triggers of democracy, 49
  judicial strategies and roles, 73–74
  overview, 78–83
  procedural creativity during, 31
  strategic decisions of judges during, 33
ordinary French courts, in French judicial system, 297–301
organizational leadership, Dutch Hoge Raad, 193–194
originalism, in Constitutional Tribunal of Chile, 127–129
origins of South African Constitutional Court, 97–99
Orthodox stream of Judaism, 327
Osmonov, Kurmanbek, 85, 86
Otero Formula, 149

pacification politics, Dutch, 183–184
Pakistan
  changing judicial roles in, 64
  legal complex in, 343